THE DEVELOPMENT OF THE TOP 40 RADIO FORMAT

This is a volume in the
Arno Press collection

DISSERTATIONS IN BROADCASTING

Advisory Editor
Christopher H. Sterling

See last pages of this volume
for a complete list of titles.

THE DEVELOPMENT OF THE TOP 40 RADIO FORMAT

David R. MacFarland

ARNO PRESS
A New York Times Company
New York • 1979

Publisher's Note: This book has been reproduced from the best available copy.

Editorial Supervision: Andrea Hicks

First publication 1979 by Arno Press Inc.

DISSERTATIONS IN BROADCASTING
ISBN for complete set: 0-405-11754-X
See last pages of this volume for titles.

Manufactured in the United States of America

Library of Congress Cataloging in Publication Data

MacFarland, David T
The development of the top 40 radio format.

(Dissertations in broadcasting)
Originally presented as the author's thesis, University of Wisconsin, 1972.
Bibliography: p.
1. Popular music radio stations--United States.
I. Title. II. Series.
PN1991.67.P67M3 1979 338.4'7'62 78-21726
ISBN 0-405-11765-5

THE DEVELOPMENT OF THE TOP 40 RADIO FORMAT

BY

DAVID T. MACFARLAND

A thesis submitted in partial fulfillment of the
requirements for the degree of

DOCTOR OF PHILOSOPHY

(Communication Arts)

at the

UNIVERSITY OF WISCONSIN

1972

ACKNOWLEDGMENTS

After writing so comparatively many words in the text of this work, the few allotted here to express the author's thanks for the help he has received seem all too meager. As in so many other aspects of both broadcasting and scholarship, it should be understood that there is no necessary correlation between quantity and quality.

First there must be a special note of gratitude to Charlotte MacFarland, the author's wife, whose love, patience, and belief motivated this work at times when no other incentive prevailed. In the gathering and the writing of this research, as in all the other hours of the past five years, Charlotte is *sine qua non*.

Next, Dr. Lawrence W. Lichty merits special praise for the manner in which he advised the author in this research. Dr. Lichty offered counsel and guidance when called upon at all hours, yet never intruded into the author's own design or basic conclusions. Thus, where the method, content, style, and conclusions reached in this work are appropriate and correct, much of the credit is due to the help of Dr. Lichty; where they fail, the shortcoming is certainly the author's.

To Dr. Richard Lawson and to Dr. Ordean Ness go the author's grateful thanks for offering to read the manuscript in less than perfect form. They, along with Dr. Charles Sherman, have provided the scholarly nurture and the social support that any student would count himself lucky to have. Mr. Tom Hoffer, who was completing his dissertation concurrently with this one, also provided advice and insight at times when they proved most useful.

The Department of Communication Arts and the University of Wisconsin have the author's gratitude for their many resources and helpfulness, and for their benign neglect when that was also appropriate.

Outside of the University of Wisconsin, there are even more people to whom the author owes much in the writing of this work. Dr. Christopher Sterling and Dr. David Leroy both believed in the author's capacity for such research long before the author did. So did David L. and Jean MacFarland and John and Marge Kutz, the author's parents and parents-in-law, who provided both verbal and financial encouragement.

Two men in broadcasting have been helpful to the author and his wife in the conduct of this research beyond any reasonable measure, and most of the primary material that is quoted or reproduced herein was supplied through them. The generosity of Bill Stewart and Edd [sic] Routt can really never be repaid.

Gordon McLendon and Ken Dowe have been no less important to this work than Bill Stewart and Edd Routt because it was McLendon's decision that opened the McLendon Policy Books to the author's inspection for several days, and Dowe's implementation of that decision that helped the research to proceed smoothly. Ken Dowe also granted a lengthy, comprehensive, and altogether valuable interview, and at one time even offered the author an honest job.

Others who took time to have an interview with the author and who merit thanks for their help in this regard are Jerry Bartell, George W. Armstrong, Robert Rounsaville, Arnold Kaufman, Don Keyes,

Pete Thomas, Bill Meeks, Wilson Northcross, Tom Merriman, Scott Blake, Garrett Haston, Hub Atwood, Joe Bankhead, Sol Rosinski, Donald Meyers, and Bill Stubblefield. The background they provided in every case proved to be of great help.

Carolyn Richmond at McLendon headquarters in Dallas has to be the most helpful secretary in broadcasting. The people at KLIF who helped Charlotte with stacks of Xeroxing also have our thanks.

Jon Wolfert provided much help in Dallas, and Jeanne and Brian Svikhart offered friendship, lodging, and an invaluable map to Casanova, Virginia, where we found Bill Stubblefield. Lee Whitney and Ken Devoe both provided tapes which proved useful to the author, as did Miss Winnie Bell and Dr. Raymond Muncy at Harding College. Ken Costa, Grahame Richards, Ross Bevel, Victor Sack, and Jack Thayer all provided correspondence or other material which the author also gratefully acknowledges.

The research was supported in part by a grant for travel from the Graduate School of the University of Wisconsin. The grant made possible the interview with Bill Stewart and the extensive perusal of the McLendon Policy Books, and the author most gratefully acknowledges this financial help.

THE DEVELOPMENT OF THE TOP 40 RADIO FORMAT

David T. MacFarland

Under the supervision of Professor Lawrence W. Lichty

The radio broadcasting term "Top 40" refers both to a list of the 40 or so most popular records to be played on a station, and also to a general radio format and specialized formula incorporating the 40 or so most popular records as an essential ingredient. The term has come to be synonymous with a type of radio broadcasting which enjoyed wide popularity in the 1950s and early 1960s but which is now commonly referred to as "contemporary" or "popular music" radio. Previous treatments of this era have concentrated either on the music and recording stars or on disc jockey personalities, none of which was as influential in determining the content and style of Top 40 radio as were station owners, managers, and program directors. The latter group of decision-makers are the focus of this research.

In the 1950s, suburbanization, increasing affluence, decreasing median age plus the post-war baby boom were among the general social changes which produced a climate in which Top 40 radio could develop. In the broadcast industry, the rapid rise in the popularity of television caused both listeners and advertisers to abandon evening radio programs for TV, and led to a dwindling supply of entertainment programming from radio networks. Decreasing radio time sales, profits, and station selling prices, along with increasing numbers of daytime-only stations also competing for audience and advertisers are explained in detail, as are the growing numbers of radio sets (especially transistor and auto radios), and new studies which began to discover that listening was taking place in new locations, in new attention-modes, and to new stations. A comparison of the programming of network and of independent stations demonstrates how the radio networks generally fought a doomed "holding action" in continuing their old-style shows in direct competition with television, while music and news stations found growing audience- and advertiser-acceptance as the only kind of radio programming which was filling an audience need for non-demanding entertainment of a consistent type. A number of the most popular disc jockey programs (such as those of Martin Block on WABC and Alan Freed on WINS) which were offered on radio networks and syndicated to local stations are explored, as are TV record shows such as Dick Clark's American Bandstand.

The management philosophies, station acquisitions, and programming policies of four Top 40 group owners are set forth in the central section of the research, with reproduced documents and quoted memoranda providing detail about the responses made by Storz, McLendon, Bartell and the Plough group to the emerging new patterns of radio listening. All were determined to program objectively, filling audience needs and tastes rather than their own. All four believed in the necessity for program considerations taking precedence over sales factors, and all felt that programming should "fill a void" rather than being a duplication of already available fare.

Detailed analysis is provided of the three most crucial Top 40 programming policies--music, monitoring, and promotions--including discussion of the limited playlist, music selection, music content, competitive and feedback monitoring, stunts, treasure hunts, rating hypos, call letter repetition, and case histories of diffusion of various promotions. Policies on news gathering and presentation, commercial production and presentation, and deejay chatter are also explored. Top 40 management's policies on group organization and executive promotion, station acquisition and operation, and investment in hardware, software and personnel are explained, as are such facets of group operation as membership in trade associations, affiliation with certain station representative firms, the placement of trades advertising, and efforts to improve the image of Top 40 radio. The Top 40 format is placed in perspective by examining its acceptance by audience, advertisers, and the radio industry in general, and by discussing such other specialized formats as all-news, all-ads, and other music-based formats such as country-and-western, "good-music," etc. A comparison between the early Top 40 style and that promulgated by Bill Drake and other modern programming "refiners," who represent the maturation of Top 40 from a "maverick" operation in the 1950s to adult big-business today, concludes the text.

TABLE OF CONTENTS

Page

INTRODUCTION

When the reader reaches the conclusion of this work, it is hoped that he will have come to understand the term "Top 40" to mean far more than an arbitrarily-limited number of popular records. The term is used purposefully because it is no longer an accurate description of a radio format (if it ever were), but is still denotative of an era in which the first "formula" broadcasting by independent stations took place. To knowledgeable broadcasters and scholars, the term "Top 40" today refers to both the era and the management philosophies which sprang from that era to shape radio in the 1960s and beyond. This research attempts to explore both the literal meanings surrounding the term and the even more important legacy of attitudes that have become staples in radio management.

A number of books have been written about the music and the life-styles that prevailed in the 1950s when Top 40 radio was being evolved. For the most part, they focus on musical performers, song writers, or teenage idols, all of which might be of some interest to the "popular culture" historian. But all such books--even ones about disc jockeys which purport to show the influence such personalities had upon the musical taste and life-styles of the times--fail to appreciate that the music that was heard, the performers that became idols, and the disc jockeys who became household words all depended to an extent on the policies of the owners and operators who managed the Top 40 stations. It is the purpose of this research to supply that missing perspective by setting forth the principal accomplishments of management in developing a format that since the mid-1950s has commanded the attention of more radio listeners than any other type of programming fare. If only because of the sheer size of its audience right up to the present, the development of the Top 40 format would be worthy of examination.

The author knows of no books or extended articles whose subject is Top 40 station management. There is also a scarcity of other written materials on the subject. In some cases, material exists but station ownership refuses to let a student see it. In other cases, the broadcasting company claims that nothing exists at all. When asked about the Bartell group's "Blue Book" of programming policies, Gerald Bartell told the author "Nobody ever saw it, and you won't ever see it" (Bartell interview). Asked about the roles of program directors and music directors at the Top 40 pioneering Storz stations, executive vice president George Armstrong replied in the interview:

Armstrong: We have some processes, and I did not say that we did not have some procedures involved. What else?

Author: Did you want to talk about what those procedures were?

Armstrong: No.

No primary material was supplied by either Bartell or Armstrong (for Storz). Only the McLendon group admitted having policy books and other archives and indicated a willingness to let the author use them in this research. Undoubtedly, the McLendon operation was not in every way typical of Top 40 management policies, and the omissions and biases of both the McLendon Policy Books and the author's selections from them may have further distorted the actual picture of what transpired in the

Top 40 era. However, the McLendon Policy Books are the only source available to the author (or to anyone else, apparently) concerning these early days of decision, and thus become especially valuable to the student in their uniqueness. At some points in the work, the reader may feel that a letter or memorandum for the McLendon Policy Books is being quoted at excessive length, but he is asked to keep in mind that part of the motive for doing so may be the hope of preserving documents whose originals might be destroyed or withdrawn from use by students. Care has been taken by the author to ensure that material that might prove of a sensitive nature to the McLendon interests either be excluded from this work or else be accompanied with a qualifying explanation. The author presumes to act as a spokesman for the McLendon interests in asking that any quotation that may be made of such material should be made wholly in context and should include any qualifying explanation, as doing otherwise might cause some future student to be denied the use of an extremely valuable resource for studying recent radio history.

Every attempt was made to interview those persons directly in charge of the most important companies which operated Top 40 stations in the 1950s. Of the three men most often associated with Top 40 pioneering--Todd Storz, Gordon McLendon, and Jerry Bartell--Todd Storz is dead, Jerry Bartell has sold his interests in the radio stations he once owned, and Gordon McLendon was unavailable for an interview on two separate visits to Dallas. Jerry Bartell did grant an interview, as did George Armstrong, today the chief executive officer in Storz Broadcasting.

The author also arranged interviews with the national program director of both the Storz and the McLendon stations, since program directors and station owners worked together in developing the Top 40 format. Other disciples, imitators, and persons employed in industries related to the development of Top 40 radio were also contacted by the author for their insights. A total of 18 personal interviews were conducted.

In the chapters that follow, little attempt is made to explain to the novice how Top 40 radio actually sounded as it was received by the listening public. Any attempt to render in mere words the total aural milieu that was Top 40 was considered to be futile. Those who must read what follows without a listening knowledge of Top 40 are advised to listen to off-the-air recordings made in the late 1950s or early 1960s or to recreations such as the "Cruisin'" series of long-play records. As the latter are likely to be more generally available, it seems worthwhile to recommend in particular the following albums: "Cruisin' 1956" (Increase Records INCM 2001) for its contrasts between rhythm-and-blues-oriented music and some old-fashioned production and commercials; "Cruisin' 1961" (Increase Records INCM 2006) for its pubescent-voiced host Arnie Ginsburg, the tight production, and the use of noises and jokes; and "Cruisin' 1962" (Increase Records INCM 2007) for an example of how McLendon's KLIF sounded in the evenings when "Weird Beard" Russ Knight used all of the electronic sounds at his command.

CHAPTER ONE

SOCIAL, MEDIA USAGE, RADIO AUDIENCE, AND RADIO INDUSTRY TRENDS

The changes in radio programming which resulted in the Top 40 format are not easily grasped without an understanding of the trends which affected the entire radio industry in the period between the end of World War II and the beginning of Top 40's success. These radio trends, which are the subject of the latter portion of this chapter, in turn cannot be fully appreciated without some knowledge of the changes taking place in society in general.

Social Trends and Media Usage Trends Prior to Top 40

General Social Trends

In the post-World War II period, a number of general social changes became widely recognized as trends. Among them were decreasing median age of the U.S. population, a concomitant development of the youth market for goods and services, and a general increase in affluence.

Decreasing median age

Recent interest in the environmental crisis known as the population explosion has made the concept of population doubling more widely understood. In each population doubling, the median age of the general population decreases (since doubling reflects a birth rate which far outstrips the death rate). Thus at the present time in the

United States, more than half of the population is under 30 years of age. According to the President's Commission on Population Growth and the American Future, 70,000,000 of the 1972 U.S. population of 209,000,000 are under 18 years of age.[1] According to estimates of the U.S. Census, by 1975 nearly 50 percent of the total population in the United States will be under 25 years of age.

Development of the youth market

The lowering of the median age of the general population can be most easily understood when some span of time is considered. For example, in the 15 years between 1960 and 1975, the population in this country that is 24-years-old or under will have increased by 31,000,000, while the population above 25-years-of-age will have increased by only 18,000,000.

The median age of the population was decreased an extra amount in the United States by the World War II "baby boom," which resulted in a greater number of births during and especially after the war than would have been predicted by doubling alone. This simple "bulge" in the birth rate became an increasingly more lucrative market for goods and services as the "boom" babies' purchasing power grew along with increasing age. The children of the "baby boom," along with the normal lowering of the median population age, made the development of a specialized youth market a reasonable possibility.

Increasing affluence

An important factor in the development of the youth market was

---

[1]"The Crucial Math of Motherhood," Life, May 19, 1972, p. 48.

the increase in the spendable income of the average family. Part of this increase in "uncommitted" income was turned over directly to young people in the form of wages or allowances. Other portions were spent by the family on goods or services used by young persons that the latter would otherwise have had to supply for themselves. In either case, the result was more money being spent on nonessentials by families in general and by young people in particular. A significant portion of this new spendable income was used by both the family and by young people on the entertainment media, as will be seen later.

Suburbanization

The Post-War era saw the expansion of the suburbs at an increasing rate. In the period from 1950 to 1960, cities increased population by 8% while suburban areas increased 47%.[2] As new population clusters sprang up around the central cities, new business often followed. The shopping center, partly because of its proximity to the new population clusters, came into fashion. At the same time, workers often continued to be employed in the central cities, necessitating transportation to and from the job. Whereas while living in the city, a short walk or the use of mass transit could convey the worker to his job, the suburban situation made travel by automobile the most flexible and convenient. Suburbanization thus resulted both in an increase in the number of cars on the road, and also in an increase in the number of hours they were employed in driving to and from a job. As will be

---

[2]"Radio has the Facts and Figures," Broadcasting, September 28, 1964, p. 68.

shown later, this facet of suburbanization would eventually be exploited by radio as "drive time."

Suburbanization also affected the usage of certain communications and entertainment media, as will be discussed below.

Media Trends

Print media

The dispersion of population into suburban clusters and the fragmentation of markets by age groups had the greatest negative effect on the print media, which, partly because of the weight of tradition, and partly because of more difficult problems, were slower to adapt to the new conditions.

Newspapers

Big-city newspapers, the first American mass media, were especially hard-hit by suburbanization and the rise of TV's popularity. As both readers and advertisers moved to the suburbs, city newspapers found it increasingly more difficult and expensive to get their editions distributed. Even retail sales outlets were dispersed and few in number. As suburbs grew beyond rail lines and railroad commuting declined in favor of automobile travel, circulation suffered still further. Additionally, travel by automobile created a ready audience for the radio advertiser, since radio was the only medium available to the driver. And unlike train commuters, bus commuters did not gather at a central location to board their buses, so another sales point was eliminated.[3]

---

[3]"Special Report: Mass Media Head Into Era of Crucial Change," Business Week, May 27, 1961, p. 104.

Even more troublesome for city newspapers than the dispersed reader was the problem of the dispersed advertiser. For a suburban advertiser ten or twenty miles east of the central city, it would be unreasonable to expect to attract customers from a suburb ten or twenty miles west of the city. Yet, until regional editions were developed, if the advertiser wanted to buy newspaper space at all, he had to buy the entire distribution area and pay the correspondingly high rates. Few suburban advertisers did so, leaving city papers to rely on the "downtown" city advertisers, who found a dwindling response to their advertising as similar goods and services became available in suburbia.

Finally, city newspapers faced increasing competition for both readers and advertising from new suburban newspapers and "shoppers" which offered local news appeal, local circulation, and lower rates.[4]

Magazines

The magazine industry suffered some of the same problems as the city newspapers, but for different reasons. While the city newspaper's main competition for advertising was from radio and other suburban papers, the magazine found its greatest enemy in television, since both needed the same national advertiser. Yet because the feature content of most national magazines was (and was expected by readers to be) national in scope, magazines did not have to establish regional editions for editorial content, as newspapers did. (Many have established regional editions for advertisers, but the editorial content is usually the same.) Magazines offered one feature that television, until

---

[4] Ibid., p. 109.

recently, could not match: color. Only recently has color TV set saturation passed the 50% level.

In regard to readers, the magazine industry as a whole was quicker than the newspaper industry to take advantage of the specialized markets developing within the total population, by developing specialized publications to match them. Many of the publications which today have a "mass" circulation among a specialized audience began in this Post-War era. Playboy is a good example of a magazine which appeals to the young, affluent male. The "teen" magazines are examples of the same magazine marketing principles, as applied instead to a younger, generally female audience. "Fan" magazines, appealing to persons interested in a specialized pastime or hobby, also sprang up during this period. The most phenomenally successful of these has been TV Guide, which has always had regional editions. Another successful "fan" magazine is Hot Rod.[5]

Broadcasting

As has already been pointed out, the broadcast media were in some cases agents for change in the usage of other media. At the same time, the broadcast media themselves were also being transformed from forces both within and without.

Television, which profoundly affected advertising in mass circulation magazines, and which cut into both the readership and the advertising lineage of city newspapers, also had a deep effect on radio. Radio, to most people, meant "network" radio, and with television's

[5] For a discussion of other TV magazines of the middle 1950s, see "Fan Magazines" in Broadcasting, November 22, 1954, pp. 43, 50.

increasing need for programming in the late forties and early fifties, many of network radio's stars and programs were transferred to television, where increasing numbers of viewers and advertisers eagerly awaited them. Whereas the loss of national advertising could be made up by radio broadcasters by turning to local advertising, the loss of radio network personalities and programming to television was much more difficult for radio to rectify. One of the programming answers was Top 40.

Phonograph records

A mass medium not noted previously in this review of trends is the phonograph record. Its background must be mentioned because the pop record was such an integral part of the "music and news" format from which Top 40 was derived. The record industry is, in turn, only one of the "publishing" arms of the music industry, which must thus be the starting point for this discussion.

Music publishing industry

Music had been published in the form of sheet music for many years before radio began to broadcast much live or recorded music. In the days before radio, songs were debuted and popularized via live performances in broadway shows, vaudeville, and so on. Publishing houses employed song pluggers whose job it was to convince top vocalists and orchestras to perform a particular song. The inducement was usually in the form of a payment--thus, "payola" existed quite openly long before it became an issue in radio. Radio stations did not play recordings regularly until electrical pickup cartridges were developed, because of the poor reproduction derived from a microphone pickup of an acoustical phonograph. (Even with this, radio networks banned transcribed music for many years because of its presumed lack of fidelity.) For a while, the playing of records on radio was regarded by music publishers as just another way to bring their music to the attention of the public.[6] Then publishers realized that repeated exposures of certain songs by radio stations were increasing sheet music sales.[7] It was at that point that the song pluggers began to become record promotion men instead, and the industry turned from being almost totally concerned with sheet music publishing to being heavily involved in recording.

In 1914, the American Society of Composers, Authors and Publishers was formed as a voluntary association to protect members' economic rights in their music. ASCAP was alone in its music-licensing function until BMI (Broadcast Music Incorporated) was formed in 1940 with the financial backing of broadcasters who had balked at a rate increase asked for by ASCAP. BMI began with a virtually empty catalog, as compared with ASCAP's hundreds of thousands of songs. ASCAP had traditionally set high standards for its music, and depended heavily on Broadway and Hollywood shows to supply "high-class" new material. According to a table produced by D. Duane Braun in his The Sociology and History of American Music and Dance, between 1920 and 1930, about 25% of all hit songs were supplied by Broadway shows. Then, as film sound was improved, films grew to account for between 20% to 30% of

---

[6]Hazel Meyer, The Gold in Tin Pan Alley (Philadelphia: J. B. Lippincott Co., 1958), p. 128.

[7]Ibid., p. 128.

each year's hits, while Broadway dropped to about 15% during the 1930s. During World War II, films accounted for nearly 30% of all hits, while Broadway's share was only 5% to 10%, but immediately after the war, Broadway rebounded and films dropped proportionately so that in the years 1946 to 1956, Broadway shows and Hollywood films each accounted for about 15% of each year's hits. From about 1956 on, the share of hits produced by each dropped closer to 10% (and in films for the years 1958 and 1959 it dropped to 2.2% and 3.3% respectively) probably reflecting both the rise of BMI hits being produced outside of Broadway and Hollywood, and the audience's increasing attention to TV, which reduced movie box office receipts generally and curtailed the production of musicals.[8]

While ASCAP frowned on country, western, and Negro or "race" music, because BMI needed to develop a catalog the latter encouraged songwriters in these fields.

> The folk tune, cowboy lament, barbershop ballad, polka and gospel chant of a scornful yesterday became, almost overnight, a potential hit. People liked this music.. They would have liked it earlier, no doubt, if ASCAP publishers had considered it commercial.[9]

ASCAP publishers had come to agree that it took a big name in a big production plus good plugging to make a hit.[10] BMI didn't have big names or big productions, but it did have access to good plugging through its radio station ownership. Disc jockeys were encouraged by

---

[8] D. Duane Braun, The Sociology and History of American Music and Dance (Ann Arbor, Michigan: Ann Arbor Publishers, 1969), Table Two, pp. 164-65.

[9] Meyer, The Gold in Tin Pan Alley, p. 94.

[10] Ibid., pp. 113-14.

BMI to play increasing numbers of BMI songs to "keep the profits in the family" and were reminded that ". . . the public selects its favorites from the music it hears and does not miss what it does not hear."[11] In 1940, this would have appeared as a subversion of the public's taste, except that the public was eager to hear types of music it had largely been denied by ASCAP. Not until BMI had thoroughly dominated the rhythm and blues and "teen" music markets and teenage and rhythm and blues records came to dominate the airwaves in the 1950s did a major public outcry occur as will be shown later.

Record industry

A parallel with the ASCAP-BMI competition exists in the record industry. For many years, dating almost from the beginning of the industry, a few companies known as "majors" dominated the production, pressing, distribution, and plugging of records. "Major" record companies included Victor, Decca, and Columbia prior to the 1940s when Capitol joined the list. All of the majors had made their fortune with ASCAP music, and most continued that affiliation even as independent record companies began to produce hits licensed by BMI. "Indies" had been recording western, "race" and country music for years, but now with BMI promoting such records to disc jockeys, a nationwide hit from an independent company became more likely.

The availability of increasing amounts of such BMI music on the radio coincided at first with the growing affluence of the general public following World War II, and then later with the first of the

---

[11] BMI Pamphlet of 1940, quoted by David Dachs in Anything Goes (Indianapolis, New York: Bobbs-Merrill Co., Inc., 1964), p. 219.

"baby boom" teenagers who seem to have been both seekers after--and a target audience for--a music of their own.

The Post-War boom economy helped the record industry immensely. In 1940, record retail sales were $48 million. By 1946, sales had quadrupled to nearly $200 million, and by 1957, they had doubled again to $400 million.[12] Part of this enormous growth in consumer acceptance was because of the introduction of the LP and the 45 discs, which offered greater fidelity and more convenience in handling and playing than the old 78s. Part was also due to new marketing methods, such as mail order record clubs, rack jobbing in stores, and discount record shops and departments.[13] Beginning as a new business in the mid-1950s, rack-jobbing expanded to account for a third of all record dollar sales in 1963.[14] Rack jobbers even developed a record vending machine.[15] Record club and discount store sales have also increased, although not as spectacularly.

As well as new marketing techniques, the record industry enjoyed the growth of two specialized markets in the 1950s. One was the growth of jukeboxes. There had, of course, been jukeboxes that played 78s, but the new, smaller 45s allowed jukeboxes to hold more selections and afforded better fidelity. By 1962, jukebox operators were buying 49 million 45s and LPs a year, and were easily the record

---

[12] Sidney Schemel and M. William Krasilovsky, This Business of Music (New York: Billboard Publishing Co., 1964), p. XVI.

[13] Ibid. [14] Ibid.

[15] "Supermarket Disk Vending Machine," Billboard, April 18, 1960, p. 3.

industry's best customer.[16]

The other specialized market had grown to become the record industry's next best customer: the teenager. In the late 1950s and early 1960s, teenagers had earnings and allowances of between nine and ten billion dollars yearly.[17] With that money, they became major consumers of records and transistor radios. The nonbreakability, ease of carrying, and small size of the 45 rpm record, coupled with its introduction just shortly before the great rise in rhythm and blues and other (primarily) BMI music may have given teenagers of the time the feeling that the 45 rpm disc was the medium for their own music, whereas the LP was for "adult" music. Some of the early independent companies never released LPs, so that their artists' performances were available only on 45s or the increasingly obsolete 78s. Tastes and artist popularity changed so rapidly that producing 12 songs for an LP instead of two for a single was financially risky.

In an effort to assure the acceptance of its 45 rpm format, RCA offered the cheapest possible record players, including one widely-sold model that plugged into a TV-set phono-jack, and had no amplifier or speaker of its own. The low price of such units probably also helped to meld the teenager with the 45 rpm record industry.[18]

---

[16] Dachs, Anything Goes, p. 137.

[17] "Teenage Population Boom is Disk Industry Boon," from Cash Box, quoted in Dachs, Anything Goes, p. 30.

[18] According to Quaal and Martin's Broadcast Management, the teenage population in the U.S. "is expanding three times faster than the total population. Teenagers have a spendable income of some thirteen billion dollars annually. They own one-fifth of the automobiles and spend a billion and a half dollars a year on entertainment......By 1970 teenagers will constitute one fifth of all the people in the country and

Radio Audience and Radio Industry Trends Prior to Top 40

Audiences and Ratings Services

Radio audience trends

In the immediate Post War years, Americans demonstrated that radio as it had been before and even during the war was as much in demand as ever. Tens of millions of new receivers were produced yearly, and almost 97 percent of all U.S. homes had a radio. Revenues from sale of time climbed steadily, and so did the number of network affiliates. But after 1948, television began its great era of expansion, which became even more accelerated in 1952 when the FCC lifted its "freeze" on new TV licenses. With more and more listeners becoming viewers, radio ratings and revenues both dropped. Between 1948 and 1952, average ratings of network radio's ten most popular programs were cut almost exactly in half. As a result, by 1952, television's yearly revenue figures were almost equal to those that radio had enjoyed in 1948, as will be demonstrated later.

Television, obviously, was the greatest factor in the decrease in American radio audiences in the early 1950s, but there were other reasons. As has already been shown, the audience itself was changing, in composition by age groups, in life-style and place-of-residence, and in the amount of money and time it had to spend on entertainment media. Radio broadcasters, and especially network-connected radio broadcasters, were understandably slow in grasping the significance of

---

their annual spending power at that time is predicted at about twenty-one billion dollars." Ward L. Quaal and Leo A. Martin, Broadcast Management (New York: Hastings House, 1968, p. 72.

some of these changes since they had for so long been accustomed to a relatively stable and well-defined population using the radio medium in an also stable and well-defined manner. The panic of the early and middle 1950s was a result of a superficial understanding of how audiences were using radio and TV. Superficially, it appeared that audience gains for TV had been made almost directly as a result of losses from radio. As it concerned evening network radio in direct competition with evening network television, the superficial judgment was generally correct. But almost everywhere else, radio was holding its own or even improving its audiences in some cases. Radio sets continued to sell. National and local spot sales continued to rise even as network revenues dropped. Stations programming music and news continued to hold or even improve their ratings, especially during daytime hours. In time, all of these facts would become evident, but in the early and mid 1950s, these and other changes concerning radio's audiences were under-reported and under-interpreted. With hindsight, it is quite easy to see the trends developing, but at the time, with glamorous television expanding even more rapidly than radio had, it is understandable that the majority of radio broadcasters were more absorbed by the bad news than the good.

Program preference trends

As was pointed out earlier, in the late 40s and early 50s, both programs and advertisers were moving to television. For a time, there were a number of "simulcast" programs--that is, programs which were aired at the same time on both radio and TV. In other cases, the audio portion of a TV program was recorded for radio and played at a later time. Neither of these were long-lived measures, however, as prime-time radio audience continued to become prime-time television audiences. Putting TV programs on radio did not bring people back to nighttime radio, but only succeeded in cutting program production costs.

When radio's top personalities moved their shows to television, taking much of the radio audience with them, the program preferences of the audience that remained to radio became of crucial importance. In the early 50s, when television was not yet available in many parts of the country, it was natural to find program preferences very much as they had been in the 1940s. But as set penetration continued to increase as the 1950s went on, the preferences of radio's audience changed.

Even before television became the dominant prime-time medium, there were program preference surveys which, with hindsight, pointed to the ultimate solution radio would find.

In 1944, NBC began a study of its 9:00 a.m. to noon network program schedule in an effort to see if different offerings would attract a larger audience. The research was directed primarily at women, and was most interested in the reasons for non-listening. The study found about a third of the female radio audience who listened regularly to the serials that were the networks' main concentration, another third who listened to other programming and another third who did not listen at all. The report urged the networks and local stations to pay most attention to these who were listening to other fare instead of soap opera, and to try to win them with programming that was soothing, cheerful, and diverting, rather than suspenseful or tense.

Personalization and human interest were found to be strong appeals, as was the availability of useful (but concise) concrete information. Of all standard program fare, music was the most desired.[19]

In 1948, the NBC radio network launched an investigation of urban teenage listening habits. A survey of 1,242 teenagers in New York, Chicago, Philadelphia and Pittsburgh was made in the ensuing year by the Gilbert Youth Research Organization, using high school and college students as the pollsters. In 1949, NBC released the report, titled "Urban Teen-agers as Radio Listeners and Customers." After pointing out that teenagers had a buying power of six billion dollars, the report went on to list 64% of both boys and girls as having radios of their own, to which they listened most often between 6:30 and 7:30 p.m. (pre-TV). Generally, boys favored comedy programs and girls favored popular music. Specifically, the survey ranked "Your Hit Parade" as eighth in popularity with 13-to-15-year olds, second among 16- and 17-year-olds, and first among 18- and 19-year-olds, among both boys and girls.[20]

In 1953, a study of young (6 to 17 years old) listening as it had been in Champaign County, Illinois in 1949, was published.[21] The survey area included Champaign and Urbana, 19 villages, and rural farm area, and as such reflected a much more rural audience than in the NBC

---

[19]Paul F. Lazarsfeld and Helen Dinerman, "Research for Action," in Communications Research, ed. by Paul F. Lazarsfeld and Frank Stanton (New York: Harper & Bros., 1949), pp. 107-08.

[20]"Tastes of the Teens," Newsweek, 33 (May 9, 1949), 57.

[21]Donald G. Hileman, "The Young Radio Audience: A Study of Listening Habits," Journalism Quarterly, 30 (1953), 37-43.

study. Television was not available in 1949 to the 377 youngsters whose diaries comprised the sample. The study showed that peak listening periods were due to one or two specific programs,[22] that girls listened more often than boys (and to specific programs)[23] and that age had more bearing on listening to a specific program type than either sex or area of residence, which would seem to coincide with the NBC survey which showed Your Hit Parade increasing in popularity among urban teenagers when age was the only variable.[24] But with the rural and suburban Illinois sample, news, religious, and musical programs were notably absent from the list of favorites. This may have been partly caused by the younger median age of the sample, but was more likely the result of the absence of these programs on the radio dial. Virtually all of the programs selected as favorites were network programs. In some cases, they were received through a local affiliate, while in others they came by tuning a 50,000 watt Chicago network affiliate. The survey generally showed tuning to particular programs rather than to stations as is common today, but it did point up that listeners near the local station were more likely to tune there for network programs while rural listeners tuned the Chicago station.[25]

The absence of "Your Hit Parade" or any similar program from the list of 25 favorite programs among this young rural audience at the same time it was eighth, second or first among urban teenagers in the NBC survey is notable, and serves to show that in 1949 there apparently was a real difference in music program preferences between urban and rural teenage audiences--a difference which is all but gone today.

---

[22] Ibid., p. 38. [23] Ibid., p. 39. [24] Ibid., p. 40. [25] Ibid.

In 1951, The English Journal published the results of a survey taken by a Metuchen, New Jersey tenth-grade English teacher (Lieber Anker) who wanted to discover "how much of an inroad television is actually making upon the school schedule." The teacher's main object was to see how 84 sophomore boys and girls (32 college-preparatory and 52 nonacademic) were responding to literature content since television had become available (Metuchen, New Jersey is only about 25 miles west of Manhattan, and virtually all New York City radio and TV signals are available there). After showing that television was indeed of vital interest to sophomore English students, the teacher/author appended a list of favorite radio and TV programs, apparently not rank-ordered.

Favorite radio programs were: Make Believe Ballroom, Home-Town Frolic, Lux Radio Theater, Requestfully Yours, My Friend Irma, The Lone Ranger, Arthur Godfrey's Talent Scouts, Your Hit Parade, and Jack Benny's program.

Favorite television programs were Texaco Star Theater (Milton Berle), Arthur Godfrey's Talent Scouts, Paul Whiteman's Teen-Age Club, Lights Out, Toast of the Town (Ed Sullivan), Cavalcade of Stars, and ahead of all others, sports programs.[26]

It is instructive to note in the list of radio programs that at least three (and possibly four) of the nine favorite shows were popular music programs. In the television list of seven favorites, one program was primarily popular music while two of the others (Godfrey and Sullivan) placed emphasis on popular music and performers.

---

[26] Lieber Anker, "Television, Here I Come!", English Journal, 40 (April, 1951), 218-20.

New York area teenagers (including Metuchen, New Jersey) in 1951 had seven channels of VHF television available, plus eight 50,000 watt AM stations (seven of which are easily receivable in Metuchen) and a 5,000 watt AM station at 570 which is also easily receivable. From the great variety of programming thus available, it seems significant that popular music programs were selected as often as they were.

In 1954, Broadcasting published a report of an audience study of the Tulsa, Oklahoma market for the years 1950 through 1952 whose purpose was to discover the types of radio programs which could best withstand the onslaught of television.[27] The report analyzes the results of seven city-wide surveys, in which a total of more than 240,000 calls were made.[28] Tulsa had six AM radio outlets, and their one VHF TV outlet during the period went on the air in the fall of 1949. The report, which covered all stations (not just music stations) says:

> As television became available more hours per day, and regular programs were offered for viewing first in the evening, then in the afternoon, and finally in the morning, the radio program preferences reacted with each successive expansion of television service. In each case there was a shift to music. When plotted against a time base it is possible to date the arrival of television in each segment of the day by noting the upturn in the music "share of audience."[29]

The report went on to show that the rating for music shows increased while total sets-in-use was declining generally. While there was an

---

[27]Storm Whaley, "Music on Radio Holds Own Against TV," Broadcasting, February 1, 1954, p. 82.

[28]The size of this figure indicates that the method used was telephone-coincidental.

[29]Whaley, "Music on Radio Holds Own Against TV," p. 82.

attempt to determine if the type of music had any bearing on music programming's success against TV, "no significant pattern was apparent."[30]

A study a year later by Advertest Research among 756 New Yorkers owning both a radio and a TV also demonstrated the power of the "music-and-news" format in maintaining audiences against television competition.[31] The interviews found 70% of the radio audience describing music as "very important," plus another 17% finding it "somewhat important." News was listed as "very important" by 62.4%, after which came sports with 22.9%. The usual staples of network radio--drama, comedy and education--did not, even when combined, equal the popularity of music or news among the radio audience. This suggested to Advertest that the radio audience was getting enough drama, comedy and education from sources other than radio (primarily TV), while TV was not supplying enough music and news.[32]

The survey also asked interviewees to describe their favorite programs. Advertest found that although New York had had TV for six years when the survey was made in late 1954, 60% of all listeners (all had both radio and TV) listened regularly to radio favorites. However, the top favorite was not a network radio program but Make Believe Ballroom on music-and-news WNEW, which polled 13.9% in first place as against 6.7% for the second choice, the CBS network Arthur Godfrey show.[33]

---

[30] Ibid.

[31] "Radio's Hold on Music and News (TV Weaknesses) Reflected in Major Advertest Audience Study," Variety, 197 (January 19, 1955), p. 24.

[32] Ibid. [33] Ibid., p. 40.

Advertest also asked the radio-and-TV owners if they were planning to continue listening to the radio in spite of increased TV programming. More than 80% said they would continue radio listening. Of that number, 39% said their main reason for continuing was that they could listen "while doing other things, and don't have to sit and watch."[34] Second in importance was the availability on radio of music-and-news. Other reasons for keeping radio were relaxation, companionship, and portability.[35]

The Advertest study as reported does not make mention of the demographic makeup of their 756-person New York sample, except to call the interviewees "radio and tv owners." Although radio ownership among teenagers was already high in 1955 (85% of all high school students owned radios by 1957)[36]--a sample not including many teenagers seems likely in the Advertest study. With this in mind, and with the results of the Tulsa survey at hand, it is easy to make a case that music-and-news, which was the format forerunner of Top 40, was already an accepted and increasingly popular program preference among urban audiences in the early to mid-1950s, and was especially favored by urban teenagers.

Listener types

In November 1954 NBC commissioned the Bureau of Applied Social Research of Columbia University to conduct a study to determine the place of radio in the television era. The resulting 156-page report

---

[34] Ibid. [35] Ibid.

[36] "Media Vie for Teen-Agers' Time," Broadcasting, March 25, 1957, p. 39.

titled "Future for Radio" was excerpted and condensed by Broadcasting in January of 1956.[37] One of the quoted chapters began "All leisure-time media and particularly broadcast media are peculiarly vulnerable to encroachments on their time."[38] Later, the report queried, "Where is radio to find the time to survive?" and then proceeded to describe the listening of a salesgirl and a housewife, who listened to radio for only a quarter or a half-hour a day, while they were primarily doing something else. The housewife had turned on the radio for "just soft music, low volume. I don't know what station, perhaps WLW, but I can't say for sure . . . No special program, just music and news. They come on and I don't know what station or what recording it is most of the time [but] I always enjoy music when I work or rest."[39]

The NBC report asked its readers to

> imagine millions of people behaving in such ways--which are random with respect to time or program or station, or random in all three respects. Then among these people the broadcaster is getting not a large bloc of assured time and attention from a loyal, regular audience. Instead he is getting a kind of low-order probability, say a nearly random chance of about 1/100th of any one individual's listening in any one hour to his station. Yet the total available "traffic" is enormous, both in terms of the numbers of people coming in and out of the radio audiences like this and also in terms of the number of hours per day, week, and year available for them to do so. The cumulative possibilities are huge.[40]

Turning from the random listener, the report then described what it termed a "reference" listener, who tuned in at specific times for specific features (such as news). The reference service function of

---

[37]"Radio and the Fight for Time," Broadcasting, January 16, 1956, pp. 84-86.

[38]Ibid., p. 84. [39]Ibid. [40]Ibid.

radio was compared to the classified advertising and weather maps in a newspaper.

The report went on to equate the random and the reference listener as part of the same short-listening phenomenon, and concluded that radio would have to find ways to serve such listeners in the aggregate, without actually needing much time from any one individual.[41] The primary suggestion in this direction was to provide programs that did not call for much specific attention to radio, since radio was the one medium that could accompany almost every type of activity. In the report's words, "the one medium everyone feels so sorry for is in fact the only medium with large and realistic opportunities for expansion outside of the orbit of the leisure-time squeeze."[42] Where radio once had been a leisure-time "reward" after a day's work, television was now occupying that role. Radio had come to be viewed less as a treat than as a kind of "companion" to some other activity. As the report put it, "It is one of the paradoxes that the less people pay attention to radio, the more useful it becomes!"[43] The report also made a reference to the effectiveness of music-and-news in serving the otherwise-occupied listener:

> Note, incidentally, that the long hours of listening are associated with a certain kind of programming (disc jockeys) suitable for the activity. . . . Thus, radio's expansion possibilities in the direction of shared time or multiple-activity listening are intimately connected to its programming, which, with the exception of disc jockeys, has probably not really responded to the opportunity.[44]

The quoted report also mentioned the increasing availability of radio sets, both in homes and out-of-home. It pointed out that the popularity

---

[41] Ibid., p. 85. [42] Ibid. [43] Ibid., p. 86. [44] Ibid.

of clock radios would not only mean more listeners, but listeners in a different room and at a different time. In regard to car radios, the report concluded:

> The generation that grew up in the 1920s or before treated cars with awe and respect, as difficult to drive and dangerous not to give full attention to. Similarly, radio listening was a full-time occupation. Naturally, the two were not mixed. In the current generation, a not uncommon pattern is, as one young California woman put it, for the radio "to go on with the ignition." Not only are automobiles treated as more routine conveniences, but especially radios are becoming routine accompaniments for any and all kinds of activities. . . .[45]

In 1955, the Radio-Electronics--TV Manufacturers Association (RETMA) statistical department released figures showing set production of various types of radios between 1947 and 1954. While the general trend for the span was down, owing mostly to the phenomenal number of radios bought immediately after the War, the acceptance of "specialty" sets was up. The Association's charts showed an increasing share for clock radios each year since 1951, and a steadily increasing demand for auto radios. The projection for 1955 was that the number of car radios produced would be double the previous year's output.[46]

Listening trends--time and place

As has been shown, in the early and mid-50s, the music-and-news format had become the one that most closely adapted itself to the new ways in which radio was being used. To understand why, it is necessary to look more closely at the times and places radio has come to be most used.

---

[45] Ibid.

[46] James D. Secrest (Exec. V.P., Radio-Electronics-TV Mfrs. Assn.), "Radios, and More Radios," Broadcasting, September 19, 1955, p. 187.

In July of 1953, the station representative firm Henry I. Christal Co. began releasing parts of a report conducted by Alfred Politz Research, Inc., and commissioned by the eleven stations Christal then represented.[47] The report studied radio entirely in TV markets, and was based on 4,985 personal interviews which were representative of the nearly 62 million people fifteen years old or over then living in those TV markets. Of the sample, 72% had TV sets, but 95% had one or more working radios, 32% had two sets, and 23% had three to seven sets. Fifty-two percent, or about 32 million people, had radio-equipped cars in 1953. The home sets were found to be scattered throughout the house. Thirty-three percent were still in the living room, where radio had been the family gathering-point for many years, but 31% were now found in bedrooms. Another 23% were in kitchens, and the rest were in miscellaneous locations. Seventy-five percent of all the home sets were either table models (64%) or portables (12%). In addition to giving the location of the set, the report also gave the location of the listener at various times of day. During breakfast, for instance, 81% listened in the kitchen as against only 7% in the dining room. But during supper, only 65% listened in the kitchen while 19% listened in the dining room.[48]

The Politz/Christal study also went on to study radio listening outside the home and to chide the ratings services for ignoring this segment of the audience:

---

[47] "Politz Study Affirms Penetration of Radio," Broadcasting, July 27, 1953, pp. 31-32.

[48] Ibid., p. 31.

> Radio's out-of-home audience is large enough and important enough to constitute a major advertising medium. . . . But advertisers have never known the true values of this audience. The exclusion of the audience from the regular ratings has reduced out-of-home listening to a less important position than it should have in evaluating the medium. As these data show, in the single time segment between breakfast and lunch, 26% of the listeners--almost 4,000,000 people--are in radio's uncounted audience outside the home.[49]

The careful methods and documentation employed in the Politz Christal study helped it to become one of the landmark audience studies of radio "crisis days." It was one of the first to point believably to the ways in which radio listening had changed, especially with regard to set location. Such new information was much appreciated by station owners, reps and advertisers alike, who were by now grasping at straws to find out if radio were going to survive.

Later studies confirmed the growing importance of the out-of-home listener. A study released by The Pulse, Inc. in 1954 compared summer and winter out-of-home listening in fifteen major markets and concluded that the expected increase in out-of-home listening was not confined to summer months but was occurring in the winter period as well. The average gain in out-of-home listeners between the summer of 1952 and that of 1953 was about 0.25 percentage points, while the gain between the winter of 1952 and the winter of 1953 was about 0.3 percentage points. These gains amounted to an increase in the size of the out-of-home audience, however, of from 15 to 26% in summer and from 12% to 22% in winter.[50]

---

[49] Ibid., p. 32.

[50] "What Will the Out-of-Home Audience Add to Radio in Summer Months?" Sponsor, March 8, 1954, p. 57.

In a "Study of Qualitative Factors" among the "Out-of-Home Audience", Pulse found that 55.5% of the summer, New York market out-of-home audience was between 20 and 44 years old, while only 12% was between 14 and 19 years old. In summer, about 60% of the out-of-home audience was male and 40% female, while in winter those figures were reversed. Over 61% of the out-of-home audience reported summer listening in cars, as compared to 55.6% listening in winter. The number of radio-equipped cars, The Pulse noted, had risen from 50% in 1948 to 60% in 1952. Twenty-five percent of out-of-home summer listening was done at work, while only 5% was reported done with portable sets.[51]

In May of 1954, The Pulse reported that not only had out-of-home listening risen 14% over the 1952 level, but that for the first time, the level of out-of-home listening was unchanged between summer and winter figures. The growth in out-of-home audience had come not only from auto listening, but also from listening at work, in public places, and during visits, according to Pulse.[52]

A study by Forest Whan of Kansas State College for WHO, Des Moines published in 1954, made the following points about the automobile radio audience in Iowa:

> About two-thirds of the women and three fourths of both interviewed and diary-recording men (in families owning cars equipped with radios) ride in those cars on an average weekday.
> Men are more likely to ride than women.
> Better than half of the riders use the car radio each day, with younger riders more likely to use it.

---

[51] "How Does Out of Home Audience Break Down by Qualitative Factors?" Sponsor, March 8, 1954, p. 60.

[52] "Radio Audience Up Outside the Home," Broadcasting, May 3, 1954, p. 38.

> About one-third of all riders use the car radio within the first five miles.
>
> Better than half use it within the first 25 miles.
>
> Three out of four use it within the first 50 miles.
>
> Approximately 11 of 12 use the radio when riding more than 100 miles on a given day.
>
> Place of residence (urban or rural) seems to have little consistent effect on the use of the car radio.[53]

The importance of a study such as the preceding one is not so much in the now-outdated figures, but in the fact that at the time, very little was known about the behavior of the auto radio audience. The auto radio audience had never before appeared to be a significant part of the total radio listenership, and so there had not seemed to be much reason to measure car listening. By 1954, the trends were obvious. In September of 1954, A. C. Nielsen announced the availability of national automobile audience ratings, and promptly signed CBS radio to a two-year contract.[54] The following April, CBS ran a two-page advertisement in Broadcasting with the words "Extra" repeated twice in large type, and with the following text:

> EXTRA radio listeners every hour of the day and night--Nielsen's now counting the audience in cars! His first reports to CBS Radio show that motorists add as much as 33 percent to the radio audience. And to the advertiser these listeners come absolutely free. When you tell your story to the 75 million radios people have at home, you get the 26 million sets in cars EXTRA![55]

CBS, which in 1954 had been forced to cut nighttime radio rates to the daytime level, ran the advertisement quoted above in the same month in which NBC announced plans for Monitor (which essentially was a network

---

[53]"Radio Lives with TV in Iowa--Whan," Broadcasting, January 11, 1954, p. 36.

[54]"CBS Buys Nielsen Auto Radio Report," Broadcasting, September 20, 1954, p. 50.

[55]Advertisement in Broadcasting, April 18, 1955, pp. 12, 13.

spot-carrier , designed for appeal to both the "reference" and the "random" listeners). CBS meanwhile was continuing to sell full programs that generally required "foreground" attentiveness. The CBS advertisement should be read with this in mind. Note that the 33 percent increase that auto listening is claimed to add to audience levels is not necessarily claimed for CBS programming.

In September 1954 A. C. Nielsen released a report showing that the size of the early morning (6:00 to 8:00 a.m.) radio audience had climbed 25% since 1950, and that in the summer of 1954, daytime audiences were larger than nighttime radio audiences.[56] A month later, Dr. Sydney Roslow, director of The Pulse, Inc., announced that out-of-home summer listening added an average 23.8% to the at-home audience, an increase of 6.5% over three years. The size of this "plus" audience had caused Pulse to decide to issue combined in-home and out-of-home ratings in future reports, beginning in October, 1954. Dr. Roslow also made it clear that applying an arbitrary across-the-board percentage figure to in-home listening to derive a both in-home and out-of-home figure would almost always result in a serious rating error, because the percent added by the out-of-home audience "varies widely from station to station."

> In New York, for example, the "plus" represented by out-of-home listening averaged 27.1% for all stations. Yet, for one broadcaster, it came to 10% while for another 50%.[57]

What this meant was that some types of programming were better suited to

---

[56]"Morning Radio Up 25% Since 1950," Broadcasting, September 20, 1954, p. 52.

[57]"Out-of-Home Listening Sets Record," Broadcasting, October 11, 1954, p. 32.

out-of-home listening than others. As has been shown, the major progra preference trend was to music-and-news.

Also in October of 1954, the Mutual Network released the first information from what came to be called the "MBS-Ward" study, which abbreviation stood for "The Mutual Broadcasting System-Ward Daily Livin Habits Survey." The study was designed to show prospective advertisers (for the first time) just what activities the average listener was engaging in between 6:00 a.m. and 11:00 p.m. each day, so that products could be sold at a time when the listener was most likely to think about using them. The survey showed, for instance, that gasoline and tire accounts would do better to buy morning and evening drive times than the typical 6:00 p.m. newcast they had been sponsoring. It also pointed out to prospective food advertisers that while buys had traditionally been made throughout the day, only 3% of women radio listeners were actually preparing food between 2:00 and 3:00 p.m., whereas 30% were doing so between 11:00 a.m. and noon.[58] Again, the interesting point about such studies was that they were offering new, otherwise unavailable information on the changes in radio listening. The MBS-Ward study, by emphasizing activities while listening, was a step in the direction of the breakouts in current radio ratings which count listeners in terms of the number of buyers for various product categories.

In December of 1954, the Cunningham & Walsh advertising agency issued the final report on its seventh annual "Videotown" survey. For

---

[58] "Pinpointing the Radio Audience: New MBS-Ward Study Shows How," Sponsor, October 4, 1954, p. 46.

the first time, the 1954 report included a radio set census among both TV and non-TV homes.

Cunningham & Walsh had been documenting the growing impact of television in a suburb of New York City (New Brunswick, New Jersey) since 1948. In past years, they had sought to discover what effect TV ownership was having on radio listening. They found morning radio listening in TV homes rising from 10% in 1951 to 15% in 1952, while in non-TV homes, morning listening went from 11% to 21% in the same span. A smaller rise in both groups had occurred in afternoon radio listening. The report also showed the sharp drop in radio listening in the evening in TV homes, and the slight dip radio also suffered in non-TV home evening listening.[59] By 1954, morning radio listening among all people in TV homes had gone from the 15% of 1952 to 23%, while afternoon and evening listening had gained slightly.[60]

The radio set census which was included in the final 1954 Videotown report showed TV homes averaging two radios each, while non-TV homes had only 1.7 radios. Additionally, in multiple-radio TV homes, radios were about evenly distributed among the living room, the bedroom and the kitchen. But in single-radio homes with TV, 43% had the radio in the kitchen, 32% in the living room, and 18% in the bedroom. In non-TV homes, 75% still had the radio in the living room, with the other 25% locating it in the kitchen. The report said "This change in placement of the radio set helps explain the increase in the number

---

[59] "Growing Up with TV in Videotown, U.S.A.," Broadcasting, October 5, 1953, p. 88.

[60] "The Lesson of 'Videotown': More Time for Radio and TV," Broadcasting, October 11, 1954, p. 27.

listening to radio in TV homes."[61] Expanding on that point, it seems that the "heavy media user" who would become a commonplace entity later had been caught by Cunningham & Walsh in the act of planting more radio around his house to support his habit. But the migration of the radio set caused by TV was clear: radio was supplanted in the living room by the TV set, whereupon it went to the kitchen. After that, it also appeared in the bedroom(s).

In the fall of 1956, the advertising agency Batten, Barton, Durstine & Osborne released a report titled "A Discussion of Radio" which listed five areas in which radio continued to be vital: 1, to reach the majority of housewives in the daytime; 2, to reach teenagers and young people in and out of the home; 3, to reach non-TV owners; 4, for the speed with which it could cover news; and 5, for its ability to appeal to specialized audiences.[62] The report also noted radio's shift away from "program-listening" to "station listening":

> While it is a universal medium, reaching almost everybody at some time during the day and in the course of the broadcast week, no more than a small percentage of these people is ever tuned in to a particular program at any one time (5%).[63]

The report noted that this trend meant that advertisers would have to schedule their messages with greater frequency in order to be sure of reaching the audience.[64]

In the mid-1950s, with radios proliferating in homes, cars, and

---

[61] "C&W Count Shows Videotown's Radios," Broadcasting, December 13, 1954, p. 37.

[62] "BBDO Releases Major Study on Radio in Television Era," Broadcasting, October 1, 1956, p. 27.

[63] Ibid. [64] Ibid.

at the beach, they also began to turn up in much more unlikely places. In 1955, The Huffman Manufacturing Co. of Dayton, Ohio placed the Huffy-Radiobike on the market. The built-in portable set was claimed to pull in stations 100 miles distant. The battery was carried in the luggage rack, and the set itself was shockproof.[65] By 1957, do-it-yourself bicycle radios had appeared, and Bob Tait, owner of Tait's Southdale Square Super Value [grocery] Store equipped 18 of his supermarket's shopping carts with the sets and claimed a nationwide first for the service.[66]

Ratings trends

Development of radio ratings services

The bicycle- and the supermarket-cart radios that appeared in the mid-1950s were just two of the many "new" audiences that the ratings services found themselves faced with. For years, the A. C. Nielsen Company, the CAB (Cooperative Analysis of Broadcasting), and C. E. Hooper had all provided national network radio ratings. In addition, the Hooper company developed local ratings for individual stations, using the telephone coincidental technique. In 1946, the CAB retired from the ratings field, after also having adopted Hooper's technique. In 1950, Hooper sold its national ratings services to the A. C. Nielsen Co. and agreed not to compete in national ratings for five years, during which time the company concentrated on market ratings instead. The Pulse, Inc., which had been founded in 1941, in the 1950s was issuing

---

65 (No title), Sponsor, August 8, 1955, p. 112.

66 "Radio in Rare Form," Broadcasting, March 11, 1957, p. 105.

monthly local major-market radio reports. In September of 1953, Trendex entered the local radio rating field in 45 major markets.[67] On February 1, 1954 Hooper announced that it was resuming radio ratings in the top 50 markets after having been dropped there earlier by subscribing stations. One week later, A. C. Nielsen announced that it was also entering the local radio ratings field, using its Audimeter device along with diary-keeping. The projected "Nielsen Station Index" reports, which were not to include automobile or other out-of-home listening, would provide listening data in terms of homes (rather than percentages) for 3-different-sized geographical areas surrounding the station sites: a 50 mile radius including most radio listening except to the most powerful stations, a "total" area including all listening to powerful stations, and a "metro" area as defined by the U.S. Census. C. E. Hooper countered the same day with announcement of an automatic "Hooperecorder" that was supposed to be even faster and more accurate than Nielsen's Audimeters.[68]

In July, 1954, Dr. Sydney Roslow, director of The Pulse, Inc., announced their own instantaneous ratings device, to be known as DAX. As with the Hooper device, it transmitted tuning information immediately over lines to a central office.[69]

In September of 1954, CBS became the first to sign for A. C.

67"Trendex Enters Radio Rating Field," Broadcasting, September 14, 1953, p. 48.

68"Nielsen Plans Local Rating Report," Broadcasting, February 8, 1954, p. 31.

69"New Instantaneous Rating System, 'DAX' To Be Offered by The Pulse," Broadcasting, July 19, 1954, p. 44.

Nielsen's new national auto listening report, mentioned earlier. The following month, Nielsen announced completion of an "improvement plan" to recognize in its national radio ratings the effects of multiple-set listening (including auto-listening), and of population shifts.[70]

In March of 1955, C. E. Hooper and ARB announced a partnership arrangement whereby each firm would assist the other by providing pooled talent in research, production and sales while remaining fiscally separate. In addition, ARB, which had contemplated expanding into local radio ratings agreed to limit itself to TV, while Hooper, which had begun TV reports, agreed to confine itself to radio.[71]

In January of 1956, the top executives of Hooper, Pulse, and Nielsen joined together to explain to advertising agency timebuyers and media department executives that any one of the ratings services was ready and able to supply audience composition data upon request, and at extra expense. Agency people had previously been critical of the services because such data were thought to be unavailable.[72]

In July of 1957, Sindlinger & Co., which was then measuring weekly attention to all media nationally, announced that for the week of June 23-29, 1957, 35.3% of all hours spent listening to radio were spent listening to auto radios. In the same week, total radio listening by those over twelve years of age nearly matched TV viewing: 57.4% had

---

[70]"Nielsen Completes 'Improvement Plan,'" Broadcasting, October 18, 1954, p. 54.

[71]"ARB, Hooper Divide Radio-TV Ratings as Pact Involving Stock Takes Effect," Broadcasting, March 21, 1955, p. 31.

[72]"Audience Composition Data Available, Hooper, Pulse, Nielsen Tell N.Y. Group," Broadcasting, January 23, 1956, p. 33.

listened to radio in the week, 57.6% had watched TV.[73]

By 1959, a study by the Adam Young representative firm showed that the leading station in 39 out of the top 60 markets was an independent rather than a network affiliate, its figures being based on Pulse data.[74]

Criticism of ratings services

When 39 of the top 60 markets were shown to be dominated in 1959 by an independent rather than a network station, it was quite natural for both the affiliated stations and the networks to claim foul play, and their first target was the ratings services. Actually, ratings had been under attack for many years for a number of reasons, some relating to discrepancies between the results shown by competing services, and others in regard to what were usually temporary and localized aberrations. In the early 1950s, however, as first television made inroads on the nighttime network radio audience and then independent stations began to erode and eventually overtake the daytime lead of network affiliates, the outcry increased.

Of the several companies in the radio ratings field, the A. C. Nielsen organization received by far the heaviest criticism. In retrospect, it seems that some of the criticism was deserved while other protests were merely "sour grapes" after publication of the truth. One of the often-criticized weakness of the Nielsen reports was their infrequency outside of the best markets, which in a volatile radio

---

[73] "Missing Measurements," Broadcasting, July 8, 1957, p. 5.

[74] "Indies Rate High in Top Markets," Sponsor, August 8, 1959, p. 42.

programming situation made them inaccurate quite soon although they (often unfortunately) continued to be used. Another weakness was the company's reluctance to include out-of-home listening for several years when this part of the audience was obviously increasing rapidly. But however conservative the company was in regard to changing listening habits, it remained in high regard for its <u>business</u> practices. While other services could easily be accused of being "bought" because their surveys were often individually-ordered by the station which seemed always to turn out to be the highest-rated in the market, Nielsen always rated all the stations in a market and had no special financial ties to any of them since they derived the bulk of their revenue from marketing studies. (Of course, a station was not allowed to use a Nielsen rating to its sales advantage without subscribing to the service.) The trust in which the Nielsen service was held may have accounted for its popularity in spite of infrequent reports--and it certainly accounted for the intensity of the criticism heaped upon the company when a station showed up badly.

The first two "Nielsen Station Index" reports, which covered listening in Los Angeles and Philadelphia homes prior to March 1955 when the studies were issued, were criticized in both cities for showing generally far less audience than reported by other services. In some cases, prominent stations were shown with audiences too small to measure.[75]

In the week following the issuance of the first two NSI reports,

---

[75]"Stations Protest NSI Data, Claim Radio is Sabotaged," <u>Broadcasting</u>, March 14, 1955, p. 32.

the Station Representatives Association's research committee met to examine the ratings books and concluded tentatively that the first two reports showed "evidence of instability of the measurement due primarily to inadequate sample size." Nielsen spokesmen answered that their probability sample was meticulously chosen, that they were supplying satisfying new data to radio, and that they were not plotting to short-change radio in favor of TV.[76] The company also chose that time to release its first auto listening report, which was described earlier. Some of the deplored "missing" audience was thus restored by adding the auto report to the NSI report.[77] However, the "Auto Plus" report supplied only overall auto listening levels for a market, and was not broken down by stations. Pulse figures cited earlier have shown the possible inaccuracy of this system.

In April 1955 Sponsor magazine attempted to answer its question "NSI: Can It Measure Today's Radio Audience?" Two important points in the controversy emerged in this symposium. First, it was shown that reporting homes in the NSI were not confined to metropolitan areas as were those of Hooper and Pulse, but reached far beyond the city.[78] Hooper and Pulse eventually were forced to expand their samples out of the city as well, and the results to Top 40 stations were sometimes emphatic, as will be shown later.

---

[76] "SRA Joins Battle Over NSI Report," Broadcasting, March 21, 1955, p. 32.

[77] "Nielsen Releases First Auto Listening Report," Broadcasting, March 21, 1955, p. 32.

[78] "NSI: Can It Measure Today's Radio Audience?" Sponsor, April 18, 1955, p. 108.

Second, the symposium pointed out a shortcoming of the NSI that even the "Auto Plus" couldn't hope to correct; the increasing tendency toward smaller, battery-operated sets which did not easily adapt themselves to the use of metering equipment or to coincidental diary-keeping.[79]

It is worth noting that at the height of the controversy over the NSI in comparison with other services, Todd Storz's WHB ran a trade ad on the December 5, 1955 front cover of Broadcasting which capitalized on the issue. The ad showed a man holding a "fan" of ratings books, with the caption, "Name your survey! Hooper? Nielsen? Pulse? Trendex? All have WHB FIRST! WHB has run away with Kansas City's radio day!"[80]

In a meeting of agency and ratings executives (mentioned earlier) in which audience composition data were offered by all services including Nielsen, Hooper president James L. Knipe spoke of "the remarkable station managerial ability being demonstrated in so many cities around the country." Although Knipe did not mention WHB by name, it was to stations with WHB's type of management to which he had reference.[81] Knipe went on to say that between 1951 and 1953, stations in major cities cancelled their Hooper service because it showed radio declining during TV's growth period, and that the Hooper ratings did not conceal that impact. But he said the service also did not "'protect

---

[79] Ibid., p. 110.

[80] Front cover ad, Broadcasting, December 5, 1955, p. 1.

[81] "Audience Composition Data Available, Hooper, Pulse, Nielsen Tell N.Y. Group," Broadcasting, January 23, 1956, p. 33.

the lethargic timebuyer' nor 'cover up the deteriorating position of a station, as its programming goes dead on its feet.'"[82] Ratings reports, he went on,

> ". . . are not meant to be soporifics--lulling advertisers to sleep with reports so lacking in sensitivity as to conceal all the progress and retrogression which are continually going on in the station field, especially now that programming is essentially a city-by-city matter rather than a network decision."[83]

The pattern of criticism surrounding the release of the Nielsen Station Index ratings reports continued with the release of the new Nielsen Coverage Service Report No. 2 in December of 1956.[84] Again, the major complaint was the sharp drop in listening when compared with other services or with NCS No. 1 (which had been released four years earlier). Ward Dorrell, vice president and director of research for John Blair & Co. criticized NCS No. 2 because it appeared to him that the data for it had been collected in the same way as for NCS No. 1, even though the characteristics of radio listening had changed enormously in the interim. He was reported as saying that the modern music-and-news programs had listenership but because they were unspectacular and lacked the "single program identity" that characterized network radio shows, listeners would be likely to "fail to mention

---

[82] Ibid. [83] Ibid.

[84] The Nielsen Coverage Service reports did not provide ratings for individual programs or time periods on each station, but instead attempted to show the audience delivered in a station's total coverage area. Maps were provided showing the percentage (from 10% to 100%) of the market's audience that tuned a given station days and/or nights, which revealed the station's general popularity with audiences, rather than program popularity. The results were valid until a station in the market changed format, which happened often in the 1950s.

specific tuning unless interview technique was adapted to fit these new patterns. . . ."[85]

A month later, in January, 1957, the station representative firm Adam Young, Inc. became the first to formally and publicly air its complaints about NCS No. 2, in an analysis titled "NCS--Its Uses and Abuses."[86] Listed below are four limitations reported by Broadcasting from the Young analysis:

> 1. The study was made in March-May 1956 and accordingly is already seven months old--and out of date insofar as many markets are concerned. "While there are markets in which listening patterns have remained relatively stable over long periods of time," the report asserts, "there are also many markets in which the introduction of new program formats, together with intelligent promotion, have changed the entire audience picture in less than six months. . . . In such dynamic areas the validity and consequently the applicability of NCS No. 2 diminishes rapidly with the passage of time."
>
> 2. The 10% cutoff--that is, the practice of crediting a station with coverage of a given county if at least 10% of the radio homes in that county listen to the station at least once a month--appears to be "reasonable," but there are areas where less than 10% coverage is of "great importance" to national advertisers because of the size of the markets involved. Moreover, later audience surveys in certain areas show substantial listenership where NCS No. 2, because of the 10% cutoff, implies none at all.
>
> 3. "Intelligent timebuying requires that advertisers know the size (and in many cases the age and sex) of the audience they reach with their program and/or spot announcement," but "NCS No. 2 does not provide this data. Only regularly scheduled rating surveys (Pulse, Hooper, NSI) supply adequate audience data so necessary to the selection of an effective advertising schedule. Only in those markets which are not regularly surveyed by the various rating services could NCS No. 2 be used as a guide to the relative popularity of competing stations."
>
> 4. NCS No. 2 does not measure out-of-home listening, although "Nielsen itself has stated that the auto-plus audience can amount to an additional 40% bonus to in-home listening." Further,

---

[85] "First Returns from New Nielsen Cause Alarm Among Radio Interests," Broadcasting, December 17, 1956, p. 9.

[86] "Adam Young Claims Flaws in NCS No. 2," Broadcasting, January 21, 1957, p. 44.

"it is not realistic to assume that stations enjoy the same relative popularity with auto listeners as with home listeners, since programming on some stations is geared more to the driver's desires than programming on others."[87]

The first of the Adam Young criticisms of NCS No. 2--its alread being out of date when issued--was echoed in some of the trades advertising placed for the Storz stations in 1957.[88] The first ad of its type showed a man holding a file marked "Nielsen 1956" as he spoke to his secretary, apparently. The caption read, "Toss em! These may be all right for somebody who doesn't know what WDGY has done to Twin Cities radio."[89] The ad did not specifically mention NCS No. 2, but did employ the March 1957 NSI to show how WDGY had risen. However, in June, an ad ran in Sponsor and Broadcasting for Storz's WQAM in which NCS No. 2 was ridiculed by name. The identical ads showed a man in a suit and hat and with an umbrella[90] kneeling on a sandy beach next to a radio and asking "Hasn't anything happened in Miami since March, 1956?* The asterisk referred to "* Date of NCS # 2." The text below the picture detailed the rapid rise of WQAM to dominance and concluded, "Next time somebody quotes NCS # 2 about Miami, yell for a Blair man, or get in touch with WQAM General Manager Jack Sandler."[91]

In July of 1957, Broadcasting reported that ABC (then ABN) was

---

[87] Ibid.

[88] Adam Young then represented Storz's KOWH and WTIX, although the ads were for WDGY and WQAM.

[89] WDGY trades ad, Broadcasting, May 13, 1957, p. 6.

[90] The man so attired became WQAM's trades ads "mascot."

[91] WOAM trades ad: in Sponsor, June 22, 1957, p. 22, and in Broadcasting, June 17, 1957, p. 8.

seriously considering dropping its subscription to Nielsen services, primarily because the network felt the rater short-changed radio in treating out-of-home audiences as a bonus. NBC was thinking of following suit because it too was dissatisfied with "horse and buggy" techniques it said Nielsen was applying to modern radio.[92]

ABC was still denouncing Nielsen radio ratings in 1962 prior to the beginning of Harris House Subcommittee Hearings on the ratings industry in 1963, and the network finally did drop Nielsen service, even though in the meantime Nielsen had announced the expansion (to twice yearly) of its network radio ratings to cover auto and portable set listening.[93] The Nielsen company finally overhauled its radio ratings in March, 1963 by increasing the size of the sample and by building out-of-home listening into each rating report.[94]

In December of 1962, The Pulse, Inc. signed a consent order with the Federal Trade Commission restricting some of its former practices. The service had claimed, for example, to measure all radio listening, but admitted after signing the consent order that it had only listed subscribers.[95] The Pulse was only one of the services accused of either poor methodology or plain fraud by the Harris Subcommittee, whose investigations brought an improvement in the accuracy and fairness of radio ratings.

---

[92] "Closed Circuit," Broadcasting, July, 1957, p. 5.

[93] "Like the Cows, People Do Come Home--Roslow," Broadcasting, June 4, 1962, p. 32.

[94] "Surrounded by Critics, Nielsen Expands Radio Ratings," Broadcasting, March 11, 1963, p. 66.

[95] "Is Pulse Running a Con Game?", Broadcasting, March 25, 1963, p. 44.

Radio Industry Economic Trends

Causes of decreasing radio revenue

Television

By the mid-1950s, much of the radio industry was in serious economic trouble. In 1954, radio time sales failed--for the first time since 1937--to show a customary annual gain. As Broadcasting colorfully described it:

> The experience of radio since the advent of television is the experience of a well-conditioned but cocky boxer who takes an unexpected belt in the jaw: First the stunned surprise, second the instinctive retreat into self-defense to give the mind a chance to clear, third the recovery.
>
> A fighter lives the experience in seconds. Radio has been going through it nearly seven years. There is evidence that at last radio has reached the third stage, with its wits restored and with muscles in its legs instead of rubber.[96]

Cautioning that not all sectors of the radio industry were recuperating at an equal rate, Broadcasting continued the analogy:

> All have survived the first stage of stunned surprise. Some are still ducking punches and hoping for their second wind. Some have got their wind back and are fighting skillfully (but with a change in style). Still others are ring-fresh and frisky because they have yet to take the first blow. These are the independents. They have gained with the growth of TV because they had nothing to lose.[97]

The Broadcasting article continued by citing three major areas of decline: network time sales (off 43% in 1955 from the 1949 peak), network programming quality and quantity, and network compensation to affiliates, which in what was described as a typical case, had dropped in 1955 to a quarter of the 1948 level.[98] To make up for this loss, stations had been forced to increase their local sales efforts.

---

[96]"Curve Starts Up," Broadcasting, September 19, 1955, p. 51.

[97]Ibid. [98]Ibid., p. 54.

By 1959, a curious paradox had developed. The trend in revenues and profits for the average station was still going down, but the selling price for radio station facilities was continuing to rise. Charles H. Tower, the NAB's manager of economics and broadcast personnel in 1959 offered several reasons for the puzzling situation; among them, uneven competition and aggressive operators anxious to try to beat the average.[99] Among the other factors Mr. Tower mentioned were increasing numbers of stations competing for a more-slowly expanding advertising budget, resulting in dwindling revenues. Each of these phenomena deserve further investigation.

Growth in the number of stations

In the period between the end of World War II and about 1960, there was tremendous growth in the number of AM radio stations. Note the following table:

STATION TYPE:	YEAR:					
	1940	1945	1950	1955	1960	1965
Daytime--non-directional	68	78	649	1017	1484	1666
Daytime--directional antenna	n.a.	n.a.	11	61	215	335
Total daytimers	68	78	660	1078	1699	2001
Total fulltimers	684	880	1649	1831	1905	2057

Source: based on data from Broadcast Yearbook, 1940, 1946, 1951, 1956, 1960 and 1966, compiled by L. W. Lichty and Christopher H. Sterling.

---

[99] "Competition is Tougher," Broadcasting, October 19, 1959, p. 80.

The table above emphasizes the growth of daytime-only stations because these were by far the more important ones during the years of Top 40's development. As can be seen, the greatest growth in fulltime stations occurred between 1945 and 1950, when the number nearly doubled. Between 1950 and 1955, about 200 more fulltime AM stations were added, and then about 100 more in each of the following five year periods.

The number of daytime stations also burgeoned between 1945 and 1950, but note that the daytime figures start with a much smaller base figure. The striking fact is that daytime stations <u>continued</u> to grow at very nearly the same rate from 1945 onward, adding no less than abo 300 stations in any five year span. By 1965, the number of daytime stations was very nearly equal to the number of fulltime facilities.

The early lack of growth and the later boom in daytime station is explained almost entirely by radio's "prime time" being shifted from nights to days by the acceptance of television. Before TV, a daytime-only station had difficulty surviving because it missed servin the large nighttime audiences. But when the majority of those audienc were watching TV in the evening and radio programming began to reorien itself to serving a daytime audience, a daytimer had the potential of being nearly as profitable as a fulltime station. Of course, the easi built fulltime facilities were taken first, so that by the 1960s, abou the only way to avoid the expense of using a directional antenna on a fulltime station was to build only a daytimer in the first place.

Note also from the table that the total number of AM stations on the air in 1945 was 958; only five years later the total was 2,309. This AM "station boom" in its later years coincided with the growth of

:V, so that there were not only more radio stations competing for the advertiser's dollar, but also more and more TV stations competing. More .mportant still for radio programming was the fact that there were only :our national radio networks.[100] The radio networks had long ago affil-.ated with powerful big-city stations which served vast areas of the :ountry, and thus had little reason to switch affiliation to the new stations which were generally confined to regional or local coverage. :f the new stations had a network affiliation at all, they were likely :o pay for it rather than be paid for carrying it. The majority of new stations were thus by necessity, independents. As such, they were seeking a form of inexpensive locally-produced programming that would bring them good revenues in the face of increasing competition for the istener's attention. Many of them would adopt Top 40 or a form of it .s their programming answer.

:osts of buying or building a station

With increasing numbers of new stations going on the air, and 'ith TV growing quickly, the selling price of radio stations was fast o react. Station prices sank to their lowest point as early as 1950, even though the revenues from station operation continued to drop generally into the mid-50s. By 1955, the trend toward selling off radio roperties had been reversed and for the first time there were more uyers than sellers.[101] The selling price of a station in the mid-50s 'as generally set at five to seven times its earning before taxes, or

---

[100]There was a fifth during part of the period.

[101]"The Going Price is Going Up," Broadcasting, September 19, 955, p. 62.

seventy-five percent to 80% of its gross earnings.[102] The following are some representative sales prices reported paid for established, medium-to-small market AM stations during the months of January and September, 1954:

KSIL, Silver City, N.M.--250 watts fulltime on 1340 kHz, CBS affil., est. 1946, single station in town. $110,000.
WGAA, Cedartown, Georgia--250 watts fulltime on 1340 kHz, independent, established 1941, single station in town. $39,000.
WINI, Murphysboro, Illinois--500 watts daytime on 1420 kHz, independent, established month of sale, single station in town. $22,000.
WHOT, South Bend, Indiana--250 watts fulltime on 1490 kHz, ABC net., established 1944, multiple station market. $140,000.[103]

In the above list, note that KSIL and WGAA have exactly the sam physical facilities, and that the lower-priced station also had had fiv more years in which to build up advertising accounts. Both were also in single-station towns. The difference in selling price here must the be accounted for by the revenues so far produced and expected in the future from the market area.

WGAA and WINI have very nearly the same facilities, again are the only stations in their towns, but WINI because it had not built up any accounts (it was sold apparently at the time of completion of construction) sold for less than WGAA.

For comparison the list includes WHOT which has the poorest physical facilities of the four stations listed. It also had competition from two other AM stations in town, plus powerful Chicago stations next door. Yet it brought $140,000 for its established accounts in a prosperous market. To illustrate further the importance of a thriving market, note the sale price in January 1955 of WPAT in Paterson, New

---

[102] *Ibid.* [103] *Ibid.*

Jersey (a New York City suburb), which operated on 930 kHz with 5,000 watts: $300,000. In comparison with that price, the $450,000 received in 1954 for WINS, New York, with 50,000 watts on 1010 kHz seems low.[104]

In 1954, the cost of building a new daytime, 1,000 watt station in a small market (WWIT, Canton, North Carolina) was put at just under $50,000. Of this amount, about $14,000 each went into buildings and broadcast equipment, another $12,000 into land improvements and tower construction, a little over $3,000 for furnishings and office equipment, and $4,000 more for preliminary organizational expenses.[105]

In December of 1955, when the station just described had been on the air for about a year, it showed an income of just over $6,100 for the month, and costs of about $4,500, leaving a monthly gain before taxes and depreciation of $1,600. Salaries, utilities, maintenance, office supplies, license, legal, accounting, programming, sales, insurance, and agency commissions accounted for the expenses. The station did not carry network service, but a sister station that did paid $250 a month additional for that privilege.[106]

An NAB survey showed that the typical (median) radio station in 1956 had revenues of $99,800, all but $200 of which was from the sale of time. Against that, the typical station showed $89,500 in expenses, for a profit of $10,300. The typical station paid $11,400 in technical expenses, $29,600 in program expenses, $14,300 in selling expenses, and

---

[104] Ibid.

[105] "Madison Avenue to Main Street," Broadcasting, May 14, 1956, p. 77.

[106] Ibid., p. 76.

$34,200 in general and administrative costs. Only $100 of its revenue from the sale of time came from networks, $12,700 came from national and regional spot, and $86,800 came from local advertisers.[107]

Radio revenues and rates

Network revenues

In 1947, radio received the largest share it ever had of national advertising expenditures--13%. After 1947, that share constantly decreased until by 1954, radio was receiving only a 7% share (while television was getting 9.8%).[108] The source of that share of the national advertising dollar also changed. In 1948, radio network revenues were near $134,000,000, and accounted for 32% of the industry's income. Local revenue in 1948 was $171,000,000 or 41% of the industry's income, while the remaining 27% of income came from $111,000,000 in national spot business.[109]

Just five years later, in 1953, radio network revenues were down to $89,500,000 or 18% of total industry income, local sales were up to $257,000,000 or 52% of total income, and spot sales had increased to $151,000,000 or 30% of the industry's total income.[110]

Network rates and compensation

CBS was the first of the four major radio networks to ask its affiliates to allow a rate cut, in April, 1951. NBC and ABC followed

---

[107] "Stations See Profit Increase," Broadcasting, August 5, 1957, p. 28.

[108] Richard P. Doherty, "Radio Joins the Business Cycle," Broadcasting, September 19, 1955, p. 136.

[109] Ibid., p. 138. [110] Ibid.

suit to stay competitive. Instead of cutting rates, Mutual increased discounts, which amounted to the same thing.[111] In 1953, Mutual proposed to affiliates that it limit option time to five hours a day and pay affiliates in programs rather than in cash.[112] The plan, which was begun October 1, 1953, was discontinued three months later due to heavy affiliate opposition.[113]

Also in 1953, ABC adopted a single daytime and evening rate for its owned-and-operated stations. In May of 1954, CBS announced a 20% reduction in nighttime rates, which it achieved through extra discounts rather than actual changes in rate cards. A month later, NBC followed suit.[114] The effect was to give the networks a single rate for both days and nights. -In 1955, Mutual also went to a single rate.[115] In an advertisement Mutual ran in Broadcasting the network pointed out that with its new rate, the quarter-hour air-time cost for each station was down to just $5.34, or $1.78 per commercial minute.[116]

In the fall of 1955, CBS reduced its compensation to affiliates

---

[111] "Radio's Rate Trend Since TV's Advent," Broadcasting, September 19, 1955, p. 194.

[112] "MBS Affiliates Offered 'Revolutionary' Policy," Broadcasting, July 20, 1953, p. 76.

[113] "MBS Shelves Affiliate Plan Effective Dec. 31," Broadcasting, November 9, 1953, p. 27.

[114] "NBC Radio Ready to Ask 20% Nighttime Rate Cut," Broadcasting, June 7, 1954, p. 31.

[115] "Mutual Fixes Single Rate for Day, Evening, Plus Single Discount Table," Broadcasting, June 27, 1955, p. 103.

[116] Mutual Broadcasting System advertisement in Broadcasting, July 25, 1955, p. 15.

by 20%, while NBC asked for a 25% cut.[117] By 1957, the totally-downwar spiral of radio network sales had rebounded with daytime advertisers, and in February of that year, CBS raised its daytime rates 5%. However the network lowered its nighttime rates by another 33%. The changes put CBS's hourly rate at about $15,750 for daytime, and about $10,000 for nights.[118] ABC was already planning to increase daytime rates in April of 1957.[119] In March of that year, NBC also announced plans to increase daytime rates and drop nighttime charges.[120] In April, the Petry station representative firm urged its stations to do the same, since it had found that nighttime sets in use was only 55% to 60% of the daytime level.[121]

The increasing number of stations on the air also affected the revenue realized by each station. In 1947, when $374,000,000 was spent in radio advertising among 1,522 stations, the "average" share per station was theoretically $246,000. By 1952, although total radio advertising expenditure had risen to $464,000,000, with 2,391 stations dividing it, the theoretical average share had dropped to $194,244.[122]

As has been shown, the great majority of the new, mostly

117"Radio's Rate Trend Since TV's Advent," p. 194.

118"CBS Radio to Price Day Over Night," Broadcasting, February 25, 1957, p. 28.

119Ibid., p. 27.

120"NBC Radio Plans Day Increases," Broadcasting, March 4, 1957, p. 100.

121"Petry Urges Night Radio Slash," Broadcasting, April 22, 1957, p. 103.

122"'52 Radio Time Sales Reach $464 Million," Broadcasting, January 26, 1953, p. 28.

independent radio stations had to turn to increasing local sales to survive. But in larger markets, where audiences were sizeable enough to be attractive to large advertisers, national and regional spot business also provided increasing revenue.

Growth of National Spot and Station Representation

Background

The increase in national (and regional) spot buying came hand-in-hand with the growth (in both numbers and in influence) of the station representative firms. An additional aid to growth was the improvement of the electrical transcription (and later the use of pre-recorded tapes and cartridges).

In 1932, the first two station representative firms appeared: Edward Petry & Co., and Free and Sleininger. The latter eventually became Peters, Griffin & Woodward.[123]

By 1934, producers of electrical transcription shows (not spots) were also selling time and charging commissions both from ad agencies and from stations.[124] Time brokers, who were not retained by stations as reps were, but who acted as middlemen between agencies wanting to buy time and stations wanting to sell it, also appeared between 1932 and 1934.[125]

As station reps gained in their importance to stations in the sale of time to national and regional sponsors, they also gained in influence over the programming in many cases. Much of the audience

---

[123] "Spot Radio's Pioneer Days," Sponsor, November 16, 1957, p. 42.

[124] Ibid. [125] Ibid.

data that reps need to sell advertising clients is the same sort of data that is useful to a station in making its programming most popular with the potential audience. Besides such audience data, reps also provide stations with their sales promotion and presentation material for the station's own use. Additionally, reps have come to take an active part in rate setting, in audience measurement, and even in billing and collection.[126]

Participating sponsorship

In 1953, the change from program to participating sponsorship was already taking place on radio networks, and a concerted effort to promote the use of spot radio was under way among station representatives. In February of 1953, Billboard reported that in radio, ". . . the trend definitely is away from the former practice of identification with key personalities and properties, and a move toward diffusion of programming which results in maximum frequency of impressions."[127] Among the companies that had pioneered the move toward participating network buys were Procter & Gamble, R. J. Reynolds, General Mills, and

---

[126] "Broadcasting's Hidden Power: The TV-Radio Reps," Saturday Review, December 13, 1969, p. 68. In 1957, the Katz station rep firm announced the availability to its stations of Mr. John Pearson, formerly program manager at Storz's WHB, Kansas City, as a roving programming consultant. Katz claimed a first in making such a trouble-shooter available, saying that the increasing emphasis on local programming had made the rep firm's role as merely a seller of what was once a fairly standardized product obsolete. Mr. Pearson would be available to do such un-rep-like activities as setting up record libraries, auditioning program tapes, examining logs for better block program schedules and so on. "Katz Hires Pearson to 'Trouble-Shoot,'" Broadcasting, June 10, 1957, pp. 100-01.

[127] "Radio-TV Sponsors Evolve New Patterns for Time Buys," Billboard, February 28, 1953, p. 1.

Emerson Drug. Lever Brothers was also reported to be selling three different products on a show that had formerly been identified only with one.[128] The article concluded with proof of the effectiveness of such buying:

> The value of multiple exposure is shown by the A. C. Nielsen research figures for the week of December 6, 1952, when the three top-rated radio shows, according to Nielsen charts, were Jack Benny (12.6) with 5,510,000 homes reached; "Amos 'n' Andy" (11.0) with 4,810,000 homes reached; and Edgar Bergen (11.1) with 4,860,000 homes reached. By comparison, and at much lower cost, sponsors buying the NBC tandem [participation plan] got a cumulative rating of 13.7 with 6,000,000 homes reached and those riding the CBS power plan [participation plan] gained a 13.1 cumulative rating with 5,730,000 homes reached. Consequently, sponsors of the various multi-program plans not only attracted a larger audience than any of the highest-rated single programs did, but reached different kinds of audiences spread all over the radio week.[129]

The advantages of buying "participations" on network radio that are so clearly stated in the Billboard article were quite obviously among the reasons why networks changed over to participating sponsorship. Meanwhile, station representatives were readying presentations to advertisers that demonstrated the greater flexibility, lower cost, and variety of programming available through national spot buys.

Spot sales

In 1953, the Station Representatives Association began its "Crusade for Spot Radio," which was an effort to supply to advertising agencies general information about the effective employment of spot radio. The first year, 318 radio stations paid one-half the one-time daytime minute announcement rate per month, for one year, to support the Crusade. Among the resulting activities were a series of Spot

---

[128] Ibid., p. 3. [129] Ibid.

Radio Clinics held between the Station Representatives Association and various advertising agencies.[130] The SRA also planned a series of studies of audience composition of spot programs as compared to network programming.[131]

The station representative firm of Peters, Griffin & Woodward made its own representation to agencies, via a special booklet they prepared which explained radio's coverage and frequency. Said Frank Woodruff, radio research director for PGW in a Business Week article in 1957, "The job was first to get money allocated for radio generally. . . . Then we could worry about how to get our own stations their share."[132]

In the period between June 1954 and June 1955, national spot sales were down in all markets except those over 1,000,000 in population.[133] In the case of national spot, the large-market stations were the leaders. Only seven months after a spot rate boost in August of 1955, Chicago music-and-news independent WIND announced another 20% increase in Class A time.[134] Even network flagship owned-and-operated stations such as WCBS in New York could announce a 20% increase in

---

[130] Advertisement in Broadcasting, April 27, 1953, p. 137.

[131] "Spot Radio: From Morning to After-Midnight, Business is Good," Sponsor, July 12, 1954, p. 206.

[132] "Lot of Life in Radio Yet," Business Week, February 9, 1957, p. 132.

[133] "The Sales in 1955: Record & Outlook," Broadcasting, September 19, 1955, p. 59.

[134] "Radio Rates Rise," Broadcasting, February 6, 1956, p. 5.

daytime rates.[135] Other large-market stations at this time were also boosting daytime rates, equalizing their daytime and nighttime rates, or discounting nighttime rates.

The 1954-55 drop in national spot buying was the only one of major size suffered in the ten years between 1947 and 1957. For further details, see "Radio Time Sales, 1947-1957, which is reproduced below from Broadcasting, February 9, 1959, p. 65.

Spot advertising grew and succeeded for a number of general reasons, many of which are the same reasons why independent--rather than network affiliated--stations also grew and succeeded. The following points were made by Sponsor magazine in a 1954 article:

National spot (and independent stations) made up in daytime audiences what they lost to television at night.

More detailed audience data allowed spot buyers to be at least as certain of success as network buyers were. Locally-produced programs that gathered the desired size and type of audience also allowed the advertiser greater selectivity than did network buying.[136]

The spot rate structure was both more responsive to audience changes than were network rates, and also offered a greater range of choice in the size and length of the schedule ordered.[137]

Independent stations of the music-and-news Top 40 type became so healthy in the late 1950s that one anonymous major station

---

[135] "20% Boost in Daytime Rates Effected by WCBS New York," Broadcasting, November 26, 1956, p. 83.

[136] "Spot Radio: From Mornings to After-Midnight Business is Good," Sponsor, July 12, 1954, p. 208.

[137] Ibid., p. 210.

RADIO TIME SALES 1935-1958

Year	National Network	% change from previous year	Regional Network	% change from previous year	National Non-Network	% change from previous year	Local	% change from previous year	Total	% change from previous year
1935 [1]	$ 39,737,867	...	[1]........	...	$ 13,805,200	...	$ 26,074,476	...	$ 79,617,543	...
1936 [2]	....	...	....	...	....	...	....	...	....	...
1937	56,192,396	+41.4	$ 2,854,047	...	23,117,136	+67.4	35,745,394	+37.1	117,908,973	+48.1
1938	56,612,925	+ 0.7	[2]........	...	28,109,185	+21.6	32,657,349	— 8.7	117,379,459	— 0.6
1939	62,621,689	+10.6	[2]........	...	30,030,563	+ 6.8	37,315,774	+14.2	129,968,026	+10.7
1940	71,919,428	+13.1	1,869,583	...	37,140,444	+23.8	44,756,792	+20.0	155,686,247	+20.5
1941	79,621,534	+10.7	2,752,073	+47.2	45,681,959	+23.0	51,697,651	+15.5	179,753,217	+15.4
1942	81,744,396	+ 2.7	3,444,581	+25.2	51,059,159	+11.8	53,898,916	+ 4.2	190,147,052	+ 5.8
1943	99,389,177	+21.6	6,256,508	+81.6	59,352,170	+16.2	64,104,309	+18.9	228,102,164	+20.0
1944	121,757,135	+22.5	7,612,366	+21.7	73,312,899	+23.5	84,960,347	+29.3	287,642,747	+26.1
1945	125,671,834	+ 3.2	8,301,702	+ 9.1	76,696,463	+ 4.6	99,814,042	+17.5	310,184,046	+ 7.9
1946	126,737,727	+ 0.8	8,043,381	— 3.1	82,917,505	+ 8.1	116,380,301	+16.6	334,078,914	+ 7.6
1947	127,713,912	+ 0.8	7,012,689	—12.8	91,581,241	+10.4	147,778,814	+27.0	374,086,636	+12.0
1948	133,723,098	+ 4.5	7,329,255	+ 4.3	104,759,761	+14.4	170,908,165	+15.6	416,720,279	+11.4
1949	128,903,467	— 3.6	5,994,858	—18.2	108,314,507	+ 3.4	182,144,301	+ 6.5	425,357,133	+ 2.1
1950	124,633,089	— 3.3	6,897,127	+15.0	118,823,880	+ 9.7	203,210,834	+11.6	453,564,930	+ 6.6
1951	113,984,000	— 8.5	8,481,000	+23.0	119,559,000	+ 0.6	214,519,000	+ 5.6	456,543,000	+ 0.6
1952	102,528,000	—10.0	7,334,000	—13.5	123,658,000	+ 3.4	239,631,000	+11.7	473,151,000	+ 3.6
1953	92,865,000	— 9.4	5,192,000	—29.2	129,605,000	+ 4.8	249,544,000	+ 4.1	477,206,000	+ 0.9
1954	78,917,000	—15.0	4,767,000	— 8.2	120,168,000	— 7.3	247,478,000	— 0.8	451,330,000	— 5.1
1955	60,268,000	—23.6	3,809,000	—20.1	120,393,000	+ 0.2	272,011,000	+ 9.9	456,481,000	+ 0.7
1956	44,839,000	—25.6	3,585,000	— 5.9	145,461,000	+20.8	297,822,000	+ 9.5	491,707,000	+ 7.7
1957	47,951,000	+ 6.9	3,709,000	+ 3.5	169,511,000	+16.5	316,493,000	+ 6.3	537,664,000	+ 9.3
1958 †	47,181,810	— 1.6	3,834,014	+ 3.4	168,714,703	— 0.5	311,904,519	— 1.4	531,635,046	— 1.1

[1] Nationwide and regional networks combined.
[2] Data not available.

* Figures prior to this date not comparable in all categories.
† 1958 figures estimated by BROADCASTING.

representative was soliciting national spot buys for one of its stations with this offer, reported by Broadcasting:

> If station doesn't turn up No. 1 in next Pulse survey, there'll be no charge for spots; if station does make No. 1 position, as rep predicts it will, business will be billed at regular rates. "You can't lose either way," say rep's letter of solicitation.[138]

---

[138] "Radio Roulette," Broadcasting, May 5, 1958, p. 5.

CHAPTER TWO

RADIO PROGRAMMING PRIOR TO TOP 40

Network Programming Trends

In September of 1953, Brigadier General David Sarnoff, Chairman of the Board of RCA-NBC, appeared at the network affiliates meeting in Chicago and said that the principal problems facing radio were the three R's: ratings, raiding, and rebates.[1] The General criticized ratings for having the appearance of accuracy while they failed to measure multi-set homes and other extra-set listening, and he deplored the making of deals and concessions as a "blight on the radio business."[2] He was not reported as having much to say about the raiding of radio talent for use on TV, perhaps because NBC had been so heavily victimized by CBS's talent raids. But the General lent a note of stability and confidence to a meeting in which 28 "new" fall programs were explained to increasingly-nervous affiliates. Operating Vice President Ted Cott explained NBC's new block-programming concept, in which each night of the week would concentrate on a particular kind of programming: Monday, music; Tuesday, mystery and adventure; Wednesday, comedy; Thursday, comedy and audience participation; Friday, all comedy; and Saturday special programs followed by hillbilly music.[3] Earlier, Cott had

---

[1]"Radio 'Rehabilitation' Is Sarnoff's Pledge," Broadcasting, September 21, 1953, p. 29.

[2]*Ibid.*, p. 30. [3]*Ibid.*, p. 31.

announced that the 28 new programs would be mass-premiered, saying "We're going to overwhelm the public with such a collection of new programs that they won't dare tune anyplace else for fear of missing something new and wonderful."[4] Among the new programs was a "Sunday Newspaper" concept, with both news and supplement-type features, to run two to three hours Sunday afternoons, and to be called Weekend.[5] A similar long weekend program, Monitor, would be unveiled by the network in 1955. But the generally old-style programs set for the fall of 1953 were sometimes sold on a new basis. Fibber McGee and Molly was one of three programs which was being opened to participating sponsorship. The new Weekend program would be a spot-carrier, as would The Big Preview, which was a Saturday morning two-hour show featuring new record releases.[6] In both programs, eight participations per hour were available at fixed rates.[7] In January of 1954, NBC added four more participating weekend hours with the debut of Road Show for motorists, from 2:00 to 6:00 p.m. on Saturdays.[8]

The long show had not been invented by NBC for network use. ABC had run three 1 1/2- to 2-hour programs in the 1952-53 season, one each on Saturday, Sunday and Monday. The Saturday show was Saturday Night

---

[4]"NBC Radio's Cott Says Overhaul to Bring 'New, Wonderful' Shows," Broadcasting, August 17, 1953, p. 88.

[5]Ibid.

[6]"New NBC Radio Sales Plans," Broadcasting, September 21, 1953, p. 30.

[7]"NBC Radio Cuts Sustainer Hours," Broadcasting, January 11, 1954, p. 74A.

[8]Ibid.

Dancing Party, the Sunday program was American Music Hall, and the Monday offering was American Concert Studio.[9] CBS had also had a long weekend show in the summers of 1952, 1953 and 1954 called On a Sunday Afternoon.[10]

In May of 1954, ABC Radio aired the first of its new "music and news" evening programs called Just Easy, which appeared Monday through Friday between 8:00 and 9:00 p.m.[11] ABC was reported to be attempting to become the first nighttime "music and news" network, in order to offer the "relaxation" that television was not providing. The radio network noted in its announcement that independent "music and news" stations were currently attracting a larger share of the nighttime radio audience than any radio network.[12] ABC had correctly deduced that nighttime audiences were receiving plenty of drama and excitement from TV, but not enough relaxing music. The network emphasized that the new format was for nighttimes only--daytime programming was not seen as being in trouble. The initial show, Just Easy, was not a records program, but rather one comprised of live, regular performers and guest stars.[13]

ABC had already begun feeding a records program to affiliates at the beginning of 1954 when Martin Block went on the network, Monday through Friday from 2:35 to 4:00 p.m. eastern time. More will be

---

[9] Alfred J. Jaffee, "The New Radio: Are You so Close to it You Can't See the Changes?" Sponsor, April 19, 1954, p. 143.

[10] Ibid.

[11] "ABC Night Format to be Music, News," Broadcasting, May 24, 1954, p. 64.

[12] Ibid. [13] Ibid.

reported on network disc jockeys such as Block later in this chapter.[14]

In July, Sponsor magazine listed six "Network Radio Trends" for the fall of 1954. Sponsor predicted that there would be more nighttime strip programming because of lower costs, larger cumulative audiences, the ability to sell strips as spot carriers, and the ease with which audiences could remember them.[15] The magazine also predicted more spot carriers throughout the day, with Mutual trying for morning and afternoon strips, NBC adding a night spot carrier, and CBS selling seven-and-a-half-minute segments.[16]

Monitor

In April of 1955, NBC announced plans for Monitor to begin regular service on June 18 of that year, running from 8:00 a.m. Saturday continuously to midnight Sunday. Program content was to include music, news, weather, "interviews, debates, audio tapes of TV shows, simulcasts, drama vignettes, etc."[17] Monitor was clearly intended as a network spot-carrier, with availabilities of one minute, 30 seconds, or six-second billboards, with ten of the latter selling for $3,000. A one-minute announcement was to be priced at $1,000 and a 30-second spot at $700.[18]

---

[14] "Web Radio's Transcribed Disc Shows," Billboard, November 13, 1954, p. 27.

[15] "Network Radio Trends," Sponsor, July 12, 1954, p. 37.

[16] Ibid.

[17] "NBC Begins Major Revision in Radio Selling, Schedules," Broadcasting, April 4, 1955, p. 27.

[18] Ibid.

NBC was reported by Broadcasting as having given the following description of a typical hour to affiliates:

> The first segment of a trip through Paris with Monitor's roving European correspondent. (Succeeding segments would be positioned throughout the rest of the day.)
> A dramatic highlight from a current hit Broadway play or movie.
> Live or taped performances by people at the top of the news that weekend.
> Comedy of all types, including live and pre-recorded routines by stars from all fields of show business; jokes and stories.
> A Monitor exclusive--which might be a dive with the atomic-powered submarine, the Nautilus; firing a rocket at White Sands, or visiting Birdland, New York's Mecca of jazz.
> Plus, of course, Monitor's basic news, time, weather, sports, and local features.[19]

NBC President Sylvester (Pat) Weaver was quoted as saying "You'll never get a 20 rating in radio again," but that the Monitor plan was to build a large cumulative audience. He expected this audience to come not from TV but from other radio stations.[20]

Affiliates and audiences were generally enthusiastic over Monitor programming, although CBS Radio Sales Vice President John Karol described it as "a seemingly endless succession of unfinished bits and pieces, interspersed by beeps and boops and the pleading admonition to 'take one.'"[21] The complaints against the new program were mostly directed against the low rates at which it was being sold. The Station Representatives Association said that Monitor's rates posed the threat of depreciation for the entire radio industry because the national

---

[19] "NBC Radio Tells Plans for Monitor, Its 40-Hour Weekend Program Service," Broadcasting, April 11, 1955, p. 52.

[20] Ibid.

[21] "Looking at Monitor," Broadcasting, September 19, 1955, p. 89.

advertiser had to pay only one-quarter to one-third as much to advertise on *Monitor* as to buy at the local station's card rates.[22] However, to balance this threat, many larger affiliates were reporting their local cutaways completely sold out.[23]

On Friday, June 17, the night before the first full weekend of *Monitor* was to begin, NBC began feeding a one-and-a-half hour record show aimed at teenagers between 8:30 and 10:00 p.m. A live audience in New York danced to the records, and each half hour a recording star appeared to talk with fans by telephone.[24]

In June, Mutual announced that it was beginning a new "companionate radio" concept in July with a program called *Mutual Morning* which was to feature "interviews, short stories, preview of the day's sports, simulated broadcasts of events of the past, baby and child care tips, among other features."[25] Although the program was originally scheduled only for 11:00 to 11:25 a.m. Monday through Friday, plans were to expand it into the afternoons and evenings, with other shows to be called *Mutual Matinee* and *Mutual Evening*.[26] It is quite apparent that the "bits and pieces" approach pioneered by *Monitor* on radio network programs was being adopted by Mutual.

In September 1955 NBC announced plans to expand the *Monitor* format into weekday periods, retaining soap operas and other

---

[22] *Ibid.* [23] *Ibid.*, p. 90.

[24] "NBC Radio Teenager Show Planned for Friday Nights," *Broadcasting*, May 23, 1955, p. 120.

[25] "MBS to Revise Program Concept," *Broadcasting*, June 27, 1955, p. 104.

[26] *Ibid.*

currently-sponsored shows. Affiliates were to be given a five-minute cutaway per hour, plus 70 seconds at the hour station break, as in weekend Monitor, which was felt by many to be too little local time on weekdays.[27] At the same time, NBC planned to increase the number of nighttime programs which would be sold on a participating basis,[28] as CBS had just announced it would do.

ABC's "New Sounds for You"

Also in September, ABC announced that it was in the process of revising its nighttime programming.[29] In November, the new approach was revealed to affiliates and the public. The basis was a series of short five- and ten-minute shows which collectively were known as "New Sounds for You."[30] The short segments were non-musical, and were intended to overcome what ABC felt was a tendency of music-and-news audiences to listen with only "half an ear," thus depriving the commercial of its full impact.[31]

In late November, ABC ran an advertisement called "This is the Radio Schedule that TV Built," which listed the programs available each night on "New Sounds for You."

---

[27] "NBC, CBS and Affiliates Mull New Radio Formulas," Broadcasting, September 12, 1955, p. 31.

[28] Ibid.

[29] "New Look for ABC," Broadcasting, September 19, 1955, p. 90.

[30] "Is Radio Overdoing Music-and-News Programming?" Sponsor, November 14, 1955, p. 144.

[31] Ibid., pp. 144-45.

"Events of the Day"

7:30 Today's Sensational Story (the top tabloid story of the day)

7:35 Inside Washington (controversial news from the nation's capital)

7:40 Transatlantic Interview (tabloid story of the day from Europe)

7:45 Personality of the Day (hero or heel of the headlines, profile, interview)

7:50 The News and You (farm, financial, medical, industry, labor, science)

7:55 News

"The World and You"

8:00 Arrivals and Departures (on spot interviews with famous people)

8:05 Let's Visit (on spot visits to famous cities and landmarks)

8:10 Yesterday at Midnight (on spot recordings with interesting people in interesting places during the late hours)

8:15 America at Work and Play (close-ups--factory, farm, beach, ballpark)

8:20 Elm Street to the Great White Way (visits backstage, Broadway to front row, town meeting)

8:25 News

"Your Better Tomorrow" (except Mondays at 8:30, The Voice of Firestone)

(and Tuesdays at 8:30, Bishop Sheen's Life is Worth Living)

8:30 Part 1--Words To Live By (words to live by from spiritual leaders)

8:35 Part 2--Advice on Your Marriage and Family (practical, expert advice on problems that touch everyone)

8:40 Part 3--Improving Your Personality (how to be a more popular, happy person)

8:45 Part 4--Your Success (how to be more attractive, more successful)

8:50 Part 5--Advice on Your Home (do-it-yourself for kitchen, workshop, house and garden)

8:55 News

"Sound Mirror"

9:00 Sounds of Yesterday (stories, readings and voices that make the past come alive)

9:05 Sounds of Today (sounds of modern life)

9:15 Sounds of No Importance [no explanation given]

9:20 Soundings (short editorial-type features. Soundings of people)

9:25 News

"Offbeat"

9:30 Offbeat Humor [no further explanation]

9:35 Futurescope (sound picture of the future, science fiction, new music for tomorrow's tomorrow)

9:45 Soloscope (readings by expert storytellers and authors themselves)

9:55 News[32]

ABC was careful to point out that its new nighttime programming was different from any other in being "bite-size" and in being "regularly-scheduled."[33] The network claimed each program attracted its own regular listeners, although one must doubt how much special tuning such short programs could generate. The shows could be bought

---

[32] Program titles from "This is the Radio Schedule That TV Built," Advertisement in Sponsor, November 28, 1955, p. 73. Content explanations from "Kintner on ABC Radio's Future," Sponsor, October 17, 1955, p. 38.

[33] Ibid., p. 73.

individually or as a strip, with five minutes on the full network costing $800.[34] The intention, according to ABC President Robert Kintner, was to establish a theme in each 25-minute period, but to subdivide it so that a listener would not have to be "glued" to his radio, yet at the same time retain "the basic strength of radio" in regular scheduling.[35]

CBS Radio did not make substantial changes in its programming in 1955 or 1956, but rather concentrated on new ways of selling the old shows. In 1956, CBS claimed that its ten weekday serial dramas, aired between noon and 2:30 p.m. was "the strongest lineup in all daytime radio," with a weekly cumulative audience of 20.5 million and a monthly cumulative audience of 31.7 million.[36] Mutual, meanwhile, was pointing to its affiliates' differences with music-and-news independent stations in an advertisement with the headline "The record you can't buy anywhere else."[37] The "record" being referred to was a list of special services and features, including the new guaranteed cost-per-thousand rates for advertisers. The ad concluded with the following sentence: "Your advertisers know you're a good buy because you have that something more to offer that only a network station can give . . . <u>not just a service of records</u> . . . / <u>but a record of service</u>."[38]

---

[34] *Ibid.*

[35] "You *Can* Make Money in Network Radio," *Broadcasting*, October 31, 1955, p. 54.

[36] Advertisement in *Broadcasting*, October 8, 1956, pp. 16-17.

[37] Advertisement in *Broadcasting*, September 10, 1956, pp. 54-55.

[38] *Ibid.*, p. 54.

Survey of Affiliate Needs

Early in November of 1956, Broadcasting sent a questionnaire on networks to all U.S. radio stations except network owned-and-operated stations. Of the 3,000-odd questionnaires sent, 1,267 were returned. Those stations retaining network service were doing so primarily because it provided programming not otherwise available.[39] Stations were asked the programming which they depended on their networks to supply. Special events were first with 90.0% approval, followed by news commentary with 80.0%, sports with 72.3%, news at 67.7%, drama at 48.8%, public service at 34.0%, and music at 27.0%.[40]

The survey also posed the following question:

> The suggestion has been made that the present plan of radio network operation, which includes both programming and sales, be replaced by a service whose sole function would be to supply programs to station subscribers on a fee basis, in much the same manner that news services like AP, UP and INS supply news and features to subscribing newspapers and broadcast stations, with all sales left to the station and its representative.
>
> If your network were to offer you a choice: Would you (a) take this proposed service in preference to your present network service; (b) prefer to retain the network service you now receive; (c) change to completely independent operation?[41]

The following table shows how network affiliates answered:

---

[39]"The Radio Networks," Broadcasting, November 26, 1956, p. 32.

[40]Ibid., p. 33. [41]Ibid.

Network Affiliation	Prefer:			
	"Press assn"-type service	Present net	Independence	Total response
ABC	42 (28.6%)	77 (52.4%)	28 (19.0%)	147
CBS	20 (20.2%)	72 (72.7%)	7 (7.1%)	99
MBS	111 (50.5%)	83 (37.7%)	26 (11.8%)	220
NBC	33 (42.3%)	39 (50.0%)	6 (7.7%)	78
Dual	12 (33.3%)	21 (58.3%)	3 (8.4%)	36

Source: "The Radio Networks," Broadcasting, November 26, 1956, p. 32.

Note from the above table that the affiliates of ABC and NBC were about evenly split between staying with their present network as against either going independent or affiliating with a "press associa-tion" type of network, with about 50% electing to stay with their current network. ABC affiliates were about two-and-a-half times as likely to choose independence as were NBC affiliates (19.0% and 7.7% respectively), while a little over 40% of NBC stations found the "press association" alternative attractive. At the same time, nearly three-quarters of the replying CBS affiliates chose to keep their network, with about the same low percentage opting for independence as NBC stations had (7.1%), and the fewest among all affiliates in choosing the "press association" scheme (20.2%). The loyalty which CBS enjoyed in the survey found its exact opposite among Mutual affiliates, only 37.7% of whom preferred to retain their present network if a "press-association" type of service were offered. A full 50.5% of replying

Mutual affiliates preferred the "press association" operation, and preferred it four-and-a-half-to-one over going independent. Most important to the Mutual network, Mutual affiliates were the only ones more willing to have the "press association" service than they were to remain with the present network (50.5% to 37.7%).[42]

With such opinions from its affiliates as to the desirability of retaining its service, it was probably inevitable that Mutual announced in January of 1957 that it was considering a network service centered almost entirely on news and commentary.[43] In April of 1957, Mutual announced details of the new service, which included a newscast on both the hour and the half hour (one being sold by the network and the other by the local station), and the retention of commentators such as Fulton Lewis Jr. and Cedric Foster, "Queen for a Day," and an 8:00 to 9:00 p.m. mystery strip.[44] The remainder of the time was to be filled with recorded music, which might also be described as "a service of records."

Meanwhile, the ABC Radio Affiliates Advisory Board, in a letter published as an advertisement in Broadcasting, had deplored what they called the "will o' the wisp of independent station rating superiority [which] has been publicized by a few instances of recent network

---

[42]The same sort of question asked of independent stations, to find out if they would be interested in subscribing to a "press association" type of operation yielded 64.4% saying yes, 35.6% saying no. Ibid., p. 33.

[43]"MBS Considers Heavy News Format," Broadcasting, January 28, 1957, p. 64.

[44]"MBS Affiliates Hear Details of Planned Music-News Format," Broadcasting, April 15, 1957, p. 40.

disaffiliation which we believe were ill advised."[45] The letter concluded, "As network affiliates who endorse the network concept of broadcasting enthusiastically, we refuse to operate like a juke box."[46]

Network Record Programs

The fall opening of the 1954-55 radio season saw a sharp rise in the number of phonograph-record-based network shows. Among the most unusual were the integration of recorded music into the *Edgar Bergen and Charlie McCarthy Show* over CBS Sunday nights at nine, and *Amos 'n' Andy*'s "Kingfish" turning up as a disc jockey on the renamed *Amos 'n' Andy Music Hall* Monday through Friday at 9:30 p.m.[47]

In November of 1954, *Billboard* took note of the rise in transcribed music programming on radio networks and compiled a complete list of all shows then being aired. That list is reproduced below.

NBC:

The Frank Sinatra Show (records and chatter), Wednesday and Friday, 8:15 to 8:30 p.m.

The Dave Garroway Show (records and live music), Friday, 8:30 to 9:00 p.m.

Road Show (records and commentary), Saturday afternoons, four hours, with Bill Cullen as M.C.

Serenade to Romance (poetry and records), Saturday, 9:30 to 10:30 a.m., with David Ross as M.C.

Two Hour Special One-Shots on Record Personalities (special commentary), guest stars, records, Sunday afternoons, twice monthly.

CBS:

Edgar Bergen and Charlie McCarthy (records, guests and chatter), Sunday, 8:00 to 10:00 p.m.

Amos 'n' Andy's Music Hall (records and situation comedy), Monday through Friday, 9:30 to 9:55 p.m.

---

[45] Advertisement in *Broadcasting*, December 3, 1956, p. 77.

[46] *Ibid.*

[47] "Star Record Shows Woo Web Listeners," *Billboard*, November 13, 1954, p. 27.

On a Sunday Afternoon (records and live music), Sunday, 4:05 to 5:55 p.m.
Juke Box Jury (panel rates new releases), Saturday night, Peter Potter, M.C.

MUTUAL:
The Ted Steele Show (records and chatter), Monday through Friday, 1:30 to 2:00 p.m.
The Ruby Mercer Show (records and chatter), Monday through Friday, 3:00 to 4:00 p.m. and Saturday 1:30 to 2:00 p.m.
Bruce Eliot and Dan McCullough (records and chatter), Monday through Saturday, 4:30 to 5:00 p.m.

ABC:
The Martin Block Show (records and chatter), Monday through Friday, 2:35 to 4:00 p.m.
Pop Concerts (records), Saturday, 11:05 to 11:30 a.m.
Brown Derby Record Room Show (records and interviews), Wednesday, 9:30 to 9:55 p.m., Al Gannaway, M.C.
Sammy Kaye's Serenade Room (records and chatter), Monday, Wednesday, Thursday, and Friday, 9:00 to 9:25 p.m.
Sammy Kaye's Sunday Serenade (records and chatter), Sunday, 3:05 to 3:30 p.m.
Big Jon and Sparkie's No School Today (kiddie records, chatter), Saturday, 9:00 to 10:30 a.m.
Living Room Frolics (records and chatter), Sunday, 7:30 to 9:00 p.m. and 9:30 to 9:55 p.m., Jimmy Nelson, M.C.
The Vincent Lopez Show (records and chatter), Monday through Friday, 5:45 to 6:00 p.m.
Platter Brains (panel show rating new releases), Saturday, 5:15 to 5:30 p.m.
American Music Hall (classical records and chatter), Monday, 8:15 to 8:30 p.m., Milton Cross, M.C.
Opera Albums (classical records and chatter), Sunday, 9:05 to 9:30 a.m., Milton Cross, M.C.[48]

Note in the list that the preponderance of the recorded-music programs being fed by the four national networks in 1954 were not typical disc jockey shows. Instead, there was a reliance on "stars" and "names," including those of the "big band" era and others. Additionally, note that most of the programs were still of the old, short variety, some only fifteen minutes in length. Finally, notice that of

---

[48] "Web Radio's Transcribed Disk Shows," Billboard, November 13, 1954, p. 27.

the 23 programs listed, only six were scheduled five-a-week or six-a-week. It is evident that the networks had made a start toward adapting music-and-news to its lineup, sometimes even grafting the new form onto an old show. But the consistency-of-product which local independent music-and-news stations were already offering was missing. A New York listener could tune WNEW and leave the dial set, while the networks continued to change their programming throughout the day.

One of the longer five-a-week programs, The Martin Block Show, was difficult for ABC to clear with affiliates at first, because most stations already had their own disc jockey show and feared network competition. However, stations which did carry the show received ratings increases, and by July of 1954, 90% of ABC's affiliates were clearing some segments of the show.[49]

ABC's live music

In May of 1957, ABC announced that it was eliminating all programs employing phonograph records in a move toward eventually featuring nothing but live music and personalities on the network. In making the announcement, ABC Radio Network President Robert E. Eastman said, "There is no good reason why a network should ever play phonograph records."[50] Ironically, at the same time that it was signalling the end of record shows (such as Martin Block's) on ABC, the network announced the appointment of Bill Morgan, Jr. as programming vice-president. Morgan

[49]"ABC Sold on Music-News Formula as Means of Strengthening Radio," Broadcasting, July 19, 1954, p. 50.

[50]"New Program Deal at ABC Radio," Broadcasting, May 27, 1957, p. 56.

had recently left his position as vice president of the McLendon Corporation and general manager of KLIF, Dallas, one of the nation's top-rated independent music-and-news/Top 40 stations, which played nothing but phonograph records.[51]

The first of the new live-music programs on ABC Radio was the Herb Oscar Anderson Show, aired five times a week from 10:00 to 11:00 a.m. EST, beginning September 2, 1957. Singer Carole Bennett, baritone Don Rondo, the Satisfiers vocal group, and Ralph Herman's Orchestra all also appeared live each day.[52] As part of ABC's promotion for the show, the network ran an advertisement in Sponsor magazine which included ratings charts for Mr. Anderson's shows in Minneapolis and New York.[53] In 1956, Anderson had been morning man on Storz's newly-acquired WDGY, Minneapolis. ABC's ad quoted a Pulse survey showing a 379% increase in program ratings for the year for the 6:00 to 9:00 a.m. time period.[54] (What ABC failed to mention was that the spectacular rating increase on WDGY was not the result of programming live music, and perhaps not even the result of programming Mr. Anderson. WDGY had been very nearly last in the Minneapolis ratings, so that any substantial increase would show up as a large percentage. But most important, WDGY under Storz ownership was programming their evolving Top 40 format, which relied on phonograph records exclusively.)

---

[51] Ibid.

[52] Advertisement in Sponsor, August 31, 1957, pp. 23, 24.

[53] Ibid., p. 24.

[54] A Pulse survey for WABC, New York for the four-week interval between July 8 and August 7 which showed a 20% increase for the same 6:00 to 9:00 a.m. time period was also quoted. Ibid.

Also in September of 1957, ABC (then calling itself the American Broadcasting Network) ran an advertisement in Broadcasting with a photograph of a wrinkled old lady with her gray hair pulled back on her head, wearing a lace-trimmed dress, a cameo, and wire-rim glasses, who with finger pointed and eyes glaring asked accusingly in the caption, "Young man, what have you done with my soap operas?"[55] The text of the answer follows on page 82.

Other ABC "live" shows included The Johnny Pearson Show, The Merv Griffin Show, The Bill Kemp Show, and The Jim Backus Show.[56]

Meanwhile, in August of 1957, CBS Radio announced at last that it was going to program something for the 14-to-24-year-old audience at night, if sponsors could be signed. Mitch Miller, who had produced many of Columbia's top selling recordings, was to be in charge of developing the format for the two-hour Monday-through-Saturday evening program. Remote pickups of special bands and of jazz festivals in various parts of the country were envisioned. The program was thought to have "great appeal" for the target age group, yet be "different from the usual disc jockey fare. . . ."[57]

Other network music service

One of the more intricate phonograph-record shows provided by a radio network in this transition period was Mutual's sustaining

---

[55] Advertisement in Broadcasting, September 2, 1957, p. 45.

[56] "Radio Networks Are Sizzling with Promotions," Broadcasting, December 2, 1957, p. 28.

[57] "CBS Radio May Add Youth Night Block," Broadcasting, August 12, 1957, p. 50.

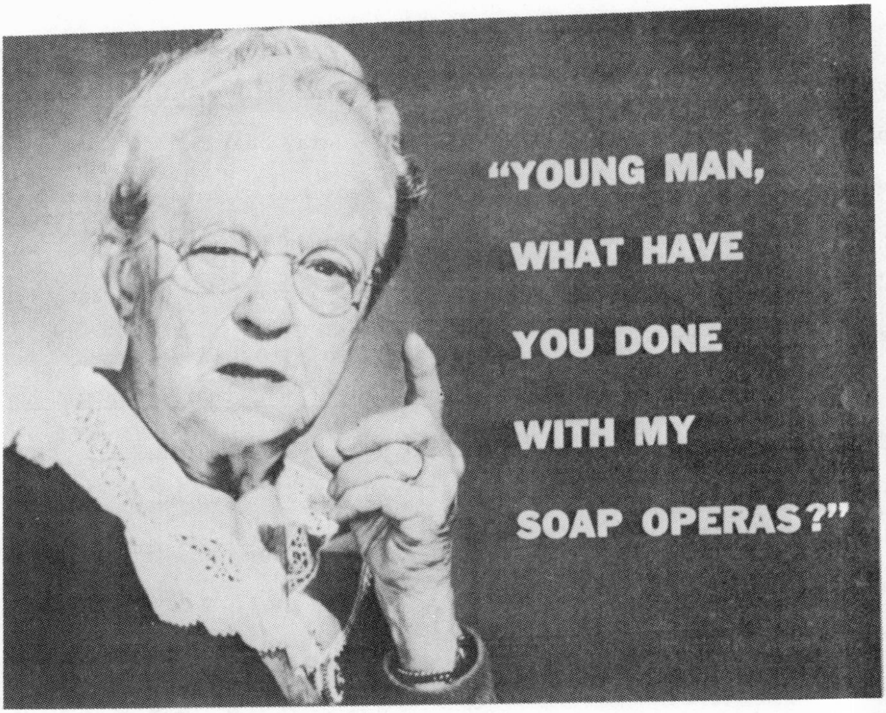
"YOUNG MAN,
WHAT HAVE
YOU DONE
WITH MY
SOAP OPERAS?"

We're sorry, ma'am. You've been a faithful listener for years. But there just wasn't any room for them in our plans for the future. At American Radio we're programing for today's new audience—the on-the-go housewife who's busier than ever, and who has formed new listening habits. So out go soap operas.

"**What's taking their place?**" you ask. **Live** music, that's what—and here's why:

1. Soap operas have dropped 37% in share of radio audience.*
2. 60% of today's housewives listen to music, while only 34.8% listen to soap operas.**
3. Night TV satisfies the demand for drama.***

That's why at American Radio we're programing **live** radio **exclusively.** That's why we're sold on the new **live** Herb Oscar Anderson Show, 10-11 every weekday. It's **live,** top tune music . . . **live** singers . . . **live** orchestra. It's fun radio, and it's what today's young housewife wants.

*A. C. Nielson
**RAB Survey of Radio and Housewives, March 1957
***Pure logic

the live one is

AMERICAN
BROADCASTING
NETWORK

America's Top Tunes. Begun in June of 1957 with 40 clearances, by the end of August it had 200. The program originally concentrated on repeating Top 40 records, but expanded the music to include jazz, country, show tunes, and LP selections after affiliates objected to the "sameness" of the Top 40 tunes. The interesting thing about the program was that it was a combination of music programmed by the network and introductions and commercials provided by local disc jockeys. Exactly one-and-one-half minutes were allowed between records for the local announcer. In order to know what the next record would be, the network prepared cue sheets a month in advance and got them to local stations ten days ahead of the program date.[58]

Mutual's music programming service was not a true network disc jockey show in the way Martin Block's had been on ABC. There were never very many network disc jockeys, since local announcers were plentiful and there were only four national networks that could offer national deejays. Radio networks in the 1950s used singers and even comedians as "star" disc jockeys, as discussed earlier, but the number of network deejays who were only disc jockeys remained few. In 1954, which seems to have been the peak year for network deejays, ABC had Martin Block, CBS had Peter Potter, and Mutual had Ted Steele.[59]

---

[58] "Top Tune Service Gets Bigger Play," Billboard, August 26, 1957, pp. 39, 54.

[59] "Star Record Shows Woo Web Listeners," Billboard, November 13, 1954, p. 1. For an excellent discussion of Martin Block's career up to 1944, see "Profiles: Socko!" in The New Yorker, July 29, 1944, pp. 27-30.

Syndicated Music Programming

By 1954, the syndicated disc jockey program had assumed an importance in radio programming at least commensurate with that of the network disc jockey. The same two approaches to hosting record programs employed by the networks--using "stars" or using real disc jockeys--also prevailed among syndicators. Ziv in 1954 was offering The Hour of Stars, with Ginger Rogers, Tony Martin, Peggy Lee and Dick Powell each hosting their own fifteen minute segment of the hour record show daily.[60] Most such programs did not supply complete programs, but only "star" chatter and introductions for insertion between the records which were selected and played locally. Thus, the actual title of the song was not mentioned, and not much comment about the music was possible.[61] Nevertheless, The Hour of Stars was bought in 400 markets in its first year.[62] Billboard credited the success of the ten disc jockey series being sold in 1954 to independent stations "looking for big-name platter shows to meet the new network competition in the heretofore strictly local disk jockey field."[63]

The syndication of "real" disc jockeys was at first largely confined to those specializing in rhythm-and-blues music. In September of 1954, Billboard reported that Alan Freed of WINS, New York, Hunter Hancock of KFVD, Los Angeles (later KPOP, later still KGBS) and Zena Sears of Atlanta all were taping their regular programs for play on other stations. WNJR, Newark, ran shows from all three deejays every

---

[60] Ibid., p. 27. [61] Ibid. [62] Ibid.

[63] Ibid.

day. Most of the tapes aired were not more than a week old.[64] Bill-board reported that until Freed left WJW in Cleveland in August 1954, the program he had taped there was carried on about ten stations. WINS in New York, his new employer, was planning on 100 stations eventually carrying tapes of Freed's program.[65] Billboard found the success of such programs baffling:

> No one knows why r&b deejays have been successful with syndicated shows when so many pop deejays have failed to make much impression in any town besides their own--with a few notable exceptions.
>
> Most tradesters have felt that jocks could become big in a city only by concentrating on local affairs and catering to local tastes and custom, and that this automatically limited them to that city alone. Many unsuccessful network jock shows gave strength to that argument.
>
> The r&b jock syndicated shows, however, are not on network stations, but are carried on indie stations. This, some claim, helps a lot, since the indie station listeners are prepared for a deejay, and as long as the jock plays the tunes they want, the show can go over.
>
> The growth of the syndicated shows, if it continues, can mean much to the r&b business, and perhaps eventually to the entire record business. It presages the time when the same record can be played on many, many stations by the same jock within a week's time.
>
> This great exposure in such a limited time period could help break thru a record quickly and result in big sales. This, of course, is only a surmise, but the increase in taped deejay shows lends support to the possibility.[66]

Billboard's predictions about syndicated music programs are surprisingly accurate in view of the syndication business at the present time. It is also surprising, therefore, that the magazine failed to see that rhythm and blues syndicated programs were increasingly popular precisely because they were unlike the low-key network disc jockeys or the

---

[64] "Syndicated Deejay Shows Expanding," Billboard, September 18, 1954, p. 11.

[65] Ibid. [66] Ibid.

anachronistic star-studded-but-impersonal nationally syndicated shows. The music and the personalities featured on the rhythm-and-blues shows were new, exciting, and not duplicated elsewhere. Such shows "filled a void."

By January of 1955, syndication had grown so popular that Variety called it a "threat," not only to musicians, but to local disc jockeys, record librarians, and even to time salesmen.[67]

Special Music Program Forms

Two other network popular music program forms must be mentioned in this discussion of the forms which pre-dated independently-programmed Top 40. One of the forms is characterized by a single program: Your Hit Parade. The other is characterized by many variations on the idea of televising a disc jockey and his audience, with American Bandstand the most notable example.

Your Hit Parade

Your Hit Parade began in 1935 with the premise that audiences nationwide would be interested in hearing the seven or so most popular tunes of the week. Your Hit Parade did not play phonograph records, but rather offered song stylings by its own orchestra and cast of singers. In the 1940s, the addition of young Frank Sinatra as a new "regular" brought the program increased listenership, and it lasted in a TV version until 1959. Variety ran the following "obituary" in April of that year:

67"Deejay Syndication Threat," Variety, January 19, 1955, p. 54.

Hit Parade Dies as Rock 'n' Roll Takes
Its Toll of Longrunner, 24

Your Hit Parade, 24, popular musical series, died in New York Friday, on CBS-TV, after a long battle against the challenging trends of the music business. For the past several years the series had been trying to hold an audience through its close to quarter-century-old format of playing the country's top tunes, but the mushrooming popularity of rock 'n' roll finally delivered the *coup de grace*.

Show was on its last legs last season on NBC-TV, but CBS took it over last fall and attempted to breathe new life into it via a more showmanlike format of integrating the clicko rock 'n' rollers with standards. It can be chalked up as a good try but it still failed to draw the kids who wanted their disclicks delivered by the "original" performers, or the adults who didn't want the current pops in any way, shape, or form. Show was fighting a losing battle from its CBS-TV fall teeoff despite the efforts of such personable song sellers as Dorothy Collins and Johnny Desmond.

The final outing Friday mixed the current clicks "Come Softly to Me," "Venus," and "Pink Shoelaces" with some reliables from (end p. 37) the first April, 1935, show like "Lookie, Lookie, Lookie Here Comes Cookie," "Isle of Capri," "It's Easy to Remember," "Lovely to Look At," "Lullaby of Broadway," and "Soon." Warren Hull, who was announcer on the first show, was on hand for the bowoff to build the nostalgic mood.

Long associated with the American Tobacco Co., the series was once known as the *Lucky Strike Hit Parade*; show was sponsored by Hit Parade cigs in its last season.

Surviving are the American Tobacco Co. [Even American Tobacco Co. didn't survive. It is now American Brands. Hit Parade cigarettes have also disappeared.], CBS, and NBC, among others.[68]

The *Variety* "obituary" emphasizes the role of rock 'n' roll music in the demise of *Your Hit Parade*, but there were other factors. One was the fact that while in 1950 an estimated 80% of all music on TV were standards, by as early as 1954 *Billboard* reported ". . . the ratio is almost all current hits."[69] In other words, television itself was already supplying plenty of exposure to hit music, as of course radio

---

[68]"*Hit Parade* Dies as Rock 'n' Roll Takes Its Toll of Longrunner, 24," *Variety*, April 29, 1959, pp. 37, 44.

[69]"Video's a Song's No. 1 Hit-Maker," *Billboard*, February 27, 1954, p. 27.

was doing increasingly.

Second, there was a problem of lack of familiarity. In 1959, the lifespan of a hit song was very much shorter than it had been in the 1930s or 1940s. There were more songs being recorded, more exposure was being given to them, and audiences were satiated sooner than before. A "newcomer to the survey" so far as adult listeners were concerned was already a "golden-oldie" to the teenage audience.

Finally, the point about "original" performances that Variety made must be explained by the fact that by 1959, "cover" versions of hit songs had all but disappeared. (A "cover" was another version of the song, released after the original, and designed to cash in on its popularity. White "covers" of black groups' rhythm-and-blues records were especially important in the early and mid-1950s in establishing rock 'n' roll among white teenagers, but as teenage record personalities were developed, the supposed necessity of releasing a "cleaned-up" version was lessened.) Ten years earlier, Russell Armes might have done a fair job at covering a Bing Crosby hit, but there was no way he could duplicate Elvis Presley. The Hit Parade regulars were the equivalent of the band singers--the Sinatras and Doris Days--who simply went out of fashion in the 1960s.

TV record shows

In November of 1954, Billboard ran an article titled "Disc Jockey Move to Video is Still a Long, Hard Trip," in which the successful local TV deejays of the day were listed. Billboard found more successful TV deejays in Hollywood and Chicago than in New York. The article claimed that the "first really successful record show on networ

TV was the Paul Dixon-Dotty Mack disk pantomime series which originated from Cincinnati more than four years ago."[70]

In November of 1956, Billboard announced the results of its disc jockey survey which showed an increasing number of local TV disc jockey shows. Billboard's poll found 51 local disc jockey shows, representing 44 cities and 26 states. Sixty percent of the programs were scheduled on a daily basis, with almost all the others weekly. Of the weekly shows, 85% were aired on Saturdays, to attract the teenage audience.[71] Billboard declared that the biggest problem in TV record shows was what to take a picture of while the record was playing. Only the larger markets could attract recording-star guests, and only the biggest markets could afford to pay guest talent scale for the usual lip-sync singing appearance.[72]

In Billboard's listing of local TV disc jockey shows, about two-thirds of the 51 programs listed were in medium-to-small-sized markets (such as Washington, North Carolina; or Dothan, Alabama).[73] Among the list was WFIL-Philadelphia's Bandstand, which Dick Clark was hosting locally between 2:30 and 5:00. p.m.[74]

---

[70]"Disk Jockey Move to Video is Still a Long, Hard Trip," Billboard, November 13, 1954, p. 2. The Paul Dixon Show, now more like Breakfast Club than a deejay program, was still aired over WLWT-TV, Cincinnati, in 1971.

[71]"TV D.J.s' Status Up at Local Level," Billboard, November 10, 1956, p. 62.

[72]Ibid.

[73]"Directory of Local TV Disk Jockey Shows," Billboard, November 10, 1956, p. 78.

[74]Ibid.

In late July, 1957, James T. Aubrey, Jr., then ABC-TV vice president in charge of programming, announced that the network would carry the renamed American Bandstand between 3:00 and 4:00 p.m. EST beginning August 7. The network claimed the new show was "in line with the network's new emphasis on live music and personalities."[75]

A week after American Bandstand's debut, Broadcasting published its review of the program. While it praised Dick Clark for being "personable, self assured" and for "blend[ing] in well with the youngsters, who undoubtedly consider him a hep oldster," the review found the music already too teen-oriented, and concluded "It is not likely many housewives (unless they're hep to 'crazy,' 'oh, yeah,' 'I'm with you,' and 'ah, too much') will tune in these summer afternoons."[76]

American Bandstand turned out to be a solid and immediate ratings success. The local program had been number one in Philadelphia in its time period before going on the network,[77] and in the September Trendex, it was already number one between 3:00 and 4:30 p.m.[78] Billboard reported "The show chalked up a 5.7 rating, with a 35.6 share of audience--62 percent higher than CBS and 35 percent greater than NBC. [T] Bandstand share-of-audience figure was more than double that chalked up

---

[75]"ABC-TV's American Bandstand," Broadcasting, July 29, 1957, p. 94.

[76]"In Review: American Bandstand," Broadcasting, August 12, 1957, p. 24.

[77]Advertisement, "American Bandstand Kayos CBS and NBC Combined!" Sponsor, October 12, 1957, p. 1.

[78]"TV Jock Finally Comes Into Own," Billboard, October 7, 1957, p. 28.

by the web in the same time period in August. . . ."[79] The October Trendex showed Bandstand with a 33.2 share-of-audience.[80] While record promoters were glad to get simultaneous exposure for their discs on the 65-station Bandstand lineup, they pointed out that generally, the record was only played once in a week, while local deejay radio programs often gave multiple-play exposure each day.[81] At its peak, American Bandstand was aired on 105 stations and reached 20 million teenagers a day.[82]

The ratings success of American Bandstand led to its being cleared by 84 markets.[83] The popularity Bandstand enjoyed in station clearances resulted in over 100 local TV record shows being aired by March 1958,[84] and caused NBC-TV to consider airing a TV deejay show of its own.[85]

There was also a "syndicated" TV record show series called Top 10 Dance Party, packaged by Victor & Richards. A local M. C. employed

---

[79] Ibid.

[80] "TV Spinners as Strong on Network as on Local Air," Billboard, November 11, 1957, p. 30.

[81] Ibid.

[82] Richard Goldstein, "Master of Mediocrity," in Goldstein's Greatest Hits, Englewood Cliffs, N.J.: Prentice-Hall, Inc., 1970, p. 202.

[83] "Bandstand Hypes Local TV DJ Rush," Billboard, March 31, 1958, p. 12.

[84] Ibid., p. 4.

[85] "NBC Mulls Deejay Rival for Clark," Billboard, March 24, 1958, p. 36.

the prizes and programming ideas which were supplied by the syndicators.[86]

In 1960, Billboard published the results of a study of 74 TV record dance shows, and found that 48 of them were aired weekly on Saturday afternoons. All of the Monday-through-Friday shows were aired between 3:00 and 6:00 p.m. to coincide with the availability of teenagers.[87] The article stated that the oldest TV record and dance show was the original Bandstand, which began with Bob Horn as host on October 13, 1952, over WFIL, Philadelphia.[88]

There is no doubt that TV record dance shows were an important factor in late-afternoon local programming in the mid-50s, and that they served to spread styles and images by the examples they presented. It can be argued that TV record dance shows were important enough to deserve a study of their own. On the other hand, TV record dance shows should not be viewed as an outgrowth of the developing Top 40 radio format. TV record dance shows were entirely different from Top 40 radio in their style of presentation, their less-limited playlist, their lack of promotion and of station recall devices and jingles, and in their use of guests and interviews. TV record dance shows' points of commonality with Top 40 radio were only in the use of disc jockey hosts, the playing of current popular records, and (to a more limited extent) the appeal to teenagers.[89] Most importantly, there was a difference in the reasons

---

[86] "Billboard Profiles TV's Disk Dance-Party Shows," Billboard, April 11, 1960, p. 22.

[87] Ibid. [88] Ibid., p. 3.

[89] TV record shows often carried such titles as Teen Canteen or Teen Dance Party, while Top 40 programs seldom sought to identify their most likely audience, for reasons that will be detailed later.

r which the two genre were begun: for TV, video record shows were an periment carried out during a healthy period of daytime program expan-on; for radio, Top 40 was the only programming form that seemed to ke money when everything else was failing. Finally, TV record shows ve survived as a program form, but not in anything approaching the mber of examples as used to be available. Top 40, meanwhile, not ly endured as a program form, but became identified as an entire ation format--many radio stations today program nothing else. One an scarcely imagine even a single TV station in the country programming othing but record dance shows all day long. Viewed in this light, the istinction between the TV record shows and Top 40 is more apparent.

Radio Network Affiliates' Local Programming

This study has already shown some of the changes that were aking place in radio network programming in the early and mid-1950s. t is appropriate now to turn to the local station level to see how hose programming changes were affecting the affiliate. (The last ortion of this chapter will deal with programming at local independent stations.)

Pete Thomas was a program director at CBS affiliate WKOW in Madison, Wisconsin in the early and mid-1950s. The CBS radio network, as has been shown previously, was the slowest to adapt to new listening patterns. Moreover, Madison, Wisconsin has never been a particularly representative market since it is both the site of the University of Wisconsin and within range of radio signals from some of the powerful stations in both Milwaukee and Chicago. Thomas's observations quoted below are thus to be applied only to the Madison market at the time, although virtually the same conditions prevailed in countless other markets.

The role of the program director at WKOW in the early and mid-1950s was either to accept or reject network offerings and to design programs to fill the times when the network did not offer satisfactory programming. The local programs in that era were not concerned with fitting a format or an overall station sound, but rather were primarily designed to produce a certain amount of revenue. A particular program was accepted or rejected for a particular time period by weighing the production charges and talent fees against the incoming revenue. Since a generalized audience was wanted, a program of general interest is what usually resulted.[90] "The assumption was a program was a program and as long as it had a fair appeal and was produced competently, it was okay."[91]

Because network programming did not change very rapidly, neither did that of affiliated stations. In the case of CBS, which dropped its long list of soap operas and other programs one by one, the increase in the amount of time which had to be programmed locally was gradual. Until about 1956, WKOW was following network patterns and programmed fully-scripted shows on Sundays, for example. In these shows, music was secondary to topical subjects which personalities discussed. By 1957, music was dominant.[92]

Throughout this period, the concept of a single format for a

---

[90] Interview between the author and Pete Thomas, Madison, Wisconsin, April 27, 1972.

[91] Ibid. [92] Ibid.

tation was anathema.

> . . . the attitude in a station was to cover as wide a spectrum of audience as you could attract . . . in other words, the philosophy that's on TV now. The idea of a station narrowly restricting itself was just alien. When stations went to heavy sports, for instance--which was one of the first things that happened--that was kind of repugnant to those of us who worked with the big network affiliates because it restricted your potential audience.

The Madison market was rated only once or twice a year according to Thomas, and true demographic information was not part of the report; thus again there was little movement toward programming for specific audiences. A program could be tailored to an advertiser if the station were lucky enough to have one waiting for it, but most often programs were designed to have general audience appeal, which in turn would have advertiser appeal. Since the ratings were so infrequently taken, they were not very important as a sales device. What was important was the "ability of the salesman to believe that the program was attracting listeners, and to convey that same feeling to the advertiser."[93]

Even before CBS started dropping its programs, WKOW was running a limited number of record programs during times when the network did not provide service at all. There was an early morning farm program, followed by a seven to nine a.m. record show which was a spot-carrier. Then the network programming began. In that era, there was not another record show on WKOW until 4:30, which filled until the network newscasts began at five.[94] One night a week, there was a show which played the

---

[93] Stations also often sold time on the basis of power and mail-pull instead of programming. Ibid.

[94] Ibid.

top ten records in Madison for a half hour, but the records and the program both appealed to a general audience at that time. "It wasn't specifically a kids' market. The records were generally the same sort you would have found on the Lucky Strike Hit Parade."[95] From 10:30 p.m. to midnight, there was an all-request-dedication show, and that was the extent of the record programming.[96]

As stated before, WKOW carried scripted programs until 1957, when the station turned to straight music-and-personalities to fill around network offerings, with the amount of music increasing as the suitable network programs diminished. The pattern in the case of affiliate WKOW is clear: local programming imitated network programming, even as network programming was failing at holding audiences. There was little attempt to develop programming to fit a certain segment of the market or even the new listening patterns. Older program forms, older selling methods, and old-fashion notions of what was "proper" prevailed. (It was not, for instance, considered proper to air a recording unless absolutely necessary--even for news feeds to a network report, wires were run for a live insertion.)

Independent Stations' Music Programming

As has been shown earlier, the great majority of independent stations programmed some form of music-and-news format, although the type of music and the amount of time devoted to various other program elements varied widely.

As early as the middle 1930s, a few independents were pioneering long blocks of recorded music interspersed with

---

[95] Ibid. [96] Ibid.

regularly scheduled newscasts and managed to compete successfully with network affiliates in their markets. Among these pioneers, and credited by many as <u>the</u> pioneer was WNEW, New York.[97]

<u>ponsor</u> magazine identified the early WNEW format as characteristic of at it called the "pre-TV format."[98] The elements of this format were:

> (1) a wide variety of music, perhaps 300 to 400 tunes; (2) strong personalities with something to say and who commanded fierce listener loyalty; (3) regular newscasts dealing with events of national or international significance; (4) an awareness of public service.
>
> The programming was smooth and professional. Station promotion was conservative. This sound has survived and prospered and will be around for a long time.[99]

<u>Sponsor</u> found the distinguishing characteristics of the post-TV ormat to be (1) "a narrower variety of music," usually just the Top 40 unes; (2) local, mobile news coverage; (3) "personalities who are ubordinate to the music they play"; and (4) a "growing interest in ublic service."[100]

WNEW

In 1934, Arde Bulova of the watch manufacturing family and ilton Biow of the then-famous (now defunct) Biow advertising agency ounded WNEW. By 1949, independent WNEW was billing nearly $3,000,000 year under the general managership of Bernice ("Tudie") Judis, and as already regarded as the nation's number one independent in terms of

---

[97]"Radio in Transition: Music and News are Only Building locks," <u>Sponsor</u>, September 7, 1957, p. 39.

[98]<u>Ibid</u>.

[99]<u>Ibid</u>. Notice that the early WNEW format called for a large umber of songs with little repetition.

[100]<u>Ibid</u>., p. 40.

prestige, programming, and income.[101]

Bernice Judis seems to have been the first independent station manager to realize some of the strengths of music-and-news programming, and some of the requirements to put it across. However whimsically she may have said it, Miss Judis was right in pointing out that by tuning WNEW, "you can leave the room and, when you come back, you've missed nothing."[102] Miss Judis also early understood the value (necessity) of some station promotion: there were shocking-pink rate cards, full page New York Times advertisements, and call-letter reminders printed on the backs of laundry tags.[103]

WNEW was succeeding while network radio was still healthy, and it continued to succeed during the TV invasion by "filling a void"--by doing something different or by doing the same thing better than any other station was doing it. For instance, WNEW did not try to compete in kind with the evening network radio programs, but instead aired inexpensive programs not really intended to offer a challenge. By so doing, WNEW saved its resources--especially its personalities--for the daytime hours when network programming was not so strong. And the station was early to specialize in doing what radio could do better than TV: play music almost continuously, and offer the news briefly but often.[104] Announcers were hired for their ability to sound intimate and personal--especially in ad-libbing commercials--rather than distant

---

[101] "The Stepchild," Time, April 18, 1949, p. 63.

[102] Ibid. [103] Ibid.

[104] "WNEW New York: Radio's Little David Doesn't Fear TV," Fortune, October, 1952, p. 133.

and impersonal, as the typical network announcer had been. The most famous WNEW announcer was Martin Block, who began with a 15-minute show and eventually became so popular that he did three and a half hours daily.[105] Block's programs were sold on a semi-participating (segmented) basis, which allowed many sponsors to be sold in a single high-rated show.[106]

There were plenty of features about WNEW in its pioneer days that distinguished it from the later Top 40 station. For one thing, the music varied both with the time of day and with the personality on whose show it appeared. The disc jockeys selected their own music at WNEW, while in Top 40 stations, management would select it. At the same time, WNEW resisted "jitterbug" songs--a nine word memo from Bernice Judis is said to have read "Effective immediately: No more screamers are to be played."[107] Finally, commercials in those earlier days at WNEW were always soft-sell and personalized rather than hard-sell and produced as they would later be on Top 40 stations, with the exception of the use of jingles for program feature introductions and public service announcements.

In August of 1955, WNEW ran an advertisement in Broadcasting which showed it ahead of all of New York's network stations, with a 21.4% share as against an 18.6% share for the top network station's best showing.[108]

---

[105] Ibid., p. 224. [106] Ibid. [107] Ibid., p. 227.

[108] Keep in mind that at this time most "ratings" were simple "head counts" of the listening audience. A share is the number of people listening to one station expressed as a percentage of all listening. Advertisement in Broadcasting, August 1, 1955, p. 11.

In 1956, WNEW reported that its average quarter-hour ratings were one-third higher than in 1947, before TV.[109] A study by the station based on Hooper ratings showed independent stations were in first place over network competition in 1956 in New York (WNEW), Chicago (WIND), Boston (WHDH), Pittsburgh (WWSW), and Cleveland (WERE).[110]

WNEW increased its audiences through shrewd programming, as already discussed, but also through the use of careful and extensive audience research. As Broadcasting put it in a 1955 article,

> Perpetually holding hands with WNEW's program department is the station's research department under Mrs. Mary McKenna. In research, WNEW does everything everybody else does but a little more and a little different. Mrs. McKenna is equipped at the drop of a figure to advise the program department that the out-of-home listener wants more traffic reports, that a quicker tempo in music garners more listeners of a Saturday morning, or that a new DJ is paying off with the teenagers. . . .[111]

Note that the product of the research department at WNEW was not used just as a sales tool, but as feedback to the programming department. There was an aggressive interest in serving to the audience what it wanted most, and extensive and careful "internal" research accomplished that end.[112]

WNEW's success was so phenomenal that the station became one of the most often-sold in the business. In 1954, Bernice Judis Herbert

---

[109] "Indie Time Buying Up," Billboard, November 10, 1956, p. 20.

[110] Ibid., p. 20.

[111] "The Stylish Stylus," Broadcasting, September 19, 1955, p. 170.

[112] "Internal" research is that which a company uses for its own private purposes. "External" research is that which is used primarily in public, often as a means of selling or promotion. Detailed ratings could be used both ways, but many stations employed them only as "external" research.

and her husband Ira sold the station for about $2,000,000 and retired.[113] When the station was sold again in 1955, the price was $4,000,000. In 1957, the station brought the highest ever paid (to that date) for a radio station: $7,500,000.[114]

The success of WNEW was widely reported, and there is little doubt that WNEW was for many years the "model" independent radio operation. At the same time, there were other noteworthy approaches to the question of how to program and operate a successful independent radio station.

WINS

WINS was another New York City radio station, and had an even longer history than WNEW, having gone on the air in 1924. However, WINS's history of success was not as steady as that of WNEW. WINS had been bought by the Crosley Broadcasting interests in 1945 from Hearst Radio, Inc., for $1,700,000. In August, 1953, Crosley Broadcasting sold the station to J. Elroy McCaw of Gotham Broadcasting Corporation for just $450,000.[115]

Under new management, the station began to stress "personalities." The first to be hired were Bob & Ray, for a morning show that began in March of 1954.[116] But in the fall of 1954, WINS hired its

---

[113] "The Stylish Stylus," p. 170.

[114] "DuMont Pays $7.5 Million for WNEW," Broadcasting, March 25, 1957, p. 31.

[115] "McCaw Group Pays $450,000 for WINS," Broadcasting, August 10, 1953, p. 70.

[116] "Leder Revamps WINS, Names New Personnel," Broadcasting, March 15, 1954, p. 88.

best-known personality among the increasingly-important teenage audience: Alan Freed.

Freed had run a request show on Akron's WAKR from 1946 to 1950, when he moved the show to WXEL, Cleveland, where it failed.[117] But Cleveland record dealer, Leo Mintz, convinced Freed against the latter' instincts that "a steady diet of gospel groups, blues singers and saxed-up instrumental combos would have the kids listening, buying--and dancing--in no time at all."[118] That "diet" is what Freed played on his Moon Dog Show (later The Moon Dog House Rock 'n' Roll Party) on Clev land's WJW, and between the consistency of the music and the sincere fre of his style, Freed became the most-sought "teen-appeal" deejay in the country. By May of 1955, Freed's program on WINS had increased the program period's ratings 200% in six months,[119] and five daily one-hour programs per week were being syndicated (under the title The Original Alan Freed Rock 'n' Roll Party) to stations in Baltimore, Kansas City, St. Louis, and elsewhere.[120] By December of 1955, WINS was claiming a 77% increase in share of audience and a 138% jump in ratings in two years for the 6:00 a.m. to midnight Monday-through-Friday time period.[121]

By 1956, the term "rock and roll" was well-entrenched as the

---

[117] Arnold Passman, The Deejays (New York: The MacMillan Company, 1971), p. 176.

[118] Ibid., p. 177.

[119] Advertisement in Sponsor, May 16, 1955, p. 126.

[120] Ibid.

[121] Advertisement in Broadcasting, December 5, 1955, back cover.

coverall description for the rhythm-and-blues-based music that was popular among teenagers, and Alan Freed, as its foremost proponent, had to begin defending the genre. In May of 1958, Freed was arraigned in Boston on charges of inciting a riot there with an anti-police remark made during a concert. On the same day, WABC announced the hiring of Freed for a nighttime show,[122] as Freed had quit WINS for failing to back his "policies and principles" the week before.[123] On November 21, 1959, WABC fired Freed because he had refused to sign a statement saying he had never received gifts or money for playing records.[124] In 1960, in Los Angeles, Freed was indicted on commercial bribery charges (payola) and in 1962, while working at Todd Storz's WQAM in Miami, he pleaded guilty to a portion of the indictment and received a suspended sentence. (Later, Freed was also indicted for income tax evasion.) According to Passman, Freed's last radio job was as a jazz deejay on KNOB-FM, Los Angeles.[125] Passman claims Freed took "the biggest fall in the payola scandals . . ." and died ". . . a penniless drunk January 20, 1965."[126]

WINS, meanwhile, was doing well. In 1960, Storer Broadcasting bought the station for $10,000,000.[127]

---

[122]"Freed Goes to WABC," Billboard, May 19, 1958, p. 8.

[123]"Rock 'n' Riot," Time, May 19, 1958, p. 50.

[124]Passman, The Deejays, p. 237.

[125]Ibid., p. 238.

[126]Ibid., p. 176.

[127]"WINS Purchased for $10 Million," Broadcasting, August 1, 1960, p. 76.

Other Stations

KLAC

What was considered to be the "first all-disc-jockey station with identifiable personalities,"[128] began in Los Angeles in March of 1946 over KLAC, formerly KMTR.[129] Al Jarvis and Peter Potter were both lured to the station from KFWB.[130] With these personalities, mostly hit music, and a minimum of commercials at the outset, the station became number one in the market in three months.[131] The various disc jockeys were not all the same in personality, but every program was a disc jockey program, and the novel consistency paid off.

There were developments in music-and-news programming in markets other than New York and Los Angeles as well.

WITH

WITH, Baltimore went on the air in March of 1941 with just 250 watts at 1230 kHz.[132] (By comparison, WNEW began with 10,000 watts and then increased to 50,000 watts at 1130 kHz.) WITH's signal radiated only about 15 miles, but that was sufficient to cover most of the 1,300,000 people clustered in the central Baltimore market area. WITH even made a sales pitch out of its lack of power in its frequent trades ads, one of which is reproduced here.[133] In 1952, this tiny station

---

[128] Passman, The Deejays, p. 115. [129] Ibid., p. 114.

[130] Ibid., pp. 114, 115. [131] Ibid., p. 116.

[132] "Those Riches in the Indies," Broadcasting, January 26, 1953, p. 80.

[133] Advertisement in Broadcasting, April 1, 1957, front cover.

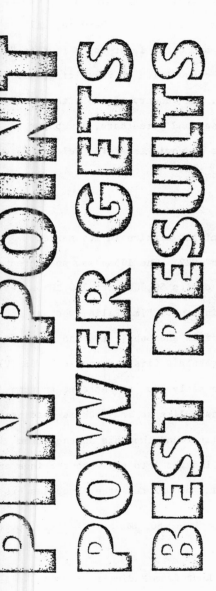

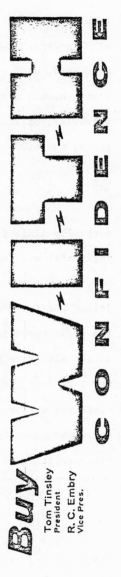

had gross time sales of $806,652.[134] Since its inception, the station had programmed music, news, and sports continuously around the clock. Only in the late hours could "hot jazz" be played; otherwise, all the records were music "that anybody can hum or at least tap a foot to."[13 WITH, unlike WNEW, refused to do any copywriting or re-writing, but like WNEW, WITH used heavy promotion. In January of 1953, the promotion schedule included ads on 350 buses and streetcars, newspaper schedules, billboards, advertisements at movie theaters, Welcome Wagon gifts, and 4,000,000 matchbooks a year.[136]

WSB

WSB, Atlanta has been the dominant station in its market virtually since it went on the air in 1922. The 1950s saw an increasingly affluent audience within range of its 50,000 watt 750 kHz signal, and yet WSB's audiences were dwindling. Elmo Ellis, who had joined WSB in 1940 as director of scripts and publicity, and who left the radio operation in 1948 to put Atlanta's first TV station (WSB-TV) on the air, came back to WSB radio in early 1952 to "attempt to pump new life into a fine radio station that--like so many others--had been neglected because of TV."[137] Mr. Ellis found that his absence from radio had given him a more objective insight into the "shortcomings an potentialities of the industry,"[138] and he offered other broadcasters

---

[134]"Those Riches in the Indies," pp. 80, 81. [135]Ibid., p. 8

[136]Ibid.

[137]Elmo Ellis, "Removing the Rust from Radio Programming," Broadcasting, February 2, 1953, p. 80.

[138]Ibid.

some conclusions about what they should do to keep radio a dominant medium.

> 1. Neither daytime nor nighttime radio will die. A multitude of people is still waiting to be entertained by "good radio." But only a cockeyed optimist would blithely conclude that radio is now going through a competitive period from which it will emerge unscathed and unchanged. Radio is suffering from the assaults of TV and, like it or not, it is undergoing a transformation. The regrettable fact is that the staffs of numerous radio stations are letting circumstances alone reshape their future. In many operations, salesmen are doing the programming, program directors are doing traffic, and the manager is doing the worrying. Proper teamwork could remedy this hapless condition.
>
> 2. A stack of records and a turntable do not make a radio program (nor a radio station), even though many broadcasters persist in that belief. But the simple addition of a sound format, a good script and capable production will turn a record show into a listenable and salable commodity. In other words, ingenuity is more important than dollars in building sound radio policies, and every broadcaster (including network and agency moguls) should learn this basic lesson.
>
> 3. A program director can't sit high in an ivory tower and decide arbitrarily what listeners want to hear and what is best for them. Why not consult the audience? Advertisers and agency men may not like to hear this, but the fact is that listeners know more about what a station should put on the air than most sponsors. Besides, the average listener likes the idea of being asked his program preferences and he is quick to cooperate by giving his opinions. Progressive stations are proving it. WSB's dominance in the Atlanta market is a direct result of giving the audience what it wants.
>
> 4. You can't obtain radio response by reviving old programs and older personalities.
>
> 5. You can't prosper by simply riding the coat-tails of a network. This job has to be done by you in your own backyard.
>
> 6. You can't snare an audience by imitating television or by presenting simulcasts.
>
> 7. You can't buy listeners by giving away autos and refrigerators or by hiring a Hollywood personality to headline on an otherwise dull and tasteless half-hour.
>
> 8. You can't build good shows with ad lib remarks (Godfreys are rare); nor can you present good newscasts by merely tearing copy off a teletype.
>
> 9. The future of radio does not lie in pursuance of the same programming methods that proved popular a decade or two ago.[139]

---

[139] _Ibid._

The points listed by Elmo Ellis in 1953 might well have been the guiding principles behind the programming of the Top 40 stations that would appear later, but for WSB, they resulted in a basic music-and-news format that added the dimensions of "distinctiveness" and "freshness." WSB became different from both TV and from other radio stations--it developed a distinctive sound of its own.[140] The "freshness" dimension was also an Ellis contribution. Station breaks were changed every week or two, for instance, so that none became overly-familiar.[141] Some Top 40 stations also adopted this element later.

Ellis also listed six questions that a program director should ask himself:

> 1. Are you playing the music your audience wants? Our close study of music has led us to play not what disc jockeys prefer, but what we have reason to believe listeners want at specific times. Every music show is built around an idea and the tunes are picked at least a day ahead of airing. . . .
> 2. Are you placing proper emphasis on your newscasts? At a time of general retrenchment, we have increased our news staff and revised news formats, to provide multiple voices for better news coverage, special sound and musical effects . . . and carefully integrated commercials. We cover beats, augment stories by phone, and spice up newscasts with interviews and locally-taped features.
> 3. Are you getting full benefit from radio's flexibility? Tapes and telephone lines give radio a big advantage of ease and speed over TV. . . .
> 4. Are you selling radio short on glamor? There's still a lot of potential magic in words and voices. We attempt to sprinkle a bit of star dust. . . .
> 5. Do you encourage steady listening? It may seem a small point to emphasize, but our station never says goodbye. We

---

[140]It was possible even in 1972 to tune across the radio dial in the Atlanta market and be struck by the distinctiveness of WSB's sound. It might best be described as "densely varied." There are so many features, phrases, musical bridges and other elements that there is no mistaking WSB.

[141]Ellis, "Removing the Rust from Radio Programming," p. 81.

hope and expect our listeners to stay with us for many hours, during the day and night. . . . Consequently, we conclude our show, not with an adios, but with a reminder to stay tuned for the next program following on the 750 spot.

And instead of merely mentioning the program that is to follow, we prepare for our announcers intriguing teaser lines. If the succeeding show is a popular record program, the announcer might end with something like: "Listen to the most popular song in America. It'll be played on the Music Room, coming up next on WSB Radio."

6. Do you promote and publicize your programs? No radio station should overlook the many ways it can publicize and promote its service other than over the air. . . .[142]

The six points listed by Ellis for program directors to consider n 1953 all became important elements in the Top 40 formula: careful usic selection to match audience tastes, more varied and lively news overage, mobile and on-the-spot reporting, glamor (as accrued to the tation and its personalities), lengthening the listening period, and rogram (and station) promotion through all available means.

BIG

KBIG, Catalina Island, California began broadcasting in June of 952. It was the 23rd radio station to enter the Los Angeles county arket, which also already contained seven TV stations. Although the tation's studios were in Hollywood, KBIG's transmitter was on atalina Island, which gave its 10,000 watt signal at 740 kHz greater han usual coverage because of the salt water ground system. Still, ith 22 other radio stations in the market, the competitive position of ny new station was apt to be a rugged one.[143]

By the third month on the air, KBIG was operating in the black.

---

[142] Ibid., pp. 81, 82.

[143] Robert J. McAndrews, "Out of Red Into Sun," Billboard, pril 25, 1953, p. 39.

Their 41 charter advertisers were mostly first-time radio buyers--none was taken from other radio stations.[144] Their sales staff simply decided to sell new prospects first, not clients already on the air elsewhere. But that is not the entire reason for KBIG's success, only a part of it. Robert J. McAndrews, commercial manager for the John Poole Broadcasting Company, owners of KBIG, analogized the introductior of a new radio service to the introduction of some more tangible produc by a manufacturer, and listed five well-known steps in the decision-making process:

> (1) market research to determine if there's a need; (2) product research to attain perfectability of the item; (3) advertising; (4) promotion; (5) salesmanship.[145]

The market research which KBIG carried out before going on the air included interviews with a cross-section of 5,000 Los Angeles area residents.

> They told us they wanted middle-of-the-road popular music, mixing the melodic hits of today with those of yesterday and yesteryear and leaving the extremes of be-bop, hillbilly and classical for other stations with more definitely limited appeals. So we give them their music--55 minutes of it each hour.
>
> They said they wanted to be kept up on the news but not be beaten over the head with too much of it, so we give them five minutes of news each hour. Three or four times an hour we insert extra news items.[146]

As Mr. McAndrews put it, "on the basis of their statements we laid out a program formula."[147] Again, management had gone to a cross-section of listeners to find out what they wanted to hear.

KBIG advertised itself in the broadcasting trades, initially spending ten percent of the first year's gross, then settling on five percent of revenue as the regular expenditure. But it spent even more

---

[144]*Ibid.* [145]*Ibid.* [146]*Ibid.* [147]*Ibid.*

n station promotion to the public, buying space in all 50 Southern alifornia daily papers, using billboards with a giant clock, and bench, ransportation, and theater advertisements. For the opening period, the tation even bought time on other radio and TV stations.[148] As at WNEW nd at WSB, KBIG's format was basically music-and-news.

Other Developments

Elsewhere in the country, music and news stations were suddenly howing up well in the ratings, especially as network listening continued to drop. WCPO, Cincinnati, ran an advertisement in Broadcasting or July 20, 1953 which carried the headline "Nix To Nets At Night--say incinnati radio listeners--Hooper survey shows WCPO with music-news-ports programs FIRST in listener preference."[149] The average quarter our rating for WCPO against the four other stations it listed was just .8, but the fact that it was garnered by a music-and-news independent as significant.

A poll of radio station managers conducted by Billboard in 1953 evealed that the average AM station devoted nearly half of its air ime to disc jockey and other recorded music shows, with the average ime per week at 113.2 hours.[150] There were no significant differences n the growth of recorded music programming nor in the current amount f such programming among stations of various wattages and market

---

[148] Ibid.

[149] Advertisement in Broadcasting, July 20, 1953, p. 60.

[150] "National Poll Pin-Points Radio's Disk Show Growth," illboard, February 28, 1953, p. 1.

sizes.[151] Nearly 60% of all stations also noted an increase in the number of sponsors for disc jockey shows.[152] Nev Gehman, who wrote th Billboard article cited above felt that the increase in recorded music programming "has been accelerated by rising operating costs and the growing impact of television. . . ."[153]

One suspects that the success of music-and-news operations was a source of irritation to the broadcasters who in the middle 1950s wer clinging to other formats while their stations continued to decline in popularity and in revenue return. The term "electronic jukebox" was a favorite expletive for the music-and-news station, even before Top 40 came into vogue. While in January of 1955, WIOD in Miami boasted of 7 requests in the hour-and-a-half that its Teenage Jukebox program was aired between 9:30 and noon on Saturdays,[154] less than two years later Donald H. McGannon, president of Westinghouse Broadcasting, felt compelled to defend music-and-news stations like his own from the "electronic jukebox" accusation. Mr. McGannon was quoted as saying he was "'not at all reluctant to indicate that the music and news format is a completely sound and proper method, in my judgment, of operating a rad station.'"[155] Mr. McGannon was quoted further as saying "'It is being met with tremendous acclaim on the part of the public. Nobody likes music and news but people.'"[156] Westinghouse Broadcasting a month

---

151 Ibid., p. 16. 152 Ibid. 153 Ibid., p. 1.

154 Advertisement in Broadcasting, January 10, 1955, p. 81.

155 "Defense of Music-News Made Before N.J. Assn.," Broadcastir November 12, 1956, p. 106.

156 Ibid.

reviously had announced the purchase of Chicago's highest-rated music-nd-news station, WIND, for $5,300,000,[157] and earlier in the year had ropped their affiliation with NBC in order to operate as independents ith their other radio stations.[158]

FCC Program Requirements

While stations and group owners programmed increasing amounts f the popular music-and-news format, few were bold enough to run usic-and-news to the exclusion of other types of programming. Until 965, the FCC required that all radio stations schedule some programing in each of seven prescribed categories: entertainment, religious, gricultural, educational, news, discussion, talks. In March of 1958 he Commission made its first challenge of music-and-news stations by ending letters of inquiry[159] to nine Atlanta radio stations whose icenses were due to expire April first. The FCC wanted to know why he preceding year's composite program logs of stations WAKE, WAOK, EAS, WERD, WGKA-AM-FM, WGST, WQXI and WTAM all showed little or no rogramming in the educational, religious, or agricultural cateories.[160]

---

[157] "WIND Sold for Record $5.3 Million," Broadcasting, September , 1956, p. 27.

[158] WBZ, Boston; KYW, Cincinnati; KDKA, Pittsburgh; WBZA, pringfield, Mass.; WOWO, Fort Wayne, and KEX, Portland, Oregon. KEX as an ABC affiliate, but also dropped its network. For a discussion f the Westinghouse switch to an independent music-and-news operation, ee "How Its Independent Move Paid Off for Westinghouse," Broadcasting, uly 8, 1957, pp. 98-103.

[159] Not McFarland letters, which are notifications of reasons hy a renewal hearing might be necessary.

[160] "Is Music Enough?" Broadcasting, March 31, 1958, p. 5.

The FCC's categories were not altogether logically-defined, which allowed most stations to exercise considerable latitude in assigning programs to the categories. Sports broadcasts, for example, were supposed to be listed as "talk."[161]

Prior to the entrance into the Atlanta market of the Bartell formula in 1955, stations WAOK and WERD programmed for the Negro listener, WEAS ran rural and religious material, WGKA programmed a heavy schedule of classical music, and the formats of WTAM and WYZE apparent varied with the composition of the audience remaining for them to serv WGST was an ABC affiliate, but was licensed to the Regents of the University System of the State of Georgia. WQXI, owned then by the Rounsaville Radio Stations, had been programming a successful but not startling form of music-and-news, relying heavily on personalities. WQXI "owned" Atlanta for this type of programming (except for WSB, which was always the number one station) until WQXI was challenged by Bartell's tiny 250-watt WAKE. WAKE was barely receivable to the city limits in the daytime, and succumbed to interference beyond the downtown area at night. Yet, the Bartell formula (to be described later) was such a magnet to listeners that they sought out the station in spi of its poor signal, and boosted its ratings enormously. Except for WS which was doing well, and WAGA and WYZE which were not, all the other AM stations in the Atlanta market "converted in some degree to formula music-and-news broadcasting" during the 1956-57 period in order to

---

[161] This citation, and the balance of this section adapted from Thomas interview, supplementary written material, n.p., n.d., except a otherwise noted.

mulate the Bartell formula appeal.[162]

WAKE did attempt some small amount of programming in all seven f the prescribed categories, but tried to schedule it in the very early orning hours so it wouldn't drive listeners away. WAKE was questioned y the FCC for the scarcity of its agricultural programming, even though o farmers lived within the city limits.

Some of the Commissioners were aware of the problem in Atlanta nd other multi-station markets where specialized stations (rather than rograms) were becoming common. At the May, 1958 meeting of the ational Association of Broadcasters, Commissioner Ford was reported by roadcasting as feeling that "'balanced programming' for a 20-station rea is different from that for a one-station market. He thought it as 'valid criticism' to say FCC had set up a program pattern into which ll stations must fit."[163]

The FCC did not grant license renewals to the Atlanta stations or more than a year, during which time none of the broadcasters equested a hearing or moved to make an industry case for specialized adio programming. Bartell, who failed to get renewals for WOKY, .lwaukee, and WYDE, Birmingham, because of the Atlanta situation, sold oth WAKE and WYDE. WGST, WAOK, WERD, and WGKA all agreed to carry ubstantially greater amounts of programming in the disputed categories.

---

[162]The massive changeover to one form by so many stations in e market may have been what called the FCC's attention to the situa- on, but this is speculation. However, note that the FCC did not ask e stations to explain why they were all airing essentially the same ogramming, but rather why they had failed to air enough in the three escribed categories.

[163]Broadcasting, May 5, 1958, p. 104.

The same condition was stipulated in the transfers of WAKE, WTAM and WQXI to their respective new owners.

A revised renewal form to allow station programming specializa tion was not issued by the FCC until August of 1965, although with the 1960 En Banc Programming Policy Statement, the willingness to allow su a shift was apparent. However, it is important to note that in the period when music-and-news--and then Top 40--were growing most rapidly they were doing so at the peril of their licenses, since until the 196 Statement, specialized programming was officially a violation of FCC regulations.

Program Services

In addition to the syndicated programs mentioned earlier, ther were many other program services and production aids available to the broadcaster. Most had existed prior to the growth of music-and-news, but some forms (such as jingles) became especially popular during the period.

Transcribed Spots and Programs

Lewis H. Avery, in a speech before New York City's Radio and Television Executive Society in 1957, noted that electrical recording (via discs) was developed in 1926, was used in 1929 to record the firs fifteen-minute program, and was employed in 1930 to broadcast 75 commercially-sponsored programs.[164] These programs undoubtedly followed standard network practice of the time which sold the entire program tc

---

[164]"Spot Radio's Pioneer Days," Sponsor, November 16, 1957, p. 42.

one sponsor (rather than to several "participating" or "spot" advertisers.)[165]

In 1927, C. P. MacGregor quit the Brunswick record company to begin what he called an advertising record business,[166] which eventually became a producer and distributor of transcribed programs such as the Army's Proudly We Hail.[167]

In 1928, Sam 'n' Henry became Amos 'n' Andy, and for about a year (until they went on the NBC network) their show was distributed on transcriptions to other radio stations by WMAQ, which was owned by the Chicago Daily News, the latter already being in newspaper syndication.

It was not until 1935 that short (20 second), fully-produced transcribed national spot announcements began to be inserted by local stations between network programs. The first such "station break" featured one George Givot who was famous at the time as the Greek ambassador. Such nationally-distributed "spots" were the brain-child of Cecil Whiddifield of the Schwimmer and Scott Advertising Agency.[168] In 1938, the World Broadcasting System, producers of transcribed radio programs, formed the first transcribed spot announcement network, beginning in October with 28 stations.[169]

---

[165] Other sources say the first transcribed half hour program was aired in 1927. See "Birth of the ET," Broadcasting, March 4, 1957, p. 16.

[166] "Transcription Boom," Newsweek, January 19, 1943, p. 58.

[167] Ibid.

[168] A. Carpenter, "Wizardry of Radio's 'Spot' Programs" (condensed from an Address), Science Digest, January, 1946, p. 17.

[169] "Forms Spot Network," Business Week, September 24, 1938, p. 18.

Early transcriptions were often of poor technical quality, so that networks and many local stations banned the playing of transcriptions as being below their standards. This attitude remained even when transcription quality was vastly improved. In 1946, Bing Crosby demanded that NBC allow him to transcribe his shows instead of doing them live. NBC refused flatly. Crosby then went to ABC who were so glad to get him that they agreed to the use of recordings, provided Bing's rating did not drop as a result.[170] A survey by Philco, Crosby's new sponsors on ABC, showed that 82% of people asked did not know what "transcribed" meant.[171] CBS and NBC still opposed recordings, but in 1948, with tape recording having been perfected by Ampex with Crosby's backing, the networks adopted recording for the delay of daylight saving time broadcasts.[172]

On December 5 of 1946, the FCC allowed broadcasters to drop the previously-required transcription identification announcement for material running one minute or less. This change made it much simpler for stations to air transcribed announcements.[173]

In 1948, the Keystone Broadcasting System, which supplied transcribed programs to rural stations that were usually without network service, listed 325 small-town subscribers. Fourteen shows on Mutual

---

170"Recordings for Crosby Show," Broadcasting, September 2, 1946, p. 16.

171"Crosby Rating Is Up Again; Philco Satisfied with Sales," Broadcasting, November 18, 1946, p. 14.

172Harry Sova, "A History of the Magnetic Recorder and Its Inclusion into Network Radio Broadcasting" (unpublished paper, The University of Wisconsin, Madison, March 18, 1969), p. 6.

173"Transcription Boom," p. 58.

nd ABC were on transcriptions, and there were more than 170 companies roducing the discs.[174]

Prior to the mid-1950s, the great majority of transcription utput was in the form of complete transcribed shows. While in the late 940s many companies were still offering dramatic shows on disc, by the arly 1950s the trend was toward music featuring big-name talent. In ay of 1952, RCA's Thesaurus announced that its three most popular ranscribed programs were Wayne King Serenade, Phil Spitalny's Hour of harm, and Music by Roth.[175]

Transcription Libraries

By 1953, the transcription companies that specialized in complete programs were in trouble, while those that offered libraries of roduction aids were doing well. According to a report in Billboard,

> . . . Chief factors in the decline of many transcription firms have been the increasing use by radio stations of records--both long play and singles. Time was when the firms could argue that their product was superior, that their product was specially engineered for radio. This argument scarcely is valid, owing to the finer quality of records, the top talent on records, etc.[176]

One of the transcription firms, World Broadcasting System, nnounced in August of 1953 that it was planning to "emphasize more and ore merchandising programs designed for local spot business and local

---

[174] Ibid.

[175] "RCA Thesaurus Sales," Broadcasting, May 19, 1952, p. 6.

[176] "Publishers Okay 3 Per Cent Rate for Transcription Library irms," Billboard, March 28, 1953, p. 20.

sales. . . ."[177] World claimed that a telephone quiz program, You Win, accounted for more than $3,000,000 in billings to its subscribers.[178]

Also in 1953, a new service for disc jockeys called "Show Stoppers" was begun. "Show Stoppers" were transcribed comedy characters that were supplied to local deejays along with scripts indicating suggested use, with 20 new cuts per month to be released. The service was sold on an exclusive (one-to-a-market) basis. Storz's KOWH in Omaha was one of the first subscribers.[179] In a later advertisement for the service, "Show Stoppers" was claimed to have 300 comic sketches in 17 dialects with over 60 character voices, "from torrid senoritas to bashful bobbysoxers, from Irish washwomen [sic] to Park Ave. matrons, from two-gun desperadoes to poet lecturers, from pesky kids to crotchety grandpas."[180]

With the rise in disc jockey programs and the increasing number of spots they carried, it was probably inevitable that the industry would come up with a way to play both more music and more commercials. In June of 1954, Standard Radio Transcription Services, Inc. announced its new "Shorty-Tunes" service, which provided ten current pop songs and ten standards per month to each subscriber on two long-play records. Each song was just one-and-one-half minutes in length.

177"WBS Tailors to Spot Buying," Broadcasting, August 31, 1953, p. 62.

178Ibid.

179Advertisement in Broadcasting, August 31, 1953, p. 63.

180Advertisement in Broadcasting, May 10, 1954, p. 16.

> Abbreviated, yet complete. . . . Tailored to fit smoothly into time-tight program schedules. . . . Eliminates breaking into middle of tune as often happens with ordinary 2 1/2 or 3 minute recordings. . . . Lets you squeeze in that precious extra minute or more you need for an extra commercial without double or triple spotting![181]

One of the orchestras featured on the first releases was Lawrence Welk's.[182] By 1957, Standard was offering David Carroll, Buddy Morrow, and Les Brown along with Andy Powell, Jimmie Blade, Bobby Christian, Dan Belloc and other lesser lights, and the service was priced at just $5 per month.[183]

The Shorty-Tunes concept may have been a good one from a sales and revenue viewpoint, but from a programming and audience perspective it was bound to fail. As has been pointed out, the increasingly-younger audience was decreasingly satisfied with "cover" versions of popular songs--they wanted the original performances, and would seek out the station that played them. This audience was not interested in "standards" at all, so that half of each Shorty-Tunes release was irrelevant. Thus, potential buyers for Standard's service were only among the dwindling number of stations that were not attempting to appeal to a more youthful audience.

By May of 1954, the number of companies offering all-purpose transcription libraries to stations had dropped to three from the original group of six. Lang-Worth, RCA Thesaurus, and World remained in active production, while Associated had ceased production of new

---

[181] Advertisement in Broadcasting, June 14, 1954, p. 59.

[182] Ibid., p. 59.

[183] Advertisement in Broadcasting, August 5, 1957, p. 57.

releases (but continued to rent the extant library), and Capitol and Standard were selling their regular libraries outright.[184] Libraries were generally rented on a three year contract rather than sold, with the average monthly rental between $60 and $350, according to the size of the market, the station, and the given library.[185] At this time, a typical transcription library consisted of:

> . . . about 5000 musical selections plus monthly pressings of new songs; scripts to accompany the records; hundreds of recorded jingles to use as lead-ins for commercials; detailed tips on selling radio to local advertisers; merchandising material for local advertisers; complete programs up to an hour in length . . . (these are built out of the library's selections plus "voice tracks" by recording stars); promotion and publicity kits for each show.[186]

In 1954, the programs that could be built out of the three continuing companies' libraries included the following:

> Lang-Worth: _Rhythm Rendezvous_ (Patti Page and Ray Anthony); _The Allan Jones Show_; _Russ Morgan_ (doing a d.j. show); _Mantovani_ (well known semi-classicist).[187]
>
> RCA Thesaurus: _The Hour of Charm_ (Phil Spitalny's all-girl orchestra); _The Sammy Kaye Show_; _Music Hall Varieties_ (featuring great names of the gay 90s); _Date in Hollywood_ (with Gloria DeHaven, Eddie Fisher, Hugo Winterhalter).
>
> World: _The Lyn Murray Show_ (includes guest stars); _Forward America_ (Walter Huston in dramatic readings surrounded by orchestra and chorus); _Freedom Is Our Business_ (dramatic readings by Robert Montgomery with music by David Rose); _Chapel by the Side of the Road_ (with reading of the Bible by Raymond Massey); . . . _You Win_, a quiz which station builds locally using a manual of questions and format furnished by World; _Whose Birthday Is This?_, a show for announcement of local birthdays with format and continuity furnished in a World manual.[188]

---

[184] "Music Libraries: What Do You Know About Them?" _Sponsor_, May 17, 1954, p. 50.

[185] _Ibid_.

[186] _Ibid_.

[187] _Ibid_., p. 51.

[188] _Ibid_., p. 132.

Sales Service Libraries

Programs, however, were not at the heart of the surviving libraries, but rather emphasis was on an expanded sales services. In September of 1954, for instance, RCA Thesaurus announced the addition of "Echo Attention Getters" to its library. Words such as "new" "refreshing" or "bargain" were echoed with diminishing volume in the repetitions, thus adding "a big production sound to local commercials."[189]

In 1955, World announced the addition of musical selections by Peggy Lee, the Sauter-Finegan Orchestra, the Four Freshmen and George Shearing to its catalog, while RCA Thesaurus added Nelson Eddy, Gale Sherwood, June Valli, Eddie Fisher and Frank Luther.[190] Lang-Worth was offering its music on tapes for programming as background music.[191] Lang-Worth had also entered the copyrighted customized commercials service field, and were reported as succeeding well in that venture.[192] RCA Thesaurus expanded its sales aids section in 1955 by adding a quarter-hour Do-It-Yourself show for the handyman, and a Weekend Shoppers Special designed to speak to that select audience.[193] RCA began in 1956 supplying what it called "Sell-Tunes" to Thesaurus subscribers,

---

[189]"RCA Thesaurus Adds 'Attention Getters' Aids," Broadcasting, September 6, 1954, p. 72. Equipment to produce a repeated echo (rather than just reverberation) was not available to most stations on a commercial basis until the late 1950s.

[190]"Radio Program Services," Sponsor, May 16, 1955, p. 64.

[191]Ibid., p. 104.

[192]"Program, Sales Services," Sponsor, July 11, 1955, p. 161.

[193]Ibid.

which were jingles keyed to certain holidays or to categories of goods and services. The service also included "specially written opening and closing themes for DJ and personality shows."[194]

By April of 1956, RCA Thesaurus had acquired the "Show Stoppers" series mentioned earlier and had added a five-minute program called Great American Women, narrated by Basil Rathbone.[195] Lang-Worth was also offering five-minute programs designed to be sold as strips. The Featurette series included weather, mystery, and western shows and one called What's the Word?[196] World announced the addition of Doris Day, Victor Young, Russel Armes, Bobbie Hackett and Mimi Martel to its music lineup.[197]

In July of 1956, Sponsor featured an article summarizing the offerings of the major program service companies. Ziv, the well-known TV program packager, had been producing dramatic radio shows on transcriptions for years, but did not enter the comedy program field until the 1955-56 season with the Red Skelton Show, which they claimed was a great success. The company had just signed Eddie Cantor to a seven-year contract to make both TV and transcribed radio shows.[198] RCA Thesaurus announced a growing interest in transcribed soap operas (since the networks were dropping them). They offered 1,000 episodes of Dr. Paul, 605

---

[194] Advertisement in Broadcasting, March 26, 1956, p. 101.

[195] "Radio Program Services," Sponsor, April 16, 1956, special Convention issue (special pagination), p. X.

[196] Ibid. [197] Ibid.

[198] "Transcribed Shows," Sponsor, July 12, 1956, p. 210.

of Aunt Mary, and 390 of Betty and Bob.[199] World announced The Betty Grable-Harry James Show, which was different from previous library programs in several ways: it was designed for daily rather than weekly play, it was designed for 15 participating announcements (12 one-minute, 3 half-minute) rather than full sponsorship, and it was designed for use with virtually no local announcer necessary--Betty and Harry did all the introductions on the transcription, while the local station played the given record (listed on the transcription label) on another turntable.[200] Lang-Worth's Russ Morgan Show was set up to operate the same way.[201] RCA Thesaurus also was rearranging its shows to allow participating sponsorship.[202] Perhaps most important was the announcement by Lang-Worth that its new Russ Morgan Show was being marketed individually--to both subscriber and non-subscribing stations.[203] For years, the library services had added "bonus" programs to their services to try to attract new clients and hold old ones, but the move to sell individual programs seems tantamount to an admission that the full-service program library was on its way out--which it was.

In August of 1956, Capitol Records entered the music library field by offering to sell at least 70 of its popular music albums a year to stations for the nominal fee of $15 per quarter.[204]

In November of 1956, Standard Radio Transcription Services

---

[199] Ibid., p. 212.

[200] "Program, Sales Services," Sponsor, July 12, 1956, p. 210.

[201] Ibid., p. 216. [202] Ibid. [203] Ibid.

[204] "Capitol Music Library Offered to Radio-TVs," Broadcasting, August 27, 1956, p. 9.

announced that it was at work on two new background music libraries for the J. P. Seeburg Company. The company had already produced four such libraries in the past.[205] Associated Program Service, another music library packager, was owned by Muzak to begin with. The two companies would later be absorbed and disappear from the station library service field.

In 1957, World announced a new audience participation sound effects quiz called Sound-O, and RCA Thesaurus announced its version of a Lawrence Welk show, as well as a nostalgia program featuring Paul Whiteman called I Remember When.[206] Lang-Worth added more jingles for local merchants, plus a series of program intros, effects and teasers called Airlifts.[207] James D. Langlois, president of Lang-Worth, stated that the company was developing this area in response to the "strong, almost unanimous move in radio . . . toward the music-and-news format. Thus--in addition to maintaining Lang-Worth Music library and feature programs--we have concentrated on a new service that aids and complements the radio station's music-and-news pattern, program and sales-wise."[208]

Specialized Program Services

A number of other program services also existed or were suggested in the period prior to and during the development of Top 40.

---

[205] "Standard Radio Producing Libraries for Seeburg Co.," Broadcasting, November 26, 1956, p. 87.

[206] "Radio Program Services," Sponsor, April 6, 1957, p. 26.

[207] "What Are the Important Trends in Radio Transcription Services?" Sponsor, September 14, 1957, p. 56.

[208] Ibid.

One which did not last was The Thoroughbred Broadcasting System, Inc., which planned to broadcast the "Race of the Day" from major race tracks Monday through Saturday beginning September 28, 1954.[209] The specialized audience this program required, plus the conservative stand of the NAB against broadcasting events in which betting was involved, no doubt doomed the TBS.

Other "audio-network" services fared better. Today, when broadcasters and listeners alike are so accustomed to hearing "actualities" and voice reports from services such as UPI Audio, it is hard to imagine that before 1954 no such service existed on a national scale.

In July of 1954, S. R. Sague, president and general manager of WSRS, Cleveland Heights, Ohio, proposed a plan to "feed live voices of White House and Capitol Hill officials to radio stations throughout the country," to James C. Hagerty who was then White House News Secretary."[210]

> Although he has not checked the technical or economic feasibility of his plan with anyone, Mr. Sague said he felt that such a service might cost subscribing stations about $100 a month.
>
> "Voices are our business," Mr. Sague said last week, "just as the printed word is that of the newspaper. The more we can broadcast the actual words spoken by the one who is making the news, the more effective will we make our medium."
>
> Part of Mr. Sague's thinking is that there would be fixed microphone facilities at various important news fronts in the capital. . . . These could be "opened" any time occasion arose and the resultant broadcast recorded at a wire service's bureau headquarters. These would be collected and at a specified hour each day would be transmitted over broadcast quality lines to subscribing stations. At present, of course, network affiliates get this service on national network newscasts.

---

[209] Advertisement in Broadcasting, September 6, 1954, p. 72.

[210] "'Wire Service' Feed of Voices Suggested," Broadcasting, July 5, 1954, p. 35.

> The idea, Mr. Sague said, is an extension of WSRS's technique in covering the 1.5 million population of greater Cleveland. Station has a microphone installation in the Cleveland City Hall and the city halls of nine suburban communities. A line feeds them all into the WSRS studio where any public announcement can be taped for use by the station.[211]

Spokesmen for AP and UP were said by Broadcasting to be doubtful that most stations could afford such a service. The Associated Press seemed to reject the idea, while United Press said it would put the plan into effect if stations would pay for it.[212]

In a letter published as an advertisement in the October 4, 1954 issue of Broadcasting, S. R. Sague invited stations to join the new "National News Network," and claimed that it would provide "Washington coverage and national events Not Now Provided by any network or news service."[213] The letter was addressed to "Radio Wisemen, Eastern States, USA," so apparently the network was to be fed only in the more populous regions of the country.[214] Virtually the same service would later be provided by both AP and UPI Audio. UPI Audio, however, did not penetrate into parts of the Southeast until the mid 1960s, even with resources vastly greater than Sague's.

In July of 1957, Broadcasting announced (buried back on page 70) that a new national radio network was being formed, to be called "Audio-Radio for Modern America."[215] In a promotional letter sent to stations, Kenny A. Green, president of Green Enterprises-Advertising of

---

[211] Ibid. [212] Ibid., p. 36.

[213] Advertisement in Broadcasting, October 4, 1954, p. 55.

[214] Ibid.

[215] "Audio-Radio Network Formed to Sell Music, News Programs," Broadcasting, July 22, 1957, p. 70.

Tulsa said the new network would program music and news 24 hours a day, would not sell time, and would not have or need option time.[216] Green called it "the beginning of the hottest radio set in all America and the answer to present day radio headaches."[217] The promotional letter was said to describe the proposed network as

> . . . a production service selling its programming by wire. Cost to stations will be $10 per day, with stations paying line charges from the nearest network terminal point. Programming includes 10 one-minute and 10 30-second "slots" per hour where stations can insert commercials.[218]

Programming was to start as soon as 100 stations had affiliated, which was expected within 60 to 90 days.[219]

As if to underscore their dubious attitude about the venture, _Broadcasting_ listed some of Mr. Green's other long-range plans:

> . . . ownership of seven TV stations for a proposed video network; building of Golden City, a multi-million dollar real estate venture; production of a feature movie based on news, and ownership of seven radio stations.[220]

Green's Audio-Radio network probably did not need _Broadcasting_'s scepticism to help it fail since, as pointed out earlier, music-and-news programming was becoming increasingly available on the regular networks. Additionally, many of the smaller stations that might have been interested in such a service could hire several disc jockeys for Green's cost of $10 a day plus line charges, so the trend toward economy in programming worked against the network. Finally, as also pointed out before, radio was becoming a more local medium in its programming, with networking by definition contrary to local origination.

---

[216] _Ibid._ [217] _Ibid._ [218] _Ibid._

[219] _Ibid._ [220] _Ibid._

The foregoing discussion of program services sought to highlight some of the programs and production aids from which the broadcaster of the early and mid 1950s had to choose to develop his programming. (Older forms, such as script services, teletype news service, live remotes and so on were purposefully excluded.) The big libraries, having a heavy investment in the long-form program, were relatively slow to adapt to the needs of music-and-news programming. None of the large libraries have survived to the present. Instead, companies like Lang-Worth have gone increasingly into jingles and commercial production aids. The libraries that are sold today by Pepper-Tanner and others do not contain music for entertainment purposes but only music (and jingles and other effects) for selling purposes. Libraries today are a production and sales aid rather than a program source.

Jingles

The shift to local and to national spot advertising that affected the sales and content of the program/production libraries also stimulated the growth of the generally quiescent jingle industry. Jingles are so prevalent today as station identifiers, mnemonic devices in commercials, and as introductions and closes to programs that it is difficult to imagine how quickly the industry has developed.

Background

Many early radio programs featured bands, some of which had their own "band themes." Some people feel that the jingle industry began with the adoption of a certain "theme song" for a radio program.[221] After months of being heard at the opening and close of a program, the theme music became part of that program's "signature." Gradually, the sponsorship of the program infiltrated the theme music, so that in some cases themes became commercials of sorts in themselves. However, so long as full sponsorship was the rule, the exposure given to such a theme--even via a national radio network--was limited to once or twice a day.

In the mid-1930s, with the introduction of the transcribed spot announcement, a music spot became a possibility. But it was not until Allan Kent and Herbert Austen Croom-Johnson collaborated on new lyrics for the old English hunting song "John Peel" that jingles received much notice nationally. Their famous "nickel, nickel" jingle for Pepsi-Cola was first aired in late 1939, and by late 1944 had been played more than 1,000,000 times.[222] The jingle had even been made into a popular record, as the "Chiquita Banana" song would be later on.

The Kent-Johnson Pepsi-Cola jingle set the trend for commercial jingles in several ways. First, the jingle was designed to last no more than fifteen seconds, based on the theory that it would take that long for the average listener to get up and retune his radio, by which time the jingle would be over.[223] Johnson credits Pepsi-Cola president Walter Mack as being "the first man to have the courage of his convictions about the musical commercial. . . . He spent enough money to give

---

[221] Al Graham, "Jingle--or Jangle," New York Times Magazine, October 29, 1944, p. 26.

[222] Ibid.

[223] Thomas Whiteside, "I Can Be Had--For Pelf," New Republic, February 16, 1948, p. 22.

it the necessary incidence to really register with the listener."[224] A second rule was thus established--a jingle must be heavily repeated for it to gain acceptance. Kent and Johnson learned the third rule the hard way--they sold the Pepsi jingle outright, instead of leasing it and collecting royalties for each use.[225]

In 1944, with the commercial jingle in its relative infancy, only about 15% of the national output was produced by specialist companies such as Kent-Johnson, with the rest being made by advertising agencies with their own talent.[226]

In 1944, WNEW was said to average 80 singing commercials per 24 hours, which was thought then to be a phenomenal figure.[227]

Also in 1944, what were apparently the first political campaign jingles for radio were produced for President Roosevelt by Mack Shopnick.[228]

In 1947, the firm of Carr & Stark offered stations rhymed singing weather forecasts.[229]

By 1953, RCA Thesaurus was offering the "Ullman Jingl-Library" of 1600 commercial jingles to its station subscribers under the new title of "Thesaurus Jingl-Library." The commercial jingles were said to cover 71 product and service categories.[230]

---

224 Ibid. 225 Ibid.

226 Graham, "Jingle--Or Jangle," p. 27.

227 Ibid.

228 "Specialist," The New Yorker, October 4, 1947, p. 27.

229 "Jingle Tingle," Newsweek, August 18, 1947, p. 55.

230 "New Jingle Library," Broadcasting, April 6, 1953, p. 9.

In 1954, the American Federation of Musicians negotiated their first transcription contract rate for jingle production.[231]

By 1956, the commercial jingle had become so prevalent that KTFS in Texarkana, Texas-Arkansas ran a 25-minute Jingle Hit Parade daily during the month of June. The audience called in to vote for their favorites. One day at least 97 people did.[232]

By 1959, with a great increase in the number of companies preferring singing commercials, a survey showed that only 20% of advertising agencies contacted still produced their own jingles, while the other 80% were now referring them to "specialists."[233]

In 1960, Sponsor published a study showing that commercial jingles could be bought from as little as $38 for an "assembly line" production to as much as $5,000 for a fully-produced national spot.[234] The low price came from The Jingle Mill, Inc., which employed already-written tunes and the technique of recording many spots at once with a single orchestra and recording session to keep costs down.[235] The expensive figure came from the use of a band with 21 musicians, five vocalists, four hours of studio time, and $3,000 in creative, arranging and copying fees for the nationally-distributed spot.[236]

---

[231] "Music Spots Grow Into Big Business with TV, Films," Billboard, September 4, 1954, p. 4.

[232] "Jingle Hit Parade," Broadcasting, June 18, 1956, p. 18.

[233] "Most Agencies Buy Singing Commercials Outside, Study Finds," Advertising Age, November 30, 1959, p. 54.

[234] "Things to Know in Buying Jingles," Sponsor, February 27, 1960, p. 36.

[235] "June-Spoon-Moon-Tunes," Newsweek, August 31, 1959, p. 72.

[236] "Things to Know in Buying Jingles," p. 38.

Musical Commercial Producers Association

By 1962, the producers of jingles had banded together in the Musical Commercial Producers Association "in an effort to set industry standards, better the musical commercial climate, and upgrade the relationship between its members and the advertising agencies."[237] One of the aims of the group was to encourage agencies to utilize the independent producers more often, but another was to ". . . revise inequitable thinking that expects top level producers to submit creative ideas on speculation or for free."[238] This phrase makes reference to the then-prevalent practice of the "demo" disc or tape, which was submitted on request by many jingle companies, and which, in order to be competitive, had to be virtually as good as the final product, thus incurring huge unpaid costs to the producers of all but the winning presentation. In reply to a letter from the author inquiring about the current activities of the MCPA, the Association's secretary, Victor Sack wrote:

> It is only fair to tell you that the Musical Commercial Producers Association, to all intents and purposes, no longer exists. We formed in time of great crisis to present a united front to persons and organizations who, through lack of knowledge of our industry, were on the verge of doing us harm. At that time we represented all of the major music people in New York, Chicago, and Hollywood. Now, through no continued need, we are nothing but a mail box.[239]

Station ID jingles

As the musical commercial came to be not only an accepted but a

---

[237]"Tip Top Jingle Money Makers," Sponsor, April 30, 1962, p. 50.

[238]Ibid.

[239]Letter to the author from Victor Sack, Secretary, Musical Commercial Producers Association, New York, September 9, 1971.

protected form in the forties and fifties, so also did the station identification jingle. By 1942, Kent-Johnson, Inc. had expanded into areas beyond the usual musical commercial and were producing time signal jingles, station identification jingles, and program segment intro jingles for an all-night musical show on New York's WJZ.[240] These may have been some of the earliest station identification jingles produced. Note, however, that they were done on a custom basis--recorded exclusively for the station ordering them. Later, in the early 1950s, Johnson was teamed with Eric Siday.[241] Together the new team produced a set of custom station identification jingles for an east coast radio station[242] that came to the attention of Gordon McLendon, who at the time was the recent past head of the Libery Network, and currently owner of KLIF, Dallas.[243] Tom Merriman, president of T.M. Productions, says:

> . . . And Gordon said to me, did you ever hear anything like this for a station? And I said no, I don't know anything about it. And he said, I wish you'd make me a few of these things. So I got some musicians together and we did these jingles. This was long before Bill Meeks ever knew about jingles. That's not to say that we didn't maybe do them at the same time. But there wasn't anybody in town who had the facilities to even do them. . . .

Merriman pointed out that McLendon's Dallas station KLIF had a room which was set up to play back movies for screening, since the McLendons were also in the theater business.

---

[240] Graham, "Jingle--or Jangle," p. 27.

[241] Siday is more recently known for his work in electronic music such as the CBS Eye animation signature.

[242] Probably WFBR, Baltimore.

[243] Tom Merriman, president of TM Productions (jingle producers), private interview held in Dallas, Texas, November 6, 1971.

. . . A guy by the name of Les Vaughn, who was their engineer there, rigged up a system whereby we could record on two systems at the same time and in effect we could sing over a background--which nobody had ever done at that time. Everything at that time was just straight out: you just got everybody together and sing it. Now, all we did there was to take a monaural tape and transfer that tape to another monaural machine and sing at the same time and mix it all together. . . .

For this set of jingles, Merriman rented a church in which to record backgrounds, and paid the musicians $15 each for the recording session. Merriman wrote the backgrounds for these jingles, which he believes were the first.

Now, Bill Meeks probably originated the organized jingle company as we know it today, because I was still messing around with trying to teach school and direct church choirs. . . .[244]

Bill Meeks is the President of PAMS, Inc., which, as Tom Merriman must have meant to say, is probably the first organized <u>station</u> jingle company. Meeks claims to have made the first station identification jingles for KLIF in 1947. He gives the air date of these as November 11, 1947.[245] A group of live musicians were gathered at KLIF to play, "and in the course of everything else, and making jingles for the local advertisers, we made jingles for the radio station."[246] These early jingles did not just identify the station, but sold the merits of the station.[247] Meeks is not sure whether it was he or Gordon McLendon who decided to do the KLIF station ID jingles in 1947, but it was McLendon who encouraged Meeks's idea of syndicating jingles to other stations in 1951.[248]

---

[244] <u>Ibid</u>.

[245] Bill Meeks, President of PAMS, Inc., private interview held in Dallas, Texas, July 28, 1971.

[246] <u>Ibid</u>. [247] <u>Ibid</u>. [248] <u>Ibid</u>.

In 1951, Meeks had opened an advertising agency.[249] One of the ccounts he had was Tenel-Hist, a nasal spray.[250] Merriman says that eeks may have created the station jingles in order to have a product o trade for the placement of Tenel-Hist advertisements on the tation.[251] In the case of the jingles he did for KLIF, Merriman says, . . . the instrument for this thing was McLendon. There wasn't any-ody else who wanted them. There was no demand for it."[252] This might xplain why Meeks may originally have had to create an artificial demand or his station ID package. However, Meeks states a different motive:

> . . . as an advertising agency, I had come to the realization that the ratings services didn't really reflect who was listening. Because, you could advertise on KLIF and get darn good results and they had no ratings. And you advertised on another radio station that had good ratings and you'd get no results. And I realized then that people would say they were listening to say, NBC, when they were listening to ABC, or whoever. . . . And I still feel that there is better recall and better retention and better association with a singing ID than a spoken ID. You know, it was like the same old thing of, why say it when you can send roses. And to me, music was a way of sending roses. So we did IDs for these radio stations, and the first eleven radio stations I sold ended up with extremely good ratings, which further proved my point. Most of the radio stations, though, that I would see, weren't really interested in the IDs. They were more interested in buying commercial jingles through us, or having us produce local jingles for their local accounts.[253]

Merriman says that even in about 1953, there was still not uch demand for station ID jingles.

> And after we did it, McLendon said, hey, I'll send it to a few of my friends, and he sent it out to guys who were in the broadcast business. After all, independent radio was hardly established at this time.[254]

---

[249] Ibid. [250] Merriman interview.

[251] Ibid. [252] Ibid.

[253] Meeks interview. [254] Merriman interview.

When Meeks began turning out his station ID series, there were no set rules and scales for musicians working in the new medium either. Meeks says,

> There were no scales for musical jingles, and the musicians didn't know how to do it or what, and the president of the local musicians union didn't know exactly how to handle it. And really it was against all sorts of union regulations to do what they call "tracking," so we did it anyway. ["Tracking" is recording a master track with musicians once, then using the recording as the background for later singing overdubs, sans orchestra.] And we called Petrillo and he told the local president here, I told you to run that union down there and quit bothering me. So that's how we got started with it. . . . Then about 1963, the Federation decided that we'd been doing it wrong and tried to make us turn around and do it a different way. At that point, the musicians union said, no, Dallas will continue as they're now doing it. . . . So, at that point, the musicians in Dallas backed us, and said that if need be they'd resign from the Federation, just to continue doing this type of business.[255]

The foregoing passage explains why so many of the jingle and commercial recording companies have continued to make their base in Dallas.

In 1956, Tom Merriman formed a company with Hoyt Hughes called the Commercial Recording Corporation (CRC). Hughes apparently entered the partnership on the basis of owning a great deal of recording equipment, which according to Merriman he did not own.[256] Eventually, Hughes left the company. In 1957, John Coyle purchased a controlling interest in the company.[257] Then Merriman left the company, went with Peter Frank and the Allman company, returned to work for CRC for a while, and then founded Tom Merriman (and later TM Productions),

---

[255] Meeks interview.

[256] Merriman interview.

[257] "Tailoring Local Spots with 'National' Sound," Sponsor, May 25, 1964, p. 42.

eginning about 1965.[258] Merriman describes CRC as "a <u>strong</u> ompany."[259] He believes the company was finally forced into bankruptcy ore by mismanagement than by inferior products.[260] CRC had been, like AMS, very much involved with the syndication of station ID packages, nd was one of the major jingle companies of the 1950s.

The other important pioneering station jingle company was Pepper tudios, now Pepper-Tanner, Inc. The company was not organized until 959, and there is evidence that its initial growth was closely tied to he success of Top 40 programming.

se of IDs by stations

As was pointed out earlier, stations (especially independent tations) had made increasing use of station identification jingles to et their stations apart from each other and from network affiliates. JZ and WNEW of New York may have been leaders in this regard. But in 955, four years after the formation of PAMS, and two years after Tom erriman got into the business on an informal basis, the use of a usical station ID was still a distinct novelty. In late 1955, roadcasting ran the following stories on their "Programs & Promotions" age:

WWDC 'IDENTITUNES'

> WWDC Washington has integrated a library of specially produced "Identitunes" into its 24-hour service. Varying from 10 seconds to 1 1/2 minutes, the tunes will be used as themes for all types of programs. They were written and produced for WWDC by Austin Croom-Johnson and Eric Siday in collaboration with Norman Reed, WWDC program director. Music was performed by a

---

258 Merriman interview.

259 Ibid. 260 Ibid.

20-piece orchestra and nine-voice choral group. Styles range from swing and blues to concert arrangements.[261]

KBIG USES MUSICAL ID'S

ID jingles were premiered Thanksgiving Day at KBIG Catalina, California. Claude Gordon's Orchestra and station vocalists cut the jingles at Capitol Records, using original music based on Avalon and Catalina themes. Alene McKinney, KBIG music director, with Cliff Gill, operations vice president, and Program Director Alan Lisser collaborated on the new identification production.[262]

Note that in both the articles above the jingles were produced on a custom basis, even though syndicated packages such as PAMS's existed. Note too that in the case of the WWDC package the styles of the music varied, probably to coincide with different styles being played on the station, as against Top 40's emphasis on a single musical style and audience.

Wilson Northcross, Executive Vice President at Pepper-Tanner, feels that it was the rise to prominence of Top 40 stations that helped jingle companies most.

> So what I'm saying is, with the advent of Top 40, which was a listenable thing, something people wanted to listen to, they started listening to the station that played that thing. . . . A lot of subtle things happened about that time, such as pushbutton radios and all this sort of thing--but it became a station medium. Station thus-and-so was the station where you could hear these Top 40 records all the time, and that was the significant change. That was the change, really.[263]

The station jingle, in summary, was originally just a part of

---

261"WWDC 'Identitunes,'" Broadcasting, December 12, 1955, p. 88.

262"KBIG Uses Musical ID's," Broadcasting, December 12, 1955, p. 88.

263Mr. Wilson Northcross, Executive Vice President, Pepper-Tanner, Inc., private interview held in Memphis, Tennessee, July 8, 1971.

the programming, in much the same way that a theme song might be. Gradually, as independent music-and-news stations sought to distinguish themselves from network affiliates that used spoken IDs (with the exception of NBC's chime logo), they adopted musical identifications. These tended to be long, sometimes almost songs in themselves, which often also sold the station to its new listeners. Contrary to Wilson Northcross's conclusions, it seems that the music-and-news stations were already well on the way to making radio a station--rather than a program--medium, and that jingles were already flourishing on such outlets. However, it cannot be denied that the popularity of Top 40 and its rapid adoption among broadcasters produced a great new surge in the growth of the station jingle business. With Top 40 radio, jingles at first sold the new sound, and then, as competitors arrived, sought to differentiate one from another. A certain musical logo and a set of phrases about the station came to be considered not just part of the programming, but essentials of station promotion. In the sense that ID jingles complemented the Top 40 music and enriched the station's promotional efforts, they can be seen as contributors to the two main ingredients in the Top 40 success formula.

Program Production Equipment

It can be argued that the equipment that is used to produce radio programming influences the type of programming that is produced, in much the same way that small portable receivers influenced the ways in which audiences listened. It is thus necessary to understand the capabilities and restrictions of radio production equipment to fully appreciate the programming that resulted in the 1950s.

The tape recorders that Ampex built for Bing Crosby in 1947 were the beginning of a revolution in production equipment. Not only did the radio networks adopt tape recording, as mentioned earlier, but inexpensive recording equipment eventually reached even the smallest station. With tape recording allowing fidelity equal to live performance, and with lower costs and better quality than disc recordings, the future of broadcast production clearly lay with tape equipment. However, the changeover was surprisingly slow, and the several reasons for that are worth further investigation.

It is difficult to trace the resistance to use of tape recording because the story is protracted, stretching over at least 15 years. It is much easier to describe the attitudes toward an innovation when it is completed in a short span of time. For radio broadcasting, such a case exists in the forced introduction of the 45 rpm record, which occurred almost entirely in 1954.

Adoption of 45 RPM Speed--Case Study

Unlike the situation with tape recording, where there was no other equal or competitive system claiming to accomplish the same thing the 45 rpm record was always clouded by the fact that it was RCA's answer to Columbia's enormously-successful 33 rpm LP. Some stations may have rightly felt that one slow speed was enough, especially since the 45 was not capable of holding very much more time per side than a 78. But in June of 1954, Columbia, RCA Victor, Capitol, Decca and Mercury announced that as of the second week in July, all pop singles hipped to disc jockeys would be on 45s instead of 78s.[264] The record ndustry had wanted to make the changeover for two years, but were eluctant to do so because they feared the reaction. Easier shipment, ess breakage, better fidelity and smaller size were all cited as dvantages of the 45 by the record companies, but the major reason they anted to make the change was the one of reduced cost.[265] Forty-fives ould be air-mailed for less than the cost of ordinary first-class mail or 78s.[266] Moreover, the cost of producing disc jockey records on a 8 rpm vinyl disc was put at between 18¢ and 25¢ each, while the cost or a 45 rpm version was only 14¢.[267]

Ross H. Beville, who was then chief engineer of WWDC-AM-FM in ashington (and who would later invent the Spotmaster cartridge tape ecorder for broadcast use) was one of the first engineers to complain hat 45s were harder to cue and that conversion of turntables would be xpensive.[268] Mark L. Hass, described as "director of KMPC Los Angeles" ad a longer list of complaints for Broadcasting:

> . . . "To convert this equipment to handle 45s would cost us well over $3,000," he said. "In addition we would have to build filing cabinets at further expense."
> "Multiply this by the 2,500-3,000 stations in a similar position," he continued, and it becomes obvious that record

---

264"Majors and Subsids Switch to 45s for Pops to Deejays," illboard, June 5, 1954, p. 14.

265Ibid.

266"DJs Air Pro & Con on 45 Shipments," Billboard, June 19, 954, p. 17.

267"Equipment Jam Develops as Stations Swing Over to 45s," illboard, July 17, 1954, p. 42.

268"Record Companies Plan to Supply Stations with 45 RPM Discs nly," Broadcasting, June 14, 1954, p. 44.

> manufacturers "are imposing a penalty of many millions on the radio industry--and incidentally, providing a mighty attractive melon to be cut up by the manufacturers of 45 equipment." [Some stations managed to convert to 45 for a $15 investment in an RCA "Little Nipper" changer, designed to be played through a phono-jack. The changer made tight cues impossible.)
> . . . "The small records are difficult to cue up, there is a tendency for the needle to skip the shallow grooves, the small records do not stack as well as do the larger 78s, the records are difficult to handle."[269]

The record companies did not take such criticism--and even outright refusals by some disc jockeys to handle 45s at all--without a rebutting sales pitch of their own. Frank M. Folsom of RCA declared that the record industry had been revitalized due to the interest in the 45 rpm record.[270]

> "The 45 records now represent more than 50% of all single records sold," Mr. Folsom said. "The older 78-rpm records are obsolete. In 1949, when RCA introduced the '45' system, record industry sales totaled $160 million. This year, because of the interest the system has generated for all types of records, the sales volume for the industry should be greater than $225 million--and the quarter-billion-dollar figure is only a matter of time."[271]

Folsom's unconvincing parochialism in boosting the 45 as the reason for increased record sales was mitigated by an almost simultaneous announcement that RCA Victor was preparing a list of 200 records from all field from which stations could choose 50 free 45-rpm versions to fill out their libraries and reduce speed--and stylus--changing.[272] Columbia,

---

[269] Ibid., p. 48.

[270] "200 Million '45s' Sold in Five Years--Folsom," Broadcasting, July 5, 1954, p. 36.

[271] Ibid.

[272] "Stations to Get 325,000 45 RPM Records Free," Billboard, July 3, 1954, p. 3.

Capitol, and Mercury were readying similar deals.[273] Capitol was also supplying a cueing disc to stations to aid in cueing and handling the 45s,[274] and later Columbia also developed a cueing mat.

On July 17, WMGM and WCBS New York were reported as ready to install equipment to play 45s, thus joining WNBC and WOV which already had the capability.[275] The move also applied to all other CBS owned-and-operated stations.[276] But two days later, Broadcasting reported that Westinghouse Broadcasting announced that it had found the 45 to be unacceptable for broadcast use, and a "backward step."[277]

Caught between disc jockeys who refused to handle 45s and the need to get their songs publicized, the song publishers found that they sometimes had to make as many as 175 acetate "direct cuts" of a new record at a cost of $2.40 per record.[278]

Even when disc jockeys were willing to play 45s, oftentimes during the summer months of 1954 they were prevented from doing so by lack of equipment. There were backlogs of hundreds of orders at those

---

[273] Ibid., p. 11.

[274] "DJ Reaction to 45s Better Than Hoped," Billboard, July 10, 1954, p. 14.

[275] "CBS and WMGM Join Stations Using 45 Discs," Billboard, July 17, 1954, p. 12.

[276] Ibid.

[277] "Witting Says WBC Won't Use 45 RPM," Broadcasting, July 19, 1954, p. 54.

[278] "45-Less DJs Prove Costly to Publishers," Billboard, October 2, 1954, p. 19.

companies offering conversion equipment for older turntables.[279] This bottleneck in the changeover was the one factor that the record industry had failed to reckon with closely enough in its advance planning.[280] As an interim measure, the record companies allowed their distributors to supply 78 rpm versions of current records to those stations that had ordered 45 rpm equipment but had not received it.[281] But by November of 1954, a survey by Billboard showed that 89.1% of the stations replying were already able to play 45s.[282] By the fall of 1954, both Westinghouse and the ABC network, which had also opposed 45s for a few months, had relented.[283] By the end of the year, the conversion was nearly complete, and the "battle of the speeds," so far as radio stations were concerned, was over.

In the case of the relatively rapid adoption of the 45 rpm speed there were several factors operating in favor of the changeover. The already-mentioned fact that it was "forced" was one. Another was that there was evidence that the public preferred 45s to 78s for single records, which gave broadcasters the assurance that 78 would be the orphaned speed, not 45. Finally, record companies were financially strong enough to be able to offer considerable inducements and "good-will" items to broadcasters to sweeten the expense of the changeover.

---

279 "Equipment Jam Develops as Stations Swing Over to 45s," p. 12.

280 "Move to 45 Backed by Thoro [sic] Survey, But There Was a Slip," Billboard, November 13, 1954, p. 76.

281 Ibid. 282 Ibid.

283 Ibid., p. 100.

Disccs Versus Tape

In the case of the adoption of tape recording equipment, there were a number of factors operating aginst it.

First, the new equipment was expensive. Ampex's first portable professional machine cost $545, for example.[284] And while a half hour reel of tape cost only about $4, even in 1948 when there was still a volume business a half-hour blank recording disc cost about $8.[285] Many stations paid the higher rate for blank discs, however, because they already had the recording (and playback) equipment.[286]

Second, use of tape equipment was unfamiliar. Disc equipment had been around for years, and it offered few surprises to engineers or announcers. No new maintenance or production techniques had to be learned.

Third, the typical station's on-the-air studio was not set up physically for easy addition of tape playback equipment. Often, in order for tape to be fit in, a trusty turntable had to be removed.

Finally, tape equipment was initially less-easily cued, harder to insert on-time (because tapes had to come up to speed) and noisier in use than disc equipment.

Basic to all of the problems mentioned except that of high cost

---

[284] "Hi-Fi That's Just for the Trade," Business Week, July 10, 1954, p. 165.

[285] "Tape for the Networks, Newsweek, May 3, 1948, p. 52.

[286] Keep in mind that the product of a disc recorder could be played back on most station turntables, while a tape recorder set up for production would usually require others set up for playback, meaning a double investment.

was the one of unfamiliarity--that which is not well known is suspect. An innovation is resisted simply for being an innovation. This was the case with the changeover from discs to tape, just as it was the case in the changeover from either discs or tape to cartridges. It must be kept in mind that stations which did not feel the need to do "tight" production were among those who adopted reel-to-reel tape playback for commercials and other program elements. But as the pace of the show became progressively faster as Top 40-type programming developed, the use of reel-to-reel machines became less practical. Discs simply remained easier to use.

Typical Production Facilities

The typical Top 40 station in the 1950s employed a four-turntable setup, with three of the turntables devoted to the playing of locally recorded acetates and the fourth available for the music. This was the setup at Bartell's WAKE in Atlanta in 1956, and at McLendon's KTSA in the same era. WAKE's production manager in that era, Pete Thomas, describes the plant at WAKE:

> . . . they really wanted to come out of their news as fast as possible and into their next program as fast as possible and ID the individual jock as fast as possible but as tightly as possible. And there were no cart machines or tapes then. And it just took an awful lot of time to produce. And the methods for doing this: at that time, four turntables were about the limit that a guy could handle--and they weren't about to put engineers in there, which would have been the alternate route. Some stations which were heavily unionized could simply put engineers and a producer in there and with enough turntables and getting enough competent people, you could do it. They weren't about to do that. [Also, engineers from network radio days tended to do slow, loose production.] They built consoles just for the operation in the deejay studio. And four turntables really represented the upper limit that a guy could handle. He could load two, have one ready, and have one playing. And that involved also getting a filing system back there where he

could drag stuff out awfully fast. I think in this case the playlist was contained on just one of these little wire racks, numbered from one to whatever. And that was the least important thing.[287]

According to Thomas, WAKE had a policy of doing production on everything possible, so that a minimum amount of air time was devoted to live non-produced material.[288] The spots which did not lend themselves to production were still transcribed. "They figured it would cut down the amount of make-goods, and it sounded a little slicker."[289]

WAKE and stations like it thus did a great volume of production, and almost all of it, even if the original had been made on tape, was played back for the air from a disc. Recordings made on discs wore more rapidly than those made on tape. At WAKE, the cutting head was "set up as high as we possibly could. I think the response was probably greater than we could broadcast through the transmitter."[290] As a consequence, discs wore even faster, and had to be recut frequently.

> But the other thing was those acetates--<u>that</u> was another thing probably for this perpetual changing for freshness--we were recutting acetates all the time anyhow. And why not, if you're going to have to recut it, why not redo it another way? Or make it tighter or make it different. You may have hit right there one of the biggest reasons for that continual changing--it had to be done all the time anyhow.[291]

Thomas points out elsewhere that the manager of WAKE was restless to keep experimenting anyway, but the point still emerges that since the physical disc had to be renewed periodically, there was a greater likelihood that the content would also be changed. It is ironic that the easily-erased and reusable tape cartridge, because it

---

287 Thomas interview. 288 *Ibid.*

289 *Ibid.* 290 *Ibid.* 291 *Ibid.*

also maintains its fidelity over long periods, may have resulted in airing of the same program elements for literally years at a time.

Development of Cartridge Tape Equipment

The development of the cartridge tape deck for broadcasting proceeded from the invention of the heart of the equipment, the tape cartridge.

Both the forerunner of the enclosed tape cartridge in use today and the "open" loop cartridge which was threaded onto a regular reel-to-reel tape player were invented by Bernie Cousino of Toledo, Ohio.[292] The open-loop model was sold under the name Audio-Vendor, and was used as a message repeater in point-of-sale store displays. The enclosed unit developed by Cousino was an outgrowth of the Audio-Vendor.[293] Billboard, in reporting the development, predicted that "A newcomer to the tape recording scene, the tape cartridge, may prove as beneficial to that field as the Dixie Cup was to ice cream."[294] The Cousino enclosed cartridge apparently had a sealing system to prevent contact with tape when the cartridge was out of the playback unit, and was a little more complicated than present-day designs.[295] In 1956, Sound Electronics Laboratories, a division of G. H. Poulsen & Company, also of Toledo, announced the development of the Fidelipac cartridge which was apparently essentially the same design as that of modern cartridges The Fidelipac system used a simple drive mechanism and was "designed fo

---

[292]"Big Potential Seen in New Gadget Manufactured by Chicago Company," Billboard, March 26, 1955, p. 17.

[293]Ibid., p. 146. [294]Ibid., p. 17.

[295]Ibid.

economical mass production."[296] At the time, the big news was that 30- and 60-minute designs had been developed, whereas other systems being manufactured could not accommodate more than 15 minutes of material.[297] Obviously, the major market envisioned for such equipment in 1956 was the home hi-fi consumer rather than the broadcast industry.

In 1959, using the Fidelipac cartridge as the basis of the system, Ross Beville introduced the first broadcast-designed cartridge deck, the Spotmaster. The Spotmaster was basically a cartridge recording or playback deck with one important extra feature--a short tone was added on a separate track from the audio signal upon commencing recording that allowed the machine to re-cue the cartridge at the exact starting position ready for the next play. With the cue tone, an operator only had to decide when to <u>start</u> the cartridge, since each was already cued and ready to run. Eventually, other cue tones would be applied so that in effect one cartridge machine signalled another machine when to start, eliminating the operator completely.[298]

In response to several questions from the author, Ross Beville, the inventor of the Spotmaster, explained that machine's development. The letter Beville sent is reproduced here:

---

[296] "SEL Develops LP Cartridge," <u>Billboard</u>, March 17, 1956, p. 16.

[297] <u>Ibid</u>.

[298] The use of sub-audible or separate tones to start and stop tape equipment was not pioneered by Spotmaster, but by Ampex. In 1955, Ampex made its first large-scale demonstration of reel-to-reel automation equipment. Two years later, only 5% of stations questioned by Ampex were using any automatic programming equipment--about 150 stations. See "Automation Off to Slow Start, But Those That Use It Like It," <u>Broadcasting</u>, January 21, 1957, p. 68.

BROADCAST ELECTRONICS, INC.
— A FILMWAYS COMPANY —
8810 BROOKVILLE RD. • SILVER SPRING. MD. 20910 • PHONE 301-588-4983 • CABLE "SPOTMASTER"

Ross Beville
5000 Kirby Road
Bethesda, Md. 20034

July 17, 1972

Mr. David T. MacFarland
115 Chestnut Street
Lodi, Wisconsin 53555

Dear Mr. MacFarland:

Sorry to be so long in replying to your letter of June 14th but I have just returned from an extended trip and your letter arrived while I was away.

Regarding your specific questions:

(1) The development period of Spotmaster tape cartridge equipment was during the years of late 1958, 1959 and 1960. At the time I was Vice President and Chief Engineer of WWDC, Inc., Washington, D.C., a position I held for some twenty five years beginning in 1943. As in all radio stations during this period, we were plagued with scratchy acetate disc recordings on which commercial and other spots were recorded. This was a continuing problem and although we experimented with various forms of reel to reel tape, automatic and otherwise, none afford a satisfactory solution.

When the endless loop tape cartridge appeared on the scene, accompanied by a rather rudimentary transport, we began a program of refinement of the transport (solenoid operation and more rugged construction) and development of electronic circuitry with the objective of utilizing the cartridge in broadcasting.

The key to a broadcast system, of course, was the endless loop tape cartridge. But, equally important was the automatic electronic cueing system which utilized a ½ second, 1000 Hz cue tone which was automatically recorded on a separately designated cue track coincidentally with the recording of the program track. Thus, when the tape was reproduced and the message completed, the tape continued to run until the electronic sensing circuitry detected the presence of the 1000 Hz cue tone at the beginning of the message and stopped the tape at that precise point. The cartridge was then ready for immediate re-use. The advantage in this is that spots are always cued and ready for use, essentially at the push of a button. It also eliminates the ever present danger of running spots at the wrong speed as is the case with disc recordings.

As you probably know, the system revolutionized spot reproduction in broadcasting. Moreover, broadcasters were quick to recognize its potential in other areas of tape recording, as well. Top 40 stations are a good example of this.

Spotmaster

(2) The equipment was first offered for sale in early 1959. A number of stations in this area saw the equipment and expressed interest but the first to receive one of our early commercial models was WQSN of Charleston, S.C. Shortly thereafter, WLAN of Lancaster, Penna. bought a number of units as did WGH, Newport News, Virginia. It goes without saying that WWDC, Washington, D.C. was loaded with them from the very beginning. Yes, there were some bugs in this first equipment but by the end of 1959 we had shaken most of them out. In gratitude to our pioneering stations we voluntarily replaced all of their original equipment with new and improved models a year later. Thereafter, our sales figures grew from year to year.

By 1962 we were shipping on a worldwide basis. Australia was our first foreign shipment and this country, which is so much like our own, developed into a large market for us. Next came Canada, Mexico and then BBC which was a big plus factor for us. Swedish radio (Government owned Sverga) gave us a substantial boost on the world wide market as did Norway. Now our sales files include most of the countries of the free world.

(3) Early sales resistance centered on our being a new, very small company. Although broadcasters were intrigued by this new concept in tape reording, they were hesitant to buy from us for fear that we might be out of business next week. Also, there was the wait and see attitude of the cautious, principally the very large stations. The large networks, CBS, NBC, ABC and MBS, were the worst of all. We had hoped to place our equipment with these companies because of the prestige value but, as it developed, they were among the last to fit their installations with any type of cartridge equipment. The small and medium sized independent stations were our principal market-God bless them - and we decided early in the game to concentrate on them. There were many more of them anyway.

There was one other area of resistance that developed. As more and more stations became equipped with cartridge equipment of various manufacture, New York advertising agencies began to express concern that the spots they had carefully recorded on disc were not always properly dubbed to tape. Some even want so far as to forbid re-recording to tape but this had little effect as most stations ignored the order. The reason for their concern was the lack of industry standards - primarily quality control and equalization curves. Their concern was not entirely without reason. During the early years, a number of equipment manufacturers, noting the increasing acceptance and growth of cartridge tape equipment, entered the market with equipment of their own. There being no industry standards, such as those usually supplied by NAB, they devised their own. The result was that not all equipment was compatible. Fortunately, the NAB had also recognized this need and in late 1961 had organized an industry committee to study and recommend cartridge tape standards for the broadcast industry. I was Chairman of this committee and its membership included all equipment, tape and cartridge manufacturers, the principal broadcasting networks and a number of independent radio stations. We completed our work in 1964 and the standards were adopted by the NAB in the same year. Following this, agency resistance largely disappeared.

I hope the foregoing provides the information you need. If you need to communicate with me further, please send any mail to the address shown below. It will reach me more quickly.

Ross Beville
6000 Kirby Road
Bethesda, Md. 20034

Very truly yours

Ross Beville

Ross Beville

Will appreciate knowing of any publications that result. RB

In August of 1959, MacKenzie Electronics of Inglewood, California was advertising its MacKenzie Program Repeater, which employed tape "magazines" rather than enclosed cartridges.[299]

Other Playback Systems

By the early 1960s, there were other designs being introduced to compete with the cartridge tape system. Gates developed what it called the SpotTape system, which employed a single 13-inch wide tape on which up to 101 90-second announcements could be selectively erased, recorded or played back by moving the head across the width of the tape to the proper track. Between the end of one announcement and the beginning of the next, there was a recycle period during which the machine cued up for the next selected spot. As with cartridges, two or more machines were required for tight production.[300] A similar device, allowing 64 announcements on a 4-inch wide tape was being sold in 1962 by Automated Electronics Inc.[301] By 1965, Ampex had developed a system which had some of the advantages of the cartridge system (especially rapid and individual selectivity of content) but without the use of cartridges. Their Cue-Matic used magnetic-oxide-coated flexible mats which resembled records except that the grooves merely transported the record-playback head across the surface to be recorded or played. In the use of cue tones at the end of the message (the beginning was cued automatically by being at the outside edge of the

---

[299]Advertisement in Broadcasting, August 17, 1959, p. 73.

[300]Advertisement in Broadcasting, November 7, 1960, p. 79.

[301]Advertisement in Broadcasting, April 2, 1962, p. 103.

mat), the system resembled cartridge deck design. However, the Cue-Matic was limited to 3 minutes and 45 seconds by the size of the mats.[302] By this time, cartridges of lengths up to an hour had been perfected for broadcast use where multiple cuts of the same general type would be most convenient in one package (as for public service announcements). As of September, 1965, Ampex announced that over 450 Cue-Matics had been ordered. The price for the recorder-reproducer was $1,395, which was about the same or slightly higher than the price of a cartridge record-play deck. However, blank mats for the Cue-Matic cost only about 45¢ each.[303]

That 450 Cue-Matic machines could be sold in 1965 at prices as high or higher than competing cartridge systems points to a lack of confidence in cartridge equipment. The scepticism was not entirely ill-founded. The early cartridge decks were described as "really dubious looking pieces of equipment."[304] Besides not appearing very substantial from an engineering viewpoint, the decks "clanked and thudded and everything else and you could see some obvious disadvantages to putting them in a room where a guy was on the air--you could imagine those clanks going through the air mike."[305] There were also problems with carts jamming, with refusing to run, with slowing down or dragging at some parts of the tape, and with "flutter." Many of these problems were caused by infrequent or improper maintenance or lack of experience

---

[302] Advertisement in Broadcasting, May 24, 1965, pp. 72-73.

[303] "Ampex Cue-Matic Goes Into Production," Broadcasting, September 27, 1965, p. 60.

[304] Thomas interview. [305] Ibid.

in using the machines among air personnel. In 1963, a number of advertising agencies became vocally concerned over what they felt was an all-too-frequent degradation of quality in making transfers between the transcriptions they supplied and the cartridges used for playback. One agency timed one of its 60-second spots at 64 seconds via cartridge.[306] A survey of 476 larger stations found six different systems in wide use, plus several other less popular designs, making the adoption of technical standards of compatibility difficult.[307] In September, the J. Walter Thompson agency requested that all of its clients' announcements be played directly from the disc supplied by the agency rather than from a cartridge copy.[308] By February of 1964, several technical committees of the NAB engineering department had developed criteria for both discs and cartridge tapes plus a set of guidelines for the technician making the transfer.[309] The disc standards were the first new ones in eleven years, while those for cartridges were the first eve set.[310] With at least manufacturing standards developed, some of the problems of cartridge tapes were eliminated.

It is interesting to note that the 1963 survey of 476 of the nation's top stations conducted by the D. P. Brother advertising agency

---

[306]"Tape or Disc for Commercials?" Broadcasting, June 3, 1963, p. 34.

[307]Ibid.

[308]"JWT Blames Quality Loss on Cartridges," Broadcasting, September 30, 1963, p. 46.

[309]"Disk to Tape Problem Solution," Broadcasting, February 17, 1964, p. 62.

[310]Ibid.

ound 406 of the stations using tape cartridges for commercials.[311] is means that among the larger stations, which could generally be ssumed to have adequate engineering and maintenance staffs, cartridge apes were the dominant medium of playing commercials in 83% of the ases. Yet as late as 1962, Top 40 stations in smaller markets were ontinuing to use discs. "No, the acetate held its own until somebody ame up with cartridge decks that were silent and rugged and proved hemselves on the air. . . . I've never seen a piece of radio equipment et that could be sold without the stations satisfying themselves. It oesn't make any difference how many tests the guy has done."[312]

In buying equipment or program services, most radio station anagement in the 1950s hesitated to try the unfamiliar or adopt the nproven. The owners and managers of the Top 40 stations to be examined n the following chapters are notable precisely for being exceptions.

---

[311]"Tape or Disc for Commercials," p. 34.

[312]Thomas interview.

SECTION B--RESPONSES TO NEW PATTERNS

CHAPTER THREE

INTRODUCTION TO FOUR TOP 40 GROUP OWNERS

The names of four independent station group owners began to appear more frequently in the trade press in the mid-1950s as the stations they owned grew to be phenomenally successful. All four came to be identified with the Top 40 format. The four were Todd Storz, Gordon McLendon, Gerald Bartell, and Harold Krelstein for Plough Broadcasting. Todd Storz was president of Mid-Continent Broadcasting Compa and Storz Broadcasting Company; Gordon McLendon headed various broadcasting corporations such as Trinity, Texas Triangle, NoeMac, the McLendon Stations and the earlier Liberty Network; Gerald Bartell was president of the Bartell Group of stations; and Harold Krelstein was president of the Plough Broadcasting Company which was owned by the Plough pharmaceutical firm. Each man and/or each company made a substantial contribution to the development of Top 40. The efforts of so were more fully-reported than others, and trade press coverage was not always commensurate with the magnitude of their accomplishments. However, all four group owners gained a share of notoriety, and through publicity about the success of their stations they were influential in spreading the Top 40 format throughout the country. Of the four men, three remain. Robert Todd Storz died in his home in Miami Beach on

April 13, 1964 at the age of 39 of what was believed to be a cerebral hemorrhage.[1] It was in the years at the mid-point of the 1950s that Top 40 group owners made the majority of their station acquisitions. In order to clarify for the reader the welter of transactions that took place during a relatively short time, two tables are offered. One lists the stations bought by the principal Top 40 group owners by the year in which the station was bought; the other lists the acquisitions by Top 40 group.

Stations Acquired by Top 40 Group Owners--By Year of Acquisition

Year	Group	Station	Number Held After Acquisition
1945	Plough	WMPS	1
1947	McLendon	KNET	1
		KLIF	2, then 1
	Bartell	WEXT	1
1949	Storz	KOWH	1
1950	McLendon	KELP	2
	Bartell	WOKY	1
1952	Bartell	WAPL	2
1953	Storz	WTIX (old)	2
	Plough	WJJD	2
1954	McLendon	WRIT	3
	Storz	WHB	3

[1] The New York Times Obituary Index incorrectly lists the date of the obituary as August 14, 1964, instead of April 14.

Year	Group	Station	Number Held After Acquisition
1955	McLendon	WGLS/WTAM	4
	NoeMac (McLendon consulted)	WNOE	-
		KNOE	-
	Storz	WDGY	4
	Bartell	KCBQ	3
		WAKE	4
		KRUX	5
1956	McLendon	KTSA	5
	Storz	WQAM	5
	Plough	WCAO	3
		WCOP	4
1957	McLendon	KILT	6
		KEEL	6
		WAKY	7
	Bartell	WBMS/WILD	5
		WYDE	6
1958	Storz	KOMA	5
		WTIX (new)	5
	Bartell	KYA	6
1959	Bartell	WADO	6
	Plough	WAGA/WPLO	5
1960	Storz	KXOK	6

Year	Group	Station	Number Held After Acquisition
1962	McLendon	WYSL (Amherst)	7
		WGES/WYNR/WNUS	7
1969	McLendon	WYSL (Buffalo)	7

Stations Acquired by Top 40 Group Owners--By Owner

Owner	Station	Year Bought	
McLendon	KNET	1947	
	KLIF	1947	
	KELP	1950	
	WRIT	1954	
	WGLS/WTAM	1955	
	(WNOE)	1955	(NoeMac)
	(KNOE)	1955	
	KTSA	1956	
	KILT	1957	
	KEEL	1957	
	WAKY	1957	
	WYSL (Amherst)	1962	
	WGES/WYNR/WNUS	1962	
	WYSL (Buffalo)	1969	
Storz	KOWH	1949	
	WTIX (old)	1953	

Owner	Station	Year Bought
Storz	WHB	1954
	WDGY	1955
	WQAM	1956
	KOMA	1958
	WTIX (new)	1958
	KXOK	1960
Bartell	WEXT	1947
	WOKY	1950
	WAPL	1952
	KCBQ	1955
	WAKE	1955
	KRUX	1955
	WBMS	1957
	WYDE	1957
	KYA	1958
	WADO	1959
Plough	WMPS	1945
	WJJD	1953
	WCAO	1956
	WCOP	1956
	WAGA/WPLO	1959

Storz

Robert Todd Storz was born in Omaha March 8, 1924, the son of Robert H. Storz, vice-president of the Storz Brewing Company. At the age of eight, Todd built his first crystal set. At sixteen he had a ham operator's license.[2]

Storz attended Omaha public schools, the Choate School in Wallingford, Connecticut, and (for one year) the University of Nebraska at Lincoln. He then spent three years in the U.S. Army Signal Corps which he claimed gave him the balance of his education.[3] During those three years, Storz never operated a radio. Instead, he was a cryptographic officer, stationed at Miami and at Warren Hills Farm in Pennsylvania.[4] When Storz left the army in 1945, he attended a 12-week summer institute in radio sponsored by NBC and Northwestern University, and then joined KWBW, Hutchinson, Kansas as a jack-of-all trades. Storz claims that he announced, engineered, sold, wrote copy, and swept the floor there.[5]

In 1947, Storz returned to Omaha and went to work for KBON there, which was then the Mutual outlet. This job, which included a late-night disc jockey show, lasted about a year. He was criticized by some listeners for not playing the esoteric swing and bop that his

---

[2]Bill Stewart, Program Director, WNOE, printed material received in a private interview held in New Orleans, November 4, 1971, hereafter referred to as "Printed Stewart interview material."

[3]"Our Respects to Todd Storz," Broadcasting, September 19, 1955, p. 26.

[4]"Printed Stewart interview material."

[5]Ibid.

predecessor had,[6] but instead playing mostly popular records. During 1948, Todd worked in local sales for KFAB, Omaha.[7]

Storz Station Acquisitions

KOWH

Todd and his father Robert were said to have often discussed the possibility of opening a new station in Omaha, but had always decided against it. Then in 1949, Todd's father heard that KOWH was for sale. KOWH had been operated for the preceding ten years by the World Publishing Company, publisher of the Omaha World-Herald. The father and son bought it for $75,000.[8] Father Robert Storz put up $30,000 to own 60% of the new Mid-Continent Broadcasting Company and was president, but Todd was vice president and general manager of the station. For his share, Todd had mortgaged a farm he owned in Iowa to contribute $20,000 while the remaining $25,000 came from a bank loan.[9]

When the Storzes bought KOWH in 1949, the station was neither going broke nor making money.[10] Two television stations (WOW-TV and KMTV) also went on the air in Omaha in August and September of 1949.[11]

For the first few weeks of ownership, Storz remained cautious and made few changes. Then, he converted from a polyglot format (an hour of popular music, then an hour of classical, then an hour of something else) to one concentrating strictly on popular music. Storz is

---

6 Ibid. 7 "Our Respects to Todd Storz," p. 26.

8 "Printed Stewart interview material."

9 Ibid. 10 Ibid.

11 1972 Broadcasting Yearbook (Washington, D.C.: Broadcasting Publications Inc., 1972), p. A-36.

quoted as saying "It was basically the music-and-news formula, although we have refined it since. . . ."[12]

At the end of its first year of Storz ownership, KOWH-AM showed a profit of $84.[13] The companion FM station had been sold in the meantime. However, it did not take a full year for the new programming to have an effect. It was only about six months after Storz took over that KOWH came up first in ratings in the afternoon among the six stations in the Omaha market, and the station required only about two years to gain leadership in all time periods. Prior to Storz management, the station had been sixth out of six in Omaha.[14]

As early as November, 1951, KOWH was claiming some firsts, but by 1953, KOWH was firmly established as the number one station in the Omaha area. For the period October 1951 through January 1953, Hooper said it had the largest share of audience (35.9%) of any Omaha station.[15] The January 1953 Hooper found KOWH with the largest share of audience in any individual time period, of any independent station in all America![16] At this time, KOWH was running a full-page ad in Broadcasting nearly every week, using novel new copy as often as possible to retell the ratings story, since ratings reports in Omaha in 1953 were not very frequent.

In November of 1953, KOIL, an ABC affiliate in Omaha on 1290 kHz with 5,000 watts fulltime (as compared with KOWH's 500 watts on 660

---

[12] "Printed Stewart interview material."

[13] Ibid. [14] Ibid.

[15] Advertisement in Broadcasting, March 16, 1953, p. 8.

[16] Ibid.

daytime only) went on sale. KOIL would later become KOWH's only Top 40 competition, and being a better facility, would eventually overtake KOWH in ratings. It might have been smart for Storz to buy KOIL, but in August, the company had bought WTIX New Orleans for $25,000, and the company's policy was always to pay off one station before buying another.[17]

KOWH's ratings, however, continued to climb. The November 1953 through February 1954 Hooper average showed KOWH with a 50% share of audience during 33 weekly quarter hours.[18]

In July of 1954, KOWH announced the appointment of H-R Inc. as their national representatives, replacing the Bolling Company. At that point, KOWH had completed its 32nd month in first place in Omaha.[19] In November, 1954, KOWH was boasting that of 40 daytime quarter hours, 36 rated by Hooper showed KOWH in first place, tied for first in one, and second in only three.[20]

In March 1955 KOWH ran a particularly attractive and effective trade ad with the title "A Good Time is Had By All!" The ad was almost entirely composed of clocks, with each one's hands at a different daytime quarter hour, with the ratings given. The message was, no advertiser gets a bad time on KOWH (see page 167).[21]

By July of 1955, Don Burden's KOIL was going after the KOWH

---

[17]"Printed Stewart interview material."

[18]Advertisement in Sponsor, March 22, 1954, front cover.

[19]Advertisement in Broadcasting, July 5, 1954, p. 6.

[20]Advertisement in Sponsor, November 15, 1954, p. 93.

[21]Advertisement in Sponsor, March 7, 1955, p. 3.

A GOOD TIME IS HAD BY ALL!

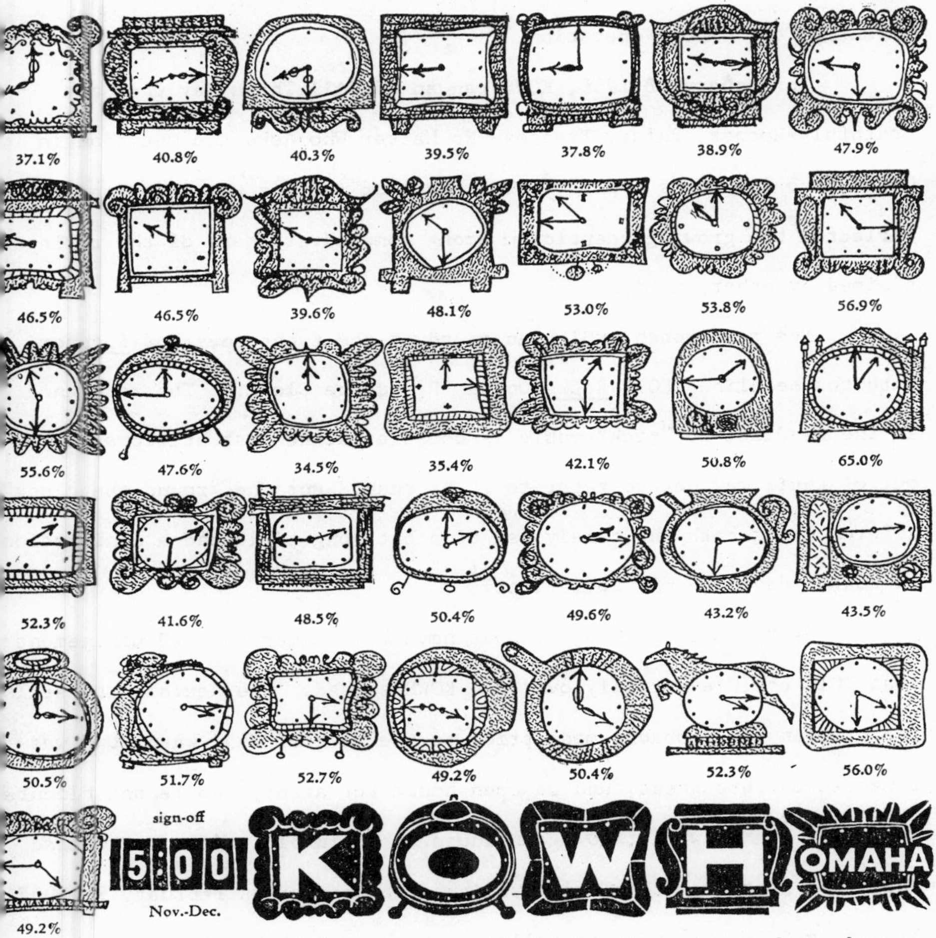

No advertiser gets a bad time on KOWH, proud dominator of every single daytime ¼ hour. Lowest average quarter: 34.5%. Highest: 65% RPT 65%.* A.M. average: 45.3%; P.M. average: 47.6%; All-day: 46.7%. (Next station 21.3%.)

The time was never better for a chat with the H-R man, or KOWH General Manager Virgil Sharpe.

Hooper Continuing Measurements, 8 a.m.-6 p.m. Monday-Saturday, Oct. '54-Jan. '55.

MID-CONTINENT BROADCASTING COMPANY

President: Todd Storz

**WHB, *Kansas City*
Represented by
John Blair & Co.**

**WTIX, *New Orleans*
Represented by
Adam J. Young, Jr.**

**KOWH, *Omaha*
Represented by
H-R, Reps, Inc.**

audience. The format was basically a copy of KOWH, but with the added advantage of 24-hour operation.[22]

In January of 1956, KOWH ran an ad "All Three Say the Same Mouthful--Hooper, Pulse, Trendex--No Matter Who Asks the Question in Omaha, the Answer is KOWH."[23] The theme of ratings unanimity may have reflected the growing scepticism among some advertisers of the ratings claimed by other stations.

The next month, KOIL ran an ad on the front cover of Sponsor with the headline "KOIL Rocks Omaha 'Round the Clock." The reference in the headline to "rock" music is notable, since most stations went out of their way not to refer to it as such. But the "round the clock" reference was both the timely use of a hit song title and a denigration of KOWH's daytime-only operation.[24]

By the end of 1956, it must have been clear to KOWH management that KOIL could eventually overtake KOWH's lead. The decision to sell the station was probably made prior to the fall of 1956 when KOWH was redecorated throughout, and an open house for agency people and clients was held.[25] Meanwhile, KOIL continued to claim big gains. A KOIL ad "Just One Step from the Top!" published in Sponsor on February 9, 1957 brought a KOWH rebuttal the following week, and then a KOIL rebuttal to

---

[22] Advertisement in Sponsor, July 11, 1955, p. 187.

[23] Advertisement in Broadcasting, January 23, 1956, p. 6.

[24] Advertisement in Sponsor, February 6, 1956, front cover.

[25] "KOWH Holds Open House Party," Broadcasting, November 26, 1956, p. 99.

e rebuttal (see pages 170 to 172).[26]

In March of 1957, Broadcasting reported that KOWH was to be sold to William F. Buckley, Jr. publisher of the National Review and owner of National Weekly Inc.[27] In headlining their report "Capital Capital Gain," Broadcasting underscored the phenomenal price to be paid for a 500 watt daytimer. The final selling price was $822,500.[28] According to former Storz Program Director Bill Stewart, the selling price was the highest price ever paid to that date for a daytime-only station.[29] Also according to Stewart, Buckley tried to sell KOWH for $300,000 beginning about 1959, and finally succeeded in selling it in 1970 for $10,000.[30] Asked if Buckley and associates thought that Stewart and the other personnel would stay with KOWH when it was sold in 1957, Stewart replied in the negative and said

> They thought it was just going to keep perking along. It's just like most of these dingbats who own stations think that it will just keep perking along. But they don't. Somebody has to be there to perk 'em along, to stay on top of them.[31]

Almost immediately after the sale was effected, KOIL began claiming an all-day number one position in Omaha,[32] and by May was claiming an "undisputed" number one rating.[33]

---

[26]Advertisements in Sponsor, February 9 and 16, 1957, front covers; and February 23, 1957, p. 17.

[27]"Closed Circuit: Capital Capital Gain," Broadcasting, March 25, 1957, p. 5.

[28]"Storz Sells KOWH for $822,500; Seven Other AM Stations Sold," Broadcasting, April 1, 1957, p. 128.

[29]Stewart interview. [30]Ibid. [31]Ibid.

[32]Advertisement in Sponsor, April 13, 1957, p. 17.

[33]Advertisement in Sponsor, May 4, 1957, front cover.

ust One Step from the Top!

It's a success story, like the best of Horatio Alger. A mere 18 months ago, KOIL claimed only fifth place in Omaha's six-station market. Today, a year and a half later, the *new* KOIL has risen to *dominant* second position!* First place is a single short step up. KOIL IS ON THE WAY TO THE TOP!

*(Both Hooper and Pulse prove it.)

KOIL's success formula means that *only* KOIL in Omaha has higher and higher ratings *continuously.* It shows again that: Nothing succeeds like success!

Now, it's all over town that advertisers get bigger and better results on KOIL than with any other Omaha station. The fact is, *more local advertisers use KOIL than all other Omaha stations combined!*

KOIL is built on success! That's why so many agencies and advertisers are guaranteeing the success of their campaigns by selecting KOIL — Omaha's *success station!*

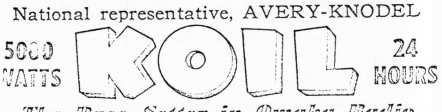

National representative, AVERY-KNODEL

5000 WATTS **KOIL** 24 HOURS

The Pace-Setter in Omaha Radio

RADIO STATION KOWH
THE STORZ STATIONS
OMAHA 2, NEBRASKA

WDCY { MINNEAPOLIS ST PAUL
KOWH OMAHA
WHB KANSAS CITY
WTIX NEW ORLEANS
WQAM MIAMI

KILPATRICK BUILDING
ATLANTIC 2228

February 16, 1957

Mr. Chick Crabtree
Co-Manager
Radio Station KOIL
Omaha, Nebraska

Dear Chick:

We have read your ad on the cover of February 9 Sponsor, and we believe there are several inaccuracies.

1. You say, "A mere 18 months ago, KOIL claimed only fifth place in Omaha's six-station market."

   The fact is that in the August-September, 1955 Hooper, KOIL showed up a very strong THIRD.

2. "Today, a year and a half later, the new KOIL has risen to dominant second position. Both Hooper and Pulse prove it."

   The fact is that December Hooper figures showed KOIL to be THIRD; KOWH, in first place. The two most recent Pulse ratings show KOIL to be a VERY WEAK THIRD.

   In the September Pulse you were just 0.8 of a point ahead of the 4th station and the December figures show KOIL again to be a WEAK THIRD while KOWH has almost twice your rating. (Monday-Saturday, KOWH 32%, KOIL 16.5%).

3. "KOIL's success formula means that only KOIL in Omaha has higher and higher ratings continuously."

   The fact is that only KOIL of the big four stations has shown a decline in the last three PULSE reports.

4. "More local advertisers use KOIL than all other Omaha stations combined."

   Not only is it a fact that KOIL does NOT have more local advertisers than OTHER OMAHA STATIONS COMBINED; actually, KOIL doesn't have more local advertisers than KOWH ALONE. A notarized air check made the week of December 17, 1956, showed that KOWH had 112 while KOIL had only 93.

Cordially,

Virgil Sharpe

Virgil Sharpe
General Manager

cc: Federal Communications Commission, Washington, D.C.
Dr. Sidney Roslow, Pulse, Inc., New York
Frank Stisser, C. E. Hooper, Inc., New York
Norman Glenn, Sponsor Magazine, New York
Harold Fellows, NARTB, Washington
Omaha Better Business Bureau, Omaha
Omaha Advertising Club
All Major Omaha Advertising Agencies
Legal Counsel, KOWH
Legal Counsel, KOIL

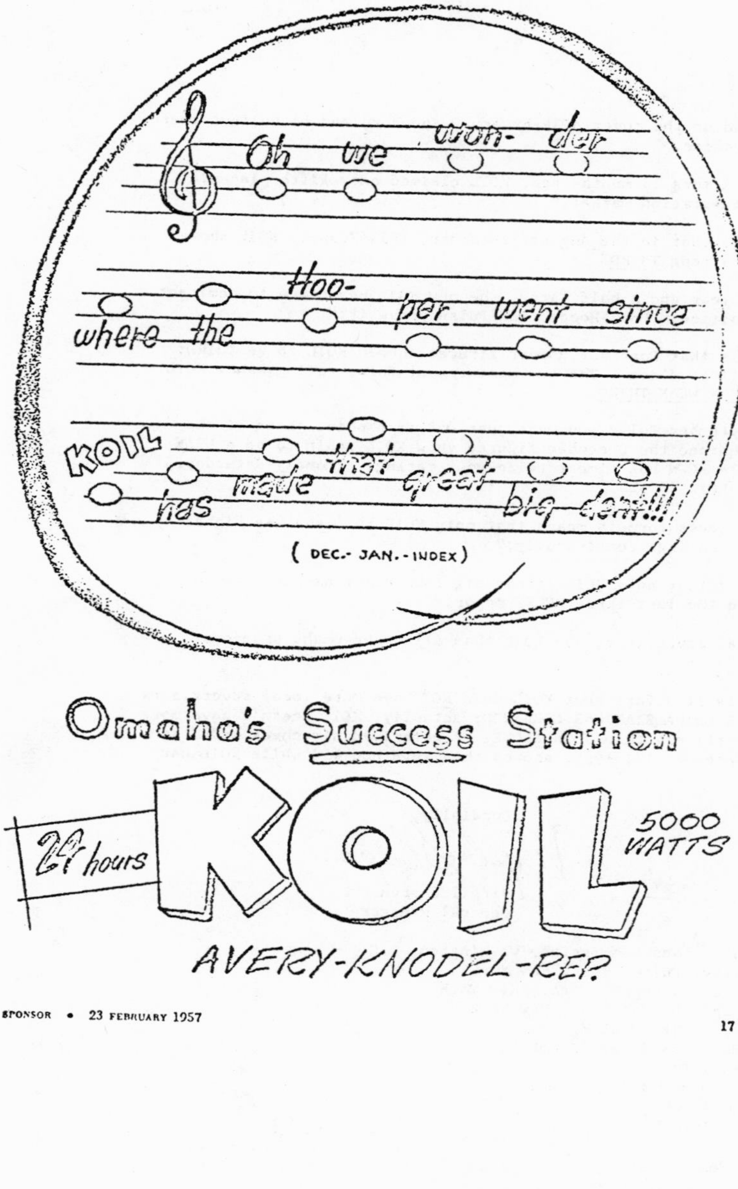
Oh we won- der
where the Hoo- per went since
KOIL has made that great big dent!!!
(DEC.- JAN.- INDEX)
Omaha's Success Station
24 hours
KOIL
5000 WATTS
AVERY-KNODEL-REP.

WTIX

By 1953, KOWH was firmly established as the number one station in Omaha, so in August of that year, Mid-Continent bought WTIX, New Orleans, for $25,000.[34] At the time of the filing, Todd was listed as Vice-President and Secretary of Mid-Continent and as a "manufacturer of advertising displays."[35] The WTIX which Storz owned then was only 250 watts at 1450 kHz. As would be the case with Bartell's WAKE in Atlanta (outlined earlier), WTIX's signal barely reached beyond the city limits of New Orleans. Yet, with Storz's type of music-and-news programming, WTIX went from eleventh among eleven stations in September of 1953 to first place in share of audience in July of 1954.[36] By January of 1954, WTIX was ahead of six other independents, and by March of 1954, only one network station was ahead in the morning, only two in the afternoons.[37] By July, WTIX had an 18.5% average share-of-audience from 7:00 a.m. to 6:00 p.m. as compared with the network station in second place with a 15.4%.[38] In the very same issue of Broadcasting in which an ad for WTIX appeared announcing the new figures, WWL, which was likely the second-place station, ran a trade ad saying "New Orleans has 746,000 people, 11 radio stations--but only one WWL--according to the mostest of the listeners. . . . It's been that way for 32 years!"[39]

---

[34] "For the Record: Ownership Changes: WTIX, New Orleans, Royal Bcstg Corps," Broadcasting, August 31, 1953, p. 103.

[35] Ibid.

[36] Advertisement in Broadcasting, September 6, 1954, front cover.

[37] Ibid. [38] Ibid.

[39] Advertisement in Broadcasting, September 6, 1954, p. 26.

However, WTIX was destined to remain firmly in first or second place up to the present.

In 1955, WTIX's license was renewed over the dissent of Commissioner John C. Doerfer who said, "I cannot find that the renewal of the license of WTIX is in the public interest. The licensee has not met the minimum program standards required by the Commission. He has failed to include any religious, educational, or discussion programs."[40] With these remarks, Commissioner Doerfer raised the sort of complaints which would culminate in the Atlanta Balanced Programming cases of 1957, but in 1955, WTIX's license was renewed on a regular basis.

By January of 1956, WTIX's daytime share averaged 21.2%, while the second station (now identified in WTIX advertising as a "50,000 watt net" and obviously WWL) had an average 18% share.[41] By summer, WTIX had increased its average daytime share to 26.0% against the next station's 14.1%.[42] By October of 1957, WTIX had 200 out of 220 first place Hooper quarter hours.[43] All of this was done with 250 watts on 1450 kHz.

In December of 1957, Broadcasting's "Closed Circuit" announced that Storz was in the final stages of negotiating to buy a full-time regional station in New Orleans to replace the feeble WTIX.[44] In April

---

[40]"WTIX Gets Renewal," Broadcasting, September 22, 1955, p. 90.

[41]Advertisement in Sponsor, February 6, 1956, p. 18, and in Broadcasting, January 30, 1956, p. 6.

[42]Advertisement in Broadcasting, August 6, 1956, p. 6.

[43]Advertisement in Sponsor, October 19, 1957, p. 13.

[44]"Closed Circuit: Storz Upgrading," Broadcasting, December 23, 1957, p. 5.

of 1958, Broadcasting announced that Storz had acquired WWEZ in New Orleans, a 5,000 watt station at 690 kHz for $490,000 conditional on the disposal of WTIX. Rather than sell the old station, Storz made a gift of it to the Orleans Parish School Board which planned to use it as an educational station with reduced hours.[45] Bill Stewart, who was at one time National Program Director for the Storz Stations, points out that, by giving the old WTIX to the local school system, Storz was able to take a tax write-off of about $500,000 while at the same time eliminating potential competition for the new WTIX.[46]

On May 7, 1958, at 6:00 p.m. WTIX moved from 1450 with 250 watts to 690 with 5,000 watts and immediately added both 1,000,000 potential listeners and nighttime operation.[47] Even before the change, WTIX was "more popular than the next three stations combined" according to Hooper,[48] so that with the vastly improved facility, WTIX became nearly invincible.

WHB

In April of 1954, Storz purchased WHB in Kansas City from the Cook Paint & Varnish Company, in a complicated four-way deal which required the divestiture of the station by its original owners because of the acquisition of another Kansas City radio station (KMBC). In

---

[45]"Changing Hands: WTIX, WWEZ, New Orleans, La.," Broadcasting, April 7, 1958, p. 76.

[46]Mr. Bill Stewart, private interview held in Slidell, Louisiana, November 4, 1971.

[47]Advertisement in Broadcasting, May 19, 1958, front cover.

[48]Ibid.

several ways, the purchase of WHB set a pattern for all later Storz acquisitions. First, the station was a prime facility: 10,000 watts days and 5,000 watts nights on 710 kHz. Second, it was an old, established station with well-known call letters, having been founded in 1922. (The same factors--good facility and established call--were also taken into account in the later purchase of WDGY, Minneapolis, and WQAM, Miami, as will be shown later.) By this time, the price of good facilities was back on the way up, and Storz had to pay $400,000 for WHB.[49]

Along with WHB, Mid-Continent inherited a Mutual network affiliation. By September of 1954, about four months after the purchase, WHB announced it was dropping its affiliation effective in October although relations with the network had been amiable.[50] The rationale for the change was stated in a joint announcement made by Storz and by WHB general manager George W. (Bud) Armstrong, which said that they believed the future of radio lay with the "aggressive and intelligently-programmed independent station."[51] They pointed out that, at that time, the company's two other independents, KOWH and WTIX, had the "'largest audience of any station in their respective cities according to the latest Hooper audience reports.'"[52]

On October 17th, WHB dropped Mutual affiliation and promoted the fact on the front covers of the next day's Sponsor and the

---

[49]"WHB-AM-TV Buys Church's KMBC-AM-TV; WHB Acquired by Storz Family," Broadcasting, April 26, 1954, p. 62.

[50]"WHB, WHCC Drop MBS Affiliations," Broadcasting, September 27, 1954, p. 50.

[51]Ibid. [52]Ibid.

November 1 issue of Broadcasting.[53] In those two advertisements, the identical copy read "Now WHB has 24 full hours a day to transmit the kind of radio which has already started the big switch in Kansas City listening."[54] But a later ad in Sponsor was more forceful. Using the same "Big Switch!" headline, this advertisement said,

> Unburdened by a lot of programs only some people want to hear, WHB now fills 24 hours a day, 7 days a week with what most people want to hear. The result: A steady switching of Kansas City dials to 710 kcs., where new studios, programming, personalities and ideas are making K.C.'s oldest (1922) call letters--K.C.'s most talked about call letters.[55]

By the end of November, a two-month Hooper was completed and WHB could advertise real figures. The first ad in Broadcasting was December 20, 1954, and was headlined "Double Take-Over! June 1954, Mid-Continent Took Over WHB . . . And now . . . WHB Takes Over Kansas City."[56] The copy read:

> It happened in Omaha and it happened in New Orleans! Now Kansas City makes three leaders for Mid-Continent! Hooper says WHB is first in the morning, first in the afternoon, first all day with 35.7% of the available audience, twice the next station's share. All this since June when new ownership-management brought new ideas, new programming, new concepts to Kansas City's oldest (1922) call letters. . . .[57]

By January, WHB's Hooper showed it had a daytime share of 38.1% to the next station's 18.8%.[58] By February, WHB had increased to 43.5%,

---

[53] Advertisements in Sponsor, October 18, 1954, front cover, and in Broadcasting, November 1, 1954, front cover.

[54] Ibid.

[55] Advertisement in Sponsor, November 29, 1954, p. 23.

[56] Advertisement in Broadcasting, December 20, 1954, p. 6.

[57] Ibid.

[58] Advertisement in Broadcasting, January 24, 1955, front cover.

while the second station was down to 17.4%.[59] And in March of 1955, WHB ran an ad saying "Nearly half of Kansas City is yours on WHB."[60] The text read:

> 48.9% (Hooper) to be exact. The other half is shared by seven other radio stations, in amounts descending from 17.1% to 1.7%. Note that WHB's share of audience is nearly 3 times that of the second station.[61]

This also seems to be the first ad for a Storz station in which figures from other ratings services were compared for corroboration. A Trendex of 42.8% share and a first in Pulse, both in-and-out-of-home were also quoted.[62] By October of 1955, Nielsen was also added to the list, with a 39.2% all-day average.[63] The text of this ad introduced the phrase "WHB is running away with Kansas City's radio day" and stressed the unanimous firsts accorded WHB by all services.[64]

In March 1956, WHB ran an ad in Broadcasting saying "It's WHB's Region Too," which quoted an Area Pulse and an Area Nielsen as again putting WHB first.[65] This approach seems to have been in response to a notion that WHB was reaching only metro area listeners. Increasingly, WHB's trades advertising focused on particular potential objections and answered them. In November of 1956, the Meredith Stations' KCMO, a CBS affiliate ran an ad in Broadcasting which hit directly at WHB's

---

[59] Advertisement in Sponsor, February 21, 1955, p. 61.

[60] Advertisement in Sponsor, March 21, 1955, front cover.

[61] Ibid. [62] Ibid.

[63] Advertisement in Sponsor, October 31, 1955, p. 18.

[64] Ibid.

[65] Advertisement in Broadcasting, March 26, 1956, p. 6.

presumed audience composition. The ad said "In Kansas City if you want to sell the rock-n-rollers, there's a place to go . . . but if you want to sell the whole family, it's KCMO radio."[66] By March of 1957, WHB was running a rebuttal (see page 180).[67] Later in the year, WHB actually answered a KCMO blast a week in advance. On December 7, 1957, Sponsor ran WHB's "Coverage? Yes . . . but who's listening?" in which a man holding a microphone seems to be speaking to a grandstand of vacant bleacher seats. The caption read, "In WHB's 96-county world, it's a WHB Pulse!"[68] It was not until the following week that KCMO's accusatory ad appeared. It said "In Kansas City, why settle for Podunk power? Get 50,000 watt coverage on KCMO."[69]

WHB also attempted to speak directly to advertiser's scepticism about sales results. An ad in January 1957 showed two men riding in a taxi with the caption "Ratings make them sign the first time--But it takes results to make them renew . . . at WHB . . . 87% renewal." The ad claimed this figure to be a higher percentage of local and national renewals than any other Kansas City radio station.[70]

WDGY

The WHB purchase in 1954 was Storz's last until the late fall of 1955, when he was reported by Broadcasting to be acquiring WDGY,

---

[66] Advertisement in Broadcasting, November 12, 1956, p. 8.

[67] Advertisement in Sponsor, March 23, 1957, p. 13.

[68] Advertisement in Sponsor, December 7, 1957, p. 28.

[69] Advertisement in Sponsor, December 14, 1957, p. 45.

[70] Advertisement in Sponsor, January 12, 1957, p. 13.

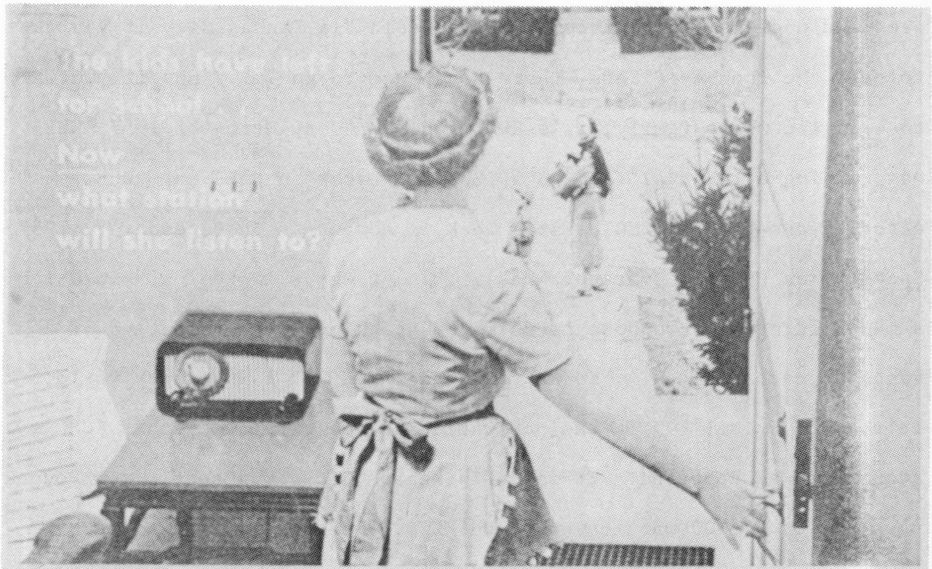

All new surveys show again:

When the youngsters are away . . . Kansas City radios stay . . . with WHB

Let's look between **9 a.m. and 4 p.m. Monday through Friday**—and see what happens to Kansas City radio listening when "all those teen-agers" are at school. WHB continues its domination! According to every major survey, everyone of the 140 quarter hours from 9 to 4 belongs overwhelmingly to WHB. This, mind you, when there are no teen-agers available. No wonder WHB carries regular schedules for virtually every major Kansas City food chain—including **A & P, Milgram's, Thriftway, A & G, Wolferman's and Kroger.** Let the **Blair** man tell you WHB's dramatic 9 to 4 story. Or, talk to General Manager **George W. Armstrong.** And while you're at it, get the whole day and night picture!

WHB 10,000 watts, 710 kc.
KANSAS CITY

WHB—FIRST 140 OUT OF 140 1/4 HOURS BETWEEN 9 and 4!

AREA NIELSEN. WHB in first place 140 out of 140 quarter-hours.

HOOPER. WHB in first place 140 out of 140 quarter-hours.

PULSE. WHB in first place 140 out of 140 quarter-hours.

WHB's share of Area Nielsen Total Station Audience: 40%.

The Storz Stations
Today's Radio for Today's Selling

TODD STORZ
President

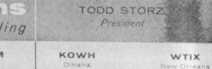

WDGY	WHB	WQAM	KOWH	WTIX
Minneapolis-St. Paul	Kansas City	Miami	Omaha	New Orleans

Represented by John Blair & Co.　　*Represented by Adam Young Inc.*

Minneapolis-St. Paul.[71] The reported selling price of the 50,000 watt day--25,000 watt night station on 1130 kHz was about $350,000.[72] The actual selling price, as recorded in the FCC transfer grant in January 1956 was $334,200.[73] Storz promoted Steve Labunski from sales at WHB to be WDGY general manager, and moved Don Loughnane from program director at WTIX to the same position at WDGY, announcing the shifts and beginning Storz programming just seven days after FCC purchase approval.[74]

In March 1956 ads boasting of the rapid rise of WDGY in the ratings began to appear. One in Broadcasting, March 12, 1956, was headlined "It's Happening Fast . . . in Minneapolis-St. Paul! Just 2 Weeks of Mid-Continent Programming Have Increased WDGY's daytime audience 133%."[75] The figures were from a February Hooper which showed another principal station also up (WCCO), while the others including a 50,000 watt network outlet went down in ratings.[76] By March 19, WDGY was advertising in Sponsor that its share of audience was up to 16.3%, as compared to the third place station's 15.7% and "Station A" (WCCO) with 26.0% according to a March Hooper.[77]

---

[71] "Closed Circuit: WDGY to Todd Storz?" Broadcasting, November 7, 1955, p. 5.

[72] Ibid.

[73] "WDGY Change Among FCC-Approved Sales," Broadcasting, January 23, 1956, p. 66.

[74] "Labunski, Loughnane Moved to WDGY by Mid-Continent," Broadcasting, January 30, 1956, p. 62.

[75] Advertisement in Broadcasting, March 12, 1956, p. 6.

[76] Ibid.

[77] Advertisement in Sponsor, March 19, 1956, front cover.

In May, WDGY ran an ad titled, "Much Ado . . . About Something," with the following text:

> Four Minneapolis-St. Paul radio stations, not fully satisfied WDGY was <u>really</u> in second place, hired a local market analyst to study the audience.
>
> WDGY wasn't expected to make a showing. WDGY wasn't invited to take part . . . but WDGY turned up . . . in <u>2nd</u> place. That's what Hooper said in the first place, and says again for March-April.
>
> Newest Area Nielsen shows WDGY gained 93% over the previous Nielsen audience share.[78]

However, the 93% gain by WDGY is not so spectacular as it might seem, since WDGY was not a ratings leader before Storz. The figure is put in perspective by an advertisement placed in <u>Sponsor</u> for May 28, 1956 by the number one Twin Cities station, WCCO. According to the same March Nielsen, WCCO's share of audience was 56.1%, the largest share garnered by any station in the 27 major markets Nielsen was then measuring. In comparison, "Station B," according to WCCO figures, which were for the total day and total week, came up with only a 9.3% share.[79]

In June, WDGY ran an ad titled "Second Thoughts" which claimed that "WDGY has momentum. New Hooper shows gain again--to 19.1% all-day average."[80]

By October, WDGY was claiming some first places. The August-September Hooper had WDGY first among all Twin Cities stations on an all-day Monday-through-Saturday average, while the June Nielsen showed WDGY second on the same basis but first among Twin Cities independents, and the July-August Pulse put WDGY second by only four points weekday

---

[78] Advertisement in <u>Sponsor</u>, May 14, 1956, p. 18.

[79] Advertisement in <u>Sponsor</u>, May 28, 1956, p. 49.

[80] Advertisement in <u>Sponsor</u>, June 25, 1956, p. 16.

daytimes, but first Saturday afternoons and first among independents during the daytime.[81]

By January of 1957, Trendex was claimed by the station's ads to be showing it first in Monday-through-Saturday daytime audience.[82]

In the summer of 1956, WDGY had changed representatives, dropping Avery-Knodel for Blair, who also "repped" WHB. In February of 1957, Blair executive vice president Robert E. Eastman defended the rising rates of some stations and Blair's advocacy of only six months rate protection in a letter to Sponsor, which used WDGY as an example.

> As you have observed in many markets, the radio picture has changed in an amazingly short span of time. In Minneapolis, for example, in less than eleven months, WDGY moved up from last position to first position in audience. They accomplished this with a tremendous investment of work, ideas, creativity and money. It would be unfair for them to have to wait the better part of a year for adequate returns.[83]

By May of 1957, with a March 1957 Nielsen to talk about, WDGY ran an ad telling advertisers to throw out their 1956 Nielsen figures with the headline, "Toss 'em! These may be all right for somebody who doesn't know what WDGY has done to Twin Cities radio."[84] WDGY claimed to be first all day in Trendex and first in afternoons by Pulse and Hooper.[85]

By October, WDGY was claiming first place by having won more

---

[81] Advertisement in Broadcasting, October 8, 1956, p. 6.

[82] Advertisement in Sponsor, January 26, 1957, p. 13.

[83] "49th and Madison: Radio's Rising Rates," Sponsor, February 16, 1957, p. 25.

[84] Advertisement in Broadcasting, May 13, 1957, p. 6.

[85] Ibid.

Pulse quarter hours than any other station.[86] Still, even Hooper found the station's average share to be 31.9%, which put WDGY behind front-runner WCCO.[87] Generally, WDGY failed to overcome the long-established (and well-deserved) listenership to WCCO. WCCO, like WSB, Atlanta, had always had the power and had always been intelligently programmed, and it "owned" its market area. By 1961, WCCO was claiming an all day 7-day share of 62.1% according to Nielsen.[88]

WQAM

The other station bought by Mid-Continent in 1956 was WQAM, Miami. Unlike the WDGY transfer, which went relatively smoothly, the WQAM switch to Storz ownership almost didn't take place at all.

WQAM was Florida's oldest station. It went on the air in May of 1921. At the time of sale, WQAM was operating with 5,000 watts daytime, 1,000 watts night, but at its 560 kHz frequency and with salt-water grounding, the station had coverage comparable to some 50,000 watt stations. For years, Knight Newspapers, Inc., publishers of the Miami Herald, had been the sole owners of WQAM. The Biscayne Television Corporation, a contestant for Miami VHF TV channel 7, was owned in large part by principal owners of WQAM. For example, John S. Knight, president and 50.3% owner of Knight Newspapers Inc. (WQAM licensee) was a vice president and 17.5% owner of Biscayne.[89] Other stockholders in

---

[86]Advertisement in Sponsor, October 12, 1957, p. 30.

[87]Ibid.

[88]Advertisement in Sponsor, February 20, 1961, p. 8.

[89]"Biscayne TV Bid Would Buy WIOD, Sell WQAM," Broadcasting, November 30, 1953, p. 61.

the Biscayne Corporation were among the owners of Miami's other major newspaper, The Miami News, which in turn owned Miami station WIOD. In 1953, the Commission had sent a pre-hearing McFarland letter to the Biscayne Corporation, questioning what it was going to do about the (illegal) ownership of two radio stations in the same city if the Corporation won the TV grant. Biscayne replied that it would "buy" WIOD (essentially from itself) and sell WQAM to "strangers."[90] In January of 1956, the Biscayne Corporation did receive the Channel 7 grant, necessitating the sale of WQAM. The FCC stipulated that WQAM would have to be sold to interests completely separate from Biscayne prior to the commencement of testing on the new TV channel.[91]

The sale of WQAM was unlike that of most stations in being both forced by the FCC and being public knowledge. Instead of being offered by a broker, WQAM was put up for competitive bids. Among the other independent music-and-news station owners bidding were Ralph Atlass, then the owner of WIND, Chicago, and Plough Broadcasting which already owned WMPS, Memphis, WJJD, Chicago, WCOP, Boston and WCAO, Baltimore at the time.[92] Broadcasting believed the $850,000 price to be a record for what it called a "regional," but as mentioned earlier, the coverage was more like that of a 50,000 watt clear-channel.

On June 4, 1956, Time magazine ran an article about Todd Storz and the Mid-Continent business and program philosophies in its "Show

---

[90] Ibid.

[91] "Closed Circuit; Newspaper Ownership," Broadcasting, January 23, 1956, p. 5.

[92] "Storz Group High Bidder for WQAM, Pays Record $850,000 for Regional," Broadcasting, May 14, 1956, p. 7.

Business" section with the heading "King of Giveaway."[93] The article is reproduced on pages 187 and 188.

Note in the article the extensive use of the word "giveaway" and the strong implication that Storz was cynical about the audience's intelligence and was only trying to "buy" them. By July, Storz was hitting back with a slam at Time's accuracy which was also an advertisement for KOWH.[94] That ad is also reproduced on page 189. Note in the KOWH ad that the Time article is described as "fulsome." The use of the uncommon word is interesting, for "fulsome" carries a positive sound while its meaning actually is negative, meaning "disgusting" or "offensive from insincerity or baseness of motive."

It is interesting to conjecture just how much influence the appearance on June 4 of the damning Time article had on the FCC's decision to send a McFarland letter to Storz on July 11 advising him that a hearing on the transfer was indicated. Bill Stewart, who had recently become National Program Director for Storz comments,

> Well, I think it was the indirect cause of it. The article focused attention on it. And then, when we bought the station, a couple of operators in Miami cited that article in their complaint to the Commission. When something like that gets in print, what happens is, the competitors in the market just cut the copy out of the magazine and mail it in an envelope to the FCC with no name on it.[95]

The FCC letter stated that the "treasure hunts" sponsored recently by KOWH and WDGY were part of a "giveaway pattern" on Mid-Continent

---

[93]"King of Giveaway," Time, June 4, 1955, pp. 100-02.

[94]Advertisement in Broadcasting, July 2, 1956, p. 6.

[95]Bill Stewart, private telephone conversation held on June 26, 1972.

SHOW BUSINESS

King of Giveaway

The fastest-rising figure in U.S. radio is Omaha's R. (for Robert) Todd Storz, 32, whose low estimate of listeners' intelligence is tempered only by his high regard for their cupidity. On the four Storz-owned stations in Omaha, New Orleans, Minneapolis and Kansas City he has found that giveaways work even better for stations than they do for individual programs. Storz shovels out jackpots in a succession of quizzes, guessing games and treasure hunts that occasionally tie up traffic when the search is on. This cash-and-harry formula is so popular with listeners and advertisers that Storz in six years has run a $20,000 investment of his own, plus $30,000 from his father, into a $2,500,000 network. Last week, in his biggest deal to date, he paid $850,000 for Miami's WQAM and prepared to test Florida's IQ.

When his listeners are not being told about a new giveaway, they get a steady serenade from disk jockeys, broken only by stunts and five-minute newscasts. Storz permits no cultural note; he allows his stations only 60 records at a time, lets them play only the 40 top tunes of the week, well larded with commercials.

Storz newscasts, which ignore the U.N. for other international bodies, *e.g.*, Anita Ekberg, are aired five minutes before every hour, so that they can catch listeners who switch off other stations' on-the-hour announcements. Last week Storz was warming the mikes in Omaha and Minneapolis for "the biggest one-shot giveaway of all time on either radio or TV." The prize: two bank drafts for $105,000, each hidden within a ten-mile radius of Storz's Stations KOHW and WGDY, which will start broadcasting clues next week. (The insurance group underwriting the prize estimates that there is only one chance in 47 that Storz will have to pay off.) If the booty goes unfound by June 17, Storz will pay only $500 consolation prizes to the hunters who eventually stumble onto the two hiding places.

"Turn the Set Off." Todd Storz first got interested in radio as a ham operator. After a three-year stint in the Army, he passed up the family brewery to take a whirl at being a disk jockey. He lasted only a short while after advising a woman who had written in to complain about his record selections: "Ma'am, on your radio you will find a switch which will easily turn the set off." In 1949, after working for another station as a salesman, Storz

Jack Clark

BROADCASTER STORZ
He stops traffic.

heard that Omaha's pioneer KOHW was on the block for $75,000. With his father he formed the Mid-Continent Co., borrowed enough to buy the ailing station.

Young Storz, who keeps tuned to his stations with a pocket-size transistor set and earpiece *(see cut)*, promptly lopped off KOHW's "minority programs," *e.g.*, classical and hillbilly music, closed down the station's unprofitable FM outlet. Aiming a barrage of popular music at "the average housewife," Storz soon concocted his first giveaway scheme. The station broadcast a street address at random, paid the occupant of the "Lucky House" up to $500 if he called the station within a minute. Storz copyrighted the idea, now earns $600 a week from other stations that he has licensed to use it. A similar Storz giveaway, in which the station selects prizewinning telephone numbers, had to be dropped by KOHW this month when the telephone company complained that hundreds of subscribers were being bombarded with idle calls from jackpot hunters.

Six months after Storz took over, KOHW was in the black. From seventh place among Omaha's seven stations, KOHW in two years went into first, last month claimed 48.8% of Omaha's total afternoon radio audience *v.* its nearest competitor's 20.4% Hooper rating. In 1953 Storz's Mid-Continent Co. paid $25,000 for WTIX, New Orleans' "good-music station." He substituted the Storz formula for symphonies and sonatas, soon had other local stations imitating him. Encouraged by Storz to try out new "refinements," *i.e.*, audience-boosting giveaways, WTIX recently assigned one of its six disk jockeys to throw away dollar bills from a downtown rooftop at rush hour. When the disk jockey was hauled off to jail for stopping traffic, 1,000 sympathetic listeners were persuaded by WTIX to go down and bail him out. WTIX fans also boosted the station from eleventh to first place in less than a year; advertisers' billings have soared 3,000%.

Traffic Tie-Up. Next stop for Storz was Kansas City. He snapped up WHB for $400,000 in 1954, in six months pushed the station's audience rating from fourth to first place, made giveaways the city's No. 1 all-weather sport; *e.g.*, one Sunday last October a $2,000 WHB crosstown treasure hunt caused such confusion that Police Chief Bernard C. Brannon said the pastime should be banned. WHB is now Storz's biggest moneymaker, grosses $2,000,000 a year.

When the giveaway king bought WDGY in Minneapolis for $334,000 last January, rival stations sent scouts to spy out Storz's stunts in other cities, have since handed out $60,000 on competing giveaway programs. Nevertheless Storz has already jacked his station up from eighth to second place, trebled advertising volume.

On every station he has bought, Storz has raised salaries and cut staffs, says: "We'd rather pay one good man three times what we'd pay for three mediocre ones." He is shopping for two more stations, to raise his bag to seven, the legal limit. Storz professes to be uninterested in TV. Says he: "Our formula is good as long as radio is good—and we think radio is good forever."

That's okay, TIME Magazine . . .

. . . you transposed the call letters of Omaha's most-listened-to radio station 6 different times in the June 4th* issue . . .

. . . but Hooper, Pulse and Trendex have it straight:

The call letters of the radio station with the biggest audience all day . . . are K-O-W-H.

Hooper says so to the tune of 44.2% of the audience.

Pulse agrees to the tune of 204 out of 240 first place quarter hours for K-O-W-H.

Trendex chimes in with firsts for K-O-W-H in every time period.

For some good TIME in the right spots, call KOWH General Manager Virgil Sharpe, or the H-R man.

* . . . in a fulsome article featuring the Storz broadcasting formula—for building and keeping audiences.

stations that indicated to the Commission that the stations were "purchasing" the listening audience.[96] Additionally, the FCC complained that the giveaways had prompted competing stations to try the same contests as counter-measures.[97] As a specific example, the Commission cited the case of WCCO which, presumably to compete with the prize contests being offered on WDGY, began a contest of its own with a potential worth of $250,000. The FCC stated, "this pattern of operation, with its apparent success, appears to be an inducement to other broadcasters to adopt similar methods" which "results in a deterioration in the quality of the service previously rendered the public."[98] The judgment that such contests "result in a deterioration in the quality of the service . . . rendered the public" seemed to Broadcasting a most remarkable intrusion into determining program content.

Storz made at least two replies to the McFarland letter inquiry. In his initial reply, he was for the most part defensive. He contended that contests and giveaways accounted for only one percent of broadcast time and were thus an insignificant programming factor, that hundreds of other stations used the same devices and spent as much or more time on them. According to the Broadcasting report, Storz complained in this initial reply that the article about his operations in Time magazine was "'full of half truths and inaccuracies.'"[99]

On July 18, Storz sent a second letter to the Commission which was much more conciliatory. One reason for this, as is indicated in

---

[96] "Program Control Threat Raised in Final FCC Actions," Broadcasting, July 23, 1956, pp. 31-32.

[97] Ibid., p. 32. [98] Ibid. [99] Ibid.

the letter, may have been that the Commission was scheduled to recess for the summer on the following day, July 19, which would have meant that no action would be taken on the WQAM transfer until after the expiration of Mid-Continent's contract, which would have amounted to what Broadcasting called a "pocket veto" of the sale.[100] Part of Storz's second letter of reply follows:

> . . . On July 12, 1956, the applicant received the Commission's "McFarland" letter of July 11 advising of the possible necessity of a hearing and promptly filed a detailed reply with the Commission on July 16, 1956.
>
> After the filing of the reply the President of Mid-Continent Broadcasting Co. discussed the subject matter of the Commission's "McFarland" letter with several of the commissioners. As a result of these discussions, the proposed transferee wishes to make the following additional showing.
>
> Until the Commission's "McFarland" letter was received on July 12, the proposed transferee was unaware that the Commission looked with displeasure upon certain types of "giveaway" programs and promotions. Mid-Continent Broadcasting Co. is of the opinion that all contests, promotions and "giveaways" carried by the applicant's stations are legal and well within the Commission's Rules and Regulations, and that its programming is in the public interest. However, since it appears that the Commission, by virtue of its July 11 letter, has some doubts on the propriety of contests and "giveaway" programs and in an effort to obtain consideration of its application before the potential termination date of the contract on August 15 we agree to abide by the apparent desire of the Commission and make the following representation:
>
> "Mid-Continent Broadcasting Co. will, upon the Commission taking favorable action on the instant application involving stations WQAM and WQAM-FM, discontinue all contests and/or "giveaway" programs designed to attract audience or influence listening over all broadcast facilities operated by it as soon as possible."
>
> Mid-Continent Broadcasting Co.
> Todd Storz, President.
> [Date July 18, 1956][101]

---

[100] Ibid., p. 31.

[101] "Whereupon He Gives Away His Giveaways," Broadcasting, July 23, 1956, p. 32.

The Commission did not base its decision on the promise made by Storz in his second letter, but on the question of whether it did have the right to consider programming.[102] By a one vote margin (4 to 3), it granted the transfer on July 19 and continued to resist active intrusion into consideration of programming. On Wednesday, three commissioners had voted for a hearing on programming, three voted against a hearing, and one (Commissioner Bartley) asked instead for a hearing on the question of multiple-ownership.[103] Thus, on Wednesday, July 18, when Storz sent his second letter, the Commission did not have a majority in favor of approving the transfer. On Thursday, Commissioner Bartley's motion for a hearing on the multiple-ownership question was voted down four to three. Then the motion for a hearing on the programming issue was considered, and it was voted down by four to three.[104] However, the Commission did decide to consider the question of how much it should be concerned with program balance and with a general investigation of giveaways and contests when it reconvened in late August. The WQAM case thus seems to have been the one which brought to the fore what Broadcasting called "the long-festering giveaway question."[105] As has been pointed out earlier in an examination of the inquiry by the FCC into the "program balance" of several Atlanta stations in 1958, the "music-and-news-only" format was no doubt also being questioned.

With the sale approved, Storz appointed Jack Sandler, a former sportscaster and salesman at KOWH and later KOWH sales manager, as the general manager of WQAM, with Dave Croninger as program director. Croninger had previously been a disc jockey at WHB and then program

---

[102] Ibid., p. 31. [103] Ibid. [104] Ibid. [105] Ibid.

director at WTIX.[106]

By December of 1956, the front page of Broadcasting was carrying the first of a series of advertisements for WQAM, showing a leap to first place in daytime ratings according to Hooper, "after less than three months of Storz programming."[107] Storz coupled this news with a letter, supposedly to the WQAM staff, praising them on their accomplishment, which was printed in Broadcasting. That letter is reproduced on pages 194 and 195.[108]

In January of 1957, WQAM's trades ads began to use the phrase "a runaway--without a giveaway!"[109] The phrase was used in trades ads at least through February, and then the word "runaway" was continued without the rest of the phrase (see page 196).[110] In May, WQAM ran a bar-graph showing "Another Hooper Run-Away Report," that had WQAM with a 34.1% share of the daytime audience, more than two times ahead of the second-place station.[111]

Meanwhile, in February, the Mid-Continent stations sent a letter to the FCC, questioning a new "pattern of operation" at New Orleans station WSMB which included giveaway promotions, and queried whether

---

[106]"Jack Sandler Appointed WQAM Miami Manager," Broadcasting, August 20, 1956, p. 97.

[107]Advertisement in Broadcasting, December 3, 1956, front cover.

[108]Advertisement in Broadcasting, December 10, 1956, pp. 12, 13.

[109]Advertisement in Sponsor, January 19, 1957, p. 22.

[110]Advertisement in Sponsor, March 2, 1957, p. 26.

[111]Advertisement in Sponsor, May 4, 1957, p. 13.

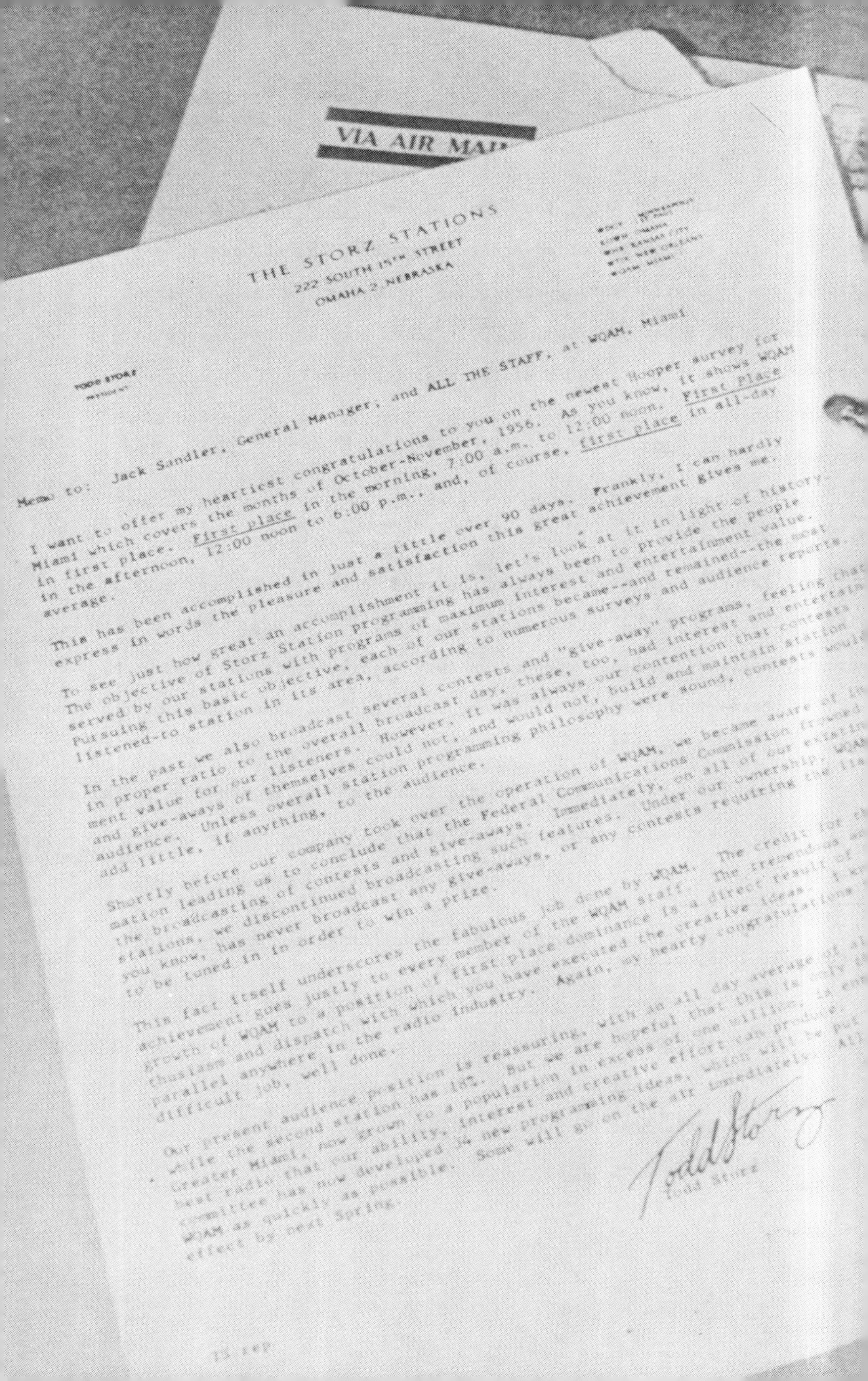

VIA AIR MAIL

THE STORZ STATIONS
222 SOUTH 15TH STREET
OMAHA 2, NEBRASKA

TODD STORZ

Memo to: Jack Sandler, General Manager, and ALL THE STAFF, at WQAM, Miami

I want to offer my heartiest congratulations to you on the newest Hooper survey for Miami which covers the months of October-November, 1956. As you know, it shows WQAM in first place. First place in the morning, 7:00 a.m. to 12:00 noon. First place in the afternoon, 12:00 noon to 6:00 p.m., and, of course, first place in all-day average.

This has been accomplished in just a little over 90 days. Frankly, I can hardly express in words the pleasure and satisfaction this great achievement gives me.

To see just how great an accomplishment it is, let's look at it in light of history. The objective of Storz Station programming has always been to provide the people served by our stations with programs of maximum interest and entertainment value. Pursuing this basic objective, each of our stations became--and remained--the most listened-to station in its area, according to numerous surveys and audience reports.

In the past we also broadcast several contests and "give-away" programs, feeling that in proper ratio to the overall broadcast day, these, too, had interest and entertain- ment value for our listeners. However, it was always our contention that contests and give-aways of themselves could not, and would not, build and maintain station audience. Unless overall station programming philosophy were sound, contests would add little, if anything, to the audience.

Shortly before our company took over the operation of WQAM, we became aware of in- mation leading us to conclude that the Federal Communications Commission frowned the broadcasting of contests and give-aways. Immediately, on all of our existin stations, we discontinued broadcasting such features. Under our ownership, WQAM you know, has never broadcast any give-aways, or any contests requiring the lis to be tuned in in order to win a prize.

This fact itself underscores the fabulous job done by WQAM. The credit for th achievement goes justly to every member of the WQAM staff. The tremendous a growth of WQAM to a position of first place dominance is a direct result of thusiasm and dispatch with which you have executed the creative ideas. I k parallel anywhere in the radio industry. Again, my hearty congratulations difficult job, well done.

Our present audience position is reassuring, with an all day average of a while the second station has 18%. But we are hopeful that this is only Greater Miami, now grown to a population in excess of one million, is en best radio that our ability, interest and creative effort can produce. committee has now developed 34 new programming ideas, which will be put WQAM as quickly as possible. Some will go on the air immediately. All effect by next Spring.

Todd Storz

TS:rep

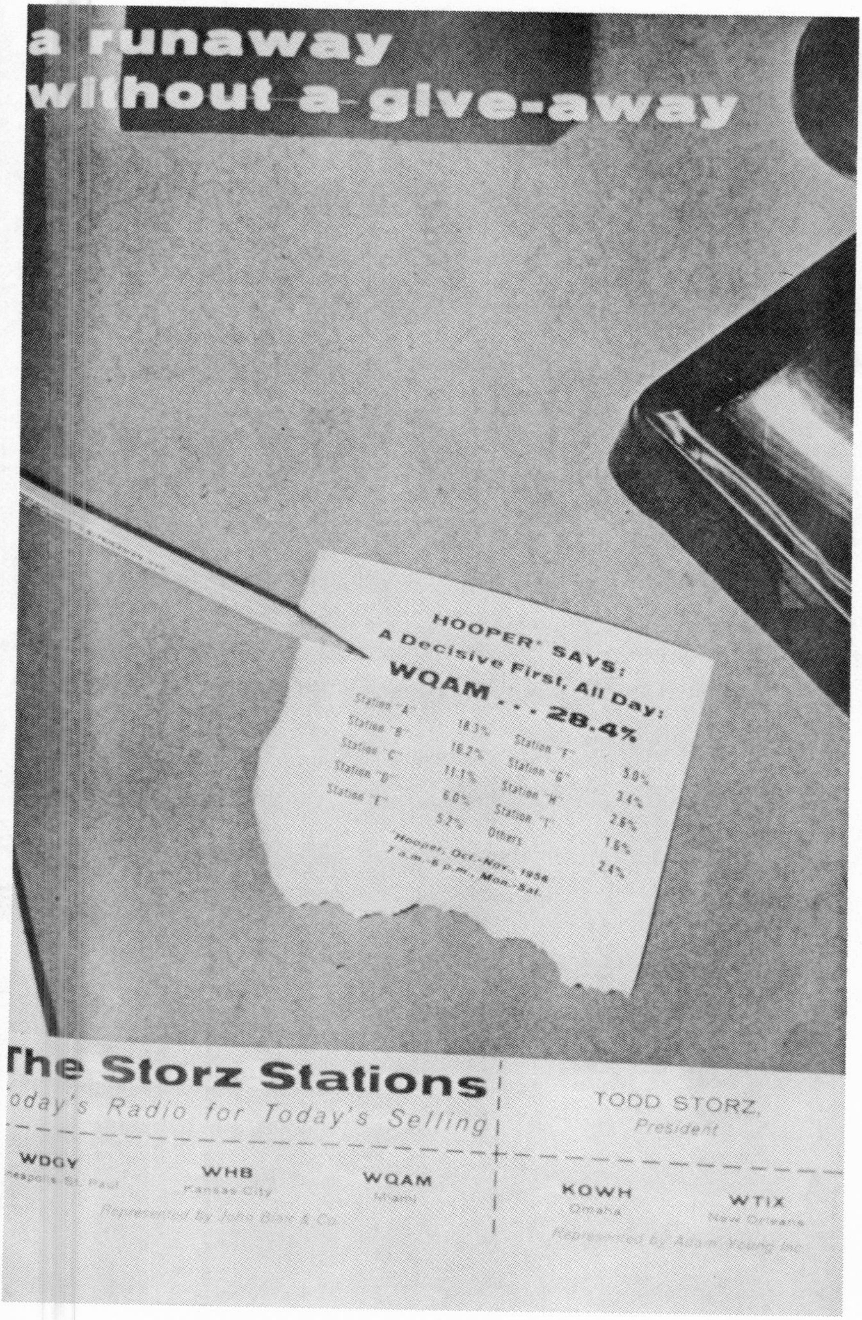
a runaway
without a give-away
HOOPER* SAYS:
A Decisive First, All Day:
WQAM . . . 28.4%
Station "A"
Station "B" 18.3% Station "F"
Station "C" 16.2% Station "G" 5.0%
Station "D" 11.1% Station "H" 3.4%
Station "E" 6.0% Station "I" 2.8%
5.2% Others 1.6%
2.4%
*Hooper, Oct.-Nov., 1956
7 a.m.-6 p.m., Mon.-Sat.
The Storz Stations
Today's Radio for Today's Selling
TODD STORZ,
President
WDGY
WHB
Kansas City
WQAM
KOWH
Omaha
WTIX
New Orleans

EAR WITNESS
TO A RUNAWAY

HEADED FOR MIAMI? DIAL WQAM (560) AND HEAR FOR YOURSELF WHY THERE'S BEEN A RUNAWAY WITHOUT A GIVE-A-WAY.

OVER 30!

WQAM	30.1%
Station "A"	15.3%
Station "B"	14.8%
Station "C"	7.7%
Station "D"	7.3%
Station "E"	6.8%
Station "F"	4.9%
Station "G"	4.6%
Station "H"	4.3%
Station "I"	2.6%
Others	2.0%

Now WQAM has jumped over the 30% mark in share of audience all day. That's what the newest Hooper says, continuing a dramatic, drastic, fantastic change in Southern Florida listening since the start of Storz Station programming at WQAM.

All this has been accomplished without so much as a single giveaway and without a single contest which required participants to be tuned in in order to win.

And . . . all this has quickly caught the eyes, ears and budgets of advertisers, who are buying WQAM, and profiting therefrom. Lend an ear yourself to the Blair man . . . or WQAM General Manager JACK SANDLER.

WQAM

Serving all of Southern Florida with 5,000 watts on 560 kc.

MIAMI

The Storz Stations

Today's Radio for Today's Selling

TODD STORZ,
President

WDGY	WHB	WQAM	KOWH	WTIX
Minneapolis-St. Paul	Kansas City	Miami	Omaha	New Orleans

Represented by John Blair & Co. — *Represented by Adam Young Inc.*

the Commission found these to be in the public interest.[112] Obviously, if Storz was to stand by his promise of not running any contests on his stations, it was in his company's best interest to see that none be run on a station competing with his WTIX.

In June, WQAM's ads commenced an attack on the outdated NCS # 2 for the Miami market. Using the headline "Hasn't anything happened in Miami since March, 1956?" the ads went on to show how WQAM now had two-and-a-half times the audience on the runner-up station, and ended by exhorting "Next time somebody quotes NCS # 2 about Miami, yell for a Blair man, or get in touch with WQAM General Manager, Jack Sandler.[113]

Ads in July of 1957 continued the theme of disregarding "old" 1956 data without mentioning Nielsen by name, and underscored the rapid shift in listening by pointing out that just since its last ad, WQAM had increased its lead to three and three-quarters the size of the second station's audience.[114] By August, Hooper showed WQAM with a 42.6% day-time share, or four times the audience of the next station.[115] In October, WQAM was running ads which read "First Anniversary as a Storz Station Finds WQAM's Runaway Complete!"[116] This ad again repeated the caution about the last Nielsen report: "Ask Blair or G M Jack Sandler why current figures are much more valid than NCS # 2, which was made in

---

[112]"Mid-Continent Questions Sale of 50% of WSMB to Radio Hawaii," Broadcasting, February 11, 1957, p. 66.

[113]Advertisements in Broadcasting, June 17, 1957, p. 8, and in Sponsor, June 22, 1957, p. 28.

[114]Advertisement in Sponsor, July 6, 1957, p. 26.

[115]Advertisement in Sponsor, August 17, 1957, p. 28.

[116]Advertisement in Broadcasting, October 7, 1957, p. 8.

Spring 1956 about a half-year before WQAM became a Storz station.[117]

In the spring of 1959, WQAM and the Miami market received some competition from a new station, WAME ("Whammy! in Miami!"). Like WQAM, the station had 5,000 watts of power, but it was at 1260 kHz and operated then in daytime only. By October of 1959, WAME was claiming to be the dominant number two station in the market with a 17.8% share according to Hooper.[118] The ad announcing the news was a parody of WQAM's, which had almost from the beginning of Storz ownership featured a man dressed in a dark suit and carrying an umbrella, who always appeared on the beach wearing a hat. The WAME parody, using a curvaceous bathing beauty, is self-explanatory (see page 199).[119]

As a daytime-only station, WAME did not stand a good chance of retaining its number two position if a fulltime station changed to the same format, which is what happened in 1960. Group owner Robert W. Rounsaville had had experience with WQXI and music-and-news in Atlanta earlier, and in 1953 he had bought WMBM, Miami Beach, which was then a 1,000 watt daytime-only station at 800 kHz.[120] Rounsaville converted the station from "hodge-podge" programming to an emphasis on Negro programming, and this is what the station ran throughout the mid-1950s. Then in the late 1950s, Rounsaville discovered that by giving up

---

[117] Ibid.

[118] Advertisement in Sponsor, October 10, 1959, p. 79.

[119] Ibid.

[120] Robert W. Rounsaville, Owner and President of the Rounsaville Radio Stations, and Arnold C. Kaufman, Vice President and General Manager, WFUN, private interview held in Miami, Florida, July 14, 1971.

WHAMM-Y-
Look What's Happened
to Miami

Heed the Call of the New Figure!

here's a NEW Number Two – WAM-E (Whamm-y) 5000 W. on 1260

r TIME BUYER friend has had a bit of a shock. ideas about the Miami radio market have been sted wide open by a hard hitting, promotion and rchandising minded new station which in just en months has roared to second place in Miami. oper says we're a dominant NUMBER TWO now h an average Monday through Friday 17.8% share udience (52% more audience than the #3 station).

Pulse gives us a 12% share, 6 a.m. to 6 p.m. Monday through Friday. And Whamm-y is NUMBER ONE when it comes to cost per thousand. We deliver thousands more listeners per dollar than any other station.

So-o-o-o, MR. TIME BUYER, take a second look at the Miami market and you'll see WAM-E. Or have a chat with our National rep, Daren McGavren; our Regional rep, Clarke Brown, or Station Mgr., Murry Woroner.

WAM-E (Whamm-y) . . . . Radio Two in Miami

WAM-E
Chamber of Commerce Bldg
Miami Florida
FRanklin 3-5533

wam-e

WMBM's 800 kHz frequency and moving to 790 kHz, he could go from a daytime-only operation with 1,000 watts to a fulltime operation with 5,000 watts day and night (nights directional). In 1960, when new transmitters and towers were ready, Rounsaville gave up the WMBM call and format and converted to Top 40 with WFUN.[121]

The distinctive call letters and the Top 40 format were decided upon because "we felt there was room for two, that one was not adequately serving the area."[122] At the time of the change, WAME was running Top 40 in the daytime, and WIOD and WCKT both ran short Top 40 type programs. Kaufman states that there were "four or five until WFUN came in and devoted full-time coverage to this, and we began to see the other stations take on other formats."[123] WFUN was a facility very near the equal of WQAM, except that its nighttime pattern was directionalized. WFUN has always been "neck and neck" with WQAM in ratings and in its early days was ahead of WQAM for 22 months, according to Hooper.[124] Since then, "We haven't beaten them decisively nor have they us. It's been a Mexican standoff. When we've beaten them it's been by decimal points, and they've beaten us the same way."[125]

KOMA

By the time Storz had acquired WQAM, the company had established a pattern in buying its stations. Don Keyes, who for a number of years was National Program Director for the McLendon stations, in early 1959

---

[121]WMBM is still on the air in Miami Beach with Black programming. It is 250 watts on 1490 kHz.

[122]Rounsaville-Kaufman interview.

[123]Ibid. [124]Ibid. [125]Ibid.

juestioned Kent Burkhart about Storz's acquisition policies. Burkhart ıad been at KOWH and was program director at WQAM for two years in 1957 ınd 1958.[126] Keyes asked Burkhart "When Todd buys a station, what does ıe generally look for? That is, power, frequency, etc.?"[127] Burkhart replied:

> His main interest has been low frequency with five- or fifty-thousand watts. That's why the KOMA buy shocked the entire company. He doesn't seem to be too concerned about competition in the town. He feels he has the horses anyway and with a good, established, old-time, low frequency operation, he can grab the ears of many new listeners. (That was the reason for the switch in New Orleans, obviously.) He converts into a fast-paced operation while still holding on to the old call letters as a prestige credit. This has been very successful! (The KOMA move is still not clear as I have not heard or seen any stock movement or offer from anyone.)[128]

As the previous correspondence indicates, Storz's acquisition f KOMA, Oklahoma City in late 1958 was a puzzle to nearly everyone, oth in and out of the Mid-Continent Broadcasting Co. It was a 50,000 att station, but it was at the high end of the dial, on 1520 kHz. It lso had a directional antenna at night. Former Storz National Program irector Bill Stewart said "The one in Oklahoma City is really not a good acility. . . . It covers all of the western part of the country, but t doesn't cover Oklahoma City that well."[129]

---

[126]Burkhart is now president of Pacific and Southern's radio ivision, which has "contemporary music" radio stations in Atlanta, enver, Los Angeles, metro New York, and elsewhere.

[127]Don Keyes, Memo on McLendon Corporation stationery, type-ritten, from the McLendon Policy Books, dated February 28, 1959, p. 1.

[128]Kent Burkhart, "Inter-Office Correspondence," on KENS, San ntonio letterhead, typewritten from the McLendon Policy Books, dated arch 9, 1959, p. 3.

[129]Stewart interview.

The broadcast industry was surprised in December of 1958 to read that Storz had decided to affiliate KOMA with NBC effective December 1. Storz claimed that the move was based on a programming study in the market which showed a desire for

> a broad type of programming service. . . . We felt we could fill this void by molding the extensive programming facilities of a major network with programs tailored to the local and regional needs of this growing market. . . . We will continue to do the intensive type of local and regional job that has marked our stations in other markets, and will control a majority of the actual hours KOMA is on the air.[130]

Uptempo music and promotion would follow that on other Storz stations. Storz National Program Director Bill Stewart said "The history of Storz . . . stations has been marked by flexibility. We believe this dramatic new step will keep pace with the policies of the Storz stations and this important market."[131] NBC, of course, was delighted.

The actual reasons for the acquisition of KOMA and the affiliation with NBC are set forth in a memo from Don Keyes to Gordon and B. R. McLendon. Between the time Keyes wrote his previously-quoted list of questions to Burkhart and the receipt of Burkhart's written replies, Keyes spent an evening conversing with Burkhart. Keyes' memo to the McLendons was the result.

> It appears that thus far no one outside of the Storz organization knows why Todd purchased KOMA in Oklahoma City, and why he is programming NBC shows. Last night I got the straight answer, which turns out to be a bit of a shocker. The Storz Broadcasting company, which has been owned entirely by Todd and his father since its conception, will be offering common stock over the counter in early spring. Burkhart told me that he first got this information from Bill Stewart, and it was later confirmed in a memo to all the managers from Todd, which Burkhart

---

[130] "KOMA Replaces WKY in Network," Broadcasting, December 1, 1958, p. 69.

[131] Ibid.

saw. This memo stated too, that the Storz managers were to economize to the bone in the operation of their radio stations. He gave instructions to thin out the DJ staffs, cancel all extra telephone lines including the various "hot lines" to the newsrooms, cancellation of merchandising efforts (Storz was following the Jumbo postcard route as we do, and even that was cut), curtailment of promotional expense, contest giveaways, etc., and the release of news personnel. . . . These economy cuts will, of course, serve to better the profit picture that will be viewed by future stock prospects. And the acquisition of KOMA, to the layman stock-buyer, will impress the fact that the profit picture not only is greater than last year, but the company is expanding as well. Of course, KOMA will be run with as much network as possible to keep the program staff as small as possible. The manager of KOMA, by the way, makes $200 a week.

This, then, is the reason for the shakeups and the changes . . . the other surprise activities within the Storz organization over the past months. This leaves only one question unanswered. Why is he doing it?[132]

A possible answer to "why is he doing it?" was supplied by Burkhart in his written replies to Keyes's written questions. Keyes had asked "Do you think that a forthcoming inheritance tax is the reason for the sale of stock this spring?"[133] Burkhart's reply was:

I haven't seen any stock up for grabs yet and, spring is here, old friend. I can't answer that question because I don't know. However, Storz doesn't like to answer to anyone so it is very unusual that stock should be opened to the public. There is obviously a reason and it could be to set stock price for future problems.[134]

KOMA's affiliation with NBC turned out to be short-lived. In July of 1959, only seven months after making the affiliation, Storz wrote to the network that "the KOMA operation as a network affiliate had been 'unsuccessful by any measure' though not necessarily through

---

[132] Don Keyes, memorandum, KLIF-Dallas stationery, typewritten, from the McLendon Policy Books, dated January 24, 1959, p. 1.

[133] Keyes memo, February 28, 1959, p. 2.

[134] Burkhart memo, March 9, 1959, p. 5.

NBC's fault."[135] Storz offered to have the network terminate the contract since KOMA had decided to clear fewer NBC programs.

KXOK

By the fall of 1960, the Storz acquisition formula was again being practiced. Mid-Continent bought KXOK, St. Louis, in December of 1960. Again, it was an old, established station (1938), at a low frequency (630 kHz) with 5,000 watts. However, the station did have directional antennas both day and night.

Note, however, that by the time of the KOMA and the KXOK acquisitions by Storz, virtually all the prime facilities had been either bought by other groups or retained and reprogrammed. By the late 1950s, the formula for a successful radio operation had been outlined for everyone by Storz and others, and it became increasingly difficult to find a failing radio station of any consequence. Thus, th KXOK acquisition was Storz's last, leaving him one short of a full complement of seven stations. In 1957 and 1958, Burkhart and Storz met on the beach at Key Biscayne in Florida many times and chatted informally Out of these conversations, Burkhart drew the conclusion that the markets Storz was interested in at that time were Cincinnati, Philadelphia Chicago, Detroit, Pittsburgh, and Cleveland.[136]

One other document illuminates the acquisition policies of the Storz organization in the mid 1950s. About March of 1956, someone in

[135] "NBC Affiliations: KOMA Cuts Network; WVET Replaces WHAM," Broadcasting, July 13, 1959, p. 54.

[136] Burkhart memo, p. 5.

the McLendon organization wrote "A Confidential Report on WHB" which is an unsigned, undated memorandum appearing in the McLendon General Programming Policy Books. (The present author has been able to supply the approximate date by tracing references in the memorandum.) The typist's mark on the last page has Gordon McLendon's initials (GBM), but the style is unlike his. It is quite like the style of the memoranda written by Don Keyes, who in the Spring of 1956 relinquished his disc jockey job at KLIF to become program director of McLendon's KTSA, San Antonio.

The author of the memorandum quite apparently had talked directly with George W. Armstrong, then vice-president of Mid-Continent and general manager of WHB, Kansas City:

> . . . Armstrong says that the first station doing the music and news formula right can maintain its dominance in the market permanently if it is the equal facility to any other station. He says that he and Storz don't want to go into any markets that they can't dominate, and dominate quickly. He says that this wouldn't be possible in a market like Los Angeles where he says the rate structure is surprisingly low, and will prevent any station from having the money to achieve more than about eight percent to ten percent of the audience. He says that San Francisco is even worse, and that he would not touch KYA at even a figure of $300,000, which is half of what is being asked, because the facility is not a prime facility, and you lay yourself open to the risk that one of five different better facilities there might be sold to the wrong man and you would be operating against a capable music and news operator who had a better facility by far.
>
> He had looked at WDOK in Cleveland and said it is a bad buy, because he didn't regard it as a prime facility, with which I completely disagree. He said that the station had a two-year contract on foreign-language programs. Further, he pointed out that WERE was doing things pretty well, and he would have to go in and buy off the top men in the market and that would cost too much. In the case of Cleveland, when you start buying the top men in the market, you're talking about $100,000 a year. He says that St. Louis would be likewise as far as buying off the top men. He says it's a far better market ratewise. He says that the stations have been able to keep their rates up pretty

> well there, and that the big trouble in St. Louis is that the union has been allowed to run away with things. He agrees completely on WGMS and the Washington market in general. He says it comes as close to being without competition as any market in the country, and that Chicago is next. He agrees that WGMS would have been one hell of a buy because of the nature of the facility. He also agrees that New York would be a good market to go into because if you can do anything at all there ratingwise, you can get $100 per spot.[137]

The Storz station lineup remains today as it was after the acquisition of KXOK, with the others being WHB, WDGY, WQAM, and KOMA. However flamboyant their programming became, the Storz station acquisition policy was a conservative one, and it seems unlikely that Storz would ever have bought a station "on speculation." As George "Bud" Armstrong is fond of pointing out, the Storz organization is an "operating" company, and under his leadership since Storz's death in 1964, the operation of the group has continued to be the only business at hand. There have been no new acquisitions nor station sales.

McLendon

Gordon B. McLendon was born June 8, 1921, in Paris, Texas, the son of Barton R. McLendon, president of Tri-State Theatres, Inc., a group of motion picture theatres in Texas, southern Oklahoma, and Louisiana. Gordon took an early interest in journalism and debating in high school. Later he went to Kemper Military School and then entered Yale in 1939, where he took an immediate interest in broadcasting. He was a sports, news, and special events announcer for the Yale radio station, WOCD. Later, he was business manager for the Yale Literary Magazine. World War II interrupted his college studies, and McLendon

---

137"A Confidential Report on WHB," typewritten, from the McLendon Policy Books, about March, 1956, pp. 2, 3.

was commissioned as an Ensign in Naval Intelligence because of his major in Oriental Languages. He spent two years in the South Pacific, translating Japanese documents and questioning Japanese officers. McLendon also did parodies of network news analysts under the nom de plume Lowell Gram Kaltenheatter for the troops listening to Armed Forces Radio Services in the Pacific Theatre. Following discharge from the Navy, he attended Harvard Law School.

McLendon Station Acquisition

In 1947, Gordon and his father Barton purchased their first radio station, KNET, in Palestine, Texas, a town of about 12,000 people at the time. In an oral history biography recorded for the Oral History Library at Harding College in Searcy, Arkansas, McLendon recalled that he paid $25,000 for his interest in the station, which was a 100-watter, but the only one in town. McLendon is grateful for the Palestine experience; "I cut my teeth in management in Palestine" he says.[138] Two things made McLendon sell his interest in KNET. One was that the way he was running the station, even if all the advertisers in town put all their money into KNET, it would go broke. The second was that the railroad, around which the town was built, was to be rerouted. McLendon thus sold his half interest in KNET back to a former owner at a loss, but claims to be grateful for the experience nevertheless.[139]

---

[138] Gordon B. McLendon, Harding College Oral History Library Distinguished Citizen Collection, Searcy, Arkansas, unpaginated (taped).

[139] Ibid.

KLIF--early

While at Palestine, McLendon applied for and received a permit to construct a daytime station in Dallas, so in early 1947, the McLendon family moved to Dallas and began the construction of KLIF. The call letters were chosen to coincide with the Oak Cliff section of the Dallas metropolitan area. KLIF was originally a daytime-only station, with just 1,000 watts of power. McLendon was asked in the Harding College oral history biography what his philosophy was in putting such a station on the air:

> I don't think I had a philosophy, but I thought I had an idea. . . . to broadcast major league baseball on a daily basis. I considered that my hidden weapon. . . . The other stations were larger, far more established, and I had to do something different. This has long been my philosophy, but I hadn't developed it quite then. The philosophy in radio that I have is to go into a market where you can do some programming of value to a sufficient number of people that other stations are not doing or are not doing as well as you believe you can do it. That is a philosophy that I have today, and it has stood me in good stead. But I had not developed it at that time, except unconsciously. I knew I would have to provide something different on this little daytime station in Dallas if I were going to make any inroads against the big 50,000 watters and other more established stations.[140]

Thus, on KLIF's first day on the air, November 9, 1947, McLendon did a "recreation" of a football game which was the forerunner of his later baseball game "recreations" over KLIF and then over the Liberty Network mentioned later. McLendon describes the recreated games as an "almost instant success."[141]

McLendon also tried to provide some other, different features on KLIF. One was a bird. An advertisement appearing in a Sunday Dalla paper on debut day introduced "Klif the Parrot" who was to do actual

---

[140] Ibid. [141] Ibid.

station IDs live and who McLendon had tried to insure for $100,000. The ad also listed the programs to be carried on the station: among the stars were Gene Autrey, Louis Jordan, and Tommy Dorsey, all with recorded programs. KLIF billed itself in this early ad as "The station of national shows and sports."[142] Quite obviously, the KLIF of 1947 was attempting to imitate the bigger national networks rather than attempting to develop a local operation.

The day after the station's debut, an article about Klif the parrot appeared in The Dallas Morning News. The article pointed out that the parrot had his own AFTRA union card, had been kept in a room hearing a playback of the word "cliff" 15,000 times so that he would learn it, and did not on opening day "break out in a rash of Portuguese cuss words," to everyone's relief.[143] By mentioning the fact that the bird could not be counted on to keep a civil beak, no doubt some listeners were attracted. This "dirty word" promotion would be used years later in another form on KLIF, so it is interesting to note that the first use came virtually with the station's first day of broadcasting.

Liberty--LBS

In 1948, what would become the Liberty Broadcasting System began to develop from baseball broadcasts over KLIF. The history of the Liberty network might alone be worthy of a dissertation, and will not

---

[142]Advertisement in The Daily Times Herald (Dallas), November 9, 1947, pp. 7--2.

[143]Frank X. Tolbert, "Parrot Does Announcing," The Dallas Morning News, November 10, 1947, Section One, p. 4.

be pursued further here.[144] It must be noted, however, that by May 1952 LBS was defunct. The network had grown primarily on the strength of its baseball programming, and when that programming was cut off at its source by the baseball clubs, the network became uncompetitive. In 1950, when it was expanded to all 48 states and nighttime service was begun, Liberty began to lose money. Its quiz programs, disc jockeys, minstrel shows, news, and talk programs were not sufficiently different from those offered on the other major radio networks (or on television) to "fill a void," a phrase that Gordon McLendon would later make famous.

In 1950, KLIF began nighttime operation and was the first station in Dallas to program 24 hours a day.[145] As flagship of the Liberty Network, KLIF naturally broadcast the network programs while LBS existed. Mr. Tom Merriman, who was musical director at Liberty says:

> . . . We had some just perfectly atrocious, gruesome shows we did for him . . . we had two or three sustaining shows throughout the day. We had a morning musical show, a variety show, and I had a noon show. We fed several shows down the line during the day.[146]

Asked if these musical programs were imitating the big band sounds on

---

[144]An undergraduate thesis, The Liberty Broadcasting System is on file in the library at Texas Tech, Lubbock, Texas. It was written by radio-TV major Beverly Callison, daughter of McLendon's long-time chief engineer, Glenn Callison, and is composed of previously-unpublished documents. Shorter, more readily-available treatments are Frank X. Tolbert, "Man Behind a Network," Nation's Business, March, 1952, pp 56-60, and an article titled "Liberty Suspends," in Broadcasting, May 19, 1952, p. 25.

[145]Advertisement in The Dallas Morning News, February 12, 1950 page number missing.

[146]Merriman interview.

the other networks, Merriman answered "They were for a while. Then they got to be more the combo things. We did a luncheon music show, for example."[147] This was live music, not recordings. ". . . Most of the stations were not playing records. And if they were, they certainly were not playing them like 24 hours a day."[148]

McLendon feels that the baseball league in refusing to sell LBS the rights to broadcast the games did him a great favor, because otherwise he might have gone on for five years trying to make the network profitable.[149] With the demise of Liberty, McLendon says he set about building "a chain of radio stations which nobody could take away from me--except the government."[150]

Trinity-KELP-KLBS

The company which McLendon formed to own his new chain of stations was known as the Trinity Broadcasting Corporation. Actually, Trinity was in existence simultaneously with the Liberty operation, and was the licensee of both KLIF and McLendon's second major station, KELP, El Paso. KELP in the early 1950s was a daytime-only station with 1,000 watts at 920 kHz. When KLIF began to program a hodge-podge of music shows after the demise of LBS, KELP followed suit but on a smaller scale. Joe Roddy, who had been program director at KLIF in 1951,[151] in

---

[147] Ibid., pp. 11, 12. [148] Ibid.

[149] McLendon, Oral History Interview, unpaginated.

[150] Ibid.

[151] "Texas Stations," Broadcasting Yearbook, 1952, p. 276.

1952 became general manager of KELP.[152]

In 1952, McLendon contracted to lease what had been KLEE in Houston and renamed it KLBS (after the Liberty Broadcasting System). Trinity Broadcasting was the licensee, but not the owner of KLBS. According to Bill Stewart, who became first a disc jockey and then program director at KLBS in the summer of 1953, "McLendon leased it on the basis that he would pay all the bills, and any profit that was made, they would get a percentage of it. . . . He really didn't want to buy it at that time, because he really didn't have anything going for him, really."[153]

Stewart says that when he joined McLendon at KLBS, McLendon had already given up on making a success of the station, and had notified the owners--Howard Broadcasting Company--that they could have the station back. Stewart also says that in the last 90 days, "I got the station kind of turned around. It started to move, and he didn't want to give it back then. But he was still gun-shy of the market."[154] However, in late 1953, the license of KLBS was returned to Howard Broadcasting Company for $100,000.[155] In 1957, McLendon would decide to buy KLBS and rename it KILT. The station was a prime facility, with 5,000 watts fulltime on 610 kHz.

McLendon's purchase of KELP and KLBS were made before KLIF in

---

[152]"Texas Stations," Broadcasting Yearbook, 1953, p. 288.

[153]Bill Stewart, private telephone conversation held on June 26, 1972.

[154]Ibid.

[155]"FCC Approves 11 Radio-TV Transfers," Broadcasting, December 21, 1953, p. 58.

Dallas had enjoyed its later phenomenal ratings successes, which began about the fall of 1953. They were also made before the KLIF programming format was firmly set. Although the details of the development of the KLIF format will be found in succeeding chapters, it must be noted here that in mid-1953, KLIF was still programming a vast variety of entertainment. Bill Stewart, who later became McLendon's (and Storz's) National Program Director recalls:

> When I went with him, he was carrying baseball games and everything else, and I told you that the ratings were nothing. And I said that the only way I would go is, I wanted an in-writing guarantee that we won't carry any more baseball, and that I will have an absolute free reign. He had a country and western guy on from eleven in the morning to one in the afternoon. I said, I'm going to change it around. He (McLendon) said, well, the guy's got the highest ratings of all. And I said, well, if he has the highest ratings--if that's the best thing--then _everyone_ should play country and western music. But I said, I want to get rid of him. So I got rid of him.[156]

Bill Stewart joined the McLendon organization in May, 1953, as a disc jockey and shortly thereafter began to consult with McLendon about programming. Clearly then, in mid-1953, KLIF had not settled into a single format, nor had the other McLendon stations. One of the reasons may have been the success of another low-power independent in Dallas, KIXL. KIXL had also been put on the air in 1947, also as a daytime-only station (it later acquired a fulltime FM channel). KIXL programmed the "quieter" popular music, mixed with semi-classical pieces to the exclusion of nearly everything else. There were no disc jockeys, no soap operas, no sports, no drama, and only 60 seconds of news headlines each hour. In other words, soothing music prevailed. However, Hooper ratings early in 1953 showed KIXL trailed only the NBC and CBS

---

[156] Stewart interview.

powerhouse affiliates in audience, and was ahead of the other five Dallas stations, including KLIF.[157]

KLIF's ratings rise

By spring of 1953, KLIF was beginning to challenge KIXL's position by playing more popular music than KIXL was playing. As Stewart pointed out, KLIF at this time did not program only music, or only the popular music, but it did program a greater ratio of popular music and began to take KIXL's audience. The following is an excerpt from a McLendon memorandum to Joe Roddy, general manager at KELP, El Paso, dated April 11, 1953:

> Here in Dallas, I sense (without knowledge of what the Hooper is, but Pulse reflects it for whatever that is worth) that we are taking the audience away from KIXL at a rapid rate--this, Joe, in spite of the fact that KIXL spends all day long on its production, has a vastly greater musical library, spends infinitely longer on its choice of music, etc. With all this, we are taking the audience slowly but steadily, and not too slowly. Of course, KLIF will never budge KIXL's highbrow fans, but then we don't want to do so. If KIXL is actually losing listeners to KLIF, why? What can you do to prevent the same thing happening in El Paso with another station?[158]

It is apparent that in April of 1953, KELP was being patterned after KIXL. Any doubt that KELP was to be an El Paso version of KIXL is erased by the following two passages. The first is from a Newsweek article about KIXL; the second is from the McLendon memo to Roddy of April 11.

> . . . nearly all of the programming is musical, mostly top-grade popular or semi-classical pieces . . .
>
> . . . KIXL is known for one nonmusical idea. At regular intervals the announcers will break in for a "Think it over,"

---

[157] "Texas Oasis," Newsweek, June 22, 1953, p. 54.

[158] Gordon McLendon, Memorandum to Joe Roddy, KELP, from McLendon Policy Books, typewritten, dated April 11, 1953, p. 1.

a sort of moral message. Segall got the idea from The Ladies Home Journal. . . .[159]

. . . . .

It seems to me that the answer to the thing lies in continually giving the people something new to talk about--something fresh on the station. The answer lies in new ideas always. Right at the moment, your "Think About It" thing is a new idea in El Paso and will give them something new to talk about, but in two or three months, you must have something new again. . . .

. . . So keep the station fresh with an occasional new idea that gets the town talking, and secondly, keep the choice of music ALIVE with enough good pop mixed with the semi-classic.[160]

Those who might read the foregoing passage and conclude that Gordon McLendon was an imitator in 1953 would be only partly right. This point will be reiterated later as more examples are shown, but it should also be made now: radio is still a small fraternity, and nearly everybody "steals" from everybody else. It is the author's conclusion that McLendon eventually contributed far more really new ideas than he borrowed.

The programming which vaulted KLIF into the top of the ratings will be examined in later pages. Note, however, that in November of 1953, KLIF was "a mediocre fifth, among eight stations. . . ."[161] By April of 1954, KLIF had become "the leading metropolitan independent in the United States in share of morning audience, third in the afternoons, fourth at night and undeniably first on Saturdays."[162] By June of 1954,

---

[159]"Texas Oasis," p. 54.

[160]McLendon memorandum to Joe Roddy, April 11, 1953, pp. 1, 2.

[161]"Objective of KLIF News Policy: Radio's First 'Newspaper of the Air,'" McLendon Policy Books, typewritten, unsigned, undated, unpaginated.

[162]Ibid.

KLIF was the number one station in Dallas in every time period[163] according to Hooper. Part of that Hooper report was preserved by McLendon in one of his personal scrapbooks. It is reproduced on page 217.[164]

The "Objective of KLIF News Policy" copy contained in the McLendon Policy Books amplifies the meaning of the rapid rise in KLIF ratings:

> Veteran radio observers simply could not believe it. Even C. E. Hooper, who called it "The most unbelievable rise I've ever known in rating history," had not believed the results of his first survey of the Dallas market in March, 1953. Incredulous, he had refused to publish the survey, changed interviewers, and surveyed again in April. Again the results were the same. From nowhere, KLIF had in 90 days gone to the top of the national rating picture. . . .[165]

The KLIF ratings verdict was far from unanimous in 1954, however. KRLD, the CBS affiliate and a longtime leader in Dallas claimed in ads in August of 1954 to have shown up in first place in total Dallas audience in an April-May Pulse.[166]

In January of 1955, perhaps to combat the increasing emphasis KLIF was putting on automobile listening, KRLD ran an advertisement headlined "KRLD . . . Dallas' No. 1 Pushbutton Station." The copy claimed that 38 out of 39 new car dealers tuned one of the buttons on a pushbutton radio to KRLD because of popular demand. The ad listed station B with 37 dealers, station C with 22 dealers, independent

---

163 Ibid.

164 Hooper Ratings for Dallas Radio Markets, June 1954, n.p.

165 "Objective of KLIF News Policy: Radio's First 'Newspaper of the Air,'" McLendon Policy Books, typewritten, unsigned, undated, unpaginated.

166 Advertisement in Broadcasting, August 16, 1954, p. 4.

HOOPER RADIO AUDIENCE INDEX

City Zone

CITY: DALLAS, TEXAS

MONTH: JUNE, 1954

SHARE OF RADIO AUDIENCE

TIME	RADIO SETS-IN-USE	570 KC (NBC)	820 KC (ABC)	KGKO	KIXL+ KIXL-FM	KLIF	KRLD+ KRLD-FM (CBS)	KSKY	WRR (MBS)					OTHER AM & FM	SAMPLE SIZE
MONDAY THRU FRIDAY 8:00 A.M.-12:00 NOON	10.0	8.4	17.5	3.7	5.8	29.5	18.2	6.1	5.1					5.6	7,343
MONDAY THRU FRIDAY 12:00 NOON-6:00 P.M.	10.9	16.6	18.3	2.5	7.4	19.9	15.2	7.0	5.3					7.9	10,665
SUNDAY 10:00 A.M.-6:00 P.M.	9.5	6.4	9.2	5.3	11.0	22.0	19.5	5.7	10.3					10.6	3,836
SATURDAY 10:00 A.M.-6:00 P.M.	9.8	3.2	13.4	1.4	11.6	31.3	15.8	6.0	9.2					8.1	3,764
SUNDAY THRU SATURDAY 6:00 P.M.-11:00 P.M.	8.5	5.0	14.0	3.2		25.4	24.8		22.3					5.3	8,486

NOTE: Radio Stations KIXL and KSKY sign off at 7:30 P.M. in June.

"Radio Sets-in-Use" is the percentage of Total Homes which are listening to the radio. Where listening to a second program over a second radio set is reported in a home, this fact is reflected in [illegible]

Where an FM station duplicates its corresponding AM station's program [illegible] the FM station [illegible] are combined with the AM station's audience.

[illegible]

station D with 18 dealers, and independent station E with 17 dealers.[167] Either station D or E must have been KLIF. In June of 1955, KRLD was still using Pulse to show it first in total circulation, with a breakdown of the highest rated 15-minute periods 6:00 a.m. to midnight seven days a week showing KRLD with 256 firsts, Frequency B (820 kc.) with 132 firsts, and station B [sic] (probably KLIF) with 39 firsts.[168] By the same time a year later, KLIF was claiming superiority with superlatives, both in numbers and in figures (see page 219).[169]

With high ratings achieved at KLIF in Dallas by the summer of 1954, McLendon began to look for stations in other markets in which he could install the same success formula. Meanwhile, the McLendon family had hedged their bets by also seeking TV licenses. In December of 1954, when the McLendons bought their next radio station, they were already the licensees of KELP-TV, El Paso and the grantees of KTLG in Corpus Christi.[170]

WRIT

The first station which McLendon bought after the huge success of KLIF was WEMP, Milwaukee. Actually, only the facilities of WEMP were bought; WEMP continued to exist. Here is the complicated story, as explained by Sponsor magazine.

---

167 Advertisement in Broadcasting, January 3, 1955, p. 4.

168 Advertisement in Broadcasting, June 20, 1955, p. 4.

169 Advertisement in Broadcasting, June 25, 1956, p. 21.

170 "Liberty Group Negotiating to Buy WEMP Milwaukee," Broadcasting, December 27, 1954, p. 7.

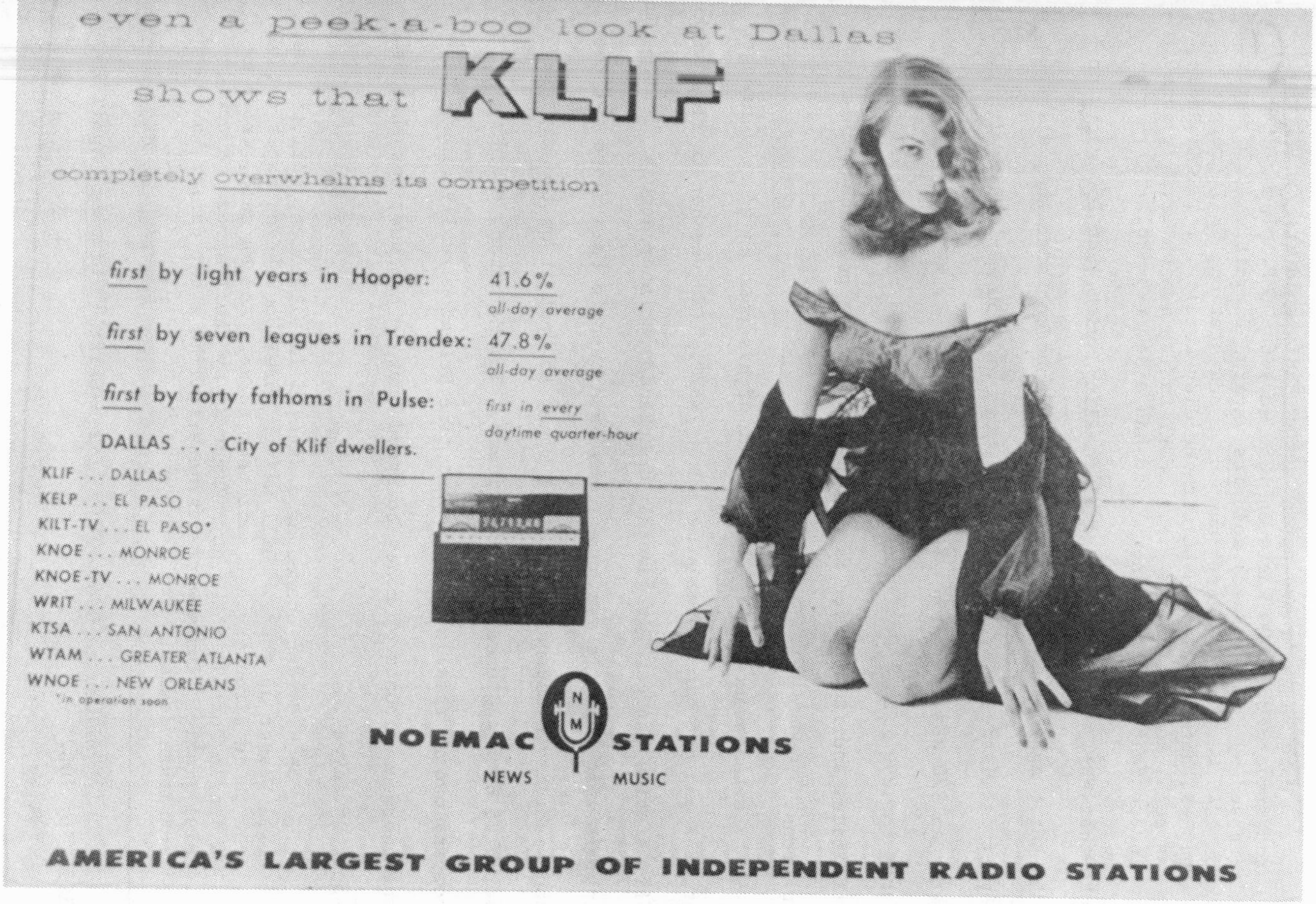
even a peek-a-boo look at Dallas
shows that KLIF
completely overwhelms its competition
first by light years in Hooper: 41.6% all-day average
first by seven leagues in Trendex: 47.8% all-day average
first by forty fathoms in Pulse: first in every daytime quarter-hour
DALLAS . . . City of Klif dwellers.
KLIF . . . DALLAS
KELP . . . EL PASO
KILT-TV . . . EL PASO*
KNOE . . . MONROE
KNOE-TV . . . MONROE
WRIT . . . MILWAUKEE
KTSA . . . SAN ANTONIO
WTAM . . . GREATER ATLANTA
WNOE . . . NEW ORLEANS
*in operation soon
NOEMAC STATIONS
NEWS MUSIC
AMERICA'S LARGEST GROUP OF INDEPENDENT RADIO STATIONS

> . . . Here we go 'round again: WCAN Radio sold its facilities and frequency (5,000 watts on 1250 kc.) to WEMP. Then, WEMP (repped by Headley-Reed) sold its vacated facilities (250 watts on 1340 kc.) to a Texas group for a new station, WRIT (repped by H-R, not to be confused with Headley-Reed). . . . WCAN Radio, as such, is off the air. . . . WOKY Radio, meanwhile, has gone independent (music and news) and has a new rep (Bolling).[171]

Note that WRIT was a very marginal facility, with just 250 watts on 1340 kHz. Against it were four other independent stations, all with better facilities: WEMP with 5,000 watts at 1250 kHz, WOKY with 1,000 watts on 920 kHz, WFOX with 250 watts on 860 kHz, and WMIL with 1,000 watts on 1290 kHz.[172] Milwaukee was also served by two local network affiliates and it received fine signals from the powerhouse Chicago stations.

McLendon moved Bill Weaver out of his post as general manager at KLIF and put him in the same job at WRIT. (Weaver became the "kick-off" station manager for several of McLendon's later acquisitions.) It appears that Weaver's assignment may have been to compensate for the poor facility by spending a lot of money to "put it on the map" in terms of both audience and advertisers. Tom Merriman, the jingle company owner, recalls that at that time McLendon really didn't have the enormous amounts of money to spend that he has now, but that he spent it anyway.

> . . . when Gordon opened up a station in Milwaukee, WRIT, he sent Bill Weaver up there. Bill Weaver tore about seven pages out of the phone directory and sent them to me. And he said, write me a jingle for all these guys I put Xs by their names. A commercial jingle. These were businesses, like a car dealer, a furniture dealer. And I wrote back and said, what will you pay

---

[171] "Milwaukee Radio-TV: '1-2-3-Shift,'" Sponsor, April 18, 1955, p. 108.

[172] Ibid.

for it? And he said, what do you want? And I said, give me $250 apiece and I'll do ten . . . or fifteen or whatever it was. It was only $250 apiece--nothing. But he says, I haven't got any of these sold, but I'm going to go into that market and I'm going to go--with this new station--and present them all with their own jingle. Well, this predates Pepper and their Concept deal and everything else in this business. And he couldn't have done that unless Gordon had said, Bill, go in there and spend three or four thousand dollars on just promotion of local merchants. And for a guy to just tear out some pages from the Yellow Pages and say, I don't care which ones, pick any ones you want to do, we don't have any of them on the air anyway, so it doesn't make any difference to us and we'll just go with the ones you want to cut! [And] they went in there and they sold maybe half of them. They went in there with a $250 cost on the jingle and got maybe a $2000 account. So, it was promotion, and if they only sold half of them, they were way ahead. It's that kind of adventuresome, willing-to-take-a-shot-at-it sort that McLendon has always been.[173]

In April of 1956, as WRIT prepared to celebrate its first anniversary on the air, June Bundy reported in Billboard's "Vox Jox" column that Hooper found WRIT to be the highest-rated Milwaukee station noon to 6:00 p.m.[174] An advertisement in the May 14 Broadcasting gave the exact figure: 20.9% as against the second station's 18.9%.[175] However, such ratings were accomplished on WRIT only by Herculean effort, and as WOKY programmed nearly the same thing with a stronger signal, it was clear that WRIT would continue to require large transfusions of money to keep it on top. In September of 1956, McLendon sold WRIT to the Balaban station group for a reported $400,500, after owning the station less than a year and a half.[176]

---

[173] Merriman interview.

[174] June Bundy, "Vox Jox," Billboard, April 28, 1956, p. 52.

[175] Advertisement in Broadcasting, May 14, 1956, p. 45.

[176] "Balaban Corp. Buys WRIT from McLendon for $400,500," Broadcasting, September 24, 1956, p. 9.

NoeMac--WNOE, KNOE

In early September of 1955, Gordon McLendon joined his father-in-law, former Louisiana Governor James A. Noe, in announcing the organization of a new station group to be known as NOEMAC. Governor Noe owned WNOE, New Orleans and KNOE and KNOE-TV, Monroe, Louisiana, while at the time McLendon held KLIF, WRIT, KELP and the re-named KELP-TV, now known as KOKE-TV.[177] The ownership of the stations remained with Noe and McLendon as it had been before NOEMAC, but the new combination allowed combined sales efforts. In addition, McLendon and his staff became increasingly responsible for programming the Noe radio stations, but referred to this arrangement as a "consultant" agreement. In actual practice, McLendon included the Noe stations in his programming and promotional plans as if they were his own.

In March of 1955, WNOE, New Orleans had severed its contract with the Mutual network, with which the station had been affiliated since 1941. The contract would normally have expired at the end of the year, but WNOE chose to make the change immediately to a 24-hour-a-day music and news format.[178] The following week, James A. Gordon, WNOE general manager announced his resignation "following a disagreement over policy matters."[179] Broadcasting pointed out that WNOE had just recently changed to an independent operation, but did not say

---

177"McLendon, Noe Organize NOEMAC Station Group," Broadcasting, September 5, 1955, p. 7.

178"WNOE Becomes Independent, WTPS Takes MBS Affiliation," Broadcasting, March 21, 1955, p. 112.

179"Gordon Resigns WNOE Post Over Policy Disagreement," Broadcasting, March 28, 1955, p. 88.

directly that that switch was the reason for the resignation. Steve French was named general manager to replace Gordon.[180]

A memo written by Gordon McLendon in August of 1955, even before the official announcement of the NOEMAC group shows how involved McLendon was in seeing WNOE succeed with a music-and-news operation. The memorandum was mimeographed and sent to "All Managers, Program Directors, Sales Force"

> BULLETIN BULLETIN BULLETIN EXTRA SIXTEEN-POINT TYPE SPECIAL
> WNOE MOVES CLOSE TO FIRST IN NEW ORLEANS
>
> August Hooper in New Orleans shows WNOE 1.5% out of first place mornings, 4.9% out of first place afternoons. Great news from the Crescent City. Congratulations, Steve French and Bill Stewart [general manager and national program director, respectively]--terrific job! Now keep the pressure on and we'll be up there in first place and then they'll have one hell of a job ever dislodging us. Now if the Hooper in Monroe shows KNOE in first place, what a sales story the NOEMAC stations have to tell! And to make it just a little bit sweeter for Bill Stewart in New Orleans, WNOE knocked off WTIX in both time periods--the first time, I guess, that one of the Mid-Continent stations ever got knocked out of first place! I'm very happy for James A., and for Bill and Steve. Now, for God's sake, don't relax. This is the time a good fighter moves in for the kill, when he's got his opponent hurt. . . .[181]

Note that WNOE with 50,000 watts days and 5,000 watts nights on 1060 kHz, was challenging 250-watt WTIX at 1450 kHz for first place.

In October of 1955, James Noe's other station, KNOE, announced that it too was going to be an independent, dropping its NBC affiliation. In announcing the change to music-and-news, Noe was quoted as

---

[180] Ibid.

[181] Gordon McLendon, memorandum on WNOE, mimeographed, August 1955, from McLendon Policy Books, n.p.

saying, "It is no longer practical for a radio station to belong to a network."[182]

With the NOEMAC contract came a greater emphasis on advertising the stations in the trades, probably because it was now more economical to do so. The same memo that proclaimed WNOE's ratings rise also mentioned to McLendon's managers, program directors and salesmen NOEMAC station advertising, and the success of KELP, El Paso:

> . . . Full page ad on KELP--not a part of the NOEMAC contract--goes into next week's Broadcasting. Built around the heading "is this the highest rated station in radio history?" While not a part of the NOEMAC contract, KELP's ad lists it as a NOEMAC station and will mention the rest of you. In any ad you run in either Sponsor or Broadcasting, even though run independently, list yourself as a NOEMAC station and list the rest of the stations. It lends strength and stature to your own call letters. And by the way, if any of you care to run extra ads, full pages of Broadcasting are $345 on our 26-time rate. And any ad in this series, and preferably any independent ad, should be placed through Tom Croke at Dayton, Johnson and Hacker in Milwaukee.[183]

The ad mentioned in the above memo is reproduced on page 225.[184]

At the same time that KELP was managing such high shares in El Paso, McLendon was at work building a TV station in the same city. The target date for what was to be known as KOKE-TV, a VHF station on Channel 13, was to be December 15, 1955. Original plans called for the station to program primarily in Spanish "with possible network affiliation to be announced later."[185] Meanwhile, Noe's KNOE-TV, Channel 8 in

---

[182] "Second Noe Station Turns Independent," Broadcasting, October 10, 1955, p. 96.

[183] McLendon, Memorandum on WNOE.

[184] Advertisement in Broadcasting, August 29, 1955, p. 39.

[185] Advertisement in Broadcasting, September 5, 1955, back cover.

DOES A 63.2 HOOPER MAKE KELP THE HIGHEST RATED STATION IN RADIO HISTORY?

HERE'S THE JULY-AUGUST HOOPER

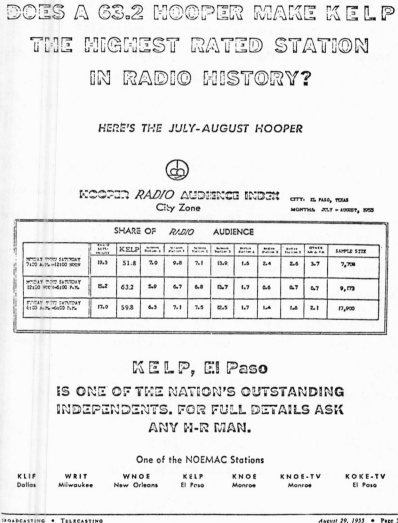

HOOPER *RADIO* AUDIENCE INDEX
City Zone

CITY: EL PASO, TEXAS
MONTHS: JULY - AUGUST, 1955

SHARE OF *RADIO* AUDIENCE

	RADIO SETS-IN-USE	KELP	Network Station A	Network Station B	Network Station C	Network Station D	[illegible] Station A	[illegible] Station B	[illegible] Station C	OTHER AM & FM	SAMPLE SIZE
MONDAY THRU SATURDAY 7:00 A.M.-12:00 NOON	19.3	51.8	7.0	9.8	7.1	13.9	1.6	2.4	2.6	3.7	7,708
MONDAY THRU SATURDAY 12:00 NOON-6:00 P.M.	15.2	63.2	5.9	6.7	6.8	13.7	1.7	0.6	0.7	0.7	9,173
SUNDAY THRU SATURDAY 6:00 A.M.-6:00 P.M.	17.0	59.8	6.3	7.1	7.5	12.5	1.7	1.4	1.6	2.1	17,900

KELP, El Paso

IS ONE OF THE NATION'S OUTSTANDING INDEPENDENTS. FOR FULL DETAILS ASK ANY H-R MAN.

One of the NOEMAC Stations

KLIF	WRIT	WNOE	KELP	KNOE	KNOE-TV	KOKE-TV
Dallas	Milwaukee	New Orleans	El Paso	Monroe	Monroe	El Paso

Monroe, Louisiana was the only station on the air in Monroe and was affiliated with all four TV networks.[186]

At the end of 1955, McLendon ran an advertisement in Sponsor listing the five radio stations he was then programming--KLIF, KELP, WNOE, WRIT, and KNOE--calling them all "thoroughbreds." "Although under separate management, each follows the same proven pattern of programming. And each of the five operates as an independent local station."[18

WGLS--WTAM

In late 1955, McLendon gained control of WGLS, Decatur, Georgia, a suburb of Atlanta, as a majority stockholder in Republic Broadcasting System, Inc. He paid just $40,500 for the station, a 1,000 watt daytime on 970 kHz. Later, the station would go to 5,000 watts of power, but continued a daytime-only operation. WGLS was listed in trades ads for the NOEMAC stations as being in "greater Atlanta."[188] By May of 1956, the call letters had been changed to WTAM,[189] to be the first of a set of two "Scottish" phonetically pronounceable call letters McLendon was then beginning on, with the other being KILT. (The KILT call would later be applied to the El Paso TV station and then to the renamed KLBS in Houston.)

According to Edd Routt, who talked with McLendon at the author's request to gather more information about WGLS/WTAM, McLendon did not

---

[186] Ibid.

[187] Advertisement in Sponsor, November 28, 1955, front cover.

[188] Advertisement in Broadcasting, April 2, 1956, p. 47.

[189] Advertisement in Broadcasting, May 28, 1956, p. 57.

perate the station. It was the first time that McLendon had ever been stockholder rather than an owner and operator. The other major tockholder was Henry Lanhan, who believed that the station could ncrease power and be a fulltime station serving the Atlanta market. 'he transfer to McLendon and Lanhan as the new majority stockholders n the station was approved, but McLendon withdrew not long after it 'as discovered that the power increase and fulltime operation would not e granted by the FCC. McLendon recalls that it was impossible to hear he station at the Atlanta airport.[190]

In January of 1956, McLendon filed three requests with the FCC. ne was to cancel the permit for a UHF TV station for Dallas, to have een called KLIF-TV. A second asked permission to change the name of he company from Trinity Broadcasting Corporation to McLendon Investment orporation. The third was an application for a new AM station to be located in Houston, to have 10,000 watts on 1070 kHz.[191]

KTSA

In March of 1956, McLendon purchased KTSA, San Antonio for $306,000, buying the fulltime 5,000 watt 550 kHz station from O. R. Mitchell, a Dodge-Plymouth dealer who less than two years earlier had bought the station for $175,000 from the publishers of the San Antonio

---

[190]Edd Routt, private telephone conversation held on July 18, 1972.

[191]"Trinity Files for New AM, Decides to Drop Dallas UHF," Broadcasting, January 9, 1956, p. 66. McLendon had sold the license of KLBS in Houston in 1953.

Express and Evening News.[192]

An unsigned memorandum titled "Timetable for San Antonio" and marked "Confidential" was written on March 30, 1956 concerning the procedures the McLendon organization planned to follow in converting KTSA to its formula. Excerpts are reproduced here:

> Application will be filed in FCC Monday, April 2. Approval will doubtless be made by FCC during latter part of April and new programming will become effective Tuesday, May 1. It is hoped that FCC approval will be given in time for us to spend a few days promoting "listen to the new look on KTSA May first."
>
> Cancellation of ABC will become final April 16. Only Mutual programs to be continued will be baseball (Eastern games only) and Fulton Lewis. Cancellation of these would mean the loss of an additional $4,333.33 per month in revenue, which we cannot stand. It was originally thought that cancellation of other off-format programming would mean the loss of $4,427.21 in net revenue but it now appears that we will probably be able to salvage almost one-half of this anticipated loss. . . .
>
> . . . We are raising local rates immediately--effective May 1 for all new business--with advertisers to be given a chance to sign on the old rate with 6 months protection if they do so before May 1 (or FCC approval). . . . National rates are also to be hiked immediately--just how much will depend on John Blair. . . .
>
> . . . Frankly, the problem in San Antonio does not look too difficult but then nothing looks difficult after Milwaukee. . . .[193]

The May 1 deadline was not met. KTSA instead began its music-and-news operation on May 21, 1956. In June, KITE, another San Antonio station filed with the FCC a protest of the KTSA sale--*after* it had been consummated, and the new programming was on the air. KITE's protest claimed that operation of KTSA by the McLendon company would unfairly subject KITE to economic injury. The complaint alluded that

---

192"KTSA San Antonio Acquired by McLendon for $306,000," Broadcasting, March 12, 1956, p. 7.

193"Timetable for San Antonio," unsigned memorandum from McLendon Policy Books, March 30, 1956.

KTSA was the eighth NOEMAC station, and that, by being part of such a large group, KTSA would have the chance to compete unfairly. KITE's protest also attacked KTSA's new programming practices which it said were designed to destroy competition.[194]

In the closing days of June, the FCC "postponed" the dates on which its grants of transfer of control for KTSA would become effective, ordered a hearing set for September 10 with KITE to bear the burden of proof, and ordered McLendon to return control of KTSA to the Dodge-Plymouth dealer.[195] In the same issue of Broadcasting in which this news appeared, KTSA was running an ad under the NOEMAC banner ("America's largest group of independent radio stations") boasting that in just three weeks of McLendon programming, Hooper had found its daytime share rising from 5.3% to 20.2%.[196]

On July 18, 1956, the same day the FCC began two days of deliberations on whether or not to grant the transfer of WQAM to Todd Storz because of the "giveaway pattern" on his stations, the Commission granted a request by McLendon that his operation of KTSA be extended until September 12. As the Commission was set to recess in mid-July, the extension, according to Broadcasting, would "allow the FCC time to consider the issues prior to the scheduled hearing." More important, the extension would not summarily take the station away from McLendon

---

[194]"KITE Protests KTSA Sale," Broadcasting, June 11, 1956, p. 76, and "KITE Agrees to Withdraw Protest Against KTSA Sale," Broadcasting, September 10, 1956, p. 82.

[195]"Protests Bring Postponements of KTSA, KVAR (TV) Actions," Broadcasting, July 2, 1956, p. 64.

[196]Advertisement in Broadcasting, July 2, 1956, p. 21.

without a hearing and would allow (as it happened) both sides time to work out their differences.

By the end of July, NOEMAC trades ads for KTSA were showing th station first in both Hooper and Pulse shares.[197] The McLendon formul apparently was working as usual in taking listeners away from the competition. But in early September, an agreement was reached by which KITE withdrew its protest. According to Broadcasting,

> . . . Associated with the withdrawal was the agreement which binds McLendon to pay KITE $1,500 as damages for infringement of copyright and as "partial" damages. It is understood that the McLendons were charged with using a promotional approach for their KLIF Dallas which had been developed by KITE. McLendon also agreed to cease using this matter.
>
> The agreement declared that some of the protest charges and counter-charges were based on misunderstandings and the knowledge that certain evidence could not be legally presented in an FCC hearing. It also provided for a $10,000 "fine" if either of the parties should publicize the agreement on their respective stations if either institutes a suit for damages against the other.[198]

By the late summer of the following year, KITE was running trades ads which emphasized its difference from the McLendon competition. One read "'The squares' (Mom) (Pop) (Adults who can buy) listen to KITE. 'Cool cats' get their kicks elsewhere. More San Antonio Mommies and Poppies listen daily to KITE than to any other station . . NCS # 2."[199] It is interesting to note that KITE had to quote the old NCS # 2 as proof of its claim.

In 1965, McLendon sold KTSA to Bernard E. Waterman for $1,500,000, which was $1,200,000 more than McLendon had paid for it.

---

[197] Advertisement in Broadcasting, July 30, 1956, p. 51.

[198] "KITE Agrees to Withdraw Protest Against KTSA Sale," p. 82.

[199] Advertisement in Broadcasting, August 12, 1957, p. 111.

LBS--KILT

In March of 1957, McLendon made his next purchase, at the same ime that he sold his El Paso stations. KELP and what had become ILT-TV in El Paso were sold together for $750,000. McLendon used most f that amount almost immediately to buy back KLBS in Houston, rather han continue to work on his application for a new AM station there. nder the Howard Broadcasting Corporation, KLBS had shown a 1956 net oss of $6,665.[200]

What was becoming the typical McLendon ratings increase story as repeated in Houston with the renamed KILT. An appealing cartoon-tyle advertisement appeared in Broadcasting and Sponsor in early July 957 telling what had happened to the station's ratings in the 30 days etween May 14 and June 15, 1957, and claiming a new world's record for oing from last to first in 30 days. The ad is reproduced on page 32.[201]

Later trades ads confirmed the first place position listing in rendex and Pulse, and introduced a name for the new programming in eferring to it as "a sensational new fun radio format."[202]

At the bottom of each of the July trades ads for KILT were the ords "affiliated with KLIF/Dallas and KTSA/San Antonio." McLendon was reparing timebuyers for the concept of "the Texas Triangle" which was a new national sales group that McLendon and Arthur H. McCoy, vice

---

[200] "FCC Approval Sought for Sales of WPFH (TV) and WIBG-AM-FM," Broadcasting, March 4, 1957, p. 60.

[201] Advertisement in Broadcasting, July 1, 1957, p. 13.

[202] Advertisements in Sponsor, July 20, 1957, front cover, and in Broadcasting, July 22, 1957, p. 38.

KILT
We really KILT 'em in Houston!
FROM LAST TO FIRST IN THIRTY DAYS: HOOPER!
Communique No. 1, OPERATION KILT, 15 June 1957. In its first public announcement since the call letters were changed from KLBS to KILT in Houston on M Day (14 May 1957), Time Buyers' Headquarters for the Greater Southwest reports complete devastation of the pre-KILT radio picture in Houston. The super-strategy of KILT's high command, headed by General Bill Weaver, developed with military precision in the tough KLIF Dallas and KTSA San Antonio sectors, has sent the opposing forces reeling. On 14 May, KILT was last in Houston with only 4.6% of the all-day average audience (May '57 Hooper). Just thirty days later, on 15 June, KILT had rocketed from last to first with 30.5% of the all-day average audience (June '57 Hooper). It's a new world's record — thirty days from last to first!
affiliated with
KLIF/DALLAS and KTSA/SAN ANTONIO
BROADCASTING • TELECASTING
July 1, 1957

esident of the John Blair rep firm announced jointly in September 57. With KLIF in Dallas, KILT in Houston and KTSA in San Antonio lus KFJZ in Fort Worth, a station also repped by Blair), the Texas iangle was claimed to have a potential audience of 73% of the Texas pulation.[203] The phrase "Texas Triangle" appeared at the bottom of ter McLendon trades ads such as another appealing for KLIT which peared on November 18 Broadcasting's back cover, reproduced on page 4.[204] Variety, in an article about the Texas Triangle, claimed that gaining a station in Texas' three major markets, McLendon had complished something other radio executives had tried to do for 37 ars.[205]

EL, WAKY

In September of 1957, McLendon acquired KEEL, Shreveport, uisiana, which at the time was known as KTBS. The facility was a ne one: 10,000 watts days, 5,000 watts nights on 710 kHz, with the ation occupying that frequency since 1922. In June of 1961, McLendon ades ads announced that KEEL was about to go to 50,000 watts.[206] In rch of 1962, the station was acquired by LIN broadcasting, which had so purchased McLendon's WAKY, Louisville in a double package. Lendon had bought WAKY in late 1957 from Northside Broadcasting rporation. The station, then known as WGRC, had been on the air

---

[203] "Texas Triangle Group Formed," Broadcasting, September 23, 57, p. 90.

[204] Advertisement in Broadcasting, November 18, 1957, back cover.

[205] "McLendon's 'Texas Triangle,'" Variety, May 15, 1957, p. 37.

[206] Advertisement in Broadcasting, June 5, 1961, front cover.

What's under the KILT?
NOTHING..
BUT THE OTHER SEVE
HOUSTON RADIO STATIONS
Everyone in and around Houston already
the answer . . . there's nothing under the KILT
the seven other Houston radio stations, lagging
behind! The new August Area Pulse proves it
a shadow of a doubt.* Not only is KILT the
one station in Houston metro ratings (any Hooper,
Pulse, any Trendex) . . . but its strong signal and
programming reaches 20% more listeners in the 53-
Houston area (Pulse) survey than the next station in the
Call your John Blair man for rates and availabilities . . .
go KILT to the hilt!
*August 19-25, 1957 Pulse Area Report covering in-home and
out-of-home audience in Houston 53-county area.
KILT HOUSTON · KLIF-KFJZ DALLAS-FORT WORTH · KTSA
represented by JOHN BLAIR & CO.
THE TREMENDOUS TEXAS

ince 1936. When McLendon bought it, WAKY had the facilities it has ow: 5,000 watts days, 1,000 watts nights on 790. McLendon programing began in July of 1958 and for three months featured a heavy chedule of promotion designed to force the station to the number one osition. This promotion schedule will be described in detail in a ater chapter, but at this point it should be mentioned that the chedule, which began on July 8, 1958, called for WAKY to announce its osition as number one on September 10th.[207]

YSL

In 1962 McLendon acquired WYSL, in Amherst, New York, a suburb f Buffalo. The original WYSL was a 1,000 watt station at 1080 kHz, aytime only. It had to compete with WKBW, Buffalo, for the target udience, and WKBW had 50,000 watts on 1520, but most important, was a ulltime operation. Realizing that a fulltime operation was essential o keeping the youth audience who listened at night, McLendon sought a ulltime facility in the market. In March of 1960, the McLendons ought the current WYSL in Buffalo proper, which is 1,000 watts days, 0 watts at night at 1400 kHz. For a while, after the success with good music" on KABL in San Francisco, this station tried to duplicate e format, but with nowhere near the success of KABL. It has since

---

[207]Don Keyes, "Confidential and Top Secret, Louisville Promoon Schedule," McLendon Policy Books, dated July 2, 1958. According Ken Dowe, National Director of Operations for the McLendon stations, was Billie Odom, long-time secretary of the McLendon corporations o came up with the call letters for the Louisville station. "She was tting around one day and said, I think that a good name for a radio ation would be 'wacky'--'WAKY.' And that's how Louisville came to be lled WAKY." Mr. Ken Dowe, National Director of Operations, the Lendon Stations, private interview held in Dallas, Texas, July 29, 71.

gone back to competing with WKBW for the AM rock audience, but has always been number two to WKBW.

The intent in Buffalo seems remarkably like that in Atlanta: buy a facility in a neighboring town for considerably less than one in the major city, but program it for the audience in the total market. Bill Stewart, former National Program Director for McLendon comments about the Atlanta experience: "Well, he wanted to get into the market. He thought he could take a fringe station and make it work, but he couldn't . . . it was even worse than a WRIT because it wasn't even licensed to the market it was hoping for."[208] That the Amherst, New York station was bought with the Buffalo audience in mind seems certa when it is recalled that McLendon later bought a station in Buffalo itself. In the fall of 1966, the McLendon corporation tried the same tactic in television, by acquiring KCND-TV, Channel 12, in Pembina, North Dakota, with the intention of beaming ABC programming into Winnipeg, Canada. The signal is not strong in Winnipeg, which makes the competitive situation difficult.[209]

WGES--WYNR

In August of 1962, McLendon took over WGES, Chicago, and almo immediately renamed it WYNR, dropping the foreign programming he had promised the FCC in his application, and aiming instead entirely for the Negro audience. The music on WYNR was more genuine rhythm and bl

---

[208] Bill Stewart, private telephone conversation held on June 1972.

[209] Ken Dowe, National Director of Operations, the McLendon Stations, private interview held in Dallas, Texas, July 29, 1971.

than white-oriented rock 'n' roll, but the station is important to this discussion for a number of reasons. First, it involved McLendon in an inquiry that lasted nearly two years, focusing on the question of whether or not McLendon had purposely misled the FCC in promising to retain 32 weekly hours of German, Italian, Polish and other foreign programming, and then, five days after taking over the station, beginning programming to Negroes 100% of the time. Representative Roman Pucinski of Illinois, who had demanded that the FCC revoke the station's license and whose insistence that the Commission should know if it had been lied to resulted in the inquiry, was accused by McLendon lawyers of bias because one of the cancelled programs was conducted in Polish by his mother, to whom time had been sold on a brokerage basis for resale. But McLendon also had to defend his promotional tactics, which like those for his Top 40 stations, included treasure hunts, mystery telephone numbers and other stunts that were claimed to cause damage to property or annoyance to citizens. Before the inquiry (to decide whether or not to hold a formal hearing) was over, even the profit motive had been found suspect. A memo from the station broker to McLendon that "this station can be turned around" to gross $2,000,000 or more annually and "make $1,300,000 before taxes" was compared with the 1961 WGES gross of $731,000 and $203,700 profit.[210] In retrospect, the "informal inquiry" seems to have accomplished its effect. As one of the more blatant forms of the FCC's "raised eyebrow" method of resolution, it sowed in McLendon both the caution that Todd Storz had

---

[210]"Informal Chicago Hearing Erupts," Broadcasting, April 15, 1963, p. 52.

acquired in a similar scrape with his WQAM transfer, and a growing distrust of what McLendon now calls "non-objective law."

The McLendon family acquired several other stations in the late 1950s and 1960s, but no others were programmed with "rock 'n' roll" or "contemporary" music. The formats and stations McLendon developed after the Top 40 era will be treated in a concluding chapter.

Bartell

Gerald Aaron Bartell was born in Chicago on May 20, 1914. He attended the University of Wisconsin, Madison, majoring in Speech, and received both a B.A. (1937) and an M.A. (1939) in that field. Between 1937 and 1939, he also acted in a Chicago radio soap opera, and even imitated a barking dog for Red Heart dog food.[211] Between 1937 and 1947, Bartell was production manager at WHA, Madison, the University of Wisconsin's educational station. In 1939-40, he attended law school, and in 1946 he became an associate professor in the Department of Speech at Wisconsin, teaching radio production. He won a Rockefeller grant to spend a summer in New York studying sales, merchandising and production at NBC.

Bartell Station Acquisitions

In 1947, Gerry Bartell founded the Bartell Broadcasting Corporation of Milwaukee, which put his first daytime station on the air. From the beginning, Bartell was joined by his brothers and sisters in

---

[211] Biographical information about Bartell is from Seymour Freedgood, "The Money-Makers of 'New Radio,'" Fortune, February, 1958, pp. 122, 123, 222, 224, 226, and Marquis, Who's Who In America, Vol. 36, 1970-71 (Chicago, Illinois: Marquis--Who's Who Inc., 1970).

supporting the operation. Lee and David Bartell were lawyers, Mel was a singer, and his sister Rosa and her husband Ralph Evans served as group executive secretary and chief engineer respectively. Together they raised $50,000 to build the first station, WEXT of Milwaukee.

WEXT, WOKY

WEXT was a daytime-only facility, with 1,000 watts on 1430 kHz. The first program director of the station was sister Rosa Evans. The profits from WEXT were not large, but were enough to buy interests in four other daytime stations. None of these made a large profit either, but in 1950 their sale provided money to build another Milwaukee station, which would become WOKY. WOKY went on the air in late 1950 at a cost of $80,000, but it was a far superior facility to WEXT, which went off the air. The new WOKY was fulltime with 1,000 watts at 920 kHz. In 1951, WOKY was affiliated with McLendon's Liberty Broadcasting System, as were many other "young" stations across the country.

The programming was not specialized nor spectacular. As of January, 1952, WOKY was ranked seventh out of ten Milwaukee-market stations by Hooper. But in that month, Bartell began programming music-and-news on a 24-hour basis. By October of the same year, WOKY was rated by Hooper among the top three Milwaukee stations 24 hours a day, and billings had risen by $10,000 a month to $38,000.[212] Bartell closed out 1952 by putting on his second music-and-news station, WAPL in Appleton, Wisconsin. WAPL is today a 1,000 watt daytimer on 1570 kHz.

By 1954, Bartell Broadcasting owned WOKY-AM and TV in Milwaukee,

---

[212]Freedgood, "The Money-Makers of 'New Radio,'" p. 226.

WAPL in Appleton, and WMTV in Madison. WOKY-TV was sold in 1954 to become the present WISN-TV, Channel 12. In December of 1954, McLendon bought WRIT in Milwaukee and prepared to challenge WOKY for ratings supremacy. In September of 1956, McLendon gave up and sold WRIT to the Balaban Corporation. John F. Box, who had been an executive vice president of the Bartell group since 1954 and who in 1954 was manager of WOKY, in 1957 became the executive vice president of the Balaban stations and in that capacity became responsible for trying to beat WOKY with WRIT.[213]

KCBQ, WBGE

In the fall of 1955, Bartell bought two of his key stations: KCBQ in San Diego and WBGE in Atlanta. KCBQ had been sold a year earlier to the parties Bartell bought it from for the same price he paid: $250,000.[214] KCBQ was a good regional facility, with 5,000 watts days, 1,000 watts nights on 1170 kHz. The agreement also included an option to buy KRUX in Glendale (Phoenix metro area) for $100,000 which Bartell would do in late November of 1955. KRUX was then 250 watts on 1340 kHz (it would later increase to 5,000 watts on 1360 kHz).

The other station bought in the fall of 1955, WBGE, was not at all a good facility. Like KRUX, it had only 250 watts at 1340. But it

---

[213]Box had come to Bartell from NBC, and served Bartell as general manager of his stations in Atlanta, Phoenix, and Boston as well as Milwaukee. His KBOX in Dallas is the only station ever to give KLIF serious competition, as will be shown later.

[214]"Bartell Buys KCBQ, WBGE in Two Sales," Broadcasting, September 19, 1955, p. 205.

was in Atlanta, Georgia, a rapidly-expanding market. Bartell changed the call-letters, and made them pronounceable: WAKE. Pete Thomas, who was production manager at WAKE in the late 1950s recalls that the reason for the change, besides being pronounceable, was that the previous format had been religiously-oriented, and Bartell wanted to completely change the station's identification.[215]

Bartell bought WBGE in 1955 for $100,000 according to <u>Broadcasting</u>, although he says the price was $75,000.[216] Bartell says he sold it for $750,000--"a very good price."[217] When bought by Bartell, WBGE showed total assets of only $44,000, of which $16,000 were current. Against those figures were current liabilities of $25,000 and an $85,000 deficit.[218]

One week following the announcement of the sale of KCBQ to Bartell, <u>Broadcasting</u> mentioned that the station was dropping its ABC affiliation.[219] In November 1955 Bartell officially bought KRUX, Glendale (Phoenix), Arizona for $100,000. At the same time, McLendon acquired WGLS, Decatur, through his majority interest in Republic Broadcasting System, Inc., for $40,500. Henry W. Lanham, a former manager and part owner of WBGE became a stockholder in and the general

---

[215] Pete Thomas, former production manager at WAKE, private interview held in Madison Wisconsin, April 27, 1972.

[216] "Bartell Buys KCBQ, WBGE in Two Sales," <u>Broadcasting</u>, September 19, 1955, p. 205.

[217] Gerald Bartell, private interview held in Madison, Wisconsin, May 24, 1972.

[218] "Bartell Buys KCBQ, WBGE in Two Sales," p. 205.

[219] "KCBQ Drops Network," <u>Broadcasting</u>, September 26, 1955, p. 7.

manager of McLendon's WGLS.[220] Once again, McLendon was up against Bartell, although Bartell this time had only been in the market a few months himself. McLendon's WGLS (later WTAM) was a more powerful facility than WAKE, but it was a daytime-only station. WAKE would continue to pull high audiences with only 250 watts after McLendon had withdrawn from WTAM.

Bartell did not make as extensive use of trades ads as either Storz or McLendon, but appeared often with news of promotions, sales, and management appointments. However, Bartell gradually seemed to increase trades advertising in early 1957 following about a year without further station acquisitions. An ad in Sponsor in February, 1957, claimed a "first in listeners, day and night" for WOKY.[221] An ad for KCBQ, San Diego, in March claimed "KCBQ now delivers more listeners per dollar than any other San Diego station," pointing out that the outlet had been acquired by Bartell little more than a year before.[222]

In April of 1957 Bartell held a 10th Birthday observance for the group's executives and announced that 1956 had shown a 225% increase in billings, with nearly $3,000,000 projected for 1957. The largest increase (300%) had been at KCBQ, but the fastest growth had been at KRUX, Phoenix. John Box, manager of KRUX, was given an award for that growth, as was Mort Wagner, general manager of WAKE for his

---

[220] "Bartell Buys KRUX," Broadcasting, December 5, 1955, p. 32.

[221] Advertisement in Sponsor, February 2, 1957, p. 65.

[222] Advertisement in Sponsor, March 30, 1957, front cover.

'original promotional and sales ideas."[223] Also in April, Bartell sold JAPL, Appleton for $100,000, and asked the FCC to increase KCBQ's power to 50,000 watts day, 5,000 watts nights, which it subsequently did.[224]

WBMS, WYDE, WILD

In May 1957 Bartell bought his first station in a year and a alf, purchasing WBMS, Boston, for $200,000. The facility was a day-imer with 1,000 watts on 1090 kHz. WBMS had played classical music arlier in the '50s, and then turned to pop music-and-news. Bill tewart had his first radio job at WBMS between February 1951 and April f 1953, when he left to join McLendon's KLBS in Houston. Stewart was irst a classical music program host and then program director of WBMS, hich Stewart said tried to compete against Boston's powerful WHDH in rogramming music-and-news.[225] With the purchase of WBMS, Bartell was ack to owning five radio stations, and one TV, but only for a brief ime. By June 1957 Bartell had acquired WILD, Birmingham, Alabama, for ore than $300,000, and had sold his only TV (WMTV-TV, Madison, Wiscon-in) for $550,000. WILD had been a Mutual affiliate on 850 kHz with 0,000 watts full-time and was a good facility--later it would go to 0,000 watts days and 1,000 watts nighttime.[226] In spite of the fact

---

[223]"New Promotion Plan Announced at Bartell 10th Birthday eet," Broadcasting, April 15, 1957, p. 74.

[224]"WBC's WAAM (TV) Buy: $4.4 Million," Broadcasting, May 13, 957, p. 112.

[225]Bill Stewart, private telephone conversation held on June , 1972.

[226]"Bartell Stations Sell WMTV (TV) to WTVJ (TV) Group for 550,000," Broadcasting, June 3, 1957, p. 68.

that WILD was already a pronounceable call, Bartell decided to change the Birmingham station's call to WYDE, effective September 2, 1957. Part of the reason was to provide a new identification for the station's new programming, but another part was the chance to stage a co-promotion with WAKE, calling the pair "the South's WYDE-aWAKE radio team."[227] The change was planned for the Labor Day weekend so that travellers who went into one of 40 restaurants in Birmingham and Atlanta and said "I want to stay WYDE-aWAKE and safe" could get a free cup of coffee. A reported 12,000 cups of coffee were consumed.[228]

Family radio

In June of 1957, Bartell announced an increase of 15% in night rates for his stations. Speaking at a conference of Bartell station managers in San Diego, Bartell also explained the success of his stations by saying that they had long adhered to a "family life" or "family participation" concept, and formally designated his stations as "family stations."[229] In the same speech, Bartell slammed "rock and roll radio operators and the news and music Johnny-come-latelys. . . . We speak out . . . against the flagrant invalidity of the 'pulpy' sensational approach to news and music. . . ."[230] "Family participation" was defined by Bartell as

---

[227] "New Call Letters for Some Bartell Stations," Sponsor, August 31, 1957, p. 89.

[228] "Bartell Promotion Plugs WILD's Change to WYDE," Broadcasting, September 23, 1957, p. 99.

[229] Photo caption, Broadcasting, July 8, 1957, p. 75.

[230] Ibid.

> . . . a captivating combination of happy musical entertainment, bright news presentation with stimulating editorial material, pleasant reminiscences, games for family fun, interesting revelations of community life, and a constant, never-ending joining of hearts and spirits, moment by moment.[231]

Being a bit more specific, Bartell claimed that the plan, which played older and nostalgic records along with the hits was designed to

> . . . keep[s] the teen-age element to a minimum, perhaps 15 percent of total audience, since their buying power represents much less. Similarly, we don't cater only to housewives, young marrieds, kiddies, or baseball fans in any time period. We maintain an all-family pattern throughout the schedule. . . .[232]

Bartell trades ads in the fall of 1957 stressed the "family radio" theme, with an ad for WYDE announcing its emergence into first place with ratings increases of up to 67% accompanied by the "radio for family life" logo.[233] A "family radio" ad is shown on page 246.[234]

In an interview with Bartell in May 1972 the author inquired, "The 'family radio' concept--was that more of a selling tool really than an actual programming sound?"

> Yeah. We were trying to take the sting off Top 40. That's what it was. When Storz came in and said "we're programming Top 40," when people said what are _you_ programming, we just said, we program "radio for family listening."[235]

Asked further if the special records for Grandma and for Dad were actually played Bartell replied,

---

[231] "Bartell Radio Format Sparks Sponsor $$," _Billboard_, March 17, 1958, p. 9.

[232] _Ibid._

[233] Advertisement in _Sponsor_, December 28, 1957, p. 8.

[234] Advertisement in _Sponsor_, October 28, 1957, p. 41.

[235] Bartell interview.

Family Radio Reaches Them All!
Ratings show Bartell Group stations FIRST . . . and reach more members of the family. "Radio For Family Life" requires talent and imagination. No short cuts. More work — but worth it!
BARTELL
BARTELL GROUP FAMILY RADIO
is based upon service and entertainment for the whole family . . . Emphasizing optimism, happiness, generosity, decency, patriotism . . . Homely virtues, basic values in family life.
Bartell It... and Sell It!
THE BARTELL GROUP
RADIO FOR FAMILY LIFE
KCBQ
WOKY
WILD
KRUX
WYDE
WAKE
Sold Nationally by ADAM YOUNG, Inc
for WOKY, The KATZ Agency
AMERICA'S FIRST RADIO FAMILY
SERVING 10 MILLION BUYERS

Aw, we said that, but it was for the people. Because, Grandma is no different from anybody else. It was just a gimmick. It's a little dishonest, but it's promotion. Its nature is slightly generalized . . . you know, and so you say. . . . I'm glad to get the hell out of it, frankly. I never felt real clean doing it. I never felt as if I were doing the best work that I could do. I feel much more competent doing other things like work in the arts and drama.[236]

he "family radio" concept, then, was only lightly adhered to in pro-ramming, but was much talked of in trades ads and to prospective lients. Bartell was upset with Todd Storz's use of the term "Top 40" nd its application to him because of the "teenage" and "jukebox" onnotations it lent to his stations.

. . . Todd Storz, who was a man who really understood beer and beer packaging--that was his father's business--thought there was nothing wrong in saying, well, we have the best ingredients in beer; we've got the best ingredients in radio--we give you the top 40 tunes! Jeez, that's just a very amateurish thing to say, but still it was picked up--naturally, by our critics--who'd say, "The jukebox king comes out for the 'Top 40.'" That's what they called me in San Francisco when I bought the station out there. "The jukebox king is in town." "The Top 40." And they just killed it. The agencies picked it up. The agencies said, you're supposed to be a cultured man--Top 40, oh. . . .

. . . I tried to use a scholarly approach on the agencies. In New York I assembled the top agencies, I got their research people, I sat them down, we had everybody there, I showed why if they were interested in another kind of programming I'd be very glad to send them records for their homes, and they could play them all they want, but if they were trying to reach this market, this was the way to get it, and I could prove it in every single market we'd been in--and they nodded their heads and refused to buy![237]

KYA

In early 1958, Bartell was negotiating to buy KYA, San Fran-isco, for $1,000,000, which would bring the group to its limit of

---

[236] Bartell interview. [237] *Ibid.*

seven stations. KYA, with 5,000 watts days and 1,000 watts nights on 1260 kHz was a good facility, and San Francisco until its entry had ha only one other Top 40 station, KOBY (10,000 watts fulltime at 1550). KSFO had been in first place for a number of years, having pioneered music-and-news in the city but adhering to a middle-of-the-road music policy when Top 40 came in.[238] By the summer of 1959, KYA and KOBY were virtually tied for second place behind KSFO.[239]

WOV/WADO

In July of 1959, the Bartells spent another $1,434,908 to buy WOV, New York, a 5,000 watt station on 1280 kHz with a directional antenna. Later in the summer, Gerald Bartell obtained 25-year exclusi contracts for new TV stations in Curacao and Aruba in the Netherland Antilles. The group had already joined with J. Elroy McCaw, owner of WINS, New York, in building a TV station in Port au Prince, Haiti. By the following year (1960), WOV had been renamed WADO, and was programm progressively more of what Billboard termed "pop-styled, Top 40 progra ming" where previously it had programmed in blocks for Negro, Italian, and Spanish audiences, separately. Billboard said, ". . . it was believed the sale was made with the understanding that the new management would continue the old WOV policy of serving these three markets."[240] In later years, WADO has concentrated more heavily on

---

[238] At one time in the early 1950s, now comedienne Phyllis Diller was KSFO's promotion manager.

[239] "Longhair Vs. Short in Bay Area," Broadcasting, July 20, 1959, p. 50.

[240] "WADO Will Alter Format," Billboard, May 23, 1960, p. 3.

Spanish programming, currently programming 155 hours of Spanish programs weekly.[241] If Bartell had planned to program more heavily to the Black population at first, he made the change more cautiously and with less uproar than did McLendon in the WGES/WYNR case of 1962.

In September of 1960, in the same week that Robert Rounsaville sold his WQXI, Atlanta, for $1,600,000, Bartell sold both WAKE, Atlanta (for $500,000) and WYDE, Birmingham (for $525,000) to Ira Herbert and Bernice Judis. Bernice Judis (Mrs. Herbert) had for many years been the general manager of WNEW, New York.

In 1961, Bartell Broadcasting was melded into the newly-formed Bartell Media Corporation of which Gerald Bartell was president between 1961 and 1963, and of which he is in 1972 still chairman of the board. Although the Bartell name is still attached to WOKY, Milwaukee; KCBQ, San Diego; WADO, New York; WMYQ-FM, Miami; and WDRQ-FM, Detroit; Bartell himself no longer owns any radio stations. Bartell says that he was involved in making programming policy only up to about 1960.[242]

Like the Storz stations and the McLendon stations, the Bartell stations were pioneers of "formula" radio in their respective cities. Like the Storz and McLendon outlets, the Bartell stations became strong ratings leaders, although their advertising did not make this point as forcefully nor as often as did that of Storz and McLendon. Bartell's trades advertising was always more concerned with the qualitative makeup of the audience, rather than its size. However razzle-dazzle was the sound of the stations, in sales approach Bartell was all business and

---

[241] Broadcasting Yearbook, 1972, p. B-142.

[242] Bartell interview.

dignity. He seems to have been plagued by the disparity between the knowledge that a successful radio station should be objectively programmed for the mass taste and the realization that to do so involved a certain pandering to a common denominator.

> You know, I was in show business all my life, in one way or another. When I was at [the University of Wisconsin's] WHA I'd be outraged if an awful lot of people who were the wrong type of people were listening to WHA. It should be the intellectual type, the more thoughtful type. I wouldn't offend them by doing the things on a radio station that was devoted to education and culture as I did on WOKY. WOKY and the Bartell group was interested in masses. And I knew that in order to attract the mass, you had to establish a number of things. The pace had to be a certain rate--I mean fast, fast, fast! And there was never to be a moment of dead air. Now, that would offend me--I don't like that myself. That's why I found it very difficult to listen to our own radio stations. . . . Why? because it was just so frantic; it just goes on. . . .[243]

Plough

Of the four groups most often mentioned as pioneers of the Top 40 format, Plough Broadcasting is by far the least reported. The Plough group might not be listed here at all except that they acquired stations in top markets at the same time the other three operators were expanding, and Plough developed a programming variation which--unlike that of the other three--has undergone almost no change since its inception.

Plough Station Acquisitions

WMPS

Plough Broadcasting Co. is a subsidiary of Plough, Inc., a drug manufacturing firm which makes St. Joseph aspirin, Mexsana foot powder, suntan lotion, and other products. The parent company was established

---

[243] Ibid.

in 1908. Over the years, Plough, Inc. had spent tens of millions of dollars in advertising, first primarily in newspapers and then later in radio, so it was not unreasonable for the company to consider the acquisition of radio stations both as outlets for its advertising but also as a diversified investment as the company grew. Plough, Inc. purchased the first of its stations, WMPS, Memphis, in March 1945, and established a subsidiary, WMPS, Inc. to administer it. Harold R. Krelstein, who today is President of Plough Broadcasting, Inc., was made a president of WMPS, Inc. WMPS today operates with 10,000 watts days, 5,000 watts nights on 680 kHz.

WJJD

In August of 1953, Plough, Inc. bought its second radio station, and set up the Plough Broadcasting Company to run it and WMPS, again with Harold Krelstein as the president. The newly-acquired station was WJJD, Chicago, a 50,000 watt limited-time independent (limited time meaning that WJJD operated directionally on 1160 Hz, the frequency of class 1-A clear-channel KSL, Salt Lake City. Since KSL operated at night, WJJD could not operate at all after sunset.

WJJD had an interesting history even before the acquisition by Plough. In 1944, WJJD was sold to Marshall Field, the department store owner by Ralph L. Atlass, Leslie Atlass, P. K. Wrigley, and A. M. Linick. Ralph Atlass and P. K. Wrigley were principal owners of WIND, Chicago, a fulltime station on 560 kHz. A fulltime operation allowing nighttime programming was crucially important to a radio station in the 1940s, so that when the FCC's duopoly rule required owners of more than one of the same type facility in a locality to divest themselves of all but one station, WJJD was the one sold for $700,000. Nine years later, in 1953, Field sold it to Plough for $900,000.[244] At the time of the sale, WJJD was an independent station, and when Plough assumed formal control in September 1953 WJJD began broadcasting a form of music-and-news which was approximately like that of WIND, which in turn was quite like WNEW, New York.[245] By 1956, WJJD had refined its format into what was described as a "Top 40" operation, meaning both a more limited record playlist than previously and other restrictions.[246] (Plough's sound will be detailed later.) WJJD was a strong success with the format until ABC turned WLS into the Midwest's top rock station in the early 1960s.

WCAO, WCOP

In 1956, Plough bought its third and fourth stations less than a week apart. In late March the company bought WCAO, Baltimore for about $600,000. WCAO, a CBS affiliate, operated on 600 kHz with 5,000 watts, using a directional antenna. As mentioned in another chapter, WITH had for a number of years been a dominant music-and-news station in Baltimore with only 250 watts. WCAO's entry would jeopardize that position. At the time of its WCAO purchase, it was announced that Plough planned to acquire its legal limit of seven stations, to be

---

[244]"Plough, Inc. Buys WJJD for $900,000," Broadcasting, August 10, 1953, p. 68.

[245]"FCC Approves Plough Buy of WJJD; 13 Station Transfers Granted," Broadcasting, September 14, 1953, p. 56, and "Plough Inc. Stations in Chi & Hub K.O. 'Top 40' for New 'Sound' Via IBM," Variety, August 15, 1962, p. 41.

[246]"Plough Inc. Stations in Chi & Hub.....," p. 41.

ocated in cities of more than 500,000 population.[247]

By the beginning of April 1956 Plough had bought its fourth tation, WCOP in Boston, from an owner of the Boston Post for a reported 450,000. WCOP which only five years before had sold for just $150,000, perated on 1150 kHz with 5,000 watts, also with a directional ntenna.[248] At the same time as it announced the sale, Broadcasting eported that Able Plough, the parent company's president, was negotiat-ng to buy WQAM, Miami (which would go instead to Todd Storz), and was also "looking over stations in Texas."[249]

Shortly after the Plough's acquisition of the Baltimore station, he CBS affiliation was dropped to make it an independent like the other three Plough stations. Obviously, speaking of WCAO, Harold Krel-stein told Broadcasting in a symposium on "Network Radio: Pro, Con":

> Some networks have done two things. First, they have taken their program service away; then they have taken their money away, but they haven't given back any of the time. Now, you talk about network revenue. I know this, that we were able to buy one station in particular only because it was a network station and its revenue had fallen apart and the people that owned it just didn't know what to do about it, and that station's income this year is about 10% of what it was some four, five, six, seven years ago, but the network, on the other hand, still has under its control the same number of hours that it had. Now, from the standpoint of pure economics something has got to give. Either the license has to go back or the station has got to get more money from the network or it has to get rid of the network in the belief that it can program that time just as well as the network did and increase its revenue. . . .[250]

---

[247] "Plough Broadcasting Adds WCAO-AM-FM to Station List," Broadcasting, March 26, 1956, p. 85.

[248] "Plough Buys WCOP, Second in Week," Broadcasting, April 2, 1956, p. 70.

[249] "Plough Inc.," Broadcasting, April 2, 1956, p. 5.

[250] "Network Radio: Pro, Con," Broadcasting, November 5, 1956, p. 61.

In the same interview, Krelstein also claimed that the programming of the Plough stations had increased the sets-in-use figures in their four cities.[251]

Plough seems to have run a regular schedule of trades ads in 1957, most of which pointed to the ratings leadership of their stations. Each featured a sleepy-eyed little cartoon man, who often was dangling a cigar from his hand as he contemplated the ratings news. In February, WMPS in Memphis claimed a first in Pulse, Hooper and Nielsen;[252] in May WCOP, Boston was billed as "fastest rising radio station in Boston!" with a second-place standing as of February 1957;[253] in October WJJD, Chicago claimed a first for weekday afternoons and a third place for mornings.[254] The WJJD advertisement concluded with the sentence, "No gimmicks, no giveaways, no promotions, just solid programming for solid listeners who really listen!"[255] An ad for WCOP, Boston in November claimed a first place in out-of-home listening, and a second place in weekday daytimes.[256]

In June of 1957, Plough ran an ad in the trades which was headlined with a bold "Notice!" and which announced the copyrighting of the Plough programming formula. A copy of that ad is reproduced on

---

[251] Ibid.

[252] Advertisement in Sponsor, February 9, 1957, p. 65.

[253] Advertisement in Broadcasting, May 20, 1957, p. 19.

[254] Advertisement in Sponsor, October 5, 1957, p. 23.

[255] Ibid.

[256] Advertisement in Broadcasting, November 4, 1957, p. 15.

page 256.[257] The ad, of course, was an attempt to call attention to the unique nature of the Plough programming formula, but it was also an attempt to decrease the outright piracy of phrases, program intros and outros, and features that by this time had become widespread, as increasing numbers of owners turned to Top 40 as the answer to increasing revenues. In July of 1957, Storz would make a similar announcement.

Joe Csida, writing in his "Sponsor Backstage" column in the July 13 Sponsor, devoted all of his space to explaining the Plough announcement and formula. Csida said that it was not clear whether the formula was indeed copyrightable, but that the company had copyrighted their "Operating Manual & Policies for the Broadcast Services of Plough, Inc." Csida had glanced through the manual and said that it ". . . spells out in the most minute detail the manner in which music, news and public service of the most practical nature are blended into an unending program sequence. The effect, in other words, of the Plough formula, is not to create blocks of programs, with little relationship one to the other, but to create a 24-hour program, all elements of which flow into all other elements."[258] This is hardly a revelation, but it is interesting to note that Plough and Bartell both managed to condense their policies into a single book. McLendon started with several in the early days and kept adding them as his holdings grew, so that today there are well over 50 McLendon Policy Book notebooks.

---

[257] Advertisement in Broadcasting, June 17, 1957, p. 19.

[258] Joe Csida, "Sponsor Backstage," Sponsor, July 13, 1957, p. 20.

NOTICE!

The success of the program formula of the Plough, Inc., Stations: **Radio Baltimore — WCAO; Radio Boston — WCOP; Radio Chicago — WJJD** and **Radio Memphis — WMPS,** is widely recognized not only by the public but by local, regional and national advertisers, and other broadcasters.

The production and method of presentation of the program formula of the Plough, Inc., Stations is fully protected by copyright. All rights are fully reserved and no portion may be lawfully used without the express written permission of Plough, Inc., copyright owner.

For information on how you may obtain exclusive rights to use this copyrighted production and program formula, contact: President, Plough Broadcasting Stations, P. O. Box 248, Memphis, Tennessee.

GA-WPLO

In July of 1959, Plough took over its next radio station--the rmer WAGA in Atlanta, Georgia. WAGA (CBS affiliate, 5,000 watts on 0 kHz) had been owned for years by Storer Broadcasting and was almost ld to Bartell to replace his 250-watt WAKE.[259] Bartell says that he ven made a handshake deal on buying WAGA, but Storer backed out when is attorneys told him that Bartell would have to sell WAKE first efore he could buy another station in the same market.[260]

WAGA was renamed WPLO (for Plough, Inc.) and became the third usic-and-news outlet in Atlanta (after WAKE and WQXI). WAKE eventually as sold by Bartell, leaving WQXI and WPLO, who fought each other for everal years. Finally, WPLO converted to a country-and-western format, s did WJJD and WCOP, but first the stations tried a "more adult" ound, adding upbeat instrumentals and swinging vocals--in effect astly expanding the playlist beyond the Top 40. Plough made much of he fact that this programming was designed by computer printout, with 0,000 recordings available to choose from.[261]

The Top 40 formula which Plough developed in the mid-1950s was nique in that it featured a minimum of deejay talk and "personality." ersonalities were so secondary to the Plough formula that they were ssigned "house names," (names such as Johnny Dollar or Clyde Coffee) hich remain with the station and the time slot no matter who actually

---

[259] Bartell interview. [260] Ibid.

[261] "Plough Programs by the Numbers," Broadcasting, August 13, 962, p. 59, and "Plough Inc. Stations in Chi & Hub K.O. 'Top 40' for ew 'Sound' Via IBM," Variety, August 15, 1962, p. 41.

does the show. Thus, disc jockeys could leave a Plough station, but the station would not suffer since the name remained. Had the jockeys been able to do much talking, the difference between the original one and his replacement might have been apparent, but talk was anathema.

With a less-talk policy, Plough stations were able to play more music, and they became known as "jukeboxes" for just this reason at that time. More than ten years later, Bill Drake, the well-known programming consultant, used the same basic approach in making the stations he represented so widely successful: less talk, more music. There are a number of other details which Drake added, as will be described later, but the "jukebox" sound was basically that pioneered by Plough stations in the mid-1950s.

WSUN

At the time of this writing, Plough Broadcasting has just announced the acquisition of WSUN, St. Petersburg-Tampa, Florida, for $2,000,000.[262] The facility is a good one: 5,000 watts on 620 kHz; but the current price for such a facility (as compared with prices in the 1950s) is remarkable. It seems likely that the station will program either country-and-western or contemporary music as do the other stations in the group.

Other Group Owners

A number of other group owners developed the Top 40 format with considerable success, and probably deserve mention. They are not

---

[262]"Plough to Pay $2 Million for Florida AM," Broadcasting, September 25, 1972, p. 32.

treated here because (1) most did not contribute very much that was new, and (2) most did not garner the attention that Storz, McLendon, Bartell and Plough received. In a later section, the process of diffusion by which contests, phrases, and gimmicks spread from one market to another is explored, but it should be noted here that informal contact, deliberate monitoring and copying, and articles and advertisements in the trade press were the three principal means by which ideas were diffused. It is simple fact that the trade press was most attentive to McLendon and Storz, to Bartell less so and to Plough hardly at all. The author believes that Storz and McLendon were given more coverage because they supplied the press both with releases of prepared copy and also (and more importantly) with new "angles"--new developments to talk about. The "angle" very often grew out of a station's promotion, so that while a station was increasing its share of audience or of advertising dollars, it also--by being reported in the trades--increased its reputation among other broadcasters. Thus, Storz and McLendon, being heavily involved in audience promotion, were more thoroughly reported, and came to be identified (rightly) as pioneers. Bartell concentrated more on advertising promotion, but was also highly reported for the imaginative merchandising campaigns conceived for both his stations and his advertisers. Plough--more corporate than personalized in image, and more conservative in its programming--was correspondingly less-reported. Smaller, still less flamboyant groups have thus remained virtually unknown to the readers of the trade press.

Four Principal Group Owners Compared

A number of differences and similarities exist among the four principal group owners of Top 40 stations described above. McLendon bought his first station in 1947, Storz his first in 1949, Bartell his first in 1947, and Plough their first in 1945. Bartell, in his own words, had "been in show business all my life,"[263] while McLendon had been connected with show business through his father's chain of motion picture theaters, for which he handled much of the advertising and promotion. Storz Brewing and Plough, Inc. were both manufacturing companies not directly connected with radio except by advertising--for both, the entry into radio was a diversification of holdings. The men who acted as heads of the four radio operating companies were all comparatively young; none was tied to the older ideas of what "proper" (i.e., network-type) radio should be like, although McLendon for a time operated the Liberty network with some typical network programs.

Of the four, only the Bartell group depended solely on broadcasting for its capital and its revenue; Plough and Storz both had their parent companies (although Storz Broadcasting operated virtually autonomously of Robert Storz's money after the beginning with KOWH), and the McLendons held numerous other corporations making money principally in oil, real estate, and movie theaters.

All four group heads were bright, educated men. Bartell had even been an associate professor at the University of Wisconsin. Curiously, the two most famous men, McLendon and Storz, share an obscur

---

[263] Bartell interview.

vocation from their service in World War II--both were cryptographers in military intelligence. It is interesting to ponder just what the aptitude or the training for that job may have had to do with their later success in developing Top 40.

CHAPTER FOUR

MANAGEMENT PHILOSOPHIES AND PROCEDURES BEHIND TOP 40

This chapter and the one which follows are concerned with the development of the Top 40 format and formula. The term "format" should be recognized as different from the word "formula." "Format" is the more generalized term, and other generalized words define elements of a format--words such as "popular music," "local news," "commercials," and so on. A "formula" is a detailed refinement of a format, and uses specific words and phrases to explain in detail how each element of a format should be interwoven to form the whole. Describing a format is much easier than describing a formula. The phrase "music and news" is a basic format description; the term "Top 40 station" is more specific as to type of music played but does not begin to describe the formula the station uses to differentiate itself from other "Top 40" stations.

As has been explained earlier, Top 40 radio grew out of the music-and-news format which had existed for a number of years. In the case of music-and-news stations, the format was virtually identical with the formula--there was very little else involved in the "sound hour" on such stations in the way of specialized and featured elements. There was a wide variety of music, there was a disc jockey host who provided commentary, there was news, there were commercials, public service announcements, and a limited number of station promotions (or simple IDs). Earlier music-and-news programs often featured full rather than participating sponsorship, so that in addition to the breaks in program continuity when news was read or station IDs were given, there were also natural breaks when the sponsorship changed. Sometimes the type of music changed when the sponsorship changed, because the sponsor had specified the kind of music he wanted.

In contrast to the music-and-news stations, the Top 40 station's formula was often built around a "clock hour" which called for certain elements to occur at very carefully prescribed times. For example, a Top 40 station might specify that the song played at the "top" of the hour be a hit from the top ten, and that its rhythm be uptempo. The next record might also be a hit, or perhaps a "hitbound" or a familiar "oldie," but whatever the variation, each different type of music to be played would be prescribed in advance. In addition, stations employing "clocks" also built in times at which certain non-musical features such as weather forecasts, traffic reports, sports scores and so on were to be given. Variations of such "clocks" are in use today at many stations that would not describe themselves as "formula" operations, but which nevertheless appeal to listeners and advertisers by offering certain program features at regular, familiar intervals.

A description of two "clocks" dealing only with what music is to be played will clarify the term. In 1956, WGTO, Cypress Gardens, Florida, was specifying that in a one hour show, jocks should play one record from the current top five list, one from the current six to ten list, four from any of the "first five" lists for the past eight years, six standards and three new releases.[1] A more confusing example is that of WAMM, Flint, Michigan, which in 1958 was beginning every half hour with a "6-T formula." First in the hour was a WAMM Tune Tip, a new record. Next was one of the WAMM Tip Top Tunes, from the top-60 list. Third, a WAMM All-Time Tune (million seller) was heard, followed next by another Tip Top Tune. Fifth came another All Time Tune, and sixth another Tip Top Tune. If the deejay got all of these completed in a half hour and could still talk, the formula was repeated.[2]

Top 40 Group Owners' Programming Philosophies

Basic Tenets

Programming before sales

It will be established that Top 40 management put programming considerations ahead of sales considerations. In so doing, Top 40 management freed itself from sponsor-dictation of music content (although the increasing use of participating sponsorship announcements also contributed). With the music out of the sponsor's control, the most important ingredient in determining the station's overall "style" became management's prerogative.

Lawrence W. Lichty has described a list of "Factors That Influence Broadcast Programming" in an unpublished paper which seeks to define categories and to build a preliminary model. Among the factors are the availability of materials for programs; economics (general, broadcast industry, and local station); competition; management policy

---

[1] Joe Csida, "Sponsor Backstage," Sponsor, January 23, 1956, p. 116.

[2] June Bundy, "Vox Jox," Billboard, April 21, 1958, p. 10.

and philosophy; sponsor policy and philosophy; the invention, imitation, and decline of programs; technical inventions and improvements; government regulation and legal sanctions; self-regulation and pressure groups; audience preferences; and social context.[3]

The present treatment has already touched on a number of the factors listed by Lichty, especially the ready availability of popular music on phonograph records, the decline in revenues in the radio industry except for those stations programming music and news, the competitive situation radio found itself in with the advent of TV, suburbanization, decreasing median age of the public, the networks' general failure to meet the new challenges, and the state of broadcast production equipment development in the period in question. Management policy and philosophy (and sponsor policy and philosophy) have not been treated in detail until now.

Management involvement

The four Top 40 group owners discussed earlier had a number of traits in common, but most important was the philosophy that management should be thoroughly involved in the development of the programming which actually reached the audience. On the surface, this may not seem a radical departure, for licensees had been responsible for their stations' programming since the earliest Radio Commissions. But in fact, most radio station owners prior to the Top 40 era did not become involved in the minutest attention to detail which characterized

[3]Dr. Lawrence W. Lichty, "Factors That Influence Broadcast Programming," unpublished paper based on Lawrence W. Lichty, "'The Nation's Station'--A History of Radio Station WLW," unpublished Ph.D. dissertation, Ohio State University, 1964.

management among the four Top 40 group owners.

One example of management's direct involvement in determining programming will demonstrate the point. In August of 1953, C. E. Hooper, President of the Hooper ratings firm, gave a talk in Dallas on his new methods of measuring out-of-home radio listening. The Trinity Policy Books contain the full text of Hooper's talk, but the text is preceded by the letter below from McLendon to his station managers:

"The Automobile Listening Audience"

> Now that we are attacking the problems of programming and getting listeners scientifically and going after ratings, I think it behooves us to know as much as possible about the sets-in-use and method of rating as it is possible for us to know.
>
> HOOPER IN A DALLAS SPEECH GAVE SOME FIGURES WHICH I THINK CAN BE ONE OF THE MOST IMPORTANT SALES AND PROGRAM WEAPONS WE HAVE EVER HAD.
>
> Before I give you his figures, let me say that all of us have known that for years radio has been giving away its out-of-home audience--the car radios, business places, hospitals, etc. In an effort to meet growing competition, Hooper is attempting to find a way of measuring this out-of-home audience. He has just about succeeded in experiments currently under way in San Francisco and I am inclined to go along with the accuracy of his method much more so than I am the recall method being used by Pulse.
>
> In order for you to get the full significance of the figures he gave, it is necessary for you to keep two important details in mind--viz., 75% of all automobiles have car radios that are in working order, and that, secondly, 90% of all out-of-home listening is done in cars. This second fact is particularly vital. It means that as much as we talk about the business places, hospitals, portables, etc., nine out of every ten people listening out of the home are listening in cars.
>
> Thus, if Hooper's figures are correct, his present measurement of homes plus the proposed added measurement of cars will give us a measurement of all but the infinitesimally small fraction listening in business places, hospitals and on portables. For all practical purposes, then, homes plus car radios will be a complete measurement. . . .
>
> * * * * * * * * * * *
>
> Add the two together and you have the following: 25.2% of the people are listening to their radios in the eight to nine

[A.M.] period. Not necessarily to one station, obviously, but the listening audience is still over a quarter of the people--actually listening.

EXPRESSING IT IN ANOTHER WAY, AT THIS HOUR MORE THAN 40% OF YOUR POTENTIAL AUDIENCE IS LISTENING IN CARS.

Between two and two fifteen in the afternoon, the percentage is even more striking. While only 8.4 of one hundred percent are listening at home, 10.1% are listening in cars, or a total tune-in of 18.6.

The figures between five and six seem strange to me, unless San Francisco people work later than elsewhere, but they still show 18.8 listening in homes and 7.4 in automobiles or a total tune-in of 26.2.

NOW, THE STATIONS WHO PLAY MUSIC AND GIVE A LITTLE NEWS ARE THE ONES WHICH HAVE THE AUDIENCE IN AUTOMOBILES. (WITH THE COMING OF TELEVISION, THEY ARE ALSO THE STATIONS WHICH HAVE THE AUDIENCE IN HOMES.)

Let's do something affirmative about capturing that tremendous out-of-home audience listening in automobiles. For one thing, I want each of the Trinity stations to put in headlines on the half-hour at six-thirty, seven-thirty, eight-thirty A.M.; four-thirty and five-thirty P.M.

Make these headlines ever so brief and emphasize that full details will be given on the next hourly newscast. I WANT EACH STATION AT SEVEN AND EIGHT A.M. AND AT FIVE AND SIX P.M. TO PUT IN A FORTY-FIVE SECOND TO ONE MINUTE SPORTS PAGE OF THE AIR AS PART OF THEIR FIVE-MINUTE NEWSCAST.

There are probably some other things we can do to nail down the audience in cars, and not lose them at home. One station in San Francisco has a program called "Car-Tunes" especially designed for this audience. We would not want to vary our program in this way but it is an example of how seriously we must begin to take this tremendous new tune-in in cars.[4]

Objectivism, filling a void

If there is any one characteristic programming philosophy that applies to all four Top 40 group owners it is objectivism. For all four, subjective tastes in programming were subjugated to objective appraisal of what the public actually desired to hear. The old presumptions about programming stars, big bands, major record labels and

[4]Gordon McLendon, "The Automobile Listening Audience," Trinity Policy Books, August, 1953, n.p.

formal or relaxed announcers were all re-examined. The results were expressed in different philosophies for different groups, but objectivism is at the core in each case.

For Gordon McLendon, a key phrase became "filling a void." In an interview with Richard K. Doan over WNEW in 1967, McLendon explained how this philosophy developed.

> Years ago when radio was at its lowest ebb and when it was kind of like the position that the British were in at Dunkirk, when our backs were to the beaches in radio, it seemed to me that if we were going to survive against that first crashing onslaught of television, that radio's only survival would have to come in doing something that television either could not do or could not do as well, i.e., furnishing to the public a utility. And as it was in 1949 or 1950, radio at that time was not furnishing to the public, by and large--WNEW, by the way, was furnishing--it was one of the very few stations, interestingly enough, furnishing the public a utility. It was furnishing music and news, something that television didn't do and certainly didn't--and can't do as well.[5]

McLendon Programming Philosophy

In a 1969 speech, which McLendon said he hoped would be his "final speech in the field of radio and television for reasons that will remain private with me," the group owner enlarged on his philosophies for the young aspiring broadcasters.[6]

> . . . I have always been a listener, concerned almost entirely with what came out over the radio. Nothing has ever happened to change me in all of those years and I feel now as then that it is the programs, which come out over radio's loudspeaker or on television's screen, that are all that matter in the end.

---

[5]Gordon McLendon and Richard K. Doan, "The Truth About Radio: A WNEW Inquiry," transcript of interview broadcast on WNEW, New York, May 14, 1967, pp. 2, 3.

[6]Gordon McLendon, "The Time Before This," a speech given before Alpha Epsilon Rho, Detroit, Michigan, April 29, 1969, p. 1.

> If those programs are good enough, you will have many listeners, thus a high rating, and inevitably excellent sales. . . .[7]
>
> But am I not reciting a mere truism? I think not. Notice, as your career progresses, the number of licensees far more concerned with sales problems, or new and ingenious ways to hold down costs, and not a few of whom are concentrating largely on the engineering end of their station. . . .
>
> I can never be anything else but a program man. I have never bought a radio station for other than one reason: because I believed I could improve its programming and make it a success. I have never bought a successful station. I have always bought sick stations, stations sick because of their sick programming, and because of their sick programming, sick in sales. I have never taken over a station and improved its programming that its sales problems did not shortly disappear. I have never owned a 50,000 watt clear-channel station that could be neglected or even abused and still shove its way, through sheer kilowatts, to a position of power. Our philosophy in deciding whether to buy a certain station in a certain market has always been: Is there some program service of utility to a large enough group here that is either (a) not now being provided or (b) not being provided as well as we can provide it.[8]

McLendon's own statement of his philosophy is corroborated by Bill Stubblefield, a longtime friend of McLendon's and a man who as a station broker both bought and sold many of McLendon's stations. Stubblefield says,

> Gordon's completely program-oriented, and I think, tends to surround himself with people who <u>also</u> are program-oriented. Gordon would rely on his attorney or myself or his comptroller for decisions that I wouldn't let anyone make for me. Given a chance to study a balance sheet on a proposed purchase, Gordon would--hell, he would much rather be in the control room recording a spot. . . . He has to <u>make</u> himself--and always has--make himself look at the sales side. His theory has always been if you program it right, and keep it on top with programming, sales will follow, or at least it will be easier to sell. And this is true. . . .[9]

---

[7] <u>Ibid</u>., p. 1.

[8] <u>Ibid</u>., p. 2.

[9] Mr. Bill Stubblefield, private interview held in Casanova, Virginia, Friday, October 8, 1971.

Asked if it was McLendon's philosophy to extend a particular format in acquiring his various stations, Stubblefield replied

> . . . We always depended on the facility. Gordon was always very conscious of whether we had power or not. . . . If he could buy the right facility, he would have gone the KLIF format in any market. But he would not take an inferior facility and try to do the job against someone who could beat him. So, he would take another format. . . .
>
> . . . I think Gordon had a pre-conceived idea every time we bought a station as to what we would do, but if it didn't start working on the profit-and-loss statement pretty quickly, we'd change it. So, I can't read into that any great carrying of a banner. . . .
>
> . . . We pretty well picked out a list of the cities we wanted to be in. This was my assignment. In other words, if you can develop something in these markets, we'll be interested in it. But I really don't think that was because he had a preconceived idea of what he was going to program in those markets. . . .[10]

Stubblefield feels that McLendon's concentration on programming--and putting programming ahead of sales and other considerations--was one of his major contributions to the radio industry. Thus, the comment about McLendon being more interested in the control room than in the profit-and-loss figures is not meant as a criticism. In fact, McLendon has characterized himself the same way:

> . . . we run a rather large chain of radio stations. Drop in some day. You'll most often find the manager entertaining the bigwigs and handling employee business. You'll find me in some back room writing a piece of copy or trying to dream up a new idea to pass on to my managers for execution. I figure the promotion, exploitation and programming of my radio stations is the most important thing I can do to help them. It may sound to you like menial work for an owner but that's not right. It's the most important work an owner can do.[11]

---

[10] Ibid.

[11] Gordon McLendon, "The Great Drive-In Theatre Robbery," a speech made before a group of motion picture theater owners, mimeographed, n.d., pp. 6, 7.

McLendon's faith in programming as the most important aspect of station operation led him to propose a completely laissez-faire approach to programming considerations by the FCC. He was particularly upset with the old FCC requirements (described earlier) which sought to have all stations air a percentage of seven different categories of programs. In a 1962 speech at the World's Fair of Music and Sound he said of the old requirement

> . . . This is done in an endeavor to force radio stations to serve the broadest possible community need. I propose to demonstrate conclusively that such a requirement is diametrically opposed to better radio, defies all laws of the free market place and, in so doing, throttles radio. A radio station today should serve not the broadest need but rather the narrowest. . . .
>
> In the free market place, where talent and imagination have freedom from fear, the good operators will drive out the bad. Any law forcing a sameness of radio, forcing a programming common denominator, acts as a protection to the talentless, a shield for the lazy, a haven for the idea thief, a legal shelter and sanction for the mediocre.
>
> Commercial announcements are also a part of programming. Any regulation seeking to limit the number of commercial announcements on any radio station operates directly to impede better radio. The forces of competition will take care of any radio station broadcasting more commercials than the public wishes to hear. At times, our own radio stations have become overly-commercial. Notice the result: listeners tune away, ratings drop, sponsors leave, and the competitive market place has quickly forced us to adjust our commercial content. The essential governing law of commercial radio is this: the radio listener will tune off any station to which he does not care to listen. . . .
>
> . . . Chairman Newton Minow's preoccupance with programming has no doubt had some beneficial side results but when the Chairman cautions "those few of you who really believe that the public interest is merely what interests the public," he is guilty of a contradiction. The only public interest is what interests the public. . . .
>
> . . . The forces of the public interest are the forces of the free market and, left unimpaired, they are operative; left absolutely unimpaired, they are absolutely operative. . . .[12]

---

[12] Gordon McLendon, "Radio: The Years to Come," a speech at the World's Fair of Music and Sound, Chicago, Illinois, September 6, 1962, pp. 2, 4, 5, 9.

To summarize, "filling a void" means programming something different from, or better than, what is already available in a market. It is based on an objective survey of the audience and the premise that the public interest _is_ what interests the public. Competition brings specialization and creates the void in the first place, but further specialization also fills the void.

It is interesting to note that the concept of "filling a void" was operative in McLendon's failure to beat Bartell's WOKY with his WRIT in Milwaukee, although WRIT's poor facility also figured heavily. Another example: when Plough bought WAGA in Atlanta and changed it to become the third Top 40 station in the market as WPLO, Bartell sold WAKE because it could not compete in terms of power, but also because with WPLO, WQXI and WAKE all running the same thing, WAKE no longer filled a void.

Finally, it should be mentioned that filling a void is not necessarily synonymous with introducing a new program form to a market. Sometimes the void seems to be there, but the introduction of the new programming still fails to fill it. The one flaw in McLendon's "fill a void" philosophy is that he seemed to feel that the _exact_ same thing that worked in one market would work in another. In a speech to the San Francisco Advertising Club in 1960, McLendon spoke about the success of the KABL (Oakland) "good music" format and said:

> Three thousand miles to the east, our company is now proving that the programming of KABL will be accepted anywhere. Along the beautiful shores of Lake Erie in Buffalo, New York, America's 14th market, our new WYSL is a virtual duplicate of KABL. In fact, the music on our Buffalo station is programmed entirely from San Francisco. As is always the case when we move into a market, we were told that Buffalo was "different." "Remember,"

our advisors said, "Buffalo is an industrial city--second largest steel city in the nation. This is the home of the awesome, endless ovens of Bethlehem Steel; Buffalo has a highly immigrant population, a polyglot of Polish and Slovak descent."

"Don't make the fatal mistake," we were told again and again, "of comparing Buffalo and San Francisco. They can't be compared. Don't assume that what will work in San Francisco will work in Buffalo.

Yet, finally, that is exactly what we <u>did</u> assume. . . .[13]

Don Keyes, who was National Program Director for McLendon at the time of the WYSL acquisition recalls the Buffalo experience:

> We were so successful with KABL, we bought WYSL in Buffalo, and decided we were going to do the same thing in Buffalo--we were going to kill 'em. Oh! Bomb!!! Jeez! We had "the sunlight glinting off the Delaware building" and the pigeons flying around, and all the Buffalonians said, "Who are you kiddin'?" Buffalo?" "Beautiful Buffalo at sunset?" "You got to be out of your mind!" These were the natives--they were laughing at us. So we finally said, I guess they're right; I guess we can't snow these folks. . . .[14]

Bill Stewart sums up the difficulty of duplicating a format in another market:

> McLendon always made the mistake, I think, of thinking that something that works in one market will work exactly the same way in another market. . . . It won't. There have to be adaptations. I know when I was with Storz, and we went into Miami, sure we did *essentially* the same thing. But you have to make some concessions to local tastes. . . .[15]

Whatever McLendon's lapses in believing that a workable format was transferable intact from one city to another, it is not disputed that he had the showman's ear for what the public would react to. As will be shown later, McLendon's unique contribution to the success of

---

[13]Gordon McLendon, "The Changing Face of Radio," a speech to the San Francisco Advertising Club, May 25, 1960, xeroxed, pp. 1, 2.

[14]Don Keyes, private interview held at WNYN, Canton, Ohio, October 5, 1971.

[15]Bill Stewart, private interview held in Slidell, Louisiana, November 4, 1971.

Top 40 was probably his firm belief in promotion. But the keystone of promotion is having an attractive product to promote, and McLendon, like the other operators, put his programming first.

Storz Programming Philosophy

Todd Storz's philosophy of running his stations also rested on the foundation of objectivism. He is quoted as saying about his stations' music policy:

> . . . The programming of music is out of our hands. It is controlled entirely by the choice of the public. If the public suddenly showed a preference for Chinese music, we would play it. We don't, for example, assume that some people like hill-billy music and therefore put on a program of that type. . . . I do not believe there is any such thing as better or inferior music. I do not think that the listener to either classical or to popular music derives greater satisfaction.[16]

What Storz meant is that station policy should avoid advocacy in the matter of public taste. Management's job is to stay aware of changing public attitudes and be ready to adapt the programming to reflect the changes. Said Storz, "We follow the trend, we do not try to lead it. If that is what is meant by 'cold blooded' then I suppose the charge is true. If we tried to educate the public to our taste, we might have no listeners."[17]

Employing an objective viewpoint in regard to public taste also led Storz to a position similar to McLendon's on sales--that if your programming is right, then sales will follow, because the audience will be there. In a talk at the University of Georgia, Storz said:

---

[16] Herman Land, "The Storz Bombshell," Television Magazine, May 1957, reprint, p. 2 out of 8.

[17] Ibid.

In so many stations today, principal effort and thought is directed almost entirely toward sales. Our philosophy that audience comes first seems to be almost unique. Yet, in almost any other business or industry their product certainly comes first. The manufacturer of a new soap product, for instance, certainly would not devote a lot of money and effort toward sales until he was convinced first that he had a product of high appeal and comparable or better than his competitor's similar product. Audience and sales are not always truly compatible. Sometimes it is necessary to sacrifice sales at least for the moment, to take the long term approach to programming, product and audience.

In order to do its best toward audience a station must retain complete control of all its programming. For example, if a station has built a highly successful block program, let's say from 12 to 2:00 p.m., and a preacher should present himself at the station with an offer to purchase from 1 to 1:15 p.m., cash in hand, the station manager's plight is obvious. If he accepts the program he knows he will hurt his 12 to 2:00 p.m. block program. If he turns down the program he knows he will be sacrificing immediate revenue. Our answer without hesitation would be "no" to any program that didn't fit our overall program schedule. We can justify the loss of immediate revenue by the firm knowledge that we will have that revenue many times over, over a period of time, by adhering to proper program standards. No matter how good a station audience is, I do not mean to suggest that the sales department can be retired. Advertisers will never be knocking down the door to buy time no matter how successful your operation. Nevertheless, with proper programming and audience, the sales resistance is greatly lessened. This is particularly true on renewals since with a large enough audience, results are virtually assured and after all, results are what advertisers buy.

We do not believe that our mission in this world is to educate people because radio is a purely voluntary listening habit--that is, the listener is free to turn the dial or turn the set off--programming cannot be based on compulsive listening. We feel that a station's public service value is closely parallel to the station's rating. For that reason, our programming is all directed to mass listening. We omit virtually all types of minority programming even though, in some cases, the minority may be large. . . .[18]

In putting programming ahead of sales, Storz was like McLendon in that he was--for most of his tenure as head of Mid-Continent

---

[18]Todd Storz, "Independent, Alive and Healthy," excerpts from a talk at the University of Georgia, no date, but between 1954 and 1956; original was mimeographed; xerox copy supplied by Grahame Richards.

Broadcasting Company--involved in developing new programming ideas. In the same way that McLendon would rather be busy writing some copy or trying out a new promotion technique, Storz liked to experiment with his stations' programming to see what worked best. Out of this came a special regard for keeping something new and different always on the air:

> In retrospect, I know we have made many mistakes but we never regretted them. Without action, a station soon decays. Doing anything at all is really difficult. It's an old saying, and very true, that a few people make things happen, many watch them happen and the majority have no idea what has happened. With enough action the time will come when listeners will be afraid not to listen to your station because they might miss something.[19]

Part of this policy of keeping things new and fresh involved the continual changing of regular program feature intros and closings. According to Storz (quoted in 1957), ". . . we try to do something new with sound each month. One month we'll start the news with news machines ticking away, the next month we'll go in for gongs or bells. The point is, it will sound different from the week before. . . . In the same way, we try to change frequently the sounds we use in our commercials."[20]

McLendon's background in show business was not matched by Storz, but Storz nevertheless believed in strong station promotion. Having been accused by *Time* of being the "King of Giveaway," Storz defended the role of promotion in aiding a station in becoming known:

> Promotion is a very legitimate advertising method. It is of service and interest to the listener, and has proven successful in television and in building newspaper circulation.

---

[19] *Ibid.*

[20] Land, "The Storz Bombshell," p. 6 out of 8.

> The promotions are based on the station's own problems. If your station is already well established, naturally you do not need promotion so badly. If you take over a station that is near the bottom, then promotion is terribly important to let people know about you.[21]

Storz realized that promoting an inferior product would not win loyal listeners; the programming had to be right first before any promotion was begun.

> Fast results are easy to get. It's easy to get a rating. If the promotion is good enough, people will be willing to try your product. After that it's up to the product to keep them coming back.[22]

George W. Armstrong, who after Storz's death in 1964 became the head of the Storz Broadcasting operation as executive vice-president, has expressed more of the general Storz philosophy in the development of programming:

> I think that in terms of people, or programming, or station operation, that there is no contradiction in terms between solidity and "keeping up with it." And, that which is most creative and most innovative and which will last the longest is that which is carefully thought out, carefully applied with objectivity, logic, and common sense, rather than with hunch, with impulse, with so-called intuition--the latter things generally tending to characterize those who feel the "free-spirit" approach--and that's a very broad over-simplification. You know the old saying: sin in haste, repent at leisure. And I think most things, even if they appear to be spontaneous, and "with it," if they are really good, they probably have been very well thought-out, and very well planned. . . .[23]

Mr. Armstrong seems to equate the "free-spirit" approach--or what he characterized elsewhere in the interview as the "seat of the pants"

---

[21] Ibid., pp. 6, 7 out of 8.

[22] Ibid., p. 7 out of 8.

[23] Mr. George W. (Bud) Armstrong, Executive Vice President, Storz Broadcasting, private interview held in Omaha, Nebraska, August 2, 1971.

approach--with the show business flair of a McLendon, from which he might have been trying to differentiate the Storz organization. Still, no matter how cautious Storz Broadcasting had become by 1971, in the mid-1950s when Todd Storz was experimenting, it was a free-spirit operation. Like McLendon, Storz was willing "to take a shot."[24]

Bartell Programming Philosophy

Bartell subscribed both to the catechism that programming comes before sales and to the belief that radio management should be willing and even anxious to try new things. Speaking at a regional conference of the NAB in 1958 Bartell told his listeners that stations, and not advertisers or critics, had to be responsible for programming:

> The moment the advertiser is permitted to tell radio how to program . . . at precisely that moment we are giving aid and comfort to every competing advertising medium.
>
> Program policies now are a local problem, and the job of building audiences must be done right in our own operations. . . . A whole new generation of program and production people are shaping the sound of radio today. They work for a valid radio audience, not for the radio critics. . . .[25]

In an interview with the author, Bartell asserted his overall willingness to "take a shot":

> . . . Broadcasters themselves never really bothered to find out anything. I mean, the way you ought to program is to really do some deep research: find out who is listening to what and why. . . .[26]

But most of what Bartell developed was not through doing formal research but through trial-and-error experimentation:

---

[24] Ken Dowe, National Director of Operations for the McLendon Stations, private interview held in Dallas, Texas, July 29, 1971.

[25] "Stations, Not Admen, Must Run Programs: Bartell," Advertising Age, October 20, 1958, p. 8.

[26] Bartell interview.

> . . . If you have a gimmick that requires a letter- or a postcard-response, plus of course the Hoopers. We had telephone coincidentals going practically all the time. If Hooper wasn't doing them, we were doing them. And every once in a while you'd run across something that would give your station a little extra identification, some little gimmick. Some little thing that you had no idea of, but that people will mention, because, they'll attach the WOKY or the KCBQ or WAKE or WYDE or WILD or whatever it is, to that particular gimmick, then you know that that's working.[27]

In trying different gimmicks, Bartell would keep track of informal public response plus the information supplied by commissioned surveys to get feedback on how effective the innovations were. As with other stations, Bartell's source for new ideas was sometimes within his own organization and sometimes outside it, but an idea was not considered "sure-fire" until it was tried on Bartell's air.

> . . . There's no other way. Otherwise, you could build a show that would be a hit on Broadway the first time, if you could computerize it. . . . Oh, there had been thousands of audience surveys on gimmicks--how a station in Tempe which had a little thing--how that worked. If they seemed to be the leading station, I'd have a tape like that--the next day--and we were listening to it, to find out if it means anything. If it meant something, we'd make a variation, put it on the air, with our personalities, and then put that into the mix and see how it worked.[28]

Bartell also had the idea that everything on the station ought to be kept fresh. According to Pete Thomas, who was production manager at Bartell's WAKE, Atlanta, in the mid-1950s, the produced openings and closes would change regularly, to keep things fresh.[29] As pointed out earlier, this was partly the result of the necessity of re-cutting worn

---

[27] Ibid.

[28] Ibid.

[29] Pete Thomas, private interview held in Madison, Wisconsin, April 27, 1972.

acetate discs, along with the attitude that if you had to make a new cut, you might as well make a new production. According to Thomas, about two months were spent in wiring-in electronic echoes, but they disappeared in a few weeks. "They were just continually changing that station. It really wasn't that solid at any one day. Now, I don't mean in concept, but in just the little niceties. And it did change perpetually."[30]

It was also Bartell's policy to try never to air a spot "live." Everything was to be transcribed, and, if possible, also done with full production:

> They figured it would cut down the amount of make-goods, and it sounded a little slicker. The news guy, as a matter of fact, was kept very busy between newscasts cutting spots. Whenever possible they put together production spots. The object was to keep it slick on the air.[31]

Thomas assesses the quest for "slickness" not as an attempt to develop the "perfect" formula, but rather as a substitute for the "professionalism" of the "old" radio.

> "THE" formula? Maybe that was one of the quiet dreams you have, you know, but I don't think that was it so much as just trying to continually make it better than it was last week. I doubt if Mort [Mort Wagner, WAKE general manager] would tell you that he had been going after <u>the</u> formula. I never heard him say that he believed there was such a thing. Again, you're talking about a guy who came out of the older days of radio, and slickness had a hell of a lot to do with it. He wasn't totally oriented toward this new stuff--probably nobody was totally oriented toward it save for some very young guys [who] . . . hadn't grown up in the older radio. I'm sure an awful lot of Mort's motivation was just the same as mine was--professionalism--it was done this way because it was inherently better because it was done this way--that same circular reasoning.[32]

Bartell, like the others, put programming first, and

---

[30] <u>Ibid</u>. [31] <u>Ibid</u>. [32] <u>Ibid</u>.

experimented to discover what worked most effectively. Promotion was also important to Bartell, but not in quite the "glamorous" way that it was done by McLendon and Storz. Bartell's promotions were based on tie-ins with his pronounceable call letters and tended to be less startling and less expensive than McLendon's and Storz's. The promotions featuring a tie-in with the call letters (such as a clock-radio sales-push in conjunction with WYDE and WAKE) were as much oriented toward advertisers as toward building audience.

Plough Programming Philosophy

Plough subscribed to all of the tenets described above, with one major exception. Plough stations did not run spectacular audience promotions at all. The Plough group believed so thoroughly in the importance of programming coming first that the company copyrighted its station operating manual on programming, supposedly to keep other stations from stealing the ideas, but more importantly to point out that their "method of presentation" was so unique that it did not require audience-building stunts to gain an audience. Plough's "method of presentation" was said to be patterned after Storz, in that it featured rigorous central control of all aspects of programming.[33] But Plough's programming differed from that of the other three in its de-emphasis of the importance of the disc jockey, because management believed that the listener wanted to hear the hit music and not the disc jockey's chatter. Thus, Plough stations developed "house names" for their jocks since, so long as the music took precedence over personality, one person could be

---

[33]Land, "The Storz Bombshell," p. 7 out of 8.

replaced with another without the public being aroused. In emphasizing music and cutting out the talk, the Plough stations became the forerunners of the "Drake" format which became dominant in the late 1960s on contemporary music stations. As such, the Plough stations sounded and acted unlike those of McLendon, Storz, and Bartell. If the music and promotion policies were the two main factors in the development of Top 40, the Plough stations participated in that development to a lesser extent than the other three owners by denying the importance of promotion.

Top 40 Group Owners' Programming Procedures

Management Methods

Central programming control

One of the program management methods common to all four Top 40 group owners was the centralization of programming control. With Bartell and Plough, the input source which determined the basic format was also generally centralized, while with Storz and McLendon, ideas were invited from throughout the organization.

As mentioned earlier, both Bartell and Plough had written programming manuals for the staff at their stations to follow. Whatever day-to-day programming might be developed on a trial-and-error basis did not affect the necessity of programming according to the basic formula supplied in written form by top-level central management. Jerry Bartell has described his central programming control:

> . . . It was in Milwaukee at that time, although we didn't reveal to Fortune [which published an article about Bartell] or to anybody else where we kept our central control. All of our . . . every single program schedule for music for each station was delivered from Milwaukee by teletype. And they

> [the local stations] could change the order, they could change the frequency, they could change a number of things, but they couldn't change the music. It had to be those records. If an individual station in say, San Diego, or Atlanta, or Boston were to send in a very hot pitch for something that is local, that is good, and that they feel they could rely on for putting into the mix, then we would let them do it. But that record wouldn't go anywhere _else_. It would stay only in the one station.
>
> All the public service formats were identical too. Everything that had to do with what we called "The Voice of the News" at that time . . . all of those formats were exactly alike all across the country.[34]

Bartell exercised central programming control for only about three years--from 1954 to about 1957. His chief reason for starting it was the lack of qualified programming manpower.

> Our chief reason for doing it was because of conservation of manpower. We realized very early in the game that there were just a few of us who had to leverage ourselves. And so we found that when we had one radio station in 1947, we had three by 1950. We didn't have top manpower in the three stations. We had _one_ group of what I considered top manpower. Then, we had seven radio stations by 1954. Well, what we did is we put _business_ people in, but not the program people. We developed our own programming group, so that all we had to do was get top _voices_, top personalities. But we gave them _no_ responsibility for programming those records. Because, I never considered that they were capable of doing this type of thing. They talked a good game, but they were usually people who were interested in jazz or interested in country and western, or something, but mostly what I wanted was their attraction _as personalities_. . . . But I didn't expect them to have the moxie that it takes to program.[35]

Bartell describes the duties of one of his program directors as being responsible for seeing that the central programming policy was carried out locally. The program director would determine in what order the prescribed records would be played and at what times various local commercials should be aired. To do this, he consulted the Bartell "Blue Book" for guidelines and the prescribed clock-hour. He could develop features of a local nature so long as they didn't interfere with the

---

[34] Bartell interview. [35] _Ibid._

overall pace of the show. The record list and the general programming mix was put together in Milwaukee by Bartell's sister, Rosa Evans, and by three other girls. This material was designed explicitly for WOKY, but was suggested for the other stations.

> . . . But nobody had to take anything else other than the asterisked items, the ones that said "must do, must do, must do." On everything else, the people could provide their own mix, but had to use our essentials.[36]

Pete Thomas disputes the claims of centralized control made by Bartell only on one point--that often decisions had to be given immediately which made "going through channels" impractical. Thus, much of the <u>day-to-day</u> decision-making still was carried out locally.

The McLendon and the Storz stations differed from Bartell and Plough in not having a unitary written programming manual. At various times, both the McLendon and Storz organizations did of course produce programming memoranda in written form, and at least in the case of the McLendon stations, these have been comprehensively saved in dozens of what are loosely called "Policy Books."[37]

Both McLendon and Storz had national program directors to oversee the programming on their stations. Bill Stewart was National PD first

---

[36] <u>Ibid</u>.

[37] Some of the McLendon Policy Books are concerned with various program elements, each in a separate volume. Others give the history of the acquisition and development of certain stations. Still others deal with regulatory and engineering problems. Taken as a whole, they are a huge, rambling scrapbook of Gordon McLendon's entire history in radio. Out of all these, McLendon and others compiled a single operating manual at various times, but these dealt more with procedures in management than in specific programming formulae. If the Storz stations had such archives, they have been well-concealed from this author.

for McLendon, then for Storz, then for Don Burden, and then later for McLendon again. When Stewart left McLendon for the first time in 1956 to go with Storz, he was replaced by Don Keyes. Keyes was National PD for McLendon between 1957 and 1966. He has described his role as "what you might call a staff advisory position."

> . . . I had no direct jurisdiction--in the sense that I couldn't call the shots, in major changes--over the individual managers at their stations. They were responsible for their station. And it had to be that way, really, because I couldn't begin to run it from Dallas, with six or seven stations, and have absolute authority. The manager had to--he was on the scene every day. I was there for more of a "resident consultant." Today we have a lot of consultants who run around to all of their stations that they take care of. I was sort of the resident consultant. I didn't consult for anybody other than the McLendon stations. But it was a consultancy type of thing. I'd go in and listen to a station and I'd raise hell if I didn't like it, or heard something wrong. I'd have a meeting with the manager. I say "raise hell"--I had a good rapport with all the guys, and they respected my judgment. And we'd have meetings: like with Bill Weaver at KILT in Houston. I'd say Bill, I've been listening for 12 hours--here's this and this and this and this, so bring in the program director and we'll talk to him. So the three of us would have a meeting. Now, let's say at the end of the meeting there were three areas that were not resolved: I couldn't get them to go my way. Well, all I'd do is go back to Dallas and talk to Gordon. Then he'd enforce it. Most of the time he'd enforce it. Because I did not have the power to directly force this down the manager's throat. But I rarely had to use it, frankly.[38]

Although the passage above makes the McLendon operation sound harshly strict with its stations, in fact it seems to have been the most democratic, in the sense that individual managers had considerable autonomy in running their stations. According to Bill Stewart, the Storz stations (at the time Stewart was with them) ran all of their stations from Omaha, sending out music lists and virtually everything else, so that the local managers were usually instruction-followers

---

[38] Keyes interview.

rather than innovators on-their-own. Whatever the differences in <u>degree</u>, it is clear that both Storz and McLendon were heavily involved in central control of their stations' programming.

<u>Decentralized input</u>

At the same time that they kept a tight rein on programming, Storz and McLendon encouraged decentralized input of programming ideas. As will be shown later, McLendon developed a special system of manager reports just to be certain that all new ideas were shared. McLendon's willingness to "take a shot," to try new ideas also encouraged creativity among managers, program directors and others on his staffs. Bill Stewart has summarized McLendon's and Storz's receptiveness to new ideas thus:

> . . . I started out in Houston for him [McLendon], and I guess after a month or so, he thought that I had good ideas and let me have my head and let me do what I wanted to do. And I think <u>that</u> more than anything is the answer to whatever success I have had. I firmly feel that there are many, many very able programming people around the country who have never worked for anyone who would give them the opportunity to do what they <u>could</u> do. And I think this is one of the reasons that McLendon and Storz have both been successful over the years. McLendon let me do what I wanted to do, once he got faith enough in my ability, and he's done that with several other people over the years. And Storz I know also operated the same way. If he trusted your ability, he'd let you do what you could do, to the best of your ability. . . .[39]

Asked if the Storz stations used to have a policy of trading ideas from one station to another on a regular basis, executive vice president George Armstrong echoed the McLendon policy of openness to ideas from anywhere.

---

[39] Stewart interview.

> Oh, sure. We've tried it in many different ways, and we still do a lot of it. We don't think that anybody has a monopoly on good ideas. We think our executives and our managers are good experienced guys, and they have good thoughts. The people who work with them do too. But they don't have any great pride of authorship on any one idea. And we have our regular meetings during the year, and I visit the stations and talk to people, and occasionally some of them are here, and they communicate with each other, so that we don't have a company that is structured on anything but an open-door, good, friendly policy with everybody.[40]

Bartell also recognized the need to discover and encourage creative thinking among station staff, pointing out that unless ownership did so, an outside group would step in and do it themselves, stealing the man away. In an article in Billboard, Bartell is quoted as saying

> You may be sure of one thing--a potentially top man will not remain in an atmosphere where his activities are circumscribed by a rigid adherence to business principles of a fading era, or will he thrive in a climate of ownership apathy.
>
> Radio is constantly besieged by a body of talented management potential striving for recognition. But they feel restricted, unfulfilled, dissatisfied--a paradox based either upon giving a man complete autonomy and no realistic goals and guidance, or little autonomy and no inspiration. It is rare management that is given a set of working conditions based upon recognition of good judgment, freedom to develop ideas, and proper rewards for success.[41]

While it is true that Top 40 management in general was most receptive to new ideas, perhaps as a result of being younger and less tied to old-line radio practices, it should also be remembered that initially, there was little to lose in trying new directions. Because they were the only ones doing it, Top 40 stations could afford in those

---

[40]Armstrong interview.

[41]Charles Sinclair, "Ingenuity Key to New Local Radio Success Era," Billboard, May 19, 1958, pp. 1, 9.

days to make some mistakes. They were thought of as mavericks anyway, so whatever was tried was not likely to darken an already tarnished image. And maverick or not, every time they tried something new--in fact perhaps <u>because</u> they kept trying new things--their stations' ratings went up. Today, when contemporary music stations consider themselves "mature" and "big business," both of which they are, the atmosphere of experimentation which characterized the developmental era is much less in evidence.

Trends in Management Control of Programming

McLendon, Storz, Bartell and Plough were of course not alone in increasing their control over programming. A poll of station managers by <u>Billboard</u> published in February 1953 showed that of the stations answering the survey, about half of their programming hours were devoted to record shows. Stations having 5,000 watts of power or less were more likely to run record shows than the larger, more powerful stations. Of all stations, 57.2% reported devoting more time to record shows than a year ago, only 5.8% less time, and 37% the same amount of time.[42] Station managers were also asked, "To what extent are your disk jockey programs supervised by station management?" and "Does station management exact more, less or about the same amount of control over disk jockey programs as a year ago?" Here are the tabulated results from these two questions:

---

[42]"The <u>Billboard</u> 1953 Station Manager Survey," <u>Billboard</u>, February 28, 1953, p. 49.

"To what extent are your disk jockey programs supervised by station management?"

	All stations	Over 5,000 watts	5,000 watts or less
Station policy partially controls programming of jockey shows	64.6%	69.6%	62.3%
Station policy completely controls programming of jockey shows	17.7%	13.5%	19.7%
Jockeys have complete freedom of programming	17.7%	16.9%	18.0%

"Does station management exact more, less or about the same amount of control over disk jockey programs as a year ago?"

	All stations	Over 5,000 watts	5,000 watts or less
More	19.5%	17.3%	20.6%
Same	74.0%	77.8%	72.2%
Less	6.5%	4.9%	7.2%

Source: "The Billboard 1953 Station Manager Survey," Billboard, February 28, 1953, p. 50.

As can be seen in the first table, about an equal number of stations believed they completely controlled disc jockey programming as believed that the jocks had full control. Both of these groups were in the minority, with 64.6% of all station managers saying they had "partial" control over such programs. A slightly greater number of larger stations exercised partial control than did smaller stations, while a greater number of small stations exercised complete control.

In the second table, the significant information is that station management in all cases exercised more control over disc jockey programs at the time of the survey in early 1953 than they had a year ago.

A third question in the same survey queried, "If station policy controls completely or partially how disk jockey shows are programmed, what specifications are used?" The answers to this question reflected the managers' role in the policy their stations used in selecting the music played. About 60% relied on trade-paper charts or listings, about 40% built shows around specific artists (a common practice at the time, and one heavily used by Martin Block and others), 22% specified certain musical types, and 7% responded to listeners' requests. Five percent programmed on the basis of "good taste," and only about 3% did a local survey.[43] It is quite apparent from this answer that the selection of records, even in 1953, was heavily influenced by national trade-papers lists. It should be kept in mind, however, that these lists were highly "segregated," with country, and rhythm and blues records almost never showing up among the list of "regular" pop hits. The pop hits list was generally dominated by big-name artists--hence the popularity of shows built around specific vocalists and bands. The infiltration of rhythm and blues and of strictly teen-appeal music into the pop hits lists had not yet occurred.

Station managers at stations of all sizes reported a general increase in the sponsorship of record shows, with a 20% to 25% increase

[43] _Ibid_.

in sponsorship the average. Billboard pointed out that the willingness to sponsor such programs had helped their growth immensely.[44]

Billboard also polled disc jockeys in a separate survey published at the same time, and asked them "Who selects the records played on your show?" A huge 94.5% said they did it themselves, refuting management's claim to complete control in about 17% of the cases. Three and three tenths percent responded that the selection was made by the "music librarian," an almost forgotten occupation today. One and two tenths percent said the "program manager" made the choice.[45] This last figure is especially significant since in Top 40, the program director would make the final choice nearly 100% of the time. The 1953 Disc Jockey poll also asked for the two sources of information deejays who programmed their own shows used in making selections. Fifty-seven and four tenths percent relied on their own tastes, 50.6% on listener requests, and 45.2% on trade paper charts.[46] A similar question asked a year later revealed a trend toward dependence on listener requests, with that source becoming top-rated (287 responses), personal opinion next with 282 responses, and trade papers third with 214 responses.[47]

In 1956, Billboard published its ninth annual Disc Jockey Poll, which showed some definite trends in music programming and management control. The average number of hours that each disc jockey was on the

---

[44] Ibid., p. 51.

[45] "The Billboard 1953 Disc Jockey Poll," Billboard, February 28, 1953, p. 41.

[46] Ibid., p. 41.

[47] "The Billboard 1954 Disk Jockey Poll," Billboard, November 13, 1954, p. 38.

air per week had risen 8% in the past years from 20.8 hours to 22 hours. The average total number of record sides played per week had risen by 44, from 184.7 in 1955 to 228.7 sides per week in 1956. However, the number of new release sides played per week had risen by only 6.2, from 1955's 33.0 sides to 1956's 39.2 sides.[48] Quite obviously, the other 38 record sides being added per week in 1956 by the average jockey were either established hits or "oldies." It should be noted that 1956 is the year in which the true "limited playlist" was established. The term "limited playlist" will be defined fully later, but for now it can be described as the consistent repetition of a select few most popular records. The increasing use of some type of limited playlist could account for the drop in the number of new releases played relative to the increase in the number of sides aired.

In 1956, the average disc jockey show had 14 more sponsors than it had at the same time in 1955. National sponsorship had increased, from 11.7 in the average 1955 show to 14.5 in the average 1956 show, but local and regional sponsorship was up sharply, from 37.5 per show in 1955 to 48.8 in 1956. The number of transcribed commercials had also increased, from 19.3% averaging all kinds of stations in 1955, to 22.3% transcribed in 1956.[49] The increase in local sponsorship partly reflected the growth of local music-and-news and Top 40 stations, while the increase in transcribed announcements reflected in part the new commercials' "style," with more music, effects, multiple voices, and so

---

[48]"The Billboard Ninth Annual Disk Jockey Poll," Billboard, November 10, 1956, p. 82.

[49]Ibid.

orth, which could not be done live.

The 1956 poll also included a section of questions to station anagement. The answers came from 179 managers participating in the urvey and as before were grouped by wattage. Stations of 5,000 watts nd over reported a big 26% increase in the number of record shows in he past year, up from 42% of all weekly broadcast time in 1955 to 68% n 1956. A smaller 15% increase was evident on the stations having ess than 5,000 watts, where the jump was from 53% to 68%. In both ases, almost the entire increase in record shows was accomplished by utting only the time allowed for network programs. Powerful stations enerally reported playing more rhythm and blues and standard pop ingles at the expense of current pop singles in 1956, while smaller tations were playing _fewer_ rhythm and blues records, about the same umber of standard singles as in the previous year, and about 20% _more_ urrent hits.[50] It seems that the idea of "playing the hits" had aught on among the smaller stations.

Asked who controlled the music programming, the station anagers replied as follows:

---

[50] _Ibid._, p. 84.

5,000 watts and over		Under 5,000 watts
26.2%	Jockeys have complete freedom in programming	39.4%
54.8%	Management sets basic rules to guide jockeys	55.5%
7.1%	Jockey selections approved by management	2.2%
11.9%	Management does all the programming	2.5%

Source: "The Billboard Ninth Annual Disk Jockey Poll," Billboard, November 10, 1956, p. 84.

It is interesting to compare the results on this question in 1956 with those from the similar question in the 1953 poll, quoted earlier. By 1956, 10% more managers at powerful stations were letting disc jockeys have complete freedom in programming music, while among smaller stations, the number of jocks having such freedom had more than doubled, from 18.0% in 1953 to 39.4% in 1956. The number of stations in which management did all the music programming had dropped for both power groups as well, with exactly 5% fewer "powerful" stations reporting total management control in 1956 as compared to 1953, and only 2.5% of smaller stations' management controlling music programming in 1956 as compared to 18.0% in 1953.

The figures quoted above seem to argue against the premise that management was exercising increasingly more program control. First, overall program control must not be confused with record programming control--the survey reported only the latter. Second, it was the era of the personality disc jockey, part of whose often-presumed capability was the knowledge of how to choose and program records. Third, since the limited playlist was only first instituted in 1956, the poll was probably conducted too soon to reflect any diffusion of the idea that management should totally choose the music. And fourth, a good many of the stations listed in the 1953 poll probably included the selection of records by a music librarian under management control, and music librarians were far more plentiful then than in 1956.

Billboard conducted a similar poll in 1957, but it is less informative because it omits the number of respondents and does not break down responses by power groupings. However, a few significant facts still emerge. When disc jockeys were asked, "Who selects the records on your shows?" in 1957, 7% replied "program manager" whereas in 1956 only 1.3% had selected that answer. The question about the total number of record sides played per week was asked again, and again the total had increased, from 228.7 per week in 1956 to 263.5 sides per week in 1957. Also repeated was the drop in exposure of new releases; the average total number of new release sides played per week in 1956 had been 39.2, but in 1957 it was only 28.8.[51] Thus, by 1957, not only the ratio of new sides to established hits was down, but also the actual number of new sides played had dropped. Clearly, it had become apparent to stations that playing the hits and only the hits was the way to program.

Trinity Programming Policy Book

Back in the early and mid-1950s when McLendon's station holdings were known as part of the Trinity Broadcasting Corporation, Gordon

---

[51] "The Billboard Tenth Annual Disk Jockey Poll," Billboard, November 11, 1957, p. 54.

McLendon compiled a manual on music-and-news programming for his stations. This Trinity Programming Policy Book, one of the collection of McLendon Policy Books, will be quoted extensively here because it is the earliest primary source available to the author which contains information from which the evolution of the Top 40 format can be traced.

McLendon began the Trinity Book with his already quoted philosophy about programming coming first, and then listed the elements of a music-and-news format:

> . . . The following six categories embrace one hundred percent of what goes on the air on a news and music stations:
> 1. Music
> 2. Deejay patter
> 3. Commercials (a real feature with us: should attract listeners if done well)
> 4. News
> 5. Public service announcements
> 6. Promotions
>
> No station can be top-rated which is weak in any one of the six categories. [McLendon treated public service announcements and promotions in separate policy books.] The first four are fully treated in this book which you must understand thoroughly as a part of your job.[52]

In trying to explain how his stations were to make a different use of the same six elements available to all other stations, McLendon related the story (without naming the station) of the previously top-rated Dallas independent station, KIXL. In making reference to how "peaceful" KIXL's sound was, McLendon was exhorting his staff to make the Trinity stations the opposite.

> This is the story of a radio station which once had a large listening audience--and lost it. This radio station still, even to this day, spends all day long with its production, has a vastly

---

[52] Excerpt from Administrative and Programming Policy Book, Trinity Broadcasting Corporation, one of the McLendon Policy Books, mimeographed and bound but unpaginated and undated.

greater musical library than most radio stations, spends infinitely longer on its choice of music, etc.

With all of this, the radio station has lost its audience slowly but steadily to other stations in its city, and is now a bad fourth or fifth in its market. This is ironic in view of the fact that the station is still the smoothest sounding station in the city. [Note that when this was written, a large music library and a smooth sound were still important.]

What is really wrong is that the station to which we are referring has become a station without life--a station which never has anything new, which never has anything which people talk about. The station is highly formatized both as to its music, playing more and more string music, and as to the tone of its announcers' voices. The station has come to resemble and sound like a beautiful, peaceful pool of still water. There is no life in the station, no movement, no freshness, no progression, no change of pace--nothing to invigorate the listener, to make him talk about the station, nothing to give him expectancy. . . .

. . . KLIF believes that the answer to maintenance of a high listening audience lies in continuously giving the people something new to talk about--something fresh on the station. The answer lies in new ideas, constant new ideas. While the station is giving the listeners something new, it should at the same time be planning four or five other new things to introduce the moment its present project is over. The station should always feature something to make people talk about its call letters--something to give the same continuing flavor of vivid wide-awakeness which now characterizes KLIF. In other words--something to make people say, as they now say, "You know that KLIF bunch is really on the ball." This is all a part of opportunism. Word-of-mouth conversation, and continuing word-of-mouth conversation are vitally important to all good stations which wish to achieve a high audience rating--and from a high audience rating comes increased sales and, ergo, increased salaries. So, it is vital to keep your station fresh with continuing new ideas that keep the town talking and, secondly, to keep the choice of music alive with enough good pop music. The station should bounce and bubble and sparkle with originality and informality.

jazzazz

. . . Within the pop music and news format lies our future, and we must do that format just as effectively as it is humanly possible to do it.

If, then, it is important that we sound as good as we can over the air, Trinity has established a policy of asking all announcers to sound alert, happy on their jobs, full of pride in working at a fine radio station. Your feeling about your job can be sensed over the air by listeners. Your voice should be full of life. You should appear to enjoy your work and give the continuing impression of alertness. We don't mean to overbear the listeners with a "happy boy" attitude but we do mean to have all of our announcers sound as though they are on the ball. This is all part of having a wide-awake, alert radio station.

> On the subject of music, it is important to emphasize that this radio station is primarily a POP music station. This doesn't mean that we play the top 20 tunes only but we want to hear at least 2 songs from the top 20 in every half hour. The juke box operators have long been noted for desiring to make money. In order to achieve this, quite logically, they put those selections on the juke boxes which they believe the people will spend a nickel to play. These top 20 tunes are reflected in the weekly _Billboard Magazine_ poll. We are merely following the lead of the juke box operators in giving the people what they want to hear. Again let us point out that this doesn't mean we don't play oldies, a few semi-classics, and lush instrumentals, but it does mean that we are primarily and basically a pop music station.[53]

Music

In the final paragraph of the passage of the _Trinity Programming Policy Book_ quoted above, McLendon made the specific recommendation that two of the records in each half hour should be from _Billboard_'s Top 20 list. A later inclusion in the _Trinity Programming Book_ titled "KLIF Music Policy" is far more explicit about what types of music should and should not be played. The author of the KLIF Music Policy memorandum is not identified, but it should be remembered that Bill Stewart was with the McLendon organization as National Program Director from late 1953 through 1956, and the passage quoted below appears to hav been written about 1955.

> KLIF Music Policy
>
> A. This music policy will apply to all record shows regardless of the time of day or night--except those specifically designated otherwise, such as all-Top Forty Shows. Absolutely no deviation from this format is permitted.
>
> B. You will be able to play a minimum of 13 records, give or take one. The 13 records will be broken down as follows:
>
> 1. 6 records from station's Top 40 list.
> 2. 2 records selected as "comers," one of which may be your predicted hit, but not yet on Top Forty.

---

[53] _Ibid._

3. 3 records from old favorites group with emphasis on those records and sides which were Top 10 in their day.
4. 1 record of either novelty, swing, or Dixieland type.
5. 1 record of either six months to a year old, or, a Latin rhythm selection.

C. No play:

1. BeBop
2. Concert
3. Classical
4. Opera
5. Hillbilly
6. Organ
7. No race artists as such playing race music--e.g., Illinois Jacquet, Cootie Williams, no play; Nat Cole, Ella Fitzgerald, etc., okay.
8. Jazz--except Stan Kenton on a few of his commercial recordings, such as "Laura," a few done with June Christy, and a very few commercial Dave Brubeck sides.

D. General Instructions:

No segments of any one artist or band. In general, do not play same artist on two successive records and do not play two instrumentals in succession. Avoid sequences of too many female artists or male artists at a stretch.

E. Your most important job is to choose your music carefully outside the Top Forty selections. [Note that the jock still had freedom to choose some of his own music at this point.] By and large, except for the artist, you'll probably find the 6 Top Forty numbers simple. You will make or break your program choosing the other 7. Don't choose just the first 7 that you run across in the library or the first 7 that come to mind. Choose carefully. For example, and strictly for example, how long has it been since you played Patti Page's "Tennessee Waltz," Cugat's "Chiu Chiu," or "Brazil," Johnny Mercer's "GI Jive," Stafford and Laine's "Pretty Eyed Baby," Tony Martin's "Valencia," Lena Horne's "Deed I Do," Perry Como's "Million Dollar Baby," Dinah Shore's "My Bel Ami," Doris Day's "It's Magic," Esther Williams' "Baby, It's Cold Outside." . . .[54]

It can be seen that by the time the above passage was written in about 1955); McLendon management was much more fully involved in etermining the music that would be heard on KLIF than it had been a ouple of years earlier when the first memorandum was written. The Top

---

[54]"KLIF Music Policy," Trinity Programming Policy Book, ndated and unpaginated.

Twenty had become the Top 40, and the number of records selected from the hit list had grown from 4 per hour (2 per half hour) to 6 per hour. There was now also a much more detailed consideration of what other music should be played, with such details part of the evolving music "formula."[55]

Surveys

Along with the "KLIF Music Policy" in the Trinity Programming Policy Book there is a section titled "Top Forty Survey" which begins by explaining--apparently for the first time--what a Top Forty Survey is and why and how to conduct one. The section then deals with other general programming reminders. Like the earlier passage, it was probably not authored by McLendon. The reference to "Dallas or Milwaukee" probably dates the passage from the period between 1955 and 1956 when McLendon owned WRIT in Milwaukee:

> Top Forty Survey
>
> Henceforth, it will be the policy and practice of all Trinity stations to assemble, mimeograph and mail each Monday a listing of the top forty records in the station's city for that week. . .
>
> The Top 40 list is vitally important, since it is the basic feature of your station's music programming. From this list, roughly fifty per cent of your station's music programming is drawn. [Note the lowness of the figure--50%.] Each disc jockey on each show, is required to play six or seven out of each forty numbers from this list.
>
> The record shops in your city will give away copies of your station's Top 40 survey at their record counters each week. Over a thousand of these will be circulated throughout your city via the record shop channels and on mailing lists and [via] record distributors, together with the commentary which you will note on Page One of the attached sample survey report. A

---

[55]The precise methods used in selecting the music played will be treated in detail later, but since the Trinity Programming Policy Book is the earliest source of material tracing the evolution of the Top 40 formula available to the author, it seems wise to quote it further here for its value as historical background.

commentary is dictated each week by the Program Director or his designate.

Regardless of its indisputable promotional value, your Top 40 Survey has a far more fundamental purpose: to give you a two to three week lead on other stations in knowledge of the public's musical taste in your city and, indeed, to scoop completely those stations depending entirely on such sources as Billboard. Suffice it to say, a "national" top forty, picked by Billboard or any other publication, does not and cannot reflect the top forty in your city. The top forty in New York or Denver is never the top forty in Dallas or Milwaukee. On our Music Policy Sheet, you are allowed three "comer" records and you and the other disc jockeys may make a leading record out of one artist's version of a popular song, while nationally another artist's version prevails. Take a fictitious number, "Red Fire" for instance. The big national side may be the Hilltoppers' version, while in your city that side may be outsold 100 to 1 by the Four Aces' version of the same song, because your station's jockeys, at an early date, thought this the best side and rode the other almost out of the market. Thus, you see, the top forty nationally may bear little resemblance to your city's top forty. [It should be kept in mind that multiple "cover" versions of a hit were still common in the early and mid-1950s. It seems remarkable that jocks in those days were encouraged to play a version different from the one that was big nationally when today almost everybody is afraid to play anything that is not big nationally.]

And think of the advantage this gives you over the other stations in your music programming!

The Top Forty Survey is all compiled, commentary written, posted in station and mailed on Monday. This requires about three hours of time from the Program Director or his designate.[56]

Other formula elements

After explaining the Top 40 Survey, the Trinity Policy Book passes on to other programming reminders; which deal with various other elements of the formula:

One of the most important considerations is the programming arrangement. All blocks of instrumental programming should be eliminated. This includes quarter-hours of a particular dance band. In general, do not play two instrumentals in

---

[56]"Top Forty Survey," Trinity Programming Policy Book, undated and unpaginated.

succession. Exception can be made to the artist rule when introducing both sides of a new record by the same artist.

In general, schedule only one instrumental record per hour. At times, it will be permissible to play two instrumentals per hour, but never more than two per hour. One instrumental should be played prior to the newscast on the hour, in the event it is necessary to fade out of the record on time.

Do not play off-brand labels, or and this is very important, unsung artists. Always stick to the major labels and major artists. The only time an off-label record may be played is when it appears on the Top 40 list or you think it should be one of your "comers" because it is going to be on the top 40. Major labels are as follows: Decca, Capitol, Columbia, RCA Victor, Coral, Mercury, Dot, Cadence, MGM, Epic, London and X.

Do not try to build new orchestras or singers. When in doubt about the arrangement to play, take the better known artist.

There will be no interview on any station program. The mobile unit will provide opportunity for all types of interviews. . . .

In general, do not plug record labels. It is permissible to mention a label now and then but do not go into any long detailed analysis. At the most, do not plug a record label more than twice per hour.

It is against the music policy of this station to talk about or to engineers on duty or other station personnel. At no time are there to be any "house jokes" given over the air. Keep your remarks confined to the studio, unless your ad libs pertain to your broadcast or that of another disc jockey's.

Do not tell jokes on the air. It is permissible to relate funny stories received over the news wire or through other sources but they should all be short and to the point. Never go into any great detail with stories, and keep all unrelated jokes off your programs.

It is recommended that you broadcast the temperature about six or eight times an hour. When you have any doubt about what to say between records, it is recommended that you give the time and temperature. [Note that the exact times for weather and time checks were not prescribed--that is, a precise "clock" was not being followed.]

It is desirable that you plug the up-coming program following your show. These plugs should be kept very short and only given during the last 15 minutes of your program. Never more than three plugs at any time . . . preferably two.

It is permissible and desirable that you mention the record after it has played as well as introduce the record. If a record is not introduced before it is played it should always be plugged after the play.

It is desired on occasion that the disc jockey introduce some records over the music background. Use the first few bars of a record to introduce it; however, never talk over a vocal. This rule applies only to instrumental records or records with instrumental openings. [Up to this time, the standard disc jockey practice was to introduce the record and then start it playing. With this recommendation the jocks are encouraged to talk over the intro of the record, which became the accepted mode. In contemporary radio, the intros and outros of records are the only time some jocks are allowed to talk.]

This policy will make the station the Number One listened-to-station in your market. It has been evolved from experience in what the public desires. This policy has been long thought out. It is not one that has been instigated simply to produce a program. There is thought behind every item. Failure to follow the music policy will be a serious deterrent to increased ratings and business, and could be cause for dismissal.

Your complete cooperation will be appreciated.[57]

Announcer instructions

The Trinity Programming Policy Book also contained explicit instructions for disc jockeys on how they should sound.

Instructions to Announcers for Color Radio[58]

1. BE BRISK AND BRIGHT. Pause here because this is the single most important thing we demand of you. Sound peppy, alert and alive. Don't sound tired, ever. Don't laze along through a sentence. Spit it out and get it over with. Sounding brisk and lively may call for talking faster, even for slight changes in your style, but we require being sharp, fast and spirited. We have no room for dull, listless and somnolent deejays--or newsmen, for that matter. Our voices must move. Don't get into inflection ruts where you pause in the middle of sentences or between thoughts. Talk about as many things as you like, talk as long as you like, but express your thought in as few words as possible--and briskly, airily, brightly. Again, this is our single most important requirement of deejays and newsmen.[59]

It is interesting that no absolute limits were imposed as to how long a deejay could talk--he could continue until he was finished

[57] Ibid.

[58] KLIF introduced "Color Radio" to Dallas in January 1956. It had already been promoted by KABC and KYA on the West Coast, and would later be the logo of KFWB, Los Angeles beginning in 1958. See Passman, The Deejays, p. 230.

[59] Trinity Policy Books, undated, unpaginated.

so long as it stayed lively. Obviously, droll, sarcastic, tired-sounding Larry Lujac, one of the country's current top deejays, would not have passed the audition.

> 2. BE INFORMATIVE OR HUMOROUS--NOT A RECORD PLUGGER--make your patter interesting and informative--things you've seen, heard, read, things that have happened to you or others, things going on around town and in the world, jokes, one-liners, quickies, asides, newskickers, news teasers, one-line cross plugs, local names, etc. Don't make the major part of your show comments about performers or the previous or succeeding record. Being informative or humorous--and deemphasizing comments about the music--is a characteristic of top-rated deejays everywhere. We like lots of humor, but no house jokes. Station has a gag file for humor, if you want it.
>
> Furthermore, we deemphasize the word "record" in our air time. Let's not point out that we are an elaborate juke box. Cut down your references to the fact that yours is a record show. Do not use record credits except occasionally.[60]

It should be recalled that Martin Block went to elaborate pains to surround his record show, "The Make-Believe Ballroom" with the feeling that the artists had come to Martin's microphone to perform, even to the extent of saying "Go ahead Ethel" and so on. This, and the McLendon directive to avoid references to records is probably partly a holdover from earlier radio industry attitudes about records being somehow inferior to live performances, and partly an attempt to divorce the station from the "jukebox" label which was usually applied as an epithet.

> By way of being informative, if you run out of anything else, you can't use time and temperature and weather too frequently. Even if you wish to use them ten times an hour, you'll find it's the one thing in radio that can't be overdone.

The preceding two sentences might well have been Bill Drake's catechism, for in programming his contemporary music stations, he has

---

[60] Ibid. [61] Ibid.

admonished his disc jockeys to give the time between every record, and the temperature almost as frequently. The term "time-and-temperature jock," meaning someone who cannot utter anything more stimulating, has been coined to describe such persons.

> We must also insist that you avoid what we call "clock watching" phrases. Don't refer to how long you are going to be on the air or how long you've been on the air. Don't say, "Now, moving into the final thirty minutes of the Bill Smith Show," or "We'll be with you for the next eighteen hours," or "We've been with you for the last two hours." Avoid these clock-watching crutches like the plague.
>
> Don't use crutches and cliches. This is rightfully part of being informative or humorous--not a dull record-plugger. Avoid pat phrases which you use every day, like "spinning the wax for you" or "hopin' you've enjoyed it," or "the latest and best in pop music." Be a little original every day. Avoid the crutches and cliches. This is another hallmark of the fine deejay. Read memos "That Weekend Feeling" and "That Spring and Summer Feeling."[62]

The memos referred to in the last sentence above were guides to developing what might be called an "on-vacation" attitude in the listener--one of fun and relaxation.

Commercials

The third of the six music-and-news elements listed by McLendon at the beginning of the Trinity Programming Policy Book, following music and deejay patter, was commercials. Bartell, it will be remembered, had the policy of recording all spots before airing, and, if possible, doing full production on them as well, with the intention of cutting the number of make-goods and enhancing the "slickness" of the station's sound. In the section of the Trinity Book on commercials, McLendon himself proposed another reason for transcribing spots:

---

[62] Ibid.

We are not making nearly enough use of the facilities at our disposal for transcribing spots and making production numbers.

In my opinion, Les Vaughn is about the finest technical production man in the United States. In addition, he has at KLIF equipment and facilities far superior to those at other stations. Furthermore, we have more announcers at KLIF than at most other properties.

If for any given account you need a production spot, you may very well wish Les to do it. If for any account you need a fresh voice, let Les transcribe same using an announcer here. We at KLIF intend to begin using some of your voices for our own commercials here.

Now, as to these production spots: you must get the ideas and you must write them and you must tell us what music you wish put into the spots and/or what special effects or sound effects. If we don't have the music or effects, we'll get them. We had at one time planned to service all Trinity stations entirely by writing and doing the production spots for you here at KLIF but the burden is simply too great. We cannot write them ourselves. But if you will just give us the cold copy and tell us the nature of the production you want, we'll get you the spots. . . .

. . . The way up in sales is production spots which are made before you go to see an advertiser. Make his spot, make it good, and then let him listen to it. You will in most cases make a sale. Get an original idea for him. They are not too difficult to get with a little thought. But you cannot continue to go to advertisers and simply suggest that they "buy some advertising." Usually they won't. Let's start ORIGINAL SELLING and let's really make full use of these big audiences we've built up.[63]

Although it was not feasible for all of the commercial production for all of the Trinity stations to be funneled through KLIF, KLIF did serve as the source for program production aids such as show intros, closings, news sounds, etc. for a number of years. For Bartell, the "flagship" station was WOKY, Milwaukee; for Storz it was KOWH at first, then WHB in Kansas City and then WQAM in Miami. In each case, the station closest to the city where the owner was then residing became the originating station.

---

[63] Ibid.

A subsection of the Trinity Book's section on commercials concerns the matter of spot separation and also supplies McLendon philosophy about the entertainment value of commercials:

> We have several contrivances to separate any necessary double spots. We have promotion spots, we have station singing jingles, we have public service announcements. We also have famous name station breaks.
>
> Let's try to do away with "the news in a few moments," or "we'll hear Perry Como in just a moment." To put it mildly, these are punch telegraphers and are verbatim things we have heard several times from our announcers. Don't occupy it with some senseless statement like those above--put one of our regular spot separators in there. Actually, it would be much more logical to say nothing than call attention to the fact that you are double spotting by saying "the news in a few moments" or "we'll hear from Perry Como in just a moment." Along this line, a little more judicious thought would eliminate some of the double spots. Last week, a show signed on with the theme, followed by a short introduction, then a Maxwell House spot before the first number. This in itself wouldn't have been so bad had it not been for the fact that before the hour was out there were four records played with no spots in between. Try to rotate your spot separators as best you can.[64]

The preceding paragraph alludes to several programming procedures which may not have been apparent on first reading. For one, double spotting was common enough to require such devices as spot separators to give the appearance of providing some kind of entertainment between commercials. Jingles, weather reports, station promos and public service announcements all were used for this purpose. It took a number of years for the notion that there was something heinous about putting one commercial right after another to die out and for the realization to dawn that the faster all the non-hit-music material was dispensed with so that music could begin again, the happier (and more numerous) the listeners. On Drake-style stations today, much of the non-musical

---

[64] Ibid.

material is read over the intros and outros of records so that only a set of commercials and a single short jingle stand in the way of more music. Also, today most contemporary stations play "sweeps" of music, where three or four or more records are played "in-a-row," with no commercial interruptions. In other words, today music is programmed in "chunks" and then commercials are programmed in other "chunks"--the opposite of the spread-them-out approach which McLendon was recommending and which was common in the mid-1950s.

It is also interesting to note that the show which was monitored played a theme to open the program. This was common practice for disc jockey shows, just as themes had been popular on network orchestral programs. The themes would gradually be dropped in favor of very short, simple recorded introductions announcing just the name of the jock, or even no announcement at all but a segue into the first record (usually a fast-paced hit) even as the news close was dying out.

McLendon's philosophy about the entertainment value of commercials follows:

> In this connection, KLIF would like to point out that it doesn't necessarily believe that commercial announcements are bad. You can overdo it, and we are required to keep within Federal Communication rules regarding spot announcements, which we do with great care. However, we have come to the conclusion on Trinity that while people may cuss commercials, they like to hear a reasonable number of well-done commercials--note that I say <u>well done</u>. By this I mean, to some extent, commercials that are funny, unusual, arresting, etc. We do not subscribe to the view of many other radio stations that the fewer commercials a radio station can have, the more listeners it will have. This is not at all true. If the commercials are well done, they can actually be a feature of the station. At KLIF, we believe that our commercials are helping build a listening audience. A lot of them are better than the records we play. Most of them are better than what some announcers say. This is a new concept in radio insofar as we know. This is a concept of having commercials build your listening audience rather than tear it down.

> It can be done and accompanying memoranda on production spots and ingenuity in copy will detail how we think it can be done.[65]

News

The fourth item in McLendon's list of six was news. Storz had developed the "fill-a-void" solution to news coverage by concentrating on local news, which McLendon would also do with mobile news units by the mid-1950s. But in the section of the Trinity Book quoted below, apparently written in late 1952 or early 1953, the local approach had not yet been developed. Instead, there was to be an emphasis on human interest stories, which Storz also used heavily:

> On Doing the News Interestingly
> . . . A lot of stories from abroad are news so repetitious that they just disinterest, bore, and/or confuse listeners. These stories are in the following categories, by and large:
> 1. Repatriation commission hearings.
> 2. Central European political developments.
> 3. The day's activity, or lack of it, in the UN.
> 4. Localized Korean fighting.
> 5. Detailed foreign aid discussions.
> 6. Highly detailed stories on administration forum and other internal problems.
>
> These are, roughly, the type of stories that will in short order, kill any newscast. Naturally, they have then destroyed listenership for your program to follow. Most of the above categories can and should be covered in one sentence or two. It is much better to leave the item out than to confuse the listener with a news service account of localized Korean skirmishing, of Dean Acheson's erudite reasoning on why the Big Four foreign ministers should not agree to deflation of the German mark and should uphold immigration quotas against three-legged Slobovian Cement workers.
>
> You say this is all the news there is? That's not true and we don't want to hear such excuses. There never was a newscast that did not have available good human interest stories or more important, stories that could be made of human interest with a moment's intelligent thought.
>
> On your news service wire for your upcoming 5-minute newscast, and among stories and features from the last 3 hourly

---

[65] Ibid.

newscasts, you will find stories of human interest like this, for example:

1. Marilyn Monroe denies she is marrying Christine Jorgensen.
2. Big Wall Street financier tells businessmen that 1953 will be a prosperous year.
3. Stocks are up quite a bit today.
4. Stalin takes another blast at the United States--he says America is "definitely preparing for war."
5. After all these long years, America has a chance to regain the Davis Cup in Australia tomorrow.
6. Ike has made another Cabinet appointment.
7. The country is snowed in--here are temperatures in some other cities.
8. Louella Parsons says Ava Gardner and Frank Sinatra are about to split up and that Sinatra will go to work for a circus.
9. Local announcer breaks his leg; is recovered by a tractor.
10. Alger Hiss cannot get out of jail; parole board says he'll have to serve his time.

Get the idea? The above mostly fictitious items are interesting. We don't want to give you the idea that we want to eliminate the international or national political news altogether, but at least play down all confusing or uninteresting stories--all stories without human interest.[66]

The human interest angle would later be expanded on McLendon stations newscasts with the addition of regular recorded appearances by Hollywood gossip columnists such as Jimmy Fidler.

Public service announcements

The fifth item in McLendon's list, public service announcements, has never been of great consequence in overall programming, so will not be covered here.

Promotions

The sixth item on the list, promotions, is the one item that clearly separated the evolving Top 40 station from the older music-and-news station, and for the McLendon chain, promotions were the vehicle

---

[66] Ibid.

by which the stations achieved high local listenership and national acclaim. Of course, WNEW and other such music-and-news stations promoted themselves via singing jingles, matchbook covers, taxi top ads and so on, but all of these were restrained, generally accepted and unspectacular methods of promotion. McLendon, with his background in promoting motion pictures for the family's theaters, understood the value of a unique, bizarre, or spectacular promotion in getting people to talk about the station to others, thus multiplying the number of impressions. Many of McLendon's promotions were much more than promotions--they were stunts, entertaining shows in their own right.

> <u>Promotions in the KLIF Program Schedule</u>
> Aside from music and news, the third and almost as important element in the Trinity program schedule is <u>Continuing Promotions</u>.
> This is another method we use to keep our station in front of the listening audience constantly--to keep their mind on our station and to keep people talking about our station. As we have observed elsewhere, in the news style book and in the general programming book, we consider it all-important to have an opportune, alert, on-the-ball station which is constantly a subject of discussion in the community. In order to achieve this objective, we believe that constant promotion, contests, etc., are vitally important.
> Many radio stations think that the best promotion they can get is an advertisement in a newspaper or trade publication. We don't believe so. Although an occasional newspaper advertisement may be a clever promotion, such as occasionally apologizing for a bust, we believe, by and large, that a radio station is its own best advertising medium and that until that radio station is perfect, any money spent in newspapers, except under the most unusual circumstance, is not being particularly wisely spent. We believe in spending it on our own medium first.[67]

McLendon always felt that his stations were in competition with the newspapers, and disliked giving them advertising money because it would seem to potential advertisers that there was, after all, a reason

---

[67] <u>Ibid</u>.

to advertise in newspapers instead of on the radio. Many broadcasters shared this belief, including Storz. George Armstrong believes he is correct in recalling that Storz Broadcasting has never bought a newspaper advertisement nor a billboard for its promotions.[68] Storz and McLendon both liked to promote their stations over their own stations.

> In this connection, it is important to note the difference between the various types of promotions.
>
> This first type of promotion is a type that merely causes comment about the station. This type of promotion does not necessarily increase the station's listening audience at the time the promotion is run. An example of this type of promotion is the business of throwing money out a window at a downtown location. [Bill Stewart was responsible for this particular promotion, to be described in detail in a later section.] This causes plenty of word-of-mouth conversation about the station but doesn't necessarily increase listening audience at all.
>
> The second type of promotion is one which not only causes word-of-mouth conversation about the station but also increases its listening audience at the same time. An example of this type of promotion is the "Mystery Voice Contest," where the people have to listen to the mystery voices in order to identify them and to keep tuned in order to get the clues, but at the same time are going to talk their heads off with neighbors in speculation on which voice is the accurate one.
>
> There are places for both types of promotion in Trinity promotions and Trinity stations.
>
> Another type of promotion is general promotional announcements about how good the station is. We believe in telling the people that we're good--letting them know it constantly. In this connection, if your station has a high rating, here are some examples of promotional announcements that might be used:
>
> 1. Now, according to the latest Hooper ratings, the No. 1 independent station in the United States during the mornings, followed by WIND in Chicago and WNEW in New York.
> 2. Now the No. 1 independent station in the United States in morning share of audience, # 3 in the afternoon and # 4 in the evening hours.
> 3. With more listeners than the other three independent stations in Dallas combined, according to the most recent Hooper ratings.
> 4. The only exclusively disc jockey station in the southwest, with music and news 24 hours a day.

---

[68] Armstrong interview.

5. With more listeners on Saturday than the top 3 network stations in Dallas combined according to the latest Hooper ratings.

The above promotionals will give you an idea of the type we make use of when we find our station high in the ratings, which it always is. You can also find many other things on which generally to promo your station.

It is impossible to list all of the various types of promotion and publicity stunts this station can get into but we will list below, without elaboration, a number of the stunts which have been pulled by the Trinity Broadcasting Corporation with success.

1. War of the Worlds. 2. Screenings. 3. Mystery voices. 4. Walking woman. 5. We give you the answer and you tell us the question. 6. Battle of the Baritones. 7. Big hits of 1954. 8. KLIF teen-age dances. 9. KLIF contest. 10. Christmas Eve trip with Santa Claus. 11. "Do you know" contest. 12. Whose voice? 13. Treasure hunt. 14. Famous recording artist breaks. 15. Contest to find a crew-cut queen. 16. Pop singers contest. 17. Cloud-seeder. 18. Old Scotchman's Vignettes. 19. Money-dropping. 20. Playing same record 3 hours in a row. 21. Contest on "Why I Hate a Certain Disc Jockey." 22. "Why a Certain Disc Jockey Should Get a Raise" contest. 23. Giving away a live baby but not mentioning it's a live baby pig. 24. Having a canary or minah bird in background of your morning announcer which bird he ultimately gives away as a prize. 25. Taking a big news event, like a trial, and building it up into a monster and promoting it constantly on the air. 26. 5-minute program called "Yesterday's Sports Page" by the Old Scotchman. 27. "This Week's Business." 28. Giving away park books. 29. Station jingles. 30. "You never hear this on KLIF." 31. Candid microphone. 32. Last baby of 1954.

The above is a bare outline of some of the contests which have been around KLIF--not only contests, but promotions. We'd like to emphasize here that in these days of big money giveaways by the networks, it is rarely the amount of cash that you give away that makes for an interesting contest. Lots of times, for instance, we've worked out due bills with distant hotels and we give trips, record players, records, etc. In other words, you don't have to give away a lot of cash to have a successful contest. You must have a prize and it must be a representative prize but it doesn't have to be the Eiffel Tower.

Another and most important use of promotion by the station is the use of its telephone facility. We at KLIF try to answer the telephone not by merely saying KLIF but by saying, "This is KLIF--fly North American Airlines" or "This is KLIF--drink Dr. Pepper," or "This is KLIF--trade at City Lincoln-Mercury." In other words, we use our telephone service which, after all, handles hundreds of calls a week, if not thousands on certain

> occasions, to promote the interests of an advertiser. The advertiser is delighted and many times has a lot of his friends call just to demonstrate our service to them. It is a real plus for the station and costs us absolutely nothing.[69]

No doubt the Trinity Programming Policy Book which has been quoted at length above tells the story of the formative years of the Top 40 format incompletely, or with some bias peculiar to the McLendon operation. As pointed out in the Introduction, the author was forced to depend on the McLendon collection because it was the only one made available for study, Bartell and Armstrong (for Storz) being reluctant to volunteer anything beyond an interview. But even if the McLendon operation had been vastly different from that of Bartell and Storz (and the author believes it was not), the Trinity Book would still be a valuable document in tracing the evolving programming for just the McLendon chain, which was after all an important factor in several radio markets.

It should be apparent at this point that the early Top 40 was not a radical nor an overnight departure from the older music-and-news format of the WNEWs and the WHDHs. Management, believing that it shoul be involved first in programming instead of in sales, paid more attention to all of the basic elements of music-and-news, and simply elaborated and improved their impact. The only element that could be considered as a new one is the strong emphasis on promotion. Promotior along with careful attention to the music played, were the two most crucial aspects of what was becoming a Top 40 formula. To make that

---

[69] Trinity Policy Books, undated, unpaginated.

ormula work, a third element was necessary: station monitoring. hese three elements--monitoring, music, and promotion--are treated in etail in the chapter which follows.

CHAPTER FIVE

MANAGEMENT DEVELOPS POLICIES ON MONITORING, MUSIC, AND "PERSONALITY" DJs

The previous chapter discussed a number of facets of the management philosophy out of which Top 40 grew. Management's involvement in programming, its objectivism, its anxiousness to put programming before sales and to fill a void all helped to nurture the new format. In this chapter, several of the most important elements of what became the Top 40 formula will be explored.

A perspective on the meaning of the word "formula" as applied to the type of radio the Top 40 stations had evolved by the end of the 1950s was supplied in 1959 by Harold Krelstein, president of the Plough Stations. Billboard considered it news that the president of one of the most tightly structuralized station groups would declare that there was no such thing as a formula guaranteed to make your stations successful:

> However, what is possible, he said is the use of certain elements "determined thru trial and error, experience and solid judgment . . . in a setting in which they belong, naturally and comfortably for their most effective use."
>
> Unfortunately, he said, most individuals who take pro or con positions on the subject of formula radio are talking about a panacea rather than "creative, imaginative, disciplined programming." Any broadcaster who has achieved success also is, "without exception," a formula broadcaster no matter what his type of programming. The other type of broadcaster, he said, operates "without plan or thought" and borrows ideas from other sources. Krelstein wound up admonishing that "there always

has been formula radio of some sort but there never has been and never will be formula radio which is good for all times or all conditions."[1]

Another point to keep in mind about formula programming is that in actual practice in many cases, the written formula operated as a guideline rather than a strict code. The exigencies of having to get something new on the air quickly, and to keep putting new material on the air, could result in violation of the formula for practical reasons. To imagine that Top 40 stations operated precisely to the standards of a given formula would be a misjudgment. However, the successful stations, as Krelstein stated, operated according to at least some kind of a "management" formula, whether or not they employed a "clock-hour" formula. With station management heavily involved in programming decisions, the development of a mechanism for making comparisons between other stations in the market and one's own--in order to reveal information both about the effectiveness of one's own formula and where it could be improved to be more competitive--was inevitable. It was for these reasons--feedback and competitive advantage--that station monitoring became a standard practice among Top 40 management.

Monitoring

Nationwide and local station monitoring services had existed for a number of years before Top 40 primarily as a service to advertisers and agencies. When the majority of important programming was network-originated and thus the same across the country, knowing the placement and frequency of spot announcements as network adjacencies or

---

[1]"No Guaranteed Success Formula, Says Krelstein," Billboard, June 1, 1959, pp. 3, 51.

on the few participating sponsorship local shows was the only information usually desired. The first company to provide such information on a regular nationwide basis was Broadcast Advertisers Reports, or BAR, which began operating in 1952.[2] At that time, there were already firms that would tape a specific program or series of commercials on special assignment, and a few such firms continue today. The tapes or reports provided could be used both as feedback and as competitive information. In 1955, agencies paid about $5,500 annually for BAR reports on radio and TV in 14 markets, while local stations paid between $250 to $500 per report (covering a week).[3]

By 1956, McLendon was advising all of his managers (by circulating a memo to Bill Weaver, general manager of KTSA in San Antonio) to "constantly monitor" the other stations in their markets. Often the McLendon station monitors were done primarily for programming purposes, but in this memo, McLendon pointed out another reason:

> Bill, something happened here [Dallas] this week to point up the necessity of constantly monitoring the other stations in S.A. [San Antonio]. We are now monitoring here twice a month--that is, we monitor each station in any way competitive on a twice-monthly basis. Reason for this is figures just released showing that in 1955, 3 million went into Dallas radio--this means if we get $600,000 and we did, the two 50 kw boys must have each down [done] around a million, and at least $666,000 each must have been in national business. So, even with our big ratings in 1955, we lost the business. We just assumed we were getting it. Let's don't assume we are getting it in San Antonio, ever. Keep a steady monitor on WOAI, KENS, and KONO, with a lesser eye on KITE. Let's take all of the business. This year, we're going to take at least 60-70% of all national business in the Dallas market and the big reason is that we monitor the

---

[2]"How to Keep an Eye and Ear on the Competition," Sponsor, October 17, 1955, p. 46.

[3]Ibid., p. 119.

accounts constantly and scream to high heaven when something appears on a competitive station and we don't have it.[4]

Station Monitoring for Programming Purposes

Station monitoring for programming feedback purposes was much in evidence among the McLendon stations in 1957. Bill Stewart, who had been National Program Director, had left to join Storz in the same capacity. Larry Monroe, who was program director at KLIF in the summer of 1957 sent a memorandum to Al Lurie, who at that time was General Manager of KTSA in San Antonio. (The major competition to KTSA at the time was KONO, which also programmed some Top 40 records.) Monroe had just visited San Antonio for the purpose of monitoring KTSA.

> Dear Al: These are my basic observations as a result of my recent trip to San Antonio.
>
> (1) One of the major problems is a definite lack of enthusiasm on the part of the DJs. Esprit de corps is at a very low ebb. I believe a long, football-coach type pep talk is in order. You can assure the jocks that we have several new men all lined up and will have some real good boys in San Antonio before long.
>
> I compare this situation with what I ran up against in New Orleans. WTIX there, our Storz competition, started slipping in many of the ways KTSA is now. At WNOE we conceived some great promotions and tightened up the operation considerably for what we thought then would be a push to number one. However, as soon as WTIX tightened up with better production and usual Storz standards they pulled far out in front again. This will be the case at KTSA.
>
> (2) Another serious fault in sound is in music. The overall selection is all right but the individual DJ selection is very bad. Lack of pacing is in evidence in almost every show. The policy of two R & B every hour should be strictly adhered to. As an example, on Ken Knox's Friday afternoon program this was one of his hour's music selection:
>
> 1. Teddy Bear
> 2. So Rare
> 3. The Blues Don't Care--Five Keys

---

[4] Gordon McLendon, mimeographed memorandum to Bill Weaver, Don Keyes, Bill Morgan and Herb Golombeck, McLendon Policy Books, n.d., n.p.

4. Billy Goat
5. Fourteen Karat Gold
6. When My Sugar Walks Down the Street
7. My Personal Possession
8. Instrumental (?)
9. I'll Never Stop Loving You
10. Charlie Gracie
11. Love in the Afternoon
12. Everybody is Going to Roll--Geo. Hamilton IV
13. Hide-a-way Heart

You will notice the first five selections have some kind of rock and roll beat in them. Numbers one and four are definite rock and roll selections. This is too many for one half hour period. There are 4 R & B in this hour, not counting those with a slight R & B beat. As you can see, Al, there is too much R & B. If this is the case with Ken's show, I'm sure it is the same with others. My notes substantiate this.

Ken sounds great on the air. The problem is his music selections.

As it happened, the competition, KONO, was operating with similar restrictions on their music. In a symposium in Sponsor magazine in 1958, KONO program director, Herb Carl, revealed that at that time only 50% of its records were "in the top pop category," they were playing a minimum of 13 sides per hour (the same as KTSA in 1957), and about five to ten percent of the records listed in national best-seller lists did not meet KONO's standards and were not played.[5] As will be shown later, these restricted records were likely to be the rhythm-and-blues numbers.

Monroe's memo on monitoring KTSA in July 1957 went on to discuss some of the good and bad points of other personality's shows, some of which are quoted below:

(3) Hal Murray

After our talk with him Friday he went on to do the best show I have ever heard him do. He stuck as close to the policy as we can ever expect. This shows me that with the proper

---

[5]"Is Music and News Still a Vital Programming Force?" Sponsor, August 9, 1958, p. 46.

guidance he can turn in a top notch job for us. As you know, I had a long talk with him Saturday afternoon. I told him to do the very best job possible on the all-night show and that we will tape portions of his show several nights a week. Please have somebody record three half hours of his program this week. I would suggest frequent pep talks with him . . . if necessary as frequently as every day. During these talks I would play the latest air checks for him and point out his mistakes. Because of his personality I would also point out as many good points as possible. He needs a great deal of encouragement. Please don't let him give the excuse that because he is on the all-night show he can run it differently than his daytime program. It might be wise to tell him that we are re-auditioning him for a daytime show which I personally believe he will do very soon.

The phrases "He stuck as close to the policy as we can ever expect" and "because he is on the all night show he can run it differently than his daytime program" show both sides of the program director's dilemma with following a formula. It is virtually impossible to do a radio program exactly "by the book" because of differences in personnel, problems in timing, etc. At the same time, a consistency-of-sound must be striven for 24 hours a day so that the listener can tune in anytime and know what to expect.

(4) Bob Drews

Music pacing problems mentioned above in evidence here to a great extent (i.e., two R & B selections in a row, then two soft ballads in a row). Our pacing, Al, should be one fast--one slow--one fast--one slow. . . .

Monroe went on to mention another jock who still sounded good on the air but who was "getting discouraged with the lack of station sparkle. . . . He is a great morning man but is very anxious to be surrounded by good men." Monroe then relayed the general feeling of the jocks as he sensed it

They feel, as I have heard by monitoring that they are getting stale and need new sparklers, gimmicks, and McLendonisms. I'm sure we owe them that. Some of my immediate suggestions are these (in addition to those previously mentioned):

(1) Mention very frequently how many Scotch Dollars have been won.
(2) Cross-promo your DJ shows on all programs. Each jock should promo every other jock at least once in his show.
(3) One line contest promos should be aired constantly.
(4) Eliminate datelines from half hour headlines.
(5) Time should be given after every record.
(6) Temperature and forecast, however brief, after every other record.
(7) [A paragraph about handling contests, quoted in a later section.]
(8) The station needs an enthusiastic sound; they should sound as if they are the happiest and most well-paid disk jockeys in the world. The results should be that they will be.
(9) I suggest that you do something about the Miss KTSA contest.

Part of the problem will be in getting the jocks in the right frame of mind to give us their best. An enthusiastic, winning attitude is the best immediate approach, as far as I can see.

Anything I can do to help you out I will do. I'll let you know as soon as possible how many new jocks we have. In the meantime let me know how many replacements you are going to make.[6]

The final paragraph of the memo quoted above makes it clear that the monitoring of KTSA by Monroe, an outsider, was to give an added opinion on how various disc jockeys sounded so that they could be either retained or fired. Virtually all of the information was intended as internal programming feedback.

Don Keyes produced a similar report on KLIF for Gordon McLendon in November of 1957. Keyes had been a disc jockey on both KTSA and then KILT when they were started, and had been away from Dallas for some time, which, he felt, qualified him to make comparisons. At the time of the writing of Keyes' memo, KLIF had just celebrated its tenth anniversary on the air, and had run an extra-heavy schedule of

---

[6] Larry Monroe memorandum to Al Lurie, July 24, 1957, McLendon Policy Books, n.p.

promotions for this event. Keyes spent the bulk of his time in the memo critiquing the morning man's show.

> Bruce's show is loose and disjointed. While the sense of humor and remarks still remain the same, the continuity of the entire show seems to have fallen apart. I think this comes from violation of three basic policies. In order they are: (a) bad music; (b) too much extraneous talk; (c) bad pacing.
>
> To illucidate:
>
> (a) There seemed to be an abundance of rock 'n' roll during the first hour. I was not familiar with the record after the seven ayem [sic] news but it was a horrible rock 'n' roll which I don't think should even be on the station; this was followed by "The Mad Martians," a novelty "space" record. "Yody Yacky" by the Drifters lead off after the seven thirty headlines and even Bruce had a few humorous remarks to say about the title; the record itself grated on my ears at that time of day.
>
> (b) The hour from seven to eight contained 18 commercials. This would not be too much of a load if handled discretely. However, only eight records were played during the entire hour. There should have been eleven in my opinion. I get the impression that Bruce thinks his chatter is more important than the music. I would quite agree with this if the chatter had been entertaining but too much of the time it was disjointed and rambling. He spoke of course of satellites, UFOs and a few kickers from UP, but for one example, what with three commercials, plus ad lib, he went for 6 minutes without music from 7:07:30 to 7:13:10. This talk was about the weather, amount of rainfall so far, year of lowest rainfall, etc. I definitely think that this information was quite good for the rainy days we've been having but it should have been meted out throughout the next few records, not in one bunch causing 6 minutes of talk. Another crutch that Bruce uses is that of humming or singing after the records or musical commercials. This too I am not against but he ran it into the ground. After a while I got to wondering just when he was going to stop humming and tell me something. Just one other item about Bruce. I vehemently protest the constant and ridiculous use of the editorial "we." This is not a newspaper and I think the use of "we," when overdone sounds positively absurd. I don't recall the connection but Bruce referred to "the nape of our neck." This struck me as being positively asinine. I have instructed my jocks in San Antonio and Houston to become people and not just voices. What is wrong with saying, "When I got up this morning" as opposed to "when we got up this morning." Unless of course, you were sleeping with someone. To me, the use of "I" is just another way of becoming a "regular guy" to the listener. A person endowed with the same joys and problems as the listener.
>
> Bruce's show is basically good but I think with observance of some basic policies it can become much better.

Keyes then went on to criticize other shows aired on through the day. For an early afternoon shift handled by George Singer, Keyes made these recommendations, among others:

> . . . All in all however, the show was a bit flat. I think Gramps should become the producer of the show rather than just a disjointed "character" who happens to be present. Joel Spivak does a similar thing at KILT that has the same effect. Gramps should have something to do with the show. I also suggest that on a cold, raw day such as yesterday, George's show should be done from the "Pine paneled KLIF Den"--talk about roaring fire-place, crackling hearth, hot chocolate, popcorn, lounge chair, warm lights, comfortable footstool, lounging robe and other things that might denote warmth and comfort on a cold day. Also consider stealing the "Crystal Studio" from WNEW. It certainly conjures a picture. George needs to turn some imagination loose on his block and develop it to a great degree. As I say, right now it sounds quite flat and void of color.

It is interesting to note just how much the disc jockeys were being encouraged to project their personalities and an atmosphere around their shows. Management had largely usurped the jocks' old prerogative of choosing the records to be played, but at this point airing other facets of the jock's personality was still being encouraged McLendon's disc jockeys were true personalities, not just time-and-temperature jocks.

Keyes concluded the memo to McLendon with "General Comments for Improvement of KLIF":

> (a) There was too much r 'n' r during the nine to three block. Regardless of a record's position on the survey, I think that it should be on the restricted list if it is at all "teenage."
> (b) We need more cute promos on the air.
> (c) I suggest we have the community bulletin board like WNEW. A production intro would precede the spot and would add a bit to our sound of "production."[7]

---

[7]Don Keyes, memorandum to Gordon McLendon, November 5, 1957, McLendon Policy Books, n.p.

Competitive Monitoring

Competitive monitoring was carried out both formally and informally. The McLendon stations used both commercial and in-house formal monitoring, some of which will be described shortly. The McLendon stations also employed a number of informal means of "monitoring" other stations to gain a competitive advantage. A common method of informal "monitoring" was the "de-briefing" of a personality or manager who was leaving one company for another. Another was to talk informally with the management of another station group and then write down the salient information for later local use. Both of these methods were used by the McLendon organization, but it must be emphasized that this fact should in no way affect their reputation. "Spying," if it may be called that, is no less common in the radio industry than in any other where there is a competitive advantage to be gained by being the first to introduce a new idea, and the McLendon group certainly did not engage in the practice unilaterally.

Informal debriefing

A transcript of a conversation which someone in the McLendon organization had about March of 1956 with George W. Armstrong, who was then vice-president of Storz's Mid-Continent Broadcasting Company and general manager of WHB in Kansas City has been quoted briefly before, in the chapter concerning station acquisitions. The writer of "A Confidential Report on WHB" is not identified, and the date of its composition has been ascertained only through tracing references in the text.

> . . . WHB presently has a maximum of 15 spots per hour. This includes only one-minute spots plus two quickie 20-second

breaks on the half-hour. In other words, 13 one-minute spots per hour, plus two 20-second quickies on the half hour. Armstrong got a little bit worried about the possible effect it would have on his audience, and the fact that KCMO was making some noises about bringing in some outside disc jockeys, so he decided to cut back to 15 spots per hour. . . .

. . . .

I pointed out to Armstrong that certain stations weren't rating very high on news in the 5:30 p.m. period and discussed with him the possibilities of format variance to include a newscast at 5:30 in the afternoon. It was his thought, and he may or may not be right, that unless <u>your own</u> rating drops at 5:15 and you can see that the news program is taking your own audience, it is not necessary to do anything about it. In other words, if the news programs at 5:30 are taking the audience from other stations rather than you, it is okay, but if they are taking the audience from you, it may be a good idea to consider it on a five-minute basis. . . .

The "it" referred to in the last sentence seems to refer to the idea of a top 40 station's instituting a 5:30 newscast of its own to compete with that offered by other stations.

As already noted in other memos, they have practically no record library. The record library consists of the Top 40 and a few old standards, and that's it. . . .

They have some new, short singing station identification breaks which the musical groups have recorded for them free. They have only one newsman. Armstrong has union problems which make him hesitant to go all out in news until he has to. He says he has a hunch that he will have to someday in spite of the union problems. They of course have union engineering and announcing departments. . . .

He says that so far, KOWH has lost only a couple of points in Hooper share-of-audience to now-independent fulltimer KOIL. KOIL is second with about 16% of the audience, but will now get a little commercial business and will begin to level off. He says that this is what has happened to us (WNOE) in New Orleans; i.e., that we went up sharply and then got some commercial business and leveled off. We were going up sharply, in his opinion, just as long as we didn't have so much commercial and WTIX was overloaded. But when both stations got to about equal and comparable business, we leveled off. I do not agree that this is the reason for the levelling-off, as I think it is a deficiency on the part of the disc jockeys at WNOE. The station he cannot understand in New Orleans is WBOK, the Negro station, which continues to have a high morning rate of audience, but with terrible Negro programming. . . .

He is still using a jukebox for operation between 12 and 6, but no talk except transcribed announcements. . . .

Storz buys stations on the formula of top facility, plus good rate market, plus Top 40 and Lucky House Number, plus no competition. They would have to have no competition in Kansas City because it is one of the dullest sounding stations I have ever heard. It just has the music and news formula in its purest form, and that is about all. WHB also has "The Nightclub of the Air" 10:30 to 12:00, a live show from a local restaurant that is really terrible. . . .[8]

As mentioned when first quoted, the writer of "A Confidential Report on WHB" is not identified, nor is the style clearly that of any one person in the McLendon organization. Whoever it was obviously talked openly with Storz executive George Armstrong, so that most of the information seems to have been freely volunteered.

Formal debriefing

A document from about three years later, 1959, is probably a representative sample of the "de-briefing" type of monitoring. Kent Burkhart had recently left a program director position with one of the Storz stations when he was questioned by Don Keyes of McLendon. Keyes asked Burkhart 21 questions, most of which were on programming policy, and all of the latter will be quoted below. Keyes' letter to Burkhart was dated February 28, 1959. Burkhart's reply was dated March 9, 1959. Keyes' numbering of questions is retained--since non-programming questions will not be quoted here, the numbering will not be consecutive.

Dear Kent,
Here are some questions the answers of which I would consider most interesting. They concern, of course, the Storz operation.
1. What policy exists on how much talking a disc jockey is allowed to do between records? What is the theory behind this policy?

---

[8] "A Confidential Report on WHB," McLendon Policy Books, n.d., n.p.

1. The "talking" policy you refer to has never been in written form; however, it is governed mostly by the various markets and their radio environments plus a general policy of "don't talk unless you have something useful to talk about." The quoted rule is pounded into the head of each disc jockey before he begins work at the station, and at every available moment, or any needed moment. However, in some cases--for example, Kansas City--it is permissible for a personality to become cleverly chummy with his audience, but not in great length. Miami, Minneapolis, and Kansas City all observe this policy. New Orleans varies, as later words will indicate. Theory: useless words are truly useless!

The whole question of just how much the disc jockey should be allowed to talk was--and is--a constant problem for management and a constant irritation for the disc jockeys whose monologues were being shortened. This aspect of programming policy will be treated in detail in a later section, as it was a major criticism that disc jockeys made of the Top 40 format.

2. How long is the record kept on the air?
2. A record is kept on the air for not more than a period of 16 weeks, or four months. A one week listing on the playlist is the minimum airtime devoted to a recording. However, as I will explain about the "familiar" or "recognizable" tunes later, I shall leave the preceding statement as it is.

It should be remembered that in the late 1950s, the "life" of a pop record was considerably longer than it is now. The four-months figure was not at the time an extraordinary one; however, the Storz stations had a policy of holding a record in the playlist longer than most other stations of the type on the assumption that it would take adult listeners longer to become identified with the song, and that in order to get and keep adults in the audience, a song had to be retained longer.

3. What is policy on frequency of use of call letters?
3. Actually, the policy on call letter mentions is up to the local management and program director. Obviously, both know the value of such frequent use of the call letters, and I believe I would be safe in assuming that at least one mention between

> records would be the minimum. In Miami, I required at least three mentions between every record during Hooper week, and at least two mentions during the other three weeks of the month. There were live announcer mentions, and did not include any ET'd ["electrically transcribed; that is, recorded] promos, singing breaks, etc. In brief, hot and heavy use. All the stations observe the same or similar mentioned ideas.

The topics of call letters, station recall, and ratings hypos will all be treated in later sections. Note here, however, that with at least two live call letter mentions between each record, plus the mentions transcribed into the omnipresent station jingles and the promo announcements, the call letters were literally always on the air. They even appeared in the middle of some records which were exclusively released to that station, to prevent other stations from taping the release off the air and playing it on their own. And virtually every physical object, from thermometers to mobile units, was preceded with the call letters when mentioned, as of course were any feature segments.

> 9. You and I discussed programming "recognizable" tunes. Can you explain this idea more fully?
> 9. Well . . . in general the idea is to play tunes that are currently popular or have been popular, not those necessarily that will be popular. After all, we're trying to entertain the people listening, not force them into something new that they may not and often do not like! KLIF follows this idea, maybe not knowing it, and so does KILT. However, KTSA sounds at times like the Hit Parade is a thing of the past. In truth, since you came down and goosed 'em, they sound a hell of a lot better. (You should do that more often.) Incidentally, this is a strong Storz belief, and I can safely say that only about five to ten new records a week are new ones. Those are selected from the obviously up-and-coming records listed in _Billboard_'s "Coming Up Strong" section.

It is remarkable that the idea of the true limited playlist that was introduced in Omaha by Storz and Stewart in 1956 had not been taken over in 1959 by the McLendon organization as a consistent policy. In the operation of the true limited playlist, not only was just _one_ version of a song chosen, but it was also made certain that it was played over and over, to the exclusion of more varied music. The idea was to provide both consistency and repetition. The limited playlist is another concept which will be explained in great detail later.

The Storz stations in 1959 were already following the "cautious" approach to programming new releases which is still very much in evidence today, with the basic idea of playing "tunes that are currently popular or have been popular" the currently-operative criterion. KTSA was apparently violating this precept by playing new releases or other non-hit music--in effect trying to program the audience's tastes rather than the other way around. The consistently good share-of-audience figures carried by Storz stations at this period when other stations were imitating the style and dividing up the available listeners may have prompted Keyes' question.

> 10. Is there a commercial limit set within a given hour of airtime?
> 10. Yes. Eight commercials, minute length, first half of hour; seven commercials, minute length second half of hour; and six twenty-second announcements, two of which are scheduled on the half-hour break, two of which are on the break before the news, two of which follow the news. All are separated by a singing station break and perhaps a time or temperature check.

The reason Keyes had to ask this question is obscure. A regular off-the-air monitor of a Storz station would have yielded the same answers quite quickly. Many broadcasters were able to copy the "skeleton" of a successful format by duplicating the placement of spots and so forth, while the philosophy behind the formula generally eluded them, which in many cases proved to be their undoing.

> 12. Does the Top 40 show in the afternoon run on all stations? Does the disc jockey start out playing # 40 and go through to # 1 each day?

12. At the time of my leaving, the Top 40 was being run from either three to six or four to seven at all the stations. This has been the most popular radio program, in whole, for the Storz stations. The idea was stolen from Bob Howard's Top Twenty in New Orleans years ago. . . . [Over WDSU--"The Top Twenty at 1280." When Storz bought WTIX in New Orleans, as a competitive move they instituted the Top 40, the thinking then being the more records the better. Obviously, the records near the 40 mark were far less of a hit than those in the Top 10.] Let me point out that the format for each Top 40 program will vary with the individual stations. Experimentation is used to find out whether 40 through 1 or a rotating record show will better identify a larger audience. In Miami, Monday-Wednesday-Friday, it's 1 through 40, and Tuesday-Thursday-Saturday and Sunday, it's 40 down to 1. Kansas City, I believe is still rotating the records in any order. The same applies for the Minneapolis station; again, I'm not too sure about the New Orleans station. When I was in Omaha, I actually ran the first 40-down-to-1 every day type of operation. It was a success there. We had 50 and 60 percent of the audience; however, we found a drop in Kansas City, etc. Depends on market.

In answering this question, Burkhart brings up several interesting facts about the Storz operation. First, there was no dedication to the idea that what would work in one city would work exactly the same way in another. Second, there was actual experimentation to see which method would work best in each city. Such experimentation would finally show that playing the list in order was something of a "tuneout" when the bottom numbers were being played, so that in the ratings some quarter hours suffered while those containing the big hits did very well. There were only three ways out of this dilemma. One was to play nothing but the top ten or so songs--the <u>most</u> popular records. The author recalls hearing WMCA, New York, doing this about the early 1960s, and also recalls being thoroughly bored the third time through. The other, more successful method, which is the one used today, is to shorten the list in actual practice by playing the big hits more frequently and the lesser hits just enough to provide variety. When WQAM took an enormous lead in Miami soon after it became a Storz station, without using giveaways, one of the factors was public reference to the playlist as the Top 40" while in actual practice the top 25 tunes received most of the play.[9] Tightening the playlist in this way is what Bill Stewart refers to as the best method of "limiting your mistakes."

14. Is there any pattern within the hour on the use of time, temperature, weather?
14. I required temperature and time between every record, weather forecast every 15 minutes, plus twice on the hour; however this is up to the local Program Director. There is no set pattern as such.

Again, this question could have been determined by Keyes through off-the-air monitoring. The reasons for such placement would have been more important to know.[10]

15. How important does Todd consider sports scores to be? News, especially local?
15. Sports scores have really never been stressed except in a Kansas City (major league). They are generally carried on the :25 mark, and if a big score comes in, it will be given immediately. But, in general, no promotion is given. The Storz stations try to build news reputation by spending a little money, and by promoting the news director alone . . .

---

[9] Stewart interview.

[10] An interesting sidelight concerning timechecks is provided by Grahame Richards, who was National Program Director for Storz after Stewart left in 1959. In a letter to Richards, now Vice President and General Manager of KFAC, Los Angeles, the author commented that he was especially intrigued with a news close used on WQAM in the early 1960s (during Richards' tenure) which featured a hyperthyroid vocal group chanting the phrase "Ahead . . . of . . . the world . . . W-Q-A-M time!" at which time the disc jockey gave the time and "banged in" with the first record of the new hour. Richards wrote: "Your comment relative to 'ahead of the world, WQAM time! . . .' generates additional detail for your information. The fact of the matter was that all of WQAM's clocks were set ahead one minute so that in effect we were indeed ahead with WQAM time." Cited from a letter to the author from Mr. Grahame Richards, Vice President and General Manager, KFAC, Los Angeles, March 14, 1972.

(always the A.M. man). Mobile units are too expensive according to Omaha so most of the units have been done away with. The News Director tries to get close to the desk sergeants by sending them a fifth every now and then . . . but no real money is spent on news at all. Matter of fact, the recent "economy wave" kicked out one of the news services plus the special news telephone ("hot line news tips") plus the weather and Western Union machines.

There is an interesting comparison here with the McLendon operation, where news was (in the early days) considered of equal importance with the music in attracting and holding an audience. McLendon, being personally intrigued with news anyway--as was Don Keyes--backed his interest with both money and equipment. The Storz "economy wave" was thought to be motivated by the sale of stock to the public, as has been mentioned earlier; McLendon could afford to show less of a return on investment because all his stations were owned by the family.

16. What is the most successful promotion the Storz stations have ever run in their markets? Why?
16. Well, I think I have to say the Treasure Hunt gimmicks and the Appreciation Night gimmicks, both of which you're familiar with, I'm sure. Results: a lot of talk around town . . . and something to blow about. Big crowds, etc.

The promotion policies of all Top 40 group owners will be treated in greater detail in a later section. Again here, note that the motive for the promotion was simply to get the station talked about.

18. How do you explain the difference in sound of WTIX and other Storz stations? Why is it so much tighter and faster and more formalized?
18. This is very simple. WTIX is the Siberia of the Storz stations. He now sends his worst men there. They are instructed to say nothing but the time and temperature, read the plug board, comment on another disc jockey, etc. They are told to move quickly--fast pace. Since there isn't much chatter anyway, this produces a quick, tight, fast operation. That sounds ridiculous, but has so far been doing OK. Fred [Berthelson, WTIX General Manager] is a big one for screaming and hard pitch on the air also. Now you can see.

Again, the differences between Storz stations from market to market is apparent. WTIX was being used as a place to send jocks who at that time were considered "his worst men" because all they had to do was be a "time-and-temperature" disc jockey instead of projecting personality. It is likely that the WTIX sound at this time resembled that of the Plough stations, which had also de-emphasized personalities. It is ironic that Storz would send his worst men to WTIX and still beat the McLendon-programmed WNOE in the ratings.[11]

The 11 questions of the 21 asked Burkhart that have not been quoted here had to do with topics other than programming. The questions quoted either reveal a surprising lack of information about basic Storz programming policies, or else they were asked with full knowledge of those policies with Burkhart's answers to be used as a check for accuracy. However, such questions as "You and I discussed programming 'recognizable' tunes. Can you explain this idea more fully?" seem to suggest that Keyes really did not understand the concept. To state that he was unaware of it would be pure conjecture, but generally the two documents just quoted suggest that Storz programming ideas were "ahead" of McLendon's at this time in the sense that Storz was already using them and McLendon, via Keyes, would adopt a number of them later. (However, the question of who was "ahead" of whom is finally a fruitless one in Top 40, because it can be effectively argued that each of the groups contributed some factor before the others had it.) For this

[11]Don Keyes, memo to Kent Burkhart, February 28, 1959; and Kent Burkhart, memo to Don Keyes, March 9, 1959, both from McLendon Policy Books, n.p.

discussion, the importance of the Keyes-Burkhart "de-briefing" lies not so much in the particular facts gathered as in the fact that such occurrences took place. Again, it must be emphasized that the McLendon stations were far from alone in the practice. One can imagine the glee with which Storz debriefed Bill Stewart after he left McLendon the first time, or Don Burden gleaning what he could when Stewart left Storz for the Star stations. It can be argued that Stewart's peripateticism among the two most-reported group owners heavily influenced the spread of the Top 40 formula.

Costs of monitoring

A document directly concerned with station monitoring, and concentrating on the cost and content of the practice, appears in the McLendon Policy Books as a carbon copy of a memorandum to Bill Morgan, General Manager of KLIF, with carbons going to all other station managers. The memo was written November 25, 1962 by Gordon McLendon.

> Some of the material has begun to filter in from other stations regarding commercial monitoring charges of our various stations. I give you this for your own personal information in the thought there may be some real economies you can achieve in this direction since you are presently spending $1,920.00--almost $2,000.00--a year on this item.
>
> From Weaver comes this information: "My commercial or music monitors cost me $8.00 per station per day. I usually monitor three stations at a time for a total of $24.00. This is for a 12-hour monitor."
>
> Art Holt has reported that his monitor charges at WYSL are $20.00 per month. To be precise, here is the exact language of his report: "Current monitoring allowance for WYSL is $20.00 . . . or two monitors monthly. Our normal plan is to monitor WGR and WKBW one month and WBEN and WEBR the next . . . although in some of the months of the year we go below this by monitoring only one station . . . WGR, for example, has so few local accounts that we usually can cover it through having the salesmen listen when they are in their cars and they can easily remember the few local accounts heard."

> You will note that Weaver's commercial monitor is also a music monitor, which is interesting.
>
> The San Francisco broadcast audit cost $71.00 per month.
>
> You yourself [Bill Morgan, KLIF General Manager] pay $160.00 per month for monitors. If you wish, and where this memo does not make it clear, you might wish to contact the individual stations and find out what they exactly receive. I have the feeling, as you yourself have suggested that you suspect, that you may be getting more information than you really need. On the other hand, I am the last one in the world to want to eliminate sales expense that bears fruit. It seems to me that 20 monitors per month might be excessive.

Apparently the last sentence was not intended sarcastically. Perhaps Morgan, who had been in a programming executive position at ABC since leaving KLIF's general managership the first time in 1957, had become used to disposing of large sums of corporate money.

It can be seen that, in 1962, McLendon's stations had a general policy of doing regular commercial and music-monitoring, with the first for competitive sales purposes and the second for programming purposes. The volatility of the market in both aspects appears to have determined the frequency of monitoring which the local general managers ordered.

By 1964, the practice of monitoring had been taken up by advertising agencies. By August of that year, the Dancer-Fitzgerald-Sample agency had collected half-hour airchecks from more than 300 stations to act as an aid in buying markets where ratings were close, or in markets where ratings were infrequent or not available at all.[12] The tapes were, however, produced and provided by the stations, and were likely (from the author's own experience) not to be truly representative. However, with each station in a given market "putting its

---

[12] "Tape Library Becomes Buying Aid," Broadcasting, August 3, 1964, p. 50.

best foot forward" on its tape, at least a general idea of the "personality" of the station as it might be at its finest hour could be obtained, and an overall comparison of one "formula" versus another could be made.[13]

Station monitoring was one of the principal agents in the diffusion of Top 40 formula ideas, but more importantly it was the means by which the effectiveness of each addition or change in the formula was judged. At a time when music popularity varied much more from market to market than it does today, monitoring was especially important in developing the single most important part of a station's formula--its music policy.

Music Policy

Throughout the history of Top 40 radio, the one factor that has been of most crucial importance in making or breaking a station is its music policy. It has been said by a number of program directors and station managers that if you can get the music right, you can do almost everything else wrong and still have a competitive radio station.

Background

The "flagship" stations of the three major Top 40 group owners--Storz's KOWH in Omaha, McLendon's KLIF in Dallas and Bartell's WOKY in Milwaukee all played "popular" music early in the 1950s. KOWH had begun playing popular music exclusively about six months after Storz bought the station in 1949. However, there is a vast difference between

---

[13]In a letter replying to the author's question of what became of these tapes, a Dancer-Fitzgerald-Sample representative said the tapes had just recently been destroyed.

playing popular music and playing the hits; there is another gulf between playing the hits and playing only the "best" version of the song; there is a gap between doing that and playing only a certain number of hits such as 40 or so; and finally there is a difference between playing a Top 40 list and in playing a true limited playlist where the most popular records are heard far more frequently than the less-known sides. Here is the progression of the development of the Top 40 music policy shown as a list, for easier comprehension:

Pre-1949 (and also after, on non-Top 40 stations) . . .	Currently popular music mixed with other types
Late 1949-early 1950	KOWH concentrates on popular music
About 1953, with purchase of WTIX, New Orleans, and also put on KOWH, Omaha--the first "Top 40" show . . .	Block programming of current hit tunes (but sometimes different versions); otherwise popular music
About 1954 on KLIF	Playing from the Top 40 hit list outside of the "countdown" program block
Done on McLendon stations in late 1955--early 1956 . . .	Selecting one "best" version of a hit song
1956, KOWH and then other Storz stations--Stewart and Storz . . .	The true limited playlist--biggest hits heard most often; non-hits avoided

By 1956, the true limited playlist was in use on the Storz stations. Its two main points were consistency and repetition, consistency meaning that the station could be relied on to play the hits all the time, not just during a "Top 40 countdown" show at a certain hour, and repetition meaning that the most popular records were repeated more often than the less popular ones. The concept of the true limited playlist has changed almost not at all since 1956, when Todd Storz and Bill

Stewart instituted it on KOWH.

The music-and-news stations such as KOWH, WNEW, and WHDH, had been playing popular music for years. Your Hit Parade had been on radio for years as well, each week listing the top songs in the nation. There were even block-programmed local "hit parade" shows, such as Bob Howard's Top 20 at 1280 on WDSU in New Orleans, which WTIX doubled to the Top 40 in 1953. In 1953, the Storz stations were playing popular music throughout the day, but were playing the Top 40 hits only in a three hour block, usually in the afternoon to take advantage of the after-school teen audience. While they confined themselves to running the Top 40 in a program block, the Storz stations were not appreciably different from the many other stations that ran their own "hit parade" shows. It was only when the idea of playing the best version of the hit tunes all day long was adopted that a new format was begun. There probably is no exact date for when this was done, but it obviously occurred between 1953 and 1956. Since no date turns up in any printed material available to the author, it seems likely that the shift was a gradual one rather than something that was instituted suddenly and with dramatic effect. This conclusion is borne out by tracing the evolution of the McLendon stations' music policy.

Evolution of Music Policy at McLendon's and Storz's Stations

In 1953, Gordon McLendon wrote an already-quoted memorandum to KELP (El Paso) General Manager Joe Roddy, in which McLendon seemed somewhat puzzled that KLIF was taking the audience away from the long time independent leader in Dallas, KIXL. McLendon concluded that the reason this was happening was that KIXL was too calm and placid, while KLIF was fresh and exciting. Speaking of the difference in music policy between KIXL and KLIF, McLendon said,

> Here in Dallas, I sense (without knowledge of what the Hooper is, but Pulse reflects it for whatever that is worth) that we are taking the audience away from KIXL at a rapid rate--this, Joe, in spite of the fact that KIXL spends all day long on its production, has a vastly greater musical library, spends infinitely longer on its choice of music, etc. . . .

At this point McLendon explained his theory of why KLIF was taking KIXL's audience, and then continued about the music policy.

> In addition to these new ideas, there is the important problem of the choice of music. There is considerable popular music that can and should be played on KELP. By and large, KIXL just doesn't make any consistent use of popular music. I want us to do so. You should definitely not use old or new pop numbers out of tune with the type of station we are running but there are just one hell of a lot of bright, racy tunes that can fit right in with our pattern. I believe that we should not be more than 70%, and preferably, about 60% of KIXL. The Les Paul, Mary Ford daring stuff, a lot of Como's stuff, even Joni James has frequent records that fit in.
>
> So, keep the station fresh with an occasional new idea that gets the town talking, and secondly, keep the choice of music ALIVE with enough <u>good</u> pop mixed with the semi-classical.[14]

It should be remembered that the intent with KELP initially was to make it into an El Paso version of KIXL, with the sort of soothing background music that television could not provide. With this memorandum, McLendon was urging the inclusion of more <u>popular</u> music. Note that he does not specify the playing of <u>current hit records</u>, and in fact cautions against the use of "old or new pop numbers out of tune with the type of station we are running. . . ."

A little more than a year later (July 1954), McLendon wrote to

---

[14]Gordon McLendon, Memorandum to Joe Roddy, April 11, 1953, four pages, pp. 1 and 2 quoted, from the <u>McLendon Policy Books</u>.

Roddy again, this time apparently answering a request from Roddy for some suggestions that would make KELP more like KLIF, which was beginning to enjoy a huge success and which had displaced KIXL among top-rated independent stations.

> KLIF is a bit different than KELP and, by way of doing some constructive thinking about KELP improvements, I've tried to analyze what we'd have to do to make KELP another KLIF. These are the big differences between the stations as I see them now:
> 1. KLIF has disc jockeys in every time period and emphasizes names. KELP doesn't.
> 2. KLIF is built heavily around the top 20 tunes.
> 3. KLIF has a mobile news unit and goes in heavily for local news.
> 4. KLIF goes in for constant promotions, contests, etc. Right now, for instance, we have hired our own cloud-seeder to make rain over the city of Dallas. Following this, there will be a terrific Treasure Hunt. Include in our promotions all night operation.
> 5. KLIF carries six vignettes a day and these are very popular.
>
> Now, presumably if you made alterations in your format to include these five items, you'd be another KLIF. Whether it would actually happen or not, we can't know for certain but I would imagine that you'd be very much in the same situation.[15]

Note from the above quotation that KLIF had begun to be consistent at least in the use of disc jockeys throughout the day, so that listeners could tune in and find a disc jockey show at any hour.

KLIF, according to McLendon, was "built around the top 20 tunes." This statement might lead one to believe that McLendon (or someone at KLIF) had already limited the playlist, but later evidence shows this not to be the case. No doubt the top 20 tunes were played, but it is likely that they were not played repetitively. In addition, at this time it was likely that more than one version of a song would be played, as "covers" were still much in vogue.

---

[15]Gordon McLendon, letter to Joe Roddy, July 27, 1954, six pages, pp. 1 and 2 quoted, from McLendon Policy Books.

McLendon amplified the importance of playing the hit music further on in his letter to Roddy:

> Which of the five things would you like to do--or all of them. I can't make definite decisions about El Paso. That is entirely up to you. I can only speculate. It does seem to me that if you turned to disc jockeys you've got more trouble in the prima-donna department, although I doubt that your expenses would rise much in the program department. Even though we have disc jockeys, you see, all our people work their 40 hours a week. And you are paying no less for your regular announcers than you'd have to pay for disc jockeys. So, it seems to me that economically it would be feasible for you to turn to disc jockeys if you wished to do so.
>
> As for the second point, it would cost you nothing to change your musical format to equal or rather match ours. Whether you should do this is a matter for your own speculation. Certainly, the business of keeping top twenty tunes in your format is important to avoid competition in the market.[16]

It is apparent from the final sentence above that playing hit music was perceived by McLendon as an important competitive advantage for KELP, so that it is likely that he considered it so for KLIF as well. Elsewhere he mentions that KIXL also had begun to add popular music to its format, but as has been pointed out, KLIF had the advantage of playing it more consistently.

An item in Billboard's "Vox Jox" column for April 16, 1955 reveals that, at that time, KLIF was still playing a rather wide variety of music. KLIF deejay Gene Edwards had written to the column to note that fellow KLIF jock Larry Monroe "has the town going Dixieland crazy with his raccoon club."[17]

In 1955 and 1956, KLIF was a member of AIMS, the Association of Independent Metropolitan Stations, a group of independent radio

---

[16] Ibid.

[17] June Bundy, "Vox Jox," Billboard, April 16, 1955, p. 16.

stations--one in each major market--which exchanged advice, tips and ideas about programming and selling independent radio, and primarily music-and-news radio. It was a non-competitive organization in which membership was by invitation only. The Storz stations were affiliated with the group both before and after McLendon, and at one time Storz was chairman of the group. (AIMS will be discussed fully in a later chapter.) An AIMS meeting (apparently in 1955) attended by Cecil Hobbs, then general manager of KLIF, included a discussion of music policy. In a memo from Hobbs to McLendon, Hobbs remarked,

> . . . Another idea that I like was the possible air check of announcers from time to time and also the possibility of pre-selected music--provided, of course, we had someone with the ability to make the proper choice. As far as I am concerned, the choice of music is becoming more and more important.[18]

It is apparent from the foregoing that someone at this AIMS meeting (Todd Storz was in attendance) had suggested that management "pre-select" all of the music played. In spite of the burden this would place on management, Cecil Hobbs thought it a good idea, both because it was clear to him at the time that the correct choice of music could make-or-break a station, and also probably because the removal of the selection process from disc jockey control would, in the long run, produce a greater uniformity in programming and standards--both of which were likely to be management's goals.

Documents in the McLendon Policy Books show that by the fall of 1957, management control of music policy was an accomplished fact. A memo from Ken Knox, then KLIF general manager, is mostly concerned with

---

[18]Cecil Hobbs, AIMS meeting memorandum to Gordon McLendon, McLendon Policy Books, n.d., n.p., but probable date supplied by tracing references.

preparations for KLIF's tenth anniversary celebration, including a number of new production aids that were recorded on discs (ETs). Those relating to the music policy are listed below:

> 1. KLIF BOMB OF THE WEEK
> E. T. open/close in C. R. [Control Room] "Bomb" records in C. R. (picked by p. d.) [program director] Records to vary from day to day--limited to Bruce Hayes, Art Nelson and Mark Foster Shows. Ten. [Means ten cuts available]
> 2. PICK HIT OF THE WEEK
> E. T. open/close in C. R. R. A. S. [run as scheduled] on log. Record in C. R. Announce winners from sheet provided by p. d. each Friday 6 PM to Midnight.
> 3. INTRO TO SONG NUMBER 1, 2, 3, 4 and 5
> E. T. intro only. In C. R. Not logged--does not have to be used every time. Use two or more of the five intros per show.
> 4. ANNIVERSARY SONG INTRO
> 93 separate cuts. E. T. (open only) R. A. S. on log. Anniversary songs chosen by p. d. and in c. r. rack. Songs were hits during KLIF's ten years. Additional historical info from year each record was popular also provided LIVE in c. r. (thanks to Edd Routt for research) Each record will have "year" it was popular written on label.
> 5. INTO TO "TOP FORTY NEW-COMER."
> E. T. open only, in c. r. New comers to T-40 marked "new" on T-40 sheet in c. r. window. Use e. t. sparingly to avoid "sameness."[19]

Note that in the case of items 1 and 4 above, the program director was immediately responsible for selecting the music. In number 2, the program director chose the winning "pick hit" at the end of the week. (Disc jockeys often were allowed to select one record per week as their own "pick to click" so that they had some personal stake in the success of at least one record.) The determination of which records would be songs number 1, 2, 3, 4 and 5 each week (item number 3) no doubt also

---

[19] Memo from Ken Knox to "All KLIF Disc Jockeys, To GBM, Don Keyes, Newsmen," from McLendon Policy Books, n.p., date--Fall 1957--supplied.

resided with the program director, as did the determination of which songs were to be newly admitted to the Top 40 list (item number 5).

Non-hit music

Also note in the above quoted material from the fall of 1957 that KLIF was not playing only the established hits. The KLIF Bomb of the Week was the most obvious violation of the hits-only philosophy, being a record which by definition had no chance of catching on. It may have been a novel idea in regard to the total format, but was a detriment to the music policy. The use of both a personal "pick hit" and a station-determined list of "new-comers" also diluted the concentration on hit sounds. The anniversary song feature, established for the tenth anniversary celebration, was really a "golden oldie" feature, and as such did not violate the policy of playing the hits, since the older songs had been hits.

A memorandum from March 1959 which appears in the McLendon Policy Book clarifies some of the group's reasons for continuing the use of the "pick hit" program feature. The memo was from Don Keyes and was addressed to all managers and program directors.

> I have noticed lately increasing complaints from record distributors, record manufacturers, and retail record shops about the way the pick hit records are being handled at some of our stations. The common complaint seems to be that: Some of the records are not worthy of being pick hits (and with some of the horrible examples I have heard lately, I agree) and when they are made pick hits, they are played for one week and then all but disappear from the DJ shows.
>
> I caution you on this practice for several reasons. While we figure that we can do more good for a record company than a record company can do for us, it is wise to remember that we call on various recording factions for help. On numerous occasions we request a report from record shops on their sales. We request many dollars' worth of albums which are not really played

enough to warrant the expense. We obtain various pieces of equipment, record players, etc., for prizes and for our music rooms. We impose upon their promotional budget for lunches, cocktail parties, etc. We pester them to death for voice tracks of their artists. And, what's perhaps most important, we occasionally get them to commit one of their artists to appear at one of our functions for free.

Granted, many of these things can be handled within their promotional budget but it is understood that when they do an extra favor for us, we will reciprocate. Unfortunately, some of our stations have dropped the ball on this account and have put individual PDs and myself and even Gordon in some rather embarrassing positions. I merely ask that you consider your pick hit option as a definite program privilege and exercise it accordingly. I would be most selective in my selection of a pick hit to begin with because many record shops will order two or three hundred copies of a record simply because we have given our seal of approval. When you realize you have made a wrong decision in your judgment, you should still carry the record for another week or so in order that these people are not left with merchandise on their shelves.

I fully realize that our job is to entertain listeners and not to plug records, but since we do have a pick hit category, which is actually a record plug, I think it would be wise to follow through on it if you plan to continue it.[20]

Albums

A later note from the Memo from Ken Knox to all KLIF Disc Jockeys (Fall 1957) describes another detail of the music policy at KLIF:

> The music policy is clear I think . . . if you have any questions about it, please see me. There is a memo out describing exactly what we want. There is a new ALBUM program we want to try and it will be explained fully in a day or two. It simply is giving the deejay an album that he (and he only) plays for one week. He "romances" the album a bit and at the end of the week it goes into regular play or "hold" and the jock gets another album-of-the-week.[21]

The "new album program" proposed above seems to be another violation of the hits-only rationale, since, in 1957, albums were not nearly as

---

[20] Don Keyes, Memorandum on Pick Hits, March 10, 1959, from McLendon Policy Books.

[21] Ibid.

popular as they are today. But note again that the album was to be given to the deejay, rather than being selected by him. Whatever their mistakes in not playing enough of the hits, KLIF management was in control of the music policy by the fall of 1957.

The late 1950s saw a number of reports that the playing of LP albums was on the increase. Many of these reports were wishful thinking, and some were reactions to the fabulous success of Top 40 hits operations. Storz surprised the industry twice in 1958, once with the announcement in March that all Storz stations were limiting the play of teen-appeal music between 8:30 a.m. and 3:30 p.m., and were programming a few album cuts throughout the day, and again in May with the news that the Oklahoma City outlet, KOMA, was going to place its emphasis on album selections rather than Top 40 singles.[22]

Storz variations

The 1959 debriefing of Kent Burkhart by Don Keyes produced several documents which have been quoted before. One was a memorandum from Keyes to McLendon dated January 24, 1959. Portions concerned what Keyes learned about the Storz music policy are quoted below.

> I did get some valuable information concerning the Storz music setup. Like our music policy, it varies from time to time and market to market, but it is essentially this. All stations play the top 50 tunes of the Billboard weekly listings of the Top 100. Billboard also has a section on the same page of new records called "Coming Up Strong." This list is usually fewer than seven records. Stewart picks the best three of these. Local PDs may add four records of their choice and may determine from them or the "Coming Up Strong" category which

---

[22]"Storz Modifying 'Top 40' Format," Billboard, March 17, 1958, p. 1, and "Competition Spurs Key Airers to Disk Program Shuffles," Billboard, May 18, 1958, p. 1.

> one will be the station's "pick hit." There is no prescribed breakdown within the hour and the pacing of the music is left to the individual DJs. Evidently, they keep pretty close tabs on this because our music monitors a year ago showed consistent good pacing. Storz retains records on his play list a long time, even when one considers that they might be stale. His reason for this is that he is of the opinion that by this retention he will gain adult listeners because they--the adults--being slower to respond to the hits of the day, will not be tired of hearing them as soon as the teenagers will. He assumes that teenagers' _immediate_ likes or dislikes of a tune help him with the new music, but he retains the old ones as long as they are on the _Billboard_ Top 50 because of the adult audience.[23]

The "Stewart" referred to in the paragraph above is Bill Stewart, Storz's National Program Director. Note that Stewart picked three records from the "Coming Up Strong" list in _Billboard_ for inclusion on _all_ Storz stations playlists, while local program directors could add another four, probably with some urging from their local disc jockeys. But the general makeup of the playlist followed _national_ trends as established by _Billboard_, and tended to retain a record on the list after teenagers (and disc jockeys) were tired of it, in order to keep adults listening. At the Storz stations, the pick-hit was _one_ selected by the _station_, rather than one selected by _each_ of several disc jockeys. The Keyes memo continues:

> Burkhart tells me that when he was PD in Miami, the disc jockies were instructed to pace their shows by having every other tune a "recognizable" tune. I am not just exactly sure what constitutes a recognizable tune nor was Kent. It sounded like something that has a million loopholes and would have required constant close monitoring. Here is an item that I found extremely interesting in the music setup: the Storz all-night shows follow the same music policy to the letter as during the day. I think possibly our practice of not doing this is bad. Unlike Gordon, I am not of the opinion that the all-night audience is a particularly different audience than the

---

[23] Don Keyes, memorandum to Gordon and B. R. McLendon, January 24, 1959, from _McLendon Policy Books_.

> daytime people. Some Storz stations play one album cut per hour, others play one "golden record" per hour. The selection of these records and whether or not they want to use either feature is up to the local Program Director.[24]

The "recognizable" tune idea is one that has become commonplace among all sorts of music formats today, but at the time it was complementary to the hits-only philosophy in its emphasis on playing established songs. Clearly, Storz was ahead of McLendon in introducing this programming concept.

Keyes' rather contorted statement that "Unlike Gordon, I am not of the opinion that the all-night audience is a particularly different audience than the daytime people" seems to imply that Gordon McLendon felt the nighttime audience of a Top 40 station was markedly different from the daytime audience, while Keyes did not. As it turned out, both were partly right. Keyes' viewpoint might have been that the same teenagers that were available after school were also available at night, while McLendon's thinking might have been that the adults who were in the audience in the daytime went over to TV viewing at night.

It is interesting that the Storz stations in 1959 were also playing album cuts or "golden" (oldie) records at the rate of one per hour, much as the McLendon stations were doing in the fall of 1957. Note especially the last sentence of the quoted paragraph: "The selection of these records and whether or not they want to use either feature is up to the local program director." Between the national program director and the local program director, the music policy was almost completely management-controlled.

---

[24] Ibid.

Music monitors

Attached to the memo quoted above was a sort of "postscript" again from Keyes to Gordon and B. R. McLendon which also touched on the McLendon stations' music policy:

> Although this memo is pertinent to San Antonio [meaning the previously-quoted memorandum] I am not issuing a carbon to Jack Fiedler or anyone else down there because of the cries of protest that go up from our people whenever the views of an outsider are considered as a program guide for KTSA. To elucidate: Kent Burkhart, who I respect very much as a Program Director, gave me his impressions of the sound of KTSA as opposed to the sound of KONO. He points out two things: (1) our music at times is non-descript, and the pacing is often poor. (2) the jockies did not sound happy. I will go to San Antonio probably on Wednesday and Thursday of next week and check this out for myself. I wouldn't be at all surprised if Burkhart is right in his observations. He mentioned that he had heard a lot of unfamiliar records on KTSA and posed this question which was so well put and really impressed me with the seriousness of the situation, and is perhaps a good reason why we are not doing better than we are: his question was, "why be the hit station and not play the hits?" It could be that this is the result of local music programming getting out of hand. I am ordering a music monitor of KONO for Monday along with a music monitor of KTSA. I will receive these by Tuesday and will be armed with them when I sneak into San Antonio on Wednesday. No one in San Antonio knows that I am coming in.[25]

In the memo quoted immediately above, Keyes surmised that the ratings trouble with KTSA as compared to its competition (KONO) might have been the result of playing too much unfamiliar music rather than the hits, perhaps because local music programming had gotten out of hand. By comparison, both the Storz and Bartell operations at this time featured heavy national control of the music played on all of their stations, with Bartell sending out music lists for all stations from Milwaukee and Storz specifying the Billboard list plus Stewart's three picks of

---

[25] "Postscript" to Memorandum from Don Keyes to Gordon and B. R. McLendon, January 24, 1959, from McLendon Policy Books.

the new records from Omaha.

In February of 1959, Keyes sent a memo to Gordon McLendon informing him of just what his visit, projected in the memorandum quoted immediately above, had actually discovered. The four-page document covered a number of other factors as well as the music policy, but the latter category is quoted below.

> The following is a report of my findings on a trip to KTSA, San Antonio, January 28th and 29th, 1959.
> The reason for the trip was to listen to the sound of the station to see if there was any reason in my mind for the vast difference in our Pilot Survey and the January Hooper Survey.
> Generally speaking, I found the station in fairly good condition, from a program standpoint. It was the best sounding station on the San Antonio dial, but there were some loop holes in the sound, which have since been corrected.[26]

The pilot survey Keyes mentions was a ratings survey made by the station using its own interviewers, either to discover information not offered in a regular commercial survey, or to confirm or repudiate the findings of a suspect commercial survey, as was the case with the Hooper mentioned.

> 1. The music was in very weak condition, and after studying a music monitor of KTSA and a music monitor of KONO, the reason for the weakness was quite obvious. KONO was playing a few records that we were not playing and that we should have been playing. The content of each hour on KTSA was in bad condition. At one time, an hour and 15 minutes went by without so much as one record from the Top 55 Survey. The music, on the whole, had a soft sound that was not particularly commercial. Oddly enough, however, KONO sounded much the same, and it is interesting to note that, while we played approximately 156 records from 7:00 A.M. to 6:00 P.M., KONO played only 132. Our breakdown of Top 55 tunes came to approximately 3.2 per hour, while KONO's was only around 2.8. The main thing wrong about our music was that all records were not being played. New

---

[26] Don Keyes, memorandum to Gordon McLendon, February 5, 1959, four pages, from McLendon Policy Books.

records, for example, would be on the play list, but were never heard on the air.

CONCLUSION:

A. I reprimanded Fischer on the condition of the music.
B. I required music sheets to be put into effect immediately.
C. I re-established a music breakdown of four of the Top 55, five comers, three album cuts, and one "Golden Record" per hour.[27]

From the vantage point of contemporary radio programming, where "the hits keep on coming on," it is remarkable that the two hit music stations in San Antonio in 1959 played an average of only 3.2 or 2.8 hits per hour, and that for an hour and 15 minutes KTSA did not play any record from the Top 55 survey. (The number 55 was determined by KTSA's frequency, 550 kHz.)

It also seems remarkable that Keyes' solution to the "very weak condition" of KTSA's music was to demand only four hits per hour, when they were already averaging a little over three, while five new songs and three album cuts for a total of eight unfamiliar songs were prescribed. With this "solution" the ratio of "unrecognizable" to "recognizable" tunes was still at an unhealthy two-to-one.

Concentration on the hits

A memorandum from Keyes to McLendon in August of 1961 following a programming meeting at KLIF shows that by that date at KLIF, the idea of concentrating on the hits had been adopted. At the time, KLIF had just been displaced from the top of the ratings for the first time by the Balaban stations' new Dallas outlet, KBOX, named for executive vice president John F. Box, Jr. (KBOX, with 5,000 watts days and 500 watts nights on 1480 kHz was acquired in May of 1958, and by the summer

---

[27] *Ibid.*

of 1959 was claiming a number two position in the May-June Dallas Hooper.)[28] The programming meeting ranged widely over a number of topics, but in regard to the music, it was decided that KLIF should:

> . . . retain Top 60 and present music policy of six Top 30, three Klassics, remainder from bottom 30. Restrictions will no longer be observed. Deletions will be made as had been the practice previously. Playlist not to exceed 65. Klassics increased to four per hour on weekends.[29]

Previous memos pointed out the expectation that a normal hour would contain at least 13 records. Note that with only six records per hour to be from the Top 30 of the Top 60 playlist, less than half were solid hits. However, restrictions on the play of certain music at certain times of day (to prevent too much teen-appeal music from being played when adults were likely to be listening) were being lifted, perhaps in an attempt to inflate the ratings with teens. In addition, in this 1961 memo, there is no mention of any playing of "new" or "pick" hits, with established, oldie "Klassics" being the only deviation from the emphasis on current tunes. The playlist, however, was still vast, with 65 set as the upper limit. Stewart had shown in programming WQAM in late 1956--early 1957 that a station could establish itself in first place without giveaways if just the top part of the playlist were concentrated upon.

> . . . When we first went into Miami . . . we went in with I think 25 records. We never would admit it. I don't think

---

[28] "Balaban Adds Another," Broadcasting, May 5, 1958, p. 5, and advertisement for KBOX, Broadcasting, August 3, 1959, front cover.

[29] Don Keyes, Memorandum and notes from KLIF Programming Meeting of Thursday, August 24, 1961, dated August 25, 1961, to Gordon McLendon, Bill Morgan, Jack Sharp and Joe Long, from McLendon Policy Books.

> it ever got over really 30 records. We would print a Top 40. But we only played 30. And it worked. Because, again, it eliminated chance, that's the only thing it did. . . .[30]

Eventually, this concentration on playing just the top hits would become industry-wide.

Selection

It should be apparent from the preceding introductory material that the music policy was considered to be of crucial importance in the success of a Top 40 station. At the heart of the problem in working out a successful music formula was the persistent dilemma of how, and by whom, and for what effect the music should be selected.

The basic reason that music selection of some sort is necessary is that there is too little air time and too many new records competing for exposure. Paul Ackerman of Billboard estimated in 1960 that there were 130 single and 100 longplay releases each week.[31] Obviously, not all have merit, and still fewer have a chance of gaining real national exposure for reasons of distribution, obscurity of the artist or label, and so forth. Someone has to decide what ought to be played. The safest answer for many years has been to rely on the national chart listings which tell what is already popular. The problem has never been solved once and for all, for with the music business, any solution tends to be temporary. A generally good discussion of the "filtering process by which records are preselected for public consumption" is Paul Hirsch's The Structure of the Popular Music Industry, a monograph published by

---

[30] Stewart interview.

[31] "Ackerman Statement to Payola Probers," Billboard, May 9, 1960, p. 18.

the Survey Research Center of the Institute for Social Research at the University of Michigan. In this report, Hirsch makes the point that the payola scandals which culminated in the Federal Bribery Act of 1960 was the principal turning point for the music selection process in Top 40 radio.

> Before the payola scandals, there was less uncertainty in the music industry than there is today. The Federal Bribery Act of 1960 declares the secret, unannounced payment of funds to broadcast personnel in return for airplay to be a criminal offense punishable by a fine of up to $10,000 and/or one year imprisonment. Before that time, payola was tax deductible; companies could pay by check.
>
> The outlawing of this mode of preselection brought about a number of changes in the structure of Top 40 broadcasting operations. Salaries were raised in order to compensate for the loss of what had been, until then, a perfectly acceptable practice of supplementing one's income. Disc jockeys lost the prerogative of selecting the records that they play on the air; and "music committees" and the office of program director were created or expanded. The Top 40 format came to mean a rigid playlist of records selected by an individual or small group whose decisions are implemented by disc jockeys who do not participate in the selection process.[32]

There is little reason to doubt that the payola scandals accelerated the acquisition of control over the music policy by Top 40 management, but to imply as Hirsch does that such control was the result of the scandals has been shown to be erroneous by the material so far presented here. Top 40 management was already well on the way to music control for positive reasons, such as uniformity of product and a greater certainty of playing the music most wanted by the public, years before the negative fear of exposure on taking payola ever became a factor.

Other points made by Hirsch are better taken. He states that

---

[32] Paul Hirsch, The Structure of the Popular Music Industry, Ann Arbor, Michigan: Survey Research Center of the Institute for Social Research, The University of Michigan, n.d. (but references in the text do not carry dates later than 1967), pp. 62-63.

"promoter pressure, which had been diffusely applied to all disc jockeys, came to be directed solely at one individual."[33] That person was, of course, the program director. He also points out that with bribery outlawed, a program director had to become much more concerned with a record's sales figures and other indices of popularity than with how much money the record promoter could offer.[34] Hirsch also shows some of the problems with reliance on record sales as a means of selecting the records played:

> Sales can be affected by such factors as the frequency of a record's airplay by the Top 40 station. . . . This is but one of several ways in which the station program director can influence his compilation of the "Top 40's" rank order. Since the number of records sold is often quite close, the rank of two records, e. g., as numbers 10 and 15 in popularity, is quite arbitrary. The sampling procedures for ascertaining the number of records sold is frequently haphazard; the numbers reported are often subject to hyping; and in the larger cities the information on the number of copies a record has sold is often so late in arriving that it can serve to only confirm or disconfirm the program director's initial "hunch" about the record's potential popularity. This is one of the circumstances that gives rise to the question of the radio station's creating a record's popularity rather than simply reflecting it, as Top 40 stations claim to do.[35]

The "hyping" Hirsch mentions is an artificial boost to a record's sales, often by the supplying of false information about its popularity. One simple way of doing this is for the record store manager to inflate the sales figures of a certain record, for which favor he is given other free records by the promoter. Another method is to pay people to call the radio station and request the record that the record promoter wants played.[36]

---

[33] Ibid., p. 63. [34] Ibid., p. 64.

[35] Ibid., p. 67. [36] Ibid., p. 59.

National charts and newsletters

Because of the difficulties in being sure that an accurate local survey has been conducted, the majority of program directors today depend heavily on the national "charts" in such publications as Billboard, Record World, Cash Box, and Bill Gavin's newsletter. Today, most of such sources are fairly scrupulous about trying to reflect airplay, jukebox play and sales accurately. Differences among charts result partly from the method by which position is determined. In Billboard's Hot 100 for example, the positions of the records in the first 50 places are determined entirely by sales figures from dealers. The bottom 50 are determined by both sales and radio airplay. A rotating sample of 75 dealers each week is used to glean such information. Cash Box, on the other hand, gives more weight to airplay.[37]

John Kluge, who in 1959 was chairman of the board and president of what was then known as Metropolitan Broadcasting Corporation (now Metromedia), has been quoted as being skeptical of top-singles lists: "When I see one of those lists . . . I'm always reminded of the fact that man is on top of animal kingdom charts because he makes out the list. . . ."[38]

Throughout the 1950s, there was good reason for not placing too much reliance on the national charts. Record company executives were known to send people out to buy huge numbers of their own records to advance their sales positions on the charts. There is the story of a

---

[37] David Reitman, "Making the Charts," Rock Magazine, November 17, 1970, p. 21.

[38] "Metropolitan Soars with Kluge at Helm," Billboard, May 25, 1959, p. 8.

record appearing at the number 85 position on one of the charts weeks before it was released.[39] Another source, who between 1956 and 1959 was program director at WKYB, Paducah, Kentucky, has stated that one of the jocks on the station had written the song "Tragedy" and had played a version of it often on the station, to no avail. Believing that it had hit potential, the disc jockey went into partnership with another man who put up $50,000. With this money they persuaded Cash Box to sell them the number 9 spot on their charts for the song, which it did eventually attain, becoming a nationwide hit.[40] All of the national charts, as well as some specialized record programming newsletters such as Bill Gavin's have served the function of a party line for programmers, letting each eavesdrop on what others are doing. As a few of the braver programmers "go on" a new record, the charts and

---

[39] "Making the Charts," p. 31.

[40] Conversation between the author and Dr. Malachi Topping, former program director at WKYB, Paducah, Kentucky, now Associate Professor of Speech at Bowling Green (Ohio) State University, in Madison, Wisconsin, June 15, 1972. There is no question that in the 1950s payola was influential in determining the fortunes of some records which might not otherwise have been hits, and that in doing so the practice operated as part of the "selection" process. However, as has already been pointed out, management's goal was to take the responsibility for music selection away from disc jockeys and turn it over to the program or music director under management's direct control. The payola scandals story, although it concerned disc jockeys and program directors alike, does not seem to be a necessary part of the story of management control simply because it operated counter to the intent of that control. The selection processes to be explored further here all were a conscious, purposeful effort by management to eliminate the very sort of abuses which payola represented. Those wishing to read a short background of the payola problem should see "Ackerman Statement to Payola Probers," a statement by Paul Ackerman, Music Editor of The Billboard, in Billboard, May 9, 1960, pp. 8, 18. The opening round of payola hearings was interestingly covered by Broadcasting in "Harris Drums Up Payola Parade," Broadcasting, February 15, 1960, pp. 52-54, 56, 58.

newsletters note this and it becomes a record to watch. If by the next issue more programmers seem to be interested and regional or sometimes national sales show some action, the record will start to climb rapidly. The national charts use "bullets" and "stars" to denote the fast-climbing discs, which are the ones to watch. Gavin's newsletter simply says which ones to watch by listing the records in categories.[41]

Other methods of selection

The almost-exclusive reliance on national trade papers' charts seems to have occurred largely after the payola scandals and the revelation of methods by which local surveys could be "hyped." But in the formative days of Top 40, the record store and listener surveys were standard methods of determining a record's local popularity. It must be remembered that local popularity for a record was more likely in an era when local personalities could "push" a favorite disc. Where the trades failed to cover such local "action," a station's own survey was often the only means available for deciding whether to continue to play a song.

The Plough stations developed a survey method as part of their Operating Manual & Policies for the Broadcast Services of Plough Inc. in the belief that the station must be sure that it is playing the record which the local audience wants to hear. For the week of June 24,

---

[41]Bill Gavin began his newsletter in 1958 as a sort of "thank-you" to the stations that had provided him information which would help him to choose the "Lucky 10." The "Lucky 10" were the top ten songs of the week heard every Saturday night on Lucky Lager Dance Time, which Gavin programmed from the mid-1950s until its demise in 1959. For a further discussion of both Lucky Lager Dance Time and the Gavin newsletter, see Passman, The Deejays, pp. 260-63.

1957, the Plough Stations in Chicago, Boston, Baltimore and Memphis surveyed their cities and found the following records in the first five positions:

	Chicago	Boston	Baltimore	Memphis
1.	Bye Bye Love	Love Letters in the Sand	Young Blood	Teddy Bear
2.	So Rare	Bye Bye Love	Bye Bye Love	Dream Boy
3.	Love Letters in the Sand	Around the World	Over the Mountain	Searchin'
4.	White Sport Coat	So Rare	Love Letters in the Sand	I'm Gonna Sit Right Down and Write Myself a Letter
5.	I Like Your Kind of Love	Queen of the Senior Prom	It's Not for Me to Say	White Silver Sands[42]

It was pointed out that generally there are fewer differences regionally among the top five to ten records as between the lower-ranked tunes, so that the differences between the lesser hits on the Plough stations was even more pronounced, thus confirming the need for a local survey. As part of the survey of record dealers, the local Plough station each week issued to the dealers a list of 40 titles which were being played as "extras." These titles were chosen by Plough programmers; they were released to dealers so that the retailers could match their own ordering and sales efforts with the exposure being given by the station.[43]

A number of other methods of selecting the records a station plays have been tried, many of them in an attempt to avoid the usual

---

[42] Joe Csida, "Sponsor Backstage: Behind Radio's Fabulous Comeback," Sponsor, July 13, 1957, p. 22.

[43] Ibid., p. 22.

reliance on sales figures alone. WFIL convened a series of music "juries" in 1957 to help the station choose among the records it thought it wanted to play. The "WFIL Music Preference Panels," as they were called, each were comprised of ten people representing a cross section of the available audience--a high school girl, a mother of a young child, a factory worker, a retired man, etc. Each panel listened to over 100 musical selections, then rated them. Not one rock-and-roll record appeared on the list, causing WFIL to revise its format to play 50% non-rock "popular" and 50% "standards."[44]

In 1959, KING, Seattle, conducted a music survey which managed to get 10,000 listener mail responses to a sample of several different kinds of music played over the station. As in the WFIL survey, rock-and-roll records came out badly, with more people singling out the sample rock records as being disliked than four other musical categories combined.

KING was particularly proud of the size of the response it generated and the fact that the entire survey had been supervised by Dr. Stuart Carter Dodd, director of the Washington Public Opinion Lab at the University of Washington and had used an IBM computer to collate the data. The use of a computer and punchcards--then a novelty in radio research--may have prompted Broadcasting to headline the article about KING's music survey "At Last A Reliable Music Survey."[45]

---

[44]"WFIL Lets Jury Decide on Music," Broadcasting, October 28, 1957, p. 76.

[45]"At Last a Reliable Music Survey," Broadcasting, October 12, 1959, p. 33.

Unfortunately, the headline was not true. As large as the KING sample was, it was not truly representative, because it aimed only at persons over 12. A number of the respondents were not regular listeners to KING, either, having been attracted to listen and participate in the survey by a heavy promotion campaign. But the biggest problem with the KING survey, as with the WFIL "juries" that preceded it, was one of listening loyalty. In each case, the great majority of those surveyed were adults. The only trouble with using their responses as typical was that compared to their teenage children, very few of them had much of a "stake" in what kind of music was played on the station in question. They were willing to list the kinds of music they liked and didn't like, but in neither case did that necessarily correlate with how avidly they would listen to the radio station. Whatever its faults in selecting music for adult listeners, the selection and playing of the Top 40 tunes was likely to generate copious amounts of enthusiasm among younger listeners.

Concentration on Repeating the Hits

Believing that it should closely control programming, Top 40 management increasingly took control of the music policy away from the disc jockeys with whom it had previously resided. Believing that to succeed with its programming, it had to "fill a void," Top 40 management proceeded to develop what Storz executive vice-president George Armstrong calls "exclusivity of product." Before the end of its first year under Storz ownership, KOWH was concentrating exclusively on popular music. Gradually, it became apparent that "the artist didn't count as an artist to do anything that that artist wanted to do. . . .

But the artist always counted in terms of making a single record that would hit the popularity charts and go winging away."[46] The point Armstrong makes is that in the early 1950s, the individual hit was becoming more important to audiences than were particular artists. From this realization there sprang the local imitations of the Hit Parade show, with block programmed "hit tunes," rather than block programmed "popular music." Gradually, the consistency of playing the popular music became the consistency of playing the hit music, as block programming gave way to a full program schedule featuring the hits. As has been shown, these early full program schedules played many records in addition to the most popular hits: oldies, albums, pick-hits, newcomers, etc. None of these proved as popular as the playing of the most popular hits. The decision to play the most popular hits more often than anything else was the inauguration of the true limited playlist, because the third feature of Top 40 music selection was added: repetition. Most music-and-news stations had offered program exclusivity, which is one reason they succeeded even in the face of television's popularity. The stations that were evolving toward the genuine Top 40 formula offered consistency as well, so that the same programming was available at any time of day, not just in certain blocks. But it was the addition of repetition of the top hits that clearly separated a Top 40 station from all others.

Repetition

Harold Mendelsohn in his book, Mass Entertainment, offers one

---

[46] Armstrong interview.

of Freud's "fundamental law(s) of instinctual function" as one possible explanation of why repetition should be a positive rather than a negative ingredient in entertainment programming. Freud called the law the "repetition compulsion."

> . . . Here, Freud argued that the human organism tends to reproduce certain previously experienced emotional tensions, pleasurable and otherwise. Observing his patients' almost endless reiteration of experiences from the past--particularly from childhood (dominated by the Pleasure Principle), Freud arrived at the conclusion that the compulsion to reproduce emotional experiences is an innate biological function of the human organism. This basic need to repeat emotional experiences from the past has direct bearing on the experience of mass media-derived entertainment, for it is clear from a wide variety of sources that a great deal of pleasure that is derived from mass entertainment (as well as from play, dreams and fantasies, poetry, and music) stems precisely from experiencing patterns of repetitive actions, sounds, environments, situations, and so on. . . .[47]

Mendelsohn's point seems a good one to explain the appeal among teenagers of the limited playlist's repetition, and is especially strong in explaining why "golden oldies" also became an integral part of Top 40 radio.

Todd Storz and Bill Stewart together added the element of repetition. Bill Stewart says,

> . . . When I went with Storz, Storz had the idea--he was on the track of what he had in mind. And I think a lot of the refinements that I brought with me--and I'm sure one of them was the tight playlist--I know we closed the music lists, and that was one thing he was not doing--I don't think he really was aware of this idea of the same record coming up over and over again. I think that is something that we discovered together. And I remember that particular instance that has come up many times about listening--we'd go in and have a couple of beers or something and hear the waitress--or the people would be playing a particular song. You'd hear it maybe twenty times in two hours. And then the joint would

---

[47] Harold Mendelsohn, Mass Entertainment (New Haven, Connecticut: College and University Press, 1966), p. 88.

> close and the waitress would go over and put a quarter of her own money in it, and play the same song three times. And having that happen over and over again convinced both of us that people wanted to hear--that it wouldn't drive people away to play records more often. At that time, the theory was that if you played a record at nine o'clock in the morning, it didn't get played again until the next day at nine o'clock. And that experience, in our minds, killed that theory. . . .[48]

In "The Storz Bombshell" Storz is quoted as saying that he ". . . became convinced that people demand their favorites over and over while in the army during the Second World War."[49] Stewart refutes this.

> I think that is a little early. Maybe he originally got the thought at that time, but I don't think he ever put it into practice. I think it was reinforced maybe by several things like this [the restaurant experience with Stewart]. It was put into practice long after that. . . .
>
> . . . .
>
> He was not playing a limited playlist when I went there. They could play pretty much what they wanted to. [No doubt this means the jocks could select from among the hits, oldies, newcomers, pick-hits, etc., and did not then have to play hits exclusively.] I put--originally--the limited playlist in. And that was always our crutch: the deeper trouble you got in, the more limited the playlist. If ratings went down and you were playing 40 records, you went to 30 records. All it did was eliminate mistakes, that was all. That's all you hope to do. . . .[50]

Stewart recalls the date of the initiation of the limited playlist on KOWH as about February of 1956, which was three months before Stewart was officially made National Program Director for Storz, in May 1956.

Retaining the hits

Besides repeating the top hits, the Storz stations also retained the hits on the playlist longer, following a theory of George

---

[48] Stewart interview.

[49] Herman Land, "The Storz Bombshell," reprint from Television Magazine, May 1957, p. 3 of 8.

[50] Stewart interview.

Armstrong's quoted earlier that doing so would garner a larger share of adult listeners.

> . . . I always used to say that about the time the disc jockey is getting tired of the record and wants to take it off the list and change it, that's about the time the housewife is just getting familiar with the record; and about the time the disc jockey can't stand to hear it one more time, mama's now learning the words.[51]

Of this facet of the "repetition" concept, Bill Stewart says of Armstrong's theory,

> Well, that was mine or Storz's--it was not Bud's [George "Bud" Armstrong's]. I think the average person is just beginning to know the words to a song. . . . The problem with disc jockeys is that they get a record and they're playing it for four weeks before it ever gets on the Top 40. And when it comes on the Top 40, it's number 36, then next week 32, then 29. It's on the thing for ten weeks and they're not only sick of the record, but they don't have any more ways to introduce it. They've done everything they can. And disc jockeys, traditionally, are for the underdog, musically . . . the disc jockeys immediately jump for the five new records, because they want to make a hit out of it. They're sick of the old one. They don't know what they are going to do to introduce it. So, traditionally they want to go for the new record. But, a good indication of how long to keep a record on is . . . jukeboxes in a barroom. They stay. . . . It's a lot harder today than it used to be. The best way I've ever found is checking jukeboxes in barrooms. They are the great common denominator, because if they don't get dimes, they take them out. . . . Oh, you don't get the really new records, but you can tell the <u>life</u> of a record from a jukebox. . . .[52]

Stewart claims that so far as picking new records are concerned, he does not put much faith in charts and newsletters.

> They don't know any more than you do. What difference does it make if a record is number one in Decimal Point, Arkansas? . . . It really is seat-of-the-pants. I'm telling you the truth. I'm not telling you it's scientific and all that, because that's not true. You can get with guys who will tell you they take all kinds of surveys, and they bring in some guy from Badbreath,

---

[51] Armstrong interview.

[52] Stewart interview.

Iowa to do a survey of the market and they find out how many left-handed plumbers there are who go to the Presbyterian Church, and that is what determines their music list. But I don't think that is the way it really works. You have to find out for yourself. . . .[53]

By 1961, Variety was taking note of the widespread use of the limited playlist which repeated the top hits, in such headlines as "Music Biz in 'Formula' Bind."[54] The article said,

The straitjacket of formula radio is now pulling tighter than ever on the music biz. Heavy stress of the vast majority of radio stations on programming the top hits has created an imposing wall against new material as well as causing a quicker than normal exhaustion of the bestseller.

Whereas a couple of years ago, the radio outlets were covering the top 40 or top 50 songs, currently the number of featured hit songs are shrinking down nearer the top 30 mark. Under a typical formula now used by stations, the top 30 numbers are being supplemented by a half-dozen new songs each week plus an equal number of new albums for the full pop programming fare.[55]

Thus, it can be seen that by 1961, the true limited playlist had reached the practical zenith in restricting the number of records played. Stewart has already provided the best reason for repeating only the top hits: "All it did was eliminate mistakes, that was all. That's all you hope to do."[56]

Programming Music vs. Being Programmed

At WNOE in New Orleans, the station Bill Stewart was program-directing in 1971-72, there is a programming feature which suggests that the station is seeking the guidance of the listener in selecting the music the station plays. Twice an hour, WNOE runs a recording of a

---

[53] Ibid.

[54] Variety, February 1, 1961, p. 57.

[55] Ibid.

[56] Stewart interview.

telephone caller making a request for a certain song, followed immediately by that very song. Many stations across the country use or have used such a feature. It would seem that the automatically-recorded calls would provide some indication of audience interest in certain kinds of music, and in a limited way, it does provide this kind of feedback function. But the surface appearance is that the listeners to WNOE are programming the station--that they are selecting the music played. Says Stewart,

> . . . These people who call in really think they're programming the radio station, but they're not. Because, we go through the tape of 40 minutes of phone calls, and we take out the eight records that I want. The eight records I want to play, I take out. Yet they think they're programming the radio station, and everybody who hears it thinks that people who call in really are programming the station.[57]

George Armstrong, believing that no program director knows more than the public, says

> . . . when you start trying to outguess the market, I think you're doing your listeners a disservice, because they really don't want to be programmed. They want to program _you_; they don't want you to program _them_. And so it's very dangerous; it's self-indulgent . . . if you indulge in the subjective, and listen to the people that know more than the public does, that's where you run into trouble. Because they _don't_ know more than the public. Nobody does. . . .[58]

Neither Armstrong, espousing the "passive" view that the station merely reflects public taste in music, nor Stewart, promoting the active involvement of the program director in choosing the records aired, can in honesty state that music selection can be done at all without _both_ reflecting public tastes and _also_ depending upon the judgment of a program director.

---

[57] _Ibid._ [58] Armstrong interview.

The selection of music for play on the radio finally comes to this fact: the process of selection is not a democratic one anywhere along the line from artist to listener. There are, to expand on a point made by Hirsch, "gatekeepers" at every level who do the selecting. If there could be true "mass exposure" of the myriads of new recordings constantly being issued, then a true democratic selection by the listener might be possible. Lacking unlimited airtime and unlimited stations, the fact remains that the mass audience generally is allowed to choose only from those records which have already been pre-selected by a few influential men. The Gavin lists tend to concentrate on the opinions of those men; in 1965 a company called Compass began providing subscribing stations with computer-weighted opinions on brand new records that had been previewed by a number of these "influentials."[59] The point is, no matter what initial data input exists, a single man--or relatively few men--finally have to decide what to do with the data, because only one or a few can finally be responsible for the success or failure of the music policy.

The problems inherent in music selection were made even more difficult in Top 40 radio by the content of the music itself. This discussion has purposely avoided any attempt to trace the development of rock-and-roll music or its largely teenage following because these subjects have already been rather thoroughly explored.[60] It is an

---

[59]"Computers Get into the Record Act," Broadcasting, June 28, 1965, p. 72.

[60]A good general history of the development of rock and roll as a musical style can be found in Carl Belz, The Story of Rock (New York: Oxford University Press, 1969). Harold Mendelsohn in his book, Mass

inescapable fact, however, that certain types of music which tended to be played on Top 40 stations engendered a great deal of criticism for the stations, and this criticism was reflected in the music policy developed by Top 40 stations.

Public Criticism of Music Policy

It is ironic that one of the voices protesting the current music of the early and mid-1950s was Gordon McLendon. For a while, McLendon wrote a combination advertisement and commentary for Ruppert Knickerbocker Beer which appeared in the Dallas Daily Times Herald under the title "Father Knickerbocker Presents the Old Scotchman."[61] The column for July 28, 1953 went as follows:

> Well, there's good news today . . . have you ever been annoyed by the continued loud and harsh grinding of a juke box in a public place? . . . have you ever watched some drug-store jitterbug continue to feed nickels into these torture boxes? . . . have you ever seen some of the titles, like "The Jughead Polka" and "Cruising down the river because my wife's arms are getting tired of rowing" and "he don't plant cotton, he don't plant nettin, he jest keeps settin" and "I can't give you anything but what we've definitely agreed on already, baby" and "you wouldn't have such a bad taste in your mouth if you'd stop drinking Knickerbocker Beer out of your shaving mug" . . . the good news is that a very large Representative Cross Section (I forget his first name but he weighs close to three hundred) has introduced a bill which would require every jukebox to have a new and radical feature . . . from now on, by law, every jukebox would be required to have at least one nickel slot which will entitle

---

Entertainment (New Haven, Connecticut: College and University Press, 1966), deals admirably with the gratifications particular audiences receive from certain kinds of musical stimuli--see especially pp. 118-33.

[61]"The Old Scotchman" was McLendon's nickname from the days of the Liberty baseball broadcasts.

the listener to three minutes of complete silence. . . . GORDON MCLENDON.[62]

Rhythm and blues

Before the era when music was written strictly to appeal to teenagers, there was a time when the music that most appealed to teens was the rhythm and blues record, with its heavy emphasis on the beat. It was the inclusion of rhythm and blues in the Top 40 playlist that seems to have caused the most furor in the formative days of the formula.

An excellent background to the rise in popularity of rhythm and blues among teenagers was supplied by Billboard in its April 24, 1954 issue:

> Rhythm and blues records, once limited in sales appeal to the relatively small Negro market, has blossomed into one of the fastest growing areas of the entire record business.
>
> Rhythm and blues record sales last year reached an all-time high of $15,000,000. Indications are that 1954 sales will surpass this mark. The growing popularity of this music is further reflected in its wide use by disc jockeys and juke box operators.
>
> More than 700 disc jockeys across the country devote their air time exclusively to rhythm and blues recordings. Many disc jockeys who once restricted their programming only to popular records are following the change in listener tastes by including rhythm and blues selections with their regular popular offerings. . . .
>
> Teenagers have spearheaded the current swing to r&b and are largely responsible for keeping its sales mounting. The teenage tide has swept down the old barriers which kept this music restricted to a segment of the population.
>
> The present generation has not known the rhythmically exciting dance bands of the swing era. It therefore satisfies its hunger for "music with a beat" in the Earl Bostic, Buddy Johnson, Tiny Bradshaw bands or uses the rhythmically pronounced

---

[62]"Father Knickerbocker Presents The Old Scotchman," The Daily Times Herald, July 28, 1953, Section 4, p. 7, from Gordon McLendon's personal scrapbooks.

> recordings of the Clovers, Ruth Brown and others, as its dance music. . . .
>
> Juke box operators are credited with being among the first to sense the teenager swing to r&b. In noting the youngsters' preference for this music, they continued to increase its supply on those juke boxes which were exposed to teenage traffic.
>
> This in turn fostered r&b popularity as reflected in requests to disc jockeys and at record stores. Dealers who heretofore didn't stock r&b records were quick to pick up the ball and are now offering a healthy selection of r&b recordings. . . .
>
> . . . California distributors who specialize in r&b estimate that 35 percent of their sales volume comes directly from the juke box field. . . .
>
> Operators in widely scattered sections of the country have found that many r&b records have a wide enough appeal to go into boxes in any area.
>
> Indicative of the expansion of the rhythm and blues market is the large number of retail outlets which previously did not stock these platters, but have since found it necessary and especially profitable to do so.
>
> In the main, these stores and others of their type are thus far only carrying the "hit" or chart listed items, altho they are continually adding to their inventory.
>
> Where it was previously necessary for a teenager to go out of his immediate shopping neighborhood and buy a rhythm and blues recording, it is now the neighborhoods that are adding to their coffers thru stocking r&b records. . . .[63]

As a result of the growing popularity of rhythm and blues records, primarily being released by the small, independent record companies who had the Negro groups under contract, the major labels and the name artists came under pressure to produce rhythm and blues-based discs as well. Perry Como, the McGuire Sisters, Tony Bennett, Georgia Gibbs, Patti Page and others all tried the r&b approach, and although deejays such as Alan Freed refused to play their records because they were said to lack authenticity and were imitative,[64] these "white cover

---

[63] Bob Rolontz and Joel Friedman, "Teen-Agers Demand Music With a Beat, Spur Rhythm-Blues," Billboard, April 24, 1954, pp. 1, 18.

[64] Herm Schoenfeld, "R & B Big Beat in Pop Biz," Variety, January 19, 1955, p. 54.

versions" began the popularization of Negro rhythm and blues among the majority white audience. The popularity of the "covers" among white audiences helped the acceptance of the "real thing," in terms of record listening and sales. "Covers" also helped the entry of the Negro versions onto the regular "pops" charts where before such discs had been listed separately in a rhythm and blues category. Even in the South, where opposition to rhythm and blues was likely to be high among white station operators because of its origin with black performers, a vast increase in the number of r&b records requested had by 1955 forced a number of stations to program the music.[65]

Dirty lyrics

The opposition to rhythm and blues music in particular and to rock and roll in general was not confined to the South nor to causes rooted in racial prejudice alone. The fact is, rhythm and blues lyrics treated the subject of sex much less obliquely than did white moon-june-spoon-tune refrains. Playing the "off-color" or "dirty" "leer-ics," as they were called at the time, became an increasingly hotter subject of debate among record programmers as public pressure mounted.

By the end of 1954, a general feeling had developed among manufacturers, dealers, distributors, and disc jockeys that "certain double entendre records were getting a big play and sale in the r&b field at present. . . ."[66] As of early October 1954 WDIA, Memphis,

---

[65]"Deep South Jockeys Junk 50% of R&B Wax," Variety, March 30, 1955, p. 54.

[66]"Trade Views Off-Color Disk Situation with Mixed Feeling," Billboard, October 2, 1954, p. 19.

a 50,000 watt outlet that had been playing rhythm and blues almost exclusively for five years, announced that it would no longer play any record that could be considered off-color. The station screened all incoming records for suggestiveness, and immediately banned 15 discs, adding eight more a few weeks later. Letters explaining why were sent to record companies (and other radio stations), and when requests came in to WDIA to play one of the banned records, the station made this announcement:

> WDIA, your good-will station, in the interest of good citizenship, for the protection of morals and our American way of life does not consider this record (blank) fit for broadcast on WDIA. We are sure all you listeners will agree with us and continue to enjoy our programs and the music you hear every day.[67]

Im March of 1955, Peter Potter, famous for Jukebox Jury on radio and then a KLAC disc jockey, stated that all rhythm and blues records were dirty and detrimental to teenagers.[68] At this time, Variety began an editorial stand against "dirty" rhythm and blues discs which elicited a letter to the editor from Irving Berlin.

> . . . As you know, there have always been lyrics with suggestive angles and some of our greats are identified with some of these songs. However, they were confined to theatres and to personalities who put them across so that they weren't dirty.
>
> I remember during the ragtime period when "Everybody's Doin' It" was a big hit, there were some comments that the title was suggestive, but when they got to know the lyric they knew that it meant "everybody" was doing the turkey trot.[69]

---

[67] "Indie Diskers Back WDIA's R&B Bans," Billboard, October 30, 1954, p. 16.

[68] "Coast Jockeys Open Gab War on R&B Cycle," Variety, March 23, 1955, p. 41.

[69] "Irving Berlin on R&B," Variety, March 23, 1955, p. 41.

In the same issue in which the Irving Berlin letter appeared, Variety carried the following story:

> Alarmed by some disks being played over local [Houston, Texas] radio stations, the Juvenile Delinquency & Crime Commission has begun preparation of a list of objectionable records it wants banned from the air. Radio station representatives themselves asked that such a list be drawn up.
>
> It will be drawn up as soon as possible, according to L. Olshan, commission chairman, and will be mailed to managers and program directors of all the local stations. The list will probably contain at least 100 titles. It may even include several hit tunes, he said. . . .[70]

By the following week, Variety had four separate articles about the problems with rhythm and blues music. One announced that a station in Mobile, Alabama was throwing away between 40% and 50% of its rhythm and blues records because "filth in both title and words makes their destruction a must."[71] Another quoted teenagers as saying, "We have to have records we can play at church and school socials without having to be ashamed to play them." "At first we didn't notice the lyrics were off-color because we were attracted by the beat. Now we're listening to the words and it's not nice."[72] Another told its story in the headline "Chi Catholic Youth Put Pressure on DJs to Ban Off-Color Discs"[73] in which an organized mail campaign was detailed. Censorship campaigns in Boston, San Antonio, and Los Angeles were described under the

---

[70] "Houston Radio Stations Ask Crime Commission to List Indigo Disks," Variety, March 23, 1955, p. 41.

[71] "Deep South Jockeys Junk 50% of R&B Wax," Variety, March 30, 1955, p. 54.

[72] "R&B's Slip is Now Showing," Variety, March 30, 1955, p. 49.

[73] Ibid.

heading "Radio Outlets, Disc Jocks Launch Self-Policing Setups Vs. 'Leer-ic' Wax."[74]

Also in March, Broadcasting announced that WABB, Mobile, had run an advertisement in a local paper titled "Music You Won't Hear on WABB," which objected to "disguised smut" lurking in the lyrics of some records.[75]

The uproar over dirty lyrics subsided with the elimination of certain of the more explicit discs from station playlists, but the stir caused by the controversy lingered on in other forms. Program director Bill Stewart, who had a special facility for developing a striking promotion, used the question of dirty lyrics over ten years later, in 1967, in a publicity campaign to boost the prestige of the McLendon stations. However, it would be a mistake to think that the purpose of the campaign was entirely motivated by business interests. Both McLendon and Stewart had children, and they both feared the influence of certain suggestions in the music. Stewart's daughter, Sharon, provided the spark for the idea when she asked her father what the Rolling Stones' record "Let's Spend the Night Together" meant.[76] Although McLendon was in Stockholm at the time and had nothing to do with initiating the campaign, he of course got the credit for starting it since his stations were connected with it. (However, McLendon seemed happy to give credit to Bill Stewart as the originator of the idea in

---

[74] Ibid.

[75] "WABB Lashes Out Against Recorded 'Disguised Smut,'" Broadcasting, March 28, 1955, p. 88.

[76] Stewart interview.

an interview with Richard K. Doan on WNEW on May 14, 1967).[77] The advertisement Stewart placed in Broadcasting is reproduced on page 378.[78] As a result of his station's campaign, McLendon was invited to speak before the American Mothers Committee Incorporated's "Mothers of Men" Luncheon in New York on May 12, 1967, where he delivered a speech with the same title as the headline of the advertisement: "Frankly, We're Tired . . . of Raunchy Lyrics. . . ."[79]

Both the campaign and the speech received a surprisingly warm review from Time magazine in its May 26, 1967, issue. In June, Variety reported that a number of AM stations in Texas had followed McLendon's lead, with one even banning the innocuous Petula Clark hit, "Don't Sleep in the Subway," for reasons which must have been too obscure (or too ludicrous) to mention.[80] Obviously, with that kind of censorship, the pendulum had swung too far, but McLendon and others seemed pleased that at least some softening of the suggestive lyrics had taken place.

The problem of lyrics seeming too raw, threatening or suggestive to parents will probably exist as long as there continues to be a special music aimed at teenagers. The fact that the problem had to be cured _again_ in 1967 shows that the mid-50s experience was not something peculiar to the times. The content of young people's music will probably always be in some way revolutionary, and the problem of the

---

[77] "The Truth About Radio: A WNEW Inquiry," an interview with Gordon McLendon by Richard K. Doan, May 14, 1967, aired 7:30 to 8:00 p.m., xeroxed, p. 6.

[78] Advertisement in Broadcasting, April 10, 1967, p. 39.

[79] Copy of speech, mimeographed, from the McLendon Stations.

[80] "Many Texas AMers Follow McLendon in Banning Disks with Dubious Lyrics," Variety, June 21, 1967, p. 51.

AN OPEN LETTER TO: The Music Industry

Frankly, We're tired . . .

. . . **TIRED** of today's new releases coming through rife with "raunchy" lyrics, et cetra. In the past month, six records which were on the national charts far overstepped the boundaries of good taste, and we were forced to ban them.

. . . **TIRED** of "policing" your industry. It is time consuming, not our responsibility, and an outright imposition—on all broadcasters.

. . . **TIRED** of answering complaints from our listeners, civic groups, and civic leaders who blame us for your poor judgment on what is, and what is not, in good taste.

. . . **TIRED** of sincerely promising the FCC that we will do everything to elevate the needs, tastes and desires of the community—only to have one or two records threaten to tear it all down.

Therefore, we intend to

. . . 1 **REFUSE** to review effective May 15, 1967 any record submitted to us for air play unless it is accompanied by a valid and actual lyric sheet for both sides.

. . . 2 **REFUSE** to play record releases which continue, through "gimmicks" intonations, and nuances to either innocently or intentionally offend public morals, dignity or taste.

. . . 3 **REFUSE** consideration of both sides of a record if one side is adjudged unfit for airplay.

. . . 4 **URGE ALL RESPONSIBLE BROADCASTERS TO FOLLOW THIS "CODE OF RECORD STANDARDS" IN REVIEWING RECORDS IN THE FUTURE.**

Frankly, we are tired. We want to be fair. But our success, after all, is often dependent on your success as record producers; but conversely, your success is predicated on radio airplay of your product. Please, let's work together. Clean things up before some unnecessary regulatory action is taken or before the broadcasters' listening audience indignantly tunes out.

THE McLendon STATIONS

programmer, who wonders just how much to go along with the emerging new order, will persist.

Disc Jockey Criticism of Music Policy

The complaints issued by the public over the supposedly dirty lyrics of rhythm and blues records were not the only complaints being leveled at Top 40 stations' music policy. Some of the other complaints were internal--from the stations' own disc jockeys.

Disc jockeys had two basic complaints. One was that Top 40 operators were increasing their control over the selection of music, decreasing the disc jockey's traditional prerogative in that area. The other was that disc jockeys were being told more and more to say less and less. To the disc jockeys it seemed that their very personalities were being eradicated by management control and the tight format.

The disc jockeys' complaints increased in number and frequency in 1958, when many stations had adopted the winning Top 40 formula. The front page of _Variety_ for March 12, 1958 carried the headline "Deejay: Performer or Puppet?" Leaving little doubt whose side he was taking, _Variety_'s Herm Schoenfeld wrote

> The disk jockey is now in a fight for survival. Hailed as a hero in radio's surging boom in the face of television competition, the deejay now feels himself being cut down to size in the machine of "formula radio." The disk jockey--once the individualistic salesman, the personality kid--avers his hands--and his tongue--are tied in a straitjacket of "Top 40" lists, music-and-news formats and hard-sell commercials, all firmly dictated from the top by radio station management.[81]

The _Variety_ article was written immediately following the close

---

[81] Herm Schoenfeld, "Deejay: Performer or Puppet?" _Variety_, March 12, 1958, pp. 1, 60.

of the first annual Disc Jockey Convention in Kansas City, sponsored by the Storz stations, at which Mitch Miller, then an executive with Columbia records, gave a speech titled "The Great Abdication." Miller is quoted as having told the disc jockeys:

> "You carefully built yourself into the monarchs of radio and abdicated--abdicated your programming to the corner record shop, to the eight to 14-year-olds, to the pre-shave crowd that makes up 12% of the country's population and zero percent of its buying power, once you eliminate the pony tail ribbons, popsicles and peanut butter."[82]

The Variety article went on to detail the effect of Miller's speech:

> While Miller appears to be aiming his shaft at the deejays, the latter understood the speech to be directed against station management. At the windup of Miller's talk, most of the deejays gave him a standing ovation, the only speech of the two-day meet earning such a strong accolade.[83]

June Bundy, who reported on the disc jockey convention for Billboard, predicted that some of the discontent aired by the disc jockeys could result in substantial programming changes. "In the course of these complaints," she wrote, "It became apparent that many imitators and 'imitators of imitators' of the pioneer 'Top 40' type stations (Storz, Plough, McLendon, etc.) have instituted disc programming policies which are often far more restrictive than some of the originals are today. . . ."[84] June Bundy quoted Chuck Blore, program director of Top 40 station KFWB, as saying that in his station's case the formula was more flexible than most critics realized. She quoted

---

[82] Ibid., p. 60. [83] Ibid.

[84] June Bundy, "Deejay Revolt at 'Top 40' May Bring Basic Changes," Billboard, March 17, 1958, p. 2.

Blore as calling formula radio "the love child of perceptive management."[85]

In April of 1958, Los Angeles station KLAC announced that it was going to convert to a totally non-jock operation, in the sense that no live disc jockeys would be on the air--only recorded introductions and other pre-recorded productions would have announcers' voices. Otherwise, the station planned to play mostly music, and calculated that it could program 13 percent more music without the disc jockeys.[86] KLAC's decision to operate without any jocks at all may have been prompted by the fact that most of them had already quit anyway. Earlier in April jock Gene Norman had resigned, saying at the time that

> it would be inconceivable for me to desert my 15-year-standards by resorting to a "Top 40" rock and roll format, instead of playing a quality cross-section of everything from modern jazz to Broadway show tunes. Stereotype radio leaves no opportunity to be creative and interesting.[87]

In May, Billboard's June Bundy wrote a front-page feature article on the formula-versus-personality debate, noting that "in recent weeks it has proceeded at an accelerated pace. Experiments with automation, consistent rating victories by key 'Top 40' outlets, continual efforts by stations to cut costs--all these things--worry big-money 'personality' spinners today."[88]

---

[85] Ibid., p. 8.

[86] "KLAC Defends New Policy of Dropping All Deejays," Billboard, April 14, 1958, p. 9.

[87] "2 DJs Quit in KLAC '40' Row," Billboard, April 7, 1958, p. 1.

[88] June Bundy, "New DJ Radio Look Causes Concern to Personality Jocks," Billboard, May 12, 1958, p. 1.

In December of 1958, Billboard ran a "retrospective" article about the formula-versus-personality feud that had developed in the previous year, and which listed a number of the big-name deejays who had quit their jobs rather than be shackled to a formula.

> The situation was brought into sharp focus a couple of weeks ago when two veteran deejays, Martin Block, WABC, New York, and Bill Randle, WERE, Cleveland, held a joint discussion of the problem with a group of Columbia Records promotion men. Randle told the group that the name disc jockey will become as extinct as the Dodo bird if the trend toward disc programming by local station management continues to build in the industry. . . .
>
> Both Block and Randle said that they have contracts permitting them full control over their disc programming. However, Block said he had agreed to follow a top-sellers-type format at WABC. Then he deadpanned, "My ratings have never been lower."
>
> Altho many name jockeys attack "Top 40" type programming as the reason for their plight, the problem for personality jocks apparently boils down to station management programming of any kind, as opposed to personal disc selection by the jock himself. . . .
>
> . . . Meanwhile, management programming, particularly that of "Top 40"-type outlets, continues to thrive both rating and saleswise.
>
> Representing management's viewpoint, Michael Ruppe Jr., KWK, St. Louis, writes, "'Controlled music' formats are needed!" Ruppe contends that the average jockey is under such continual pressure today--because of increased numbers of releases, demands on his time for promotion, etc.--that "it's rather difficult for most personalities to keep fully-apace."
>
> "This," continues Ruppe, "then becomes management's responsibility! The trend, as we can spot it, is for more and more stations to develop an over-all music image--one that takes into consideration current music trends and those responsible for selling it on the air--the disc jockey.
>
> "Program directors are no longer what they once were. Someone suggested that the title be changed to Program Controller for that's what they appear to be doing in great quantity lately--controlling the music policy of the station as well as other activities. There is also a noticeable trend for program directors in music and news stations to be responsible for the main promotional activities."[89]

The trend toward greater program control by management described

---

[89] "Sparks Still Fly in Format Fracas," Billboard, December 15, 1958, p. 63.

in the passage just quoted prompted Sponsor magazine to query in one of its regular "symposia," "With 'controlled' programming increasing, Sponsor Asks: Does the Personality Disk Jockey Fit Into Formula?"[90] Of the four station managers queried, three defined "personality" and "formula" in such a way that the two were compatible, while the fourth said "never the twain shall meet."[91] A later "Sponsor Asks" symposium elicited thoughtful responses to the question, "Is the Personality DJ Craze on the Wane?" Chuck Blore, vice-president in charge of programming on KFWB, Los Angeles replied

> If the personality DJ is the golden-tongued, $100,000-a-year, lethargic, loquacious, self-styled music critic, the answer is "Yes."
>
> The modern DJ is a man who knows where he is going, what he is going to say, and--most important--knows why. He is a highly trained specialist, who, so unlike Stanislawski, demands motivation for any action. He realizes that only the merest minority give a damn about his pontification on the pros and cons of every record. The listener knows whether or not he likes the record and beyond that his chief reaction to anything the DJ says about it is complete indifference.
>
> The job of the DJ today is to establish his personality between records. He must say what he has to say in a brief, bright, entertaining manner. He has a reason for every remark, a motivation for every move. Will it entertain and inform? Does the listener care?[92]

Blore's programming of KFWB had resulted in a Hooper share in early 1959 of 32.4%,[93] so his thinking appeared to be paying off. Another of the participants was KLAC's president, Mort Hall. It was KLAC that had

---

[90] Sponsor, March 7, 1959, p. 52.

[91] Ibid., p. 52.

[92] "Is the Personality DJ Craze on the Wane?" Sponsor, July 18, 1959, p. 46.

[93] Advertisement in Sponsor, March 7, 1959, p. 59.

decided to drop all of its disc jockeys and just play as much music as possible. Hall commented,

> The personality DJ is far from dead. However, his role has changed.
> The modern DJ is not involved in the selling job as he once was. Gone are the long, off-the-cuff type spot announcements. Instead we find him working around a schedule of transcribed spot announcements prepared by agencies. His program has become a carrier for these announcements and adapting his personality to this type of programming is what he must learn.[94]

Bill Randle, for years the top-rated jock in Cleveland, in 1962 wrote an article for Variety in which he blasted the Top 40 formula, describing stations that programmed it as

> . . . involved in the grinding out of a rigidly limited list of mediocre, currently popular songs, tightly interspersed with insistent and incessant commercials, superimposed on a blur of monomaniacal jingles, contests, weather reports, capsule news, meaningless salutes and gimmicks, and a hodgepodge of "public service" announcements.[95]

However acutely Randle may have disliked the Top 40 formula, he was fair in placing the blame for the introduction of what he called "junk music" where it belonged.

> There is absolutely no question that the responsibility for introducing much of what is called "junk music" to general radio audiences lies not with the "top 40" formula stations but is almost entirely due to personality disc jockeys at the peak of their power.
> Subject to shifting pressures of record distributors and manufacturers, performers, teenage audiences, and ultimately radio station policies, personality disc jockeys initiated the playing and concentrated exploitation of single, currently popular phonograph records of a type that had never been generally mass-circulated in previous music business history . . . the

---

[94] "Is Personality DJ Craze on the Wane?" p. 46.

[95] Bill Randle, "Why and How Recorded Junk Music Doesn't Truly Reflect U.S. Tastes," Variety, January 10, 1962, p. 4.

> middle 50s saw a definite trend toward production of rhythm & blues and country and western music.[96]

While some saw in the new music the democratization of American music, with Negro and country performers finally being fused with more "refined" white music, Randle did not see any particular musical benefit from such a blending. He concluded,

> It is obvious that formula radio is not the final answer to the American communications problem. Success in itself is not enough. There is a distinct need for broader programming that will fulfill the real needs of larger areas of the community.[97]

Disc jockey organizations

In 1958, the year which saw the great outpouring of disc jockey discontent with management control of programming, a number of disc jockeys met at the second annual Storz-sponsored Disc Jockey Convention for the purpose of organizing a national organization--a voice for the deejay.[98] Bill Gavin, one of the initial organizers stated in a letter to Billboard that ". . . there is no thought of limiting such an association only to the 'mike men.' With the continuing trend toward controlled programming, membership would have to be open to all who participate in record programming for radio."[99]

The National Disc Jockey Association held its organizational meeting in Milwaukee in July 1959. Disc jockeys and music programmers with at least two years full-time experience, and station managers all

---

[96] Ibid., p. 49. [97] Ibid., p. 4.

[98] "Jock Meet Sows National Org Seeds," Billboard, June 8, 1958, p. 3.

[99] "Sound Off!" (letters column), Billboard, May 11, 1959, p. 3.

were eligible to join, but record company representatives were not.[100] The first annual meeting of the Association took place in Minneapolis in 1960 after the payola investigations had been started. Thus it is not surprising that a code of ethics was one of the first items of business.[101]

The DJA's code of ethics adoption release stated:

> The DJA, since its inception, has and will continue to be specifically forbidden by its bylaws to bargain with station management as to working conditions, salaries, etc. It is clearly understood that DJA is an altruistic, non-profit organization created for the sole purpose of increasing public respect for our profession and contributing whatever, whenever, and wherever possible to such altruistic and charitable activities as shall be decided upon by its Board of Directors. . . .[102]

The Disc Jockeys Association became, of necessity, a public relations effort to improve the image of the disc jockey after it was tarnished in the payola scandals. Since the payola investigation <u>confirmed</u> many broadcasters in the belief that disc jockeys could not be trusted with the selection of music, one of the motives for starting the Association in the first place was removed. Both the disc jockey conventions sponsored by Storz and the independent Disc Jockey Association are now defunct.

In the 1950s, disc jockeys ran the gamut from being considered among the "saviors of radio" in the early period to the "Judases of jukedom" at the end of the decade. The indiscretions of a powerful few

---

[100] "New DJ Assn.," Broadcasting, July 27, 1959, p. 78.

[101] Sam Chase, "DJs Adopt Code, Membership Plan," Billboard, April 18, 1960, p. 3.

[102] "Jocks' Code of Ethics Adopted at DJA Meet," Billboard, April 18, 1960, p. 3.

that led to the payola investigations were cause for broadcasters everywhere to tighten their control over the selection and programming of music, even if their general policy had been to allow the air personalities to make the choice for themselves.

As literally hundreds of new record companies sprang up and attempted to produce a hit disc in the emerging teenage market, it was perhaps inevitable that record programs and the personalities that presided over such programs would both increase in number. As the Top 40 formula of hits played consistently and repetitively evolved, and it became increasingly apparent that the audience wanted to hear the hits almost exclusively, management exerted programming control both in selecting the music to be played and in limiting the amount of talk by disc jockeys so that the wanted music could emerge. These moves by Top 40 management were taking place before the payola scandals, and probably would have happened no matter how honest the typical disc jockey. The payola hearings only served to consolidate an attitude that was already growing among radio management in general.

The control of music selection and its concomitant--control of disc jockey talk--were together one of the two important steps taken by Top 40 management in developing a unique format. The other factor in the success of the format--promotion--is the subject of the following chapter.

CHAPTER SIX

TOP 40 PROMOTION POLICIES

While the policies on music and deejay chatter that management instituted in developing the Top 40 format were the most easily discernible programming differences in comparing a Top 40 station with some other type, promotion was the factor responsible both for local ratings successes and for diffusion of the format across the nation.

The term "promotion" is widely used in radio. Very commonly, promotion means "sales promotion" rather than station promotion. When this is the case, the sales promotion should be understood as part of overall promotion of the station. As Jacob Evans says in his Selling and Promoting Radio and TV, "Every activity of the promotion department adds up ultimately to station promotion; i.e., whether programs, sales or prestige are promoted, the station as a whole benefits."[1] It has already been shown that Top 40 management generally put programming considerations ahead of sales considerations. The same is true in regard to promotion: audience promotion generally came ahead of sales promotion. The philosophy was the same as before: if you draw an audience via promotion and your programming is good, you will develop more listeners. More listeners will mean more sales.

---

[1] Jacob A. Evans, Selling and Promoting Radio and TV (New York: Printer's Ink Publishing Co., 1954), p. 215.

General Audience Promotions

Audience promotions on Top 40 stations were designed to have effects of at least three different durations. There was the promotion designed for immediate (and sometimes short-term) effect, often to "hypo" the ratings. There were promotions which continued over several weeks or months which were intended to demonstrate longer-term growth in a station's audience. And there were promotions of a continuous, non-terminating nature which served mainly to identify the station and keep its call letters in the public's consciousness, rather than to build audiences.

Evans suggests six principles of effective audience promotion:

> First: Give the promotion eye or ear appeal. Stop the person's wandering eye or ear. Gain attention. Impel people to hear you out.
> Second: Glamourize your programs. Make your promotion reflect the breath-taking excitement of show business, the magic of make-believe. Capture people's imagination.
> Third: Be specific. Give the public reasons why the program will be appealing.
> Fourth: Use newsworthy, timely copy. Offer reasons for tuning in the program today, for this particular broadcast.
> Fifth: Stick to the point. Make the copy clear, descriptive and . . . brief.
> Sixth: Move people to action. Emphasize the time of broadcast and the station's dial position.[2]

Evans' advice is given for the older radio, which *did* consist of separate, different programs rather than one continuous program, but it applies equally well to Top 40.

Audience promotion was certainly not invented by Top 40 management. It had been around for years with the other entertainment media (especially movies). However, neither radio nor motion pictures

---

[2] *Ibid.*

worked very hard at audience promotion until both began to receive competition from the growing popularity of television. The hoopla which surrounded the introduction of the numerous wide-screen and 3-D movie processes in the 1950s can be seen as the corollary of radio's promotional efforts at the same time: the "bigger and better than ever" theme was not Hollywood's alone.

Rationale for Promotions

Ted Cott was until 1950 in charge of promotion for WNEW. In that year, he went over to WNBC which, he said, "was suffering from malnutrition of excitement."[3] His philosophy in 1952 was stated as follows: "If you take a big bomb and drop it, you cause a lot of damage, but it can be cleaned up right away. I like to drop a lot of little bombs. The mess is harder to clean up."[4] The "little bombs" philosophy also appeared in one of the earliest McLendon memoranda available to the author.[5] Writing to KELP General Manager Joe Roddy

---

[3]"Little Bombs," Time, February 11, 1952, p. 69.

[4]Ibid., p. 66.

[5]At the time he was interviewed, Stewart was program director at WNOE, New Orleans, and was running an inexpensive contest in which he was going to give away several construction worker hardhats to celebrate Spiro Agnew's birthday. He used this contest to demonstrate how a simple, very inexpensive promotion (a "little bomb") is supposed to work:

> "Who, in their right mind, would want to win a hardhat? But, if someone hears it, they're liable to go to work tomorrow and say, hey, did you hear what they're doing on WNOE? They're giving away hardhats. All right, you've got a free commercial right there. On the other hand, if you give away an album, just a plain album of Frank Sinatra songs, they might want to win it--they might be more interested in winning it than the hardhat--but they won't go talk about it. So you've got to do something that will make people talk about it." Stewart interview.

in April 1953, McLendon says

> It seems to me that the answer to the thing [becoming dull and stultified] lies in continually giving the people something new to talk about--something fresh on the station. The answer lies in new ideas always. Right at the moment, your Think About It thing is a new idea in El Paso and will give them something new to talk about, but in two or three months, you must have something new again. Something to make people talk. . . .[6]

As with most radio station owners, McLendon felt that the best medium for promoting his stations was via the stations themselves.

> . . . Use your newscasts for station promotion. The newscasts should for several days carry items about the survey that we have just completed--or that the agencies have. In addition, promotional spots should be written about this survey. Station breaks should emphasize the big features of the survey. Certainly, on Sunday, we should inform all listeners that this is "KELP, which by independent survey has more listeners on Sunday than any other El Paso station" . . . that may be awkwardly worded, but you can fix it up. . . .
>
> Put on plenty of publicity blurbs when you move to your new location; make it sound like an event. Likewise, you might be putting some on when we file for nighttime. Use your station to promote all station events. If something in the station interests you, the chances are that it is good for a newscast or promotional item, or perhaps many of them. . . .[7]

Asked about how the Storz stations had promoted themselves locally, executive vice president George Armstrong said:

> Oh, well, we did clever things. Mostly on the air, by the way. We did it without ever buying a billboard or a newspaper ad. . . . I never like to say "never," but I think that for all practical purposes, it was all on the air. . . . And we never once in the development of any of the stations started any promotion until after we were set with product. No matter what kind of promotion. There's just no point in it unless you have your product set, because all you're doing is wasting money. . . .[8]

A month after McLendon wrote the memo to Joe Roddy quoted earlier, Bill Stewart joined the McLendon operation, first as a disc

---

[6] Gordon McLendon, memorandum to Joe Roddy, April 11, 1953, from McLendon Policy Books.

[7] Ibid. [8] Armstrong interview.

jockey and quite soon thereafter as National Program Director. Stewart and McLendon together were responsible for a great deal of the notoriety which surrounded the growth of Top 40. Stewart, for reasons even he cannot determine precisely, has always had a "feel" for what would appeal to an audience, be it in terms of the music played or some stunt being considered. McLendon, with his family involved in motion picture exhibition, had a "feel" of his own, both for what was glamorous and exciting, and also for promotion and exploitation as applied both to movies and radio. Just as important, McLendon had a "let's take a shot" outlook and a free attitude about finances that effectively backed Stewart's ideas with both policy and cash. McLendon and Stewart complemented each other--perhaps neither could have done alone what both accomplished together. Like McLendon, Stewart believed that the most important goal to be accomplished by any audience promotion was to get people talking about the station. Stewart says, "My philosophy has always been that you tell someone 50 times that you're going to do something. Then you do it. Then you tell him 100 times that you did it. And the least important thing is doing it."[9] Stewart also agreed with both the McLendon and Storz philosophies that a promotion was useless unless the product that you were trying to attract people to was a good one.

> . . . That's the mistake that most people make. They run all these contests, give away all this money, and they can't understand why they don't get listeners. You've got to have the product first. You've got to have the product right first, before you do anything. You can give away $1,000. People come over to win the $1,000, but if they don't hear something they like, they're not going to stay there.[10]

---

[9] Stewart interview. [10] Ibid.

Stewart's opinion is that the "product" at KLIF was a good one, basically. KLIF had introduced mobile news units, and its music was becoming increasingly more consistent when Stewart moved from the disc jockey and program director job at McLendon's Houston station (then KLBS) to program director at KLIF (and then National Program Director in the Spring of 1954). But neither KLBS nor KLIF were, in Stewart's opinion, doing very much in the way of promotion when he joined each station. McLendon corroborated this viewpoint himself in a letter to Stewart after Stewart had left KLIF to be program director at father-in-law James Noe's WNOE in New Orleans. The letter is reproduced on page 394.[11]

Evolution of Audience Promotion at McLendon Stations

"Oops, sorry"

Stewart recalls that he started the promotion of disc jockeys and of their shows in Houston just before he went to Dallas and KLIF, where he continued the name deejay buildup. But he recalls a single incident which he says "was probably the one thing that made KLIF, more than anything. That's how the original "Oops, Sorry" ad came about, too."[12] As Stewart tells the story, the KLIF mobile units were still relatively new in early January of 1954 and station personnel were not used to the technicalities involved in airing reports from them. It was, in fact, only the second night that the unit had been in use when the incident to be described occurred. Stewart had finished his

---

[11] Gordon McLendon, letter to Bill Stewart, April 26, 1955.

[12] Stewart interview.

KLIF THE McLENDON STATION

5000 WATTS ★ 1190 KILOCYCLES ★ 2104 JACKSON ★ DALLAS 1, TEXAS

April 26, 1955

Mr. Bill Stewart
Program Director
Radio Station WNOE
St. Charles Hotel
New Orleans, Louisiana

Dear Bill:

I feel that I've owed you a letter quite a long time to thank you for the wonderful work you did for us at KLIF. And it makes me feel good to know that you are still within the family.

As you know, we were open to plenty of suggestions when you came and your suggestions turned out to be uniformly good. You got us started off right on the name deejay-promotion format and that, with the addition of the news program we had, was the making of the station. Your money throw-away, teen-age record hops, Appreciation Nights, "You Don't Hear This" spots, and numerous contests stand out particularly in my memory. We might have made it to the top eventually even if you had not arrived on the scene but I doubt it; certainly, we'd have been a lot longer getting there.

By way of passing a long overdue compliment, I'd say that you ranked with the top five independent program men in the country. And, for the life of me, I can't think of the other four.

Again, many thanks. We're all grateful, as I've told you often. Now you've added another pelt to your coonskin by bringing WNOE out of the left-field and back to bat.

The very best,

Gordon McLendon

Gordon McLendon

afternoon drive air shift and was driving around with the newsman in the mobile unit.

> . . . We were driving around--just driving around--and I was showing him [newsman Dick Smith] how the thing worked, trying to tell him exactly what I wanted him to do, and we were driving in Oak Cliff [a section of Dallas]. We heard a police call, and it was about a robbery in progress at 1229 such and such. And as luck would have it, it was right around the corner from us. So we go zipping around the corner, and he's driving and I've got the mike, and I jump out. First of all, I've said "We're on our way to a robbery, stand by." So the guy at the station is alert, he's listening for us. So I jump out, and there is the guy standing on the sidewalk. And I say, what happened? And he says, well, this f*****g nigger came up, and he stuck a f*****g knife at my throat, and told me he was going to cut my f*****g throat. And I say, wait a minute, wait a minute, and I go back and push the button and I say, give it to me. So I say to the guy, now, would you tell us what happened sir? And so, he says it exactly the same way! Which was beautiful. So I go back to the station. This was at 8:45 at night. We got--we had six telephone calls that night. And that really got me mad. You know, six people. That meant there weren't too many people out there in radio-land listening. So, I went down, and ran this ad in the paper the next day, unbeknownst to Gordon or his father--or <u>anyone</u>. And they fired me. Gordon's father fired me. It was a Saturday morning. I ran the ad on the obituary page, edged in black![13]

The ad in question is reproduced on page 396.[14]

Asked why he should be fired for running such an advertisement, Stewart answered,

> Because I didn't check with anybody. And because it called attention to the fact that the guy said it. And I said, well, that's what the hell I <u>wanted</u> to do, because only six people called. And over the weekend, the telephone company had to get us to stop--to run announcements on the air--because we got about 6,000 calls in three days from people wanting to know what the guy said! And everybody was saying, well, you should have heard the words he said! You know, every dirty word that anyone ever knew! And that was what made the station. Overnight. That was <u>the</u> thing that made the station. That and

---

[13] <u>Ibid</u>.

[14] Advertisement in <u>The Daily Times Herald</u>, January 9, 1954, Dallas, Texas, from Bill Stewart's files.

Saturday, Jan. 9, 1954 THE DAILY TIMES HERALD, DALLAS

OOPS SORRY

KLIF wishes to offer this apology for the unfortunate language used on an interview during an on-the-scene broadcast of an armed robbery Friday night at 8:44 p.m.

To all of the many people who called the station, KLIF would like to say that we're sorry. But in covering news on the scene as we do, the remarks of a witness, who may be in a highly emotional state, can not be governed.

However, in all humility—KLIF tenders this apology.

BILL STEWART
PROGRAM DIRECTOR

> throwing the money out the window. And the throwing the money out the window came afterwards. If throwing the money out the window had come first, we wouldn't have had any people down there. But from that day forward, we had [listeners who could hear the station's promos]. It brought them over. We had a good product going at the time.[15]

The "throwing the money out the window" promotion will be discussed in a moment. First, it should be mentioned that the "Oops, sorry" ad turned out to have considerable staying power. On September 11, 1959, KLIF, Dallas, ran virtually the same ad again. Within a span of six weeks, four other McLendon stations (WAKY, KTSA, KEEL and KILT) ran a similar apology in <u>their</u> local papers. At the time, the managers who could be contacted all said that the indiscrete word in question had been uttered by an interviewee who was "in a state of extreme agitation, having just witnessed the plane landing." For further details, see "The Curse of Consistency," <u>Broadcasting</u>, November 30, 1959, p. 78, reproduced below on page 398. At the same time these ads were run, Stewart had just become program director for Burden's Star Stations after leaving Storz. Don Keyes was then National Program Director for McLendon.

<u>Money out the window</u>

The money-out-the-window promotion was one that Stewart "borrowed" from Storz. McLendon sent him to Omaha to look over the Storz operation. Stewart never did get to see Storz on that trip because as of that time (1954), he and the McLendon chain were relatively unknown. Stewart says that nothing intrigued him with the Storz operation then except that they had put a fellow up in a tree in a

---

[15] Stewart interview.

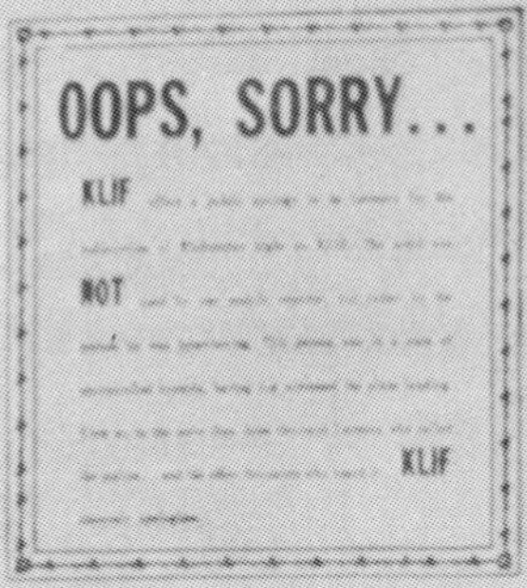
OOPS, SORRY...
KLIF
NOT
KLIF

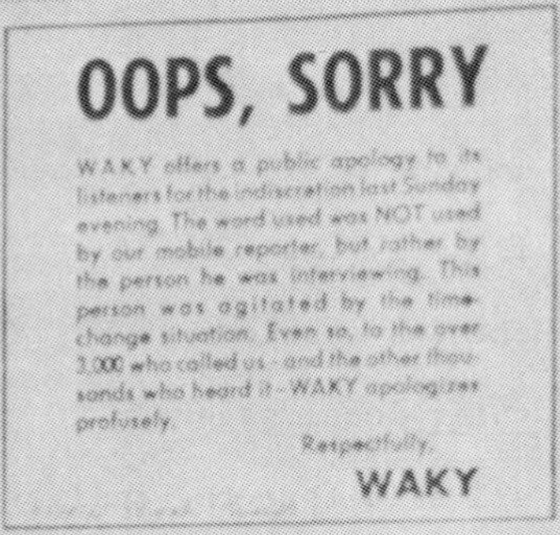
OOPS, SORRY
WAKY offers a public apology to its listeners for the indiscretion last Sunday evening. The word used was NOT used by our mobile reporter, but rather by the person he was interviewing. This person was agitated by the time-change situation. Even so, to the over 3,000 who called us—and the other thousands who heard it—WAKY apologizes profusely.
Respectfully,
WAKY

Oops, Sorry . . .
KTSA

The curse of consistency • "Oops, sorry . . ."

Under this banner, five of the McLendon radio stations have placed ads in local newspapers to offer "a public apology" for "indiscretions" on their airwaves. The ads appeared, one by each station (see cuts), over a six-week span starting with one inserted by KLIF Dallas in the *Dallas Morning News* on Sept. 11.

OOPS, SORRY...
KEEL

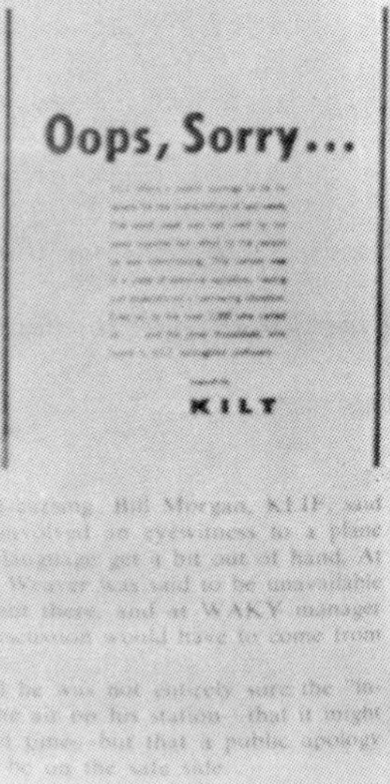
Oops, Sorry...
KILT

What were the indiscretions? In all cases, according to the ads, they were committed not by a station man but by people being interviewed at a time of emotional tension. On KLIF and KEEL Shreveport (in the *Shreveport Times*), the culprit in each case had "just witnessed the plane landing." KTSA San Antonio (*San Antonio Express*) said in its case it was somebody who had "just won a KTSA contest." KILT Houston's ad (*Houston Post*) said the person had "just experienced a harrowing situation" and WAKY Louisville's problem, the ad (in the *Courier-Journal*) reported, stemmed from somebody "agitated by the time-change situation."

All but KTSA's ad apologized to the more than 3,000 people who, they said, had called the station, and also to the "other thousands" who were listening. KTSA's apologized "to the hundreds who called us" and the other thousands who heard it."

Inquiry of McLendon vice presidents in charge of the stations brought the word in most cases that the "indiscretion" was a language lapse. Richard Wilson, KEEL, said his station's incident was a slip of the tongue on tape, fed in from "over in Texas" and somehow not properly edited, dealing with a plane in trouble. Jack Fiedler, KTSA, said deejay Pat Tallman was interviewing a woman about a contest, and cut her off the air when she started cursing. Bill Morgan, KLIF, said [illegible] involved an eyewitness to a plane landing who let his language get a bit out of hand. At KILT, manager Bill Weaver was said to be unavailable to discuss the incident there, and at WAKY manager [illegible] said any discussion would have to come from higher authorities.

One manager said he was not entirely sure the "indiscretion" got on the air on his station—that it might have been bleeped in time—but that a public apology seemed desirable to be on the safe side.

Mr. Morgan indicated that the Dallas incident was one of those things that occasionally crop up to plague [illegible] stations. Like the broadcast of the LSU-Mississippi football game a few weeks back when, he said, the game's only touchdown came when the station had [illegible] for a commercial. In that case, he said, it was not a question of public apology but of repeating the description of the winning play several times for the benefit of protesting listeners.

park, and periodically he dropped some money out of it. "All the rest of the stuff I knew" says Stewart in referring to Storz's other programming.[16] Not much more than a week later, Stewart arranged for a room in the Adolphus Hotel in Dallas, where he and some assistants put money inside of balloons which they then dropped out the window. Stewart claims that some 10,000 people were jamming the street below waiting for the money to come their way.

> When I do something, there have to be a lot of factors involved to make it right. I did it on a specific day for a specific reason. Again, it comes back to getting people talking about you. The throwing the money out the window was not that big, even though it drew 10,000 people. . . . But I did it on Good Friday [April 17, 1954] because I knew that if I did it on Good Friday, that every minister and priest in town would give us hell on Sunday from the pulpit, which they did. So we got all kinds of free publicity from _them_. And I _literally_ had to leave the country, because the police were after me. . . . And I had to leave by the service stairs, from the fourteenth floor--and I went to Mexico! I mean, they had a warrant out for my arrest, for obstructing traffic . . . they blamed _me_. Because I was the guy who signed for the room. Even though it was under an assumed name. They had me for that too![17]

Even though Storz had refused to see Stewart, after word reached him about Stewart's success with throwing money out of a hotel in Dallas instead of a tree in Omaha, Storz wrote to Stewart "You're a man of fast action."[18] From that time on, says Stewart, Storz "was a fan of mine."[19]

"You'll never hear this"

In October of 1953, WNEW began a promotion campaign with the

---

[16] _Ibid._ [17] _Ibid._

[18] _Ibid._ [19] _Ibid._

theme "You'll never hear this on WNEW." Before each of its record programs, the station presented a short satire of a TV commercial or program. The satire was followed with the words "but you will hear . . ." and then the theme for the next program.[20] Stewart used the exact theme--you'll never hear this--but he added a new twist: he mentioned the call letters of competing stations.

> I think it was the first time that any competitive call letters were ever mentioned. It was unheard of in those days. I guess it still is. I'm the only one who does it consistently. But, we ran things like--well, he mentioned that in the letter--I used to just take the paper in the morning, and we'd say, it's nine o'clock on KLIF, where you won't hear Arthur Godfrey, who is on KRLD, Backstage Wife, which is on WFAA. . . . I'd take the ridiculous ones, not all of them. Just the ones that didn't make sense for our type of audience.[21]

A letter to the editor in the June 13, 1955 Broadcasting from Stewart expresses interest in a "You won't hear this" promotion that had recently been run by WKDA, Nashville. Stewart pointed out that "I used the same campaign on KLIF in Dallas two years ago and re-used it here on KNOE two months ago."[22]

Miscellaneous Early Promotions

On July 27, 1954, McLendon wrote another letter to Joe Roddy, his manager in El Paso. The thrust of the letter was a series of answers to questions that had been posed by Roddy on how KELP could be more like KLIF. On the subject of promotions McLendon wrote,

---

[20] "WNEW Takes a Swing," Broadcasting, October 12, 1953, p. 104.

[21] Stewart interview.

[22] "Letter," Broadcasting, June 13, 1955, p. 22.

> I'm going to try to get Bill Stewart to write you a letter about promotions but among those we've pulled are: (1) the money-dropping thing; (2) playing the same "Dragnet" record for two straight hours; (3) a contest on why I hate Bill Stewart; (4) a contest for the best letters on why a certain announcer should get a raise; (5) a contest in which we gave an answer and asked the listeners what the question was; (6) the Walking Woman contest; (7) the coming rainmaker deal and (8) the coming Treasure Chest operation.[23]

The Walking Woman contest (also known later as the Walking Man contest) consisted of equipping some person with a sizeable prize to be surrendered when someone came up to her or him on the street and asked "Are you the KLIF Walking Woman (Man)?" The "rainmaker deal" referred to was not a contest but a news-type promotion--KLIF hired a rainmaker to seed the clouds over Dallas and make it rain in the late summer of 1954.

McLendon's letter continues,

> Now, besides these direct promotions, I would say that we do some other things that can be classified as promotions. We try to give news and cover special events that we feel minorities are interested in and we try to cover them in a way that we feel does not bore the majority. For instance,
>
> (1) coverage of sports events with bulletins every thirty minutes. We only try to cover in such a way sports events that are not being covered live by the networks. . . .
>
> . . . We plug these continuing bulletins several days in advance. And this reminds me that we do heavy cross-plugging of personalities. . . .
>
> . . . We make it a point never to vary our music and news format for sports coverage play-by-play. We never vary the format for anything else <u>except</u> than on election coverage--and even this is in keeping with our news format. . . .[24]

It was apparently painful for McLendon to give up sports play-by-play, especially after the Liberty experience, but as stated above, format consistency demanded it. To still provide sports coverage of a

---

[23]Gordon McLendon, letter to Joe Roddy, July 27, 1954, from <u>McLendon Policy Books</u>, n.p.

[24]<u>Ibid</u>.

sort, bulletins were carried, and then promotional spots were run to let listeners know when and where to find the bulletins--"tell them you're going to do it, do it, and then tell them you did it."

McLendon's letter to Roddy continues,

> I have not included in promotions our news intros because you also have them. I have also not included our station jingles, which will shortly be supplemented by personalized weather jingles which I'm having made for KELP also. And we have frequent one-shot promotions on the small side, like: asking a question and continuing to call people and ask the same question until it is answered; (2) giving away a live baby (not saying that it's a baby pig); (3) a canary singing in the background of our morning announcer; (4) complete coverage of the progress of Santa Claus at Christmas time; (5) recordings of local personalities which we play and ask listeners "Whose voice is this?"; (6) extensive plugging of a playing of the complete broadcast of Orson Welles' "War of the Worlds."[25]

It is apparent from the above list that in the summer of 1954, McLendon and Stewart were still concentrating on word-of-mouth promotions that involved little expense. Still, it should be remembered that however unglamorous they may seem compared to the treasure hunts and prizes to come later, they were the "only ballgame in town" at the time. The adoption of these simple promotions by other stations may have been one reason for Top 40 stations such as KLIF adopting the more spectacular promotions.

WNOE-WTIX lawsuit

In 1955, Stewart went to WNOE to try to boost its sagging ratings against the stiff competition of Storz's WTIX. WTIX had just staged its first treasure hunt in June 1955. Stewart noted that WTIX had inflated the number of people said to be attending the treasure

---

[25]Ibid.

hunts in its own post-event promotions, claiming 23,000 people had participated. WNOE's newscasts carried stories saying that WTIX's crowd figures were fabrications. A memorandum from Todd Storz, apparently to his station managers, supplies details:

> We are currently involved in a slight legal dispute in New Orleans. WTIX has filed suit against WNOE and its program director, Bill Stewart, in a $250,000 damage action. Bill Stewart, personally, has filed suit against WTIX in a $50,000 damage action. Since this is a legal action, I am hesitant about making comment on it, but for your information, the following verbatim quotation is provided from a portion of our petition for damages which was filed in Civil District Court . . . June 10th, 1955 . . . WTIX vs. James A. Noe, d/b/a, radio station WNOE <u>and</u> Bill Stewart.
>
> "That petitioner is informed and believes, and so alleges, that radio station WNOE, owned and operated by the defendant, James A. Noe, as aforesaid, on June 6, 1955, on a regularly scheduled news broadcast at 10:00 a.m. made the following statement, to wit:
>
> 'In one of the greatest hoaxes ever perpetrated upon the people of New Orleans, a local radio station yesterday claimed that over 7,500 cars and 23,000 people attended an alleged Treasure Hunt, Sunday afternoon. This, ladies and gentlemen, is the greatest lie ever perpetrated upon the people of New Orleans.'
>
> "That again at 11:00 a.m. on said date, the said Radio Station WNOE broadcast as follows:
>
> 'And here now is the 11 o'clock news from everywhere. In one of the greatest hoaxes ever perpetrated upon the people of New Orleans, a local radio station yesterday claimed that over 7,500 cars and 23,000 people attended an alleged Treasure Hunt, Sunday afternoon. This, ladies and gentlemen, is the greatest lie ever perpetrated upon the people of New Orleans.'
>
> "That petitioner is informed and believes, and so alleges, that the aforesaid statement, was prepared by defendant, Bill Stewart, who was then acting within the course and scope of his employment, as program director and assistant manager of Radio Station WNOE, by and for and on behalf of the defendant, James A. Noe, in the operation of said Radio Station WNOE. . . .
>
> . . . That although the aforesaid broadcasts did not specifically refer to petitioner's radio station by its call letters WTIX, said broadcasts, nevertheless, were obviously aimed at WTIX since WTIX was the only local station sponsoring and staging said Treasure Hunt, which fact was well known to the defendant, his agents, servants and employees, and the public.
>
> That the aforesaid broadcasts by Radio Station WNOE were false, slanderous, and defamatory and were maliciously intended by the said defendant . . . to deprive petitioner and its Radio

> Station WTIX of their good name and business reputation and to bring petitioner and its said radio station into disrepute and deprive them of the esteem and confidence which they enjoy among advertisers and the radio listening audience.
>
> That the defendant . . . including defendant Bill Stewart, well knew that said Treasure Hunt staged as aforesaid by Radio Station WTIX was not a hoax and was not an "alleged" Treasure Hunt and, therefore, acted deliberately and maliciously in so falsely misrepresenting the character of said Treasure Hunt.[26]

Anyone reading the text of the suit quoted above must be impressed with the seriousness of the action being taken. Asked by the author what this suit and his own countersuit against WTIX were supposed to accomplish, Stewart replied:

> This was one of the first--it was the thing that probably introduced me to Storz; I'm sure it was. Because, from that day on, he tried to get me to go with him.[27]

Asked if he meant to make news for WNOE by talking about WTIX, Stewart answered, "Right. It was promotion instead of a lawsuit anyway . . . I was just trying to stir up some promotion, which I did."[28] Both he and WTIX withdrew their suits. Stewart had accomplished several things in the meantime. He had planted the seed that WTIX hadn't told the truth, and that the truth was available on WNOE. And probably not incidentally Stewart also made sure that this time (unlike his trip to Omaha), Storz had heard of him. From that time on, according to Stewart, Storz tried to hire Stewart away from McLendon (which he eventually did), perhaps thinking that in a competitive situation it was better to have

---

[26]Todd Storz memorandum, xerox copy provided by Bill Stewart, n.d., n.p.

[27]Stewart interview.

[28]Ibid.

Stewart's ideas working for Storz than for the competition.[29]

Record marathons

Although Al "Jazzbo" Collins is said to be the first to conduct a "record fillibuster" with his three-and-a-half straight hours of playing Art Mooney's "I'm Looking Over a Four Leaf Clover" in Salt Lake City,[30] Bill Stewart believes that he developed the promotion in which a single record was played over and over again for a number of hours. He recalls that he first did this in the summer of 1953 at KLBS, and then again in Dallas in November of 1953. Stewart recalls playing Ray Anthony's "Dragnet" over and over again for three hours one afternoon at KLIF. The strongest reaction came from Gordon's father, B. R. McLendon, who had not been warned about the stunt, and who nearly broke the control room door down to make him stop.[31]

In 1955, at WNOE, Stewart had staged the longest record marathon to that date. Beginning on Monday, February 14, 1955 at 6:00 a.m., the record "Shtiggy Boom" was played continuously until 4:42 p.m. Wednesday for a total of 1,349 times, pausing only for newscasts, commercials and short features. Stewart arranged this marathon to promote WNOE's change to an all-night broadcasting schedule. Broadcasting reported the results:

---

[29] For further information on what Broadcasting called "The Radio Battle of New Orleans," see "Station Sued," Broadcasting, June 13, 1955, p. 7, and "WTIX Files Counter Suit in New Orleans Radio Row," Broadcasting, June 20, 1955, p. 98.

[30] Passman, The Deejays, p. 122.

[31] Stewart interview.

The promotion did not go unnoticed, as both official and public reaction evidenced. The phone company temporarily discontinued service to WNOE because of the avalanche of calls. The Police Dept. made an investigation and the FCC also inquired into the matter because of calls it had received.

When the recordthon did come to an end, "Shtiggy Boom" composer Al Jarvis was on the scene, as was Major Delesseps Morrison, who ordered a halt to the musical exhibition. Mr. Jarvis, a Hollywood radio-tv personality, earlier wired the station that he was flying to New Orleans "to plead with you to cease and desist in this murder." Mr. Jarvis, it is reported, is a good friend of Mr. Stewart.[32]

Promotion diffusion case histories

Girl on a swing diffusion case history

A famous KLIF billboard with a girl's skirt blowing up to expose a message beneath was a promotion that McLendon adapted from similar (but less spectacular) promotions on other stations. As such it serves as the first of three diffusion case histories, all intended to demonstrate how the broadcast industry "borrows" ideas from each other.

A girl on a swing is not an idea unique to broadcasting by any means, but the use of a girl on a swing as a station's "logo" or identifying symbol seems to have originated with Kansas City's WHB and WHB-TV, dating from the period before WHB-AM was acquired by Storz. Before Storz, WHB and WHB-TV were owned by the Cook Paint & Varnish Co., and it is this company that used the girl in their trade ads. The word "swing" was an important part of the promotion, for any number of phrases using the word as a verb instead of a noun were available: "Swing the Kansas City Market Your Way," "In Kansas City the Swing is

---

[32] "Record Marathon in New Orleans," Broadcasting, February 21, 1955, p. 92.

to WHB and WHB-TV," and others. The company even published a monthly "magazine" called Swing which was really a mailing to timebuyers and agencies touting WHB. In mid-1955, WHB-TV and KMBC-TV stopped their time-sharing arrangement and WHB-TV was deleted in favor of a fulltime KMBC-TV operation which had been bought out by Cook. With the change, which resulted in the sale of WHB-AM to Storz, the girl on the swing went over to KMBC-TV. If anything, the change in call letters was advertised even more extensively via the swing logo than the old WHB-TV had been. Shown on page 408 is an advertisement from the back cover of Sponsor of August 8, 1955.

In the summer of 1955, someone wrote a draft of a magazine article about the McLendon operation to that point, which rough draft was included, unsigned and undated, in the McLendon Policy Books. It contains these sentences in the section on promotion: "And KLIF has just put up a 'spectacular' on the heavily-traveled Central Expressway which is another first for the station. It pictures a young lady in a swing, with an actual skirt of flowing nylon. A special blower arrangement billows the young lady's skirt to an interesting height and large letters on the sign proclaim 'the swing is to KLIF.'"[33]

It seems likely that McLendon adapted the "the swing is to ____" idea from the prominent and frequent WHB/KMBC ads of the same type in the trade magazines. What he did was to use the premise in developing a moving billboard, with the billowing skirt certainly a new touch. Thus, part of the idea was borrowed, but the new application

---

[33] Magazine article rough draft, apparently written summer of 1955, unsigned, from McLendon Policy Books, n.p.

the SWING is to ABC and
KMBC-TV
Kansas City's Most Powerful TV Station
Now, with new and wonderful program flexibility available* on Channel 9 in Kansas City, you can buy just about any commercial handling you desire for fall and winter schedules —within programs, or between programs, designed to appeal specifically and effectively to exactly the audiences you wish to reach.
On September 28, 1955, KMBC-TV joins the Swing to ABC, the nation's most dynamic and fastest-growing television network... and introduces, daytime, a schedule of station-produced shows that will set Kansas City audiences afire!
You can sponsor these shows...buy filmed minute-participations...schedule live commercials, demonstrations, sampling or audience - participation testimonials... utilize station-breaks or IDs. Use whatever format, frequency and scheduling you require to make your Kansas City campaign just exactly what you want it to be!
KMBC-TV, in joining the Swing to ABC, will program the most imaginative daytime television ever brought to Kansas City:
KALEIDOSCOPE*—A two-hour early-morning show.
MORNING MOVIE—Feature-length, integrated with regional and local news, weather and service reports.
WHIZZO THE CLOWN*—A wonderful children's hour which will include the famous "Little Rascals."
NOON*—Studio Party for the ladies.
MY LITTLE MARGIE—Daily, Monday through Friday.
HAPPY HOME—With Bea Johnson, McCall award winner.
AFTERNOON THEATRE—Fine half-hour dramas on film.
MOVIE MATINEE—Full-length feature film.
BAND STAND—Teen-age dancing show; pop records.
To these add the new ABC evening schedule with Mickey Mouse Club, Warner Brothers Presents, MGM Parade, Wyatt Earp, Bishop Sheen, Wednesday Night Fights and Disneyland (not to mention the older ABC favorites)—and mister! KMBC-TV has it! Your Free & Peters Colonel can tell you how to get with it!
KMBC-TV
Kansas City's Most Powerful TV Station
First Vice President
Vice President and General Manager
Vice President and Sales Manager
Director of Television
Free & Peters, Inc.
And in Radio, it's the KMBC-KFRM Team
in the Heart of America
KMBC of Kansas City
KFRM for the State of Kansas

by McLendon added his own creativity. This, according to Bill Stewart, is a general rule among the big operators: to try to add something new and better to an idea gotten from somewhere else.[34] This is what McLendon ultimately did with another promotion with the theme "All I Have On Is . . ." (see pages 410 and 411).

"All I Have On Is" diffusion case history

On August 13, 1955, McLendon sent a "General Memorandum" to his managers in which he stated that the "Dallas News refuses ad 'All I Have On Is KLIF.' Naturally."[35] The "All I Have On" promotion also used a girl, but this time the handling was a bit more provocative than merely blowing up a ruffled skirt.

It seems probable that the "All I Have On" promotion developed out of an earlier and more mundane approach, which simply had people carrying portable radios and wearing sandwich boards which read "I'm listening to W____" Irv Lictenstein, publicity and promotion director in 1953 for WWDC, Washington wrote Broadcasting the following letter:

> It seems from your issue of Dec. 7 that the New York radio and tv stations went gimmick happy during the recent newspaper strike.
>
> In fact, I am now looking for a cheap lawyer to start copyright infringement suit because one of my ideas was not begged or borrowed, but stolen.
>
> The gimmick I'm referring to was the use of people listening to portable radios on the streets and wearing sandwich board signs with the inscription, "Ask me for the latest news and tune in Station . . ."
>
> My gripe is this: WWDC Washington used the same gimmick during the week of February 20, 1950--approximately three years

---

[34] Stewart interview.

[35] Gordon McLendon, General Memorandum, from McLendon Policy Books, August 13, 1955, n.p.

LISTENING TO
WWDC
Now
1260
ON DIAL

wyde
AWAKE
850
ON BUT...
wyde

WE'VE GOT NOTHING ON
"THE HERB OSCAR ANDERSON SHOW"

...the only thing she has ON today is
KLIF
THE LAZIEST GIRL IN TOWN

ago. That was the time the station picked up 5,000 watts of power and changed its spot on the radio dial to 1260. . . .[36]

Since the promotion quoted above took place in February in Washington, D.C., the lady who carried the radio and sandwich board also wore an overcoat. When McLendon and Stewart tried the same basic idea but with a change in wording to "All I Have On Is . . ." in 1955, they also changed the woman's wardrobe (or lack of it) to conform. The sandwich board was large enough to suggest that it was, indeed, all she had on.

In 1957, the ABC network (then ABN) again got around to adapting a Top 40 promotion for its own purposes, this time to call attention to its live-music Herb Oscar Anderson Show. The network hired two girls to parade in front of buildings housing prospective advertisers' executives. In another slight change, they wore rain barrels instead of just a sandwich board, but the message was the same: "We've got nothing on but . . . The Herb Oscar Anderson Show."[37]

At practically the same time, Bartell's WYDE, Birmingham, was using the girl-in-sandwich-board approach to promote that station. She also offered a cup of coffee to passers-by.[38]

McLendon made the "final" and most spectacular change in the promotion by developing a "living" billboard, featuring a provocatively-dressed (but nevertheless dressed) girl who actually lived on the billboard during peak traffic hours. As part of her "house" she had a

---

[36]"Whose Idea?" Broadcasting, December 21, 1953, p. 18.

[37]Photo captioned "The Telegram," in Broadcasting, September 9, 1957, p. 80.

[38]"Picture Wrap-Up," Sponsor, September 21, 1957, p. 66.

stool and a curvaceous chaise. One sign said, "The laziest girl in town," while another read ". . . the only thing she has 'ON' today is KLIF." By emphasizing the girl's "laziness" and the word "on," the living billboard managed to convey the idea that the damsel's appointment book was free and waiting for an invitation from some harried commuter snarled in traffic below her.[39]

Color radio diffusion case history

Bill Stewart's last major promotion innovation with the McLendon stations before he left to join Storz in January 1956 was "Color Radio." A memorandum from McLendon to all stations in December 1955 contained this information about the planned promotional push for the "new look":

> KLIF, as most of you know, has a fifty percent rate increase going into effect January first. During the latter part of December, therefore, and throughout January, we will turn on the steam program- and promotion-wise to keep everybody talking about KLIF.
>
> In the next week or so, we'll begin announcements, "Don't miss the new look on Cliff January third." Then, in the week between Christmas and New Years, when we also plan to have a Walking Man promotion going, we'll hit with all sorts of live and transcribed promotionals about the fact that KLIF IS GOING COLOR RADIO effective January third. This idea is original with us--we've been thinking about doing a color radio promotional since late July. Built up properly, with an atmosphere of mystery surrounding same, I believe we are going to create tremendous word-of-mouth conversation. We'll keep telling our listeners it's the newest development in radio.
>
> Among the things we're going to do: change virtually all deejay schedules, change all formats, discontinue Rear Windo [sic] until fall and substitute another contest--probably Lucky Telephone Numbers; new news formats; news will be done with two voices instead of one; we will institute Bill Stewart's trick of having newscasts sponsored by various disc jockeys, there'll be dozens of new promos and I.D. lines, at least one new disc jockey, a taxi-back campaign on color radio, new

---

[39]"Zany Stunts Put Radio Chain in Clover," Business Week, September 9, 1961, p. 124.

> Fidler intros and closes to emphasize color radio on KLIF, some special jingles on color radio, the announcement that one of our deejays is going to run for office, the announcement that at a peak traffic hour one of our deejays will give out dollar bills for ninety-five cents--reserving the right to limit the number per customer, and virtually a new promotion every day for sixty days. We're also beginning editorializing in earnest.
>
> Some suggestions to you for the Christmas and New Year season . . . give away a disc jockey for Christmas (winner to have right of choosing any deejay on station to wash Christmas dishes). . . .[40]

"Color radio," the main subject of the memo quoted above, was not a McLendon nor a Stewart original. According to Passman, the slogan "color radio" was used by KABC in 1954 and 1955 to add the image of some sparkle to its network programming.[41] Don Norman, disc jockey at KFAB, Omaha, claimed in 1956 that "I have been broadcasting radio in full compatible color since the spring of 1954, via KFAB, color radio center, in Omaha."[42] Norman's letter to Broadcasting was in response to a notice in the January 2, 1956 Broadcasting that KLIF was about to begin broadcasting "the newest entertainment miracle" and that Martha

---

[40]Gordon McLendon, General Memorandum, either December 12 or December 18, 1955--date unclear, from McLendon Policy Books, n.p. Rear Windo was a promotional device that was widely adopted after McLendon and Stewart developed it. The station gave out stickers for pasting in the rear window of a car (or on a bumper). If the station identified a certain car carrying a sticker and the driver responded within a given time, he won a prize. This device kept drivers listening to be called, and also provided a vast amount of nearly free advertising. By September 1955 Edd Routt had reported to Harrison Lilly at Time-Life that there were 55,000 KLIF sticker equipped cars in the Dallas area.

The "Fidler" referred to in the memorandum quoted above is Jimmy Fidler, whose recorded gossip column appeared on KLIF as part of the newscast.

[41]Passman, The Deejays, p. 230.

[42]"Color Radio Red-Hot," Broadcasting, January 16, 1956, p. 15.

Hyer, Hollywood starlet, had been selected as "Miss Color Radio of 1956."[43]

Late in 1956, the ABC radio network issued a brochure promoting two of its daytime soap operas as "Color Radio."[44]

On January 2, 1958, KFWB, Los Angeles introduced "color radio" (again) to that city, this time in connection with the Top 40 station being programmed by former McLendon KELP disc jockey, Chuck Blore.[45]

The diffusion of the concept of "color radio" may not have followed the pattern of borrowing-and-embellishing quite so strongly as the "Girl on the Swing" did because, at the time, color television was the newest sensation. A radio station, competing with TV for audience, might quite naturally adapt color television promotions to radio. In the case of KFWB and Chuck Blore, however, the legacy he owed McLendon's KLIF from 1956 seems clear.

Miscellaneous Middle Period Promotions

By June of 1955, with the WNOE-WTIX lawsuit in the trades, Stewart's and McLendon's philosophy of keeping people talking about the stations was in full flower. As part of his constant feud with Dallas newspapers, McLendon's KLIF ran a contest in June giving away magnifying glasses to the 50 best letters explaining why they liked the way KLIF's program logs were listed in the Dallas press.[46] In August

---

[43] "Color Radio in Texas," <u>Broadcasting</u>, January 2, 1956, p. 76.

[44] "ABC Promotes 'Color Radio,'" <u>Broadcasting</u>, December 10, 1956, p. 122.

[45] Passman, <u>The Deejays</u>, p. 230.

[46] "Seek & You May Find," <u>Broadcasting</u>, June 20, 1955, p. 97.

of 1955 in a "General Memorandum," McLendon wrote, "WNOE, New Orleans, is really starting to hit hard with the promotions. They've got the Walking Man and the Mystery Telephone gimmick both going at the same time with a steady series of promotions coming up."[47] The Mystery Telephone contest (to be discussed later in relation to the McLendon Milwaukee station, WRIT) involved a cash prize awarded to the person who called the unannounced number of the Mystery Telephone.

On September 9, 1955, Edd Routt, longtime assistant to McLendon, wrote Harrison Lilly of Time-Life with a list of suggested topics for an article on McLendon. Among the promotions noted were:

> Giving away an island, with five thousand dollars in cash buried on said island, winner to have the right to dig with the aid of vague buried treasure maps.
> KLIF's famous name station breaks--endorsements by Dwight Eisenhower, Alfred C. Kinsey, Mickey Rooney, Douglas MacArthur, etc.
> KLIF's Appreciation Night at Plantation--brought in big-name band and big-name singers, entertaining 10,000 youngsters free.
> KLIF's famous introductions to news broadcasts: Greenwich mean time, foreign voices, etc.
> Billboard on Central Expressway with girl's skirt blowing.
> The Secret Word for today is. . . .[48]

A number of the promotions listed above were developed by Bill Stewart. The KLIF Appreciation Night was one--a promotion that was widely copied by other Top 40 stations including Storz's. The Greenwich Mean Time news intros were used for years by other stations, with Stewart developing variations as late as the mid-1960s. The Secret Word was a simple but very highly effective gimmick invented by Stewart: unlike the usual randomly-chosen secret word that if guessed brought the listener

---

[47] Gordon McLendon, "General Memorandum," August 13, 1955, McLendon Policy Books.

[48] Edd Routt, letter to Harrison Lilly, September 8, 1955, McLendon Policy Books, n.p.

a prize, Stewart's Secret Word was the mere mention of some advertising client's full name several times a day. Typically, people would stop the man on the street and say something like, "I hear you're KLIF's secret word." The man would be impressed with the size and wide range of ages in KLIF's audience and would often either initiate or increase an advertising schedule. The Secret Word was a strong tool in Top 40's campaign to convince advertisers that teenagers were not the only people listening. The famous name station breaks, Routt should have mentioned, were not done by the real famous people, but by local people with the same name, culled from the phone book.

A number of the promotions carried by the McLendon station were very simple and straightforward, designed to accomplish an objective by direct appeal. An example follows:

> Research has found that students study better with a radio. So why not apply the same to your office? Take KLIF to work with you every day. You'll find that the good music heard each day on KLIF will tend to improve dispositions . . . cheer up your fellow workers . . . and make for a better all around atmosphere. And too, Cliff News keeps you posted on what's happening in Dallas all day. So . . . get in the KLIF-at-work habit. You'll like it.[49]

In April of 1956, McLendon urged his disc jockeys to try another simple promotion using recordings from other deejays.

> Some time ago I pointed out that I would like to see some of you begin to get intros from deejays in other stations in other cities to go along with your shows. So far as I can hear, none of you has done this yet . . . not only with our stations, but with such stations as KLAC in Los Angeles, KMPC; Chicago and New York stations. I am sure that you could effect

---

[49]"Promo # 6, KLIF at the Office," dated February 21, 1956, from McLendon Policy Books, n.p.

> an interesting exchange. I do hope you will follow this up.[50]

Attached to McLendon's memorandum were some examples of what he had in mind. The first of these is quoted:

> Hi there! This is Gene Edwards, at WRIT in Milwaukee, one of KLIF's sister stations. By way of saying hello to all my old friends at KLIF in Dallas, I thought you'd like to hear the song that's Number One in Milwaukee right now. Here 'tis.[51]

By the end of 1956, it was apparent that KTSA was not making the spectacular ratings climb that KLIF and KELP had, probably because there were already several carefully-programmed stations in San Antonio when McLendon took over KTSA. A memo from Gordon McLendon to KTSA General Manager Bill Weaver and Program Director Don Keyes, written either at the end of 1956 or early 1957, contains a number of suggestions for improving the ratings situation, with most of these concentrating on promotion.

> . . . Herewith a lot of random observations:
>
> (1) Why have we dropped the "new KTSA"? This should have been kept on for at least a year. But now that we have dropped it, would suggest the "even newer KTSA" right away. . . .
>
> (4) Begin to use news teasers--I can't imagine why these were discontinued.
>
> (5) Run the Mystery Telephone Number contest again one weekend--this is one that gets plenty of talk. . . .
>
> (7) Start mentioning some towns surrounding San Antonio and even towns that are quite an area away--looking to our taking an area Pulse in January or February.
>
> (8) Run the contest on the Don French show "why should I have an extra day off from work." This is a good contest to run for a month or so. If you don't remember the details, let me know. . . .
>
> (11) Start contests to select beauty queens of each high school. This can be done simply, from pictures and interview, and without bathing suit competition. Have a panel select the

---

[50]Gordon McLendon, Memo to All Disc Jockeys, April 14, 1956, from McLendon Policy Books, n.p.

[51]*Ibid.*, attachment.

best looking girl from each high school, with the winners then competing for "Miss KTSA." But above all, leave the judging to an independent group. The prize need not be more than a trophy.

(12) Begin to plan for KTSA 35th birthday celebration (35th is the coral anniversary) and we might think of something like the KLIF Appreciation Night of a couple of years ago.

(13) Run the hidden thousand dollar bill Treasure Hunt on either Saturday, January 28th, or preferably Sunday, January 29th. This, of course, will be a real sensation. You can do it like WHB did it. If you need details, I'll send them. But you should begin to warn people now that it is coming up and that to be eligible to participate you had to have a Rear Windo sticker on your car. Incidentally, have we gotten any business from Conoco yet? My only question on this contest is whether you think it will work with a smaller amount of money (I doubt it), or whether we should hide ten one-hundred dollar bills, or five one-hundred dollar bills, or simply one one-thousand dollar bill--in other words, what is the proper consideration? With the proper buildup on the air, and if the amount is sufficient, there'll be the damndest crowd and greatest publicity you ever saw.[52]

The "news teasers" referred to in item (4) above are a brief excerpt or headline from a relatively exciting story to be covered in an upcoming newscast.

When McLendon bought KLBS in 1957 and took over the management of that Houston station for the second time, the promotions included many of the stunts and gimmicks used before. Variety reported that KILT began its promotion with the new disc jockeys visiting area high schools and giving away free records. So far as money giveaways were concerned, McLendon had no definite comment for Variety, but was quoted as admitting that "a 100G promotional budget for KILT isn't a 'far off' report."[53]

---

[52]Gordon McLendon, Memorandum to Bill Weaver and Don Keyes, no date but had to be late December 1956 or early January 1957, from McLendon Policy Books, n.p.

[53]"M'Lendon's 'Texas Triangle,'" Variety, May 15, 1957, p. 37.

On June 21, McLendon sent a memorandum to Bill Weaver and Don Keyes at KILT similar to the one he had sent them at KTSA in late 1956, although KILT was experiencing a faster ratings success than KTSA did. The portions of the memo to Weaver and Keyes at KILT relating to promotion are quoted here:

> (3) I think we should have the jocks talking about the fact that we have raised from seventh to fourth and now are in third place, and otherwise build it up. I think you can probably afford to announce about the 27th, which is a week away, that we have gone into No. 2 position and that the flagpole sitter is going to come down as soon as the official figures have arrived from the C. E. Hooper measuring agency in New York. This will give you an excuse for keeping him up there for several more days while the figures ostensibly are on their way down. . . .
>
> (8) . . . I don't hear the announcement ". . . the station which has run away with Houston's radio day."
>
> (9) Not enough mentions of "radio Houston."
>
> (10) No station IDs on the flagpole sitter that I heard.
>
> (11) Not enough frequency and saturation on promotional spots like two o'clock feeding time, "Music for Aesthetes," etc. We give these things a pretty good saturation campaign for a couple of days until we get the idea over and then cut them back. You are simply not giving these things enough exposure . . . to cause talk. For instance, twice a day is not enough talk to get people started talking about the Brooklyn Ferry announcements. They should be run once an hour for two days or at the minimum once every two hours.[54]

In the memo quoted above, it might at first seem either arrogant or deceptive to be certain of announcing that KILT was number one at a certain time. It should be recalled that by this time, McLendon (and the other Top 40 operators) had developed their programming and promotion formulas to the point where, given a market without a similar competing station, actual ratings leadership was almost inevitable. In addition, the self-fulfilling prophecy may have been at work. That is,

---

[54] Gordon McLendon, memorandum to Bill Weaver and Don Keyes at KILT, June 21, 1957, from McLendon Policy Books, n.p.

if in the case of a WNEW it was considered a good way to build audiences by reminding people that they were listening to the number one station, then telling people that they were listening to a station on the way to the top may well have helped it to reach that goal.

In July of 1957, with Weaver and Keyes running KILT, McLendon wrote to the new general manager at KTSA, Ken Knox. KONO was still giving KTSA a hard fight and McLendon's suggestions answered that problem:

> . . . Also start to get snappy recorded intros and promos, etc. Tell the announcers again to sound like they are in a hurry. KONO has a real live sound now and I want to be sure that we show no marked contrast. . . .
>
> . . . Don French, as well as the other announcers, should be encouraged to give "KTSA Time," "KTSA Weather," "KTSA News," etc. That is to say, we want to use KTSA over and over again. We want repeated identification of the call letters. . . .
>
> . . . I would run the stuff about being a copycat out of their ears with frequent changes of copy. . . .
>
> . . . I would run spots or station breaks at least, indicating how much money has been given away so far in total Scotch Dollars.[55]

Scotch Dollars were giveaway money on the McLendon stations, where everything had an "old Scotchman" connection.

Limitations on Airing Promos

It was apparent to McLendon that the number of promotions had to be controlled for programming reasons. Traditionally, when a new station went on the air, there was a light commercial load and promotions could be freely used. But when KTSA went on the air as a McLendon station, it was already anticipating sellouts a couple days of the week. McLendon wrote KTSA program director Don Keyes the following

---

[55]Gordon McLendon, memorandum to Ken Knox, July 17, 1957, from McLendon Policy Books, n.p.

memorandum of advice on how to handle promotions in such a case:

> Don, since we are going to have so very much stuff going for us in the opening weeks, I'd be careful to keep promos to one or two-liners and to be careful to keep the promos, contests themselves, gimmicks, and other promotional material in hours which are not maximum commercial. If you have anything to put into the driving hours, be sure that the driving hours can take it without overloading. That'll happen a couple of days a week, maybe. And if you do find an hour at the maximum commercially, I'd be very cautious before I put anything in--and if I did it would be a one-liner. . . .
>
> . . . Would start "You'll never hear this on KTSA" things beginning Monday and using them in hours that can take it commercially. Likewise the famous station breaks--Eisenhower, Kinsey, etc. Likewise, the "secret word for today" bit, using names of prominent San Antonio advertisers and agency people. Likewise Miss Universe promos, although I'd make them a bit shorter than you did in Dallas. Also "the new KTSA."[56]

The limitations McLendon suggested above were called for by the heavy load of non-musical programming that KTSA was carrying in its opening days. By 1959, McLendon had developed some general policies limiting the use of certain promotions to particular times of the broadcast day. The memo setting forth this policy is reproduced on pages 423 and 424.

Promotions by Other Stations

The McLendon stations were certainly not the only ones pushing hard for audiences with increasingly spectacular promotions. As mentioned in a McLendon memo, the Storz stations were sponsoring $1,000 Treasure Hunts under the program directorship of Bill Stewart. They also were developing a number of other giveaway contests which will be described later. Bartell, by his own admission, at this time was not

---

[56] Gordon McLendon, memorandum to Don Keyes, May 16, 1965, from McLendon Policy Books, n.p.

MEMORANDUM

TO: ALL MANAGERS. PROGRAM DIRECTORS. TRAFFIC DIRECTORS
POLICY BOOK. B. R. McLENDON

FROM: GORDON McLENDON

DATE: OCTOBER 3, 1959

As all of you are aware. Don and I have discussed with you the necessity for differentiating your promotions, to wit:

1) Promotions appealing primarily to teenagers
2) Promotions of general audience appeal

Category 1) promotions should not be heard at all from 9:00 a. m. to 3:30 p. m. Monday through Friday. They should be heard from 8:00 a. m. Saturday to 2:00 a. m. Sundays, and then again Sundays from 9:30 a. m until midnight. The careful choice of teenage hours is due to teenagers' late waking habits on weekends.

In addition, we now bring you another restriction, which you will welcome and which is to be strictly obeyed. Every survey evidence points to the fact that in the 6-9 a. m. period, teenagers are still a minor factor--far less important than in the 3:30 to midnight period, or during holidays, or in the summer period. Therefore, on any promotion you begin which is in your opinion primarily designed to appeal to teenagers, you will use the promos, plus an i. d., once an hour in the 6-9 a. m. period for three days only. Then drop recorded promos and sustain it with i. d.'s only in the 6-9 a. m. period. This will relieve the clutter in the morning period, keep the teenage promotion identity yet enable us to retain predominantly an adult sound. You will have established your promotion in the three days--you sustain it with i. d.'s and then, if you consider the promotion significant enough, you can double up or otherwise hit harder 3:30-midnight.

If all of you are hewing to your commercial limitation you will be no more crowded on Thursday and Friday than you are on other days so there is no use differentiating these days. But I do want to say that both Don and I recognize the fact that special event broadcasts sometimes cramp your schedule and there may be rare days when you have to de-emphasis any promotion. There's no law that says the next day you can't double up. There's no law, either, which says you can't double up 8 a. m. -midnight Saturdays, or on Sundays--or at nights. These are times when our stations are by and large weaker commercially and yet teenagers are available. If you are forced to neglect a promotion slightly in another period, think of these periods and days as an extra-hypo possibility.

Sometime ago we put out a "promotion check list". If you don't have a copy, ask us for one. Follow it where practicable.

Category 2) promotions are for use in any time segment Even here. you might wish to cut down in rare cases from 8 p m to midnight to double up on a good teenage gimmick

Please see that beginning immediately your logs reflect the instructions in this memo If your station has the alive sound it should have--and the many things going you should have--this memo is vitally important to you in these days of heavy commercial load

###

running giveaways because competition had not forced him to do so yet.[57]

Noting the success of the McLendon and Storz operations in capturing both audiences' and advertisers' attention via their stunts, a number of other stations began to try their own promotions. One of the most popular was the disc jockey marathon, in which a disc jockey stayed on the air continuously until the old time record was broken.[58] On Thursday, August 30, 1956, WMOP, Ocala, Florida set up a studio 15 feet underwater in nearby Silver Springs and broadcast there for a day.[59] In October, KDKA disc jockey Rege Cordic arranged a whistlestop campaign railroad tour for Cordic's show character Carman Monoxide, who supposedly was running for President.[60] One day in July 1957 WINS, New York gave away two tickets to _My Fair Lady_ to "the first caller whose private telephone number totaled . . . some . . . 'magic number.'" According to WINS, the calls received on the first day for the _two_ tickets totaled 50,000, and put the MUrray Hill 7 exchange out of commission. _Broadcasting_ detailed the ensuing feud between the telephone company, which wanted to deny service to WINS if the giveaway was tried again, and the radio station which _did_ repeat it, several more times.[61]

---

[57] Bartell interview.

[58] See "Titles Change Hands Quickly in Disc Jockey Marathons," _Broadcasting_, July 16, 1956, p. 103.

[59] "Funny Thing Happened On My Way to the Studio," _Broadcasting_, September 3, 1956, p. 66.

[60] "This Junket Admittedly Was for Laughs," _Broadcasting_, October 22, 1956, p. 103.

[61] "WINS Ballyhoo Ties Up N. Y. Phone Exchange," _Broadcasting_, July 15, 1957, p. 90.

WPTR, Albany, New York, was shown in an article in Life to be partial to animals in their promotions. They used an elephant to carry a sign reading, "WPTR--the biggest thing in radio," a kangaroo went with a sign saying, "WPTR--always a jump ahead," and a lion accompanied a sign which proclaimed, "WPTR--The king of radio."[62] In August 1957 disc jockey John Gregory claimed to have broken his own world's flagpole-sitting record of 21 days by staying aloft in Beloit, Wisconsin, for over a month.[63] Bartell's WILD in Boston, recently acquired and given the new call letters, put four models in a new Edsel convertible in September and drove through the streets with a sign on the side of the car reading "Get a Kiss from a Wild Gal." The kisses were candy ones.[64] Meanwhile, disc jockey Eddie Clarke on Storz's WHB, Kansas City, was running an "eat out" contest on his program, offering four married women winners eight meals each at the restaurant of their choice.[65] In October, Storz's WTIX held an "Appreciation Night" (as McLendon and Stewart had with KLIF) and drew a reported 50,000 people to the concert.[66]

One of the zaniest and also one of the best-attended promotional events was staged by San Francisco station KSFO. Broadcasting's entire

---

[62] "Radio's New Riches," Life, July 22, 1957, p. 80.

[63] "DJ Spins from Flagpole," Broadcasting, August 5, 1957, p. 105.

[64] "Programs and Promotions," Broadcasting, September 16, 1957, p. 106.

[65] "D.J. Holds 'Eat Out' Contest," Broadcasting, September 16, 1957, p. 106.

[66] "WTIX Hold 'Appreciation Night,'" Broadcasting, October 14, 1957, p. 118.

account is worth quoting.

> "Brass and Brasshats Win a War"
>
> Quiet again reigns in Stockton. A peace treaty has been signed between Field Marshal Sherwood and the beleaguered California municipality. (Field Marshal Sherwood is, of course, commander of the famous Sherwood-Harper Liberation Expeditionary Force of the Greater Bay Area Inc.)
>
> The "peace treaty" culminated events that started from a casual, on-the-air conversation. Don Sherwood, disc jockey at KSFO, San Francisco, and Hap Harper, an aviator who flies a daily weather-observing mission for the morning Sherwood show, were discussing the possibilities of bombing Stockton. Several thousand listeners, according to the station, volunteered their services. KSFO's manager, William D. Shaw, decided the idea had possibilities as a promotion.
>
> Thus was born the Sherwood-Harper Liberation etc., etc. All volunteers were issued admirals' and generals' commissions. Lapel buttons bearing the battle cry, "Scharge--on to Stockton," were distributed to 15,000 listeners. Distribution was taken over by neighborhood Shell Oil Dealers and distributors for Burgermeister beer.
>
> Highlight of the campaign was a "daring" daylight bombing raid on the city. Sherwood & Harper dropped 30,000 "surrender or else" leaflets on Stockton's streets. A second raid was cancelled when street cleaners protested.
>
> Fifth column groups sprang up in both cities. Listeners sent gifts to the "troops." A San Francisco firm printed one hundred thousand $1000 1/2 bills for invasion money. All was ready for D-Day.
>
> Lon Simmons, head of KSFO's sports department, was on hand at Stockton's Courthouse Square to keep KSFO listeners informed of the invasion's progress. Marshal Sherwood, in an M-47 tank, led the parade of jeeps and sportscars to the treaty signing. . . .
>
> . . . To the roar of gunfire (blanks shot off by the U. S. Army's 767th Tank Battalion), the peace treaty was signed. Observers included pilots of 162 light planes, 240 sportscar drivers, several hundred teen-age fans and a score of pigeons that occupy the upper levels of the courthouse.[67]

It should be pointed out that a promotion like the one just described was unusual even for a time when promotions and stunts were the watchword. There is hardly a city on earth that would allow itself to be bombed by most disc jockeys that could be named, but to be bombed

---

[67] "Brass and Brasshats Win a War," Broadcasting, October 14, 1957, p. 118.

by the unique Don Sherwood was something of an honor. A very popular personality and skillful handling by KSFO made such a potentially embarrassing episode into good fun for everybody, and certainly into more profits for KSFO.

In an article in the May 23, 1960 Billboard which detailed a number of the gimmicks and stunts being used to build audiences (most of which were quite unspectacular compared to McLendon's) June Bundy concluded that "Broadcasters . . . have become increasingly promotion minded over the last few years as the result of stepped-up competition in the local music-and-news field, but the present situation represents an all-time high for this kind of activity."[68] An article in August described what Bundy called "Jock Silly Season" and detailed such stunts as dyeing a deejay's hair green for a personal appearance and a duel between two competing jocks with cans of bug spray.[69] A further article in December 1960 described a stunt in which a disc jockey was "buried" inside a wall of cans of cranberries in a supermarket, only being released when shoppers bought enough for Thanksgiving dinners, and another who did his show from a birdcage hanging outside the studio.[70]

Miscellaneous Late Period Promotions

By the end of 1957, McLendon had instituted the policy of

---

[68] June Bundy, "Promotions Key New Radio Awareness," Billboard, May 23, 1960, p. 1.

[69] June Bundy, "Dog Days Usher in Jock Silly Season," Billboard, August 1, 1960, p. 1.

[70] June Bundy, "Deejay Stunts Grow Rougher & Tougher," Billboard, December 5, 1960, p. 1.

sending out promotional programming aids from Dallas to the other stations (KILT, KTSA, KEEL and WNOE). A memo dated December 18, 1957 directed to all managers and program directors gives details.

> On December 21, KLIF will ship to KILT, KTSA, KEEL and WNOE the following recorded material:
> 1. 1 gimmick deejay promo, recorded at KEEL.
> 2. New Year's Day greeting (KEEL).
> 3. 3 different basketball score promos (KILT).
> 4. 3 different promos for a new disc jockey (KILT).
> 5. 3 different High School Hall of Fame promos (KTSA).
> 6. 3 different Lucky Telephone Promos (KLIF).
> 7. 2 different Hula Bowl promos (KLIF).
> 8. 3 different "Citizen of the Week" promos (KLIF).
> 9. 2 different half-hourly news and weather intros (WNOE).
>
> This makes 21 different recorded cuts for each of you. In addition, we are mailing to KTSA and KILT Area Pulse promos, and to all of you a script that will enable you to record spots about your individual newsmen. Furthermore, we have earlier sent you Merry Christmas House promos recorded by KTSA and are sending you right away 8 different vignettes for use in the period of December 26-January 1st.
>
> Use your own judgment on what you wish to use. We consider all of it usable except possible Lucky Telephone and Hula Bowl for any stations which do not plan to run those events. . . .
>
> We got started late on this in December but January's mailing should be a real doozer. Please have your assignments completed on the exact day they are scheduled. No excuses about sickness, days off etc. Rotate cuts where you have several different of a particular type of promo, ala basketball. . . .
>
> . . . May I caution again that this should not prevent you from continuing to do promotions for yourself. This monthly mailing is not intended to take the place of ordinary station promotion and creativity--it better not.[71]

In February of 1958, KLIF General Manager Bill Morgan wrote to all other McLendon managers that he had a new idea for a promotion that "is the wildest yet":

> . . . Instead of hiding a check, I am going to bury a man alive, let them hunt for him seven days, and then leave him in another seven days and let spectators pay 50¢ to come and see him. . . .

---

[71]Gordon McLendon, memorandum to All Managers and Program Directors, December 18, 1957, from <u>McLendon Policy Books</u>, n.p.

. . . This will be a combination Treasure Hunt and Flag-pole Sitter in reverse. . . .[72]

In the fall of 1958, Bill Weaver came up with an idea that is still used today--a sort of "Teacher of the Week" award, in which deejays surprised teachers while class was in session with a basket of "apples for the teacher." Don Keyes, who disseminated the idea to the other McLendon managers wrote, "See no reason why this can't be logged as 100% public service." Keyes also suggested trading out the apples with a local delicatessen.[73]

On September 12, 1957, Gordon McLendon sent the memo quoted below to all of his station managers.

> One thing seems to be evolving more clearly than anything else in the confused ratings picture. That is that advertisers like to buy a station showing action.
> Many times they will buy a station that has a lot of things moving when cost per thousand or ratings simply do not justify. Thus, promotions are important--and continuing promotions all the time--to give your station the Action that impresses many advertisers.[74]

A memo two days later to Don Keyes stated, "More and more radio stations around the country, as a recent article in Sponsor indicates, are turning to public service as promotion. We need to do more in this regard. . . ."[75]

In Broadcasting for March 28, 1960, McLendon ran the stunt that

---

[72]Bill Morgan, memorandum to All Managers, February 15, 1958, from McLendon Policy Books, n.p.

[73]Don Keyes, memorandum to all managers, and all program directors, October 23, 1958, from McLendon Policy Books, n.p.

[74]Gordon McLendon, memorandum to all station managers, September 12, 1957, from McLendon Policy Books, n.p.

[75]Gordon McLendon, memo to Don Keyes, September 14, 1957, from McLendon Policy Books, n.p.

was easily the most startling to the broadcast industry. The front-page announcement is reproduced on page 432. One must look closely in the lower right hand corner to notice the tiny legend "(april fool)." The many in the industry who missed those two words certainly did what McLendon wanted them to do--talk about his stations.

Most of the McLendon Policy Books are composed of pages of memoranda, but one exception is the page which holds a red plastic ice scraper. Don Keyes wrote a note to be included in the Policy Books explaining the ice scraper. It reads:

> During a recent cold snap, with icy weather forecast, the KLIF Deejays gathered at an intersection during heavy afternoon traffic and gave away 950 of these ice-scrapers to drivers. The cost per thousand was $92.18 and we got them from the J. Hugh Campbell Co. here in Dallas.[76]

Printed on the ice scraper was the legend "Cold, ain't it?? KLIF--1190."

Dimensions, Cost, and Decline of Promotions

In the fall of 1957, a survey of 300 radio stations which produced responses from 122 showed some interesting figures on the dimension to which radio station promotion had grown. Seventy-seven percent of the responding stations reported buying newspaper space for local tune-in ads, 46% used trade paper advertising, and 24% had a full-time promotion manager. Seventy-seven percent of the stations said that their promotion schedule had resulted in bigger audiences, 82% said they had more local sponsors as a result of their promotions, and 66% said they had more national accounts. Forty-two percent planned to

---

[76]Don Keyes, memorandum, February 21, 1962, from McLendon Policy Books, n.p.

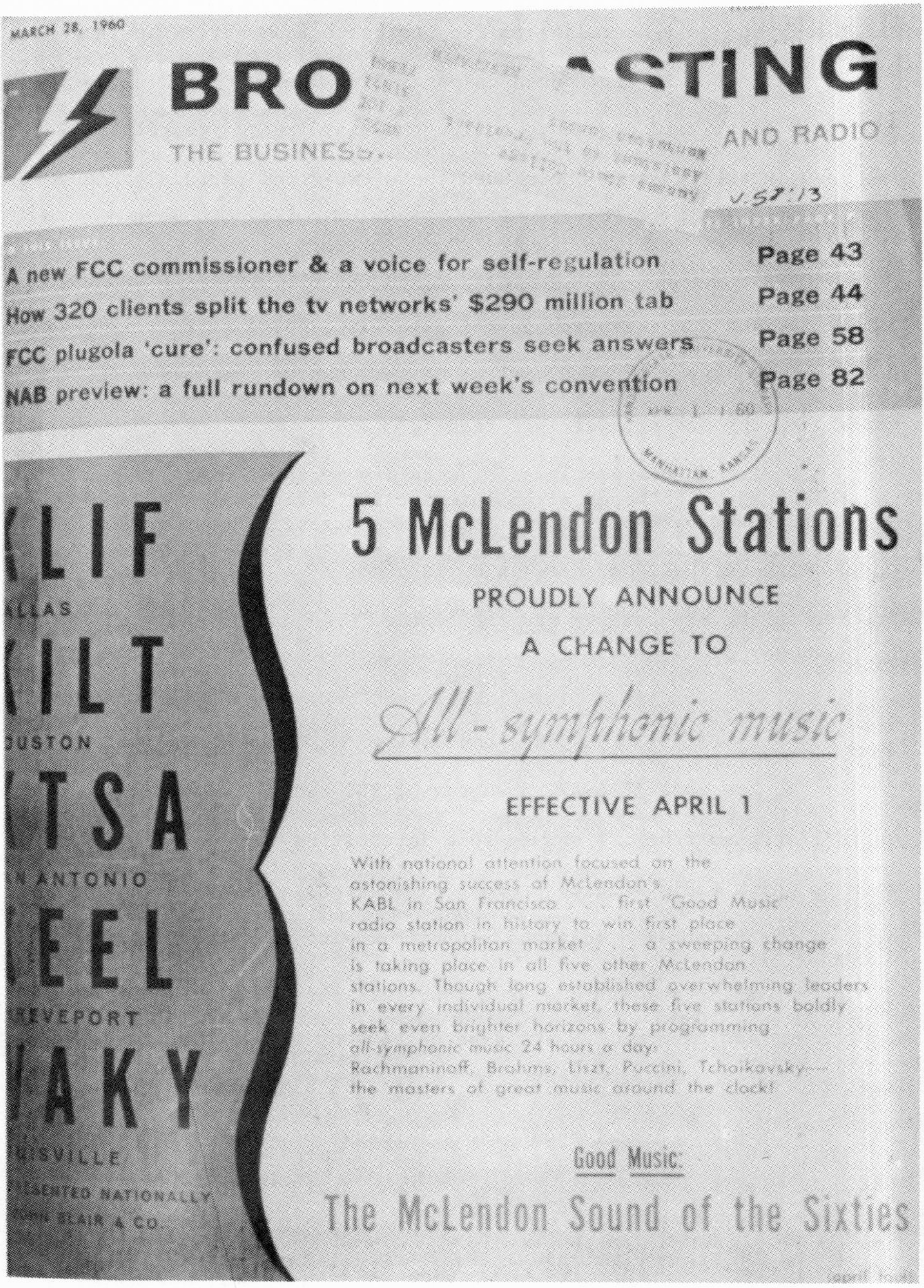
MARCH 28, 1960

BRO ASTING

THE BUSINESS AND RADIO

v.58:13

A new FCC commissioner & a voice for self-regulation Page 43

How 320 clients split the tv networks' $290 million tab Page 44

FCC plugola 'cure': confused broadcasters seek answers Page 58

NAB preview: a full rundown on next week's convention Page 82

MANHATTAN, KANSAS

KLIF
ALLAS
KILT
OUSTON
KTSA
N ANTONIO
KEEL
REVEPORT
WAKY
ISVILLE
ESENTED NATIONALLY
OHN BLAIR & CO.

5 McLendon Stations

PROUDLY ANNOUNCE

A CHANGE TO

All-symphonic music

EFFECTIVE APRIL 1

With national attention focused on the astonishing success of McLendon's KABL in San Francisco . . . first "Good Music" radio station in history to win first place in a metropolitan market . . . a sweeping change is taking place in all five other McLendon stations. Though long established overwhelming leaders in every individual market, these five stations boldly seek even brighter horizons by programming all-symphonic music 24 hours a day: Rachmaninoff, Brahms, Liszt, Puccini, Tchaikovsky— the masters of great music around the clock!

Good Music:

The McLendon Sound of the Sixties

increase next year's (1958's) promotion and advertising budget, which in 1957 had been between $1,000 and $2,000 for 56% of the stations, between $2,000 and $4,000 for 13% of the stations, between $4,000 and $6,000 for 7.7%, and over $6,000 for 23% of the stations.[77] This last figure is especially interesting, for it seemed to be the old story that it takes money to make money--and those stations that had it were glad to spend it to make more.

Also in December, Broadcasting reported that the networks were trying hard to do promotions of their own, giving away anything from silver dollars to turkeys, and working out all kinds of program cross-plugs and newspaper tune-in ads.[78] For networks, however, to try to do the same sort of promotions that local independent stations were doing would not pay off. The local stations had the advantage of a local personality and a loyal audience that identified with the station. Stunts and gimmicks could be entirely localized on a single station, while on a network, they had to suit all parts of the country. Most of all, networks could not expect to draw crowds to a single point for some event, and what they did generally was not talked about nor carried in the newspapers as were the stunts of the local independent stations.

In November 1959 Henry J. Kaufman, apparently the head of an advertising agency with the same name, spoke before the fourth annual convention of the Broadcasters Promotion Association. He revealed the

---

[77] "Radio Outlets Value Promotion," Broadcasting, December 2, 1957, p. 64.

[78] "Radio Networks Are Sizzling with Promotions," Broadcasting, December 2, 1957, pp. 28, 29.

results of a survey he had taken which showed that broadcasters urged others to buy a far higher percentage of advertising than they themselves bought. Kaufman claimed that "the average national advertising expenditure per metropolitan area, in terms of ratio to non-network, national time sales, is well under 1%." A full 40% of radio broadcasters admitted that they operated without any kind of annual promotion budget or plan, simply making decisions from "crisis to crisis."[79] In comparison, it is interesting to examine the McLendon approach. McLendon claimed in 1961 that he spent 5 to 10% of his then $3,000,000 to $4,000,000 gross on promotion. When he launched his good music KABL in San Francisco, the bill for the first 45 days of promotion was $35,000.[80]

In March 1963 McLendon explained his philosophy about spending money on promotions for an article about him in the "Pictorial Living" section of the San Francisco Examiner. His credo at that time: "$10 in promotion will result in 1,000 listeners, who will, in turn, bring back $10,000 in advertising billing."[81]

In September of 1961, Business Week carried a four page article on the McLendon stations' promotion practices, titled "Zany Stunts Put Radio Chain in Clover." The article describes the treasure hunts staged by McLendon (to be discussed later) but gives McLendon's opinion

---

[79]"TV, Radio Stations Spend Too Little for Promotion: Kaufman," Advertising Age, November 16, 1959, p. 8.

[80]"Zany Stunts Put Radio Chain in Clover," Business Week, September 9, 1961, pp. 126, 131.

[81]Jack Setlowe, "Gordon McLendon," in the "Pictorial Living" section of the San Francisco Examiner, March 31, 1963, three pages, from Gordon McLendon's personal scrapbook.

as of 1961 that "today, you do not have to give away vast amounts of money to attract attention--The $64,000 Question made it hard to come up with a significant enough amount of money to pull." Business Week stated McLendon was shifting instead to "ideas that catch the public fancy . . ." such as a contest in which a listener sends in $125,000 and the station sends back 25 words or less.[82]

But just as the day of the big-money giveaway was over, so was the day of the spectacular stunt coming to a close. In September of 1962, Broadcasting reported the case of radio station WLLE vs. the FCC. The transfer of ownership to the new company (WLLE) had barely been granted because of the type of promotion the station had used to call attention to the change. Said Broadcasting,

> All broadcast licensees were put on official notice by the FCC last week that the next station which utilizes "repetitious playing of one record, interspersed with an off-color story, discordant sounds and other vagaries" will be in serious trouble. . . .
>
> . . . A letter from the FCC admonishing WLLE will be sent to all stations before "taking further regulatory action in an individual case." . . .
>
> . . . WLLE pointed out that several stations had engaged in similar one-day programming in the past for a special promotion. . . .
>
> . . . The commission said that it had no wish to "stultify exuberance" in licensees, but the WLLE actions do not qualify "either as inventive or as in the public interest." Rather, the agency continued, such programming was obviously designed to serve the new owner's private economic interest by shocking the community.
>
> While past industry promotion practices are no excuse, the FCC said it is taking no further action against WLLE because "the licensee may have been influenced by a belief that such methods were acceptable."[83]

---

[82]"Zany Stunts Put Radio Chain in Clover," p. 131.

[83]"Stiff Warning to Stations," Broadcasting, September 17, 1962, p. 52.

The worst of the so-called "off-color" or "smutty" remarks that *Broadcasting* could find was this one: "Did you hear about the goose that got on the subway and got peopled five times before he got off?"[84]

This case shows the beginning of what McLendon has referred to as "non-objective law" being applied to broadcasting. Ken Dowe, who is today National Director of Operations for the McLendon Stations, was asked by the author if what Dowe had characterized as an aggressive attitude on the part of the FCC in examining programming had decreased the showmanship that had been the hallmark of the Top 40 era. Dowe replied "Oh, sure. That's one of the reasons."[85]

It does seem paradoxical that by "raising its eyebrow," the FCC may have indeed taken some of the exuberance out of radio programming by stifling the free-wheeling promotions that in the Top 40 days were such an integral part of the entertainment. It is quite literally true that between his news broadcasts and his promotions, McLendon's Top 40 stations were ones that you were "afraid to turn off because you feared you'd miss something." This is no longer the case with the typical music-and-news station today. In addition to the changes in the regulatory climate at the FCC in recent years the "mavericks" and "take-a-shot" people have become both middle-aged and wealthy. Top 40 radio became fully "respectable" by growing to be a multi-million-dollar business. Top 40 stations today stay ensconced in the top positions in their markets by playing more music and doing less talk--and promotions--*any* kind of promotions--are not the wanted music but the dreaded talk.

---

[84]*Ibid.*

[85]Ken Dowe interview.

Prize Contests

As has already been shown, promotion took many forms, but the most spectacular and popular with the Top 40 audience was the prize contest or "giveaway." This is one form that Top 40 management definitely did not invent, for as will be shown, the giveaway program had been a staple in radio for a number of years. What Top 40 did do was to transfer the giveaway program from the radio network to the local station level where "promotion of the promotion" could be carried on most effectively.

Background

The giveaway program was in vogue on the national radio networks in the late 1940s. In February of 1948, Business Week counted 15 such programs on national networks and "dozens more on regional and local programs."[86] By 1949, Business Week reported the total at 38 shows giving away an estimated $3,500,000.[87] In most cases, the prizes were supplied free of charge to the program just for a free product mention. In 1947, the leading electrical appliance manufacturers such as Westinghouse and General Electric estimated that they received $5,000,000 in advertising for $250,000 worth of goods.[88]

In August of 1949, the FCC took upon itself the duty of interpreting the U.S. Criminal Code's lottery regulations. (In September

---

[86] "Free Gifts, Cheap Ads," Business Week, February 7, 1948, p. 42.

[87] "Giveaways Down, Not Out," Business Week, August 27, 1949, p. 31.

[88] "Radio Handouts," Fortune, November, 1947, p. 142.

1948 Congress transferred the lottery section from the Communications Act of 1934 and added it to the U.S. Criminal Code.) In a three-to-one decision, the FCC decided that giveaways were lotteries and thus illegal. Humorist and cynic Henry Morgan was quoted as saying, "First . . . they have no right to make such a ruling; second, I approve of it thoroughly."[89] The networks immediately appealed the decision, which allowed the broadcast of giveaways to continue, although it is probable that the uncertainty about the legality of such programs may have slowed their development at the local level. Finally, in April of 1954, the U.S. Supreme Court ruled that giveaways were not lotteries. One of the key findings was that "consideration" traditionally was held to mean "something of value," and that "listening to a giveaway program was not 'consideration' within the sense of the lottery statute."[90]

Some of the financially strong and prestigious local stations such as Crosley's WLW in Cincinnati went ahead with giveaway programs even before the Supreme Court decision. In 1952 and 1953, WLW gave away several Kaiser cars, and one time gave away a house.[91] Storz, too, was dropping money from a tree in an Omaha park for his KOWH. But it is interesting to note that McLendon's first big giveaway was not until April 17, 1954, the Good Friday when 10,000 people jammed downtown Dallas to catch the money being thrown from the window of the

---

[89] "Gift Horse Hobbled," Newsweek, August 29, 1949, p. 44.

[90] "Giveaways Not Lotteries, According to U.S. Supreme Court Ruling," Broadcasting, April 12, 1954, p. 34.

[91] "Station WLW Gives Away House . . . Cars, to Snag Off-Hour Audience," Business Week, July 18, 1953, p. 72.

Adolphus-Baker hotel by Bill Stewart and others. This stunt came only a week after the Supreme Court decision. In reporting the promotion, Broadcasting said, "The station ran five announcements per day during the week," which suggests that the promotion of the stunt was only for a week preceding Good Friday.[92] Bill Stewart has been quoted earlier as saying that this stunt is the one promotion that really established KLIF.

Storz Example: "Lucky House Number"

Storz, meanwhile, had begun to concentrate on one principal prize contest: the Lucky House Number. This was a very simple contest in which a street address is announced, and if the occupant of that address calls within a minute, he wins the jackpot. The prize increases each time it is not won. Storz copyrighted this idea, and in 1957 was earning $600 a week from other stations that had taken out licenses to use it.[93] In 1955, Storz executive George Armstrong told AIMS members in a letter that the station he was in charge of, WHB, Kansas City, had adopted Lucky House Number as its principle promotion.

> Briefly, the reasons we are sold on Lucky House are these. First, it in no way interferes with your regular program format. Therefore, it does not drive audience away. Second, there is, of course, no consideration, inconvenience, or thought process involved which would tend to confuse listeners. Anybody can win, simply by osmosis. Lucky House Number also lends itself to giving away large prizes which are, in my judgment, more dramatic than a lot of little ones. A third advantage to Lucky House Number is that it can be sold or not sold as the station may elect.

---

[92] "Programs and Promotion," Broadcasting, May 3, 1954, p. 74.

[93] Herman Land, "The Storz Bombshell," Television Magazine, May 1957, reprint, p. 7 of 8.

> In general, about give-away gimmicks, it is my feeling that a station should have one self-perpetuating type of give-away on which to hang its hat. However, I am against the use of a lot of different give-aways, most of which clutter the air and cheapen the station. The give-away must be put in its proper perspective. You can use a give-away very successfully as a sort of neon sign to get people into the store. But, if the product is not sound in its own right no amount of gimmicking in the world will save your neck.[94]

What Armstrong probably did not need to say but which should be recognized here is that the contest's goal was to keep people tuned to the station, and that it succeeded in that regard. (McLendon's WINDO with the KLIF sticker in the rear window of the car seems to have one big advantage--it ought to keep the large automobile listening audience tuned.)

One of the stations running "Lucky House Number" was WAPI, Birmingham. In at least two issues of Sponsor in October 1955 the station ran the following ad:

> LUCKY HOUSE NUMBER, featured on several WAPI shows, averages a winner a week. This indicates how regularly people stay tuned to WAPI.
>
> "I was ironing a dress" says pretty Nannette Parrish. "Of course I had the radio tuned to WAPI. The program was Wright with Records. Suddenly I heard our own house number called. I put down the iron (not on my dress) and called WAPI. The next day I went to WAPI and Bill Wright handed me the check. I have given 10% to my church and the rest is in my education fund." Miss Parrish is a 15-year old Junior High Student.[95]

In the "Confidential Report on WHB" which was written about 1956, the writer, who had talked to George Armstrong, noted the following:

---

[94] George W. Armstrong, Excerpt from AIMS Letter from WHB to all AIMS members, dated September 1955, from McLendon Policy Books, n.p.

[95] Advertisement in Sponsor, October 17, 1955, p. 102 and October 24, 1955, p. 66.

When stations steal the Lucky House Number Contest which Storz has syndicated, and supposedly copyrighted, Storz does not sue. He says all such suits can be beaten and there is just no use. He just lets them steal it when they want to.[96]

On July 21, 1956, Bill Stewart sent a memo to all announcers at KOWH. Stewart, as National Program Director, was directing them to drop the Lucky House Number promotion after the next winner. The reason for doing so, it will be remembered, is the promise that Storz made to the FCC that all giveaways on all his stations would be discontinued if the FCC would grant the license to WQAM. The grant was approved on July 19, two days before Stewart's letter, the text of which follows:

As soon as we have our next LUCKY HOUSE NUMBER winner, it will be discontinued, with no mention whatsoever on the air as to why it was discontinued. When we do get the winner, please be sure to use the story on the rest of the newscasts that day, but be sure to let Peggy know right away so that she can cross out the balance of the LHN's for that day and for any other logs she has made up.

The CASH FOR KIDS promotion will taper off thusly: we have been running eight a day. On Monday there will be five scheduled. Tuesday there will be two, and Wednesday it will be completely off the air. Please make no mention whatsoever on the air about its being off, and when the kids start calling inquiring about it, the switchboard operator should tell them to keep their cards and badges, and we will be announcing how they can use them at some future date.

AUTO CASH will also cease almost immediately. We have a contract with Art Miller which will have to be straightened out by Virgil (Virgil Sharpe, KOWH General Manager) who will let you know Monday or Tuesday exactly when AUTO CASH will stop.

The important thing to remember is . . . ABSOLUTELY NO MENTION ON THE AIR ABOUT THE CONTESTS BEING OFF!!!!

Regarding Appreciation Night, we have already definitely committed Russ Carlyle, Jerri Southern and Georgie Shaw, and

---

[96] "A Confidential Report on WHB," McLendon Policy Books, approximate date March 1956, n.p.

> the latest record of each is in the studio and can be played as an extra every so often to promote Appreciation Night.[97]

"Auto Cash" was virtually the same as McLendon's WINDO, involving a sticker for the rear window of the car to be spotted by a car from the radio station and mentioned on the air, at which time the owner of the sticker had a certain amount of time to call and claim a prize.

Note that all of the <u>direct</u> giveaways of cash and merchandise were being discontinued, but that promotions of a different sort--i.e., the "Appreciation Night" featuring a free concert--went on.

Treasure Hunts

<u>Storz stations</u>

The events that had forced Storz into the position of giving up giveaways in order to get WQAM were the "treasure hunts" which reached a zenith of popularity in 1956. Storz conducted the first "big money" treasure hunts in June of that year, but had been running treasure hunts with relatively small cash prizes for some time. WTIX, the Storz station in New Orleans, conducted its first Treasure Hunt in June of 1955. By September of that year, the practice had spread to smaller markets, as evidenced by a letter to <u>Broadcasting</u> from the president of KFTM, Fort Morgan, Colorado pointing out that his station had given away $1,000 cash at that time.[98]

The Storz stations were apparently well enough known in the industry for their treasure hunts that other stations asked for advice

---

[97] Bill Stewart, "Memo to All Announcers," July 21, 1956, supplied by Bill Stewart, n.p.

[98] "Open Mike--Treasure Hunts," <u>Broadcasting</u>, October 1, 1956, p. 18.

on how to conduct them, for at some time in the first six months of 1956, Storz management felt it necessary to draw up a form letter answer to inquiries about how to organize such contests. The letter was on the letterhead of the Mid-Continent Broadcasting Company (the Storz group), supposedly written by KOWH General Manager Virgil Sharpe. A copy of this letter has been provided by Bill Stewart and is reproduced on pages 444 to 446. This treasure hunt was obviously quite well thought out except for the traffic problems mentioned. Its previous success, plus the arrival of Bill Stewart in Omaha to work for the Storz organization early in 1956, no doubt prompted the decision to try a treasure hunt with a really big prize--one in excess of $100,000.

In May of 1956, Broadcasting announced that Storz would be giving away $105,000 at each of his stations in Omaha and Minneapolis with the contest to begin June 7, 1956. The reasons for choosing Omaha and Minneapolis and not also New Orleans and Kansas City were simple: WTIX in New Orleans and WHB in Kansas City were firmly established ratings leaders in their cities. KOWH had been the ratings leader in Omaha for some time but was being challenged by more powerful, fulltime KOIL. In Minneapolis, WDGY had been acquired by Storz only at the beginning of 1956 and at that time it was at the bottom of the ratings. In order to garner good shares of the spot business being placed for the fall, their late spring ratings would have to be good.[99]

In reporting the imminent beginning of the contests, Broadcasting stated, "This is believed to be the largest single prize

---

[99] Herman Land, "The Storz Bombshell," reprint, p. 7 of 8.

MID-CONTINENT BROADCASTING COMPANY

WDGY, Minneapolis KOWH, Omaha WHB, Kansas City WTIX, New Orleans

"TREASURE HUNT CONTEST"

Thank you for your recent inquiry about our Treasure Hunt Contest. Since you will undoubtedly want to modify our format to conform with local conditions I will only outline the contest plans very briefly. You are welcome to make any use you desire of this information with no obligation to us.

WHAT THE CONTEST DOES....

1. Thousands of cars in your area will have your call letters prominently displayed in their rear window. This naturally causes a lot of comment because people seeing these stickers will ask other people what they mean.

2. You will effectively demonstrate to advertisers in your area that your station has listeners, and you will show them the power of radio.

We started out with brief "teaser" announcements on the air. These announcements said in effect that there would soon be a big KOWH Treasure Hunt. We asked listeners wishing to get in on the big contest to simply send their name and address to TREASURE HUNT, KOWH, Omaha. In return, we sent them a sticker for the back of their car, and a letter of instructions. We used the brief announcements to eliminate having to go into all of the details of the contest over the air. The letter of instructions explained the contest in complete detail, and we think it eliminated a lot of confusion. The sticker that went out with the letter is a very important part of the whole contest. The stickers we used measured approximately 3 1/2 by 12 inches, and had a narrow gummed strip at each end of the sticker so they could be attached inside the back windows of the autos. We had the stickers imprinted "KOWH TREASURE HUNT." We used a special "day-glo" stock which made the stickers very eye-catching and made them readable at considerable distance. We got our stickers from the Business Printing Service, 2409 Farnam St., Omaha 2, Nebraska. The stickers were quite expensive because of the stock used, and because it was necessary to hand-gum the stickers. Our cost was approximately $45.00 per thousand. These stickers could be made for a fraction of this cost if they were done on regular stock, and if you asked listeners to stick them on their windows with scotch tape.

As soon as we started getting stickers out, we went into the second phase of the contest. This was a preliminary award system, designed to accomplish two purposes. First of all, we wanted to make sure that people would get the stickers on their cars before the big Treasure Hunt day, and second, we wanted to stimulate interest in the contest to get more entries. This second phase consisted simply of spotting a car each day that had the official sticker on it and calling that license number over the air. If the person owning that car was listening, he received a special award, which in this case was a five-dollar bill. When we spotted the car for the day we also wrote down the approximate year, color and make of the car so that when a person claiming that license called in we could double check their correct identity.

For the big Treasure Hunt itself, we chose a Sunday afternoon. We started the Treasure Hunt at Approximately 2:00 PM and it ended about 5:00 PM. We had three separate Treasure Hunts, one after the other. The first Treasure Hunt prize was $50.00, the second $100.00 and the third $250.00. We used our short wave mobile unit throughout the afternoon on the Treasure Hunt Day and all the broadcasting relative to the Treasure Hunt came from that unit. I think it would be possible to have a Treasure Hunt without a short-wave unit, but it would probably be quite difficult. At approximately 2:00 O'clock we ran several announcements as follows: "Calling all Treasure Hunt cars...Assemble in the downtown Omaha area." This tied up traffic completely in the downtown area until we directed the cars to the first treasure. The city police called out over 40 extra patrolmen to help break up the traffic jam. I'm sure you can readily see the tremendous traffic problems that a contest of this kind will create. For example, if you have five thousand entries you can easily figure that five thousand cars almost bumper to bumper would stretch in a single lane for 20 miles. The fortunate thing about this contest is that since all the people in these cars are listening to your station on their radio, you can break up the jam at will.

Make sure that you choose Treasure Hunt locations that have ample parking space and locations that preferably can be reached by several good through streets. Also make sure that you include adequate safety provisions. I'll go into that more thoroughly in the next paragraph but I might mention now that we announced throughout the contest that anyone breaking any traffic laws or trespassing on or destroying private property would immediately be disqualified from the contest.

The contest itself operated quite satisfactorily. The only place we experienced any difficulty was at our first Treasure site, and that was our fault because we had picked a location that did not have sufficient streets leading to it to move the traffic properly. As a result, even when the first treasure was found we had cars lined bumper to bumper for several miles, still on their way to the treasure site. To prevent any racing and any other traffic violations we divided the clues into two sections. The first clues were quite general and were designed to bring all the cars to the Treasure Hunt site. People were told several times that they would gain nothing by racing to the Treasure Hunt site because the specific clues would not be given until everyone had arrived. For example, our first clue for a specific contest was: "The Treasure is south of downtown Omaha." This was general enough to prevent any speeding since the contestants did not have any specific place to go. Gradually we narrowed it down until as a final clue we said: "The Treasure is near the ball park." After allowing ample time for everyone to park and get out of their cars we continued with the specific clues as to the location of the treasure. For this purpose we had a mobile public address system at the site. These later specific clues were heard by the contestants after they were out of the cars over the PA system which was simply tuned to the radio inside the PA truck. We actually had both our short wave car and the PA system at each location. The announcers in the short wave car would give the clues, and it would go by short wave to our studio pick-up, then out to the transmitter, then back over our AM station to the treasure site and through the PA speakers. For the treasure itself we hid a dummy check in a very well concealed hiding place. The check was not signed and made out simply "Treasure Hunt Winner Number 1" with the amount specified. On the back of the check we included a lot of conditions stating that the check must be found in accordance with the contest, then we honored these dummy checks with valid checks when presented at the radio station.

As you can see, the contest involves a considerable amount of work, but I think you will find it to be an excellent promotion well worth the effort. Our total expenses, including prizes, ran about one thousand dollars. This included expenses incident to the mailing of the letter and stickers as well as rental of the public address system and hiring of special police. We did not sell our contest. We already had a heavy commercial schedule on Sunday afternoon, when the actual Treasure Hunt took place, and we ran the contest simply as a station promotion. However, I can tell you that I'm sure you will find it very easy to sell if you wish to do so. Although our contest was not for sale, we had inquiries from a number of promotion-minded advertisers soon after the stickers started to appear in car windows.

If you havey any questions about the contest I will be very happy to assist you if I can.

With best wishes, I am

Very truly yours,

Virgil Sharpe
Vice President
General Manager

offered in the radio-tv industry."[100]

Bill Stewart has supplied a copy of the instructions given to all Storz personnel in Omaha and Minneapolis on the actual running of the $105,000 contests. It is reproduced on pages 448 to 450.

The $105,000 Contests" certainly created the kind of audience acceptance hoped for in spending such a large sum. If anything they were too successful. Stewart states that families in far distant parts of the country who had heard about the giveaway wrote and called the station for details because some were changing the dates of their vacations to arrive in the cities where the prizes would be hidden in the first half of June 1956.[101]

Unfortunately, with so much money at stake, the treasure hunters became quite frantic in their efforts to locate the check. Broadcasting made the following report in the Monday, June 18, 1956 edition:

> "Giveaways Create Furor in Minneapolis, Omaha"
> Two major cities--Minneapolis and Omaha--approached the weekend in a state of mild shock as radio listeners scrambled for a potential $460,000 in prize money.
> Two Mid-Continent Broadcasting Co. stations, WDGY Minneapolis and KOWH Omaha, closed separate $105,000 treasure hunts today (Monday), last chance to find checks hidden by an insurance firm. The two stations have been broadcasting frequent clues supplied by the insurer which charged fees totaling 1/47th of the prize money on a probability basis.
> WCCO Minneapolis ran a competing "Cashorama" contest offering a potential $250,000 in prizes to listeners who responded to WCCO phone calls by repeating key phrases heard on the air. This contest closed Saturday.
> Todd Storz, president of Mid-Continent, told B-T its contest had drawn searching parties from as far away as Bellingham,

---

[100] "$210,000 Giveaway," Broadcasting, May 28, 1956, p. 84.

[101] Stewart interview.

OUTLINE ON THE $105,000 CONTEST -

In Omaha and Minneapolis, we are running the $105,000 contest. The starting date is 5:15 p.m. on June 7th, and the closing date is 5:15 p.m. on June 16th. This closing date will apply to the $105,000 prize, but there will be a further explanation on the time element later in this outline.

We have contracted with a nationally known insurance company to underwrite the $210,000. We cannot, before or during the contest, identify the company. After the contest is over, we will probably want to publicize (for the sake of the record) the name of the company. However, until then, we will refer to it as "a nationally known and respected insurance company."

The company designated a man of trust who is in their employ, to hide a bank check in the amount of $105,000 in each city. If the check is found after the closing date of 5:15 p.m. on June 16th, it will be worth $500 in each city. We will broadcast two clues per day for the entire ten day period.... a total of twenty different clues. I thin we should set up at the outset, some rules that will be followed in both cities. One is in order to build sustained listening, we must stress that the clues will not be repeated after the one time they are broadcast on the air; nor will they be given by the receptionist on the phone. We also must stress that the clues will be broadcast between the hours of 7:00 a.m. and 6:00 p.m. each day. Naturally, those won't be the only two mentions of the contest during the day, but after the clue is given in the morning, the idea that we want to build up in all the following announcements is to the effect that "Everyone is still looking, and there will be more clues sometime later this afternoon," etc.. Todd has suggested that we set up an alarm clock in the studio that will be ticking all day in the background, and the jockeys can build the suspense element by saying that no one knows exactly what time the next clue will be --that the alarm has been set by the program director, and the new clues will be given when the alarm goes off. The clock can be set in a box, and the guys can say that they have no idea when the alarm is set for, because the box is sealed.

We also have to stress on the air, in all references to the contest, that the check may not be found in the ten day period, and that if it is not, we will on the eleventh day, give many direct and very pointed clues so that someone will have to find it. (It will then be worth $500.)

Let me establish also that there is only one person in the whole wide world who knows where the checks are hidden or buried. He has drawn rough maps of both locations, and one will be deposited in a safe deposit box at the Northwestern National Bank in Minneapolis and the other in a box at the Omaha National Bank in Omaha. It will be necessary to have two signatures in order to get the rough maps out after the contest is over....one being that of the insurance company representative, and the other that of Steve Labunski in Minneapolis and that of Virgil Sharpe here in Omaha. In talking over the details of this contest, many things were kicked around that may seem to trivial to be mentioned here, but they must necessarily be brought to your attention. One is that the man from the insurance company is very much afraid that if his identity were to become know, his children or family might be in danger, and that gangsters might threaten his family with bodily harm if he didn't divulge the location of the check. It is also quite possible that some of the radio station personnel might find themselves in the same position. So, it must be emphatically stated and reiterated on any air promotion, that absolutely no one at the station knows the whereabouts of the hidden check, and that the check is non-negotiable. It also must be brought out that "employees of the radio station and/or their families, are not eligible to participate, etc."

In view of the fact that we are going to have to stress hard that if the check is not found in the ten day period, the clues will be narrowed down, etc., and the prize will be $500, we are going to have to offset this in another way. One of the big ways will be to have the air men continuously pitch the optimistic approach "If you have organized a searching party of friends or members of your family, be sure that you have figured out and agreed upon how you are going to split the $105,000. We don't want any broken families, friendships or necks on account of our contest." etc. The big pitch of course will be "This is your chance of a lifetime"... "You'll never have to work again"... "You can retire to a life of ease"... "You'll no longer have to live with your mother-in-law"... "You don't have to be an expert on art or cooking or anything"... "You'll be able to have four cars, one for each direction," etc.

It might also be well to stress that the check is not hidden in the building where the station is located; nor is it located on the property of the station's transmitter; nor is it on the property of any of the station personnel. And, the following in brief, are direct quotes from the signed agreement with the insurance company, for your edification: "It is further agreed by the insurers and the respective radio stations as follows:

1. The checks mentioned are to be non-negotiable....are to be marked "Payable upon acceptance by the radio station involved" and are to be marked that they will be accepted only if presented by a person eligible under the contest rules, and who will give an affidavit that check in mention was first discovered by him, during the period from June 7th to 16th inclusive. (This clause will protect the insurance company in any eventuality such as one cited before, i.e. if a gangster were to "threaten him with bodily harm," etc.)

2. The checks are to be hidden within a radius of ten air miles from the respective radio stations' studio....are to be placed where they are accessible to the average able-bodied person....it being understood that each check will be not over fifteen feet above the ground, or five feet below the ground. It is understood that the checks can be recovered withou the use of power tools, and without material damage to any property. (This underlined portion must be stressed very hard on all the announcements.

3. One of the rules of the contest is that the radio stations concerned by notified immediately that the check is found.

I do not have to remind you that this is a tremendously expensive promotion, and in order for us to get the full benefit of such a large outlay of money, we are going to have to promote it "to the hilt." We are running teaser announcements here in Omaha now, and will step up the teasers all next week., and will start on the 28th of May to break the check angle. We have made no mention whatsoever so far as to any details of the contest. We have just referred to it as the biggest contest in the history of radio or television, etc. But, we will start to pitch the whole thing on the 28th, with at least one spot an hour for that entire week, and then, as many spots as possible in the five days preceding the kick-off time. Some of the spots can be produced, but most of them will have to be adlibbed by the jockeys. And, they will be able to build up the enthusiasm for the entire thing. It appears at this moment that we might get a very good national break on the contest. Kaufmann Associates in Washington are working very hard on Life Magazine. And, if that doesn't pan out, there are other interesting things brewing. But, the Life coverage, or any other coverage, by a national magazine will depend upon the amount of interest we can build up in advance.

Washington. Portable radios were carried by listeners and in Omaha the Sol Lewis Appliance Co. sold out its entire stock June 8, second day of the contest.

Some Omaha incidents: One of the twice-daily clues mentioning a street intersection brought a crowd of 7,500 within 20 minutes. A belief that the check was in the Commodore Hotel drew enthusiasts who tore a rug off the floor and ransacked a room--a $200 damage bill that KOWH cheerfully paid. And a bag of missing checks stolen in a recent drug store robbery was found under a bridge and turned over to police.

In Minneapolis it took 20 policemen to handle a crowd at Hennapin and Yyndale [sic] intersection and trees everywhere were ransacked in search of the WDGY prize. In both cities phony checks were planted by pranksters.

Chambers of commerce, Mr. Storz said, were delighted "with the tremendous influx of visitors from near and far," and hoped the contests would become annual affairs.

WCCO officials chuckled, they said, when WDGY repeated such prize-winning slogans as "WCCO is always first with the news," in an effort to keep listeners tuned to WDGY. This practice was dropped, they explained, after a few days.

Cash awards offered by WCCO to those who could repeat the key phrase after it was broadcast varied from $1,000 to $5,000. Fifteen calls were made per day.[102]

The incident described above wherein WDGY gave WCCO's clues so that listeners could stay tuned to WDGY and thus be ready to win <u>either</u> contest was a "first" according to Bill Stewart. WCCO, as stated in the <u>Broadcasting</u> article, did not make it easy for WDGY--the slogans always contained the WCCO name and a complimentary phrase. But WDGY aired them all cheerfully, and, according to Stewart, this very act helped endear the station to listeners and helped it be thought of as every bit the equal of long time leader WCCO.[103] However, it is also true that WDGY was forced into this position by the fact that in the case of Storz's "invasion" of Minneapolis, the other stations were ready and waiting for him. A number of the stations, including leader

---

[102]"Giveaways Create Furor in Minneapolis, Omaha," <u>Broadcasting</u>, June 18, 1956, p. 106.

[103]Stewart interview.

WCCO, studied Storz's operation and decided to "fight fire with fire." Steve Labunski, who at the time was WDGY General Manager, is quoted describing the battle that ensued:

> In Minneapolis, they were waiting for us. In Kansas City, we had used the $25 weekly news-tip successfully, WTCN started it just before we came in, so we didn't use it. WCCO began a Saturday Top 40. WLOL went into a Top 40. We went ahead with ours on the grounds that you can't imitate the name of the show--ours features the name of the disc jockey. WLOL also used the Lucky House contest. The first result was an increase in the total amount of popular music being aired.
>
> In the same 10 days during which our $105,000 buried treasure contest ran, WCCO ran a $250,000 secret word contest. We announced we would run the secret word, so that listeners wouldn't have to listen to WCCO. WCCO ran long phrases, like "WCCO is the best station in Minneapolis." We carried them. WCCO vaulted us into the big-station category. They invited us into the club.[104]

Hunts by other stations

In spite of the problems that the two Storz stations had encountered with their treasure hunts, New York station WRCA (now WNBC), the flagship station of the NBC network, decided to stage a series of treasure hunts in New York as a boost to the ratings of its morning "Pulse" program emceed by Bill Cullen. WRCA promotion manager, Max Buck, admitted that Todd Storz's stations had been the inspiration for trying a treasure hunt on WRCA.[105] The station gave away one $1,000 prize per week, beginning July 23, 1956, and by September 10--having given away $7,000 and raised the ire of city policeman and other victims--planned to keep right on hiding checks.[106] One of the prizes

---

[104] Herman Land, "The Storz Bombshell," reprint, p. 8 of 8.

[105] "What Are They Looking For? They're After WRCA's $1,000," Broadcasting, September 10, 1956, p. 108.

[106] Ibid.

was hidden behind a toll-rate card at Grand Central Station. There, Newsweek reported that telephone books were torn apart, private offices were broken into and timetables were strewn all over the floor. Another lead (false) led hordes to the New York Public Library, where frantic officials finally got Bill Cullen to call off the searchers. Said Newsweek,

> . . . Plans to plant a certificate somewhere in the Metropolitan Museum of Art were fortunately abandoned when an imaginative WRCA official was seized by a nightmare vision of what might happen to the museum's priceless paintings and objets d'art.[107]

The September 1, 1956 issue of America carried an article with the title "How to Encourage Nuisances--Treasure Hunts." The title conveyed the feeling of indignation both of the magazine and of many of the victims of radio station treasure hunts. The text described New York's experience with WRCA's treasure hunt, and concluded with the worried surmise that other stations might copy the formula for instant listenership.[108] As it turned out, this is what happened. Apparently there were a number of stations in the country that did not fear the FCC's July 1956 near-failure to grant WQAM to Storz because of his stations' "giveaway pattern." Pepsi-Cola actually became a sponsor of some such events, according to Advertising Age,[109] and even such

---

[107] "Gold at Coney Island," Newsweek, August 27, 1956, p. 55.

[108] "How to Encourage Nuisances--Treasure Hunts," America, September 1, 1956, p. 494.

[109] "Stations and 'Jukes,'" Advertising Age, December 10, 1956, p. 86.

obscure stations as WVNA, Tuscumbia, Alabama, were hiding $2,500 in Pepsi-Cola bottles in late 1956.[110]

McLendon stations

Whether or not Pepsi-Cola sponsored Gordon McLendon's biggest treasure hunt, the $50,000 prize of which was also hidden in a soda bottle is a moot question, but it is fact that McLendon's KLIF did give away $50,000 in a treasure hunt which began December 1st, 1956 and ended nine days later. The check was found by a lathe operator just six hours before its value would have dropped to $500. As with the Storz treasure hunts, McLendon had insured the find (but with Lloyds of London, for $1,250). Lloyds had to pay $45,000 of the value of the check, while KLIF had to pay only $5,000. Another $100 was paid to a local insurance company executive who, again like the Storz operation, was responsible for hiding the check and writing the clues, only two of which were given per day (a la Storz). McLendon claimed that about 7,000 people looked for the check in freezing weather.[111] Note that more people had turned out for far less money in April 1954 when the money was thrown out of the window of the Adolphus hotel.

Promotions Defended

McLendon

McLendon answered the critics of giveaways and contests in a speech before the timebuying and selling seminar of the Radio and

---

[110]"Hunt a Hit," Broadcasting, November 19, 1956, p. 119.

[111]"Return on Soft Drink Empty: $50,000," Broadcasting, December 17, 1956, p. 50.

Television Executives Society in New York on Tuesday, December 18, 1956. He said of KLIF's ratings during the hunt just described:

> In November, before the big treasure hunt, Hooper showed KLIF with 39.9% of the morning audience in Dallas and 40.9% of the afternoon audience. Our December figures show KLIF with 39.1% of the morning audience, a decrease of nearly 1% and 47.9% afternoons, about a 7% increase. We believe we'd have had this same small afternoon increase without the treasure hunt, since we had effected some other afternoon program changes that made us normally anticipate an increased share, and we dropped slightly in the morning despite a $50,000 giveaway!
>
> . . . We can prove beyond any question that most giveaways no longer have any appreciable direct or short-run effect on local station ratings. We know that a network giveaway like The $64,000 Question draws big ratings, but even so these ratings are due to its entertainment value since the audience can have no expectation of reward. We do not believe any local radio giveaways directly stimulate audience to any great extent. At one time, they did. But now, here in New York you've seen little direct effect on ratings, either short or long run, from WINS' huge giveaway, Kashbox. Neither have WRCA's hidden thousand dollar bills been able to project it into first place. Perhaps the novelty of entering such contests has worn off for a large share of the audience. Too many people have entered station contests and have not won. These local station contests and giveaways still have indirect, long-run value to the station, but not value because of sudden increases in ratings.
>
> Our station in Milwaukee, WRIT, made notable gains quicker than a peg-legged man in a forest fire--despite Wisconsin's asinine laws which virtually forbid contests of any description. In El Paso our KELP deliberately went four months without a promotion just to see what would happen. Instead of dropping, our share of audience in El Paso actually climbed 2%--to 55%. Our station in San Antonio, KTSA, maintains a solid first place position in both Pulse and Hooper and yet for the past four months KTSA has had few giveaway contests.
>
> Here in New York, WNEW leads in both Hooper and Pulse and I can't think of the last time WNEW had a contest or giveaway. WIND shows terrific command of Chicago, yet if WIND has ever had a giveaway contest I can't remember it. I can give you endless striking examples--the newest is WOAM, which bounced to the top in Miami Hooper in 90 days with no giveaways or contests at all.
>
> So you say, if local contests and giveaways do not directly increase value, why have them?
>
> The value of most contests to us is that, first, they stimulate talk, and second, lend an atmosphere of excitement and sparkle to the station. We believe that, even though some stations lead by large margins without such contests and

> giveaways, they could increase their overall general margin in share of audience by promotions (of which contests are but one type) the like of which our McLendon stations use. Mind you, I didn't say they could increase their share of audience for one period or one month, but, perhaps, show quarterly and yearly increases in share of audience. . . .
>
> . . . If anything I have said sounds like an apology for prize contests, it shouldn't. They aren't necessary to rating domination. And, furthermore--at least on the local scene--contests and giveaways have been exaggerated out of all proportion to their real significance by those low in ratings. Stations which have little audience tend to seize upon anything for defense of their humble position. It has become fashionable to defend against leading stations by falsely claiming that giveaways have led to their dominance, when the real truth is that they lead because of hard work and superior programming.
>
> Promotions have numerous collateral values. We think that the presence of certain promotions, especially continuing promotions, identifies the station in the listener's mind so that he or she is able to answer interviewers more accurately. And promotions generate public interest in and attention to radio and thus increase sets-in-use. In Milwaukee, where at least three stations aggressively promote radio, morning sets-in-use have crawled to 18.8 and afternoons to 14.1, according to Hooper. Promotion has done this. Compare Milwaukee to some other, stagnant markets where Hooper shows sets-in-use less than 10%. . . .[112]

McLendon's generally excellent analysis of the usefulness of prize contests as promotions is marred only by a slight exaggeration in the case of the Milwaukee station, WRIT, which did not do very well without prize contests, and in the statement that promotions help to identify the station in the listener's mind "so that he or she is able to answer interviewers more accurately," when "accuracy" is not really the goal.

Storz

Coincidentally, the end of December 1956 saw a statement very similar to McLendon's issued to the advertising trade by Todd Storz. Storz's defense of promotions was in the form of a letter replying to

---

[112] "Gimmicks and Giveaways," Broadcasting, December 24, 1956, pp. 36, 38.

a wide-ranging article on broadcasting in the December 10, 1956 Advertising Age. Part of that article under the heading "Stations and 'Jukes'" said:

> Without doubt the publicity champion has been Todd Storz, head of the five-station Storz chain, whose success in operating "jukebox" stations and building interest in them with local treasure hunts earned him fame as a kind of arch-devil of radio broadcasting. . . .
>
> . . . A frown from the FCC eventually buried the most sensational of these circulation-builder contests, ending an orgy of audience-buying by Storz and competitors in Minneapolis. Yet there were still enough of them going a month or two ago that a couple of ARTB meetings were impelled to warn the ratings services against any extra ratings they might produce. . . .[113]

Storz replied in the December 31 issue of Advertising Age, and in his letter echoed many of the themes McLendon had sounded less than half a month earlier.

> To the Editor:
>
> First of all, may I commend you for devoting a considerable portion of your Dec. 10 issue to the broadcasting industry, and thank you for the references you made to the Storz stations.
>
> At the same time, we seriously object to being described as "juke box" stations, a phrase invented by competitors of modern, entertaining and informative listening which today's radio audiences have found much to their liking. It is no more apt a description of us than if we referred to competitive stations using network programming as "soap opera machines"; or "do nothing specialists."
>
> Furthermore, it is simply not true that we indulged in "an orgy of audience buying . . . in Minneapolis." It is a fact that in what we felt was a proper ratio to the overall broadcast day, we engaged in several contests and so-called "give-away" programs simply as a small part of a very much larger and continuing promotion of our station WDGY in Minneapolis. It is particularly significant that we have long since discontinued all such "give-away" programs at all of our stations, and our audiences have continued to grow everywhere. The most revealing and most recent example of this success has been in Miami, where WQAM vaulted into first place in audience in approximately 90 days without the use of a single so-called

---

[113] L. S. Botts, "Big Advertisers Like It Local, Radio Finds," Advertising Age, December 10, 1956, p. 86.

"give-away" contest. The theory that contests "buy audiences" has been exploded once and for all by our WQAM experience in Miami. As a further interesting footnote, some of our competitors in Minneapolis and the other cities are still running various "give-away" contests and are generally not succeeding in gaining audience.

We are convinced that the size of a station's audience closely parallels the entertainment value of the programming content offered and the over-all service provided to the station's listening area. As an organization, we concentrate much of our time and energy in trying to assure maximum audience appeal in everything we do. . . .

. . . At times, it seems that nobody likes our programming but the listeners.

(Signed, Todd Storz)[114]

In spite of Storz's protestations that "give-aways" had been stopped, it would not be accurate to say that contests of all kinds had ceased on the Storz stations. One week after Storz's letter appeared in Advertising Age, a short article appeared in Broadcasting announcing that WQAM was offering $100 to any parakeet that could clearly say, "I like the new WQAM, 5-6-0 on your radio."[115] Perhaps the $100 was not a prize but a "talent fee."

On March 1st, 1957, Storz sent a letter to the FCC notifying the Commission that his stations were no longer going to prohibit "legitimate" promotional efforts, which included give-aways. Storz's reason was the FCC's inattention to a complaint he had filed earlier in the year against New Orleans station WSMB which Storz claimed was using money giveaways under the direction of the tentative new ownership of the station.[116] Storz did not claim that WSMB ownership had a

---

114"Programs Include Many Services, Storz Head Says," Advertising Age, December 10, 1956, p. 32.

115"No Birdbrain Here," Broadcasting, January 7, 1957, p. 88.

116"Storz Scores FCC Inaction on WSMB," Broadcasting, March 11, 1957, p. 74.

"giveaway pattern" among its other stations as the FCC had charged to Storz, and taken as a whole, his protest seems on the face of it to be mere petulance. Further, it would seem to be a means of justifying the company's re-introduction of a full complement of promotions, including giveaways, which was probably being forced upon him for competitive reasons.

Treasure Hunts were continuing across the country, but none with stakes as high as those staged by Storz and McLendon in 1956. WORL, Boston was hiding $100 a week;[117] KJOY, Stockton, California had a $25,000 hunt in July 1957 (but the prize was reduced to only $500 because it wasn't found in time);[118] McLendon's KILT in Houston staged a $25,000 hunt in August, even after McLendon's disclaimers of needing such promotions;[119] and by October 1957 WRCA had planted its 30th $1,000 check in two years of irregularly-run treasure hunts.[120] Even as late as the spring of 1958, KMYR in Denver held a $50,000 treasure hunt which resulted in "uprooted trees, tracked-across lawns, jammed streets, pulled up street signs and generally . . . a mess."[121]

---

[117]Advertisement in Broadcasting, February 11, 1957, p. 101.

[118]"KJOY Stockton Sponsors $25,000 Treasure Hunt," Broadcasting, August 12, 1957, p. 109.

[119]"'H' Marks the Spot," Broadcasting, August 26, 1957, p. 80.

[120]"City Treasure Hunt Gives Radio a Boost," Business Week, October 5, 1957, p. 44.

[121]"KMYR Goldrush Blitzes Denver," Billboard, May 19, 1958, p. 6.

Prize Contests in Decline

In February 1966 the FCC effectively "outlawed" treasure hunts by issuing a rather severe warning. Citing complaints of damage to public parks, libraries and museums, the infringement of public or private property rights or the right of privacy, annoyance and/or embarrassment to innocent people, traffic congestions and health and safety hazards, the Commission warned that "Contests or promotions which result in consequences such as these raise serious questions as to the sense of responsibility of the broadcast licensee involved."[122]

Contests with smaller prizes and less likelihood of creating a public disturbance have, of course, continued but the "big money" treasure hunts of 1956 (with lesser imitators throughout the late 1950s) have not been resurrected.

Today's prize contests are simpler, less spectacular, but more topical, such as the Spiro Agnew Hardhat contest worked out by Bill Stewart on WNOE in 1971. Besides the FCC's warning, there is the fact that the present generation of listeners is both skeptical of big money giveaways and tired of hearing about them as well. Even a "joke" contest, such as, "Send in $25,000 and we will send you 25 words or less," probably does as much to increase listenership today as the same idea worded the "right" way.

The treasure hunts and other prize contests which marked especially the Storz and McLendon operations of the mid-1950s were the most widely-reported of all of their station promotions. In the

---

[122] "FCC Eyes Complaints on 'Treasure Hunts,'" Sponsor, February 21, 1966, p. 110.

extensive "borrowing" that has always gone on among music-and-news operators, it was inevitable that the big-money treasure hunts and other spectacular promotions would be adopted across the nation as part of the overall "formula" for attracting and holding an audience, and in turn for showing prospective advertisers that the station was showing some "action." Probably too many stations assumed that the spectacular prize contest would be <u>both</u> an instantaneous and a lasting hypo to their ratings. As has been shown, such contests operated at both levels, depending on the size of the prize and on the familiarity of the listening audience with the given type of promotion.

It is curious that all of the many stations that used the big-money treasure hunt in an attempt to hypo their ratings failed to realize that timebuyers would not be likely to be persuaded by sudden and difficult-to-sustain jumps in audience share. <u>Broadcasting</u> provided ample warning when it said,

> As a rule, the timebuyer will take notice of increased audience claims as translated from a rise in ratings. But nary a one, so long as he is aware of the cause of the upswing, will plunge headlong into a buy. All of those questioned indicated they ordinarily would wait and see if a sudden rating rise could be sustained for any length of time.[123]

The statement was made in 1956.

Promotions and spectacular prize contests were the ingredients of Top 40's success "formula" that "put the station on the map" when the process of diffusion had passed beyond the Storz and McLendon innovators to the imitators in smaller markets. Often burdened with a

---

[123]"Timebuyers Cautious of 'Giveaway-Hypoed' Station Ratings," <u>Broadcasting</u>, December 24, 1956, p. 37.

high dial position seldom frequented by listeners to the low-numbered old-line network outlets, the hoopla and "show-business" glamor of audience promotion made converts to local independent stations. These "mavericks" were simply "the only exciting radio on the dial" as Bill Stewart puts it.[124] Whatever the excesses of some of the stunts, nevertheless Top 40 promotion brought radio back to the knowledge that it was, indeed, in the entertainment business--that what the public wanted was not "programs" but shows, in the sense of show business. Top 40 promotion proved to listeners and broadcasters alike that radio had a glamor and an appeal not arrogated to the distant and unknowable network star, nor usurped by the flicker of the magic new TV screen.

---

[124] Bill Stewart interview.

CHAPTER SEVEN

TOP 40 MANAGEMENT'S POLICIES ON OTHER ELEMENTS OF PROGRAMMING

As has been shown in the previous chapter, continuing talk-generating promotions were a large and important part of the Top 40 success formula. Prize contests such as treasure hunts were among the most popular of promotions and served along with other types to keep the station's call letters constantly before the public and in the trade press. The philosophy behind constant promotion was that if a station could attract more audience by being fresh and by being "the only exciting radio on the dial," it could in turn show upward action in the ratings to advertisers.

Ratings Hypos

The philosophy summarized above became a motive in the phenomenon of ratings hypos. A ratings hypo, in one restricted definition, is a device whose primary goal is to increase a station's ratings, regardless of what else it may also accomplish. It is the author's belief that the general idea of keeping Top 40 stations fresh and exciting via promotions preceded the institution of intentional ratings hypos, for various Top 40 promotions were tried in the days prior to any recorded evidence of intentional ratings hypos. It seems likely that when Top 40 management discovered what effect various promotions had on the ratings, then certain promotions were run specifically to have the desired effect.

Ratings hypos must also be understood in the context of a long (and continuing) history in broadcasting. An especially comprehensive three-part article in Advertising Age in 1958 offered a good perspective on the practice. Comparing promotions-as-hypos in radio and TV, the article said,

> Radio: Promotion in this medium tends to lead a life of its own, independent of programming except as programs become a vehicle for it. . . . Promotion supplies the local color even as it used to at the peak of the newspaper promotional wars 20 or 30 years ago. . . .
>
> . . . As the variety show of local radio, promotion becomes a pretty constant thing, and rating week promotions have to be seen as simply the periodic climax to a steady effort. For the most promotion-minded stations perhaps the distinguishing mark of a rating period is that the most competing cash give-aways are reserved for it.
>
> Television: Giveaways are apparently increasing in importance in this medium, but program promotion is still the main lever with which to raise a rating. The standard device is to arrange the programming so that the best movies and the most challenging local shows appear in the rating period.
>
> Newspaper advertising (which radio stations seldom bother with) gives these treats advance billing, as does on-the-air advertising. But the program is still the thing.[1]

Calling rating week hypos "a very old device,"[2] the Advertising Age article described some of the practices of the radio networks in the past:

> . . . In their time, the networks have all engaged in such practices as overloading variety shows with big-name talent during rating week--and correspondingly over-promoting the shows.
>
> Most of these efforts in recent years have been aimed at influencing the Trendex poll, which is based on

---

[1] "Rating Hypo Fought by Stations; Not Agencies," Advertising Age, July 14, 1958, p. 3.

[2] Ibid., p. 54.

> measurements in only 15 large cities and has the added virtue of rating on the first week of the month. One well-honored device has been the so-called "Trendex Tours," in which stars of network shows appear in the major (Trendex) markets to rev up the ratings.[3]

Ratings hypos, it should be noted, were made both possible and lucrative by the fact that, for all but a few of the top markets, it was simply too expensive to maintain continuous ratings. Therefore, all the services except Nielsen relied on the ratings as determined in a single week of the month, usually the first week of the month so that the report could be issued by the end of the given month. Nielsen supplied four-week averages, but only in the larger markets. Since the medium to small-sized markets were surveyed only two to four times a year or even only once, it was worth it for a station to spend the time and effort to hypo its rating during rating week since the inflated figure would be reflected for a long period of time thereafter. It is this fact that led a "substantial majority of stations [to] practice it wherever ratings are made."[4] It should also be remembered that ratings at this time were still fairly rudimentary, consisting usually only of share of audience or program rating expressed in terms of "bodies" rather than precisely defined demographic categories. For the most part, audience composition figures had to be obtained on special request. The Advertising Age article noted that these could be useful in exposing a hypo "since hyperpromotional stations tend to have an

---

[3] Ibid.

[4] "Rating Week Hypo Cuts Rational Buying of Time," Advertising Age, July 7, 1958, p. 38.

especially heavy share of teen-agers in their audiences."[5]

Milwaukee Case

In late December 1955 and early January 1956, a ratings-hypo battle was waged in Milwaukee between WOKY and WEMP on the one hand and representatives of seven other Milwaukee stations on the other. The group of seven had brought to the attention of both the deputy district attorney and the local Better Business Bureau certain practices of stations WOKY and WEMP. The stations were airing promotions designed to induce listeners to tell interviewers that they were listening to one of the stations, whether or not they were.[6] WEMP later claimed that it had "fought fire with fire" by running such a promotion to prove that phone surveys could indeed be rigged.[7] To WEMP's claim, Bill Weaver, manager of McLendon's Milwaukee outlet, WRIT, wrote the following reply in a letter to Broadcasting:

> WEMP's martyr-like stand for unbiased and honest surveys for Milwaukee is like the man who murdered his wife because his children were too friendly with their mother.
>
> The fact of the matter is: WEMP conducted an on-the-air gimmick specifically designed to induce Milwaukee listeners to falsify listening habits, and to influence the national survey picture in Milwaukee, and now because other Milwaukee radio stations (including the writer's) made objections, WEMP is now taking the position that they wanted to prove surveys could be corrupted, and the only way they could do this was to fight "fire with fire."
>
> The excuse behind this reasoning is because of a similar gimmick previously broadcast by WOKY, but WOKY, at least, had

---

[5] "Rating Hypo 'Cures' Bring on New Maladies," Advertising Age, July 21, 1958, p. 24.

[6] "Milwaukee Outlets Hit Rigged Phone Surveys," Broadcasting, January 6, 1956, p. 96.

[7] "A Tale of 3 Cities: Rating Rhubarbs," Broadcasting, January 16, 1956, p. 82.

the foresight to stop their promotion after the national survey companies discussed this ill-advised practice with them.

Some three weeks or more lapsed between the campaigns of WOKY and WEMP, and WEMP's stand of fighting "fire with fire" is a little belated inasmuch as the fire has already been put out.

WEMP's promotion, therefore, was totally unnecessary inasmuch as WOKY had previously proved WEMP's point: that surveys could be corrupted by unethical and dishonest endeavors.

Just for the record: let it be known that WOKY was the first culprit and WEMP was the second culprit. No other Milwaukee radio stations have deemed it necessary to resort to such ill-advised practices.

Bill Weaver, Gen. Mgr.
WRIT, Milwaukee, Wis.[8]

In a speech almost concurrent with the events in Milwaukee which led to Weaver's letter, Gordon McLendon stated to the Radio and Television Executives Society that

> I should like to distinguish between legitimate and illegitimate promotions. I could not and would not defend dishonest promotions which offer prizes to listeners for falsely stating that they have been listening or are listening to any station. Stations employing such devices should be put off the air.[9]

Rating Services Remedies

The McLendon stations do not seem to have been involved in the very direct kind of audience-buying described by both McLendon and Weaver, even though in Milwaukee and San Antonio they had to compete against stations that were using such devices. Note that McLendon and Weaver did not claim to prohibit what others called "indirect" buying of the audience through various other types of promotions and giveaways, and that in fact Wisconsin's strict lottery laws put McLendon's low-powered WRIT at a disadvantage without such promotions. In 1957, KITE

---

[8] "Milwaukee Gimmicks," Broadcasting, January 23, 1956, pp. 18, 22.

[9] "Do Ratings Hypos Help Stations?" Sponsor, January 5, 1957, p. 28.

in San Antonio was encouraging listeners to answer their telephones with its call letters while other stations in town including McLendon's KTSA presumably discouraged the practice. For so doing, Hooper omitted KITE's rating entirely from its San Antonio report because according to Broadcasting,

> . . . there is no way to tell whether a person answering the telephone in such fashion is actually listening to the station he names, or whether he only claims he is listening. On the other hand, they said, if a station conducts a promotion which in itself requires that people be listening in order to win--in contrast to only saying that they are listening--then that station's ratings are not omitted from the report.[10]

Hooper used the same tactic at the same time to combat "promotional excesses" of KOOO and Storz's KOWH, both in Omaha. Pulse approached the problem in the Omaha market in the fall of 1957 in a different way. It decided, as Advertising Age put it, to "institutionalize the individual stations' own practices of telling the advertising agencies and rating services about each other's peccadillos."[11] What Pulse did was to send letters of inquiry to all of the stations in the market about what promotions they and others were doing. Then they printed the substantiated accusations of one station made by another as a frontispiece to the ratings report. Those stations not accused by others of trying to hypo the ratings had their own statements to this effect printed. Here is the Pulse Omaha Report frontispiece as quoted by Advertising Age:

---

[10] "Hooper Omits Ratings on Three Using Local Phone Promotions," Broadcasting, December 9, 1957, p. 35.

[11] "Rating Hypo 'Cures' Bring on New Maladies," Advertising Age, July 21, 1958, p. 22.

Special Programming Efforts During the November Survey Period

KFAB--KFAB is running no cash giveaways such as those you describe in your letter of Nov. 12. Cordially, Lyle Bremser.

KOOO--As reported by another Omaha station, "KOOO is running a mystery voice worth $1,420 and giving clues throughout the day with an added bonus for the person answering the telephone with 'Hello, KOOO.' They also have a cash club with $1,000 prize to women's organizations."

KOWH--As reported by another Omaha station: "KOWH, along with the cash jackpot for 'Lucky House Number,' is giving the listener a chance to win a new 1958 automobile each and every hour of the day."

KOIL--As reported by another Omaha station: "KOIL each hour is running their 'Lucky Telephone Number' twice with cash jackpots of $200 to $500. Once each hour they have a $1,000 cash call to identify a mystery voice."

WOW--This is to certify to you that Regional Radio WOW carried no money giveaways or other artificial stimuli of any kind that might affect ratings taken during the month of November, 1957. Sincerely, Bill Wiseman.[12]

The Advertising Age article noted that "you even hear about stations which diabolically conduct their 'hypos' during the week or ten days just preceding rating week, then lay off during the week itself--'so we don't get listed.'"[13] On the other hand, the article pointed out,

> In radio, where promotion has itself become a form of programming, the problem is trickier still [than with TV]. Accuse a station manager of aiming a promotion at rating week and you'll very likely be right. But chances are he can very quickly show you a similar promotion which was not aimed at a rating week.[14]

WAKY Hypo

The McLendon stations all liked to point to the rapid ratings increases they enjoyed when converting from the programming of former ownership to the McLendon Top 40 formula. It has already been mentioned

---

[12] Ibid. [13] Ibid. [14] Ibid.

that what might at first seem a deception on the part of management in determining beforehand when a station would be proclaimed number one in the ratings was probably a self-fulfilling prophecy instead, both because of the knowledge gained in past successes and because of the audience's usual willingness to listen to a McLendon promotional "blitz." A case in point is the "Louisville Promotion Schedule" which is in effect a three-month-long ratings hypo plan. The details of the Schedule were contained in a memorandum marked "Confidential and Top Secret," which was sent by Don Keyes to Herb Golombeck and Phil Page on July 2, 1958.

> This memo shall consist of a definite schedule of events concerning on-air and off-air promotions for the new WAKY thru 14 September 1958. All promotions scheduled after that are offered as suggestions and you may change them around as you see fit. Following this schedule will be a long memo from me telling of the fine points of each factor mentioned. Since I have been through this two or three times I think it will serve as an excellent guide for you.

(Don Keyes means by the last sentence that he had launched several other stations for McLendon--KTSA and KILT--so that the promotion schedule was one recommended out of his previous experience.) The schedule continues:

8 July	approval
9 July	close, "This is WGRC in Louisville, soon to Whacky," "This is WGRC, BCJS in Louisville" starts.
10 July	Continue BCJS promotion. Continue whacky promotion.
11 July	Explain BCJS, continue whacky promotion.
12 July	Explain BCJS, continue whacky promotion.
13 July	Announce BCJS winner, continue whacky promotion.
14 July	Start record marathon, continue whacky promotion.
15 July	Continue record marathon, continue whacky promotion, "wanted" ads in paper, models on streets, record give-aways.
16 July	End marathon, NEW PROGRAMMING STARTS, mystery phone starts, "found" ads in paper, models on streets, record giveaways, balloon drop.

17 July	Mystery telephone continues, models continue, record giveaways continue, T. H. promos start [probably Treasure Hunt].
18 July	Mystery phone winner, models, record giveaways, T. H. promos.
19 July	T. H. starts, models, pop corn.
20 July	T. H., models, chili peppers.
21 July	T. H., models, picketing.
22 July	T. H., models, picketing.
23 July	T. H., models, cards.
24 July	T. H., models, cards.
25 July	[not copied]
26 July	T. H., models, jumping beans.
27 July	T. H., models, jumping beans.
28 July	T. H., models.
29 July	T. H., flagpole promos start, models.
30 July	T. H., flagpole promos, models.
31 July	T. H. winner, flagpole promos.
1 Aug.	Flagpole sitter goes up, flagpole promos continue thru flagpole stunt.
2 Aug.	"
3 Aug.	"
4 Aug.	Rear Windo promos start.
5 Aug.	[blank]
6 Aug.	Rear Windo contest starts. (Runs TFN) ['Till Further Notice].
8 Aug.	Mystery Walker promos start ($100).
10 Aug.	Mystery Walker contest starts.
13 Aug.	Mystery Walker winner.
14 Aug.	Scrambled phone promos starts.
15 Aug.	Scrambled phone contest starts. "We are now in 4th place in Louisville" promo.
20 Aug.	"We are now in 3rd place in Louisville" promo.
9 Sept.	End scrambled phone contest. "We are now in 2nd place in Louisville" promo.
10 Sept.	"We are now in 1st place in Louisville" promos. "Flagpole sitter is waiting for confirmation in writing" promo before he comes down.
13 Sept.	Flagpole sitter comes down (confirmed)
14	HURRAH! NORMAL ROUTINE OPERATION[15]

It would be a mistake to assume that the McLendon operation was the only one to have promotion schedules of this sort in the late 1950s. It would also not be correct to assume that the schedule was followed "to the letter" in regard to such things as when the various contests

---

[15] Don Keyes, "Louisville Promotion Schedule," McLendon Policy Books, dated July 2, 1958, n.p.

would actually have winners. At a program directors meeting held November 14, 1959, McLendon discussed prize contest policy with the men, and the memo of notes from the meeting issued by Don Keyes corroborates the view that McLendon's contests were not "fixed":

> 1. Gordon emphasized the extreme need for the proper handling of our contests and promotions in the light of the current FCC activity along these lines. We all know that all of our promotions have been carried out in a manner above reproach, but he emphasized the fact that extreme pains must be taken effective immediately in the execution of all contests and promotions where any kind of prize is involved. There have been reports of carelessness in our past promotions where a winner did not get a prize or the prizes were late in coming. This situation should be policed immediately and the prize winners should receive their prizes with the least possible delay. Some stations outside of our company are in the habit of having false winners on contests. Gordon urged that this never be allowed to happen within our organization, and we all know that it never will.[16]

In the very same memo, the following paragraph also appeared:

> 4. I briefed all Program Directors on the format and the operation of "The Spelling Bee" contest which Gordon would like all stations to run as a major Hooper contest the first week of December. You will be receiving formats and instructions from me on this contest within the next few days.[17]

It is important to understand that while McLendon policy was strictly against the fraudulent contest, the ratings hypo was such a way of life for all Top 40 stations that a contest to hypo the ratings was not felt in any way to be against the public interest. The fact of the matter was that in most good-sized markets, the station which did not hypo was in the minority, and suffered accordingly.

Besides the use of prize contests and other gimmicks in ratings

---

[16] Don Keyes, Memorandum to All Managers, McLendon Policy Books, dated November 20, 1959, n.p.

[17] Ibid.

weeks to act as ratings hypos, there were two other devices that were used increasingly into the late 1950s: pronounceable call letters and the station jingle. Both aided the station's ratings by supplying the casual listener with an easily-recalled station name if he were interviewed for ratings purposes.

Mnemonic Devices

Pronounceable Call Letters

Both McLendon and Bartell believed in pronounceable call letters. In 1947, each man put a station on the air with a pronounceable call--McLendon's KLIF and Bartell's WOKY, both obliquely referring to their cities (or sections thereof).[18] Asked if he named WOKY strictly for station recall, Jerry Bartell replied,

> Oh, sure, yeah. Like, "WOKY-in-Milwaukee." That made WOKY. One of the things that made WOKY was "WOKY in Milwaukee." "WOKY walkie-talkie." . . . We used the same gimmick on the trade, too. We had WYDE, WAKE, and WYLD. You know, wide-awake-and-wild. That was for the advertising community. Many of our orders would go, WYDE, WAKE and WYLD. Just like that. . . .[19]

According to former WAKE production manager, Pete Thomas, WAKE was the first station in Atlanta to consistently pronounce its call letters.

> . . . I don't know as we ever gave a legal station ID. I'm not sure. We were going to ask for a clarification and then decided why ask, maybe we aren't. So the station was always identified as "wake."[20]

---

[18]Some others of this type: WACO, Waco, Texas; WARE, Ware, Massachusetts--suggested by Charles W. Godwin, vice president, Mutual Broadcasting System in "More on Call Letters," Broadcasting, November 25, 1963, pp. 29-30.

[19]Bartell interview.

[20]Thomas interview.

At the time, Rounsaville's WQXI was not "quicksie," as it later became, but just W-Q-X-I. Thomas explained that since the station was aware that the ratings were derived from interviews,

> . . . a lot of the station promotion was aimed at making it very easy to remember the station. So they pumped out the call letters every chance they got. And the pronounceable call letters--I don't know who had the inspiration to do that. . . . They actually negotiated for that set of call letters. Before Bartell owned it, the Atlanta station had been religiously-oriented, so he wanted some way to get it completely un-identified with its previous format.[21]

Thomas also pointed out that the first station in the market to do audience promotion with pronounceable call letters had an advantage in the ratings when other stations copied the format: "People may be listening to somebody else, but if they all sound the same, they'll report the one they know the best."[22]

Pronounceable call letters today are somewhat less in vogue, perhaps because so many ways of promoting stations besides pronouncing the call have been developed. Sol Rosinsky, Vice President and General Manager of KOIL in Omaha (one of the Don Burden stations that includes KISN and WIFE), was asked what importance pronounceable call letters have today. He replied,

> . . . Maybe in the beginning when you are trying to establish yourself, it's really helpful. But I can't imagine that in our operation, for instance, that we would be any worse off if our call letters were KXXX. We'd <u>make</u> something out of that. We'd promote it. We'd make something out of it. It's a little easier maybe with a set of memorable call letters.[23]

In modern times, call letters have come to be descriptive of dial position and of format. K-IOI is a West Coast FM station at

---

[21] *Ibid.* [22] *Ibid.*

[23] Rosinsky interview.

101 kHz. WTSO is located at ten-seven-oh on the dial. McLendon's KABL in San Francisco was a smart choice for a city famous for its cable cars, while K-ADS was a good call for his experimental all-classified ads station in Los Angeles, now renamed KŌST-FM (long O). Perhaps the finest marriage of call and format came in Don Keyes' naming of McLendon's first all-news station based in Tijuana, Mexico, which thus had an X prefix. Keyes chortled when he recalled for the author how he beat McLendon to thinking of the perfect call letters: XTRA.

Jingles

The other way--and, according to Bill Stewart, still the most palatable way--to get the call letters known and remembered is via jingles. The station ID jingle industry, it will be recalled, developed rapidly in the middle and late 1950s as a result of the need for stations to differentiate themselves from each other, and to get the call letters before the public more often but in a pleasant way. Under Grahame Richards' Program Directorship, Storz's WQAM in Miami had jingles made for every conceivable Miami temperature, so that instead of a jock reading the temperature, a jingle sang "WQAM mercury says it's 77 degrees," thus slipping in another WQAM mention. In late 1959, McLendon introduced Spanish jingles on his KTSA in San Antonio.[24] Other stations serving large Spanish speaking populations also used some Spanish jingles. The author recalls hearing WQAM, shortly after Cuban refugees began to flood Miami, airing "Este es la estación

---

[24] Don Keyes, Memorandum to All Managers, November 20, 1959, from <u>McLendon Policy Books</u>, n.p.

numera una--es la favorita!" ("This is the number one station--it's the favorite!")

Repetition of Call Letters

It should be pointed out that the use of a singing station identification jingle was only the most palatable, but not the most frequently-used method of getting the station call letters in front of the audience. An analysis of the programming of Bartell's WOKY, Milwaukee, was made in 1961, by Edward F. Douglass as part of the research on his Master's thesis, A Case Study of Formula Radio. Douglass recorded the programming of WOKY for various hours of the broadcast day in April 1961. In a Sunday morning segment (9:00 to 10:00 a.m.), he found that while fifteen singing station IDs were used, "There were 60 occasions when the word "woky" or the letters W-O-K-Y were used."[25]

Station self-promotion via repetition of the call letters in various production elements eventually led to complaints from advertisers that Top 40 stations were spending more time talking about themselves than about the products that supported them, with what was thought to be a corresponding decrease in attention to advertising. Benjamin J. Green, who in 1962 was Vice-President of Arthur Meyerhoff Associates in Chicago, wrote in Advertising Age:

> In the early 1950s when a few stations first hit on the device of using their time signals, weather reports and other station-owned time to help identify their call letters, the little-known or less popular station was in keeping with the

---

[25] Edward F. Douglass, A Case Study of Formula Radio (University of Wisconsin, Madison, Master's Thesis, 1961), p. 41.

> times. Music, news and weather formulas were harder to identify than soap opera.
>
> In the readjustment of listening following the advent of television, it was to be expected that radio broadcasters needed weapons to fight with. Now, any station with the unsold time and ingenuity can hypo its rating regardless of its real position in the listener's market. It can do this to the point where it's impossible to separate the selling messages for products of paying advertisers from the self-adulation messages of stations fighting for extra rating points. The result is a watering-down of the authenticity of the ratings to the point where they may become completely useless. How much is the station damaging itself when its sponsors have to fight not only against their competitors, but against overpowering station identification messages, too?
>
> If all unsold time on a station is employed to drive home the importance of the station call letters, the broadcaster is giving himself far more promotional weight than any advertiser is able to buy on the station. Until recently, it was generally supposed that it was nature's weather, not Station GLOM's weather. It was supposed that time was a universal measurement and not something that was a private possession of Station DUBB.[26]

A 1958 McLendon memo on the use of call letters shows graphically how station management was working to make the call letters unavoidable. It might almost have been the basis for Green's argument. The memo is reproduced on page 478.

What was claimed by RAB and NAB to be the first study ever conducted of the degree to which people knew what station they were listening to found in 1964 that 83% of listeners could identify the station they were listening to at the time of the call, and that 91% of these responses were correct.[27] It would seem likely that the great emphasis placed on call letters and station recall by Top 40 operators and their imitators, plus the growing differentiation of

---

[26] Benjamin J. Green, "Radio Stations Killing the Goose?" Advertising Age, March 12, 1962, p. 94.

[27] "83% of Listeners Know What Station They're Hearing: NAB-RAB Study," Advertising Age, August 24, 1964, p. 8.

USE OF CALL LETTERS BY McLENDON STATIONS
1/6/58

From now on, station call letters, either pronounced or spelled out, will be used a minimum of ten times in each newscast--including intro and close. You can accomplish this by inserting a couple of times "KTSA Dateline Berlin," or "Special to KTSA from Hong Kong," or "KTSA exclusive--Paris," or in innumberable other ways. You could just say "KTSA from Paris," or "Stuttgart to KTSA," and otherwise let your imagination run riot. It will be interesting to see what individual PD's do in this department.

The same saturation use of call letters is to be carried through into disc jockey progr and recorded promos themselves. As you know, all promos should have the station call letters in them seven times. In addition, the disc jockeys themselves are to use the call letters continuously during their show.

To wit:

It is never "the time," It is "KILT time," or "Kilt time."

It is never "the temperature." It is "Klif temperature," or "KLIF temperature."

It is never "the Weather." It is "Keel weather," or "K double E L weather."

It is never "the John Smith Show." It is the "KTSA John Smith Show," or "The John Smith Show on KTEA."

It is never "the news." It is "kilt news," or "KILT news."

It is never "the headlines." It is "klif headlines" or "KLIF headlines."

It is never "the basketball scores, or the football, or the baseball scores." It is "the KEEL scoreboard," or "keel scores," etc.

It is never "the Top Forty." It is "The KTSA Top Forty."

These are but a few of the ways in which we should absolutely brainwash our men. Every time they violate one of the above, or other standards which you will think of, they should be corrected until it becomes an absolute habit and automatic pattern. Again, you will think of many other ways to use the call letters in the deejay show pro You may even wish to set certain rigid standards about how many times the call letters may be used between records but I believe that if you achieve the above standard uses o call letters, plus whatever number the deejay will throw in naturally--plus promos--we will be on our way. And, as covered in the Dallas meeting, deejays are assiduously to avoid an extreme use of the word "I" or "my." Your call letters are the proper substitution.

Okay, you are now flying the airplane.

Gordon McLendon

GBM:bp

stations as they pursued specialized audiences, were responsible for the relatively high percentage of listeners being able to identify a station.

News Policy

The "contemporary music" station that yesterday's Top 40 station has become today generally treats news as something of a step-child. Current thought concludes that since the primary attraction to the listeners lies in the music played, news is therefore a "tuneout" and should be minimized. It is interesting to note that in the formative period of Top 40, Storz and McLendon were quite opposite in their thinking concerning the role of news in Top 40, Storz's view being close to the current one (news is a "tuneout") while McLendon favored a greatly expanded news effort. As will be shown, both were partly right.

Storz's Thinking

In a talk given between 1954 and 1956 at the University of Georgia titled "Independent, Alive and Healthy," Todd Storz explained how his stations' news policy had been derived:

> . . . Radio has long been known as an excellent medium for news. We use one newscast each hour, "five minutes before the hour." We feel sure that our listeners want news and although they have shown signs of crossing us up in the past, I think we now have a common meeting ground with them on our news. At the beginning of the Korean War, the rating on all of our news showed a substantial increase over the program preceding and following the news. But, in early 1951 this trend was completely reversed and we realized that something was wrong with our news policy. Realizing that we could only find out from the listeners, we decided to call approximately 100 of our listeners who had recently sent mail of one sort or another to the station [KOWH, Omaha]. Several of us made these calls and had long discussions with each person called whenever possible.

> While admittedly 100 people represent a very small sample for any survey, the response we obtained was unanimous and we thought the sample was truly significant. Almost without exception, the listeners asked us to stop all news completely.
>
> They didn't like our news--they only endured it to get to our next music program. Summing up their comments, we found that their interest in news was very low, practically negligible, except for a reasonable amount of interest in local news and a great deal of interest in what I will kindly refer to as human interest stories, more particularly Hollywood divorce scandals and the like.
>
> Confronted with this information, we gave serious thought to discontinuing our news, but for many reasons, not the least of which was the fact that our news was very successful in a commercial sense, we decided to make one last try at salvaging our news and making it interesting to the listener. Two additional wire services were ordered, which gave us the facilities of all three of the major wires--AP, UP, and INS. Newscasters stopped their "beat" and instead were asked to spend all available time preparing each newscast by using, virtually without rewrite, wire stories. Knowing what the listeners wanted, we gave it to them in large doses. The truly important news happenings of the day were summed up in a 30-second spot bulletin type summary of the important national and international happenings. The rest of each 5-minute newscast was devoted to the local news, the sensational news they wanted, and weather which was also of considerable interest. Needless to say, there was a great deal of reluctance on the part of the newscasters in following this policy. However, we felt that if we had continued our policy of straight news we would soon have few news listeners at all. As it is at present, we have very high news listening and occasionally, we can sneak in a truly informative news story and our listeners have listened to it before they realize it.
>
> On-the-scene reporting of local news seemed to us to be a good path to pursue. We constructed a mobile unit which had a complete shortwave installation making it possible for us to broadcast from any spot in the area on short notice. These broadcasts are principally of disaster or casualty type stories such as plane crashes, drownings, fires, etc. We interrupt our regular program to broadcast these direct stories.[28]

The material quoted above from Storz's speech is an excellent example of Top 40 management taking an active role in planning programming

---

[28]Todd Storz, "Independent, Alive and Healthy," a talk given at the University of Georgia between 1954 and 1956 (the xerox copy of mimeographed manuscript supplied by Grahame Richards was undated), pp. 3, 4.

that gives the public what it wants rather than what a broadcaster thinks it ought to have. What Storz alludes to in the difference he discovered in KOWH's ratings between the time of the Korean War and the quieter period afterward, is a combination of news-seeking behavior on the one hand and news avoidance on the other. Apparently, the majority of the KOWH audience in the early 1950s avoided national and international news except when it was of such a threatening nature that they might be personally affected by it, in the same way that they might be affected by a garbage collection strike in their city. Hollywood personalities and others with whom the audience identified also had this personal affectiveness dimension, which seems to the author a more precise and descriptive term than mere "local" news.

McLendon's Thinking

While Storz says in the speech excerpt quoted above that "we gave serious thought to discontinuing our news . . ." Gordon McLendon was working throughout the early '50s to increase and expand KLIF's news coverage. It was McLendon's belief that news was the one format factor that kept a music-oriented station from becoming a jukebox. Even if the very same records and commercials were repeated endlessly, the news was ever-changing. By definition, news was constantly fresh and novel, and thus an asset to a station that wanted to make people afraid to turn it off for fear of missing something.

McLendon believed that KLIF's news coverage was the one format factor most responsible for the success of the station. While it is likely the music and its presentation were more important, it is probably true that KLIF's efforts in local news enticed a great many adult listeners to stay tuned to a station they might otherwise have been glad to ignore. Top 40 news as developed by both Storz and McLendon became an asset to the station by complementing the music, personalities and promotions, all of which caused Top 40 to be "the only exciting radio on the dial."

Local Emphasis

Mobile units

Top 40 radio seems to be the first format which specified that emphasis in coverage be placed on local rather than national stories. In a 1953 speech before the Kansas Association of Radio Broadcasters, Jim Reed, executive editor of the Topeka Daily Capital, quoted a time-buyer for a large advertising agency as telling Reed the following:

> Probably the biggest complaint I have against radio newscasts is this: The powerful, metropolitan stations with good news departments frequently put too much of their emphasis on purely local news that is not of real interest to their entire listening audience. Local stations, with limited news staffs, frequently put too much of their emphasis on purely national and world news. It occurs to me that the one thing a local station can do, that its outside competition cannot touch, is to lean heavily on news of a purely local nature . . . news that would not be of sufficient value or interest for coverage from the outside. On the other hand, it occurs to me that some of the larger stations could increase the effectiveness of their statewide coverage by trimming their purely local news and increasing their area of regional coverage.[29]

By the time Jim Reed made the speech from which the quote above was excerpted, McLendon's KLIF in Dallas already had its first mobile unit on the street covering local news. The first one at KLIF was a Ford "Courier" panel truck which was painted bright red. It housed

---

[29] Jim Reed, "What's Right and Wrong with Radio News," Broadcasting, November 30, 1953, p. 94.

shortwave equipment for sending transmissions back to the studio to be put on the air "live." By July of 1954, McLendon had had enough experience with the mobile news unit to be able to write to KELP manager Joe Roddy describing both its cost and its value:

> The third item is the news truck. Including payments on the truck and equipment, this would cost you around $600 a month--that would include a newsman, gasoline and oil and maintenance and the whole works. I can't tell you how important our mobile news unit is to us. It is just indescribably valuable.[30]

It is interesting to note that mobile news units were a highly imitated piece of broadcasting equipment. For a while in the late 1950s, virtually every radio station in the country had some kind of vehicle painted up as a "news cruiser." A substantial number of these had no more equipment inside than a salesman with a dime for the telephone, but they served as effective rolling advertisements for the station. A station that did not at least pretend to have some kind of a local news car was just not "with it."

Selection of stories

The news cars provided the means to cover local news, but management supplied the incentive for doing so. If an exciting sound was the goal, then the question of what generated the most interest in a newscast had to be determined. Todd Storz is quoted in 1957 as having said:

> "We try to lead off with a local item. Our view is that the average person is more concerned with the auto accident that happens around the corner than with the United Nations I came to this view from newspaper readership studies which

---

[30] Gordon McLendon, letter to Joe Roddy, July 27th, 1954, from McLendon Policy Books, n.p.

show that interest in local news is higher than in national or international events.

"However, we definitely do cover national and international news, though we usually give it headline rather than detailed treatment."[31]

In "The Storz Bombshell," author Herman Land defended Storz from the charge that his newscasts were loaded with "sensationalism" by providing a list of the items aired on the 8:55 a.m. newscast of KOWH on April 11, 1957 (in order):

Winner of Mrs. Nebraska contest
Mid-western fugitive returned to Tennessee for prison term
Reform school escapees held for stealing automobiles
Iowa murder arraignment
Davenport barmaid cleared of jail break connection
Kansas State Prison warden refuses to resign
Evacuation of Pennsylvania families in face of spreading chlorine gas fumes
Eisenhower budget director on post office financial crisis
Hearing of newsmen's protest of State Department's ban on travel to Red China
Senator Sparkman on foreign aid
Izvestia on U.S.-Israel plan to construct new Mediterranean port
Saudi-Arabian warning to Israel on Gulf of Aqaba
Israeli report on Jordan crisis.[32]

It is apparent from the list above that roughly the first half of the newscast was devoted to news of regional interest, while the second half dealt more heavily with national and international affairs. An in-state story led the newscast, with a gradual widening of focus through to the international news.

Sensationalism

As to the charge of sensationalism, it at one time had both a basis in fact and was also a result of the manner in which the news

---

[31]Herman Land, "The Storz Bombshell," reprint, p. 7 of 8.

[32]_Ibid._, p. 6 of 8.

was presented, in a staccato, rapid-fire manner. Land quotes Storz as saying

> "We don't emphasize sensation as much as we did at the beginning. But we still go in for what would be more correctly described as human interest, as well as Hollywood material. As with our music, our policy is guided by what the audience wants to hear."[33]

McLendon also was emphasizing Hollywood stories. Hollywood reporter Jimmy Fidler was a taped regular feature of McLendon newscasts. In 1954, McLendon wrote in his letter to Joe Roddy, "And let's not forget that we have a standing rule--no fewer than twelve items must go into any four and a half minute newscast and that one item on every newscast must be a Hollywood story."[34]

The Hollywood columnist of the air continued to be popular on Storz and McLendon stations into the late 1950s. In 1957 Storz said,

> We pretty much do things we are sure will be acceptable to the mass of the people. We know the average housewife is more interested in a Hollywood divorce case than a roundup of United Nations news. We run the UN news, but in a very supplementary way. We may favor the Hollywood story for length.[35]

In June of 1957, the Storz stations went into the syndication business with an exclusive contract with Hollywood columnist Mike Connolly, who was due to tape 63 short news inserts per week for subscribing stations. All of the Storz stations (except KOMA, not then acquired) were subscribers.[36]

---

[33] Ibid.

[34] Gordon McLendon, letter to Joe Roddy, July 27, 1954, from McLendon Policy Books, n.p.

[35] Printed information derived from the interview with Bill Stewart, material dated June 1957, n.p.

[36] "Storz in Syndication with Connolly Series," Broadcasting, June 3, 1957, p. 61.

News Tips

A feature of Top 40 news that has lasted even longer than the emphasis on a Hollywood gossip column is the news-tip award, by which a listener who telephones significant news information to the station wins a dollar or more for his efforts. This was not an original idea with Top 40. WCKY, Cincinnati, for one, had the news tip system in effect in 1947.[37] Storz began using it in 1949 with KOWH.[38] WWDC, Washington, D.C., managed to get over a full page in Broadcasting in 1957 describing the news tip system that it had started to use a year earlier. The report elaborated on the WWDC gimmick as if it were something new. Various stations said that the news tip typically produced from five to 60 news tips per day, with the cost per year running far less than the salary of one fulltime newsman.

Presentation

Storz began a practice that has become almost universal with Top 40 and contemporary music stations: the placement of the newscast at five minutes before the hour. The reason for this is simple--those for whom news is a "tuneout" and who are confronted on the hour with news on some other station will find the Top 40 station playing music when they turn the dial, and may stay tuned.

The news was not read in the rather straightforward manner generally found today, but was delivered with much "personality" on the part of the newscaster, who spoke in the same rapid, staccato style

---

37. "Dollars for News Tips," Broadcasting, January 23, 1956, p. 91.

38. Herman Land, "The Storz Bombshell," reprint, p. 6 of 8.

that the disc jockeys employed. Very often, on smaller stations, the disc jockeys were the newscasters because of lack of air personnel. In such cases, the disc jockey often had to select, edit and rewrite the news himself. In a small operation without an engineer to run the hand-cued transcriptions, there was seldom time for such amenities, which led to the "rip-and-read" approach: rip the newscast off of the teletype machine and read it "cold," hoping that all of it had been sent ungarbled. The "rip-and-read" label was applied to many Top 40 stations even though the practice generally was confined to the small stations in small markets. McLendon, Storz, and Bartell all had actual news staffs and did not use the jock to read news. Because the pace of Top 40 required such an output of energy and exuberance from the disc jockey, he generally needed five minutes an hour to recuperate anyway.

Almost all stations, regardless of the size (or even the existence, or lack of it) of their news departments, promoted their news operation. The mobile units were one example. "News teasers"--headlines from a story to be reported later in the hour--were another, and one that McLendon especially liked his stations to employ. Jingles and catch-phrases also extolled the virtues of the station's news effort.

Any deficiencies in the actual substance of the news provided by small-time Top 40 stations were likely to be overlooked because of their imitation of the manner in which large Top 40 stations "showcased" their newscasts. Regardless of the fact that a bone-tired jock was hoarsely delivering the news exactly as UPI had sent it, sentence fragments and all, the many special effects injected into the typical Top 40 newscast caused it to sound like the most exciting and urgent information ever spoken. Typically, a newscast would open with some kind of attention-getting device: an explosion, a gong, a bell, a siren or perhaps a mere news jingle.[39] Then a sound effects recording of teletype machines or typewriters might be inserted in the background to let listeners know that this was the newsroom. (Live pickups of actual teletype machines could not be counted on because sometimes the press wire did not send anything while the newscast was being read, in which case a dull humming was all there was to be heard.) If the news were given with datelines, several devices could be brought in to handle these. One was a reverberation unit which gave an added authority to the name of the city where the story had originated. Another was the use of a high-pass filter, which effectively cut off all the bass and most of the mid-range frequencies of the announcer's voice, simulating a telephone's frequency response. The author worked at a Top 40 station in 1961 which used an old earphone (wired as a microphone) which was taped next to the regular air microphone to accomplish the filter effect. The filtering was so complete that at times the disc jockey really did sound like another person giving the datelines. The filter was also used for the concluding weather forecast, to give the effect of a direct report from the weather bureau without the weather bureau's generally unsatisfactory voices. Stations also used <u>two</u> voices on newscasts, so that before the first had finished his concluding sentence, the other was already beginning another story.

---

[39] Bill Stewart says that he developed the <u>produced</u> news intro/outro at KLIF in 1954.

The total effect of all of the devices and practices just described was to create excitement, or as McLendon National Program Director Don Keyes described what he wanted in 1959, "blood and thunder."[40] Station KWIZ, in Santa Ana, California, in 1955 admitted that its news style was designed to be "tabloid journalism."[41] WOKY, Milwaukee, formerly Bartell's flagship station, still has newscasts which can be most directly compared to the tabloid approach of The New York Daily News.

News As a "Tuneout"

By 1960, two emerging factors began to cause stations to decrease their use of news "production," although many smaller stations continued the practice for a number of years. One was the growing importance of adult listeners, who presumably were not as enthusiastic about the noises and gimmicks as were teenagers. The other was the fact that news itself had been discovered to be a tuneout for the majority, no matter how well done it was. In 1959, speaking of the recent vogue for mobile news units and the practice of breaking into a record with a report, Bill Stewart said "There are good reasons why these mobile news units haven't really caught on. . . . Much of the novelty has been dissipated."[42] In 1961, with its first real challenge of ratings leadership coming from KBOX, the Balaban's Dallas outlet,

---

[40] Don Keyes, Memorandum to Gordon McLendon on KTSA, February 5, 1959, McLendon Policy Books, n.p.

[41] Pat Michaels, "How to Scoop the Field with Radio," Sponsor, June 13, 1955, p. 92.

[42] "A Programming Expert Evaluates Radio," Television Magazine, November 1959, p. 63.

McLendon's KLIF held a series of programming meetings, one of which produced the following policy on Mobile News Reports:

> (a) Mobile News Unit Reports are to be brief and to the point. Written out before going on the air except in situations dictating immediacy. (b) More emphasis to be placed on first-person interviews . . . eyewitnesses. (c) Repetition/rebroadcast of mobile reports will be done when story and timeliness of report dictate need. In most cases, they will not be because story will be updated through the day. (d) More attention needs to be given to localizing of national stories. (e) Policy on story qualifying for mobile coverage eliminates traffic accidents and holdups unless of an unusual or interesting nature.[43]

The thrust of the quotation above is to try to eliminate "chatty" news and to concentrate instead on the unusual and the spectacular. This same theme is reiterated in a 1964 memo from Keyes to all managers, program directors and managing editors, about which news stories should be "billboarded"--or talked about in advance of their being reported. The first memo, dated June 7, 1963, is reproduced on pages 491 and 492.[44] In the second, dated January 8, 1964, Keyes supplied a list of nine stories which did not qualify, and then explained again what he wanted:

> . . . the following stories do not qualify for billboarding.
> 1. Pope's visit to the Holy Land
> 2. Commissioners' Court budget hearing
> 3. Adenauer's resignation
> 4. $1,000 winner in Mystery Home Buyer Contest
> 5. Plan . . . for "Freedom Day" school boycott
> 6. Exceptionally warm weather and record drought
> 7. Kennedy's planned visit to Army-Air Force game and cancellation
> 8. President Johnson's pledge to act on Civil Rights
> 9. President Johnson at the Texas White House
>
> A story to be billboarded must be, as pointed out previously,

---

[43] Don Keyes, Notes from KLIF Programming Meeting, August 24, 1961, from McLendon Policy Books, n.p.

[44] From McLendon Policy Books, n.p.

MEMORANDUM

TO: ALL McLENDON STATION MANAGERS

cc: All Managing Editors

FROM: DON KEYES

DATE: JUNE 7, 1963

I wish to remind you about the practice of what we choose to call "billboarding", which a few years ago was a vital mainstay of our on-the-air sound. For those of you who are relatively new to the operation, I will take a moment to explain what this is.

It is the constant and frequent mention (whether by ad lib or by prepared live copy) by your disc jockeys on a subject of relatively great magnitude or immediacy, in which some of your listeners might be interested. Billboarding applies to usually two sources--promotions that require, by their nature, continuing emphasis, such as Scotch Dollars, Rear Windo, Flagpole Sitter, Mystery Telephone, etc; and news stories that are:

a.) Sensational and immediate, such as the hourly developments in a trial that is of extreme local interest; a news story, let's say, of a plane crash that would require frequent reports from the scene; etc.

b.) News stories that are not being carried by other media. Usually you will know of these in advance, such as (and this particular story we have used many times in the past) the Davis Cup tennis matches; an important football game that is not being broadcast locally (Notice this should not be just any game, but an important game); etc.

There may be other types of stories you will wish to apply to this business of billboarding but, basically, this pretty well outlines what you should look for as a billboard subject.

After you have chosen the topic to be billboarded, there should be a specific place set aside in your control room for the posting of billboard material--suggested lines to use, ad lib suggestions for your disc jockey to pick up on--and this place should be inviolate. That is, it should never be used for any other purpose. KILT in Houston, for example, has a blackboard hanging in the control room upon which is written in chalk the items worth billboarding.

(continued)

- 2 -

Now that you know what is to be billboarded, and how it is to be presented to the announcers, there are only two other facts to cover, both most important:

1.) The copy must be kept fresh and in many instances, literally up-to-the-minute.

2.) Announcers should be instructed to bill-board an item after every other record.

Without the latter, particularly, you cannot begin to gain the immediacy and the excitement which you are trying to generate.

Don Keyes

ys
3/7/64 (re-issued)

> sensational and immediate or, at least, exclusive. The above stories, obviously, are none of these things. I take this opportunity to caution you on this subject because the type of stories mentioned above can only add more talk to your station without injecting any excitement.[45]

When Madison, Wisconsin station WKOW hired Capital Cities executive Mike Josephs as a programming consultant in 1968 to boost the station's low ratings, Josephs introduced a number of changes in the presentation of the station's news. Although WKOW at the time was clearly a middle-of-the road station musically, it is interesting to note how many of the changes suggested by Josephs for news presentation are directly attributable to Top 40:

1. Insert WKOW identification phrases in stories, such as WKOW News, . . . 1070 News, etc. . . . Average one ident per minute.
4. Average one to three actualities in a 3 minute cast, and one to five in a 5 minute newscast. Any story can be translated into a beeper.
7. Give news according to importance, but follow local, regional, state, national, world pattern, with biggest stories first.
9. Keep production at tight pace. Keep bright, interested, enthusiastic. Project, yet do not scream. Mature and moderate pace in voice and delivery. . . .
12. Average 9 items to a 3-minute newscast, 15 items in a 5-minute newscast. This includes beepers and features.
13. Only use important news. Namedrop locally. Use much human interest. Use people news, de-emphasizing intellectual and routine political and legislative news. Give news that interests the little people. Who and what are they talking about now--and what will they talk about? Talk about news that affects people personally.
15. Watch pace. Do not read slow. No long pauses during or after item. Just a short breath. Omit dead air.
16. Local news--local news---local news---local news![46]

---

[45]Memorandum from Don Keyes to all managers, program directors and managing editors, January 8, 1964, from McLendon Policy Books, n.p.

[46]"WKOW News Techniques," dated February 1968, supplied by the station, mimeographed, n.p.

In spite of the fact that news is still a tuneout for the majority of the contemporary music audience today, news staff sizes have increased at the larger stations since the Top 40 era, according to both Ken Dowe, speaking for McLendon stations, and George Amrstrong for Storz. Disc jockeys no longer also double as news announcers, partly because most stations can now afford the real thing, and partly because the disc jockey is now so used to talking for only a few seconds at a time that he might not be able to do a satisfactory newscast today. Armstrong sums up the change as the same kind of specialization that has happened in football, with different platoons performing different functions.[47]

It should be noted that the news function of a Top 40 station came under the control of the program director, the same as did music, disc jockey talk and other elements. This fact is one of the reasons why, for a time, news presentation went through the same "production showcasing" as all the other format elements on the station. Some of this was mere noise and fluff, but such things as the use of recorded actualities (which the Bartell stations used heavily on their "Voice of the News")[48] did introduce a new standard to local newscasts whereby listeners came to expect to hear actual voices rather than quotations. This change in the expected standards came about mostly by accident, merely as the side effect of the program director's desire to bring as much vitality and variety as possible to his station's newscasts. As Pete Thomas put it, speaking of using such actualities, "you don't do

---

[47] Armstrong interview.

[48] Bartell interview.

it to improve the reporting of the news--you do it to make it sound better."[49] That might well be the capsule statement for all of Top 40 news in the 1950s.

Commercials Policy

It is only recently that the number, placement, and style of the commercials aired on contemporary music stations has become an important consideration. Bill Drake, with his "more music" policy, not only cut down on deejay talk, but also limited the number of commercials that could be aired in a given time period and specified the optimum placement of commercials of various types: straight talk before dramatic, dramatic before musical, and so on. Drake attempted to avoid tuneout by clustering commercials into sets, with both the time and the number of different spots in a set limited, and within that set he decreed that the more thoroughly-produced, more entertaining commercials would be saved for the end of the set.

In the Top 40 era, there was little emphasis on avoiding tuneout by tinkering with fine shades of differences between commercials. The simple fact was that in most medium to small communities, if you wanted to hear the Top 40 records, you had little choice about the station you listened to--there was usually only one. At that time, tuneout, if the phrase were used at all, would have referred to turning off the set entirely rather than changing to another station. The people who liked Top 40 tuned it in then regardless of the station's

---

[49] Thomas interview.

commercials policy (or lack of one) simply because there was nowhere else to hear the same music consistently.

The commercials policies which developed in the 1950s were not nearly so much concerned with programming (as they are today on Drake-consulted stations) as with getting the commercials sold. The early Top 40 period is characterized by difficulty in selling commercials, the middle period (about at the beginning of the 1960s) displayed a generally oversold condition just prior to the time when other stations began counter-programming to re-attract an audience to themselves, and the late (or current) period is the one in which Drake led the way in limiting and placing spots using "psychology."

Difficulty in Selling

There was a time when Gordon McLendon would trade a spot on KLIF for a haircut.[50] In the early days, it was difficult to convince most advertisers that the audience of a Top 40 station was not limited to teenagers. Bill Stewart's "Secret Word" promotion was a fine method of proving to an advertiser that adults were listening, since adults would continually tell the person, "Hey, I hear you're KLIF's secret word." It was one of the few tools a station had to demonstrate to a prospective advertiser that there were adults among the high shares the station was garnering according to the simple, non-demographic ratings then available. Still, the more conservative advertisers refused to buy Top 40. Donald Meyers, General Manager of WAKY,

---

[50] Ken Dowe interview.

Louisville, for LIN Broadcasting recalls the problem as it was even in the early 1960s:

> . . . everyone thought of us as having no one under the age of -- because all their kids listened to the radio station, so they figured well, this is a teen radio station. So we fought this for many years. We couldn't get the banks on the air, the savings and loans. We got all the movie business and the soft drinks and the beers and all that stuff, but we couldn't get what you might call the 52-week, or the more substantial type of advertiser, like the banks and the savings and loans. Well, this we've beat down--they finally understand that our listeners have grown up, and contemporary music has a sound that's not like it used to be. . . .
>
> . . . .
>
> A contemporary station measures its success by ringing cash registers. Most of our clients for many years were cash register clients. In other words, a savings and loan is not. A bank is not. But the man selling an automobile, or a department store, or somebody with sporting goods--you ring their cash registers on Thursday, Friday, and Saturday. This is how you prove you have people listening.[51]

Sunday problems

In the era when the majority of Top 40 stations' revenue came from "ringing cash registers," Sunday became a major problem in selling time, since in those days few businesses had Sunday hours and thus could not benefit directly from a sales message. A memorandum from McLendon, after an AIMS meeting, to all his station managers and to his sales people at KLIF, written October 26, 1955, mentions some of the problems of selling Sundays (and other times).

> Bud Armstrong is selling Sunday by creating an "artificial shortage" of time. When an advertiser calls wanting spots on Friday and Saturday [traditionally the two most heavily-subscribed days] or perhaps on Saturday only, Bud will tell that advertiser that he just doesn't have the 20 spots that the advertiser requests on Friday and Saturday--even though he may have all the free time in the world those two days. But, he says to the sponsor, we can give you 7 on Friday, 7 on

---

[51] Meyers interview.

Saturday, and 6 on Sunday. The sponsor, more correctly the agency, invariably takes it because he already has an okay from his client on buying that many spots on your particular station. It takes a lot of nerve to begin with to refuse spots when you've got the time available but once you get the sponsor accustomed to Sunday advertising, he gets results and you are okay to get him over that phobia against Sundays which harks back to the days when the networks had the thing sewed up with Benny, McCarthy, Skelton, Allen, etc. [who prevented listeners from tuning independent stations, another reason for not buying Sundays on a WHB or a KLIF]. Now, that just isn't so but the hangover persists and Sunday is our weakest day. A weekend-package deal is a possibility but has not been too effective in many places. Another procedure for selling Sunday which has worked for several stations is to quote seven day availabilities and only that. It was pointed out that Robert Hall will buy on Sundays. In this connection, I am going to urge from now on that we accept no ROS ["Run-of-Schedule"] package deals which do not give us 7-day privileges.

Armstrong now has a no-protection rule on auto accounts. He guarantees no separation at all, just as newspapers.

Dave Morris getting excellent results by distributing to all agencies a printed breakdown of the listenership of KNUZ at all hours, i.e.: 7:00 a.m.--33,461 listeners--13,378 adult males, 12,502 adult females, 3,409 teenage females, 2,880 teenage males, etc. The figures are my own for purposes of illustration. This gets around--with actual figures--that old argument that "most of your listeners at that time are just teenagers." Or, "you don't have any colored listeners on that show." Pulse can give you these figures.[52]

A memorandum from McLendon to his station managers apparently written a year later in 1956, demonstrates the persistence of the problem of selling Sundays. At one point in the memo he answers one of his managers thus:

I do not agree with you about Sunday programming. Our Sunday programming must be fine because we have 55% of the audience. And with higher sets-in-use Sunday becomes terrifically valuable. The only reason you would need better programming is to attract more audience, and we've already got more audience than on weekdays. Yet the sales problem remains, and I still think it will eventually be solved by forced

---

[52] Gordon McLendon, General Memorandum to all station managers and KLIF sales people, October 26, 1955, from McLendon Policy Books, n.p.

weekend buying when the weekdays get jammed up. We will have to create an artificial shortage on Sundays. I don't think a gimmick is the answer unless it is something pretty startling. . . .[53]

Lack of ratings credibility

In the mid-50s, the problem of selling Top 40 radio for any day of the broadcast week was complicated by a lack of credibility toward many of the ratings offered. The solution quoted in the section on "Sunday Problems"--which described station KNUZ's supplying of actual numbers of people to go with the shares expressed in percentage--was a new idea in 1955. Bill Stewart feels that stations such as this one were, however, less responsible for the evolution of true demographic ratings than were advertising agencies, which demanded more information on what the ratings actually meant, since they were buying stations they really didn't know about other than through the numbers they produced. Before the more sophisticated demographic breakdowns became available, the Bartell stations used the agencies' own skepticism about Top 40 station ratings to build credibility for the ratings of their own chain. Pete Thomas recalls a campaign for WAKE in which promotional mailings were sent to prospective national clients with the theme that there obviously had to be some mistake in the ratings:

> The gist was, if you are looking at our current ratings, you may be impressed by the fact that no station could have achieved this position in the market in this few months. And we said we were inclined to agree with that. In other words, the whole thing tended to build credibility for the rating

---

[53] Gordon McLendon, memorandum to Bill Weaver, Don Keyes, Bill Morgan, Herb Golombeck, probably written 1956, from McLendon Policy Books, n.p.

because we cast some slight doubt on it in the same way that a timebuyer would have.[54]

Anti-Top 40 bias

As well as supplying corroborating numbers for certain categories of listeners to complement the "share" information supplied by the typical rating, Top 40 stations also had to convince prospective timebuyers that their programming was not limited to just the playing of popular music, as the latter was automatically equated with an audience consisting only of teenagers. Arthur H. McCoy of the John Blair station representative company sent a letter to Gordon McLendon on March 10, 1958, outlining this problem and suggesting a solution.

> Dear Gordon:
> As you know, we like to use tapes to sell agency executives on the exciting sounds of Spot Radio. We feel that there are probably two different kinds of tapes which we should have on file--one which shows all the fast-moving sounds of the station, including the top pop music, and another which would be designed for the main purpose of pointing out the community service functions of these same leading stations.
> In our Chicago meeting, Chuck Fritz brought up the Dodge problem. It isn't isolated. We are going through a similar type problem here on Sinclair refining, and in our Sales Meeting last Tuesday here, I realized all over again that personal opinions on the part of some of the key media people are likely to affect our billing adversely unless we come up with a new effective sound that will impress them.
> Certainly KLIF does an outstanding news job, editorializes like no one else, handles public service more interestingly than anyone else, and can fit the description of the "friendly necessity" better than any other station in Dallas. I believe that if you were to give us a ten-minute tape showing specific examples of these and other important points, we can do a lot about putting the focus on this phase of your operation--and take some of the spotlight away from the top pop problem which arises in certain areas.
> I don't have to tell you any more what I have in mind--I am sure you get the idea. I know that Chuck would be able

---

[54] Thomas interview.

> to use it immediately in Detroit, and we would like to have a copy here. Likewise, Cliff would need a copy.[55]

Whether or not KLIF and other McLendon stations responded to the suggestion that seems to be made in the letter from Blair (that the station supply one tape to sell one kind of client and a different type to sell another) is not so important as noting that such practices--on the part of both reps and stations--were prevalent. By 1962, the RKO-General stations felt that some further assurance that their tapes were genuine was necessary and so asked the Broadcast Advertisers Reports (BAR) monitoring service to make their own tape of RKO stations to verify that the one sent to agencies by RKO was representative.[56]

Meanwhile, the criticism that Top 40 stations catered only to teenagers continued. In 1957, KIXL, the Dallas station that McLendon at one time thought was unbeatable with its "beautiful" music, was running trades advertising with the slogan "Buy the audience that can afford to buy" (see page 502).[57] At the time, Bill Morgan--who had been at KLIF, gone to the ABC radio network, and would later again be KLIF General Manager--was the General Manager at KIXL. Quite obviously, Morgan was utilizing some of the criticisms most often directed at a station like KLIF to attract sponsors to KIXL.

By March of 1958, Pulse was servicing agencies--generally at

---

[55] Letter from Arthur H. McCoy, the John Blair Company, to Gordon McLendon, dated March 10, 1958, from McLendon Policy Books, n.p.

[56] "RKO Starts Monitoring Service for Proof of Radio Programs," Broadcasting, August 13, 1962, p. 30, and "Program Tapes Now Get Official Seal," Sponsor, August 13, 1962, pp. 44-45.

[57] Advertisement in Broadcasting, December 9, 1957, inside front cover.

Buy the Audience that can Afford to buy
IN DALLAS IT'S
KIXL
THE STATION THAT DELIVERS
THE GREATEST ADULT AUDIENCE
AT THE LOWEST COST PER THOUSAND
FOR COMPLETE DETAILS
CALL OR WRITE
BILL MORGAN, GEN. MGR.
Wonderful
KIXL
Radio
To The Discriminating Adult Listener
REPRESENTED BY H-R and CLARKE BROWN IN THE SOUTH

their request--with audience composition figures for each hour in certain radio markets among the Top 25 (such as New York, Washington, Birmingham, and Atlanta), with Cleveland, Boston, Baltimore and Detroit about to be initially covered in this way.[58] With such data being regularly ordered by agencies, the actual number of teens and adults listening (assuming an accurate survey) could be told. Typically, agencies in 1958 were looking for no more than 12% to 15% of the audience to be teenagers.[59]

In spite of the availability of objective audience composition data, such agencies as Guild, Bascom and Bonfigli were so willing to side with more conservative advertisers against Top 40 that they summarily declared, "If the top juke box records dominate a segment--or the entire musical programming for a station--you've got the baby-sitting set."[60] That quotation comes from a strong indictment of Top 40 programming by the vice president of Guild, Bascom and Bonfigli, Ernest J. Hodges. His critique was printed in Broadcasting in April 1958, and is reproduced on page 504.[61]

What Broadcasting accurately described as "a spirited defense of 'modern radio'" was issued in a 24-page report in June 1958 by the Adam Young station rep firm. The facts presented from--and about--the

---

[58] Charles Sinclair, "Madison Ave. to D.J.s: 'Get an Adult Audience,'" Billboard, March 24, 1958, p. 13.

[59] Ibid., p. 34.

[60] Ernest J. Hodges, vice president of Guild, Bascom and Bonfigli (agency), "Critique on Rock and Roll Radio: We're Not After the 12-year-olds," Broadcasting, April 14, 1958, p. 113.

[61] Ibid.

from **ERNEST J. HODGES,** *vice president, Guild, Bascom & Bonfigli*

Critique on rock and roll radio: We're not after the 12-year-olds

A baby-sitting society has taken over the musical programming of hundreds of American radio stations. As a result, millions of advertising dollars are being spent to reach an audience interested not in products or services but in (as one critic put it) "bad grammar set to bad music."

Rock and roll as an art form is of no interest to our agency except as a purely private irritation. We are not concerned in a corporate sense with the problems of a group of juveniles who require constant noise as a background to nearly every waking moment. We *are* concerned when radio—one of our most useful means of communicating with people—presents us with an audience composed mainly of 12-year-old minds, not in the cynical sense but literally. As advertising men we *must* be concerned when any pressure group takes control of any measurable portion of any American mass medium.

By what obscure logic can agencies justify attempting to sell an item of interest primarily to adults or a commodity for use by the whole family on a program or on a station which is playing music selected almost exclusively by youngsters? If anyone doubts that the giggle set controls the radio set on "top 40" programs, let him listen to one of the stations which accepts telephone requests with an open key. If he has the courage and fortitude, he could listen to stations which broadcast conversations between d.j.'s and teen-agers — conversations which usually have a background concerto of popping bubble gum.

Our good friends the radio reps will now grab their rating charts and audience composition studies. Don't try to confuse us with either of those. Leaving aside the validity of ratings, radio can, like television, be committing "ratingside."

The standards of ratings, power, cost-per-thousand and station promotional material are not enough; they do not provide all that a media director needs when he is hundreds or thousands of miles away from a market. These statistics may provide a defensible position for a media director—after all, he "bought the most popular station." And he can, at the same time, be doing a perfectly lousy job for his trusting client.

You can figure audience compositions until your slide rule steams but plain common sense will tell you that any station which uses juke box sales or telephone requests as its standard for musical popularity is being strongly controlled by a vocal minority. These are teen-age tastes being reflected as a result of teen-age pressures. The fact that studies will show a third of even these program audiences as being adult, in years anyway, does not alter the fact that a minor portion of the population is exerting disproportionate pressures on a mass medium.

NOT BIG-MONEY SPENDERS

Teen-agers *do* buy millions of dollars worth of soft drinks, lipstick, hair dressings and other American products each year. But teen-agers are not representative of the American family in today's purchases of very much of the food, the automobiles, the homes and services which are the backbone of radio income.

At Guild, Bascom & Bonfigli we are attempting to communicate with people who are *listening*. Our vision of our prospect for a sale is not a juvenile doing homework. At least that is what some of them claim they are doing while they sprawl across a table with a phone cradled on their shoulder while waiting for some radio station to accept a request for this week's version of "Jailhouse Rock" or "Great Balls of Fire." Maybe they are doing homework. They do have a textbook propped against a ketchup bottle. And maybe they *are* listening to advertising. It's hard to guess.

But there is a test for audience programming which doesn't need to be a guess. You don't need to guess at a station's personality either. You don't need to read the trade press accounts of Bob Convey's rock 'em and break 'em at KWK in St. Louis, or even study Henry Untermeyer's mail poll (90% against rock and roll) at KCBS in San Francisco. You might simply examine a musical log for stations you plan to buy—one of our routine procedures at GB&B. If the top juke box records dominate a segment—or the entire musical programming for a station—you've got the baby-sitting set. And you've got an audience which should be labelled for what it is. It's an audience you wouldn't settle for in a family newspaper or in any magazine unless you were trying to reach teen-agers. And it's an audience, too, that you wouldn't pick for adult products on television.

And as a purely private solace, there may be one other hope: My 15-year-old daughter informs me that "rock and roll is dull. We're tired of it."

Ernest J. (Buzz) Hodges, b. June 7, 1917, Boston. After stint as trade magazine writer, joined Cleveland Press *as reporter. Enlisted in Army Air Corps 1942. From 1946 to 1948 was copywriter and later copy group head in J. Walter Thompson's San Francisco office. With Russell Pierce, formerly head of JWT's San Francisco office, started public relations firm of Hodges, Pierce & Assoc. Clients included Guild, Bascom & Bonfigli. Joined GB&B in September 1952, was made vice president three months later. Now is account supervisor on Ralston-Purina Co. business placed by that agency.*

Adam Young report are as realistic and measured as was the attack by Hodges (quoted earlier) distorted. Broadcasting's account of the Adam Young report is reproduced on pages 506 to 508.[62] Also in June of 1958, the NBC network published the results of a poll of a panel of 258 timebuyers (from 203 different agencies) who were asked how they bought various radio formats. The questions and overall design of the survey were quite obviously biased against Top 40 stations, which at one point were categorized as "Music-rock 'n roll or 'Top 40.'"[63] In almost all cases, what was called the "standard music & news station" showed up best.

In the July 7, 1958 Broadcasting, Todd Storz, Gordon McLendon, Gerry Bartell and Harold Krelstein (for Plough) were among a group of seven who replied to the NBC survey. (Adam Young of the Adam Young station representative firm, Arthur McCoy of the John Blair rep company, and Morris Kellner of Katz station representatives were the other three.) Todd Storz commented that he was unaware of any group or station in the country which programmed only the Top 40 tunes and nothing else, as the survey category suggested. Then to demonstrate the continued and growing popularity of Top 40 and other independent operations, he recited a list of cities in which the independent station had from three to eight times the share of the local NBC outlet.[64] McLendon, like Storz, disavowed running Top 40 stations,

---

[62] "A Spirited Defense of Modern Radio," Broadcasting, June 2, 1958, pp. 77-78.

[63] "The Top 40 Formula--Under Fire," Broadcasting, June 30, 1958, p. 36.

[64] Ibid., p. 28.

A spirited defense of 'modern' radio: Adam Young report testifies that it works

A 24-page study designed to dispel the "myth" that "modern radio" caters mainly to rock 'n' roll-loving teenagers is being released today (Monday) by Adam Young Co [AT DEADLINE, May 26].

The special report on "The Audience of Modern Radio"—based on a Pulse study conducted last fall in 10 major markets—contends that: (A) the audience of "modern" radio stations is predominantly adult (84.9% as against 11.7% teenagers and 3.4% children); (B) "modern" radio stations reach more adults than "oldline" network affiliates (50% more in the 6-9 a.m. period, 80% in the 9 a.m.-3 p.m. period, 60% in the 3-6 p.m. period); (C) "modern" radio stations reach more impressionable younger women than "old-line" network affiliates (85% more).

Markets in which the Pulse study was conducted were Los Angeles, New York, Chicago, Minneapolis, Cincinnati, Milwaukee, Atlanta, Miami, New Orleans and Seattle. Only in the latter market did the Young companies pick on a "compatible affiliate," KING Seattle—a station that, says President Adam Young, programs "similarly to independent stations." KING is an ABC Radio affiliate. In the nine other markets the study contrasted an independent with a network affiliate.

"We picked Pulse," Mr. Young said last week, "because in most agencies station buying is done according to Pulse. We felt their [Pulse's] findings would impress agency buyers."

Mr. Young further explained that while his report concentrated on major markets, sample surveys conducted in smaller markets (e.g., Greensboro, N. C.) tended to bear out his feeling that listening habits don't change very much in non-metropolitan areas.

The Young companies represent stations in five of the 10 markets analyzed but the findings in those five were not confined to client stations, Mr. Young points out.

In releasing the study, Mr. Young said he resents the "muddled thinking" that equates modern radio with rock 'n' roll music. Although his personal tastes in music don't include R & R he maintains a Voltaire-like attitude towards it. He will defend to the death a station operator's right to include R & R in his music selections assuming such programming can be justified in terms of the broadest mass audience appeal and, through it, advertiser impact.

MR. YOUNG

"Our salesmen found," he explained, "too many agency timebuyers who picked stations not on up-to-date market and audience factors but on reputations the stations had built over a period of years. Apparently it made little difference to these buyers that their image of stations had long been shattered by the arrival of modern radio."

Rock 'n' roll, according to Mr. Young, is but "one small facet of modern radio today." Granted, he said, that the single most important element of modern radio is the kind of music that inevitably determines station popularity, by itself music is not the total answer to the development of modern radio. A modern station, as opposed to "traditional" independents and network affiliates, also will stress local public service and news programming and will innovate "where others have feared to tread," Mr Young asserted. In the realm of news broadcasts, a modern radio station will open with local news—usually delivered by on-the-spot reporters—and will rely as little as possible on wire service copy, he said.

Another thing, according to Mr. Young: modern radio station management must control music policy to the very last record "unless it wishes to surrender program dictates to the likes and prejudices of its various disc jockeys." A traditional radio station, said Mr. Young, will depend almost primarily on the Top 40, thus wind up with a station that has no personality of its own. People today must have a reason to turn to any given station; "people no longer listen to stations *per se* . . . they pick a station because they expect something."

Not only does Mr. Young feel that Top 40 is a misnomer when thought of as R & R ("After all, the No. 1 hit at WINS New York last week was the non-R & R 'All I Do Is Dream' . . .") but that it is a complete fallacy that stations can buy audiences by means of gimmicks.

"No station has enough money to buy its audience . . . Furthermore, in the final analysis no station can keep its audiences—assuming for a minute that it *can* buy listeners—unless it services their likes and needs."

As regards the rock 'n' roll controversy, Mr. Young feels that it has been "fostered by the trade press and a certain radio network vice president" whom he identified as NBC Radio's Matthew J. Culligan. Also serving as targets for Mr. Young's slings and arrows: Columbia Records' artists and repertoire director Mitch Miller ("who is against R & R because he's pushing album sales and sees Columbia and the other big firms being murdered by the new single-disc firms . . .") and Cunningham & Walsh's Jerome Feniger ("who in a recent talk [ADVERTISERS & AGENCIES, May 19] criticised the people who were implementing the very things he recommended at the outset . . .").

The severest critics of modern radio, Mr. Young went on, "fail to realize that programming today is no mere hit-or-miss proposition; programming today is based on long and careful study for how else do you explain that when a modern radio operator enters a new market, sets in use increase by a fantastic percentage?" These critics, he contends, "are those who have never had the problem of running a station or of building local audiences."

Much of the anti-modern radio fire emanates, Mr. Young charged, "from the networks who in olden days of radio were the 'haves' and today find themselves playing the part of 'have-nots' in terms of audiences. These are the men who are accusing independent station operators of doing the same things they themselves tried to do . . . but unsuccessfully. The successful affiliate operators today are those who on station time emulate their independent rivals."

One reason Mr. Young gives for the "passions" inherent in the current controversy is that "rock 'n' roll does not allow indifference; people either love it or they hate it." He believes those operators who are currently playing R & R "to the hilt" (and "R & R is just a passing fad . . . look at the Top 40 today as against the Top 40 of six months ago . . .") exercise a "censoring eye" on the more blatant and vulgar selections. He also dismisses the "tired refrain" that R & R programming is a contributing factor to the alarming growth of juvenile delinquency: "I feel that tv shows that glorify crime should take most of the blame . . . if any blame is to be apportioned to broadcasting."

Mr. Young questioned the "hypocrisy" of some people who charge R & R is catering to a distinct minority, thereby ignoring the wants of most listeners: "What do you think WQXR (New York) and other classical music stations are doing but catering to a distinct minority, I ask you?"

YOUNG'S PREMISES

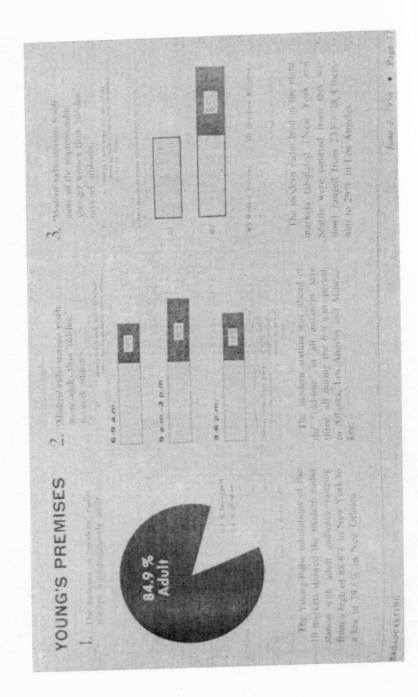

1. The audience of 'modern' radio stations is predominantly adult.

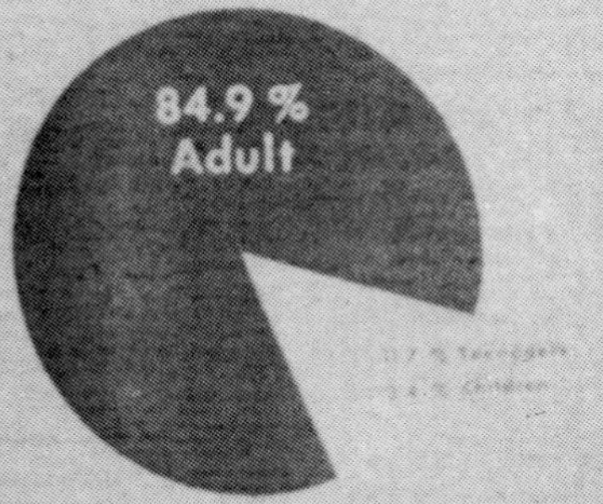

The Young-Pulse tabulations of the 10 markets showed the modern radio station with adult audience ranging from a high of 88.8% in New York to a low of 79.6% in New Orleans.

2. 'Modern' radio stations reach more adults than 'old-line' network affiliates.

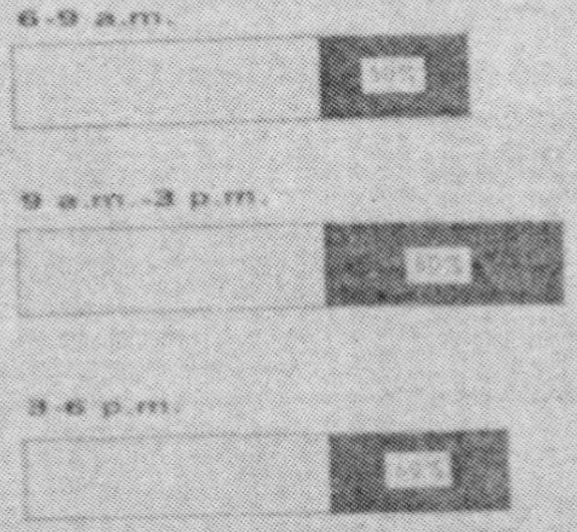

The modern station was ahead of the "old-line" in all instances save three, all during the 6-9 a.m. period, in Atlanta, Los Angeles and Milwaukee.

3. 'Modern' radio stations reach more of the impressionable younger women than 'old-line' network affiliates.

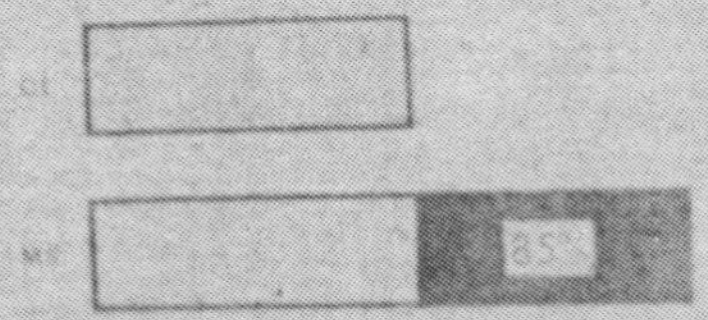

The modern radio lead in the eight markets tabulated (New York and Seattle were omitted from this section) ranged from 233% in Cincinnati to 29% in Los Angeles.

claiming that his stations also programmed standards along with the hits.[65] Harold Krelstein noted that ". . . most network stations in this country, regardless of their affiliation, are completely mimicking their non-network brethren when they themselves are required to program locally. . . ."[66] Gerald Bartell made several points in rebuttal:

> . . . It is difficult to evade the conclusion that networks are no longer capable of capturing the dominant radio audience and network affiliates have not been quick to compete on local terms. Because of many years of reliance upon the networks they have atrophied by the disuse of the creativity they may have possessed. . . .
>
> . . . Radio's best people--in management, programming, talent--are now in modern radio. Network radio has been pauperized of personnel. The networks wrote off radio during television's ascent and networks never since have been able to attract top manpower.
>
> Any survey geared to a predetermined conclusion adds nothing to the body of competent research.[67]

Adam Young continued his company's defense of modern radio by writing,

> . . . To sum this up, NBC is still in the radio business because with their usual efficiency they forgot to bury the body.
>
> There are some top-notch NBC affiliates today and we never underestimate them. They are good, however, because of their own local programming which is similar to that of the modern station operator.
>
> NBC's obvious rigging device in this survey has been to over-simplify very complex problems of programming. Thus, the questionnaire divides radio stations into three categories: as NBC labels them, Top 40 or rock-and-roll, standard programming and varied programming.
>
> This seems the most obvious bias and fallacy of the entire study. Modern radio, as we champion and sell it, cannot be characterized by a one-word or one-phrase description. Modern radio is a combination of many different elements. Modern radio is based on the concept of programming under the absolute control of astute management. This means that the public is not allowed to dominate the station's programming through Top 40 lists, nor are air personalities permitted to impose their taste on the public.[68]

---

[65] _Ibid._, p. 29. [66] _Ibid._

[67] _Ibid._, p. 30. [68] _Ibid._

This very same factor--management control of programming--was pointed to by Blair's Arthur McCoy as being far more important than partially-accurate labels of any sort. Wrote McCoy:

> Timebuyers who are up-to-date on the complicated business of local programming look first of all for a very important ingredient not even mentioned by NBC--the station ownership and management. All considerations for depth understanding of the business under study must start there. The sounds that come out of a station are a direct reflection of the manager. And the ability of the manager to really reach his market (the masses the advertiser needs to move enough merchandise to affect his profit statement) is shown in circulation figures like Pulse, Hooper and Trendex. If a buyer gets caught in the web of a prejudiced survey and buys only a small circulation station with "varied programming" he likes, he will more than likely end up with (a) an unhappy client, (b) a broke client, (c) no client at all.[69]

Morris Kellner for Katz also criticized the loaded wording of the questionnaire and pointed to management as the single most important element in making a successful radio station.[70]

Spot Scheduling, Production, Load and Rate Increases

The vehemence of the wording of the rebuttals to NBC's "survey" by Top 40's apologists demonstrates that by this time, in 1958, they felt themselves to be at last on the offensive rather than fighting defensively as they had been doing for so long. Spot sales were continuing to increase, the reputation of independent stations generally was continuing to improve, and objectively-accomplished audience composition studies showed a gratifying number of adults listening to Top 40. The attacks and accusations of being mere "jukeboxes" would continue for a number of years, but by 1958 at least some national

---

[69] *Ibid.*, p. 31. [70] *Ibid.*

advertisers were beginning to believe that the best way to sell mass-appeal products on radio was via radio that attracted a mass audience, which meant the Top 40 station. In the decade between KOWH's acquisition by Storz and 1960 when sales resistance to Top 40 had largely subsided, Top 40 stations had experienced a true "rags-to-riches" growth in the number of advertisements they carried. Until the diversification of programming by other stations brought on a fragmentation of the Top 40 audience during the decade between 1960 and 1970, the Top 40 station was forced to cope with scheduling an increasingly heavy load of spot announcements by virtue of being "the only ballgame in town." For the program director, the problem became how to fit the many spots into the format and still keep a lively sound, and ultimately when to plead with the manager to stop selling altogether.

Scheduling

From 1951 through 1955, Storz experimented on KOWH with various levels of commercial load to determine at just what point the station had the maximum number of announcements without losing listeners in the ratings. According to George Armstrong, the optimum limit seemed to be about 18 minutes, a figure that was settled upon before the NAB decided to codify the same number as an upper limit for all stations.[71] As of the summer of 1971, Storz station WQAM in Miami was still operating at 18 minutes of commercials per hour against two other AM Top 40 stations (WFUN and WINZ) which were airing only 12 minutes, but was

---

[71] Armstrong interview.

holding its traditional first place in the ratings (sometimes tieing with WFUN).

In 1953, Gordon McLendon wrote to Joe Roddy suggesting how Roddy might try to handle an increasing commercial load on KELP, El Paso. Again, McLendon's model was the successful Dallas daytime "good music" station, KIXL.

> Now, as you begin to get more and more commercials on the station, the problem is how to handle these commercials without disturbing the smooth continuity of the station. First of all, I have come to the conclusion that while people cuss commercials, they like to hear a reasonable number of well-done commercials--note that I say, well-done. A station without them is apt to sound rather dullish. In order to get your commercials in and not to lose the continuity of your music, study carefully the devices KIXL has used. . . . They will play about three musical numbers in a row, sometimes only two, without interruption, and then have three commercials in a row. Yet it doesn't sound like triple or quadruple spotting. They give a commercial after a record, then a station break, bring up some music or give a chime or two, fade and go into another commercial, and then bring up some more music, give a Think It Over, and follow with another commercial and then bring in two numbers without interruption save for announcement of titles. Done smoothly, this can still give you the effect of not interrupting your station constantly for commercials. A heavily-commercial station can use this device to sound as though it is making a deliberate effort to be non-commercial.[72]

A little more than a year later when McLendon wrote to Roddy again, this time to explain how KELP might emulate KLIF's growing success, it was apparent that McLendon had not taken his own advice about uninterrupted music and clustered commercials. This time he told Roddy:

> About the only difference between KLIF and KELP worth listing is the fact that we accept about any type of commercial, no matter how strident, and KELP doesn't. And we make no attempt at uninterrupted music. As you can see, it doesn't seem to hurt

---

[72] Gordon McLendon, letter to Joe Roddy, April 11, 1953, from McLendon Policy Books, n.p.

> us. Our listenership seems to go up every time we add another spot. And reflecting, I can't see that KFJZ's old habit of triple and quadruple spotting has hurt their listenership any. I am beginning to change a little and wonder if people don't like considerable talk on a station along with the music to break the monotony. . . .[73]

Production

By the Spring of 1955, McLendon had translated his "wondering" quoted above into a positive statement that commercials were indeed attractive to an audience:

> More and more every day, we are becoming convinced that one of the main reasons for KLIF's big listening audience is the entertainment value of our spot announcements. This is in direct conflict to what most radio stations think, i.e., that spot announcements drive away listeners. We believe that the commercial announcements here at KLIF actually increase our listening audience because they are well produced and very entertaining.
>
> A lot of our announcements are gimmick commercials, some are very funny commercials, many are singing jingles, but all in all we think our commercials are one of the big features of the station. We have tried to analyze and determine what it is that KLIF has that no other radio station in Dallas has. We all have to some extent the same music, although we only do it better; several of them have disc jockeys and although we think ours are better, they do have them; and all of us have news although we think our system is better on news, also. Still if we have one thing which is outstandingly different from any of the other stations, it is our commercials, our recording setup and our recording engineer, Les Vaughan, gives us an immense advantage in this department. I hope to see all of you have the same outstanding type of commercials that KLIF has since we think it is going to increase everybody's Hooper Rating.[74]

Surely the memorandum just quoted overstates the case for commercials being part of the entertainment. Obviously, well-produced commercials

---

[73] Gordon McLendon, Letter to Joe Roddy, July 27, 1954, from McLendon Policy Books, n.p.

[74] Gordon McLendon, Memo to all Managers, April 18, 1955, from McLendon Policy Books, n.p.

would not have as deleterious an effect on building an audience as would poor ones, but the very fact of their repetition must still have been irritating. However, the point must also be conceded that the use of gimmicks and full production on commercials made locally was often only being accomplished at this time by the Top 40 station in a given market. Often, only the Top 40 station had all of the talent, the facilities, and the software to produce a really good local spot.

An AIMS membership mailing in September 1955 found George Armstrong talking about the production of local spots in Kansas City at Storz's WHB:

> To my knowledge there hasn't been a new announcement gimmick in the last ten years. Singing commercials, sound effects, echo chambers, voices recorded at various speeds--all of these things are standard equipment for stations and agencies. Frankly, we use them all in our own recording. However, it is only fair to say that as of this writing most of our spot business is being done by agencies.
>
> Perhaps this would be a good paragraph to point out what is currently the most popular type of announcement gimmick in the Kansas City market, not only on WHB but on other stations as well. It seems that No. 1 on the spot hit parade at the moment is the screaming, two-voice pitch spot. This, as you know, involves two announcers racing at breakneck speed through a series of short sentences with every third or fourth line being a repetition of the client's name, slogan, or current lowest price. These spots may or may not incorporate an attention-getter at the outset.
>
> This style seems to be particularly appealing to the appliance boys and the automotive dealers. I suspect that this style of spot is pretty universally popular this year as I have heard a lot of the same thing in other markets.
>
> By contrast to the above, I think there is also a tendency on the part of more advertisers than ever to give ad lib privileges to personalities and to take greater advantage of the stylized personal approach of each disc jockey.[75]

For some reason, only one type of advertiser has continued to use this

---

[75] George Armstrong, from an AIMS Newsletter mailing, September 1955, from McLendon Policy Books, n.p.

type of two-voice "screamer" spot up to the present time: the drag-race promoter. Typically, these spots begin with two voices yelling, "Sunday! Sunday!" with awful urgency while mighty engines roar in the background. The "screaming" two-voice spot was just another way to add urgency and a sense of speed to the Top 40 sound. However, it and the style of some of the disc jockeys' delivery within their programs earned the Top 40 station the nickname "screamer" among those who disliked the sound.

Spot load and rate increases

To those who might think that Bill Drake developed the idea of cutting back on the spot load in order to retain more listeners, it will come as a surprise that George Armstrong was doing it on WHB in 1956. The writer of "A Confidential Report on WHB" states,

> WHB presently has a maximum of 15 spots per hour. This includes only one-minute spots plus two quickie 20-second breaks on the half hour. In other words, 13 one-minute spots per hour, plus two 20-second quickies on the half hour. Armstrong got a little bit worried about the possible effect it would have on his audience, and the fact that KCMO was making some noises about bringing in some outside disc jockeys, so he decided to cut back to 15 spots per hour.[76]

As this cutback in spot load came at a time when business at Top 40 stations was really beginning to boom, it is important to note that rates were constantly being raised as the selling difficulty decreased. In addition to raising rates, there were other methods of increasing the value of time or even of producing new time where it before had been sold out. The writer of "A Confidential Report on WHB" continues,

---

[76] "A Confidential Report on WHB," McLendon Policy Books, n.p.

> Because he feels he did not raise his morning rate high enough on a local basis, Armstrong has now made his end rate [largest possible buy] locally ROS. Class A spots bought at $23 and Class B spots bought at $16.50 can only be bought on a ROS basis, unless the client agrees to daily or five-times-a-week use. If he buys a year's contract, but it is not used on a regular daily or five-days-a-week basis, it is ROS. He can, however, avoid ROS placement if he does use it daily or on a five-times-a-week basis. This ROS business applies only to the end rate on the rate card.[77]

In May 1957 Bartell both raised national rates and created new time categories. His stations at that time began offering class "AA driving times" in morning and afternoon peak listening periods.[78] Pete Thomas recalls the typical spot load at WAKE, Atlanta, at about this time as follows:

> . . . of course you are always oversold in those periods [drive times]. And they didn't count spots at that time like they do now. You could sell as many spots as you could put in there. They didn't put a quota on spots. If you had one in there, that quarter hour was logged as commercial. So you might as well load the damn thing up with as many as you could put in there. Quarter hours is what the FCC counted, not the number of spots. And in the morning, one of the real marks of talent was getting through this heavy load of spots and make it sound reasonable. A good station would cut them back to maybe seven or eight per quarter hour. But I've certainly seen times at a station where they would take up to thirteen in a quarter hour. And of course what they would do is fudge--the live spots wouldn't run a minute.[79]

Traditionally, as a Top 40 station has been faced with competition by a similarly programmed station, it has done what WHB did in 1956, and what Drake did ten years later--cut the spot load. Bartell sold WAKE before he had to make very drastic changes in this regard because of

---

[77] Ibid.

[78] "3 Bartell Stations Hike Rates, Create Class AA 'Driving Time,'" Broadcasting, May 20, 1957, p. 76.

[79] Thomas interview.

competition from WQXI and then WPLO. Stations without such competition, however--especially ones in smaller markets--often were able to keep their top position in the ratings despite an incredibly heavy spot load. The 1,000 watt regional Top 40 station at which the author was a disc jockey in 1962 (WKKO, Cocoa, Florida) at that time carried at least two minutes of commercials between each record, with these being broken by a jingle or short feature segment such as a weather report, salute to a citizen, etc. The ratio of music to non-music on WKKO in 1962 thus was about 50-50, which was not atypical for a station of its type in a small-to-medium sized market. An unidentified Los Angeles Top 40 station was found in 1959, however, to have about the same ratio of music to commercials, with 12 minutes 41 seconds of music, 1 minute 45 seconds of news, and 15 minutes 34 seconds of commercials in a half hour.[80]

The important point to remember about Top 40 commercials policy was that it was always related to the condition of the rest of the radio industry that made Top 40 "the only exciting radio on the dial." When other stations began to imitate the pioneer Top 40 outlet in the market, and later when other specialized formats were developed, Top 40 operators responded by decreasing the spot load and paying more attention to the placement and production of commercials. Until this took place, Top 40 commercials policy was determined by the conditions prevailing in a seller's market, and however undesirable it may have been from the standpoint of the listener, the fact that Top 40 stations could

---

[80] William O'Hallaren, "Radio Is Worth Saving," Atlantic Monthly, October, 1959, p. 70.

sell time when other stations could hardly give it away impressed broadcasters everywhere with the idea that at least this type of low cost, high-profit operation could make money for them, too. There are many broadcasters today who feel that radio might not have survived the economic doldrums of the 1950s if Top 40 operators had not led the way back to profitability. Thus, one must weigh the harm to the public interest from the overselling of commercial time against what some feel was the salvation of local radio for that same public.

CHAPTER EIGHT

TOP 40 MANAGEMENT DEVELOPS NON-PROGRAMMING POLICIES

While its attention to programming was easily the most important contribution to modern radio made by Top 40 management, these operators also developed a number of other, non-programming policies which influenced programming indirectly and also were adopted by the broadcasters who sought to imitate Top 40's success.

Management Policies

Organizational Patterns

Storz, McLendon, and Bartell all developed their own patterns of organization for their group operations. The chief differences among them centered on the degree of autonomy which the local General Manager of the station could exercise and the degree to which the "home office" determined local programming. Generally, McLendon seems to have allowed more local authority in both of these areas than did either Storz or Bartell. For example, both Storz and Bartell sent out music lists from the central office for use on all stations with a few local insertions allowed. McLendon let his stations each conduct their own surveys and compose their own lists, which sometimes resulted in local problems with music selection as memos quoted previously have shown. General Managers in all three groups had to make regular reports to the central ownership but all also had the mandate to make local decisions as they needed to, since they were "on the scene" and could appraise the given situation most accurately. McLendon's directives to his General Managers which are contained in the McLendon Policy Books most often take the form of suggestions rather than orders. Meanwhile, Storz (according to Stewart) and Bartell (by his own claim) were more likely to prescribe than to suggest. Sometimes directly and sometimes through their national program directors, all three men were heavily involved in determining the total sound which radiated from their stations. Of the three, McLendon was most directly involved in on-the-air work, being heard in commercials and promos supplied to his group both in recordings and via copy he had written. McLendon paid for this involvement by being less interested than were Storz and Bartell in the financial policies of his stations.

None of the three men seem to have gotten into Top 40 with the express goal of developing a Top 40 station group. In all three cases, they simply added stations as they found it advantageous to do so, and later "discovered" that they had a station group. The major new factors in running a station group rather than a single station are the conservation of manpower and the diffusion of information. Bartell points out that he foresaw the chief difficulty in running a group of stations would be that of securing enough good programming people, and so he early decided to make his operation a centralized one in terms of programming. As a Top 40 pioneer, Storz found himself being imitated almost as soon as he had innovated something, and for that reason he, too, decided on central programming of such things as the larger contests and promotions. In the Storz case, the problem was the <u>unwanted</u>

diffusion of information that could allow a competing station to be running a Storz promotion before the Storz station did, unless all his stations began it simultaneously. National control solved this problem. McLendon's operation illustrated the positive aspect of the diffusion of information: McLendon instituted a newsletter or "weekly programming report" to which all of his stations were expected to contribute news of what they were doing locally. The goal was the stimulation of new thinking or at least the supplying of ideas that could be adapted for local use without the need for long and original creative effort.

Weekly reports

The McLendon organization was proud of its establishment of weekly reports, and found it inconceivable that other station groups could operate without such a system. The writer of "A Confidential Report on WHB" says,

> All accounting is done in Kansas City for WHB and likewise for all Storz stations in each station's home city. The only contact between WHB and the home offices in Omaha is a monthly profit and loss statement which is sent to Omaha for purposes of overall corporate accounting. There are no weekly or daily reports. . . .[1]

On July 19, 1960, McLendon National Program Director Don Keyes sent a memorandum to "All Managers, All Program Directors" in which he made the following points:

> A year or so ago, I became well acquainted with an ex-Storz Program Director who told me that one of the frustrating things about that organization was that there was no exchange of ideas among the Storz Stations.

[1]"A Confidential Report on WHB," McLendon Policy Books, n.p.

> I have seen evidence lately that we are falling into a similar rut. On contacting some of our stations recently, I accidentally picked up some good promo ideas in idle conversation.
>
> I would remind the Program Directors here that our "Policy Book" did not materialize out of thin air. They are ideas compiled over the years and I would like to see them get fatter.
>
> I would like to hear from each station periodically concerning not only what's going on in your station but anything from your local opposition as well. I don't want to shackle the Program Directors down to a weekly report but it would be good for all stations if they'd drop me a few lines every so often.[2]

By 1963, the McLendon organization had instituted a weekly digest of ideas, which were sent in by individual group stations and then mimeographed and sent back out to all stations in the group. Gordon McLendon circulated the memo reproduced below on July 25, 1963, in order to explain the handling of these weekly digests. The memorandum was addressed to all managers, with carbons to Don Keyes and to Bill Stewart.

> I want to be sure that all of you understand explicitly that each member of your executive staff is supposed to read our weekly digest and read it the minute it comes in. I refer to your News Director, Program Director, Sales Manager and the General Manager, as well as anyone else you think wise. The reason we are sending you one single copy only is because we do not want these reports circulated around the United States, and if we start sending four copies to every station we will find them being mailed all over the country to friends.
>
> All of this brings me to something that I don't think I have stressed before, but now is a good time to do it. These reports are for our own use and for nobody else's. They are NOT to leave our stations.[3]

The author's own perusal of the weekly report digests collected in the McLendon Policy Books yielded the following list of categories

---

[2] Don Keyes, Memorandum, July 19, 1960, McLendon Policy Books, n.p.

[3] Gordon McLendon, Memorandum on the Weekly Digests, July 25, 1963, McLendon Policy Books, n.p.

(no significance to order of listing): Critiques of practices at stations; Station Breaks; Competitor's Commercials; Saturday and Sunday Sales; Competitor's Promotions; Promotion; Hot Klimbers [(records)--later "Hot Comers"]; Public Service Ideas; Rejected Commercials; Copy Approaches; Best On-The-Air Promo Ideas; Merchandising; Accounts Sold; Increased Efficiency; News Format; Objectionable Songs [later]; PSA Approach; Equipment Problems; Functional Difficulties; and Building Station Image.

Chain of command

In the Storz, McLendon, and Bartell groups, the "chain of command" seems to have been from the named owner, sometimes through his national program director (if any) and other times direct to the local general manager and/or local program director, and from there to the employees of the local station. Engineering, sales, and accounting matters followed separate chains directly from the chiefs at group headquarters to their local station counterparts. It is interesting to note, for example, how few of McLendon's memos to his general managers are concerned directly with sales, accounts, and revenue matters. Partly this was McLendon's distaste for such work, but partly it was a reflection of the typical Top 40 management pattern which separated sales from programming in order to concentrate first on the programming. Of the three organizations, McLendon displayed this separation most strikingly while Storz had more interest in financial aspects and Bartell worked on sales promotions almost as avidly as he experimented with the programming.

Promotion of personnel

The separation of sales from programming produced one other interesting effect: in Top 40, promotions in rank were more likely to come to programming personnel than to those in sales, where, traditionally, new management talent had been tapped. McLendon's two best-known national program directors, Bill Stewart and Don Keyes, both started as disc jockeys. Kent Burkhart and Steve Labunski both started as Storz deejays and both became station managers. Of course, promotion from programming into top management was not always feasible or desirable, and sometimes was actually spurned by the prospective promotee. Ken Dowe, who is now the powerful National Director of Operations for the McLendon stations, actually turned down several requests to give up his deejay position at KLIF and go into top management before he was finally persuaded.

The McLendon stations' policy of promoting those who made constructive contributions to the operation of the group, regardless of background or department, was in operation as early as the days of the Trinity Broadcasting Corporation in the mid-1950s. The following unsigned, undated statement is from the Trinity Broadcasting Corporation Policy Book (mimeographed):

> Ideas
> This radio station is peculiar in that it likes ideas. It wants you to use your brain; it wants you to think. It likes criticism. We like to have our employees come in to the appropriate department heads and present any constructive criticism or any complaint they may have which needs to be remedied. We like them to come in and give us ideas, tell us what they hear from listeners and from accounts. Don't ever feel reluctant to express a criticism or offer an idea. You will not be censured nor will you receive notice. If your criticism is good, it will be acted on and your idea will be welcomed, good or bad. It is this sort of employee, who presents constructive

criticisms and ideas, who advances to the executive jobs in this corporation. The employee who sits back and "does his job" without unusual thinking or without offering criticism to the management, is an employee who not only is not going to advance in the corporation but is likely to be with the corporation only a short time. Therefore, the long and short of it is, we wish you to speak your mind and speak it as often and freely as you wish.

This corporation wants new employees to get ahead just as badly as you probably want to get ahead. The main problem that we have is finding good people to fill executive capacities. We are looking for them constantly. The answer to your advancement rests entirely with you. Those people who have advanced in this corporation are those who have shown ingenuity and who have used their mind continuously while they are on the job and many times when they were not on duty. Let me emphasize that nobody wants you to advance any more than this corporation does because we spend thousands of dollars looking for men and, Lord knows, if we can take them right out of our own employ, it is simply wonderful, both for us and for you. In this connection, we might note that most of the executives have indeed been lifted from our own staff.[4]

Financial Policies

Station acquisition

The three Top 40 group owners differed widely in their station acquisition (and divestment) policies. Storz was easily the most conservative. Storz never sold any of the stations he bought (except KOWH in Omaha and the frequency and power trade with WTIX), and he never bought another station until the last one purchased was well on the way to being paid for. All of the stations the company has today are prime facilities or nearly so (KOMA is less than perfect) and all are in medium-large markets (Oklahoma City is again a possible exception). Storz did all of his station buying by 1956 with the KOMA exception.

Bartell has now sold his interest in all of the stations which

---

[4]"Ideas," Trinity Broadcasting Corporation Policy Book, n.d., n.p.

used to bear his family's name. Bartell and McLendon each bought their first station in 1947, two years ahead of Storz, and in both cases it became the flagship of the group (WOKY and KLIF, respectively). Bartell was not as worried about having a prime facility as was Storz--he set the pace in Atlanta for several years with 250-watt WAKE. Still, stations with better coverage eventually forced him to sell WAKE (at an enormous profit). Bartell operated all of his stations long enough that he cannot be accused of "trafficking" in stations, but now that he is out of the business (while the Storz and McLendon operations continue), he can be seen as the pioneer "defector" from the business of buying operating Top 40 stations. His last buys were made in the early 1960s.

While McLendon continues to own and operate a Top 40 station (WYSL, Buffalo) he has turned his interests to developing other formats such as "good music," all news, all advertisements, etc. Of the three operators, McLendon was least convinced of the need for a good facility, probably because he was most convinced of the attractive power of good programming. A number of times, he has bought or sought to acquire stations in suburban communities in an attempt to serve a larger metropolitan one (WGLS/WTAM, Decatur (Atlanta); the original WYSL in Amherst (Buffalo); WCAM in Camden (Philadelphia); KROW/KABL, Oakland (San Francisco); sales rights to XTRA, Tijuana, Mexico (Southern California); and KCND-TV, Pembina (Winnipeg, Canada). Of the three groups, McLendon is also the Top 40 owner most often accused of "trafficking" in stations because he would sometimes sell a station off after he had made it successful with his programming, reaping a large profit in so doing. There is no doubt that McLendon enjoyed seeing his stations become successful and that when he saw a chance to sell one for an exceptionally good profit, he did so. However, the number of stations he has sold after holding them for less than the now-prescribed three years is still only a fraction of the number he has held continuously, and fewer than the number of new formats he has introduced. Some of McLendon's imitators deserve the "trafficking" label far more than he does.

Station operation

Hardware investment

All three operators believed in investing heavily in quality program production equipment, whatever the shortcomings of their transmitting facilities. Since all of their stations made money, it was easier for them than for other radio station owners to spend money for new and better equipment, but given their belief in the necessity for fresh, exciting programming before all other considerations, it was also partly inevitable. For example, while most owners would have pondered the merits of buying an echo or reverberation machine, Top 40 owners were having them installed because they would provide another novel sound for their stations.

Software investment

Money spent for such software items as jingles, production libraries, program services and news wires followed the same motive as expenditure for new programming equipment: the desirability of better production, and a "slicker" sound for the station. As has been shown, jingles added further identity to the station, and program services such as Jimmy Fidler's Hollywood gossip reports and multiple news wires added new dimensions to news, but the overall goal was simply a better total sound.

Personnel investment

It has already been shown that Top 40 management felt it was vitally important to have top-notch people in charge of programming. Bartell has said that he realized quite early that really good programming personnel would be scarce, thus necessitating a centralized program control for his stations. In believing that obtaining good programming people was crucial, it naturally follows that Top 40 operators actively recruited programming personnel. After securing one national program director and several local PDs, the big problem was in finding enough suitable disc jockeys. Disc jockeys were secured in two ways: by direct recruiting, and by stealing them from other stations.

Deejay recruiting.--In 1955 and 1956 as he expanded into Minneapolis and into Miami with two new stations, Storz placed display ads in the classified section of Broadcasting in an attempt to secure new disc jockeys. McLendon also placed some very similar-looking advertisements to recruit deejays for *his* expansion efforts. A selection of some of the ads in Broadcasting is reproduced on pages 529 to 531.

With good disc jockeys in short supply in the mid-1950s, direct recruitment was not always successful in producing all of the talent a

DISC JOCKEYS— IMMEDIATE OPENINGS!

If you're interested in being with America's most "program-minded" radio group, send your tape. We're expanding again—adding WDGY, 50,000 watts, in Minneapolis, subject to FCC approval. Openings available immediately in all of our markets. We are particularly interested in disc jockeys with a smooth selling ability. If you have a personality identity such as singing, piano playing, voice characterizations, impersonations, etc., so much the better. If you're good we want to talk business. Every tape carefully auditioned, and promptly returned. (Be sure to include address *inside* box.) Send all tapes to: Todd Storz, President,

MID-CONTINENT BROADCASTING CO., OMAHA 2, NEBRASKA

KOWH Omaha   **WHB** Kansas City   **WTIX** New Orleans

WANTED: DISC JOCKEYS WHO THINK THEY'RE EXCEPTIONAL—AND HAVE THE TAPES TO PROVE IT.

That's right. We said "Exceptional." If you're not, don't bother. You'll only waste your time and ours. But . . . if you are exceptional, rush us the tape that proves it. Immediate openings in 4 markets with America's most program-minded radio group. Latest addition: WDGY, 50,000 watts, Minneapolis. Our idea of an exceptional disc jockey features smooth selling ability. If you have a personality identity such as singing, piano playing, voice characterization, impersonations, etc., so much the better. Every tape carefully auditioned, and promptly returned. (Be sure to include address inside box.) Send all tapes to Todd Storz, President,

MID-CONTINENT BROADCASTING CO., OMAHA 2, NEBRASKA

WDGY   KOWH   WHB   WTIX

DISC JOCKEYS: Want to join Noemac?

There are now openings for top-flight men in several of the top-rated NOEMAC stations. NOEMAC stations are KLIF, Dallas; WRIT, Milwaukee; WNOE, New Orleans; KELP, El Paso; WGLS, Greater Atlanta; KNOE and KNOE-TV, Monroe, Louisiana and KTSA, San Antonio, Texas—the latter subject to FCC approval.

If you are good—especially if you have a "different" style—send us a tape and prepare for advancement in the expanding NOEMAC group. Send tapes to:

Gordon McLendon
2104 Jackson Street
Dallas, Texas

Wanted: Top deejays and newsmen at

BAGHDAD ON THE BAYOU

KLBS IN HOUSTON

Here's your chance to be in on the ground floor with another of the nation's coming great independents—KLBS in Houston. We need **top** disc jockeys, with good voices and gimmicks or different styles, and also top radio newsmen. If you fit in either category and want a top opportunity, send your audition tape and background information today, to:

Gordon McLendon
2104 Jackson Street
Dallas, Texas

NEED THREE HEADED DISC JOCKEYS

Means just that! Must have mental capacity—originality—and alertness because you'll find that things are always "right side up" on the STORZ STATIONS. The STORZ STATIONS are expanding again. WQAM-Miami has just joined the fold KOWH-Omaha; WTIX—New Orleans; WHB-Kansas City and WDGY-Minneapolis are all *the* TOP RATED stations in their respective markets. We need strong personalities for several of our markets to cover the expansion. TOP PAY to TOP MEN. If you're interested only in the "sunshine of Miami" or the "leisurely living" of New Orleans, save your time and ours by contacting the Chamber of Commerce in those cities. But, if you're interested in joining the NUMBER ONE FAMILY of Independent stations—send a representative tape with a short resume of your background. If you sing over records or whistle while humming counterpoint at the same time—let us hear it. All tapes returned promptly.

MAIL TAPES TO: Todd Storz-President
THE STORZ STATIONS
Kilpatrick Building
Omaha, Nebraska

"IF"*

IF *you pride yourself on being expert at spotting "off label" songs with great potential . . .*

IF *you think Elvis Presley is the greatest thing since Daylight Saving Time and aim to prove it on the air . . .*

IF *you know the square root of Bill Haley's Social Security number, OFF-HAND . . .*

IF *you're deeply enthralled by what you hear on your headsets while you're doing your show—and if your conception of a "great" show is a soft and dreamy type . . .*

IF *you're adept at tearing 5 minute news summaries from the machine and reading them cold with no more than 5 or 6 fluffs . . .*

IF *you're more interested in getting your listings to Variety and Cash Box each week than in preparing your show . . .*

IF *you feel that you have to let "VOX JOX" know every time you have a headache . . .*

IF *you think Frank Sinatra's latest release is Ava Gardner and that Tommy Leonetti is an r & b trio . . .*

IF *you need a teleprompter to say, "Hi there folks" . . .*

IF *your answer to all of the above is in the affirmative—then stay where you are —YOU'VE FOUND A HOME.*

HOWEVER

IF none of your answers to the above were in the affirmative and *IF* you'd like to become a part of America's fastest growing radio organization—let us hear what you have to offer. We're looking for disc jockeys who are alert enough to *sound* alert on the air. *IF* you have any gimmicks, *IF* you sing along with the records, all the better. We can offer you top pay, a chance to grow along with a growing organization, many employee benefits and the benefit of the years of Mid-Continent know-how.

Send all tapes to: Todd Storz, President
Mid-Continent Broadcasting Company
Omaha 2, Nebraska

Please include brief history and return address inside tape box.

WDGY	KOWH	WHB	WTIX	WQAM*
Minneapolis-St. Paul	Omaha	Kansas City	New Orleans	Miami

*Pending FCC Approval

station needed. For this reason, and to gain a competitive advantage over other stations in the market, it became common practice for a Top 40 station to "steal" a disc jockey by buying him away from his former employers. For example, Storz (through Armstrong) considered buying station WDOK in Cleveland in 1956, but decided against it both because it was not a prime facility and because in order to make it number one, the two top men in the market would have had to be bought away from WERE, which would cost about $100,000 a year.[5] It was quite typical to attempt to steal the top disc jockeys in a market for your own station. When McLendon was setting up KTSA in San Antonio in March of 1956, an unsigned writer of a memo to McLendon offered the following appraisal of the jocks that might be bought there:

> There are only three even passable deejays in the market--Stan Nelson on KITE, Howard Edwards and Herb Carl on KONO. By way of comparison, I don't believe any of the three could make it at KLIF although the first two might be nighttime men. Even so, it will probably be wise for us to lift Nelson if we can. The other two are relatively new but Nelson is well-known and apparently, for lack of much competition, well-liked. He has been with KITE since it began as a morning man and for some time now has been PD. Bud Lutz guesses that, with bonus plans, he is making around $600 per month. . . .[6]

According to Bill Stewart, Storz did exactly the same kind of monitoring of the local talent before he moved into a market with a new station. Stewart was the man who did the scouting for the acquisition of WQAM in Miami. He said:

> . . . We would go into a market, and I would go in about a month before we took over. My <u>ear</u> was programmed. If I walked into a room and there were 19 naked girls in there and the radio

---

[5]"A Confidential Report on WHB," <u>McLendon Policy Books</u>, n.p.

[6]"Timetable for San Antonio," March 30, 1956, <u>McLendon Policy Books</u>, n.p.

was on, the first thing I would pick up was, what station the radio had on, and then I would start checking the physical attributes of the girls. And I would go into a market, and I would check the cab driver on the way in from the airport; I'd ask the bellboy what station he listened to and why; I'd ask the girl in the coffee shop; I'd ask the guy behind the desk. And everyone I would run into, I would ask. Then I would sit down and call every record store in town, and ask them what the hot radio station was, and who was the hot disc jockey. And I would tabulate it up who the hot disc jockey was, and we would go after him, and get him no matter what it took. And Miami was a strange market. It was the strangest one I ever ran into. Because, it was the only market where of the--we'll say 60 calls I made to 60 record stores, I got 60 answers that were the same, for the station and the guy. It's the only station where that's ever happened, and I've done it in maybe 40 markets. . . . It was WINZ, and it was guy by the name of Jerry Wishner. So we hired him. He worked for WINZ seven days a week for 85 bucks a week. . . . And I think I gave him 125, and he thought I was The Savior. We broke the pattern down there. It still isn't the greatest paying market in the world, but it used to be awful. It used to be a dollar an hour and all the sunshine you could drink. . . .[7]

Deejay contracts.--The prevalence of the practice of stealing disc jockeys by buying them away from a competing station was a trick not peculiar to only one or two Top 40 operators. Knowing that any operator could do the same thing to them, Top 40 management tried to develop a disc jockey contract that could not easily be broken. Most found this to be impossible. Instead, the operators decided to use a simple "pledge" either on the length of their employment or on other terms. This memorandum to "All Stations" from Gordon McLendon was written in February 1956 in an effort to solve the difficulty:

> Henceforth, new disc jockeys hired into our organization will be employed only after we have reached a gentlemen's agreement with them on the terms of their employment.
>
> The gentleman's agreement is a fair one: that in consideration for us hiring them, they will agree to the following--that if we let them go for any reason at all, they have the privilege

---

[7]Stewart interview.

> of going to any station anywhere, including the same city. But, if they should choose to leave us for any reason, they cannot work in the same city for a period of two years.
>
> This rule works even for disc jockeys who say, live in Dallas, but want to work at KLIF. They needn't worry about security under the rule. After all, if we fire them, they can go right to work for a competitive station in Dallas. The only way they can lose security with us is through their own choice, a choice to leave us--which is always their privilege. As consideration for our having hired them and built up their names and following, they agree not to use us as a stepping stone to another station <u>in the same city</u>.
>
> Would urge you to follow this same agreement without exception. It is a legally-binding verbal agreement and furthermore it is the sort of agreement only the most foolhardy jockey would attempt to violate. After all, somewhere down the line in his career somebody will check references with our organization and one of the most damning things that can be said is that a person broke both his contract and his word. But even more than the mere matter of checking references, the word would get around in the trade and the man's reputation for integrity would be completely impaired.[8]

Kent Burkhart's answers to Don Keyes's question to him as a former Storz employee in early 1959 reveal that Storz used a similar "pledge."

> . . . Seems as though individual state laws play an important part in the situation. They [Storz] are pleased with the number of people they have scared into staying with them because of the contract, however. Program Directors have signed contracts whether they are on the air or not. Also Commercial Managers. Also the managers are all asked at one time or another to sign a pledge to the company--not a contract, but a pledge.[9]

Keyes' question to Burkhart about Storz's policies on deejay contracts may have been prompted by growing numbers of disc jockeys who were leaving McLendon for other stations, regardless of their pledge to the company. In November 1959 McLendon announced that he was filing suit

---

[8] Gordon McLendon, "On Hiring New Disc Jockeys," February 13, 1956, <u>McLendon Policy Books</u>, n.p.

[9] Kent Burkhart, Letter to Don Keyes, March 9, 1959, <u>McLendon Policy Books</u>, n.p.

against a disc jockey who had gone to a Portland, Oregon station in breach of his contract. At the same time, he announced that he was going to sue stations for luring away his personnel with what he called "fabulous offers" which the station owners knew they could not "possibly hope to sustain."[10]

The recruiting of disc jockeys by whatever means are necessary has not subsided in the present day. Top disc jockeys such as Larry Lujac in Chicago and Don Imus in New York continue to be the subject of much persuasion to move to more lucrative and prestigious positions.

Group Operation Policies

Trade Association Investment

Perhaps because they were for a time the only radio station owners who were clearly making money, while at the same time the old-line operators castigated Top 40 owners as mavericks and opportunists, Top 40 management generally displayed a willingness to participate in trade organizations whose goal was the economic betterment of independent radio.

RAB

The Radio Advertising Bureau, which originated in the early 1950s as the Broadcast Advertising Bureau (BAB), concentrated its efforts on the promotion and sale of radio advertising. A subscription to RAB was like a subscription to NAB in that subscribing was voluntary. However, rather than being a lobby group and information dissemination

---

[10] "McLendon Files Suit, Hits Contract Jumping," Broadcasting, November 9, 1959, p. 81.

point like the NAB, the RAB gave subscribers printed materials that they could use to sell clients locally. RAB also was radio's apologist with agencies at the national level. However, in Top 40's formative years in the mid-1950s, RAB's chief, Kevin Sweeney was vehemently anti-Top 40:

> It's clear to me that there's a limit to how long people can be interested in a medium that plays the McGuire Sisters in "Sincerely" 39 times a day and whose standard approach to something as vital and important as the news is five minutes of bulletins torn off the wire. . . .
>
> Here's this great potential medium. Ninety-nine percent of the families have it. They listen to it continuously. So what do we elect to do? We become a jukebox without lights. . . .[11]

Sweeney's and RAB's anti-Top 40 bias may have been one reason why George Armstrong refused to let the Storz stations subscribe to RAB in 1956, but the writer of the "Confidential Report on WHB" offers another:

> Bud refuses to let his stations subscribe to RAB; said he doesn't want his salesmen taking time to read all that stuff that they send out. They should be out on the street selling. . . .[12]

In spite of Sweeney's bias against Top 40, RAB still could not avoid in its sales-aids mailings such facts as the one that was the subject of a four-page folder: radio disc jockey shows were heard in 1954 by more families than were reached by all consumer magazines combined.[13] In 1954, Sweeney also urged radio broadcasters to develop programs not provided by other media, which is exactly what Top 40

---

[11] Kevin Sweeney, "Radio: That Dip Isn't a Trend," Broadcasting, March 28, 1955, pp. 40, 41.

[12] "A Confidential Report on WHB," about 1956, McLendon Policy Books, n.p.

[13] "BAB Report Stresses Pull of Radio Disc Jockey Shows," Broadcasting, March 22, 1954, p. 38.

operators did. His plan, which followed Top 40 management's philosophy of increasing sales by drawing larger audiences (as a result of improved programming) contained three points:

> "(1) Hit 'em where they ain't. Put on the type of entertainment and information that is not now being provided by other media. Develop new radio personalities that are exclusive to radio and not available, for better or worse, to any tv channel including your own.
> "(2) Expand news coverage. We can cover the news hours ahead of newspapers but we don't exploit our advantage by providing the deep coverage of individual stories, especially local stories, that most people want. We should make it unnecessary for anyone to go elsewhere for all the news. . . .
> "(3) Buy ourselves four or five program geniuses to develop programs exclusively for radio. Pay them enough so they won't be tempted to go over to TV, rent them an ivory tower and get from them the diversification we need in our program structure."[14]

It does seem ironic that Top 40 group owners accomplished all three of Sweeney's points--providing a service not available elsewhere, expanding news coverage and making it more locally-oriented and vital, and giving authority to program directors and others to really develop new program ideas--but still were regarded by RAB as "jukeboxes without lights."

AIMS

The AIMS organization was a group of independent metropolitan stations (Association of Independent Metropolitan Stations) who programmed primarily music and news and who believed that independent station operators could benefit from each others' broadcast experience. AIMS was established in 1948, well prior to Top 40, but its membership in the early and mid-1950s included all of the Storz stations for several years and the McLendon stations for a short time. One of the

---

[14]"Sweeney Urges Radio Program Development," Broadcasting, April 12, 1954, p. 84.

requirements of membership was a regular contribution to a circulating newsletter forum. The association also provided meetings at which station personnel discussed policies on sales, deejay recruiting, music, billing, and so on. A memorandum to Gordon McLendon from Bill Morgan, general manager of KLIF in 1956 is reproduced on pages 539 to 541 to show the wide range of information that could be received from attendance at a single meeting.[15] Certainly, AIMS was a very valuable aid to stations which were not among the pioneers as Storz and McLendon were. Storz and McLendon probably learned progressively less from AIMS meetings and newsletters as their own level of competency increased, but in the formative period, just the corroboration of their own practices that the group provided must have been of considerable worth.

Station representation investment

All but the smallest stations in the smallest markets had had station representatives for a number of years prior to Top 40, since it was the most economical means of making themselves known to national advertisers. The success of the Top 40 format brought about two changes in policy regarding station reps. First, as Top 40 owners prospered, they changed representation from lesser known companies to the larger, "big-name" station representative firms. Then, when the controversy and invective about the Top 40 format began to spread and nearly everyone in the radio industry began to "take sides," the Top 40 owners realigned themselves again, this time favoring firms such as Blair, Katz, and Adam Young, who were in turn favorable to Top 40. These

---

[15] From McLendon Policy Books, n.p.

MEMORANDUM

KLIF — DALLAS

TO: Gordo[illegible] DATE: October 12, 1956

FROM: Bill Morgan SUBJECT: AIMS Meeting, Tuesday, Wednesday, Thursday, October 9, 10 and 11th

The meeting was attended by 30 people which I imagine is about the best attendance the AIMS group has ever enjoyed. Dave Morris was elected the new chairman for the coming year and conducted a very thorough meeting. I am going to give you the report as I jotted down items of interest so if this appears a little at random, please bear with me.

Of interest to all of you is the first item on the agenda, compensation to managers, and almost entirely this was a fixed salary plus a percentage of the net profit. Most stations, I have found, have written contracts with their managers. This, of course, is good from the station's standpoint if they have a good manager and fine from the manager's standpoint if he is not too sharp.

One station is charging 5% each month of their accounts receivable for bad debts and waiting until the following year to charge back what excess they have. Of course, we are charging 1% and this is always more than we actually lose, but it is a thought as far as income tax is concerned.

If you have anyone on your payroll that is not a bonafide employee, you will be in for trouble on next year's income tax. You must show the percentage of time on a weekly basis. The definition of an employee has definitely been changed to cover this and it is something that should be watched.

Several stations have an insurance plan where they insure their executive personnel and the station is paid the benefit of the policy in the event the employee should become accidentally killed or die of natural causes. In the event he does live to the maturity of the policy, it becomes a retirement fund for the executive. This is possibly something that could be looked into as I understand the premiums are a tax item.

Almost all stations have eliminated notarization of affidavits. They only send affidavits now to national accounts and the majority of the larger stations find that this is no problem as far as the national agencies are concerned. This is something I think we should go into immediately as it will certainly save a lot of time and trouble.

On our next program logs I intend to have more printed in as far as the format of our shows is concerned as it will be saving us quite a bit of typing. For instance, we know the news is going to be on each hour and this can be printed in and the sponsors name merely typed in.

All of you should check your taping equipment and the wiring in your control rooms as equipment is added constantly using different kinds of wiring and it tends to cut your efficiency. Also, be sure that your chief engineers are making field checks each week to see that you are getting the maximum efficiency on your power. All the wiring in your control room should be protected. If not, this should be done at once. We are also checking into a technical change called Low Fi instead of Hi Fi which allows most radios to pick up the lows instead of the highs and makes your station sound much louder and more powerful. You will receive a further memorandum on this. If you have an extra transmitter you should be sure that it is licensed as an alternate and not an auxiliary as this allows you to substitute at anytime without notifying the FCC.

Here is something that is certainly of value: From now on, on all public service announcements that we run, we are sending the recipient of the announcements, i.e., Community Chest, Boy Scouts, YMCA, a paid bill at card rates of the number of announcements that they have run. In this way we think that they will appreciate much more the time that we are giving them as it will mount into quite a sizeable figure over a year.

I understand that KXYZ in Houston has been cited by the FCC monitoring station for carrying a record with suggestive lyrics and I urge you to watch this and pass on to your program director. Be sure that records of this type do not get aired.

In SRDS you can get a heading over your station's call letters of "Independent". It costs just a little but I think we should all write in and have this put on. Also, I think it advisable that we have some kind of a trade ad in SRDS calling attention to the combo for the Texas stations we now own and operate.

A little something extra that WHB is doing which I like is on their time and weather intro they put in between records, they use the phrase "The time in WHB-Land is so and so and The Weather in WHB-Land is so and so". This is a little extra instead of saying "Dallas". It will give them a little deviation from the same pattern.

Also, something that will help you which I definitely am going to do — on all newscasts that are not sold I have instructed my traffic department to put a spot in the newscast, preferably a national spot, and this lightens your load for the coming half hour. The account is not given a lead-in or lead-out. No credit for sponsorship of the newscast is given but it gives you an opportunity to get rid of one spot in an otherwise lost portion of your hour.

Several stations are now charging extra for Thursday and Friday time. I know that we have the problem of Thursday and Friday availabilities as most independent stations do and this will make a client buy across the board and if he does buy a strip Monday through Friday or Monday through Saturday he does not have to pay the extra charge for the Thursday and Friday times

Check and see if Curtiss Publishing Company has any trucks in your area. If so, they will work a trade-out with you and let you put signs on the sides of the trucks for a few announcements for Saturday Evening Post and Ladies Home Journal and it will not interfere with any schedules you have. Through BBDO on these publications.

Several stations give $25 a week for the best news tip of the week and I believe this to be excellent. It seems that most of the time these are furnished by members of the Police Department which also keeps them working very closely with your station.

A little different form of merchandising rather than the usual jumbo postcard is used in this manner: If a client buys 50 spots a week on a firm 13 week basis and you spread these spots, one in each of your programs during the day, you agree to make for him 500 phone calls in this 13 week period. You have each disc jockey make one phone call per day for this client to either the druggist or food store on his list and in this way you get your 500 calls over within about 10 or 11 weeks. It actually gets a lot of people in your city talking to your personalities and works two ways, as well as being a wonderful merchandising feature for your clients.

I find that a lot of stations are using Jimmie Fidler for all kinds of promotion spots which do not have anything to do with his regular programs. Also, he will cut commercials for you if they are in any way connected with any of the programs he is on.

This is something you can keep in your backlog as you may need it someday. One of the AIMS stations used the phrase "The station most listened to". Two other stations started using the same slogan, which of course cut down the value of such an announcement. Our AIMS member came back with the following and consequently the other two stations quit using theirs: "The station more people listen to than all the other most listened to stations put together".

One station is sponsoring a cooking school - merely promoting it, nothing on the air and it is put on by the American Meat Institute and it sounds like a fine gimmick for the housewife. I am going to check into this and will give you details later.

I think the AIMS meeting this year was quite successful although I could not pick up too much information from most of the stations as they are doing practically what we have been doing for some time. However, I do think this - that the independent station is in line for the national business, every market either first or seconds with most agencies and I think that the year 1957 should be a very fine year for us all.

cc: Herb Golombeck
Bill Weaver

changes definitely paid off for Top 40 groups such as Storz. Income from national spot sales increased from 13.8% of total in fiscal year 1953-54 to 22.5% of total in 1954-55. By 1955, income from national spot for the Storz chain (which had added two more stations to its original KOWH) was 30 times what it had been in 1950.[16]

Ratings service investment

As has already been shown, Top 40 owners employed ratings information both as a sales tool and also as internal feedback on the effectiveness of programming. In the summer of 1953, McLendon learned from a speech given in Dallas by C. E. Hooper just how important the automobile listening audience in cars could be to a station's ratings, and made plans then to change KLIF's programming to appeal more to the driver.[17]

Both Storz and McLendon used ratings figures extensively in their national trades advertising, since their stations--being top-rated--could afford to boast. The favorite services were Hooper and Pulse, for a number of reasons. For one, both surveyed frequently--much more often than did Nielsen. For another, neither regularly provided audience composition data, which was available then only at extra cost to the ordering client. The absence of audience composition data (until its introduction by Nielsen in the 1960s) helped the credibility of early sales claims that phenomenally high share figures

---

[16] "Case History # 3 of Sponsored Advertising," a special self-advertising insert in Sponsor, August 31, 1957, pp. 55, 56.

[17] Gordon McLendon, "The Automobile Listening Audience," written in the summer of 1953, McLendon Policy Books, n.p.

were composed mostly of buying-power adults. While Pulse was often felt by agency timebuyers to be more reliable than Hooper, Hooper seemed to produce the highest share figures most consistently. The writer of the "Confidential Report on WHB" says of Armstrong's feelings about the ratings services in 1956:

> Armstrong said that Hooper is his Bible, and he believes it completely and implicitly, and that other services are useful to him only for sales purposes if he shows well, and he does.[18]

Trades advertising investment

The trades ads of Storz, McLendon and Bartell have already been displayed a number of times in a previous chapter on the growth of the station groups. The examples do not convey the heavy frequency with which such advertising appeared or the impact that it had compared to other, less daring, more conservative station ads being placed at the time. Sponsor and Broadcasting both had standing orders from McLendon and Storz at one time, so that an advertisement appeared almost every week. All of Storz's, McLendon's, and Bartell's station advertising utilized full pages, and Storz and McLendon used the front (and rear) covers relatively often.

In 1957, Sponsor magazine published an insert on special heavy paper in its August 31, 1957 issue which was the third in a series of success stories for Sponsor advertisers. This insert sought to show how the growth and success of the Storz stations paralleled the growth of the group's placement of station advertising in Sponsor. Sponsor

---

18"A Confidential Report on WHB," written in 1956, McLendon Policy Books, n.p.

admitted that Storz in 1957 used three other magazines for his messages, but pointed out that Storz's placement of 100 pages in Sponsor in 1957 reflected a budget for that magazine nearly equal to the other three publications combined.[19] Sponsor printed the following table in support of its claim (see page 545).[20] The two pages following the table displayed copies of letters to Sponsor magazine from station representatives Adam Young and John Blair, from Todd Storz, and from the Harry J. Kaufman advertising agency that had prepared the striking Storz advertising. These are also reproduced here on pages 546 and 547, as they explain the importance to Storz of his trades ads campaign.[21] There is reason to believe that the glowing reports of the success of the Top 40 format which McLendon's and Storz's trades advertising supplied must have been a leading factor in the process of diffusion by which Top 40 spread from the pioneers to the small-market imitators--a side effect which was probably not intended by either Storz or McLendon.

Image improvement investment

Bartell, McLendon, and Storz all recognized the need for improving the "maverick" image that Top 40 had. The three took differing approaches to making their format more respectable, and in a special way, these three different approaches are representative of the three different philosophies each had about running a station group.

---

[19]"Case History # 3 of Sponsored Advertising," p. 56.

[20]Ibid., p. 57.

[21]Ibid., pp. 58-59.

"Here's the Storz Story

in dollars-and-cents."

Fiscal Year Ending June 30	SPONSOR	Magazine "B" *	Magazine "C" *	Magazine "D"	Storz National Spot Revenue	% Spot Is of Total Revenue
1950	—	$ 9,000	—	—	$ 11,000	7.4%
1951	$ 280	9,500	—	—	23,000	10.1
1952	4,233	10,000	$ 840	—	28,000	9.4
1953	6,077	10,000	925	—	52,000	14.3
1954	2,796	10,500	925	—	62,000	13.8
1955	9,118	14,400	1,600	—	332,000	22.5
1956	24,132	23,200	2,800	—	723,000	27.6
1957	38,317	27,750	4,470	$13,500	1,622,000	34.5

*Appropriations for Magazines "B" and "C" approximated for years prior to 1957.

KOWH	WTIX	WHB	WDGY	WQAM
Omaha 1949-1957	New Orleans August, 1953	Kansas City May, 1954	Minneapolis-St. Paul January, 1956	Miami May, 1956

"SPONSOR . . . 'must' reading for all in the broadcast and advertising field"

ADAM YOUNG

Adam Young Inc.

RADIO STATION REPRESENTATIVE

3 EAST 54th STREET, NEW YORK 22, N. Y. • TELEPHONE PLAZA 1-4848

June 12, 1957

Mr. Norman Glenn
Sponsor
40 E. 49th Street
New York, N. Y.

Dear Norm:

I have always been a firm believer in the value of trade paper advertising. It is the obvious way to reach our prime prospects in selling broadcast facilities.

If I had needed any further convincing, the success of Todd Storz' campaign in Sponsor would have done it. Every Storz ad in Sponsor has attracted attention, comment, and - what is most important - interest. I believe that Todd's insertions in your magazine have been a definite aid in our spot sales efforts.

Obviously, the advertisements alone would have been of little value if the editorial content of Sponsor had not made the magazine "must" reading for all of us in the broadcast and advertising field. Every issue is vital and important, and this vitality and importance add impact to the advertising.

Congratulations on the fine job you are doing for the sponsors - and for your advertisers.

Cordially,

Adam

Adam Young

"When we write Storz ads for SPONSOR, we know we'll be seen by a lot of somebodies"

HARRY LONDON

HENRY J. KAUFMAN & ASSOCIATES
Advertising & Public Relations
1410 H STREET, N.W. • WASHINGTON 5, D.C.
AFFILIATED OFFICES IN MAJOR U.S. & CANADIAN MARKETS

June 3, 1957

Mr. Norman Glenn
SPONSOR Magazine
40 East 49th Street
New York, New York

Nearly three years ago, Norman . . .

. . . we were appointed as advertising agents for three Storz Stations, WHB having been acquired just a few months previously. Even at that juncture, Todd Storz was a major trade press advertiser, and SPONSOR was playing a significant role in Storz Station growth.

At this writing, there are five Storz Stations. It takes a word like "phenomenal" to describe what has happened, as you can see from the progressive billings figures supplied to you.

Those intervening years have been marked by a sharp increase in Storz trade promotion. The Storz Stations are now among the biggest users of the industry press. I don't have to tell you how greatly SPONSOR has shared in this increase.

The rapid growth of Todd's expenditure with you should be ample and gratifying evidence of the fine job SPONSOR has done.

All I have to add is this: Certainly no single advertisement or series of ads -- however arresting or convincing -- can hope to make a point unless there is somebody to see it. When we write Storz ads for SPONSOR, we know we'll be seen by a lot of somebodies.

Kindest personal regards.

Cordially,

HENRY J. KAUFMAN & ASSOCIATES

Harry London

HL:hd

"SPONSOR has certainly played a vital role in our development"
TODD STORZ

THE STORZ STATIONS
222 SOUTH 15TH STREET
OMAHA 2, NEBRASKA

May 25, 1957

Dear Norman,

In the relatively short history of the Storz Stations, hardly a month has passed which hasn't demonstrated with great impact — the importance and value of our national spot promotion in the trade press.

We feel this importance and value in our phenomenal growth in national spot billings — now running at $200,000 per month.

Without trade promotion, which relies heavily on Sponsor, all our other efforts could have failed to bear fruit. I refer to the tremendous amount of energy and thinking which we devote to the creation of a fresh, listenable, attractive sound. These efforts have brought to each of our stations the big audience in its market. These big audiences have enabled us to place in the hands of our national representatives powerful selling tools.

But even the most powerful story in the hands of our competent and resourceful reps, cannot be driven home with full force unless our prospects are exposed to a continuous preconditioning — both as to the Storz concept of selling-via-radio, and what the individual stations have accomplished in their markets. Our experience has been that when we (or our reps) call on a time-buyer, he already knows the Storz story.

That's all we've ever asked of our trade promotion — and we've been getting just that from Sponsor, in full measure.

I can't help but think back to our first days in radio. We were just beginning to create a new kind of radio, and you were just starting out to create your special kind of industry publication. It's interesting to note the parallels in our growth and yours. I don't know to what extent you can credit the Storz Stations with your development — but Sponsor has certainly played a vital role in ours.

Cordially yours,

Todd

Todd Storz

TS/rep

"Your good publication has been the recipient of a substantial portion of this investment since the first issue"
JOHN BLAIR

PLaza 3-4250

JOHN BLAIR & COMPANY
National Representatives of Radio Stations

NEW YORK 17, NEW YORK

May 28, 1957

Mr. Norman R. Glenn,
Editor
Sponsor Magazine
40 East 49th Street
New York 17, New York

Dear Norm:

Probably the best testimonial we can give to the effectiveness of trade paper advertising in the broadcasting field is our own continuous use of our industry trade papers for our company advertising over a period of more than 24 years. Your good publication has been the recipient of a substantial portion of this investment since the first issue.

What is true of our company should similarly be true for radio stations. A well operated radio station always has a sound, consistent sales story to present to its clients, and trade paper promotion represents an opportunity to keep the story before the trade on the same basis that makes good consumer advertising successful - consistency and continuity.

Best personal regards,

Sincerely,

John

John Blair

/av

Storz

As has just been shown, Storz was a strong believer in consistent use of business-like, straightforward, fact-filled trades advertising. His advertising to the trades always talked about high ratings, sales campaign successes, a high rate of renewal, the number of housewives who listened or some other aspect that would demonstrate the station's (or the group's) substantiality.

The Storz sponsorship of the disc jockey conventions in the late 1950s was another attempt to improve the image of the business by attempting to make disc jockeys--whom Stewart called "our stock in trade"[22]--seem more respectable and professional, in turn transferring those qualities to their stations. According to Kent Burkhart's memo of answers to Don Keyes's questions, Storz did not spend much of his own money on the disc jockey conventions. According to Burkhart, the 1958 Deejay Convention in Kansas City cost Storz only $3,000, with the record companies paying the rest of the expense. The organization of the conventions was left to Bill Stewart, who was already on the payroll, thus avoiding the expense of hiring further personnel.[23]

A portion of the program given to jocks attending the 1958 Kansas City convention, and a copy of the front page of Broadcasting for February 1958 saluting the disc jockey, are reproduced on pages 549 to 552.

---

[22]Printed material from Stewart interview.

[23]Kent Burkhart, letter to Don Keyes, March 9, 1959, McLendon Policy Books, n.p.

12:30 "The Future of Radio" Grand Ballroom

Norman Glenn
Editor and President
Sponsor Magazine

John Meagher
Vice Pres. National Association
of Broadcasters

1:00 Luncheon—Host: RCA Victor Records
John Y. Burgess, Jr.

G. W. ARMSTRONG
Vice President
and
General Manager
W H B

"Welcome to the First Annual Pop Music Disc Jockey Convention." In fact, let me extend two welcomes: one on behalf of Radio Station WHB and her sister Storz stations ... the other on behalf of all the citizens of Kansas City.

Both the Storz Stations are very proud to be in the forefront of this great DJ Convention, and WHB is extremely happy to be your host. We feel that this Convention and Seminar is a sincere and deserved tribute on the part of the music and broadcasting industries to you men and women who contribute to making their success.

The American disc jockey is today as much an integral part of our national scene as hot dogs, ham and eggs, or the right of free speech. You disc jockeys are many wonderful things to business men, housewives, GI's and young folks. You are friend and entertainer, companion and public servant. WHB and all the Storz Stations salute you and welcome you to this, your first convention.

There are also a million members of the Kansas City family who extend their welcome and greeting to each disc jockey attending the convention. For weeks they have been told of the coming event and have been making plans to insure that you all have a good time and take back many fine impressions of our city. The official city "red carpet" is out in a big way. The Chamber of Commerce, the Mayor's Office and the Police Department, to name a few, have extended themselves in every way possible to cooperate with us on every aspect of the convention.

So DJ's ... make yourselves at home. You are Kansas City's for this convention weekend, and we are so proud of you, your accomplishments and your contributions to American life.

Welcome to Kansas City and good luck always!

THE DEEJAY . . . . . AN AMERICAN INSTITUTION

TODD STORZ

by TODD STORZ
President
THE STORZ STATIONS

For a great many years, the Disc Jockey was regarded as a sort of "Barnacle on Radio's Ship of Progress." He was a little-regarded young man, working feverishly with residual audiences on stations which, for the most part, commanded no respect in the broadcasting industry. How the DJ's overcame this lowly origin and emerged as radio's most celebrated stars, is the story of Post War American Radio, and its amazing growth.

Our story, however, has its start before the war ends. A handful of Independent stations in extremely large cities had begun to find out that popular music and the DJ were a business winning combination against the high-rated network operations. The idea, nonetheless, did not expand substantially until post war radio station construction populated the country with more stations than the networks could accommodate as affiliates. This situation created a legion of independent stations, wholly responsible for their own programming. Thus, the stage was set for the birth of another great American Institution — The Disc Jockey.

For some time, Independents, though more numerous, still did not achieve importance or influence in radio's overall picture. Then came the revolution! Television entered the picture and panicked the network concept. A.M. stations as previously conceived and operated, lost ground steadily, as T.V. took over the living room and orthodox network programming.

Enter here the new era of radio — paced by the heretofore lowly Independent stations and their Disc Jockeys. These stations, whose faith in radio's future held firm, provided the American public with entertainment unavailable on TV: popular music, latest news and local service features, both desirable and necessary to the communities served by the stations.

The first successful years were rewarding for the DJ in his new-found glory, and for the stations too. But with more importance came more responsibility, greater competition, and an increased obligation on the part of Disc Jockeys to listeners, advertisers, and station.

Today the Real Disc Jockey is called by many names — "Air Salesman" — "Personality" — "Companion." But the one factor that sets him apart in our industry is his "Professional Approach."

This is what we look for and demand in our DJ's. Storz Station Disc Jockeys are mature-minded men with a deep rooted understanding of radio, gleaned from years of experience. They are men who approach every minute of every show as a challenge to their talent, and as a serious responsibility to fulfill. No open mike is treated lightly, no audience treated flippantly.

Storz Station Disc Jockeys know that all segments of their audience deserve full respect and courtesy. Our DJ's are invited guests in thousands of homes every day, and they owe their hosts and hostesses the consideration of "Conduct Becoming a Gentleman." In performance they owe our listeners maximum effort, both in entertainment and in service.

Our stations also feel that the Professional DJ is also a fulltime member of the community he serves. He responds readily to civic and public affairs, both on and off the air. He rings doorbells for charity, addresses school groups to help combat juvenile delinquency, and sells the Community Chest on his show as hard and as effectively as he sells automobiles, cigarettes and soap.

This "Professional Man" concept of the DJ is, in our opinion, the main element in perpetuating his popularity. Application of these Professional Principles will increase the integrity, influence and importance of Disc Jockeys everywhere.

DISC JOCKEY . . . . CONVENTION OBJECTIVES

BILL STEWART

by BILL STEWART
National Program Director
THE STORZ STATIONS
Convention Coordinator

Radio's spectacular re-birth has been due in a large measure to the individual we refer to as a disc jockey. In the beginning, the term "disc jockey" referred to an announcer who talked between playing recorded music. This individual has changed in concept and importance over the years. Today's disc jockey is first of all a talented artist. He has become a part of the community which he serves. He is friend and confidant to the young and old alike. He is the always welcome guest in home, automobile, sick room, at a beach party or business place. He is a reflection of public taste. His very program denotes planning, but most of all, he is an entertainer.

In the past years, many have attempted to organize the group known as disc jockeys, but in most cases these organizations have failed. Many have failed because the disc jockey is basically an individualist, and although his name applies to a group, no one person is representative of that group, either in appearance, personality, delivery, salesmanship, voice intonation or approach to a basic program.

In planning the first Disc Jockey Convention and Seminar, we are not attempting to organize, but rather to formulate ideas concerning the work and the success of disc jockeys, radio stations and the music industry. Only by bringing this great array of talent together in a free exchange of ideas and convictions can we grow as an industry. If two men would exchange dollar bills, each would still have one dollar. If two men exchange ideas, they are both richer, for then they each have two ideas. Multiply this hundreds of times, and you can easily see that after our convention, the disc jockeys of America will be richer in creative ideas, which is the backbone of our industry.

The disc jockey of today is faced not only with the problem of his own progress in his own particular market; he must be made aware of trends of music, industry problems, of rating services, of promotional ideas, of public service to his community. None of us is so big that we can handle all of these problems without the advice of and consultation with others. No one man will ever control the thoughts, ideas and motivation of the disc jockey. No one man will organize, will ever be able to dictate to the disc jockey as an individual or as a group. For this is America's and the disc jockey's greatest attribute — INDIVIDUALITY.

In fostering the idea of a disc jockey convention, the Storz Stations are in a small way attempting to present an open, frank and courageous discussion of industry problems and trends.

We are confident that the First Annual Disc Jockey Convention will bring great rewards to those who participate in panel discussions, floor discussions, and all interested bystanders.

See Back Cover for
Fabulous List of
Attendance Prizes

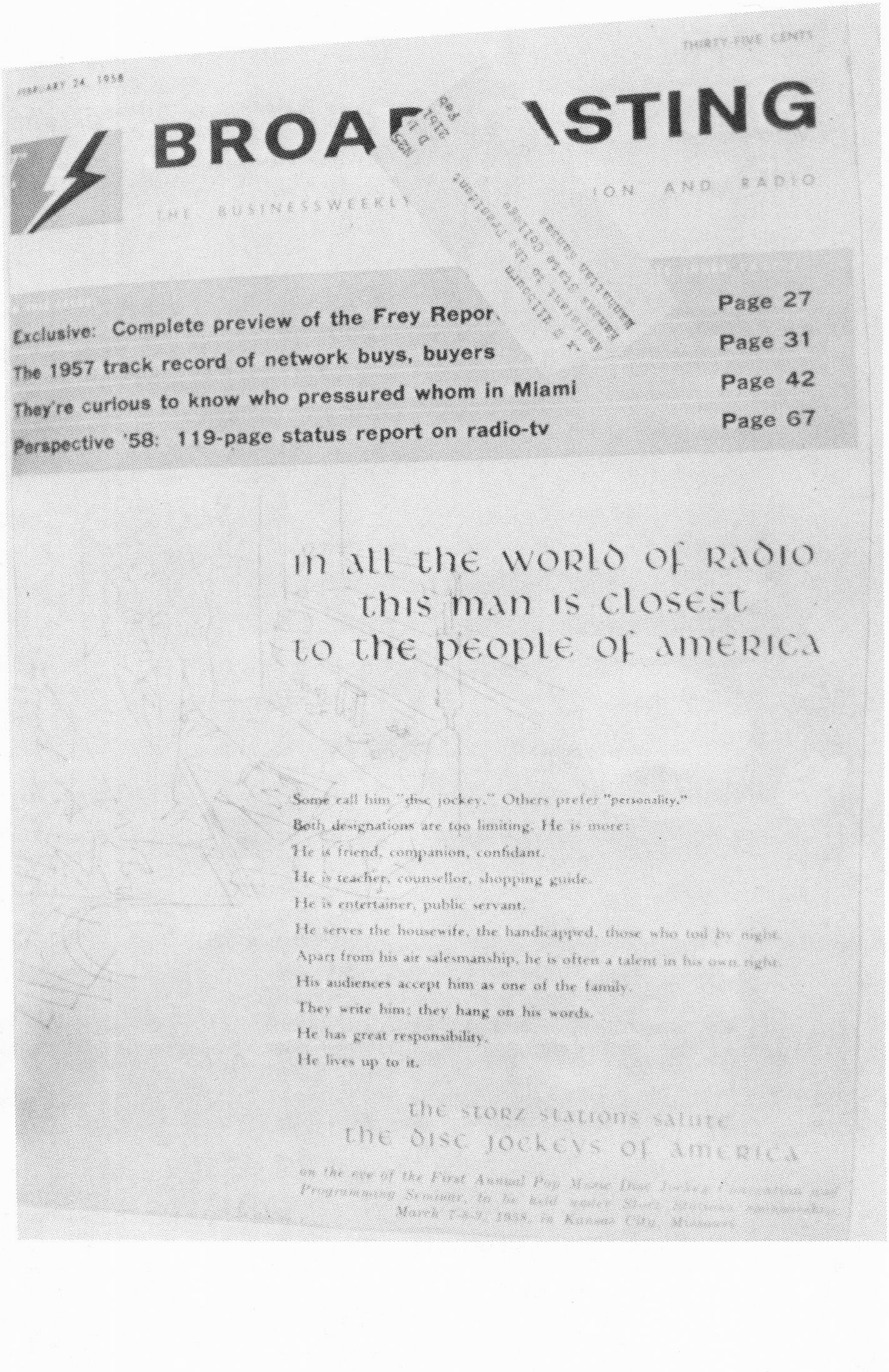

FEBRUARY 24, 1958

BROA… STING

THE BUSINESSWEEKLY … ION AND RADIO

Exclusive: Complete preview of the Frey Report	Page 27
The 1957 track record of network buys, buyers	Page 31
They're curious to know who pressured whom in Miami	Page 42
Perspective '58: 119-page status report on radio-tv	Page 67

McLendon

McLendon's approach to improving his stations' image seems to have been tied to his background in promoting movies for his family's theaters. Thus, McLendon's trades ads and his other efforts at improving Top 40's image were usually tied to his delight in developing promotions. News about the McLendon stations--especially their stunts and contests--appeared frequently in the trade press. These releases, coupled with flamboyant trades advertising often using an attractive young lady in a bathing suit or gown, combined to surround the McLendon stations with an aura of showmanship and sparkle. El Paso was hardly the equivalent of Kansas City in terms of its value as a market, but McLendon's advertising made it seem so by asking if KELP were the highest-rated independent station in radio history, thus bringing a "bigness" to the station which it only partly represented. The movies had a phrase that might well have been McLendon's as well: "the movies are bigger and better than ever."

To offset the razzle-dazzle, McLendon sought to emphasize the more substantial elements of his programming: superior news coverage, frequent, regular, and hard-hitting editorials, and (more recently) a campaign against suggestive lyrics in some records.

Bartell

Bartell's main effort at image-improvement centered around his effort to divorce Top 40 from the "teenagers-only" stigma by supplying a new selling phrase for the format: "Family Radio." All of Bartell's trade advertising contained the phrase, and the copy complemented it by emphasizing the varied composition of the audience. Bartell admits now that "Family Radio" was more a selling tool than a programming reality, but at the time perhaps some prospective advertisers were convinced that Bartell's version of Top 40 did not have an appeal limited only to teenagers.

It is curious that Bartell's choice of call letters in some cases seems to have worked against the "family" image he was working for. While WILD and WOKY were easily pronounceable and simple to remember, they might have had somewhat of a teenage "slang" sound to them that could have worked against the "family radio" image.

Storz, McLendon and Bartell seem to have believed that the radio format they were trying to sell to advertisers would really do a good job of moving merchandise--regardless of the audience composition--because at the time it was the only radio that was really being listened to. The themes of substantiality, sparkling showmanship, and family listening thus were all employed to induce advertisers to at least consider the stations in their buying plans rather than automatically ignoring them because of personal dislike for the programming.

CHAPTER NINE

LATER DEVELOPMENTS--TOP 40 IN PERSPECTIVE

It is hardly necessary to mention that the Top 40 format was highly successful. Its acceptance by audiences, advertisers and diverse factions of the radio industry led to the format's diffusion into markets of all sizes, so that for a time in the late 1950s, many AM stations were airing music-and-news, or other specialized formats with elements of the limited playlist. Some stations block-programmed the Top 40, while others converted their entire schedule to the format. The mass-adoption of Top 40 as the singular answer to many stations' programming needs was followed rather quickly by defections from the format by those stations (especially small-market imitators) that had attempted to duplicate the form without understanding the necessary philosophy that motivated Top 40. The failure of these and other, larger stations to attract an audience to their version of Top 40 may have accelerated the trend toward further format and audience specialization which itself began with Top 40.

Defections

In 1957, a report issued by the Adam Young station representative firm showed that regional and local (Class III and IV) stations had bypassed clear channel (Class I and II) stations in share of audience between 1952 and 1956, thus suggesting that a powerful signal was of less consequence in attracting an audience than was programming.[1] But even as the adoption of Top 40 was spreading down to the small-market stations in 1957 and later, a new trend was beginning among some of the large-market innovators: defection from Top 40. The music-and-news pioneer, WNEW, was one of the first to drop the Top 40 limited playlist (in September of 1957). Broadcasting reported,

> . . . the move was viewed last week as "radical," since more and more stations reportedly are featuring the "tops in pops" as a staple diet of programming. WNEW was a pioneer in this format.
>
> WNEW Program Manager Hall Moore conceded the "top 40" lists "serve a most useful purpose by showing trends and other pertinent information," but added that "such data should be treated as a source of information for a program rather than constituting the program itself." Furthermore, noted Mr. Moore, the music business has changed so much over the past few years--with the advent of the "LP" album--that single discs do not reflect the true status of U.S. musical tastes today, but rather a "restricted picture."[2]

It took other stations and programmers several years to come to the same conclusion as Moore reached in the article quoting him above, that album sales were too large to play only singles. Progressive rock stations, which sprang up in the late 1960s, concentrated almost entirely on albums.

In 1958 and 1959, other stations defected from the Top 40 format, often with more flamboyance than WNEW used. KWK in St. Louis in January of 1958 marked the end of the playing of a limited list of rock and roll records by playing each one more time and then breaking the disc

---

[1]"Young Questions 'Power' Radio," Broadcasting, June 17, 1957, p. 90.

[2]"WNEW Dropping 'Top 40' Hits to Keep 'Creative Urge' Free," Broadcasting, September 23, 1957, p. 90.

on the air.[3] KAVI in Rockyford, Colorado did the same thing a year and a half later,[4] again demonstrating the lag in the diffusion process between large-market innovators and small-market imitators. In 1960, Sponsor's regular "Sponsor Asks" symposium feature inquired in February, "What Factors Did You Consider in Switching From Top 40?"[5] with the title indicating that the trend was an accepted one. Herb Golombeck had become the General Manager of what had been KOWH after Storz sold it, and in the Sponsor article Golombeck describes how KOWH's call was changed to KMEO to reflect the station's playing of "cameo music" which was Omaha's only "good music" format.[6] In November of 1961, Record Source Incorporated, a firm which provided low-cost record service to small stations not given discs by the record companies announced that more stations were subscribing to the "easy listening" package than to the "Hot 100" (rock and roll) package, and more stations were buying album plans than single plans.[7] In March 1963 the top-rated station from 3:00 p.m. to midnight in New York, WINS, announced it was giving up rock and roll because of a "growing client resistance" to the format, which was especially difficult in New York

---

[3] "St. Louis Station Smashes Records to End the Sway of Rock 'n' Roll," Business Week, January 25, 1958, p. 78.

[4] "Take Rock Out of Rockyford," Billboard, July 13, 1959, p. 1.

[5] "What Factors Did You Consider in Switching From Top 40?" Sponsor, February 6, 1960, pp. 48-49, 71.

[6] Ibid., pp. 49, 71.

[7] "Trend to Variety in Radio Programs Seen," Broadcasting, November 27, 1961, p. 69.

because the agencies could monitor the station.[8] Meanwhile, Sherman P. Lawton's second study of changes in radio programming had been briefly quoted in Broadcasting under the headline "Study Finds Radio Programming 'More Conservative.'" Lawton's survey of about 300 scattered stations revealed a drastic drop in the number of stations that called themselves "top tune" outlets: from 27.2% in 1960 to only 9.3% in 1962, with a corresponding increase in the number of "good music" stations.[9] The switch back to a more conservative sound may have helped the fortunes of the radio networks, which by about 1960 had generally realized the futility of supplying expensive dramatic programs having few listeners, and instead began turning to supplying music-and-news, and finally just news and features. In 1960, the NBC radio network showed its first profit in eight years, and Mutual announced the same good news two years later.

In October of 1961, RAB announced that the average daily radio audience had increased 15.6% in the four years since 1957, from 68,354,000 to 79,003,000, while the U.S. Population had grown only 6.2% in the same period.[10] While the growth in the average daily radio audience could not be attributed directly to Top 40, it should be

---

[8] "R&R Will No Longer Dominate, Opines WINS Program Director Ted Steele," Variety, March 21, 1962, p. 53.

[9] "Study Finds Radio Programming 'More Conservative,'" Broadcasting, January 28, 1963, p. 64. See also Sherman P. Lawton, "Changes in U.S. Radio Programming, 1960-61," Journal of Broadcasting, 6, No. 4 (Fall, 1962), 327-334. An article summarizing the changes in the New York market in 1962 is "Radio's Changing Sounds," Sponsor, April 30, 1962, pp. 35-37, 51, 62.

[10] "Population Explosion Misfire Compared with Radio's Growth," Broadcasting, October 30, 1961, p. 25.

remembered that the period was the one in which the format spread virtually throughout the radio industry.

Format Specialization

Good Music

In the move away from rock and roll and the dominance of the Top 40 format, stations quite naturally adopted what seemed to be the antithesis of Top 40's "screaming" music, which was "good music." Gordon McLendon had phenomenal success with this format also, notably with his KABL ("cable") in San Francisco, beginning in 1959. Unlike the "good music" stations of the past, which had an austere, stuffy sound, KABL was lively with promotions, exotic non-commercials, and love-poems to the city of San Francisco. The promotions were not the treasure hunts and cash giveaways that had been popular on Top 40, but more sophisticated, urbane contests like winning one of the world's most valuable jewels to wear for a week. Don Keyes, who was then McLendon's National Program Director, admits that the promotion and the style of announcing were the only new ingredients added to the good music formula that had been derived much earlier in Dallas by Lee Siegal, owner of KIXL--the station that McLendon at one time thought was unbeatable. Keyes states that the policy of playing only "familiar" or "tuneful" music was developed by Siegal, along with a quiet logo for the station--a harp glissando, which KABL also used. According to Keyes, "KIXL was listened to in <u>the</u> homes in Dallas, <u>the</u> cars, <u>the</u> Cadillacs in Dallas. It was the first station I've ever run across that had snob appeal."[11]

---

[11] Keyes interview.

McLendon and Keyes realized that the self-image that San Franciscans had could also be responsive to a station with "snob appeal," which KABL supplied by its constant adulation of the city. KABL very rapidly became a ratings success, at one time claiming to be the first good music station in history to be number one in its market. Since then, KABL has consistently been in about the number three position, which with all the stations in San Francisco is still a good place to be. "KABL music" as it became known, "filled a void" in San Francisco and continues in popularity there at this writing.

McLendon saw an opportunity to put the same format on the air in Buffalo, New York, with the original WYSL ("whistle"), again buying a facility in a suburb to cover a major market as he had done with KABL. (KABL had been KROW in Oakland, across the bay from San Francisco; WYSL was licensed to Amherst, New York, a Buffalo suburb.) The same "romancing" of the city of Buffalo was tried on WYSL. Don Keyes has already been quoted (p. 273) on the unsuccessful result there. But in other cities, the good music format evenutally succeeded. When McLendon bought WGES, Chicago in 1962, he first tried programming better-quality Negro music (renaming the station as WYNR). Later, he tried all-news, this time changing the call to WNUS. Finally, WNUS, still so named, became a good music outlet, like KABL. KOST-FM in Los Angeles, which was McLendon's former all-advertising station (KADS) is also airing "good music" at this writing.

---

[12] _Ibid._

All News

All-news and all-ads were also McLendon format innovations. In the case of the all-news format, the idea was not necessarily original, but nobody else had programmed it as widely nor promoted it as heavily before McLendon. All-advertising seems to have been a totally new idea for radio, but one not far removed from the concept behind the community "shopper" circulars which carry both paid display advertising and free classified advertising by individuals.

Whether or not McLendon was aware of it is unknown as of this writing, but in 1955, Kevin Sweeney of RAB recommended that some broadcaster try an all-news format:

> . . . you don't need, in a community where there are eight stations, eight disc jockey stations. Somebody has got to look and see what the areas that need exploitation are, has got to enter those areas and do a merchandising job and a selling job. May I suggest one area? There are 1,500 or 1,600 daily newspapers in this country. Sure, they merchandise "Joe Palooka" and "Li'l Abner" and astrology lessons and classified ads and people read them because Bergdorf Goodman or Lord & Taylor or the Hecht Company has advertising in them. But their basic commodity is news.
>
> Now, they can whip us on some aspects of the news. But there's one thing: while they're still thinking about sending news down from the city room in the chute, we can put it on the air. Point out once for me, one outstanding news job being done by a radio station in the country. I'd like to see it, where news is their primary commodity. Is there room for it? I don't know. Maybe. If it costs you in the metropolitan area five-six million dollars to get into the business of selling news that you print, for a few hundred thousand dollars you could get into news-on-the-air. Is it an impractical idea? Why doesn't somebody find out? Then he has something specific to sell that is not "Sincerely" or "Sh-Boom," or what everybody else has got.[13]

The budget considerations that Sweeney mentions were important

---

[13]Kevin Sweeney, "Radio: That Dip Isn't a Trend," Broadcasting, March 28, 1955, p. 40.

ones in the case of McLendon's first all-news station, X-TRA. McLendon had acquired the sales rights to XEAK, a station in Tijuana with 50,000 watts, clear channel. At the time, XEAK was being programmed with rock and roll by making tapes in studios at the Mission Valley Inn in San Diego and then physically carrying them across the border to the transmitter. Keyes points out that with fast-breaking news, this was not feasible. Instead, lines had to be run from Los Angeles, including ten teletype wires at one time. Keyes recalls that the station had a staff of twelve announcers, also a high figure. The expense of these largely excluded the use of mobile reporters in southern California cities, but since XTRA had no competition for a while, they were not considered essential. When KFWB dropped Top 40 and began an all-news format which included reporters on the street, McLendon decided that the cost of competing from Mexico was too high, so he reverted back to a less-expensive good music format on XTRA (AM), complementing the music on KOST-FM.[14]

Although XTRA billed itself as the "world's first all news radio" when it went on the air May 6, 1961, in fact San Francisco station KFAX had gone on the air a full year earlier as "the nation's first newsradio station."[15] KFAX did not program only news. It featured a 15-minute newscast on the hour, a 5-minute summary on the half hour, and commentaries, analyses, editorials and features in between.[16] This is the basic format that most so-called "all news"

---

[14]Don Keyes interview.

[15]"Tuneless Air Format Bows," Billboard, May 16, 1960, p. 18.

[16]Ibid.

stations actually follow today. It is also the format that KLIQ, Portland, Oregon followed in launching what it claimed was "the world's first all news radio station," in April of 1959, eclipsing KFAX's claim by one year and XTRA's by two.[17] McLendon's XTRA (and later WNUS) were literally all news--there were no features, but only newscasts repeated over and over. The format originally called for two 7 1/2-minute newscasts in each 15-minute segment. According to Keyes, this was found to be too short an interval, "especially for commuting Los Angeles, where it takes you 40 minutes to get to work, at least."[18] Keyes and McLendon expected to have a complete audience turnover in 30 minutes, because after that everything being heard was essentially a repeat of what had just been said. But apparently there was enough updating to keep avid news-seekers tuned all day long, according to Keyes. In 1962, Pulse found the average listener tune-in to XTRA lasting only 18 minutes.[19]

When, in 1964, McLendon turned Chicago station WYNR into WNUS to become that city's first all-news station, the station used a quarter-hour newscast format, being repeated 24 hours a day. Eventually, the station also went to a 30-minute format before repeating. In Chicago, McLendon did use mobile units on the street (with electric signs for spelling out news bulletins visually on their roofs), but there were still no features or other content in addition to the "hard"

---

[17]"KLIQ," Sponsor, April 25, 1959, p. 69.

[18]Don Keyes interview.

[19]"Pulse Makes Quarter-Hour Studies," Broadcasting, November 19, 1962, p. 98.

news. WNUS, like XTRA, changed to "good music" programming in March 1958.

McLendon's all-news stations relied more on wire services than on original reporting.[20] Since McLendon's withdrawal from all-news, some CBS owned-and-operated stations, and several of the Westinghouse stations have been highly successful with the news-plus-features version of the all-news format.

All Ads

McLendon also pioneered the first all-advertising station in this country. The qualification "in this country" is made because again, there were forerunners of the idea. An item headlined "Classified Radio" appeared in Broadcasting on June 11, 1956 explaining how, in Afghanistan, radio advertisements were sold as newspaper classified ads were, with the announcer reading one right after another with no other entertainment intervening. However, the Afghanistan station did not broadcast classified ads continuously, but only for a period after two daily news broadcasts.[21]

When McLendon proposed to the FCC in 1965 that Los Angeles FM station KGLA be converted to an all-advertising format, the Commission was in the midst of developing some new policies on over-commercialization. Broadcasting listed a number of questions the FCC would have to answer about commercialization before acting on the proposal:

---

[20]For further detail about McLendon's (and other operators') all-news formats, see "News and Nothing But the News on XTRA," Broadcasting, June 19, 1961, pp. 108-09; "McLendon All News at Chicago Station," Broadcasting, August 24, 1964, p. 68; "All News Format is Winning Friends," Broadcasting, June 27, 1966, pp. 100-03.

[21]"Classified Radio," Broadcasting, June 11, 1956, p. 99.

> Are commercials, for instance, always or even usually considered an intrusion by the listener? Do they serve only the private needs of stations and advertisers? Or can a station, at least in a city like Los Angeles that is practically drowning in a sea of radio signals, serve a public need by acting as an audible want-ad page virtually all day long?[22]

The Commission eventually did grant the transfer to McLendon with the proviso that he would have to apply for license renewal in one year (instead of three) so that the FCC could determine if the station were operating in the public interest. McLendon acquired the station in July of 1966, and began the all-ads format in November of that year. By the summer of the following year, with license renewal requiring a report, McLendon decided to give up the new format. For a detailed report describing the development of this station, see James A. Kushner, "KADS (FM): Want-ad Radio in Los Angeles," Journal of Broadcasting, XVI, No. 3 (Summer 1972), 267-76.

Other Formats

A number of other formats were developed in the period beginning in the 1960s when scores of stations dropped Top 40 in favor of what were felt to be more "adult" formats. A few stations began to program "sing along" music, encouraged by the popularity of Mitch Miller's sing-along records and shows. Such a development must have been sweet to Miller, who had been a vehement critic of Top 40 radio, but the format was not widely adopted. Other stations tried all-talk, in which guests in the studio or callers on telephones were aired generally more for human interest value than for any substantial

---

[22] "A Gordian Knot for the FCC," Broadcasting, December 27, 1965, p. 34.

information that might be imparted. A few stations in larger markets found it profitable to program jazz or classical music, while in smaller, rural markets country and western music became extremely popular. By 1965, the country and western trend was large enough that Plough's WJJD, Chicago, which had been trying to compete with rock station WLS, decided to switch to country and western, beginning a trend toward the development of C & W stations in large cities as well as in the country. Religious and gospel music stations also grew in number in the 1960s, as did the number of stations playing music appealing to Blacks, which became known as "soul" stations. In cities with large populations of foreign-language-speaking persons, stations turned to serving those audiences in their native tongues. And middle of-the-road and music-and-news stations continued to attract wide and varied audiences. It is interesting to note, in regard to these other formats, that when a good facility was programming one of the new forms, then smaller, less powerful stations suffered in the ratings and often had to give up the specialized format for something more general. This same phenomenon is happening as this is written with progressive rock stations--those with the better signals are overtaking the pioneers with lesser facilities. Note also that in the case of country and western stations, the format was proved in the middle markets before it was tried in the large top markets, exactly as had been the case with the adoption of Top 40.[23]

---

[23]For a long and detailed report on the diversification of formats by 1964, see "One Best Format for Each Station," Broadcasting, December 14, 1964, pp. 57-101. Another account, comparing 20 radio markets in 1965 is "Radio's Changing Landscape," Variety, July 28, 1965, pp. 39, 42, 46. A good discussion of the growing popularity of

By about 1964, a great diversification of formats and a striking re-appropriation of audiences had taken place. The specialization of Top 40 just ten years before had proved that the radio audience could be attracted not just to various individual programs of different types but also to a single continuous program (thus, to a station) of one type. Just as music-and-news stations had led the change in listening habits from networks to local independents, so Top 40 stations had led the shift from program tuning to station tuning. Having acquired the habit of listening to a station for a consistently-offered kind of programming with Top 40, audiences were easily persuaded to listen to other stations providing other kinds of entertainment in later years.

Late Top 40

What happened to Top 40 after the imitators defected to other formats can be summed up in two words: refinement and maturation. The great champion of refinement has been programmer Bill Drake, while the process of maturation has occurred both because of advertiser pressure and because of the simple passage of time.

Drake

Bill Drake--real name Philip Yarbrough--in the late 1960s and early 1970s became the country's best-known contemporary music station programmer because of his initial success with boosting the ratings of such powerful stations as KHJ (Los Angeles), CKLW (Detroit market), and

---

the country and western format is "Growing Sound of Country Music," Broadcasting, October 18, 1965, pp. 69-91. Also see a Broadcasting "Special Report" titled "One Best Format for Each Station," published December 14, 1964.

KFRC (San Francisco). Drake's most important contribution was the concept of a "tuneout"--anything that is aired that makes the audience turn the dial. Everything Drake did to increase ratings was aimed at eliminating tuneout. The wrong music is the biggest tuneout, so Drake was careful to have his stations play a very limited playlist. Too many commercials are a tuneout, so Drake-programmed stations aired only about 12 or 13 minutes of commercials in an hour. These commercials were carefully arranged in sets with the longest, most boring first, progressing to the shortest most interesting spot just before the set ends, so that the pace of the commercial set was quickened as boredom was setting in. Interruptions to the flow of music were minimized so that records were often played in "sweeps" of three or four or more in a row. And the disc jockey was allowed to say something only over the intros or outros of the music, usually just the time and temperature.

Maturation

Today, contemporary music radio is respectable. It is big business. It is serious about itself, and cautious to preserve the status-quo which generally finds contemporary music stations at the top of both ratings and billings. For the most part, the maverick Top 40 station has become the good neighbor pop music station, and in larger cities contemporary music stations have even taken over the low end of the AM radio dial where the prestigious network affiliates used to be. The "mavericks" today are in FM, where what used to be called "underground" radio has become "progressive" rock or "free-form" programming. With experimentation and pioneering now expected on FM, the AM contemporary music station can relax and concentrate on just playing the hits and keeping the order-takers by their telephones.

Stanley N. Kaplan, who in 1968 was owner of contemporary music station WAYS in Charlotte, North Carolina (now president of SIS Radio, Inc.), gave a speech at the 1968 NAB convention in Chicago titled "Whatever Happened to Top 40 Radio?" Portions of the text of Kaplan's speech, reproduced on pages 570 to 574, explain with some wistfulness in just what ways Top 40 has matured.[24] While the author must disagree with Kaplan's choice of names for a list of "copiers" of Top 40 (page one of text)--since Jerry Bartell and Bill Stewart have been shown in the present work to have been innovators, not imitators--Kaplan's emphasis on Top 40 having contributed a "management attitude" of greater importance than any notion about the size or selection of the playlist seems eminently correct. It seems appropriate, too, for Kaplan to call "the operator in any market that puts blood and guts and money into the basics of production, promotion, and people" a "Top 40 operator no matter what he programs." The development of the Top 40 format did give to all of radio in the 1950s the formula for immediate survival and the principles on which to build future success.

---

[24] Stanley N. Kaplan, "Whatever Happened to Top 40 Radio?" a speech presented at the NAB convention in Chicago, Illinois, 1968.

WHATEVER HAPPENED TO TOP 40 RADIO? WE CAN'T ANSWER THAT QUESTION....OR EVEN ASK IT INTELLIGENTLY....WITHOUT FIRST AGREEING ON WHAT TOP 40 MEANS. OF COURSE THE TERM ORIGINATED WITH REFERENCE TO A PARTICULAR TYPE OF MUSIC SELECTED BY A PARTICULAR METHOD. BUT CERTAINLY TODAY THE IMPLICATIONS OF WHAT THE TERM HAS COME TO STAND FOR INVOLVE A LOT MORE THAN A CHOICE OF RECORDS.

FIFTEEN YEARS AGO WHEN RADIO WAS CONSIDERED IN ITS DOLDRUMS, WHEN THE MAJOR EXECUTIVES IN RADIO GOT INTO TELEVISION AS QUICKLY AS THEY COULD, AND WHEN THERE WERE 650 STATIONS IN THE COUNTRY AS OPPOSED TO THE 4,000 OR SO WE HAVE TODAY, EVERYBODY WAS BEEFING ABOUT THE GOOD OLD DAYS OF RADIO AND REMINISCING ABOUT HOW THINGS USED TO BE WHEN YOU PLUGGED INTO THE NETWORK AND THE MONEY ROLLED IN. BUT SOMEWHERE AROUND IN THE WOODWORK THERE WERE SOME YOUNG, CREATIVE GUYS WHO LIKED RADIO BETTER THAN TELEVISION, WHO DIDN T GIVE A DAMN ABOUT ANY PRE-CONCEIVED NOTIONS. THEY WERE ABLE TO SNEAK INTO THE RADIO BUSINESS BECAUSE NOBODY WANTED THE FREQUENCY THEY WERE AFTER.

THIS WAS A BAND OF UNKNOWN, IMPOSSIBLY COCKY GUYS WHO WENT AT IT AS THERE WAS NO WAY TO LOSE. TWO OF THEM, FOR EXAMPLE, WERE TODD STORZ AND GORDON MCLENDON. THEY AND OTHERS LIKE THEM SPAWNED A GLITTERING BAND OF INTELLIGENT PIRATES WHO ARE TODAY RUNNING MAJOR STATIONS AND NETWORKS ALL OVER THE COUNTRY. MEN LIKE STEVE LABUNSKY AT NBC, RALPH BEAUDIN AT ABC, BOTH STORZ GUYS. BUD ARMSTRONG, WHO NOW RUNS THE STORZ STATIONS, ART CARLSON OF WSBA. MCLENDON PROTEGES LIKE CHARLIE PAYNE AT WESTINGHOUSE, KENT BURKHARDT AT WQXI, BILL WEAVER WHO RUNS WKBW IN BUFFALO. IN ADDITION TO THE FORMER EMPLOYEES OF STORZ AND MCLENDON THERE ARE THE ADMIRERS WHO WATCHED FROM A DISTANCE, COPIED EVERYTHING THEY COULD FIND, AND WENT HAPPILY DOWN THE ROAD TO SUCCESS. PEOPLE LIKE DON BURDEN, JERRY BARTEL, HERB MENDELSON, HAL NEAL, JACK THAYER, RALPH BEAUDINE, RUTH MEYER, JOHN BARRETT, BILL ARMSTRONG, BILL STEWART, BILL MORGAN AND MANY MORE.

THE ONE THING THAT NEARLY EVERY ONE OF THESE MEN HAD IN COMMON IS THAT NONE WERE ENGINEERS. A FEW WERE SALESMEN AS MANY OF THE EARLIER LEADERS OF RADIO HAD BEEN. MOST OF THESE GUYS WERE PROGRAMMERS, DISC JOCKEYS, PROMOTERS....AND THAT PROBABLY HAD A GREAT DEAL TO DO WITH THE FACT THAT THEY CHANGED THE FACE OF RADIO. INDEED, THEY PROBABLY SAVED RADIO ALTOGETHER. CERTAINLY THEY HAVE GIVEN IT THE FORWARD THRUST THAT IT NOW HAS.

OUT OF THIS CHANGE AND THRUST EMERGED SOMETHING CALLED TOP 40 RADIO. IT HAS BROUGHT A LOT OF SUCCESS TO A LOT OF PEOPLE. NOW SOME OF THOSE SAME PEOPLE WHO RODE THIS BANDWAGON ARE WONDERING WHAT HAPPENED TO IT. MAYBE THAT'S BECAUSE THEY DIDN'T REALLY UNDERSTAND THE SECRET OF THEIR OWN SUCCESS.

TEN YEARS AGO THE OLD-LINE STATIONS IN ANY MARKET WOULD NOT EVEN CONSIDER SUCH FUNNY THINGS AS JINGLES. MANY, IN FACT, STILL HAD STUDIO ORCHESTRAS. ALL WERE GENERALISTS TRYING TO APPEAL TO ALL PEOPLE WITH ALL THINGS. THEY NEITHER PROMOTED NOR PRODUCED ANYTHING....AND A CONTEST?.......FORGET IT!!!!!

TODAY THE OLD-LINE STATIONS THEMSELVES HAVE SUB-DIVIDED INTO 5 OR 6 SPECIFIC CATEGORIES. IF AN OLD-LINE STATION IS A MUSIC STATION TODAY IT PLAYS A LOT OF MUSIC. IT HAS JINGLES AND CONTESTS AND GOOD PRODUCTION. IT PAYS SOME ATTENTION TO THE MUSIC IT PLAYS. IT TRIES ITS VERY BEST TO BE CONSISTANT. IT WORKS HARD ON ITS LOCAL NEWS. IT NO LONGER PROGRAMS FOR SALES. (RADIO BEFORE THIS REVOLUTION PROGRAMMED ALMOST EXCLUSIVELY FOR SALES, BUT THE ADVENT OF MANAGEMENT FROM THE PROGRAMMING SIDE AS OPPOSED TO SALES AND ENGINEERING MAKE THIS A NO LONGER FEASIBLE PURSUIT). SOME OLD-LINE STATIONS HAVE DECIDED TO GO TALK. THEY ARE ALL TALK. THESE INCLUDE WBBM IN CHICAGO, WKAT IN MIAMI, SOME OLD-LINE STATIONS HAVE GONE INTO THE GOOD MUSIC AREA. THESE INCLUDE KABL IN SAN FRANCISCO, WPAT IN NEW YORK AND WEEZ IN BOSTON, WIOD IN MIAMI, WAIT IN CHICAGO.

SOME OF THE OTHER STATIONS HAVE GONE TO VERY SPECIFIC MARKET SEGMENTS.....NEGRO, COUNTRY & WESTERN, CLASSICAL. THE NET RESULT IS THAT A MAJOR MARKET TODAY MIGHT HAVE AS MANY AS 8 TO 10 VERY WELL PROGRAMMED STATIONS IN DIFFERENT FORMATS COVERING

-3-

THE FULL SPECTRUM. ALL OF THEM ARE BETTER THAN THEY EVER WERE BEFORE. EACH HAS SLIGHTLY HIGHER AUDIENCE SHARES THAN EVER BEFORE. EACH IS CUTTING INTO THE ONCE DOMINANT TOP 40 STATIONS IN THAT MARKET. SOME TOP 40 OPERATORS HAVE PANICED. THEY ARE SAYING THINGS LIKE "THE PEOPLE ARE NO LONGER INTERESTED IN OUR KIND OF MUSIC." THINGS LIKE "THERE AREN'T ENOUGH KIDS."

WHAT IN FACT HAS HAPPENED IS THAT THE TOP 40 GUY BEGAN TO PROGRAM FOR SALES, BEGAN TO SOFTEN HIS MUSIC; CUT BACK ON HIS PROMOTION. SOME OF THESE TOP 40 OPERATORS HAVE BECOME THE GENERALIST OF THE 60'S AND NOBODY'S GENERALIST IS GOING TO WIN. YOU CANNOT BE ALL THINGS TO ALL PEOPLE. THESE VERY SAME TOP 40 OPERATORS PROVED THIS A DOZEN YEARS AGO AND NOW THEY HAVE FALLEN VICTIM OF THE VERY SAME DISEASE. THEY ARE DOING ALL KINDS OF FAKE THINGS FOR ALL KINDS OF FAKE REASONS....NONE OF WHICH ARE RELATED TO THEIR AUDIENCE. THERE ISN'T ONE DAMN THING WRONG WITH TOP 40 PROVIDED IT IS THE KIND THAT SPAWNED THIS WHOLE ERA OF RADIO, PROVIDED IT IS IMAGINATIVELY PACKAGED, MAGNIFICENTLY PRODUCED AND EFFECTIVELY PROMOTED AND PROVIDED THAT AN EARNEST EFFORT IS MADE TO FIND OUT WHAT INDEED ARE THE 40 OR SO MOST POPULAR TUNES IN YOUR MARKET. INSTEAD OF LAMENTING THEIR FATE AS NO LONGER BEING ABLE TO ACHIEVE 50% OF THE AUDIENCE WE SHOULD BE GRATEFUL FOR THE FACT THAT IN BOTH TECHNOLOGY AND POPULATION A REVOLUTION HAS INCREASED THE TOTAL LISTENING AUDIENCE OF RADIO. AS THE RESEARCH HAS IMPROVED WE ARE NOW ABLE TO DEMONSTRATE THE REMARKABLE REACH OF RADIO. TOP 40 OPERATORS NEED NOT SELL DEFENSIVELY AS THEY HAD TO 10 - 15 YEARS AGO. HUNDREDS AND THOUSANDS OF ADVERTISERS ARE ANXIOUS TO PURSUE TEENAGERS, TEENY BOPPERS, ALL TEENS, 18-24 YEAR OLD ADULTS AND ESPECIALLY 18-34 YEAR OLD ADULTS. MAYBE IT IS NO LONGER POSSIBLE TO GET ALL OF THE AUDIENCE ANYWHERE. BUT THE NUMBERS ARE SUCH AND THE DIVISION OF AGE GROUPS ARE SUCH THAT EVERYTHING IS TILTED IN THE FAVOR OF THE YOUTH ORIENTED. RADIO STATION. AND WHAT THEY NEED TO DO IS TO PAY RELIGIOUS ATTENTION TO PURSUING THE UNDER 25 AUDIENCE WITHOUT COMPROMISING AND WITH FULL UNDERSTANDING THAT IF IT TAKES THREE OR FOUR STATIONS TO MAKE FOR A SUCCESSFUL ADVERTISING CAMPAIGN IN

-4-

THEIR MARKET .....AS IT DOES IN VIRTUALLY EVERY MARKET IN THE COUNTRY....THEN THIS IS NOT A LIABILITY AT ALL. BECAUSE IN THIS BILLION DOLLAR BUSINESS OF OURS THE DOLLARS ARE THERE FOR ANYONE WILLING TO EARN THEM.

THE BETTER A STATION IS PROGRAMMED, WHATEVER THE FORMAT, THE MORE DETERMINED IT WILL BE NOT TO PROGRAM FOR SALES. NOT ONLY DOES THIS MEAN THAT THE AUDIENCE WILL NOT BE SACRIFICED ON ANY DOLLAR SCALE, BUT IT MEANS THE STATIONS WILL NOT BE OVER COMMER-CIALED.....NOT BECAUSE OF THE NAB CODE BUT BECAUSE OF THE ECONOMIC NECESSITY TO BE COMPETITIVE. AS ALL STATIONS DIMINISH THE AMOUNT OF COMMERCIALS THEY WILL CARRY THEY WILL RAISE THEIR RATES ACCORDINGLY. AND THEY WILL DELIVER A BETTER PRODUCT TO ANY ADVERTISER.

* * * *

SO WHATEVER HAPPENED TO TOP 40 RADIO? MAYBE THE PEOPLE WHO ASK THAT QUESTION DON'T REALLY KNOW WHAT TOP 40 REALLY MEANS. IN MY OPINION, TOP 40, AS A TERM DESCRIBING A SUCCESSFUL BRAND OF RADIO, MAY HAVE VERY LITTLE TO DO WITH MUSIC ALTOGETHER. IT HAS MORE TO DO WITH PROGRAMMING AS A WHOLE, PROMOTING, GIVING THE AUDIENCE AND THE CLIENTS THEIR MONEY'S WORTH. AND REFUSING TO COMPROMISE THE INTEGRITY OF YOUR FORMULA...AND IT CAN BE ANY ONE OF MANY DIFFERENT FORMULAS, SOME PROBABLY NOT EVEN DREAMED UP YET. AND IT HAS TO DO WITH NEVER LETTING UP IN YOUR EFFORTS TO DO WHAT YOU SET OUT TO DO THE VERY BEST IT CAN BE DONE, AND NOT DILUTING THOSE EFFORTS BY LOSING SIGHT OF WHAT YOU HAVE SET OUT TO DO.

THESE ARE THE PRINCIPLES WHICH ARE BEING APPLIED IN MANY CASES TO SO-CALLED MIDDLE OF THE ROAD' STATIONS, TALK STATIONS, ALL KINDS OF STATIONS, WHILE THE GUY WHO THOUGHT HE WAS THE TOP 40 OPERATOR HAS GOTTEN FAT AND COMPLACENT AND FORGOTTEN HOW HE GOT THERE IN THE FIRST PLACE.

* * * *

I DON'T INTEND TO LOSE SIGHT OF THE BASIC LESSONS THAT I BELIEVE I HAVE LEARNED FROM THOSE PIONEERS OF THE NEW RADIO. ONE WAY YOU CAN LOSE SIGHT OF THE BASICS IS BY GETTING BOGGED DOWN IN DETAIL. YOU CAN FIND YOURSELF MAKING DECISIONS WHICH AFFECT THE TOTAL OPERATION, BUT BASED ON SOME MINOR MATTER OR PROBLEM WHICH IS

RELATIVELY INSIGNIFICANT. THIS IS ONE OF THE HAZARDS OF SUCCESS, AND ONE OF THE PROBLEMS, I SUSPECT, OF SOME OF THOSE PEOPLE WHO ARE WONDERING WHATEVER HAPPENED TO TOP 40.

* * * *

I PERSONALLY TRY TO POSITION PEOPLE SO THAT I CAN BE THE TROUBLE SHOOTER. IT REMINDS ME OF A STORY TOLD OF A VERY, VERY SUCCESSFUL HOUSE OF ILL REPUTE IN SOUTH CAROLINA. A FRIEND OF MINE, ONE OF ITS REGULAR CUSTOMERS, WAS AMAZED TO FIND ONE DAY WHEN HE WALKED INTO THIS PLACE THAT THE MADAM HAD LINED UP ALONG WITH HER GIRLS. WHEN HE ASKED HER ABOUT IT SHE SAID TO HIM THAT SHE WAS JUST SICK AND TIRED OF ADMINISTRATION. ME TOO! I HIRE EXCELLENT ADMINISTRATION. AND THEREFORE I AM GOING TO BE FREE TO THINK ABOUT THE LARGER PROBLEMS AND PAY ATTENTION TO THE AUDIENCE.

WE ARE GOING TO CARVE OUT A NICHE IN EVERY MARKET, AND WE ARE GOING TO PLAY TO THAT NICHE LIKE THEY WERE THE DRIVEN SNOW, WHICH THEY ARE. WHERE WE HAVE A ROCK STATION WE ARE GOING TO BE A ROCK STATION WITH NO COMPROMISE, NO APOLOGIES, AND NO EXCEPTIONS. I AM ABSOLUTELY CERTAIN THAT AS RESEARCH BECOMES MORE SOPHISTICATED, AND THERE IS MUCH EVIDENCE THAT THIS IS ALREADY HAPPENING, EACH OF US WILL BE DAMN LUCKY TO HAVE A FINGER HOLD ON A GIVEN SEGMENT OF A GIVEN MARKET. MAYBE IN SOME OF THE HEAVILY STATIONED MAJOR MARKETS THE GREATEST ECONOMIC SUCCESS WILL GO TO THE STATION THAT OWNS THE AUDIENCE UNDER 25 AND DOESN'T HAVE A SINGLE SOUL OVER THAT AGE. IN THE NEXT 5 YEARS OR SO INSTEAD OF THE AGENCY SLIPS TO THE REPS SAYING WE WANT 18-49 OR 25-50 THEY WILL SAY "WE ARE GOING TO PUT 35% OF OUR BUDGET 18-24 AND 22% OF OUR BUDGET 45-51%, ETC." IT MAY BE SOME DAY SOON THAT SOME STATION WILL SPECIALIZE EXCLUSIVELY IN UNDER 14 AND DO IT SUCCESSFULLY. THE ONE THING THAT IS CERTAIN IS THAT NO ONE EVER AGAIN IN MOST MAJOR MARKETS CAN EVER BE A GENERALIST. THERE ARE NO DOUBT FORMATS YET TO BE INVENTED. THEY WILL SWITCH 4-5% FROM THE GENERAL AUDIENCE. BUT THE SPECIFIC, TRIED AND TRUE PRINCIPALS OF MANAGEMENT WILL PREVAIL. THE OPERATOR IN ANY MARKET THAT PUTS BLOOD AND GUTS AND MONEY INTO THE BASICS OF PRODUCTION, PROMOTION, AND PEOPLE........HE IS THE WINNER. AND I FOR ONE INTEND TO CALL HIM THE TOP 40 OPERATOR NO MATTER WHAT HE PROGRAMS.

SUMMARY

Background

The changes in radio programming which resulted in the Top 40 format were one portion of the new trends in media usage which in turn were but one part of a set of changes taking place in the American society as a whole. Among the general social trends of the post World War II era were decreasing median age, a concomitant development of the youth market, a general increase in affluence, and a migration from the cities to the suburbs. Suburbanization dealt a heavy blow to the big city newspapers, and the arrival of television hit picture magazines equally hard. Television also caused radical changes in the radio industry, by replacing the radio in the living room, by usurping radio's former prime time in the evenings, and by adopting radio's stars and programming personnel. Meanwhile, the music and record industries were also changing. The entrance of BMI into the music licensing field, with its willingness to promote country and western and "race" music, broke the Broadway and Hollywood show-tunes-only pattern of ASCAP. The more specialized BMI music was often recorded by independent record companies rather than the "major" labels, and in the recording field, these "indies" gained an increasingly larger share of the market. The introduction of the 45 r.p.m. record by RCA found a ready acceptance in the youth market because of its low price, its portability, and the teen-oriented content it increasingly contained.

Independent Music and News Stations

Only some of the changes which took place in the audiences available to radio were directly attributable to television. The social trend of suburbanization gave rise to the phenomenon known as "drive time," in which radio had an audience in cars all to itself in early morning and late afternoon. In the home, radio listening became a diversion from other activity rather than the activity itself (just listening). As a "companion," radio sets began to turn up more frequently in the kitchen, the bedroom and the bathroom, and portable sets were carried on picnics and outings more often, too. The listener also changed his demands on the medium. As he grew to depend on TV for entertainment, radio became the place he turned for weather, time, traffic information and other news, as well as the music he liked. The star-studded, highly-produced show that had been the staple prime-time fare of the radio networks began to receive less audience and advertiser attention than did a local service provided by an independent (non-affiliated) station emphasizing music and news. Music and news fit in perfectly with the "background companion" role that radio was assuming, and stations programming this format continued to rise in the ratings, even as network stations were continuing to fall off. As ratings services began to include sampling of the vast out-of-home audience, and as "metro areas" rather than city limits came to be the basic survey area, music and news stations ranked even higher than before, while again network affiliates did not fare well. For the first time, the local, low-power, independent radio station found itself capable of competing with the powerful city-based network affiliates in regard to audience and advertising revenues. Daytime-only stations became almost as valuable a property as a fulltime outlet, and many more daytime-only stations were built in the late 1940s and early 1950s.

Shift from Network to Local

In reflecting their loss of audience to television and to local independent stations, networks cut the rates charged to advertisers, both to reduce the overall price and also to lower the price of evening time (since daytime was now radio's prime time). Networks also cut their compensation to local affiliates, and this plus the success of local programming encouraged the development of national spot buying and the growth of station representative firms. Station reps helped spot buying on local stations to be almost as easy as buying national spots on a network, and as a consequence, the participating spot announcement (rather than the fully sponsored program) became the norm in radio by about the mid-1950s. The reasons for the growth in spot sales and for the use of the participating announcement parallels the reasons for the success of independent music-and-news stations. Both spot buys and independent stations made up in daytime audiences what they lost to television at night. Locally-produced programs that gathered a particular size and type of audience allowed the advertiser greater selectivity than did network buying, while the spot rate structure was more responsive to changes in audience makeup than were network rates, and offered a greater range of choice in the depth and length of the schedule ordered as well. On the other hand, because the national advertiser went into television, an increasing number of radio stations were left with the problem of developing the loyalties of <u>local</u> sponsors, and this shift was thus also responsible for radio becoming a _local_ medium in the 1950s.

Disc Jockey Shows

The radio networks at first sought to fight the rise in popularity of music-and-news stations by offering more of the same programs that had been offered for years. As these failed to develop a following, ABC and NBC began to experiment with new forms. The most innovative of these was NBC's _Monitor_, launched in June of 1955, which was obviously designed to be a carrier for network-sold participating announcements. Following the magazine format, ABC announced a series of (usually) five-minute-long evening programs called "New Sounds for You." In 1957, ABC attempted to revive bands and singers by converting almost all of its programs to live music. Meanwhile, Mutual was experimenting with network disc jockey programs (which became increasingly popular in the mid-1950s) while CBS carried on much as it had before. The early network disc jockey programs tended to feature "stars" and "names" who merely were on hand to introduce the records and provide chatter. However, the phenomenal success of Martin Block's deejay program pointed the way for other networks and program syndicators to try their own non-name deejay shows. For example, deejay Alan Freed did a syndicated show aired on about ten stations before he moved to WINS in New York. Syndicated deejay shows featuring the rhythm and blues music popular with teenagers succeeded in the mid-1950s, while those shows featuring just popular music did not fare as well. In 1959, the TV version of _Your Hit Parade_ went off of television, partly a victim of too much rhythm and blues music and the preferences of the teens for the "original" versions of the hits. Meanwhile, local TV disc jockey shows of the type epitomized by ABC-TV's American Bandstand were flourishing, so that by 1958, about a year after Bandstand's network debut, over 100 local TV record shows were being aired.

Program Services

As disc jockey programs flourished, a number of companies which had formerly been in the business of furnishing transcribed programs turned to providing programming aids such as jingles, sound effects, and shortened versions of pop songs. Several attempts were also made to establish specialized networks, including a forerunner of news actuality services as currently exemplified by UPI Audio. The station identification jingle became popular in the middle and late 1950s as increasing numbers of music-and-news formats were adopted, each vying for special recognition from a part of the audience. Bill Meeks' PAMS was probably the first company to specialize in station identification jingles, while Tom Merriman with his Commercial Recording Corporation provided a sales aids service as well as IDs. Pepper Studios (now Pepper-Tanner, Inc.), was formed in 1959 and has grown rapidly to be the world's largest producer of station ID jingles and other commercial music. The increasing use of such short programming elements as jingles and spot announcements created a need for such equipment as the MacKenzie Spotter, Ross Beville's Spotmaster and Ampex's Cue-Matic--all designed to handle individual bits of programming quickly and automatically.

Station Acquisition by Top 40 Group Owners

There is rather wide variation in the station acquisition policies of the Storz, McLendon, Bartell and Plough groups.

The Storz group had a policy of never buying a new station until the previous acquisition had been largely paid for. Storz also bought the very best facility he could find, on the belief that the first person in the market to do Top 40 with a decent facility would be very hard for later challengers to dislodge. Storz's experience with his own KOWH, Omaha (500 watts) and the original WTIX, New Orleans (250 watts)--the only two stations the group has ever disposed of--may have been responsible for this philosophy. The Storz station lineup today remains as it was at Storz's death in 1964: WHB, Kansas City; WDGY, Minneapolis; WQAM, Miami; KOMA, Oklahoma City; KXOK, St. Louis. George "Bud" Armstrong likes to define Storz Broadcasting under his leadership as an "operating" company, and this seems an apt description.

The station acquisitions of the McLendon organization were the most extensive of the four group owners examined. McLendon did not always purchase a top facility as did Storz, and in some cases bought stations licensed to cities adjacent to the one he intended to serve. Over the years, McLendon has held under his own license ten stations which programmed Top 40 music, plus numerous others which have run other formats such as all-news, and good music, and still others which he helped to program under the license of his father-in-law, James A. Noe. At the present writing, McLendon owns only one AM station which is programming Top 40: WYSL, Buffalo.

Bartell was at various times during the mid-1950s, owner of a total of eight AM stations which programmed Top 40. Like McLendon, Bartell did not always purchase a top facility, but often enjoyed great success anyway. Bartell attempted to take the "sting" off of the term Top 40 by calling his programming "Family Radio" and by claiming to play music of interest to various members of the family. Like McLendon, Bartell sought to name his stations with pronounceable call letters to help them be remembered (especially for ratings purposes).

The acquisitions of the Plough group were the least extensive of the four groups examined. Plough's station buys were made slowly and unspectacularly with the exception of one week in 1956 when both WCAO, Baltimore, and WCOP, Boston, were acquired. Plough bought good facilities, as did Storz, and like Storz, did not change the original call letters but simply reprogrammed the stations. Plough has largely converted its stations to the playing of country and western music in recent years.

The Top 40 Formula

The Top 40 formula grew out of the earlier music-and-news format. While music-and-news stations generally featured a wide variety of music and a rather relaxed mixture of other elements, Top 40 stations often employed a "clock hour" which specified (in formula fashion) exactly when certain elements were to occur. Most important in the formula was the selection and placement of the records played, after which consideration was given to the best position for other featured elements.

It is impossible to describe exactly what Top 40 was. However, the departures that Top 40 practitioners made from the earlier music-and-news format can be outlined. The most important of these concerned the selection and presentation of the music. A summary of the development of Top 40 music policy is as follows:

Pre-1949 (and also after, on non-Top 40 stations)	Currently popular music mixed with other types
Late 1949--early 1950	KOWH concentrates on popular music
About 1953, with purchase of WTIX, New Orleans, and also put on KOWH, Omaha--the first "Top 40" show	Block programming of current hit tunes (but sometimes different versions); otherwise popular music
About 1954 on KLIF	Playing from the Top 40 hit list outside of the "countdown" program block
Done on McLendon stations in late 1955--early 1956	Selecting one "best" version of a hit song.
1956, KOWH and then other Storz stations--Stewart and Storz	The true limited playlist--biggest hits heard most often; non-hits avoided

Even before the establishment of the true limited playlist in 1956, Top 40 stations owned by Storz, McLendon, and Bartell were enjoying phenomenal local ratings, in part because of the other major element in the Top 40 formula: promotion. News, commercials, disc jockey chatter and other programming elements summarized later here, were also designed to maximize listener attention and thus garner higher ratings. Neither Storz nor McLendon nor Bartell "invented" Top 40 as it was constituted when it became widely imitated by stations across the country. Instead, each company contributed a certain few elements, which were then "borrowed" by the other major practitioners, and which, in turn, were then imitated by smaller-market stations. The long and spectacular success enjoyed by the major Top 40 group owners was not always matched by their imitators, who sometimes attempted to duplicate the outward forms without understanding the reasoning and the experimentation behind them.

Programming Philosophy

A number of programming philosophies held by the major Top 40 group owners influenced the programming turned out by their stations. Among these were the belief that programming considerations should come ahead of sales considerations, that management should be thoroughly involved in the development of programming, that subjective tastes in programming should be subjugated to objective appraisal of what the public actually desired to hear, and that in programming a station every attempt should be made to "fill a void" by programming something new or something not being done as well. The major Top 40 group owners also used several management methods to see that these philosophies could be realized. One method common to all four was the centralization of programming control. With Bartell and Plough, the input source which determined the basic format was also generally centralized, while with Storz and McLendon, ideas were invited from throughout the organization. These were often collected and disseminated via programming Policy Books such as the ones developed by McLendon.

Monitoring

The management of the Top 40 groups discussed also developed very specific mechanisms for monitoring their own and competing stations, for determining the type of music played, and for controlling the amount of disc jockey chatter. Competitive monitoring included simple listings of the music and commercials played on competing stations (plus notations as to which deejays might be worth having), but also extended into the area of some "corporate spying" to better determine the reasons for format variations, station acquisitions, etc. Station management also monitored its own station's output ("air-check") in order to help air personnel to see the errors they were making and to check the overall sound of the station.

Music Policy

As mentioned before, the type of music played was a crucial part of a Top 40 station's sound, so that careful attention was paid to it. Special "music monitors" were sometimes ordered, to be sure that no important record being played by the competition was being overlooked. In addition, methods of selecting new records from among the many received each week were developed. Simple surveys of local phone calls and record sales were subject to "hyping" by dealers and distributors, so considerable trust was placed in national charts and newsletters showing nationwide "action." "Payola" was also a factor, but Top 40 management's move to keep control of the music for itself ran counter to the situation payola depended upon, which was the old system of allowing each deejay to choose his own records. In addition to selecting the records played, management also developed policies on how often they were repeated (the true limited playlist) and how long they were retained on the hit lists (in order to gain more adult listeners). These attempts to manipulate popularity were not the ones generally criticized by the public, however. As reported by the trade press, the public seemed far more concerned about the "dirty lyrics" and the "offensive" beat of the rhythm-and-blues music which had won the popular approval of teenage record listeners. In the mid-1950s, a number of stations (in widely varied parts of the country) found it prudent to ban some of the current R&B records from their playlists, because of "suggestive" lyrics.

Disc Jockey Policy

Disc jockeys also were unhappy with Top 40's music policy, but, again, for different reasons than those held by the public. First, disc jockeys were unhappy that station management had usurped the deejay's traditional prerogative of selecting his own music, and they were also unhappy at management directives to delete chatter in favor of playing more music. In 1958, disc jockey discontent with management control reached a peak and resulted in a call for a national Disc Jockey Association. However, just as the DJA was being formed, the payola scandal became headline news and the organization was forced to assume a defensive public relations role rather than an offensive stance against management. The payola hearings served to consolidate management's extant attitude that it had to control music programming.

Audience and Station Promotion

Audience and station promotion were factors contributing to both local ratings successes enjoyed by Top 40 stations and also to the diffusion of the format across the nation. Some audience promotions were designed to have immediate, short-term results, and often were meant to be ratings "hypos." Others were designed to demonstrate longer-term growth in a station's audience. Still others were more or less continuous and intended to identify the station and keep its call letters in the public consciousness. All were designed to get the audience talking about the station so that the station's reputation would spread. The success of any of these types in building larger audiences encouraged other broadcasters to copy the promotions for their own use, thus diffusing them widely. Storz was forced to introduce all promotions simultaneously on all his stations so that an idea pirated from one of his stations would not already be playing against him on a competing station in another market. Such situations demanded a National Program Director to coordinate the programming. Promotions eventually became so prevalent that stations had to devise policies to limit their use to certain times of the day so as not to drive away listeners with too much talk. The most spectacular and most-imitated promotion was the treasure hunt prize contest. Storz ran two of the largest (with a $105,000 prize) in both Minneapolis and Omaha in 1956, and had so many requests from other stations wanting to know how to run a similar contest that a form-letter explanation was prepared. McLendon's stations also staged big-money treasure hunts, and for a time, even more conservative network owned-and-operated stations such as WRCA (now WNBC), New York were scheduling treasure hunts. The public outcry at the traffic tieups and damage to property that these caused eventually prompted the FCC to issue a warning against such contests (in February 1966). However, the success of flamboyant promotions and spectacular prize contests proved to broadcasters everywhere that the public was still interested in a <u>show</u>--in the unusual and the glamorous--and that radio could fill that interest as well as the movies or television.

Ratings Hypos

The philosophy behind constant promotion was that if a station could attract more audience by being fresh and by being "the only exciting radio on the dial," it could in turn show upward action in the ratings to advertisers. In the case of the ratings hypo, this philosophy became a motive. One of the most widely-used ratings hypos was the offer of a prize to those who answered their telephone with the station's call letters. This ploy was supposed to encourage listeners to respond to ratings service callers by giving the station's call letters. By 1958, such gimmicks had become so widespread that the ratings services were forced to precede their reports with lists of "special programming efforts" which were compiled by competing stations. Regardless of this, Top 40 stations continued to employ all available means to gain a top audience position, including the self-fulfilling prophecy (when combined with a series of stunts) that a station just going on the air would become number one in a matter of weeks. Given past experience and a proven set of stunts, top ratings were almost inevitable.

Call Letters

Top 40 stations also were careful to use all the mnemonic devices at their disposal in order to be easily identified among the audience. A favorite device was the pronounceable station call letter, used by both Bartell and McLendon, but not by Storz nor by Plough. The repetition of call letters was also a matter of importance, and was accomplished by the use of singing jingles, by recording the call letters into production themes and bits, and by offering prizes to the disc jockey who made the most mentions on his show.

News Policy

Management also developed policies on the gathering and delivery of the news. It is interesting to note that in the formative period of Top 40, Storz and McLendon were quite opposite in their thinking concerning the role of news in Top 40. Storz's view at that time closely paralleled modern thinking which says that news is a tuneout, while in the same early days McLendon favored a greatly expanded news effort and believed news was as important as the music in the success of his flagship station, KLIF. Mobile news units were widely adopted, partly for their glamor and partly because they helped to gather the locally-affective story that was being sought. Local stories were featured first on Top 40 news, and the presentation often included numerous sound effects and other attention-getting devices to lend an air of excitement.

Commercials Policy

The commercials policies which developed in the 1950s were not nearly so much concerned with programming (as they are today on many contemporary music stations) as with getting the commercials sold. Those institutions which thought of themselves as appealing only to adults especially avoided Top 40 radio, which was thought to gather an audience comprised only of teenagers. The "Secret Word" and other name-mention gimmicks helped to cure this antipathy. The creation of an artificial time shortage on Fridays and Saturdays helped to persuade retail merchants to advertise on Sundays when their stores were closed. Persuasive sales campaigns by certain station reps helped to overcome some of the prejudices which a few national advertisers had developed as a consequence of their contact with the more conservative radio networks. Meanwhile, Storz was especially active in experimenting to determine an optimal spot load for each market, and eventually settled on about 18 minutes per hour (long before it became an NAB standard). McLendon and Bartell concentrated on making their announcements as thoroughly-produced as possible, and Bartell had a standing rule that nothing would go on the air live if it could possibly be done with production instead.

Organization and Management Policies

Top 40 management developed a number of organizational patterns which complemented the effectiveness of its programming policies. While there were variations in the amount of local autonomy granted to station managers (with McLendon allowing more local control than Storz or Bartell), in all cases management's goal was the conservation of manpower via centralization, while preserving the opportunity for ideas to flow in from all levels. McLendon developed a Digest of Weekly Reports which quoted pertinent new ideas sent in from each station, but which was distributed to all stations in the group. Such encouragement of decentralized programming input had a corollary in the likelihood of personnel being advanced to a management position without need of a sales or management background.

A number of other management policies were also peculiar to the

Top 40 operation. One was a willingness to invest in both programming hardware (equipment) and software (program services). Coupled with the latter was a recruiting program for disc jockeys in which both Storz and McLendon employed novel trades ads to attract the best personalities to their expanding station lineups. Both groups tried to develop non-breakable deejay contracts, since their own practices made it plain how easy it was to buy a good jock away from his current employer.

As operators of station groups, Top 40 management also developed policies regarding group operation. The Radio Advertising Bureau was, for a time, quite unsympathetic to Top-40 operators, and membership in RAB was thus not prevalent among Top 40 groups in the format's early years. Membership in AIMS (Association of Independent Metropolitan Stations) was high among Top 40 stations so long as there was as much to be learned from others as others could learn from them. When the reverse was true (and when independent stations were at last accepted as important broadcast services), Top 40 membership in AIMS waned. The need to convince advertisers of the importance of buying the Top 40 audience encouraged substantial spending for station representative services, ratings services, and trades advertising. Trades advertising was also used as a medium in Top 40 groups' campaign to improve the image of their format. The Storz stations' sponsorship of two national Disc Jockey Conventions was primarily motivated by the desire to improve the prestige of a Top 40 operation. McLendon sought to increase esteem for his stations by emphasizing their bigness and their success image, the size of their promotions and the superiority of their programming features, while Bartell's main image-improvement effort centered around the phrase "Family Radio," which was an attempt to remove the "teen-agers only" stigma from Top 40.

Imitation and Specialization

The success of the Top 40 format among the medium-market stations owned by Storz, McLendon and Bartell inspired heavy imitation by stations across the country in the late 1950s. By the early 1960s, many of these imitators had become defectors as they found it hard to compete for audience with stations (generally powerful outlets in larger cities) which had far more programming resources at their command. At about the same time, radio networks finally decided to stop trying to win an audience to expensive dramatic programs and instead turned to supplying music and news (and finally just to news and features). As a result, radio networks began to show profits again for the first time in about a decade.

The success of the Top 40 format in gathering large audiences pointed the way for other stations to attempt other types of format specialization. McLendon introduced a lively and promotable form of "good music" on his KABL in San Francisco in 1959. All-news and all-ads were also McLendon format innovations, with all-ads a clear McLendon first. Other stations, notably the Plough group, have in recent years specialized in country and western music. Storz's stations have continued to play basically the Top 40 hit tunes, but with the refinements introduced by programmers and consultants such as Bill Drake. Attention is now paid to the number and placement of commercials and to the avoidance of tuneouts caused by long newscasts, non-hit music, and too much jock chatter. These "improvements" have kept Top 40 the format with the most listeners of any in the country, and have made it a respectable big business. The "mavericks" of radio today are the FM stations which are programming "free-form" or "progressive" formats, themselves specialized forms, of which Top 40 was the first.

CONCLUSIONS

1. Top 40 was not "invented." It grew from music-and-news, an already-established format which was rather prevalent among independent stations.
2. Unlike the case with music-and-news, disc jockeys did not have much power in determining the music played in the Top 40 format. The selection of music, and the determination of many other important programming elements, was in the hands of management which paid closer attention to programming than had usually been the case.
3. Top 40 management put programming ahead of sales considerations, and sought always to fill a void with its programming rather than to do something imitative.
4. Top 40 management was pragmatic above all, and sought to serve majority tastes no matter what previous radio practices might have dictated. Thus, music was selected by survey and news was presented as briefly and as excitingly as possible, to attract a majority audience.
5. The men who headed the Top 40 station groups explored here were all young, and none were tied to old concepts of what radio <u>ought</u> to be. Additionally, while McLendon and Bartell dabbled briefly in TV, all four group owners were primarily concerned with radio, and they bought and programmed radio properties at a time when some of radio's best talent was being siphoned off to put local TV stations on the air.

6. Top 40 developed first in the middle markets because they were the markets that (a) could support the expense of the software, hardware, and personnel investment that the pioneers believed was necessary, and (b) because large-market stations were too expensive to buy.

7. Storz always bought the best facility he could, believing that the first in the market to do Top 40 with a good facility would be able to fend off all later competition. Plough also bought prime facilities, and always in the larger of the medium markets. Bartell and McLendon sometimes bought marginal facilities, intending to overcome a lack of power or dial position with superior programming. McLendon also bought stations neighboring the market he actually intended to program to.

8. Storz and Plough, by buying prime facilities to begin with, have found it profitable to hold their stations as long as possible, while Bartell and McLendon have sold some of their lesser facilities when better-equipped competition made it most prudent to do so.

9. The greatest activity in station acquisition took place in the middle years of the 1950s (1955, 1956, 1957) after television had taken much of radio's audience, but before other broadcasters had realized how much money was still to be made with a Top 40 operation. In the 1960s, the FCC's attention to "trafficking" made frequent station-trading less desirable.

10. Stations programming music-and-news (or the Top 40 specialization of it) were never threatened by TV because they provided a service

that, unlike newspapers, magazines, or even earlier dramatic radio programs, could be appreciated without having to pay much attention. Music and news or Top 40 were used as companions or as background to other activity. The format was especially attuned to a mobile society that lived increasingly in the suburbs, and Top 40 operators eventually found that 50% of their audience was listening away from home, and programmed accordingly.

11. The development of ratings reports which more accurately reported out-of-home and other specialized audiences was encouraged by the willingness of Top 40 operators to order frequent and detailed surveys. These, in turn, helped the Top 40 operator to convince prospective advertisers that the audiences he claimed were not mythical.

12. Audiences tuned Top 40 stations because they played the music that was popular within a context which made such stations "the only exciting radio on the dial."

13. Because music was the element most important to the audience, much care was taken in determining which music was played. Beside popularity surveys to determine which records to air, "clock hours" were developed to make consistent the times at which certain kinds of records were played. Limiting the records to hits, limiting the number of these played, repeating the top hits more often, and retaining the hits after the teens had begun to tire of them, were all attempts to make the music consistent and popular.

14. After music, promotion was the next most important programming element developed by Top 40. Self-promotion kept the station's

call letters before the public, and audience promotions caused the public to talk about the station among themselves. While some promotions were intended to have long term effects, such as the maintenance of a certain "image" for the station, others were designed for short-term impact and were sometimes used to "hypo" the ratings. Big money treasure hunts were the most exciting of the prize contests designed for short-term impact.

15. The difficulty of selecting the right music and developing novel promotions made the conservation of manpower a necessity. Thus, the major Top 40 group owners all practiced some form of central programming control, in some cases sending out music lists and prepared promotions, or in other cases merely being certain that all new ideas were shared among the group (via newsletters, etc.). An important aspect of this central programming control was the use of a National Program Director, such as Bill Stewart.

16. Top 40 management made music, commercial and station monitors (air checks) more frequently, and used them more directly to determine programming than had been previous practice. In addition, the debriefing of personnel from other stations was a common practice, not so much to gain vital new information as to be certain that important practices developed by others were not being overlooked.

17. The payola scandals did not cause, but instead served to strengthen the resolve which Top 40 management already had to control the selection of records played on their stations. The payola scandals did, however, lead to a heavier reliance on national charts and newsletters instead of local surveys.

18. The rhythm and blues music which became known as "rock and roll" was adopted as <u>the</u> music of teenagers in the 1950s and early 1960s, just as 45 rpm records became "their" disc format. Much of the teenage content which characterized the pop music of the 1950s is not now to be found in most Top 40 records, suggesting that as Top 40's original audience grew up, the music content grew up with it--probably for the first time in history. The lack of teen content also confirms the "mature" image that Top 40 sets for itself today.

19. Because radio is still a relatively small fraternity, it does not take long for management in one part of the country to hear what someone in another part is doing. For this reason, because of the reporting in the trades press of the more elaborate promotions and stunts, and because of the placement by Top 40 stations of trades ads pointing to their ratings and sales successes, the Top 40 format diffused rapidly and was widely adopted by all kinds of stations. Individual promotions were also widely copied and provide a good example of the way an idea is borrowed and changed.

20. The need for station self-promotion (repetition of the call letters) in order to keep the name before the public for ratings purposes stimulated the growth of the station ID sector of the jingle industry.

21. The success of flamboyant stunts and glamorous contests in promoting a station helped radio to realize that it really was in show business, and that the public was just as avid for entertainment on radio as it was for entertainment on TV. McLendon, with his

family background in promoting movies at their theaters, was particularly attuned to making programs into shows.

22. The use of pronounceable call letters was a helpful but not a necessary gimmick to insure high station reporting in ratings surveys.

23. Top 40 stations developed the emphasis on locally-affective news. The typical order of presentation was changed to put the most important local stories first. National stories were used so long as they had a chance for some sort of local appeal, but an effort was made to limit the number and length of these. News presentation was controlled by the program director to get the overall station sound he wanted. Thus, Top 40 stations attempted to make news presentations as exciting as the balance of the hour containing the records. However, despite the novelty of presentation and content, news eventually came to be identified as a "tuneout" and was later de-emphasized on many stations.

24. Top 40's catering to the 50% of the audience that was in cars and the fact of an increasingly mobile society led to the popularity of the mobile news unit.

25. Top 40 overcame its difficulty in selling time to institutions desiring an older listener by inventing devices such as the "Secret Word" to prove the extent of adult listenership. Such gimmicks were employed until ratings were both more complete and more reliable.

26. Top 40 management (especially McLendon) was ready to spend money on almost anything that promised more entertaining programming.

Experimentation was prevalent.

27. Top 40 management believed in the need to improve the "teens only" and the "maverick" image of their stations, and spent money on trades ads, promotions, and even conventions to cure such prejudices.

28. The success of the Top 40 format in gathering a large audience encouraged other types of specialization and format experimentation.

29. The problem with small-market imitations of the Top 40 format was that the imitators often ran their shows as cheaply as possible, rather than as attractively as possible, and attempted to duplicate forms rather than trying to understand functions.

30. Critical distaste for the Top 40 format did little to dissuade the majority audience from continuing to tune in. As Todd Storz was fond of saying, "It seems like nobody likes our programming but the people."

31. Part of the freshness and constant novelty associated with Top 40 is attributable to the necessity to re-cut the acetate discs on which promotions, program intros and outros, and other segments were recorded in the early days of the format. It is ironic that the easily-erased tape cartridge appears to have brought more permanence instead of less.

32. No one person was most responsible for the development of the Top 40 format, because the development process was evolutionary rather than revolutionary. However, Bartell, Storz and McLendon all encouraged an atmosphere of experimentation, and the latter two

both employed Bill Stewart as National Program Director, from which position Stewart wielded considerable influence in determining the sound of his stations. While Stewart appreciated the importance to a station's success of playing the right music, he also was partly responsible for making the other element of the Top 40 formula--promotion--one of the major elements. But most of all, he had the backing of his employers, McLendon and Storz, who not only allowed him, but encouraged him (and others), to "take a shot."

SELECTED LIST OF SOURCES CONSULTED

Special Collections

The McLendon Policy Books

The McLendon Policy Books are a collection of the memoranda, letters, and reports which have been retained by the management of the McLendon Stations, beginning about 1947. For this research, the author examined about 30 of 50 to 60 such books which are retained at McLendon Stations Headquarters in Dallas, Texas. Among the McLendon Policy Books is one quoted at length in this text: The Trinity Programming Policy Book.

McLendon, Gordon B. Personal Scrapbooks.

The author had access to portions of these during two visits to Dallas to examine the McLendon Policy Books. The scrapbooks are a separate private collection.

Unpublished Materials

Interviews

Armstrong, George W. Private interview with the author. Omaha, Nebraska, August 2, 1971.

Bartell, Gerald. Private interview with the author. Madison, Wisconsin, May 24, 1972.

Dowe, Ken. Private interview with the author. Dallas, Texas, July 29, 1971.

Keyes, Don. Private interview with the author. WNYN, Canton, Ohio, October 5, 1971.

McLendon, Gordon B. Tape-recorded biography. Harding College Oral History Library Distinguished Citizen Collection. Searcy, Arkansas.

McLendon, Gordon, and Doan, Richard K. "The Truth About Radio: A WNEW Inquiry." Transcript of an interview broadcast on WNEW, New York, May 14, 1967.

Meeks, Bill. Private interview with the author. Dallas, Texas, July 28, 1971.

Merriman, Tom. Private interview with the author. Dallas, Texas, November 6, 1971.

Northcross, Wilson. Private interview with the author. Memphis, Tennessee, July 8, 1971.

Rosinsky, Sol. Private interview with the author. Omaha, Nebraska, August 2, 1971.

Rounsaville, Robert W., and Kaufman, Arnold C. Private interview with the author. Miami, Florida, July 14, 1971.

Routt, Edd. Private telephone conversation with the author. July 18, 1972.

Stewart, Bill, Private interview with the author. New Orleans, Louisiana, November 4, 1971.

Stubblefield, Bill. Private interview with the author. Casanova, Virginia, Friday, October 8, 1971.

Thomas, Pete. Private interview with the author. Madison, Wisconsin, April 27, 1972.

Topping, Malachi. Interview with the author. Madison, Wisconsin, June 15, 1972.

Letters

Beville, Ross. Letter to the author. July 17, 1972, 2 pages.

Richards, Grahame. Letter to the author. March 14, 1972, 2 pages.

Sack, Victor. Letter to the author. September 9, 1971.

Memoranda

Stewart, Bill. "Memo to all Announcers," July 21, 1956 (mimeographed) (xerox copy from Bill Stewart).

Stewart, Bill. "Outline on the $105,000 Contest" (mimeographed) (xerox copy from Bill Stewart).

Storz, Todd. Memorandum on WNDE-WTIX Lawsuit. Undated (circa 1955), unpaginated (xerox copy from Bill Stewart).

"WKOW News Techniques." Supplied by WKOW, Madison, Wisconsin. February, 1968 (mimeographed).

Papers

Lichty, Lawrence W. "Factors That Influence Broadcast Programming." Unpublished paper based on Lichty, Lawrence W. "'The Nation's Station'--A History of Radio Station WLW." Unpublished Ph.D. dissertation, Ohio State University, 1964.

Sova

~~Sova~~, Harry. "A History of the Magnetic ~~Records~~ Recorder and Its Inclusion into Network Radio Broadcasting." Unpublished paper, The University of Wisconsin, Madison, March 18, 1969.

Speeches

Kaplan, Stanley N. "Whatever Happened to Top 40 Radio?" A speech presented at the NAB convention in Chicago, Illinois, 1968. 5 pages.

McLendon, Gordon. "Frankly, We're Tired . . . of Raunchy Lyrics." Speech delivered to the American Mothers Committee Incorporated's "Mothers of Men" Luncheon in New York, May 12, 1967 (mimeographed).

McLendon, Gordon. "Radio: The Years to Come." Speech at the World's Fair of Music and Sound, Chicago, Illinois, September 6, 1962.

McLendon, Gordon. "The Changing Face of Radio." Speech to the San Francisco Advertising Club, May 25, 1960 (xeroxed).

McLendon, Gordon. "The Great Drive-in Theatre Robbery." Speech made before a group of motion picture theater owners (mimeographed), n.d.

McLendon, Gordon. "The Time Before This." Speech given before Alpha Epsilon Rho, Detroit, Michigan, April 29, 1969.

Storz, Todd. "Independent, Alive and Healthy." Excerpts from a talk at the University of Georgia, no date, but between 1954 and 1956 (xerox copy supplied by Grahame Richards).

Articles in Magazines and Journals

Note: For the convenience of the user, the magazine and journal articles listed here are in chronological order. Where several articles are cited from a single issue, those with the lowest page numbers are listed first. When two articles beginning on the same page of the same issue are cited, the one closest to the beginning of the alphabet is listed first. When two different journals share the same publication date, the journal name closest to the beginning of the alphabet is also given first.

1938-1952

"Forms Spot Network." Business Week, September 24, 1938, p. 18.

"Transcription Boom." Newsweek, January 19, 1943, p. 58.

Graham, Al. "Jingle--or Jangle." New York Times Magazine, October 29, 1944, pp. 26-27.

Carpenter, A. "Wizardry of Radio's 'Spot' Programs." Science Digest, January, 1946, pp. 17-21.

"Recordings for Crosby Show." Broadcasting, September 2, 1946, p. 16.

"Crosby Rating is Up Again: Philco Satisfied with Sales." Broadcasting, November 18, 1946, p. 14.

"Jingle Tingle." Newsweek, August 18, 1947, p. 55.

"Specialist." The New Yorker, October 4, 1947, pp. 26-27.

"Radio Handouts." Fortune, November, 1947, pp. 140-142.

Tolbert, Frank X. "Parrot Does Announcing." The Dallas Morning News, November 10, 1947, Section One, p. 4.

"Free Gifts, Cheap Ads." Business Week, February 7, 1948, p. 42.

Whiteside, Thomas. "I Can Be Had--For Pelf." New Republic, February 16, 1948, p. 22.

"Tape for the Networks." Newsweek, May 3, 1948, p. 52.

"The Stepchild." Time, April 18, 1949, p. 63.

"Tastes of the Teens." Newsweek, 33 (May 9, 1949), 57.

"Giveaways Down, Not Out." Business Week, August 27, 1949, p. 31.

"Gift Horse Hobbled." *Newsweek*, August 29, 1949, p. 44.

Anker, Lieber. "Television, Here I Come!" *English Journal*, 40 (April, 1951), 218-20.

"Little Bombs." *Time*, February 11, 1952, pp. 66-69.

"RCA Thesaurus Sales." *Broadcasting*, May 19, 1952, p. 6.

"WNEW New York: Radio's Little David Doesn't Fear TV." *Fortune*, October, 1952, pp. 132-133.

1953

Hileman, Donald G. "The Young Radio Audience: A Study of Listening Habits." *Journalism Quarterly*, 30 (1953), 37-43.

"'52 Radio Time Sales Reach $464 Million." *Broadcasting*, January 26, 1953, pp. 27-28.

"Those Riches in the Indies." *Broadcasting*, January 26, 1953, pp. 80-81.

Ellis, Elmo. "Removing the Rust from Radio Programming." *Broadcasting*, February 2, 1953, pp. 80-82.

"National Poll Pinpoints Radio's Disk Show Growth." *Billboard*, February 28, 1953, p. 1.

"Radio-TV Sponsors Evolve New Patterns for Time Buys." *Billboard*, February 28, 1953, p. 1.

"The *Billboard* 1953 Disc Jockey Poll." *Billboard*, February 28, 1953, pp. 33-34, 41.

"The *Billboard* 1953 Station Manager Survey." *Billboard*, February 28, 1953, p. 49.

"Publishers Okay 3 Per Cent Rate for Transcription Library Firms." *Billboard*, March 28, 1953, p. 20.

"New Jingle Library." *Broadcasting*, April 6, 1953, p. 9.

McAndrews, Robert J. "Out of Red Into Sun." *Billboard*, April 25, 1953, p. 39.

"Texas Oasis." *Newsweek*, June 22, 1953, p. 54.

"Station WLW Gives Away House . . . Cars, to Snag Off-hour Audience." *Business Week*, July 18, 1953, p. 72.

"MBS Affiliates Offered 'Revolutionary' Policy." Broadcasting, July 20, 1953, pp. 74-76.

"Politz Study Affirms Penetration of Radio." Broadcasting, July 27, 1953, pp. 31-32.

"Father Knickerbocker Presents the Old Scotchman." The Daily Times Herald [Dallas], July 28, 1953. From Gordon B. McLendon's personal scrapbooks.

"Plough, Inc. Buys WJJD for $900,000." Broadcasting, August 10, 1953, p. 68.

"McCaw Group Pays $450,000 for WINS." Broadcasting, August 10, 1953, p. 70.

"NBC Radio's Cott Says Overhaul to Bring 'New, Wonderful' Shows." Broadcasting, August 17, 1953, p. 88.

"WBS Tailors to Spot Buying." Broadcasting, August 31, 1953, p. 62.

"For the Record: Ownership Changes: WTIX, New Orleans, Royal Bcstg Corps." Broadcasting, August 31, 1953, p. 103.

"Trendex Enters Radio Rating Field." Broadcasting, September 14, 1953, p. 48.

"FCC Approves Plough Buy of WJJD; 13 Station Transfers Granted." Broadcasting, September 14, 1953, p. 56.

"Radio 'Rehabilitation' is Sarnoff's Pledge." Broadcasting, September 21, 1953, pp. 29-31.

"New NBC Radio Sales Plans." Broadcasting, September 21, 1953, p. 30.

"Growing Up with TV in Videotown, U.S.A." Broadcasting, October 5, 1953, pp. 88-90.

"WNEW Takes a Swing." Broadcasting, October 12, 1953, p. 104.

"MBS Shelves Affiliate Plan Effective Dec. 31." Broadcasting, November 9, 1953, p. 27.

"Biscayne TV Bid Would Buy WIOD, Sell WQAM." Broadcasting, November 30, 1953, p. 61.

Reed, Jim. "What's Right and Wrong with Radio News." Broadcasting, November 30, 1953, pp. 94, 98-99, 102-103.

"Whose Idea?" Broadcasting, December 21, 1953, p. 18.

"FCC Approves 11 Radio-TV Transfers." <u>Broadcasting</u>, December 21, 1953, p. 58.

<u>1954</u>

"Radio Lives with TV in Iowa--Whan. <u>Broadcasting</u>, January 11, 1954, p. 36.

"NBC Radio Cuts Sustainer Hours." <u>Broadcasting</u>, January 11, 1954, p. 74A.

Whaley, Storm. "Music on Radio Holds Own Against TV." <u>Broadcasting</u>, February 1, 1954, p. 82.

"Nielsen Plans Local Rating Report." <u>Broadcasting</u>, February 8, 1954, p. 31.

"Video's a Song's No. 1 Hit-Maker." <u>Billboard</u>, February 27, 1954, p. 27.

"What Will the Out-of-Home Audience <u>Add</u> to Radio in Summer Months?" <u>Sponsor</u>, March 8, 1954, p. 57.

"How Does Out of Home Audience Break Down by Qualitative Factors?" <u>Sponsor</u>, March 8, 1954, p. 60.

"Leder Revamps WINS, Names New Personnel." <u>Broadcasting</u>, March 15, 1954, p. 88.

"BAB Report Stresses Pull of Radio Disc Jockey Shows." <u>Broadcasting</u>, March 22, 1954, p. 38.

"Giveaways Not Lotteries, According to U.S. Supreme Court Ruling." <u>Broadcasting</u>, April 12, 1954, p. 34.

"Sweeney Urges Radio Program Development." <u>Broadcasting</u>, April 12, 1954, p. 84.

Jaffee, Alfred J. "The New Radio: Are You So Close to It You Can't See the Changes?" <u>Sponsor</u>, April 19, 1954, pp. 31-33, 143-147.

Rolontz, Bob and Friedman, Joel. "Teenagers Demand Music With a Beat, Spur Rhythm-Blues." <u>Billboard</u>, April 24, 1954, pp. 1, 18.

"WHB-AM-TV Buys Church's KMBC-AM-TV; WHB Acquired by Storz Family." <u>Broadcasting</u>, April 26, 1954, pp. 62, 64.

"Radio Audience Up Outside the Home." <u>Broadcasting</u>, May 3, 1954, p. 38.

"Programs and Promotions." Broadcasting, May 3, 1954, p. 74.

"Music Libraries: What Do You Know About Them?" Sponsor, May 17, 1954, pp. 50-51, 132, 134-135, 136.

"ABC Night Format to be Music News." Broadcasting, May 24, 1954, p. 64.

"Majors and Subsids Switch to 45s for Pops to Deejays." Billboard, June 5, 1954, p. 14.

"NBC Radio Ready to Ask 20% Nighttime Rate Cut." Broadcasting, June 7, 1954 p. 31.

"Record Companies Plan to Supply Stations with 45 RPM Discs Only." Broadcasting, June 14, 1954, p. 44.

"DJs Air Pro & Con on 45 Shipments." Billboard, June 19, 1954, p. 17.

"Stations to Get 325,000 45 RPM Records Free." Billboard, July 3, 1954, p. 3.

"'Wire Service' Feed of Voices Suggested." Broadcasting, July 5, 1954, p. 35.

"200 Million '45s' Sold in Five Years--Folsom." Broadcasting, July 5, 1954, p. 36.

"DJ Reaction to 45s Better Than Hoped." Billboard, July 10, 1954, p. 14.

"Hi-Fi That's Just for the Trade." Business Week, July 10, 1954, pp. 162-165.

"Network Radio Trends." Sponsor, July 12, 1954, p. 37.

"Spot Radio: From Morning to After-Midnight, Business is Good." Sponsor, July 12, 1954, pp. 195-200, 204, 206, 208, 210, 212, 214, 216, 218, 220-224.

"CBS and WMGM Join Stations Using 45 Discs." Billboard, July 17, 1954, p. 12.

"Equipment Jam Develops on Stations Swing Over to 45s." Billboard, July 17, 1954, pp. 12, 42.

"New Instantaneous Rating System, 'DAX' To Be Offered by The Pulse." Broadcasting, July 19, 1954, p. 44.

"ABC Sold on Music-News Formula as Means of Strengthening Radio." Broadcasting, July 19, 1954, pp. 50, 52.

"Witting Says WBC Won't Use 45 RPM." Broadcasting, July 19, 1954, p. 54.

"Music Spots Grow Into Big Business with TV, Films." Billboard, September 4, 1954, p. 4.

"RCA Thesaurus Adds 'Attention Getters' Aids." Broadcasting, September 6, 1954, p. 72.

"Syndicated Deejay Shows Expanding." Billboard, September 18, 1954, p. 11.

"CBS Buys Nielsen Auto Radio Report." Broadcasting, September 20, 1954, p. 50.

"Morning Radio Up 25% Since 1950." Broadcasting, September 20, 1954, p. 52.

"WHB, WHCC Drop MBS Affiliations." Broadcasting, September 27, 1954, p. 50.

"45-Less DJs Prove Costly to Publishers." Billboard, October 2, 1954, p. 19.

"Trade Views Off-Color Disk Situation with Mixed Feeling." Billboard, October 2, 1954, p. 19.

"Pinpointing the Radio Audience: New MBS-Ward Study Shows How." Sponsor, October 4, 1954, pp. 44-46, 112-115.

"The Lesson of 'Videotown': More Time for Radio and TV." Broadcasting, October 11, 1954, pp. 27-28.

"Out-of-Home Listening Sets Record." Broadcasting, October 11, 1954, p. 32.

"Nielsen Completes 'Improvement Plan.'" Broadcasting, October 18, 1954, p. 54.

"Indie Diskers Back WDIA's R&B Bans." Billboard, October 30, 1954, p. 16.

"Star Record Shows Woo Web Listeners." Billboard, November 13, 1954, pp. 1, 27.

"Disk Jockey Move to Video is Still a Long, Hard Trip." Billboard, November 13, 1954, p. 21.

"Web Radio's Transcribed Disc Shows." Billboard, November 13, 1954, p. 27.

"The Billboard 1954 Disk Jockey Poll." Billboard, November 13, 1954, pp. 34, 38.

"Move to 45 Backed by Thoro [sic] Survey, But There Was a Slip." Billboard, November 13, 1954, p. 76.

"C&W Count Shows Videotown's Radios." Broadcasting, December 13, 1954, p. 37.

"Liberty Group Negotiating to Buy WEMP Milwaukee." Broadcasting, December 27, 1954, p. 7.

1955

"Radio's Hold on Music and News (TV Weaknesses) Reflected in Major Advertest Audience Study." Variety, 197 (January 19, 1955), 24.

"Deejay Syndication Threat." Variety, January 19, 1955, pp. 47-54.

Schoenfeld, Herm. "R&B Big Beat in Pop Biz." Variety, January 19, 1955, pp. 49-54.

"Record Marathon in New Orleans." Broadcasting, February 21, 1955, p. 92.

"Stations Protest NSI Data, Claim Radio is Sabotaged." Broadcasting, March 14, 1955, p. 32.

"ARB, Hooper Divide Radio-TV Ratings as Pact Involving Stock Takes Effect." Broadcasting, March 21, 1955, pp. 31-32.

"Nielsen Releases First Auto Listening Report." Broadcasting, March 21, 1955, p. 32.

"SRA Joins Battle Over NSI Report." Broadcasting, March 21, 1955, p. 32.

"WNOE Becomes Independent, WTPS Takes MBS Affiliation." Broadcasting, March 21, 1955, p. 112.

"Coast Jockeys Open Gab War on R&B Cycle." Variety, March 23, 1955, pp. 41, 46.

"Houston Radio Stations Ask Crime Commission to List Indigo Disks." Variety, March 23, 1955, p. 41.

"Irving Berlin on R&B." Variety, March 23, 1955, p. 41.

"Big Potential Seen in New Gadget Manufactured by Chicago Company." Billboard, March 26, 1955, p. 17.

Sweeney, Kevin. "Radio: That Dip Isn't a Trend." Broadcasting, March 28, 1955, pp. 39-42, 44, 47-48, 50.

"Gordon Resigns WNOE Post Over Policy Disagreement." Broadcasting, March 28, 1955, p. 88.

"WABB Lashes Out Against Recorded 'Disguised Smut.'" Broadcasting, March 28, 1955, p. 88.

"R&B's Slip Is Now Showing." Variety, March 30, 1955, p. 49.

"Deep South Jockeys Junk 50% of R&B Wax." Variety, March 30, 1955, p. 54.

"NBC Begins Major Revision in Radio Selling, Schedules." Broadcasting, April 4, 1955, pp. 27-28.

"NBC Radio Sells Plans for Monitor, Its 40-Hour Weekend Program Service." Broadcasting, April 11, 1955, p. 52.

Bundy, June. "Vox Jox." Billboard, April 16, 1955, p. 16.

"NSI: Can It Measure Today's Radio Audience?" Sponsor, April 18, 1955, pp. 40-42, 102, 104, 106, 108.

"Milwaukee Radio-TV: '1-2-3-Shift.'" Sponsor, April 18, 1955, p. 108.

"Radio Program Services." Sponsor, May 16, 1955, pp. 64, 104.

"NBC Radio Teenager Show Planned for Friday Nights." Broadcasting, May 23, 1955, p. 120.

"King of Giveaway." Time, June 4, 1955, pp. 100-102.

"Station Sued." Broadcasting, June 13, 1955, p. 7.

Stewart, Bill. Letter to Broadcasting, June 13, 1955, p. 22.

Michaels, Pat. "How to Scoop the Field with Radio." Sponsor, June 13, 1955, pp. 46-47, 88-90, 92.

"Seek and You May Find." Broadcasting, June 20, 1955, p. 97.

"WTIX Files Counter Suit in New Orleans Radio Row." Broadcasting, June 20, 1955, p. 98.

"Mutual Fixes Single Rate for Day, Evening, Plus Single Discount Table." Broadcasting, June 27, 1955, p. 103.

"MBS to Revise Program Concept." Broadcasting, June 27, 1955, p. 104.

"Program, Sales Services." Sponsor, July 11, 1955, pp. 160-161.

"McLendon, Noe Organize NOEMAC Station Group." Broadcasting, September 5, 1955, p. 7.

"NBC, CBS and Affiliates Mull New Radio Formulas." Broadcasting, September 12, 1955, pp. 31-32.

"Our Respects to Todd Storz." Broadcasting, September 19, 1955, p. 26.

"Curve Starts Up." Broadcasting, September 19, 1955, pp. 51-54.

"Time Sales in 1955: Record & Outlook." Broadcasting, September 19, 1955, pp. 59, 62.

"The Going Price is Going Up." Broadcasting, September 19, 1955, p. 62.

"Looking At Monitors." Broadcasting, September 19, 1955, pp. 89-90.

"New Look for ABC." Broadcasting, September 19, 1955, p. 90.

Doherty, Richard P. "Radio Joins the Business Cycle." Broadcasting, September 19, 1955, pp. 134, 136, 138.

"The Stylish Stylus." Broadcasting, September 19, 1955, pp. 168, 170.

Secrest, James D. "Radios, and More Radios." Broadcasting, September 19, 1955, p. 187.

"Radio's Rate Trend Since TV's Advent." Broadcasting, September 19, 1955, p. 194.

"Bartell Buys KCBQ, WEGE in Two Sales." Broadcasting, September 19, 1955, p. 205.

"WTIX Gets Renewal." Broadcasting, September 26, 1955, p. 90.

"KCBQ Drops Network." Broadcasting, September 26, 1955, p. 97.

"Second Noe Station Turns Independent." Broadcasting, October 10, 1955, p. 96.

"How to Keep an Eye and Ear on the Competition." Sponsor, October 17, 1955, pp. 46-47, 119.

"You Can Make Money in Network Radio. Broadcasting, October 31, 1955, pp. 51, 54, 56.

"Closed Circuit: WDGY to Todd Storz?" Broadcasting, November 7, 1955, p. 5.

"Is Radio Overdoing Music-and-News Programming?" _Sponsor_, November 14, 1955, pp. 32-33, 144-145.

"Bartell Buys KRUX." _Broadcasting_, December 5, 1955, p. 32.

"WWDC 'Identitunes.'" _Broadcasting_, December 12, 1955, p. 88.

1956

"Color Radio in Texas." _Broadcasting_, January 2, 1956, p. 76.

"Milwaukee Outlets Hit Rigged Phone Surveys." _Broadcasting_, January 6, 1956, p. 96.

"Trinity Files for New AM, Decides to Drop Dallas UHF." _Broadcasting_, January 9, 1956, p. 66.

"Color Radio Red-Hot." _Broadcasting_, January 16, 1956, p. 15.

"A Tale of 3 Cities: Rating Rhubarbs." _Broadcasting_, January 16, 1956, p. 82.

"Radio and the Fight for Time." _Broadcasting_, January 16, 1956, pp. 84-86.

"Closed Circuit: Newspaper Ownership." _Broadcasting_, January 23, 1956, p. 5.

"Milwaukee Gimmicks." _Broadcasting_, January 23, 1956, pp. 18, 22.

"Audience Composition Data Available, Hooper, Pulse, Nielsen Tell N.Y. Group." _Broadcasting_, January 23, 1956, p. 33.

"WDGY Change Among FCC-Approved Sales." _Broadcasting_, January 23, 1956, p. 66.

"Dollars for News Tips." _Broadcasting_, January 23, 1956, p. 91.

Csida, Joe. "Sponsor Backstage." _Sponsor_, January 23, 1956, p. 116.

"Labunski, Loughnane Moved to WDGY by Mid-Continent." _Broadcasting_, January 30, 1956, p. 62.

"Radio Rates Rise." _Broadcasting_, February 6, 1956, p. 5.

"KTSA San Antonio Acquired by McLendon for $306,000." _Broadcasting_, March 12, 1956, p. 7.

"SEL Develops LP Cartridge." _Billboard_, March 17, 1956, p. 16.

"Plough Broadcasting Adds WCAO-AM-FM to Station List." Broadcasting, March 26, 1956, p. 85.

"Plough, Inc." Broadcasting, April 2, 1956, p. 5.

"Plough Buys WCOP, Second in Week." Broadcasting, April 2, 1956, p. 70.

"Radio Program Services." Sponsor, April 16, 1956. Special Convention Issue. Special pagination.

Bundy, June. "Vox Jox." Billboard, April 28, 1956, p. 52.

"Storz Group High Bidder for WQAM, Pays Record $850,000 for Regional." Broadcasting, May 14, 1956, p. 7.

"Madison Avenue to Main Street." Broadcasting, May 14, 1956, pp. 76-78, 80, 82-83.

"$210,000 Giveaway." Broadcasting, May 28, 1956, p. 84.

"Kite Protests KTSA Sale." Broadcasting, June 11, 1956, p. /6.

"Classified Radio." Broadcasting, June 11, 1956, p. 99.

"Jingle Hit Parade." Broadcasting, June 18, 1956, p. 18.

"Giveaways Create Furor in Minneapolis, Omaha." Broadcasting, June 18, 1956, p. 106.

"Protests Bring Postponements of KTSA, KVAR (TV) Actions." Broadcasting, July 2, 1956, p. 64.

"Titles Change Hands Quickly in Disc Jockey Marathon." Broadcasting, July 16, 1956, p. 103.

"Program Control Threat Raised in Final FCC Actions." Broadcasting, July 23, 1956, pp. 31-32.

"Whereupon He Gives Away His Giveaways." Broadcasting, July 23, 1956, p. 32.

"Jack Sandler Appointed WQAM Miami Manager." Broadcasting, August 20, 1956, p. 97.

"Capitol Music Library Offered to Radio-TVs." Broadcasting, August 27, 1956, p. 9.

"Gold at Coney Island." Newsweek, August 27, 1956, p. 55.

"How to Encourage Nuisances--Treasure Hunts." America, September 1, 1956, p. 494.

"WIND Sold for Record $5.3 Million." Broadcasting, September 3, 1956, pp. 27-28.

"Funny Thing Happened On My Way to the Studio." Broadcasting, September 3, 1956, p. 66.

"KITE Agrees to Withdraw Protest Against KTSA Sale." Broadcasting, September 10, 1956, p. 82.

"What Are They Looking For? They're After WRCA's $1,000." Broadcasting, September 10, 1956, pp. 107-108.

"Balaban Corp. Buys WRIT from McLendon for $400,500." Broadcasting, September 24, 1956, p. 9.

"Open Mike--Treasure Hunts." Broadcasting, October 1, 1956, p. 18.

"BBDO Releases Major Study on Radio in Television Era." Broadcasting, October 1, 1956, pp. 27-28.

"This Junket Admittedly Was for Laughs." Broadcasting, October 22, 1956, p. 103.

"Network Radio: Pro, Con." Broadcasting, November 5, 1956, pp. 61-62, 64.

"Indie Time Buying Up." Billboard, November 10, 1956, p. 20.

"TV D.J.s' Status Up at Local Level." Billboard, November 10, 1956, p. 62.

"Directory of Local TV Disk Jockey Shows." Billboard, November 10, 1956, p. 78.

"The Billboard Ninth Annual Disk Jockey Poll." Billboard, November 10, 1956, p. 82.

"Defense of Music-News Made Before N.J. Assn." Broadcasting, November 12, 1956, p. 106.

"Hunt a Hit." Broadcasting, November 19, 1956, p. 119.

"The Radio Networks." Broadcasting, November 26, 1956, pp. 31-34, 36, 39, 41.

"20% Boost in Daytime Rates Effected by WCBS New York." Broadcasting, November 26, 1956, p. 83.

"Standard Radio Producing Libraries for Seeburg Co." Broadcasting, November 26, 1956, p. 87.

"KOWH Holds Open House Party." Broadcasting, November 26, 1956, p. 99.

"Programs Include Many Services, Storz Head Says." Advertising Age, December 10, 1956, p. 32.

Botts, L. S. "Big Advertisers' Like It Local, Radio Finds." Advertising Age, December 10, 1956, p. 86.

"Stations and 'Jukes.'" Advertising Age, December 10, 1956, p. 86.

"ABC Promotes 'Color Radio.'" Broadcasting, December 10, 1956, p. 122.

"First Returns from New Nielsen Causes Alarm Among Radio Interests." Broadcasting, December 17, 1956, p. 9.

"Return on Soft Drink Empty: $50,000." Broadcasting, December 17, 1956, p. 50.

"Timebuyers Cautious of 'Giveaway-Hypoed' Station Ratings." Broadcasting, December 24, 1956, p. 37.

"Gimmicks and Giveaways." Broadcasting, December 24, 1956, pp. 36-38.

1957

"Do Ratings Hypos Help Stations?" Sponsor, January 5, 1957, pp. 28-29.

"No Birdbrain Here." Broadcasting, January 7, 1957, p. 88.

"Adam Young Claims Flaws in NCS No. 2." Broadcasting, January 21, 1957, p. 44.

"MBS Considers Heavy News Format." Broadcasting, January 28, 1957, p. 64.

"Lot of Life in Radio Yet." Business Week, February 9, 1957, pp. 131-132.

"Mid-Continent Questions Sale of 50% of WSMB to Radio Hawaii." Broadcasting, February 11, 1957, p. 66.

"49th and Madison: Radio's Rising Rates." Sponsor, February 16, 1957, pp. 24-25.

"CBS Radio to Price Day Over Night." Broadcasting, February 25, 1957, pp. 27-28.

"FCC Approval Sought for Sales of WPFH(TV) and WIBG-AM-FM." Broadcasting, March 4, 1957, p. 60.

"NBC Radio Plans Day Increases." Broadcasting, March 4, 1957, p. 100.

"Storz Scores FCC Inaction on WSMB." Broadcasting, March 11, 1957, p. 74.

"Radio in Rare Form." Broadcasting, March 11, 1957, p. 105.

"Closed Circuit: Capital Capital Gain." Broadcasting, March 25, 1957, p. 5.

"DuMont Pays $7.5 Million for WNEW." Broadcasting, March 25, 1957, pp. 31-33.

"Media Vie for Teen-Agers' Time." Broadcasting, March 25, 1957, p. 39.

"Storz Sells KOWH for $822,500; Seven Other AM Stations Sold." Broadcasting, April 1, 1957, p. 128.

"Radio Program Services." Sponsor, April 6, 1957, pp. 26, 44.

"MBS Affiliates Hear Details of Planned Music-News Format." Broadcasting, April 15, 1957, pp. 40-41.

"New Promotion Plan Announced at Bartell 10th Birthday Meet." Broadcasting, April 15, 1957, p. 74.

"Petry Urges Night Radio Slash." Broadcasting, April 22, 1957, p. 103.

Lord, Herman. "The Storz Bombshell." Television Magazine, May, 1957 reprint, 8 pages.

"WBC's WAAM (TV) Buy: $4.4 Million." Broadcasting, May 13, 1957, p. 112.

"M'Lendon's 'Texas Triangle.'" Variety, May 15, 1957, p. 37.

"New Programs Deal at ABC Radio." Broadcasting, May 27, 1957, p. 56.

"3 Bartell Stations Hike Rates, Create Class AA 'Driving Time.'" Broadcasting, May 30, 1957, p. 76.

"Storz in Syndication with Connolly Series." Broadcasting, June 3, 1957, p. 61.

"Bartell Stations Sell WMTV(TV) to WTVJ(TV) Group for $550,000." Broadcasting, June 3, 1957, p. 68.

"Katz Hires Pearson to 'Trouble-Shoot.'" Broadcasting, June 10, 1957, pp. 100-101.

"Young Questions 'Power' Radio." Broadcasting, June 17, 1957, p. 90.

"Closed Circuit." Broadcasting, July 8, 1957, p. 5.

"Missing Measurements." Broadcasting, July 8, 1957, p. 5.

Csida, Joe. "Sponsor Backstage: Behind Radio's Fabulous Comeback." Sponsor, July 13, 1957, pp. 20, 22.

"WINS Ballyhoo Ties Up N.Y. Phone Exchange." Broadcasting, July 15, 1957, pp. 90-92.

"Audio-Radio Network Formed to Sell Music, News Programs." Broadcasting, July 22, 1957, p. 70.

"Radio's New Riches." Life, July 22, 1957, pp. 77-83.

"ABC-TV's American Bandstand." Broadcasting, July 29, 1957, p. 94.

"Stations See Profit Increase." Broadcasting, August 5, 1957, pp. 28-29.

"DJ Spins From Flagpole." Broadcasting, August 5, 1957, p. 105.

"In Review: American Bandstand." Broadcasting, August 12, 1957, p. 24.

"CBS Radio May Add Youth Night Block." Broadcasting, August 12, 1957, p. 50.

"KJOY Stockton Sponsors $25,000 Treasure Hunt." Broadcasting, August 12, 1957, p. 109.

"Top Tune Service Gets Bigger Play." Billboard, August 26, 1957, pp. 39, 54.

"'H' Marks the Spot." Broadcasting, August 26, 1957, p. 80.

"Case History # 3 of Sponsored Advertising." Advertising insert in Sponsor, August 31, 1957, pp. 53-60.

"Radio in Transition: Music and News are Only Building Blocks." Sponsor, September 7, 1957, pp. 38-41.

"The Telegram" (photo caption). Broadcasting, September 9, 1957, p. 80.

"What Are the Important Trends in Radio Transcription Services?" Sponsor, September 14, 1957, pp. 56-57.

"DJ Holds 'Eat Out' Contest." Broadcasting, September 16, 1957, p. 106.

"Programs and Promotions." Broadcasting, September 16, 1957, p. 106.

"Picture Wrap-Up." Sponsor, September 21, 1957, p. 66.

"Texas Triangle Group Formed." Broadcasting, September 23, 1957, p. 90.

"WNEW Dropping 'Top 40' Hits to Keep 'Creative Urge' Free." Broadcasting, September 23, 1957, p. 90.

"City Treasure Hunt Gives Radio a Boost." Business Week, October 5, 1957, pp. 44-46.

"TV Jock Finally Comes Into Own." Billboard, October 7, 1957, p. 28.

"Brass and Brasshats Win a War." Broadcasting, October 14, 1957, p. 118.

"WTIX Holds 'Appreciation Night.'" Broadcasting, October 14, 1957, p. 118.

"WFIL Lets Jury Decide on Music." Broadcasting, October 28, 1957, pp. 76, 78.

"The Billboard Tenth Annual Disk Jockey Poll." Billboard, November 11, 1957, pp. 29-32, 54.

"TV Spinners as Strong on Network as on Local Air." Billboard, November 11, 1957, p. 30.

"Spot Radio's Pioneer Days." Sponsor, November 16, 1957, p. 42.

"Radio Networks Are Sizzling with Promotions." Broadcasting, December 2, 1957, pp. 28-29.

"Radio Outlets Value Promotion." Broadcasting, December 2, 1957, p. 64.

"Hooper Omits Ratings on Three Using Local Phone Promotions." Broadcasting, December 9, 1957, p. 35.

"Closed Circuit: Storz Upgrading." Broadcasting, December 23, 1957, p. 5.

1958

"St. Louis Station Smashes Records to End the Sway of Rock and Roll." Business Week, January 25, 1958, p. 78.

Freedgood, Seymour. "The Money-makers of 'New Radio.'" Fortune, February, 1958, pp. 122-124, 222, 224, 226.

Schoenfeld, Herm. "Deejay: Performer or Puppet?" Variety, March 12, 1958, pp. 1, 60.

"Storz Modifying 'Top 40' Format." Billboard, March 17, 1958, p. 1.

Bundy, June. "Deejay Revolt at 'Top 40' May Bring Basic Changes." Billboard, March 17, 1958, p. 2.

"Bartell Radio Format Sparks Sponsor $$." Billboard, March 17, 1958, p. 9.

Sinclair, Charles. "Madison Ave. to D.J.s: 'Get an Adult Audience.'" Billboard, March 24, 1958, p. 13.

"NBC Mulls Deejay Rival for Clark." Billboard, March 24, 1958, p. 36.

"Is Music Enough?" Broadcasting, March 31, 1958, p. 5.

"Bandstand Hypes Local TV DJ Rush." Billboard, March 31, 1958, p. 12.

"2 DJs Quit in KLAC '40' Row." Billboard, April 7, 1958, p. 1.

"Changing Hands: WTIX, WWEZ, New Orleans, La." Broadcasting, April 7, 1958, p. 76.

"KLAC Defends New Policy of Dropping All Deejays." Billboard, April 14, 1958, p. 9.

Hodges, Ernest J. "Critique on Rock and Roll Radio: We're Not After the 12-year-olds." Broadcasting, April 14, 1958, p. 113.

Bundy, June. "Vox Jox." Billboard, April 21, 1958, p. 10.

"Balaban Adds Another." Broadcasting, May 5, 1958, p. 5.

"Radio Roulette." Broadcasting, May 5, 1958, p. 5.

Bundy, June. "New DJ Radio Look Causes Concern to Personality Jocks." Billboard, May 12, 1958, p. 1.

"Competition Spurs Key Airers to Disk Program Shuffles." Billboard, May 18, 1958, p. 1.

Sinclair, Charles. "Ingenuity Key to New Local Radio Success Era." Billboard, May 19, 1958, pp. 1, 9.

"KMYR Goldrush Blitzes Denver." Billboard, May 19, 1958, p. 6.

"Freed Goes to WABC." Billboard, May 19, 1958, p. 8.

"Rock 'n' Riot." Time, May 19, 1958, p. 50.

"A Spirited Defense of Modern Radio." Broadcasting, June 2, 1958, pp. 77-78.

"Jock Meet Sows National Org Seeds." Billboard, June 8, 1958, p. 3.

"The Top 40 Formula--Under Fire." Broadcasting, June 30, 1958, p. 36.

"Rating Week Hypo Cuts Rational Buying of Time." Advertising Age, July 7, 1958, pp. 1, 38.

"Rating Hypo Fought by Stations; Not Agencies." Advertising Age, July 14, 1958, p. 3.

"Rating Hypo 'Cures' Bring on New Maladies." Advertising Age, July 21, 1958, pp. 3, 24.

"Is Music and News Still a Vital Programming Force?" Sponsor, August 9, 1958, pp. 46-47.

"Stations, Not Admen, Must Run Programs: Bartell." Advertising Age, October 20, 1958, p. 8.

"KOMA Replaces WKY in Network." Broadcasting, December 1, 1958, p. 69.

"Sparks Still Fly in Format Fracas." Billboard, December 15, 1958, p. 63.

1959

"Sponsor Asks: Does the Personality Disc Jockey Fit Into Formula?" Sponsor, March 7, 1959, pp. 52-53.

"KLIQ." Sponsor, April 25, 1959, p. 69.

"Hit Parade Dies as Rock 'n' Roll Takes Its Toll of Longrunner, 24." Variety, April 29, 1959, pp. 37, 44.

"Sound Off!" (letters column). Billboard, May 11, 1959, p. 3.

"Metropolitan Soars with Kluge at Helm." Billboard, May 15, 1959, p. 8.

"No Guaranteed Success Formula, Says Krelstein." Billboard, June 1, 1959, pp. 3, 51.

"Take Rock Out of Rockyford." Billboard, July 13, 1959, p. 1.

"NBC Affiliations KOMA Cuts Network; WVET Replaces WHAM." Broadcasting, July 13, 1959, p. 54.

"Is the Personality DJ Craze on the Wane?" Sponsor, July 18, 1959, pp. 46-47.

"Longhair Vs. Short in Bay Area." Broadcasting, July 20, 1959, pp. 50-52.

"New DJ Assn." Broadcasting, July 27, 1959, p. 78.

"Indies Rate High in Top Markets." Sponsor, August 8, 1959, p. 42.

"June-Spoon-Moon-Tunes." Newsweek, August 31, 1959, p. 72.

O'Hallaren, William. "Radio Is Worth Saving." Atlantic Monthly, October, 1959, pp. 69-72.

"At Last a Reliable Music Survey." Broadcasting, October 12, 1959, pp. 33-34.

"McLendon Files Suit, Hits Contract Jumping." Broadcasting, November 9, 1959, p. 81.

"TV, Radio Stations Spend Too Little For Promotion: Kaufman." Advertising Age, November 16, 1959, p. 8.

"Most Agencies Buy Singing Commercials Outside, Study Finds." Advertising Age, November 30, 1959, p. 54.

"The Curse of Consistency." Broadcasting, November 30, 1959, p. 78.

"Competition is Tougher." Broadcasting, October 19, 1959, pp. 80-81.

1960-1972

"What Factors Did You Consider in Switching From Top 40?" Sponsor, February 6, 1960, pp. 48-49, 71.

"Things to Know in Buying Jingles." Sponsor, February 27, 1960, pp. 36-38.

"Billboard Profiles TV's Disk Dance-Party Shows." Billboard, April 11, 1960, p. 22.

Chase, Sam. "DJs Adopt Code, Membership Plan." Billboard, April 18, 1960, p. 3.

"Jocks Code of Ethics Adopted at DJA Meet." Billboard, April 18, 1960, p. 3.

"Supermarket Disk Vending Machine." Billboard, April 18, 1960, p. 3.

"Ackerman Statement to Payola Probers." Billboard, May 9, 1960, p. 18.

"Tuneless Air Format Bows." Billboard, May 16, 1960, p. 18.

Bundy, June. "Promotions Key Now Radio Awareness." Billboard, May 23, 1960, p. 1.

"WADO Will Alter Format." Billboard, May 23, 1960, p. 3.

Bundy, June. "Dog Days Usher in Jock Silly Season." Billboard, August 1, 1960, p. 1.

"WINS Purchased for $10 Million." Broadcasting, August 1, 1960, pp. 76-78.

Bundy, June. "Deejay Stunts Grow Rougher & Tougher." Billboard, December 5, 1960, p. 1.

"Music Biz in 'Formula' Bind." Variety, February 1, 1961, p. 57.

"Special Report: Mass Media Head Into Era of Crucial Change." Business Week, May 27, 1961, p. 104.

"News and Nothing But the News on XTRA." Broadcasting, June 19, 1961, pp. 108-109.

"Zany Stunts Put Radio Chain in Clover." Business Week, September 9, 1961, pp. 124-126.

"Population Explosion Misfire Compared with Radio's Growth." Broadcasting, October 30, 1961, p. 25.

"Trend to Variety in Radio Programs Seen." Broadcasting, November 27, 1961, pp. 69-70.

Lawton, Sherman P. "Changes in U.S. Radio Programming, 1960-61." Journal of Broadcasting, VI, No. 4 (Fall, 1962), pp. 327-334.

Randle, Bill. "Why and How Recorded Junk Music Doesn't Truly Reflect U.S. Tastes." Variety, January 10, 1962, p. 4.

Green, Benjamin J. "Radio Stations Killing the Goose?" Advertising Age, March 12, 1962, p. 94.

"Radio's Changing Sounds." Sponsor, April 30, 1962, pp. 35-37, 51, 62.

"R&R Will No Longer Dominate, Opines WINS Program Director Ted Steele." Variety, March 21, 1962, p. 53.

"Tip Top Jingle Money Makers." Sponsor, April 30, 1962, pp. 32-34, 50.

"Like the Cows, People Do Come Home--Roslow." Broadcasting, June 4, 1962, p. 32.

"RKO Starts Monitoring Service for Proof of Radio Programs." Broadcasting, August 13, 1962, p. 30.

"Plough Programs by the Numbers." Broadcasting, August 13, 1962, p. 59.

"Program Tapes Now Get Official Seal." Sponsor, August 13, 1962, pp. 44-45.

"Plough Inc. Stations in Chi & Hub K.O. 'Top 40' for New 'Sound' Via IBM." Variety, August 15, 1962, p. 41.

"Stiff Warning to Stations." Broadcasting, September 17, 1962, p. 52.

"Pulse Makes Quarter-Hour Studies." Broadcasting, November 19, 1962, pp. 97-98.

"Study Finds Radio Programming 'More Conservative.'" Broadcasting, January 28, 1963, p. 64.

"Surrounded by Critics, Nielsen Expands Radio Ratings." Broadcasting, March 11, 1963, p. 66.

"Is Pulse Running a Con Game?" Broadcasting, March 25, 1963, p. 44.

"Informal Chicago Hearing Erupts." Broadcasting, April 15, 1963, p. 52.

"Tape or Disc for Commercials?" Broadcasting, June 3, 1963, p. 34.

"JWT Blames Quality Loss on Cartridges." Broadcasting, September 30, 1963, p. 46.

"More on Call Letters." Broadcasting, November 25, 1963, pp. 29-30.

"Disk to Tape Problem Solution." Broadcasting, February 17, 1964, p. 62.

"Tailoring Local Spots with 'National' Sound." Sponsor, May 25, 1964, p. 42.

"Tape Library Becomes Buying Aid." Broadcasting, August 3, 1964, p. 50.

"83% of Listeners Know What Station They're Hearing: NAB-RAB Study." Advertising Age, August 24, 1964, p. 8.

"McLendon All News at Chicago Station." Broadcasting, August 24, 1964, p. 68.

"Radio Has the Facts and Figures." Broadcasting, September 28, 1964, p. 68.

"One Best Format for Each Station." Broadcasting, December 14, 1964, pp. 57-101.

"Computers Get Into Record Act." Broadcasting, June 28, 1965, p. 72.

"Radio's Changing Landscape." Variety, July 28, 1965, pp. 39, 42, 46.

"Ampex Cue-Matic Goes Into Production." Broadcasting, September 27, 1965, p. 60.

"Growing Sound of Country Music." Broadcasting, October 18, 1965, pp. 69-91.

"A Gordian Knot for the FCC." Broadcasting, December 27, 1965, p. 34.

"FCC Eyes Complaints on 'Treasure Hunts.'" Sponsor, February 21, 1966, p. 110.

"All News Format Is Winning Friends." Broadcasting, June 27, 1966, pp. 100-103.

"Many Texas AMers Follow McLendon in Banning Disks with Dubious Lyrics." Variety, June 21, 1967, p. 51.

"Broadcasting's Hidden Power: The TV-Radio Reps." Saturday Review, December 13, 1969, p. 68.

"Plough to Pay $2 Million for Florida AM." Broadcasting, September 25, 1972, p. 32.

Books

Belz, Carl. The Story of Rock. New York: Oxford University Press, 1969.

Braun, D. Duane. The Sociology and History of American Music and Dance. Ann Arbor, Michigan: Ann Arbor Publishers, 1969.

Dachs, David. Anything Goes. Indianapolis, New York: Bobbs-Merrill Co., Inc., 1964.

Douglass, Edward F. A Case Study of Formula Radio. Unpublished Master's thesis. University of Wisconsin, Madison, 1961.

Evans, Jacob A. Selling and Promoting Radio and TV. New York: Printer's Ink Publishing Co., 1954.

Goldstein, Richard. "Master of Mediocrity." Goldstein's Greatest Hits. Englewood Cliffs, N.J.: Prentice-Hall, Inc., 1970.

Hirsch, Paul. The Structure of the Popular Music Industry. Ann Arbor, Michigan: Survey Research Center of the Institute for Social Research, The University of Michigan, circa 1967.

Lazarsfeld, Paul F. "Research for Action." Communications Research. Edited by Paul F. Lazarsfeld and Frank Stanton. New York: Harper & Bros., 1949.

Marquis's *Who's Who In America*, Volume 36, 1970-71. Chicago, Illinois: Marquis--Who's Who Inc., 1970.

Mendelsohn, Harold. *Mass Entertainment*. New Haven, Connecticut: College and University Press, 1966.

Meyer, Hazel. *The Gold in Tin Pan Alley*. Philadelphia: J. B. Lippincott Co., 1958.

Passman, Arnold. *The Deejays*. New York: The MacMillan Company, 1971.

Quaal, Ward L., and Martin, Leo A. *Broadcast Management*. New York: Hasting House, 1968.

Schemel, Sidney, and Krasilovsky, William M. *This Business of Music*. New York: Billboard Publishing Co., 1964.

DISSERTATIONS IN BROADCASTING

An Arno Press Collection

Bailey Robert Lee. **An Examination of Prime Time Network Television Special Programs, 1948 to 1966.** *(Doctoral Thesis, University of Wisconsin, 1967)* 1979

Burke, John Edward. **An Historical-Analytical Study of the Legislative and Political Origins of the Public Broadcasting Act of 1967.** *(Doctoral Dissertation, The Ohio State University, 1971)* 1979

Foley, K. Sue. **The Political Blacklist in the Broadcast Industry:** The Decade of the 1950s. *(Doctoral Dissertation, The Ohio State University, 1972)* 1979

Hess, Gary Newton. **An Historical Study of the Du Mont Television Network.** *(Doctoral Dissertation, Northwestern University, 1960)* 1979

Howard, Herbert H. **Multiple Ownership in Television Broadcasting:** Historical Development and Selected Case Studies. *(Doctoral Dissertation, Ohio University, 1973)* 1979

Jameson, Kay Charles. **The Influence of the United States Court of Appeals for the District of Columbia on Federal Policy in Broadcast Regulation, 1929-1971.** *(Doctoral Dissertation, University of Southern California, 1972)* 1979

Kirkley, Donald Howe, Jr. **A Descriptive Study of the Network Television Western During the Seasons 1955-56 to 1962-63.** *(Doctoral Dissertation, Ohio University, 1967)* 1979

Kittross, John Michael. **Television Frequency Allocation Policy in the United States.** *(Doctoral Dissertation, University of Illinois, 1960)* 1979

Larka, Robert. **Television's Private Eye:** An Examination of Twenty Years Programming of a Particular Genre, 1949 to 1969. *(Doctoral Dissertation, Ohio University, 1973)* 1979

Long, Stewart Louis. **The Development of the Television Network Oligopoly.** *(Doctoral Thesis, University of Illinois at Urbana-Champaign, 1974)* 1979

MacFarland, David T. **The Development of the Top 40 Radio Format.** *(Doctoral Thesis, University of Wisconsin, 1972)* 1979

McMahon, Robert Sears. **Federal Regulation of the Radio and Television Broadcast Industry in the United States, 1927-1959:** With Special Reference to the Establishment and Operation of Workable Administrative Standards. *(Doctoral Dissertation, The Ohio State University, 1959)* 1979

Muth, Thomas A. **State Interest in Cable Communications.** *(Doctoral Dissertation, The Ohio State University, 1973)* 1979

Pearce, Alan. **NBC News Division:** A Study of the Costs, the Revenues, and the Benefits of Broadcast News and **The Economics of Prime Time Access.** *(Doctoral Dissertation, Indiana University, 1972)* 1979

Pepper, Robert M. **The Formation of the Public Broadcasting Service.** *(Doctoral Dissertation, University of Wisconsin, 1975)* 1979

Pirsein, Robert William. **The Voice of America:** A History of the International Broadcasting Activities of the United States Government, 1940-1962. *(Doctoral Dissertation, Northwestern University, 1970)* 1979

Ripley, Joseph Marion, Jr. **The Practices and Policies Regarding Broadcasts of Opinions about Controversial Issues by Radio and Television Stations in the United States.** *(Doctoral Dissertation, The Ohio State University, 1961)* 1979

Robinson, Thomas Porter. **Radio Networks and the Federal Government.** 1943

Sadowski, Robert Paul. **An Analysis of Statutory Laws Governing Commercial and Educational Broadcasting in the Fifty States.** *(Doctoral Thesis, The University of Iowa, 1973)* 1979

Schwarzlose, Richard Allen. **The American Wire Services:** A Study of Their Development as a Social Institution. *(Doctoral Thesis, University of Illinois at Urbana-Champaign, 1965)* 1979

Smith, Ralph Lewis. **A Study of the Professional Criticism of Broadcasting in the United States. 1920-1955.** *(Doctoral Thesis, University of Wisconsin, 1959)* 1979

Stamps, Charles Henry. **The Concept of the Mass Audience in American Broadcasting:** An Historical-Descriptive Study. *(Doctoral Dissertation, Northwestern University, 1956)* 1979

Steiner, Peter O. **Workable Competition in the Radio Broadcasting Industry.** *(Doctoral Thesis, Harvard University, 1949)* 1979

Stern, Robert H. **The Federal Communications Commission and Television:** The Regulatory Process in an Environment of Rapid Technical Innovation. *(Doctoral Thesis, Harvard University, 1950)* 1979

Tomlinson, John D. **International Control of Radiocommunications.** 1945

Ulloth, Dana Royal. **The Supreme Court:** A Judicial Review of the Federal Communications Commission. *(Doctoral Dissertation, University of Missouri-Columbia, 1971)* 1979